Traditional Crafts in Britain

TRADITIONAL CRAFTS IN BRITAIN
was edited and designed by
The Reader's Digest Association Limited, London

First Edition
Copyright © 1982

The Reader's Digest Association Limited,
25 Berkeley Square, London W1X 6AB

Printed in Italy

TRADITIONAL
CRAFTS
IN BRITAIN

PUBLISHED BY THE READER'S DIGEST ASSOCIATION LIMITED

LONDON · NEW YORK · MONTREAL · SYDNEY · CAPE TOWN

CONTRIBUTORS

The publishers would like to thank the following people
for major contributions to this book

PRINCIPAL AUTHORS

George Anfield

Plantagenet Somerset Fry

Jack Hamner

J. Geraint Jenkins, MA, FSA, FMA

Angela Levin

Philip Llewellin

John Manners

John Norwood

David Owen, B.Sc

Keith Spence

PHOTOGRAPHERS

Mike Burgess

John Cook

Andrew Lawson

Colin Molyneux

Malkolm Warrington

Jon Wyand

ILLUSTRATORS

Andrew Aloof

Rachel Birkett

Barbara Brown

Brian Delf

Colin Emberson

Hayward & Martin Ltd

Launcelot Jones

Norman Lacey

Richard Lewington

John Rignal

Les Smith

Steve Sturgess

Ted Williams

Contents

THE CRAFTSMAN'S ART

*An illustrated exploration into the history, traditions and
techniques of the best in British craftsmanship*

CRAFTSMEN AT WORK

A visitor's guide to craft workshops and museums in Britain

SKILLS THAT SURVIVED THE AGES

What do we mean by crafts, and what is a craftsman? Where does the line lie between tradesman, craftsman and artist? Generally, by craftsman we mean a man or woman who, through training and natural aptitude, develops the ability to produce an object or a piece of work from natural materials that is useful and, at the same time, beautiful.

The craftsman often requires only the simplest of tools, for his skills are those of hand and eye. He is a traditionalist, since most crafts have their roots deep in the past, and their mysteries have been passed from one master-craftsman to another down the centuries. But he is also creative: every true craftsman improves, however minutely, on the work of his forbears, and bequeaths his ideas to those who follow him. In this way he keeps his craft alive and adaptable, meeting the changing needs of the society in which he lives.

Craftsmanship is older than civilisation itself. As long as 35,000 years ago, men in the primeval forests of Europe were working in bone, antler, stone and wood to make harpoons, arrow heads, scraping tools and the like. But it was with the growth of towns that the craftsman came into his own – a man with more dextrous hands and a greater skill with natural materials than his neighbours, who would therefore gladly support him in exchange for his specialised labour.

And so craftsmen became inseparable from the story of mankind's development. Indeed, for thousands of years certain of them – shipwrights, masons and goldsmiths especially – were the close and trusted servants of kings and governments. By the time of the Middle Ages, the prestige and economic power of the master craftsmen and the craft guilds were enormous.

But from these heights, many crafts went into a decline. The decay came about during the last 200 years, when the industrial and agrarian revolutions altered the face of our towns and the traditional rural way of life.

The Industrial Revolution brought cheap mass-produced goods to an expanding population. New forms of transport – canals, railways and finally the motor-car – made the goods widely available.

The results were devastating. Craftsmen could not compete with the new low-cost mass-production techniques. The craftsman's shop vanished from the streets, to be replaced by the store selling machine-made goods. Poverty and the lure of quick money forced young people to work in the factories. This broke the continuity of a way of craftsmanship that for centuries had been based on a reliable system of training the next generation of skilled workers. The result was a massive decline in the number of craftsmen, particularly of those engaged in traditional village crafts.

Always, however, there was a customer somewhere who continued to believe that human hands could accomplish much more than a mindless machine. In addition, the best craftsmen adapted, as indeed they always had.

Blacksmiths turned to decorative wrought-iron work and mending tractor bars; cabinet makers and joiners built the first aeroplanes; and others, such as stained-glass workers, millwrights and wheelwrights found new life in restoration work – brought about by an increasing public awareness of the need to preserve the past.

In recent years there has been an enormous upsurge of interest, not only among those who are involved in making and doing, but also among those who want to see and learn more about crafts and craftsmanship.

The resurgence is a direct result of our dissatisfaction with the monotony of mass production. At one level we may need the products of modern technology and the Computer Age. But in our hearts we reject them, and turn to the more satisfying products of bygone days.

The vigour of the crafts revival means that such days have not been lost for ever. This book's special emphasis on living crafts will encourage the reader to see Britain in a new light. He will discover that there are distinctive styles of thatching employed in different parts of the country, and understand the reasons for these variations. He will learn how the glass etcher achieves his wonderful effects of light and shade; why, in the making of a wagon wheel, nails and glue are almost unnecessary; and how the local landscape and weather must be taken into account when building a dry-stone wall.

As the secrets of the craftsmen unfold, the reader will enter the world of the heddle, raddle and castle; of the yealm, the sway and the leggett; of belly-stuffers, mashers and bulldogs; of dummies, clew-boasters and half-moon drags. (These are terms taken from the crafts of weaving, thatching, saddlery and masonry.)

Traditional Crafts in Britain makes no distinction between artist-craftsmen, such as cabinet makers, jewellers, glass engravers and so on, and the traditional country craftsman. Nor would most skilled people recognise one. For it takes just as long for a thatcher to learn how to weave a ridge from sedge-grass, or for a dry-stone waller to know how to match the form of his wall to local topography and weather, as it does for the woodcarver to achieve his skills.

One characteristic brings all craftsmen together – individuality. The human touch – that mysterious blend of brains, hands and heart – differentiates the realm of the master craftsman from the world of the mass-production line, where the tools are master of the man.

The best way to appreciate the skill and loving care that has gone into making an object is to see the craftsman creating it. And this book does that. The regional guide, *Craftsmen at Work*, takes the reader to the workshops where he can see the experts applying their skills. The guide also list the museums which show how the goods were made by expert hands in days gone by.

Traditional Crafts in Britain places the emphasis where it truly belongs: on the here-and-now of craftsmanship, on today's living crafts which have been nurtured by a continuous stream of age-old custom and practice.

THE
ANTIQUE CLOCK
RESTORER

REPAIRING AND RESTORING YESTERDAY'S EXQUISITE
CLOCKS CALLS FOR THE SAME CONSUMMATE SKILLS
THAT WENT INTO THEIR MAKING

*T*ime, it is said, even the best of us captures, but for much of our history, any attempts at reciprocation – to capture or harness time to our own requirements – were fraught with difficulty. Nor was it particularly necessary to do so: most folk rose with the sun and went to bed when it got dark, and any further divisions of time between the two were fairly rudimentary and geared either to mealtimes or to prayer.

The Romans regulated daily life by signals at three-hourly intervals, and these periods later became the basis of the divisions of the monastic day – Matins, Lauds, Prime, Terce, Sext, None, Vespers. At each of these it was decreed that bells should be rung, and it was to arouse the ringer at the correct times that the first mechanical clocks of the Christian era were devised. These were adaptations of the old Roman *clepsydrae*, or water clocks, in which water dripping through a hole operated a train of wheels that rang a bell. They were marvellously inaccurate, however, and required constant comparison with a sundial to keep them even reasonably correct.

The search for improvement led in the 13th century to the weight-driven clock, in which a weighted cord rotated a spindle. But it was not so much in the drive, as in its mechanism, that the clock's ingenuity lay.

Arguably one of the great inventions of the western world, and certainly one of the least proclaimed, was the escapement device that operated the early clocks (see Fig. 1). Its purpose was to control the rate of movement of the working parts and transform it into a steady, regular motion that could measure the passing of time. Considering the period, it was ingenious indeed, and with adaptations and improvements the escapement mechanism still regulates all mechanical clocks today. It worked by means of a crown wheel – so called because, with its triangular teeth, it resembled a crown – set on a spindle and driven by the weight. The revolving of the wheel was constantly arrested by two pallets on a vertical rod or 'verge'. Set on opposite sides of the wheel, the pallets alternately caught a tooth and permitted it to escape, so causing the verge to oscillate back and forth and impart a steady tick-tock movement to the working wheels of the clock. The top of the verge was set into a swinging horizontal beam with weights at each end, called a foliot. This balanced the verge and the clock could be made to go faster or slower by moving the weights.

To begin with, the main purpose of these clocks was still to remind the bell-ringer to go to the belfry. Then, during the 14th century, the laity began to feel the need for a more immediate means of measuring time than calls to prayer ringing out from the nearest church or abbey. To meet this, the day was divided into 24 equal hours and many towns established public chiming clocks to help the citizens adjust to the new way of life.

The ensuing 150 years brought an ever-increasing demand for smaller, domestic clocks, suitable for hanging in hall or bed chamber. In these, the lighter balance wheel replaced the heavy foliot, and for the sake of lightness too, the working parts were cut out of brass, a skill that fell more into the province of the locksmith.

It was a locksmith, Peter Henlein of Nuremburg, who invented the spring-driven clock about 1510, making portable timepieces possible. But until some means was found to keep the power of the spring constant, whether fully wound or running down, the idea remained only an idea. The answer was provided about 15 years later by the invention of the fusee, a spirally grooved conical drum from which a gut string or fine chain ran to equalise the pull of the mainspring barrel (see Fig. 2). As the spring ran down, so the chain ascended to the wider end of the fusee, keeping the leverage on the main spindle constant as the force of the spring diminished. Though the device was recorded as long ago as 1525, the fusee is still used in the finest spring clocks and chronometers.

Clockmaking was becoming a craft in its own right, or rather, was developing into two crafts – clock and watch-making. France and Germany were producing superb, if still fairly inaccurate, timepieces, ranging from exquisite jewel-led watches to massive chiming clocks for palaces and cathedrals. Only in England was the craft neglected; there, clockmakers were blacksmiths still, and throughout the Tudor and Jacobean periods, the most stylish clocks in Britain were made by foreign craftsmen. Considering that by the early 1700s English clockmakers were acknowledged to be the best in the world, this was an oddly muted beginning.

There were several reasons for the upsurge, one of which was the marriage of the clock with the pendulum. Long ago, the great Galileo had discovered that a free-hung pendulum, following the pull of gravity, has a uniform and predictable swing, but it was a Dutch astronomer, Christiaan Huygens, who thought of harnessing it as a regulator to clockwork. An Anglo-Dutch clockmaker, John Fromanteel, brought the idea to London in 1657, and within a year was producing clocks that, so far as timekeeping was concerned, made all other clocks obsolete.

Some of the credit must also go to the inquiring spirit of the age, as given point and substance by the new-born Royal Society and its patron, Charles II. Under its banner gathered astronomers and scientists of all kinds, all of whom required, in pursuit of their experiments, ever more accurate timepieces. Out of this grew remarkable partnerships of scientist and craftsman, the most fruitful of which was that of the experimental philosopher Robert Hooke and

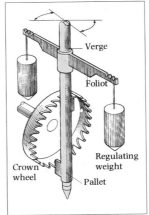
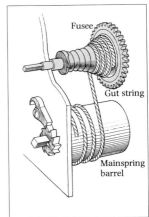

Fig. 1. *The verge and foliot escapement that regulated 13th-century clocks.*

Fig. 2. *The fusee – the 1520s invention that controls the finest modern timepieces.*

CAPTURING
THE VAGRANT HOUR

This early 17th-century ring sundial once stood in the gardens of Hardwick Hall, Derbyshire, where on sunny days at least it told the time with remarkable accuracy. The central rod was positioned according to latitude and the passage of time was recorded by its shadow falling on the figured ring.

This attractive instrument is a century nocturnal, a kind of night-time equivalent of a sundial. To tell the time, the date was set on the outer scale and the North Star sighted through a tiny hole in the centre plate. The pointer was then turned to line up with either the Great or Little Bear, and the time was shown by the position of the edge of the pointer against the hour scale on the inner plate.

THE CHALLENGE OF THE PAST

'You can get inside a clockmaker's mind by working on his clocks.' Gerald Penn, antique-clock restorer of Saffron Walden in Essex, has been doing just that for a lifetime, and the men he works with span the centuries from the Middle Ages on. With infinite patience he dissects the worn parts of their clocks, reaches for an understanding of the parts that are missing, and brings their clocks back to full life.

the clockmaker Thomas Tompion. Between them, they designed and built the anchor escapement, which, oscillated by a pendulum of 39.1 in., permitted the escape wheel to advance at the rate of half the space of a tooth each second. For the first time there was a satisfactory means of registering seconds and minutes on the dial of a clock.

About the same time, other English clockmakers such as Joseph Knibb, Edward East and George Graham were also producing clocks of great beauty and precision, much sought after not only as household regulators but as status symbols too.

To satisfy the demand, colonies of ancillary craftsmen grew up, especially in London's Clerkenwell. Fire-gilders and veneerers, silverers and engravers, fusee chain-makers, gear and wheel cutters, casemakers and finishers – theirs were the hands that built the superb timepieces that have come down to us bearing the signatures of such master clockmakers and designers as Thomas Tompion. The splendour of their workmanship is still apparent, but there is little doubt that the greatest single legacy from the golden age of English clockmaking was the development of a timepiece accurate enough to determine longitude at sea. Longitude is measured by north-south circles or meridians drawn on the globe; to discover your own longitude it is necessary first to obtain a fix on your local time by, say, observations of the sun. This is then compared with the time at some standard meridian, now internationally agreed upon as the one passing through Greenwich. The difference between the two, measured in degrees, minutes and seconds, or in time, is your correct longitude.

The problem, of course, was to find an instrument that after months at sea with the attendant stresses of damp and temperature fluctuation, would still be capable of registering the correct time.

Scientists and craftsmen strove for centuries to make one, until in 1714, the British Government, spurred by a series of maritime disasters caused by ships becoming hopelessly lost, offered a £20,000 reward for a clock that would gain or lose no more than five seconds on a voyage to Jamaica.

In 1762, it was claimed by John Harrison, the son of a Yorkshire carpenter, who after 30 years of trial and error, produced his No. 4 Timekeeper, surely one of the greatest examples of original mechanical engineering in history.

Among its many innovations were double balance wheels to compensate for the ship's motion, working parts of *lignum vitae*, a hard, permanently greasy wood, and polished brass that required no oiling, and a spring controlled by a 'compensation curb', a compound strip of brass and steel that adjusted to changes in temperature.

The instrument was entirely successful. After a six-week voyage, Jamaica lifted out of the sea on time and only 1 mile out of reckoning. Even so, he had to exercise almost as much ingenuity in getting the money out of the government as he had in making his timepiece.

Time present, time past

For Gerald Penn, clockmaker and antique-clock restorer of Saffron Walden, the old masters are his companions still. Some enthuse him more than others. The good, tough Yorkshire face of John Harrison, an innovator and lover of good machinery like himself, looks down from a portrait in his sitting-room, and he has a particular fondness, too, for the work of the old-time, unsung outworkers.

'You can get inside a clockmaker's mind,' he says, 'just by working on his clocks.' George Graham, for instance, Tompion's apprentice and successor, was a man full of ideas. He installed a special gear in his clocks to prevent them stopping during winding, and invented a mercury pendulum to compensate for changes in temperature. His fondness for gadgetry became only too apparent to Mr Penn during the two years he spent in rebuilding the Graham masterpiece now ticking away the hours in the Fitzwilliam Museum, Cambridge.

For Joseph Knibb, one of whose small 17th-century clocks lies in pieces all over his workbench, he has a special affection. Indicating a brass plate beautifully engraved in patterns of leaves and flowers, he says: 'Normally, that's covered by the case, and no one sees it, perhaps not once in ten years. But it was engraved just the same. Not many people would take that trouble today.'

Restoring a clock like this can take 18 months or more, aggravated in this case by some savage Victorian 'improvements'. For some reason, the pendulum had been changed and the repeater mechanism removed – this last, a gadget for telling the time in the dark by chiming the hours to the nearest quarter when a cord is pulled. Then there are centuries of wear and tear to contend with. 'A man buys a car, runs it two hours a day and gets it serviced every three months,' says Mr Penn, 'yet he expects a clock to run 24 hours a day for 300 years on a drop of oil.'

Restoration begins with research, in museums and private collections, for similar clocks whose parts may have survived the years better – not an easy task, for there may be only two or three other examples in the world. He takes photographs and rubbings and, armed with these and an

CLOCKMAKER TO KINGS

Thomas Tompion (1639–1713) was to English clockmaking what Chippendale was to furniture and Grinling Gibbons to wood-carving – a craftsman of extraordinary merit and originality whose work was as admired in his own day as it has been by posterity since. At first following in his father's footsteps as a Bedfordshire village blacksmith, he switched to clockmaking in his 20s. Within three years of completing his apprenticeship he was making clocks for the Royal Observatory and later, under the direction of Dr Robert Hooke, made navigational instruments and the first English spring-balance watch. With Edward Barlow he invented the cylinder escapement, a compact mechanism for use in portable timepieces, and also created new and ingenious barometers and sundials.

Thomas Tompion
Innovator and Craftsman

This splendid Tompion clock was made for William of Orange about 1695 when it cost £1,500. Decorated with solid silver and fire-gilt, it is said to be the finest spring clock in existence, and runs for a year on one winding.

intimate knowledge of the original maker's techniques, can then begin rebuilding. There are very few of the old outworkers left nowadays, so Mr Penn must make all the replacement parts himself. The tools he uses are mostly of the 18th and early 19th centuries, and over the years his tiny, two-part workshop – the lower room is reached by a trapdoor and a ladder – has become something of a clockmaker's museum. He admits that since he cannot afford the kinds of clocks he restores, he collects clockmaker's tools instead. They are all still used for the tasks they have performed for 100 years and more. There are spring winders and copying machines for reproducing watch parts; a beautiful Lancashire wheel engine of brass and polished wood for cutting the teeth on wheels; depth tools ranging from about an inch to a couple of feet long for determining the depth and degree of intersection of gears and wheels in clocks of various sizes; mandrels and lathes for a dozen tasks – everywhere brass and steel gleaming.

His work benches are like the layout in an operating theatre – literally, since he uses dental tools for oiling hard-to-get-at pivots. Beside them lies a long, meticulous row of files, whose handles of box, yew, ebony, mahogany or walnut, he turned himself out of scraps of fine wood.

Indeed, picking up unconsidered trifles is an important part of the craft of restoring old clocks. Mr Penn searches scrapyards for brass of the right age and colour to make wheels and bushes for worn spindle holes, and explores junk shops for old ivory billiard balls to make beads for repeater pulls. The cord for the restored repeater mechanism on the Knibb clock is woven from the silk ribbon of a Regency quizzing-glass. The work is meticulous and wearying – hours of gazing through an eyeglass while making endless minute adjustments. And when the interior is done, there is the exterior; the dial to be re-silvered, worn engraving to be replaced, hands to be re-blued, the wooden case to be repaired and polished. ('I never use beeswax on fine casings; always canuba – palm-leaf – wax from Brazil or Kitagumi wax from Japan.')

Examples of his work in various stages of restoration stand all around us – and in the middle distance too, since Mr Penn also rebuilt the clock above Saffron Walden's Corn Exchange. Each one places its own imprint upon time: a smooth-faced, opulent piece that marked the minutes in a Rothschild board room ... a long-case clock with a rustic cottage painted on its dial that was given by George V's Queen Mary to her favourite jockey ... a clock of 1770 on which a figure, a curious combination of the Devil and Father Time, waves a quart tankard to the pendulum's beat.

Mr Penn finds a certain amount of joy in them all, and a kinship with the men who made them, as he does with the makers of all good machinery. By way of relaxation from the minutiae of clockwork, he is rebuilding a pair of massive 1930s diesel engines intended for a narrow-boat of similar vintage. One day, too, he will establish a museum containing turret clocks, early clock machinery and, of course, the fine tools of the master clockmakers of the past.

PRECISION IN BRASS

When cutting new wheels for old clocks, Mr Penn uses scraps of antique brass picked up in junkyards in order to match the original mechanism. His wheel-cutting engine, too, is something of an antique, since it was built in 1840, as was the brass indexing plate for determining the number of teeth in the wheel. When first built, the engine was operated by an apprentice pumping a treadle; Mr Penn has replaced both with a small electric motor.

THE
BASKET MAKER

BASKETS HAVE BEEN MADE FOR AT LEAST
9,000 YEARS AND ARE STILL INDISPENSABLE. THERE
ARE NONE BETTER THE WORLD OVER THAN THOSE
HAND-WOVEN IN ENGLISH WILLOW

Willow
stripping
brake

WHITE WILLOW HARVEST

*White rods for basket making
are cut in the spring – or
sometimes in autumn, when
they are left to over-winter in
the running water of a stream.
In either event, the bark is
stripped by brakes, a pair of
springy blades that peel the rods
as they are drawn between
them.*

Basket making is an amazingly useful craft. The craftsman needs only a few basic tools, but his skills can be adapted to work in a variety of materials, from flimsy straw to stout willow. Basketwork is strong for its weight, easily repaired and pleasing to the eye. And it can be created only by human hands.

To most people a basket simply means something in which shopping is carried, or a pet cat or dog curls up. But basketry has been used to make such diverse products as birdcages and bathchairs, fish traps and footwear, and even, in more recent times, summer houses and wheelbarrows. Miners used to go down in baskets; balloonists still go up in them; and in 1875 a movement was begun to promote burial in basketwork coffins (they could still be obtained in the 1930s). For centuries it has also been used to make beautiful lightweight furniture.

'Stake-and-strand' is probably the most widely used of all basketry techniques. It involves weaving pliable rods – the strands, or weavers – around rigid uprights – the stakes – that are supported by a base. The ideal material for this is young willow growth.

Plaiting is a technique which makes use of rather more pliable materials, such as rushes, which are used in much the same way as the warp and weft of woven fabrics.

Another method – coiling – was once widespread in Britain and was used, for example, in making beehives. A thin rope of straw or other vegetable fibre was coiled round

on itself and each layer sewn to the previous one by twine, split cane or other material. This was known as lipwork.

Raw materials can also include soft fibres such as grass, creepers, straw and roots, from which baskets can be woven so closely that they resemble textiles, and may even be watertight. The method is very similar to stake-and-strand, using many fine uprights, round which the soft fibres are twisted in pairs.

Basketry is among the oldest crafts known, probably predating pottery. The earliest examples of British willow work, recovered from the lake village of Glastonbury, date from the 2nd century BC. But they are recent compared with fragments 9,000 years old found in Utah, USA. Baskets can be seen on many ancient sculptures. The 'hen basket' so fashionable as a shopping basket in the 1950s can also be seen in a 12th-century illuminated manuscript.

The willow used traditionally by British basket makers is an obliging plant, which grows rapidly near running water. Once it was cultivated or cut along many river valleys, where it grew conveniently to hand for basket makers serving local agriculture and industry. These days, however, very little willow is cut outside Somerset, where the low-lying moors have always been the main source. Here, it can still be seen growing in dense green blocks, whose tall, swaying plumes are a refreshing sight in summer.

Preparing the willow rods

Much care is given to the growing of willow, which after its first three years of life is cut every winter. The rods are bundled and stacked to dry where air can circulate freely round them. A few are used 'brown', with the bark on, after drying, but most of them are given further preparation. Bundles are boiled for several hours, then left to soak, so that the tannin in the bark stains the wood. When the bark is removed in a stripping machine, the rods emerge as pinky-brown 'buff' willows.

To make 'white' willow, bundles are stacked in shallow pits of water, or ditches, until the leaf starts to appear in spring. Stripping at this stage reveals creamy-white rods, once in great demand for baskets in the catering trades. Both buff and white willows go through a further period of drying before being sold in bundles which measure 37 in. round at a point just above the base; they are graded in lengths between 3 ft and 9 ft.

When the basket maker receives his willows, he stores them in a dry place. But before use, they must be soaked in water to bring them to a workable condition. They are then kept under damp sacking for a few hours to mellow them. The time allowed for soaking buff or white rods depends on their size – as little as half an hour for small ones, or up to four hours for large ones. Brown willows may need several days, so the craftsman must plan ahead.

All baskets – except the frame type – are made from the base upwards, and start with a structure called the 'slath'. This consists of at least four stout willows – or more, according to the diameter – known as 'sticks', cut a couple of inches longer than the proposed base diameter. These may be simply laid over each other, but more often are pared or 'slyped' in the middle with a knife, half then being passed through slits made in the others to form a cross. This is bound with a thin rod, or weaver, then opened out like a big asterisk.

To make a slath, the craftsman holds the structure steady on the floor with one foot, leaving his hands free to bind it together. As bottoms are usually worked with a simple under-and-over weave, it is necessary to insert an extra half-stick at an early stage, otherwise the weave will repeat instead of alternating. The aim is to produce a slightly domed bottom, so that the basket will stand steady.

When the bottom is complete, the ends of the sticks are cut off with secateurs, and the slyped ends of somewhat thinner rods, called 'stakes', are pushed well in, one on each side of every stick. Where it is necessary to open the weave for this purpose, the basket maker uses a stout bodkin, lubricated with tallow.

Using his knife to prick the bend, the craftsman turns each of the stakes up at a right-angle, then drops a light cane hoop over the cluster to keep them upright and out of the way. Now he settles himself down on his 'plank' on the floor, his back to the wall, with the embryo basket on a lap-board across his thighs. A lead weight inside the basket keeps it from sliding about as he turns it, always working from left to right.

Beginning the side – known as the 'upsett' – calls for special attention, not only because this junction is a potentially weak area, but also because spacing of the stakes and the basket's final shape are determined by it. So it is worked with a strong weave called a wale, in which a sequence of three or four rods go alternately behind one stake and in front of two. These 'weaver' rods are slyped at one end and pushed in next to the stakes.

When the wale is complete, the side can be worked with a choice of weaves. The simplest weave is randing, in which a single rod is taken in and out of every stake; a variant is rib-randing, going in front of two and behind one. Much quicker is slewing, when two or more rods are used together. Pairing is weaving two rods together, under and over each other, to produce a braided effect. This strong weave is applied in open-work, or fitching, to keep the stakes straight – around the sides of a cradle for example.

David Drew, basket maker of Chard in Somerset, sorts out willows and cuts stakes in preparation for a new job. Behind are some of his finished products – baskets for fruit and flowers, and even a basketry cradle.

THE TRADITIONALIST AND HIS TOOLS

David Drew makes baskets to contain almost anything – cherries and blackberries, fish, pets, logs, shopping, waste paper and long-stemmed roses. He sits on a sack, with a board for a workbench lying between his outstretched legs in the working stance favoured by basket weavers for centuries. His tools are as traditional as his products – a cowhorn filled with tallow or grease to help the bodkin run more easily through the willow; a commander and dog for straightening rods; a three-way cleave for splitting willows into three; an upright shave for taking a curl off each side of a willow to make the edges parallel; and a beating iron for packing the weave down.

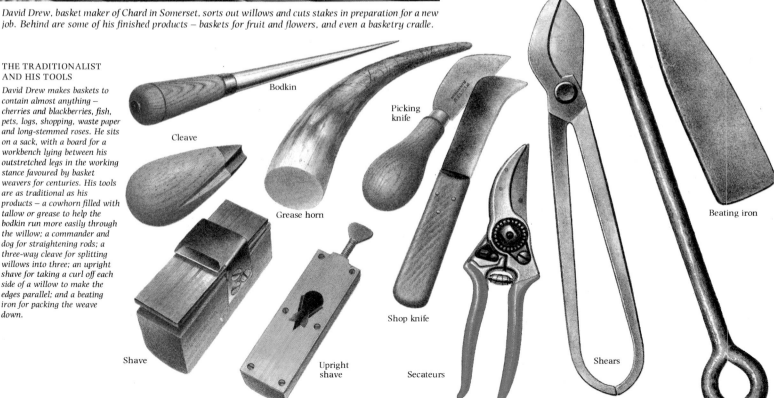

Bodkin

Picking knife

Dog

Cleave

Grease horn

Beating iron

Shave

Upright shave

Shop knife

Secateurs

Shears

BOTTOMING, UPSETTING, WALING, SIDING UP AND BORDERING – THE STEPS IN MAKING A LOG BASKET

Willow cane is light, but any notions about its frailty are swiftly dispelled when a beginner makes his first attempts to work it. These are usually attended by aching fingers and numerous cuts, for the material, with its resilience and sharp ends, seems almost to fight back. Strong hands and a thousand knacks must be acquired to master it, but once these are gained – in a matter of four or five years – then a long-lasting, heavy weight-bearing basket like this can be built in only a few hours.

Making the bottom. The first weavers are joined in.

The bottom completed, the side stakes are driven in, bent up and a four-rod upsett commenced.

The walls are built up using a four-rod slew weave. Butt ends are left inside and later trimmed with a picking knife.

Beginning a two-rod handle. One of the rods is pulled through under the wale to form a bow.

Withies, made pliable by twisting, are wound round the handle and the ends tucked away.

14

From time to time the craftsman may use a beating iron to tap the weave down tightly.

Of course, there are decorative possibilities when using say, white or brown willows as a contrast to buff. An old basket-maker's rhyme recalls some of the essentials of good workmanship:

I can rand at your command;
Put on a decent border,
Upsett tight, wale all right,
And keep my stakes in order.

And so to the 'decent border', which is generally supported by a round of waling for strength. For the simplest border, a trac, the stakes are cut off, leaving about 2 in. proud. These ends are then bent to the right, in front of one stake and tucked behind the next, so that each stake is locked by its neighbour. There are several more complicated borders, such as the four, five or six-rod plain and the three-pair plait, all of which produce flat-topped borders that lock in the top of the basket.

Basket handles are built up around a bow – a stout curved rod, often a piece of cane – with slyped ends which are pushed into gaps made for them. Round this rod are twisted several thin rods, which are brought under the basket's border at both ends, then twisted back to the other side and trimmed off where the ends will not be seen. Smaller 'ear' handles may simply be twisted on without reinforcement.

When finished, the basket is worked over with a picking knife to trim off all protruding ends. The picking knife, with its short oblique blade, is one of the trade's most characteristic tools, and features in the ancient arms of the Basket-makers' Company.

Three other tools, traditional to the basket maker, enable him to produce particularly fine work called skeining. Willow skeins are prepared from the rod by first splitting it lengthwise with a cleave, an egg-shaped wooden tool with three or four metal-edged fins – rather like an aerial bomb. The pith is removed from the skeins by passing them through a shave, a small planing tool, with an adjustable blade. To trim the skeins to even width they are pulled between the two vertical blades of another upright tool. Skeins are sometimes used for lapping round handle bows, or they may be used to make entire articles where an especially neat finish is wanted.

Two shapes of basket call for a variation of method. To make an oval one, the normal slath is lengthened as required, with extra bottom sticks inserted to allow for more side stakes. The rest of the work is as normal.

The other shape is, of course, rectangular, as for a hamper. Here the bottom is woven as a separate panel, the sticks being held upright in a simple wooden clamp fastened by two turn-screws. The finished bottom is laid flat, and stakes inserted in the weave at each end of the base, then turned up and inserted in holes made in the outer sticks

THE STAGES USED IN BASKET MAKING

- Border
- Slewing
- Waling
- Randing
- Fitching
- Upsett

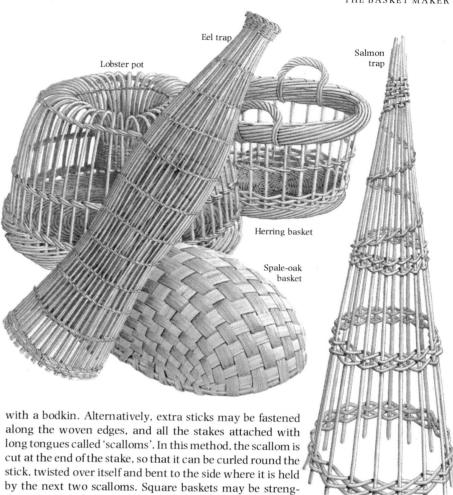

Lobster pot

Eel trap

Salmon trap

Herring basket

Spale-oak basket

with a bodkin. Alternatively, extra sticks may be fastened along the woven edges, and all the stakes attached with long tongues called 'scalloms'. In this method, the scallom is cut at the end of the stake, so that it can be curled round the stick, twisted over itself and bent to the side where it is held by the next two scalloms. Square baskets may be strengthened at the corners by additional extra-thick stakes. Lids are made like bottoms.

Modern container development has reduced demand for the basket-maker's skills, but only a century ago more than 200 specialised types of basket were being made in Britain. Few sections of the community could have done without them. East Anglian fishermen needed their crans and cockle flats, Cornish market gardeners their broccoli crates and Somerset farmers' wives their cheese baskets. Many other kinds were made for farm work, such as sack fillers, cattle-feed baskets and carrot skeps. Transporting produce called for yet more, including fruit flats, chicken crates and rabbit hampers. There was a constant demand for skeps in textile mills, and scuttles for coaling ships. Hospitals needed bottle baskets and the Brigade of Guards required basketwork frames for their bearskins, as they do to this day.

Although most British baskets are made with willow, other kinds may still be found. Perhaps the best known is the Sussex trug (see p. 204). A very rare example is the spale basket of Furness, in Cumbria. Once it was made in other areas, and called a scuttle, slop, skep, skelk, swill or wisket. Its laborious construction has doubtless hastened its decline, even though it is strong and useful. It begins with a steamed hazel rod, bent to form a circular or oval rigid rim. The woven body is made of thin wooden strips, split from oak poles which have been boiled for several hours to soften them. These strips, called spelks, are further trimmed with a draw-knife, then soaked again to keep them pliable. The stoutest spelks are woven into the thinner strips, called 'chissies', creating a deep-bowled basket.

Some work in rush and sedge is also still carried on – principally in East Anglia – producing log baskets, shopping baskets and mats. On the River Severn large conical salmon traps and bottle-shaped eel traps are worked with hazel rods, and around the coast a few fishermen still turn out traditional lobster pots of hazel and willow.

BRITAIN IN A BASKET

Having reached perfection in prehistoric times, the basic designs of many forms of British basketwork have remained unchanged ever since. Coracles and wattle fencing are of immensely ancient origin; so too are the wicker lobster and crab pots of the northern and western coasts, and the willow salmon traps of the Severn that are laid in barrages across the river to capture the fish as they are swept down on the tide. Eel traps, woven from hazel or willow, are used in much the same way in the Fens. Spale baskets, made of boiled oak strips, are mostly used by potato pickers nowadays, but have a close resemblance to the corn baskets of our Iron Age ancestors.

THE
Bell-founder

THE CONTINUING 'SWEET' THUNDER OF CHURCH
BELLS, SO INTIMATE A PART OF OUR HERITAGE, DEPENDS ON
THE OUTPUT OF TWO REMAINING FOUNDRIES

Bells chime our entrances and our exits and pace out the hours of our days; they ring out the news of great joys and victories, and solemnly tell of the deaths of kings.

Not so long ago, bells were regarded as the voice of God and credited with the ability to quell storms and dispel evil and plague. Small wonder that they were accorded personalities of their own, so that when a new bell was hung in the church it was often draped in a christening robe and baptised with holy water.

Some of the ancient bells of Britain date back to the 13th century, and their construction makes it apparent that the craft of the bell-founder is of particularly long standing. The first Christian bells, made by monks, consisted of hammered and riveted iron plates, though by the 8th century the method was superseded by casting in bronze. Three-hundred years later, and for many centuries following, secular itinerant founders wandered from church to church casting bells on site, as furnace chimneys in old church-yards bear witness. It is still a highly individual craft, combining the skills of musician and metallurgist, sculptor and antiquarian – with more than a touch of engineer and joiner thrown in.

Its practitioners are rarish nowadays. In fact, in all Britain there are only two bell-founding firms, one in London's Whitechapel and the other at Loughborough, in Leicestershire. As becomes the eternal nature of their product, both can trace their histories back for centuries.

Bells are made of bell-metal, an expensive alloy of about 77 per cent copper and 23 per cent tin. From it, Taylor's of Loughborough, for example, can construct bells weighing from a few pounds up to 20 tons. And though they have never made a 20-tonner, they are quite prepared to do so if asked. The largest they have made – the noble, deep-voiced Great Paul for London's St Paul's Cathedral, weighing nearly 17 tons – is still the biggest bell in the Commonwealth.

Its birthplace has not altered much since Great Paul set out for London behind a straining traction engine a century ago. The interior of the foundry is rather reminiscent of that of some ancient dreadnought – a row of furnaces served by ponderous machinery around which lie great open-mouthed, mortar-like shapes in dark iron. These are the cases, or copes, in which the outer shells of the bell moulds are built up. The nearly solid cores, giving the bell its inner shape, are constructed round brick foundations, and rise up

CRITICAL MOMENT At a now defunct foundry at Croydon, a cope is being lowered over a core, its great weight massively increased by a lining of polished loam. The cope will be cramped to the underlying core plate and buried in sand to await casting day, when bell-metal will be ladled into the opening in the top.

from cast-iron core plates on the foundry floor near by.

The basic material of both parts of the mould is called loam – a black-grey glutinous substance composed of black and red sand, chopped hay and horse manure – that is applied and smoothed by hand. The shape of the core is kept true by a crook, a swivelling template that carves and governs both the inner and outer curves of the bell.

The core and the cast-iron, shrouded outer case are trolleyed into a cavernous oven and baked over several weeks until quite dry. When they emerge, the rough, dull grey inner and outer surfaces of the mould are sleeked – that is, they are hand-rubbed and coaxed to a glassy dark silver with applications of mingled powdered graphite and whitewash.

When an inscription is ordered – and it generally is, since there are few longer-lived memorials than those inscribed on church bells – then a groove is cut into the case, the space filled with loam, and the inscription stamped in, letter by letter. It may record the name of the donor, or those of the vicar and wardens, together with the date and place of casting and perhaps a line from the Scriptures.

A particularly pleasant touch is added if an old bell has come in for re-casting – that is, to be melted down and the metal used to make a new bell. Then, a lead casting is made of the old inscription so that its wording may be stamped into the loam beside the new.

SOLID TO THE CORE
The core, that gives the bell its inner shape, is built up by hand over a brick foundation. The moulding material is called loam, actually a concoction of horse manure, chopped hay and sand, that perfectly holds the shape through all the processes of working, baking and polishing. The curves are kept true by a crook, or template, moving round a swivel through the centre of the core.

SIGNED WITH PRIDE
Look at most bells, and somewhere on them there will be the insignia of the man or company who made them. Such is the respect of modern founders for their predecessors that if an old bell is being re-cast, they will precede their own mark with that of the original maker. Here are three foundry stamps that span the ages.

Roger Landon, Wokingham, 15th century.

Robert Mot, Whitechapel, 1570.

Thomas Bartlet, Whitechapel, 1618.

John Taylor & Co., Loughborough, 1980.

The case is now lowered on to the core and the joint made between them – a skilled, lengthy business, since the slightest mistake will result in a poorly shaped bell and an even poorer note. Once the joint is completed, the mould is moved to a vast sand-pit in the foundry floor and gently dug in, to a depth suitable for the size of the bell.

A mould for a $2\frac{1}{2}$ ton tenor bell, for example, standing nearly as tall as a man, is buried almost to the top, while the little trebles lie practically on the surface. An entrance box, through which the molten metal will be poured, is clamped over the 1 in. aperture in the mould. Pipes are laid beneath the sand to flame off gases, and all is ready for the magic moment of casting.

Furnaces roar as the temperature of the alloy is raised to an incandescent 2,000°F (1,100°C), while not far off, though at a respectful distance, stands a group of parishioners or donors, come to witness the birth of their bell. The furnace is tapped, and a ladle filled with a red-yellow glow trundles along a gantry and halts above the mould.

Gently, gently the ladle is tipped, and a golden stream of molten metal curves into the entrance box. Smoke and

DRAMA AT WHITECHAPEL

Thoughtful faces reflect the care with which the bell-metal is poured into the runner box, from which it will penetrate into the space between the core and the cope's loam lining. Bell-metal, an alloy of copper and tin, reaches the required molten state at 2,000°F (1,100°C); a large bell may take as long as two weeks to cool.

TUNING FOR GLORY *The final, fine tuning is carried out on a turntable, on which the bell moves against a fixed lathe. This removes tiny shavings from the interior until the right note is reached.*

flame erupt as the metal passes into the mould, and a bell, with a life expectancy of perhaps three centuries or more, is born. It may be a fortnight before a large bell has cooled sufficiently to be removed from the sand, the core dug out and the case lifted away. It is then taken to the tuning shop.

The tone of a bell is determined by its shape and size; the bigger the bell, the deeper the tone. Bourdons, giants of the species, occur only in a few great belfries where they provide a low, resonant backdrop to the peal, or toll solemnly alone when popes, kings or presidents die.

But bourdon, tenor or treble, the matter of tuning is all much the same. All bells are cast slightly sharp in tone and require an infinitesimal shaving on the inside to achieve perfection. This is done in the tuning shop, where the bells move on turntables about a fixed toolpost that removes tiny curls of pale gold metal until the precise note is reached.

Electronic apparatus is used nowadays to assist in arriving at this point, but the final tuning is often tested in the old-fashioned way – with tuning forks. This must rouse special echoes in the tuning shop at Taylor's, for it was there in the late 19th century that the Taylor family rediscovered the art of accurate bell-tuning by 'shaving', which had been lost for over 200 years.

Casting and tuning are the basics of bell-founding, but it is perhaps in its variety of ancillary tasks that the sheer ingenuity of the craft shines most brightly. Whether the bells are to be hung in a space-age concrete tower in Canberra or in the bell-chamber of some little medieval church in the Cotswolds, each presents its own individual problems and demands individual answers.

Will the frame or even the tower take the strain? Bells are heavy enough in themselves, but when swung up into the vertical or horizontal, they exert a force of four times their weight.

Can a new bell be made to harmonise perfectly with its brothers, cast hundreds of years ago?

How can a steel-girder frame be installed in a bell-chamber where the only means of access is a 2 ft square trap-door or a lancet window?

CHIMES, CHANGES AND CARILLONS

The most primitive form of musical bells – indeed, one of the earliest musical instruments – was the chime, in which a set of stationary bells was struck in sequence with wooden mallets. Like so many other 'firsts', it was Chinese in origin. But by the 9th century, 4–15 bell chimes were established in many Western monasteries. In the 13th century, some forgotten genius geared chimes to play simple tunes automatically before the hours in clock-towers, and it is in this form they are best known today. *Oranges and Lemons* and *The Bells of Aberdovey* bring tears to the eyes of exiles, and the sound of Big Ben is

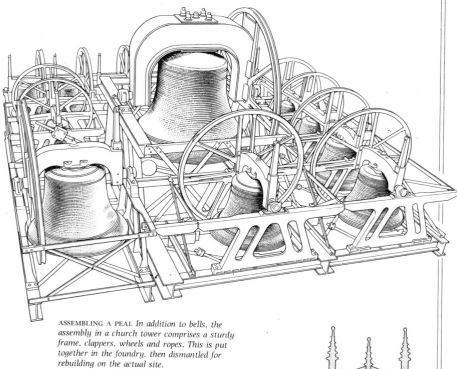

ASSEMBLING A PEAL *In addition to bells, the assembly in a church tower comprises a sturdy frame, clappers, wheels and ropes. This is put together in the foundry, then dismantled for rebuilding on the actual site.*

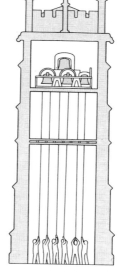

PLAYING A CARILLON *Although having two dozen or more bells, a carillon is played by a single musician – a carillonneur. He learns the art on a replica keyboard connected to tuned metal bars instead of bells.*

famed the world over as the Westminster Chime, though in fact it was composed for a church in Cambridge some 200 years ago.

A natural progression from the chime is the carillon, in which 23 or more stationary bells are played from a keyboard whose keys and pedals are wired to the clappers of the bells. The world's biggest musical instruments, with whole towns and cities for audience, carillons achieved a peak in 18th-century Flanders and Holland. where *carillonneurs* played their own arrangements of Handel, Bach and Mozart.

Melody was never so important in England, where for 300 years or so the joys of change-ringing have captivated its bell-ringers. In this, the principle is entirely different, for the bells are mounted upon wheeled headstocks and swung by ropes from the ringing chamber below. What is aimed at is not music exactly, but a series of musical sequences in which bells of different tones are rung in different order to form mathematical permutations. Obviously, the greater the number of bells, the greater the number of permutations, or changes, possible; thus, on five, six and seven bells 120, 720 and 5,040 changes can be rung, while 12 bells provide the awesome possibility of 479,001,600 changes. Each series of changes, called a method, is given a name followed by a suffix indicating the number of bells. Doubles means five bells, for instance, Triples equals seven, Major, eight, and Maximus, 12. The record number of changes actually rung was a Bob Major of 40,320 changes. The feat took 17 hours to accomplish, and was carried out by ringers at the Loughborough foundry in July 1963.

To these and dozens of other puzzles, engineering, musical, financial or doctrinal, the foundry is expected to provide solutions.

For the most part, bells are hung in one of two ways, as peals or in carillons. There are many differences between them, but basically, in a carillon, it is the clappers that move, controlled from a keyboard, while the bells remain stationary. In a peal, on the other hand, the bells swing, their movement governed by bell-ringers pulling ropes attached to wheels.

Both methods are complicated to set up and require a wide range of skills – in wiring clappers to keyboard, in making headstocks, or sliders and stays so that the bells may be rested in a 'mouth upwards' position when the

ringers' work is done; in building the wheels.

If any mistakes have been made, it is better to discover them in the foundry than in the belfry. So the whole thing – frame, stays, headstocks, bells and clappers, wheels or transmissions – is set up in full working order in the main shop. At least, this is the practical reason for doing so, but it is probably more than any craftsman could bear to dispatch, say, a 53-bell carillon to the other side of the world without hearing it at least once.

It is a superb occasion. The whole staff gathers round; there is a moment of silence, then the clapper of the 6 ton largest bell falls majestically home and its sweet thunder, designed to carry over miles of countryside, shakes the old building to its foundations.

THE
BLACKSMITH
AND FARRIER

THE AGE-OLD SKILLS OF THE BLACKSMITH REMAIN IN
SUCH DEMAND THAT TODAY'S CRAFTSMEN CAN SCARCELY
COPE WITH THE FLOW OF WORK

Alfred the Great once told a group of craftsmen that the blacksmith was father of them all, because he made their tools as well as his own. That was 1,000 years ago. Today, most craft tools are factory-made, but there is still ample scope for the blacksmith's skills. Following an ancient tradition, he is producing the heirlooms of tomorrow.

Iron-working was discovered by Hittite metalsmiths in Asia Minor (present-day Turkey) about 4,000 years ago. They melted rocks of iron ore, together with a small quantity of wood, in pit fires which they fanned with goatskin bellows – the process known as smelting. At some stage they learned that if they allowed the resulting mass of pig-iron to cool, and then re-heated it – stirring the mix to get rid of impurities – it became easier to fashion into tools and weapons. They had, in fact, discovered the art of making wrought iron, which was to be the blacksmith's basic raw material for centuries to come.

The Iron Age changed the course of history. Its sharper-than-bronze weapons guaranteed military superiority for any nation that used them. And it elevated the ironsmiths, or blacksmiths, into an élite class. The Hittites kept the iron-making process secret for centuries, but knowledge of the wonder-metal spread across Europe when their empire collapsed, around 1200 BC. It reached Britain about 700 BC, with the Celts.

By the Middle Ages, blacksmiths were the leaders of industry. Not only did they make the weapons needed for those turbulent times, and forge the spades and plough-shares that made English farming the wonder of Europe, but they also produced the working tools for other craftsmen. These included hooks and shears for thatchers, chisels and picks for stonemasons, saws and adzes for carpenters. They manufactured cauldrons, knives, tankards and toys; they made fittings for wagons, bits and shoes for horses and stirrups for their riders.

Some blacksmiths began to specialise in shoeing horses, a relatively new skill invented by the Celts in Romano-British times. These men were called farriers.

At first, blacksmiths were itinerant, touting for work up and down the land. Then, as the demand for their skills grew, they set up smithies in towns and villages, generally near woodland so that they were assured of ready supplies of wood for firing their hearths and for smelting the iron. Before long they were making intricate locks and maze-patterned keys for chapel and castle gates; scroll-work and hinge straps for cathedral doors; brightly burnished armour for knights going to the wars; and also elaborate crane

ARTISTRY IN IRON

Wrought-iron scrolls and leaf decorations form part of a magnificent ornamental screen at Hampton Court. It was made by Jean Tijou, the French-born ironsmith whose work may also be seen at Burghley House, near Stamford, and at St Paul's Cathedral. It is said that Wren, architect of St Paul's, persuaded Tijou to tone down his naturally exuberant style.

FIRE WELDING *With a resounding bang and a shower of sparks, Clive Davies, of Trawscoed, near Aberystwyth, joins two pieces of molten metal by hammering them together. Accurate judgment of heat is essential – brilliant white for wrought iron; red-white for mild steel.*

mechanisms for raising and lowering cooking pots over hot kitchen fires.

The basic methods used by blacksmiths in the Middle Ages – and even earlier – have not changed, though some of their forge equipment has become more sophisticated. Where once they burned wood in rough brick or stone-lined pits, today they use breeze (a form of coke) in better-made hearths of brick, cast iron or steel. A cowl is mounted over the hearth to funnel off the fumes. To keep the fire glowing, the blacksmith pumps air into it with mechanical fan blowers, though a few smithies still sport a pair or two of magnificent giant bellows, perhaps 6 ft across, shaped like the traditional home-fireside type.

The blacksmith no longer makes his own anvil, the crucial all-purpose work 'table' whose general shape has changed little since the 1200s. He buys one, or perhaps inherits it – most commonly the London anvil which is recognisable by its beaked end, or 'bick'. Early anvils used not to have beaks, while it is possible today to find anvils with two beaks.

Anvils are made of mild steel (or sometimes the more precious wrought iron) with a hardened steel top, or face. This is the working platform on which the red-hot iron is hammered by the smith.

At the squared end, called the hanging end, a round pritchel hole takes the shanks of various small tools. Next to it there is a larger, square hardie hole for bigger tools, such as chisels and swages. At the other end, stepped down from the face, is a narrow block, or table. This is not hardened, and allows the iron to be cut with cold chisels without damaging the chisel edge. Last comes the bick, upon which the blacksmith curls or rolls the iron when forming curved shapes.

Wrought iron is over 99.9 per cent pure iron. To achieve this purity, iron has to be smelted first with carbon (in the form of charcoal) and then re-heated and stirred to get rid of

practically all the carbon. The resulting iron is cooled and heated again with slag, and then hammered, producing an iron with a fibrous structure that can be worked at a wide range of temperatures. From the earliest times until recently, this was the only way to obtain wrought iron. But today the process has become exceedingly costly because of the stages involved, and few firms make it in Britain. It can be imported, but again only at high cost.

So, blacksmiths have turned instead to mild steel. Although this is not so easy to work as wrought iron, it has greater strength when drawn out.

The structure is granular rather than fibrous, and the range of temperatures at which it can be worked is narrower. But mild steel is cheaper. It is supplied to blacksmiths in specially shaped bars called flats, rounds and squares, in a variety of sizes.

The process of forging depends upon what the blacksmith is making and the materials he is using. Armed with a working scale-drawing made on strong brown paper (or perhaps a drawing done in chalk on a sheet of iron plate) he selects the bars he needs and cuts off appropriate lengths. Short lengths of a flat will be used for scroll-work on a firescreen, and long cuts of square or round for the uprights of a pair of gates.

Then he moves to the forge, dons the traditional full-length spark-proof leather apron (used as safety clothing for centuries) and grips the iron piece with tongs whose jaws are appropriately shaped for the particular job. Next he 'takes the heat' – that is, he puts the iron in the fire and brings the heat up to the right forging temperature, watching carefully as the colour of the metal changes. The colour range is blood-red (for easy bends), bright red (for punching shallow holes) and bright yellow (for 'drawing down', or hammering into a tapered end). There are greater heats for more specialised work.

Taking the heat is a crucial operation. If the iron heats up too quickly, it may break when hammered; if it heats too slowly, it may burn and form lumps which must be cut away, wasting time and material. The heat is controlled by careful use of the bellows or air blower.

As soon as the iron has reached the right heat, the blacksmith takes it out of the fire, removes any scaling with a wire brush and starts hammering it into shape. He re-heats and hammers it again and again, glancing meanwhile at his working drawing, until he has the shape he wants. He generally uses one or two of a variety of hammers, notably a ball-peen, with one flat and one round face, and a sledge-hammer if the job is a big one.

Later, when the metal is cold, holes may be drilled in it and the work of riveting and assembly begins.

Forging is still the blacksmith's principal working method, whether he is general smith, architectural wrought ironsmith or farrier, or a combination of the three. He employs it for every job brought to the workshop.

Today's architectural wrought ironsmith is a blacksmith who specialises in designing and making ornamental gates, door hinges, tomb grilles, house railings and balustrades, lanterns and lamp standards, fire dogs and baskets, and so on. He is the descendant of the medieval blacksmith who combined decorative ironwork jobs with simpler and more functional tool and utensil making.

Decorative ironwork began as a practical solution to a pressing social need – security. Churches had to be protected against attack, and a stout pair of oak doors covered with ornate ironwork hinges and decorated mounts made the doors practically impregnable. There is a fine early example at Uffington Church, in Berkshire, which was almost certainly created by the village blacksmith.

Castle entrances and sally ports were protected by

WHEN EVERY VILLAGE HAD ITS SMITHY

Cars and tractors had yet to make an impact on sleepy Lyme Regis when a photographer paused at Govier's Forge in 1898. The scene he captured must have been typical of numerous villages and small towns of the time. The new century saw a massive reduction in the need for farriery, while more sophisticated farm machines were less amenable to homely repairs. Yet, though Govier's – like so many smithies – has long since closed its doors, the old skills survive in the hands of craftsmen able to adapt to changing times.

Scroll form

Pritchel hole

Hardie hole

Floor mandrel

Sledge-hammer

London anvil (on elm block)

Swage block

Swage

Square

Fire irons

Ball-peen hammer

Tongs

Set hammers

Scroll wrenches

Files

Fullers

Leaf tool

Leaf hammer

Drifts

portcullises. These were grids of timber with an iron backing and iron reinforcing at the bottom, or, for smaller openings, solid iron grids, known in Scotland as yetts. Mansions that contained treasures had grilles of interlacing iron bars in front of the windows.

The need for defensive ironwork gradually faded away, but this did not put the blacksmith out of work. On the contrary, fine mansions took the place of castles, and their owners wanted ironwork as part of the building. Black-smiths were often given a free hand to experiment with ironwork decoration. Tracery, scrollwork and foliage domi-nated in gates, grilles, balustrades and screens.

The art reached its peak in Britain at the end of the 17th century under the French emigré Jean Tijou, a Huguenot craftsman driven out of France by religious persecution, who eventually settled in England under the patronage of William III. Tijou designed and made some of the finest and most intricate ironwork ever made in this country. He headed a 'school' of artist-craftsmen whose ironwork ranks with the best in Europe. These included Bakewell, whose work may be seen at All Saints Cathedral, Derby; the Davies brothers, who left their mark at Chirk Castle; and Robinson, whose ironwork adorns Trinity College, Oxford.

The tradition of Tijou continues. Today's architectural wrought ironsmiths are producing exquisite designs in contemporary and in earlier styles – grilles for banks, cresting for gates at embassies, stair railings for new universities, candelabra for new cathedrals.

The architectural ironsmith creates his designs by for-ging. A leaf, for example, is forged on the anvil by heating and hammering a cut from a flat bar, shaping it and curling the tip at bright red heat over the bick with a special leaf hammer. He makes a scroll, one of the most familiar motifs in present-day ironwork, by gripping the heated bar in a vice and bending it with a scroll wrench. The finished curves are produced across the bick.

Any blacksmith may also be called upon to repair ironwork of earlier times. A set of Tijou gates was forged in the first place and can only be mended properly with forging, and by using the same kind of tools.

Many blacksmith's tools have fascinating names –

BLACKSMITH'S BASIC TOOLS

The scroll form, used with a scroll wrench, serves as a guide when fashioning matching ornamental ironwork. The floor mandrel, a hollow cone of cast iron, is an essential aid for forming rings and hoops. Metal bars placed on the swage block are hammered to shape with the aid of swages – hand-held tools that match particular grooves or notches in the edge of the block. The holes in the block are for shaping and twisting heated rods. Set hammers are placed on a hot iron and struck with a sledge-hammer to produce a square shoulder on a forging. Fullers are round-nosed tools for drawing hot metal in a particular direction. Leaf tools and leaf hammers are for bending thin plate to shape. Drifts are punches for enlarging holes.

MAKING A SET OF HORSESHOES

Today, most farriers buy in stocks of machine-made horseshoes in several sizes. These are supplied in three basic styles: plain, stamped shoes which are flat; three-quarter fullered shoes which have narrow grooving round most of the shoe arc for containing the nail heads; and concave fullered shoes, which are grooved all round. It is the farrier's task to forge these to fit the horse.

Sometimes a horse needs special shoes that cannot be adapted from machine-made types. In this case the farrier makes a set of shoes out of four lengths of metal bar. After cutting two bars to the correct length, he first makes the front pair. He heats one bar and bends it over the anvil bick with a hammer to about 90 degrees, shaping the toe in the middle of the bar (top). Then he turns and tapers one branch to form the outside heel. Next, he re-heats the bar and stamps the nail holes at intervals along it, widening the holes with a drift (centre). The inside heel is forged and the shoe is trimmed.

The next operation is to take down the metal to make the toe clip. This is done on the hanging end of the anvil, and then finished on the bick (bottom). The completed shoe is finished with a few strokes of a rasp.

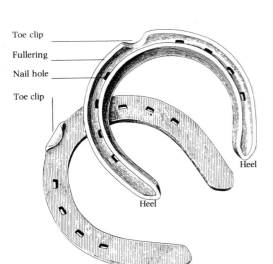

Toe clip
Fullering
Nail hole
Toe clip
Heel
Heel

SOME UNUSUAL SHOES

The appearance of horseshoes has changed greatly over the years. Designs have always been dependent upon the size and weight of the horse, the shape of its hooves and the work the horse has to do.

1 Wavy-rim Saxon shoe. Only the front feet were shod.
2 A keyhole shoe (named after its shape) from the 15th century.
3 Heavy shoe for a draught horse, with ten nail holes, from the 17th century.
4 Late 19th-century shoe with a cast bar toe clip.
5 Veterinary, or patten, shoe, with heel bar fitted to relieve pain from lameness.
6 Leather overshoe fitted for horse to pull mowing machine.

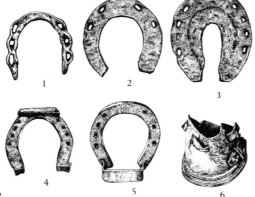

swage, fuller, mandrel, hardie, flatter, bob-punch, drift cold sett, bird-mouth tongs . . . Each has a different function, and the blacksmith generally makes his own tools, particularly when one is needed for a special assignment. The shapes and sizes have hardly altered in hundreds of years, so that Tijou would be perfectly at home in a modern blacksmith's workshop – once he had got used to electric power.

Making tools requires great skill. They have to be forged, hardened and tempered properly, or they will break. The smith forges a tool to the shape and size he needs. He heats it again, to between black and cherry-red heat, takes it from the fire and plunges it into the bosh, a water-trough mounted at the forward end of the hearth. This is called quenching, and it hardens the metal.

But a single quenching only hardens it to brittleness, so he heats it again, this time to a lower temperature, and then dips it into the bosh again. This second dipping is done more slowly, and results in tempering, which gives the metal a degree of elasticity. If one end is to be hardened and tempered but the other to remain soft, as in the case of a chisel, only the sharp tip is dipped. Then it is ground down with sandstone until a fine edge is obtained.

Until the present century, blacksmithing skills were handed down from generation to generation, to sons and nephews, and also to apprentices. Once trained, these younger craftsmen became journeymen and then masters, and sometimes started their own smithies.

Today, though the urban blacksmith is not as important a member of the industrial community as he was, the role of the smith in rural areas remains essential.

His problem is not finding work to do, but staff to help get it done. Blacksmiths' sons do not always want to carry on the business, so apprentices are often sought.

THE FARRIER

Before the Celts in Roman Britain invented the forged iron horseshoe, the Greeks and the Romans had sometimes fitted their horses with 'hipposandals' to reduce the wear and damage caused to hooves by paved roads and hard ground. These were iron cups shaped to enclose the hoof, secured with tough leather thongs. But hipposandals worked loose and let sharp stones in between the iron and the soft sole of the hoof, causing the horses great pain.

The Celtic shoe was a tremendous advance. A flat bar of iron shaped to fit the hoof and pierced for nails was pressed into position at red heat, hammered for adjustment and quenched, and finally nailed down when cold. Even in those times blacksmiths allowed for the sensitivity of the spongy V-shaped pad of flesh on the underside of the hoof, called the 'frog', which acts as a shock-absorber. The shoeing operation has not changed in almost 2,000 years, though both sizes and types of horseshoes have been greatly extended.

Some blacksmiths began to specialise in horseshoeing in the Middle Ages. They came to be known as farriers, a corruption of the Latin *faber ferrarius* (maker in iron).

Farriery is an exacting skill, and it takes years to learn to do it well. The farrier has not only to be an expert blacksmith, but must also understand horses and get to know the character of every horse he shoes. He has to understand horse anatomy, for the balance of the animal is influenced by his work on its foot. And until the recognition of veterinary medicine as a separate profession, farriers often had to be horse-doctors as well.

In the 1670s the Company of Farriers was granted a charter. By that time strict standards had been laid down for membership, standards that continue to be insisted upon today by the Company and by the National Master Farriers', Blacksmiths' and Agricultural Engineers' Association, which runs apprenticeship schemes for young people to train as farriers. More than 100 people are taking up this craft as a career every year.

Like general smiths, farriers make their own tools, many of which are peculiar to the farriery skill. The shoe nail is hammered into the hoof with a nailing-on hammer, which has a curved double claw with which to twist off the nail points sticking out of the side of the hoof. Hoof edges are trimmed with special parers (pincers with angled sharp-edged jaws). Rasps are used to smooth down the hoof after paring. These and other tools are kept in racks near the hearth in a workshop that in many respects looks the same as a general smith's.

When a horse is brought in, the farrier talks kindly to it and pats its forelegs. This reassures the horse, which will generally lift up a foreleg for inspection of its hoof. Then the farrier goes to the hindlegs. He stands with his back to the horse's hind-quarters and takes the leg, resting it in his leather apron between his thighs. This is the safest position if the horse kicks.

The farrier takes off the old shoe with a pair of pincers. He smooths and trims the hoof with a rasp, and then goes over to the hearth and takes out a red-hot shoe. On the anvil he hammers it until he thinks it is exactly the shape for the hoof, and then presses it on to the bottom of the hoof while the metal is still hot. Dense white clouds of acrid fumes billow up from the scorching hoof, but this does not hurt the horse.

If the shoe fits, the farrier cools it in the bosh and nails it down on to the hoof with great care, for there is an arc only about $\frac{1}{4}$–$\frac{1}{2}$ in. wide through which to hammer the nails without causing pain or damage. The nail ends that protrude on the upper side are then twisted off. Most farriers reckon to shoe a horse with all four shoes in just over half an hour.

Until a century ago, farriers made all their own horse-shoes. Then in the 1870s the first machines for mass-producing horseshoes were introduced into Britain from the United States. Now, the farrier buys in stocks in several basic sizes, from $3\frac{1}{2}$ to 4 in. for ponies, about 5 in. for racehorses, $5\frac{1}{2}$ to $6\frac{1}{2}$ in. for hunters and 7 to 8 in. for farm horses. All shoes are made from mild steel – except those for racehorses, which are in the lighter metal aluminium.

Like their colleagues the blacksmiths, early farriers were itinerant and visited the establishments of rich men who owned large numbers of horses, or went to a town to do a day's shoeing for anyone who needed his services. Later, they set up their own workshops.

Today, many farriers are back on the road again, this time in vans equipped as mobile smithies, with anvil, hearth and tool racks, and plenty of shoes and nails. Some of them can be found at both famous and little-known showgrounds and rural riding-club meetings. Others call regularly at private stables. Some even spend a day or two a week helping out at the workshop of another farrier with a bursting order-book.

SHOEING

After removing the old shoe, John Price, of Talsarn, Lampeter, pares the hoof with a sharp knife or hoof parer and smooths it with a rasp. Then he heats the new shoe to a dull red (left), and presses it down on to the trimmed hoof to try it for size and fit (below). If needed, he takes the shoe back to the forge to re-heat and adjust it. Once it fits, he nails it in place, leaving fragments of hoof round the shoe edge, which must be pared. A hoof grows like a human fingernail and has to be pared regularly. Racehorses are shod at least once a week; shoes on hunters and work horses can be left for about a month.

Traditional tool-kit of a travelling farrier.

THE
BOAT BUILDER

THOUGH MODERN BOATBUILDING MATERIALS HAVE THEIR
ADVANTAGES, NOTHING CAN EQUAL THE SHEER BEAUTY
OF WOOD, WORKED BY TRADITIONAL METHODS

*I*n the years before metalled roads made travel and transport swift and convenient, it was often cheaper, quicker and safer to sail from town to town around the coast, or along rivers. So boatbuilding yards flourished all over Britain, wherever there was enough water to float the finished craft; yards which could turn out anything from a rowing-boat to a man-of-war.

Every port and every estuary had one or more types of local working boat, each with its own hull shape, rig and purpose. From the twin-keeled cobles of the north-east coast to the graceful ketch-rigged sailing trawlers of Brixham in Devon, there was colourful profusion of types, most of which have all but vanished.

The larger, working boats were nearly all built by methods which evolved slowly over the centuries. Apart from the switch from sail to steam – and eventually to the marine internal combustion engine – the only real change came with the introduction of new materials in place of wood. In the last century, the first ironclad warships appeared, but these were really conventional wooden ships with an outer skin of iron plates. Towards the end of the century, however, iron and steel began to be accepted as the most suitable materials for building large ships. In time steel replaced wood, because of its sheer strength and immunity from attack by rot and marine life. But steel, too, has disadvantages: it will rust unless scraped and painted frequently, and it lacks the resilience of wood.

Later materials also have their advantages and drawbacks. Aluminium alloy does not rust, but is vulnerable to corrosion caused by the electrolytic action of salt water on the metal. It also suffers more than steel from bumps and scrapes. Concrete, a newer alternative, demands a quite different building technique. But possibly the toughest competitor to wood in the small to medium-size ship market is glass fibre – glass reinforced plastic, or GRP. It is easy to work, extremely tough, and resistant to rot, worms, rust and impact. Indeed, glass fibre has almost completely replaced wood, even in many surviving working boats, because it is relatively cheap and easy to use and repair.

Wood – the traditional raw material

Wood has become expensive – so expensive that only the well-heeled private owner can now afford this kind of boatbuilding. But there are still enough buyers with respect for the unbeatable beauty and warmth of a well-made wooden craft to provide a steady trade for the few remaining traditional boatbuilders.

Every inch of today's wooden yacht is first carefully planned on paper. Modern hull design – for performance, comfort and handling – is so critical and competitive that old rule-of-thumb methods no longer suffice. Instead of making the traditional half-model – split vertically down the centre line – the first step is to draw up the profile plan, a

detailed side-view drawing of the hull. On this plan is superimposed a series of horizontal lines called waterlines, and the one at the designed water level when the finished boat is at its correct weight is called the load waterline, or LWL. A series of vertical station lines is then drawn on the plan to complete a grid of co-ordinates for identifying every point on the hull.

The third dimension is added on a different set of drawings, called the body plan. These are a series of vertical sections from stem to stern through the hull at each of the section lines, half of each section showing the view of the hull looking forward, balanced by the other half-section looking aft. Detailed tables of figures, called offsets, are calculated to help fix the shape and position of every part of the hull in three dimensions.

CARVEL OR CLINKER?

The planks which form the skin of a wooden boat are joined together in one of two ways. A carvel-built boat has the planks butted together, edge to edge, to form a smooth outer surface. Any gaps are plugged with caulking to keep the skin watertight. A clinker-built boat has each plank's lower edge overlapping the upper edge of the plank below it. Larger boats are usually carvel built, as overlapping planks would create excessive drag as the boat moved through the water.

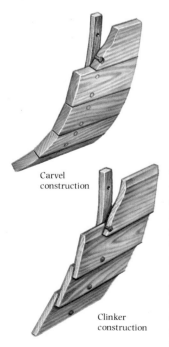

Carvel
construction

Clinker
construction

They also provide the information needed to make up the moulds – wooden patterns which will be used in turn for making the frames, or bulkheads, which shape and support the hull. These patterns are made usually in a room called the moulding loft. They are drawn to their finished size on the floor, using a set of standard curved templates, then pieces of plywood are cut, shaped and assembled into the finished moulds.

The next step is to make the frames themselves. Once, this meant using a lifetime of experience to select growing timber with the grain running in exactly the right direction to suit some very complex curves. Nowadays, most builders use more economical methods. The revolution in tough, quick-setting glues, which began in the Second World War with the production of wooden Mosquito bombers, has

made it possible to assemble pieces of timber with exactly the right grain structure, simply by steaming and bending strips of straight-grain wood and laminating them, layer by layer, into the finished whole.

The actual building begins with laying the keel. But whereas at one time most boats, particularly the larger ones, were built on slipways in the open air, now it is more common to build them under cover.

There have been other changes, too. Once the keel would be a single large baulk of timber; now it is fitted together carefully from several different pieces, often weighted with iron to provide extra stability against the pressure of the wind in the yacht's sails. The forefoot, or crook, where the keel sweeps up to the bows, has to be one of the strongest parts of the hull. It is laminated from two-dozen or more

THE UNDYING BEAUTY OF A WOODEN BOAT

Even the smallest and simplest boat has a complicated shape. This helps to provide stability, while responding readily to oars, sails or mechanical power, and to river currents or the rolling swell of the open sea. These photographs, taken in Ian Cooper's boatyard in Cumbria, show how the subtly curved planks are fashioned to form the sharply rounded stem and the broad beam of a clinker-built Shetland working boat.

STEAMING THE PLANKS

It is impossible to bend untreated planks into the right shape for the hull of a small boat, particularly for the sharp curve of the bows, without breaking them. The planks have first to be softened by steaming, then bent to shape and finally allowed to harden again. Here, a steam-heated wallpaper stripper is being used to bend the heavy gunwale of a River Dee salmon boat into the sharp curve where it joins the stem. In the old days, boatbuilders used a specially made steam chest (below). Three or four gallons of water were heated in a pot placed on bricks over an open fire, and the resulting steam allowed to rise into a chest containing the planks.

Steam chest

separate pieces of wood, matched together into a single, solid, smooth curve.

The frames are fitted one by one on to the keel, to build up the skeleton for the hull. These frames are given temporary support, and are faired up or trimmed to shape. Ribbands – strips of wood – are now nailed or screwed to the frames to stiffen up the whole structure prior to planking, and also to provide temporary support for steamed ribs to be fitted, where these are used. The ribbands are removed one at a time as planking proceeds.

The tops of the frames are joined by other timbers, called shelves, which hold the frames themselves together and provide a solid support for the deck beams which are fastened on top.

There are several ways of fitting the 'skin' of planking to the bare bones of the hull. Small rowing-boats – and some quite large yachts, like the Scandinavian folkboats – are often clinker-built, with a single layer of stout planking. Others, like the spritsail barges of the Thames and Medway, have the toughest combination of all. A double layer of $\frac{1}{2}$ in. or even thicker planks of tough timber, such as iroko or mahogany, is laid diagonally around the hull, with the second layer laid at right-angles to the first.

A lot of work also remains to be done once the hull has been assembled. Hatches and companion-ways must be fitted, and floors and bulkheads put in below deck along with galleys and bunks, auxiliary engines and lockers.

Masts, too, have to be made. At one time, selected straight-grain timber would be smoothed to shape with hours of patient work, but now the masts are invariably supplied in alloy from a specialist mast-maker. Even so, there are variations in the rig of the boat and in the type of mast fitted: its position and how it is fitted to the hull. Some designs take the mast down through the deck to butt securely against the keel for extra strength. Others fit it into a sort of box on deck, called a tabernacle, to save precious space below and make the mast easier to raise and lower.

The business of boatbuilding was very different when the spritsail barges were in their heyday. They remain perhaps the best-loved of all Britain's working boats, many of them meticulously preserved and sailed by enthusiasts to this day.

Designed to carry bulk cargoes amid the shallows and mud-flats of the Thames Estuary, the barges were solid, bluff, utilitarian boats with shallow-draught, flat bottoms which allowed them to sit out a falling tide on a convenient stretch of mud. To keep the deck clear, the conventional

wooden boom along the bottom of the mainsail was replaced by a sprit – a wooden spar pivoted at the bottom of the mast and attached to the peak of the big gaff mainsail.

This was an ideal arrangement for the barge's work. The rig allowed a large sail area to drive a heavily loaded barge at a useful speed against a powerful tide. The use of a large topsail above the mainsail meant that the barge could catch a breeze even in the shelter of tall buildings and warehouses. When the barge docked, the sprit could also be used as a derrick for shifting cargo into and out of the hold.

Barges were expected to lead a long, hard-working life, and were built with that in mind. The hull had not only to be strong, but also elastic enough to withstand the stresses of settling on to the mud as the tide fell, and being refloated when it rose again. Other stresses were imposed by loading and unloading, and it was essential that they should be really watertight if cargoes like cement or grain were not to be ruined.

But they were never planned, in the sense of being designed on paper. Instead, the boatbuilder would produce a half-model, mounted on a flat board. When builder and buyer had agreed on final details of shape and construction, and the model modified accordingly, the shapes of the full-sized timbers would be taken from it. This method was amazingly accurate with a boatbuilder who really knew his job. One Kent boatbuilder, asked to make a barge to carry 200 tons of cargo, worked entirely by eye and experience to shape a half-model. The full-size barge, when built from the scaled-up measurements, was found to carry 197 tons.

The first stage in building a hull was to lay the keel blocks – huge baulks of timber, usually lengths of oak 18 in. square – which were built up in stacks to a level where the hull could be built on top of them. Enough space was left between the blocks for men to work comfortably beneath the bottom of the hull proper. The keel itself was a wide flat plank, usually of elm, with holes cut at the ends so that the oak stem and stern posts could be mortised into position.

The floor of the barge had to be specially strong, so it was

CLENCHING *Nails hammered through from the outside fasten the steamed ribs to the finished planking of the hull. Here, Chester boatbuilder Arthur Howard rivets the copper nails over washers, called roves – a task known as clenching – to make each joint tight.*

built from several layers. The bottom layer of planks was usually Oregon pine, a middle layer of oak planks was laid transversely, with a third layer of pine on top. The three layers were held together by bolts driven right through, and often the oak would be salvaged from an old man-of-war.

The frames were oak, dovetailed into the ends of the floor timbers, and the boatbuilder would nail in temporary cross beams to hold the frames at the right distance apart while the rest of the building work went on.

Ribbands were nailed in place, and once the frames were held firmly their inner faces were shaped and smoothed with an adze – an axe with the blade at right-angles to the handle which was capable of astonishingly precise work in skilled hands.

The next step was to fit the deck beams. First an oak support called the inwale was bolted to each frame, then the oak deck beams were fastened from each frame to its opposite number on the other side of the hull, replacing the temporary cross beams. These deck beams were braced firmly in position by means of large wooden angle brackets, called knees.

Finally, the planking was built up on the outside of the frames. The bottom had an extra sheathing of 1 in. planks on the outside of the existing three layers, while the sides had two thicker layers of planking, each plank being joined to the next with a tongue-and-groove joint. Planks were fastened to frames with long dowel-like pins, made from oak cut along the grain and called treenails, or trunnels. Since these could not be hammered in like metal nails, a hole had to be drilled with an auger for each one. The pin would then be driven in with a heavy mallet. If the treenail was only slightly out of line it could break, and the broken pieces had to be carefully drilled out before the job could begin again. Finally, the end would be split and a wedge driven home to hold the pin firmly in place.

Thousands of fastenings like these held the hull together and gave it strength. But the elasticity came from a layer of tarred hair between the layers of planking. Elk hair was the best, but some barges used cow hair or even tarred felt. The outside of the hull would be tarred and painted.

A far cry from today's methods ... but one factor still holds true of any traditionally built boat. The process is long and painstaking – more than a year from start to finish is by no means unusual for a sizeable boat. And the costs are heavy. A 40 ft well-found sailing cruiser can cost anything from £40,000 to £100,000 for this standard of work.

'CHIRPING' CAULKING MALLETS

Gaps between the planks of a carvel-built boat are packed with oakum – strands of unravelled rope – carefully forced into place with a set of broad-bladed chisels called caulking irons. Too little oakum and the joints will let in water; too much and the planks may be forced apart. The irons are driven home with a caulking mallet, which has a long wooden head ringed at the ends with thick iron. Slots are cut longitudinally into the head between the handle and the end rings, so that when the shipwright swings the mallet it produces a shrill whistling note. In the days when such work was commonplace, this used to be called 'singing' or 'chirping'. One reason may have been to blanket the shattering noise of several mallets being used at the same time.

KEY TO THE MAIN PARTS

A Stem
B Mast beam
C Thwart
D Shutes
E Rising
F Hanging knees
G Thole
H Keel
I Transom
J Forward thwart
K Thwart rising
L Gunwale

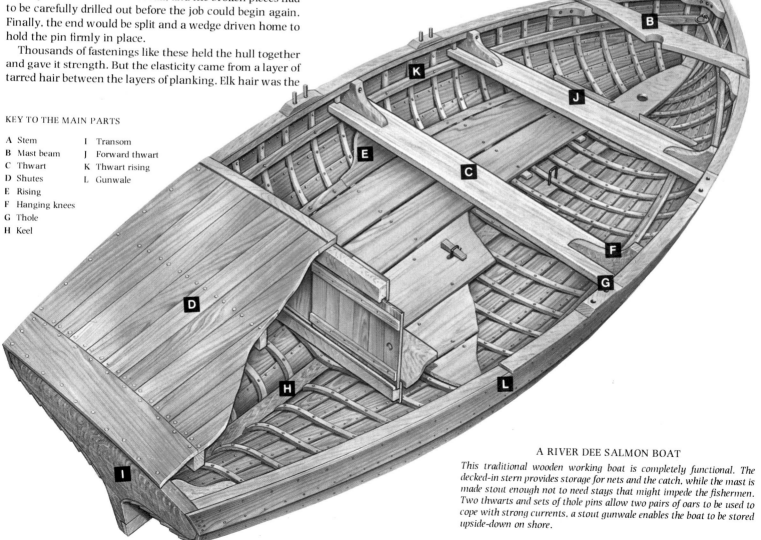

A RIVER DEE SALMON BOAT

This traditional wooden working boat is completely functional. The decked-in stern provides storage for nets and the catch, while the mast is made stout enough not to need stays that might impede the fishermen. Two thwarts and sets of thole pins allow two pairs of oars to be used to cope with strong currents, a stout gunwale enables the boat to be stored upside-down on shore.

THE TOUCH OF GOLD ON LEATHER

British bookbinders have used gold lettering and decoration since the 16th century, but it was Samuel Mearne – a 17th-century craftsman patronised by Charles II – who really made such workmanship fashionable. Egg-white albumen ('glaire') is used to make gold leaf adhere to the book. Simple stamps are used to impress letters, while the main decorative tools are known as pallets, fillets, gouges and rolls. Here, Arthur Winstanley, a bookbinder and restorer of Salisbury, Wiltshire, is using a pallet to apply gold leaf to a leather-covered spine.

THE BOOKBINDER

THE SIMPLE PERFECTION OF A HAND-BOUND BOOK REVEALS LITTLE OF THE SKILL AND LOVING CARE THAT HAS GONE INTO ITS MAKING

Today's bookbinders can trace the story of their craft back almost 2,000 years, to the days when papyrus and parchment scrolls gave way to 'codex' books with separate leaves. Britain's first binders were Anglo-Saxon and Celtic monks of the 8th century. Their religious and historical works, such as the *Book of Kells*, were written in Latin, beautifully illuminated, bound between boards of oak or beech and often embellished with ornate metalwork and precious stones. Since paper did not reach Europe for 1,000 years after the Chinese had invented it about AD 105, the leaves were of vellum – a parchment-like material produced from calfskin and specially prepared for writing.

Panel-stamped bindings made by English monks between the 10th and 12th centuries were famed throughout Europe. However, after the invention of the printing press in the middle of the 15th century, other centres sprang up in central and southern Europe and the binding of books passed from monastic to secular hands. It was the Venetians who developed the use of gold-leaf decoration on 'morocco' (goatskin) bindings – a technique believed to have originated in the Far East.

Jean Grolier, a diplomat and avid collector of books, was a leading patron of Venetian bookbinders in the 16th century. He broke with the practice of writing the title across the front edges of the book's leaves. Instead, his titles were impressed in gold leaf across the spines, and a motto was lettered on the front: '*Io Groliori et Americorum*', or 'For Grolier and his friends'.

Notable exponents of the craft in England have included Thomas Berthelet, binder to Henry VIII; Elizabeth I who, as a young princess, produced embroidered bindings, one of which is still in good condition in the Bodleian Library, Oxford; and Samuel Mearne, Charles I's binder. Under Charles II, Mearne developed the typically English 'cottage roof' style of decoration on both covers of the book.

The 18th century was a period of high excellence, too. The 40,000 volumes in the library of Robert Harley, Earl of Oxford, were serviced by the skills of Thomas Elliott and Christopher Chapman in the unique 'Harleian' style of gold centre panels on deep red morocco. James Edwards, of Halifax, created beautiful vellum bindings; on the underside of the material – and showing through it – were delicately painted arabesques, and floral and geometric designs.

Despite the sophistication of today's semi-automated, high-speed book-production methods, there is a steadily growing demand for craft bookbinders, many of whose techniques would have been familiar to the monks of Saxon England. Much of their time is devoted to binding one-off commemorative books and to restoring valuable old volumes for libraries, antiquarian booksellers and private collectors. For instance, Theo Merrett, a Gloucestershire binder, made the official visitors' book for the opening of the Severn Bridge in 1966, and has also rebound a 1632 edition of Shakespeare's works for Dame Edith Sitwell.

Arthur Winstanley, a craft binder with a business in Salisbury, Wiltshire, has a collection of 2,000 tools with which he can match bookbinding designs of 400 years ago.

But perhaps the three best-known bookbinders in England today are Sidney Cockerell, of Grantchester, Cambridgeshire, who produces the famous 'Cockerell' marbled papers; Roger Powell, of Foxfield, Hampshire, who repaired the *Book of Kells* in 1951; and Bernard Middleton, of London, who owns probably the largest private collection of books about binding in the world.

If he is making a new book, the binder starts with sheets, fresh from the printer, on which pages have been printed in multiples of four. These sheets are cut, then folded with great accuracy into 'sections', so that all the printed lines on each page register exactly – that is, fall precisely over the lines on the pages beneath – and a 'signature' is printed on the first page of each section to identify its position in the volume. The sections are sandwiched between tough endpapers, which link book and binding.

The sewing of the sections is one of the most important aspects of the bookbinder's craft, because inferior needlework can only result in an inferior book. However, the need to make the book as sturdy as possible has to be balanced against the fact that it must also open freely. One by one, each section, together with the endpapers, is secured with cotton thread. This is passed in and out of the spine fold and around each of five hemp cords spaced evenly along the spine. The cords, which will run across the back of the book, are longer than the volume is thick so that the ends can eventually be used to attach the sections to the boards. For ease of handling they are, at this stage, held firmly upright in a sewing frame.

The sewing of each section is completed with a 'kettle stitch', about $\frac{1}{2}$ in. from the extreme ends of the spine – the 'head' and the 'tail'. This allows the edges of the book to be trimmed later without damage to the sewing. The kettle stitch, from a similar-sounding German word meaning a small loop or chain, is formed by passing the needle through a loop in the thread. The knot which results secures each section to the next. The stitches nestle in light saw-cuts, or 'kerfs', made across the spine before sewing begins.

The 'gluing up' of the spine comes next. With a brush and the back of his thumb the binder works a thin gelatin glue into the spine so that all the gaps between sections are filled. He must make sure that every section along the spine is level, or the result will be a badly misshapen volume. He uses a type of glue that will not set hard, for the aim is to combine strength with flexibility.

'Rounding and backing' are second only to sewing in ensuring the durability of the book and the easy opening of the binding. Since the sewing threads and the spine folds should together have resulted in a swelling of the spine, the binder now taps the spine into an evenly convex shape. For this he uses a round hammer. An unrounded book would eventually push its central sections outwards until they extended beyond the boards along the front edge.

The rounded book is immediately placed between wedge-shaped backing boards, positioned carefully so that the section folds along both the front and back of the spine protrude a little way – a distance slightly greater than the thickness of the boards selected for the binding. Considerable pressure is applied, in a horizontal press.

The binder then moulds the spine with the same hammer that he used for the rounding process. Working outwards from the centre, he makes the section folds overlap each other. This consolidates the shape of the spine and results in the formation of a neat, 90 degree joint that precisely fits the boards to be used and acts as a hinge against which the front and back boards turn once they are attached.

THE FORWARDER'S TOOLS

Traditionally, bookbinding is divided into two phases: forwarding and finishing. Forwarding involves making the basic book, while finishing is the decorative work carried out on the spine and the cover. The forwarder's array of tools includes trindles, which are U-shaped pieces of metal used to flatten the spine when the book's fore-edge is being cut with a 'plough'. A thin, sharp awl is sometimes needed for making sewing holes, and for other fine work. A larger version is used to make holes in the boards, through which the cords of the sewing are laced. The heavy swell stick compresses the spine after sewing. The spine is later rounded with deft blows from a bookbinder's hammer with a clean, smooth, convex head. A strip of bone is used to fold the paper, converting the large, flat, printed sheets into groups of leaves known as sections.

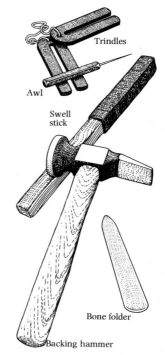

Trindles

Awl

Swell stick

Bone folder

Backing hammer

THE ANATOMY OF A BOOK

Seen through a layman's eye, even a hand-bound book may appear to be little more than a number of leaves protected and held together by a cover finished with anything from paper to the finest, gold-tooled leather. It is, in fact, a surprisingly complicated collection of parts brought together by the binder's craftsmanship. The leaves which form the heart of the volume are arranged in folded sections, ready for sewing. Endpapers, often with 'marbled' decoration, are a sort of inner cover which adds strength while also protecting the book's first and last sections. A saw is used to make the kerfs – fine cuts through which needle and thread are passed to hold the sections together. Hemp cords, very like those used by the earliest bookbinders, are traditionally left raised above the spine, but may also be sunk in saw-cut grooves. Either way, they form a series of vital links between the body of the book and the cover boards through which they are laced and secured.

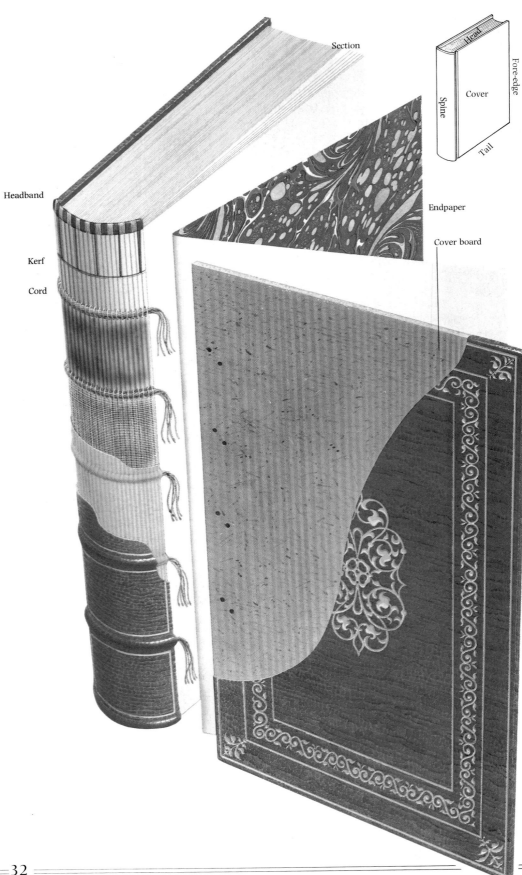

Section

Headband

Kerf

Cord

Head

Spine

Cover

Fore-edge

Tail

Endpaper

Cover board

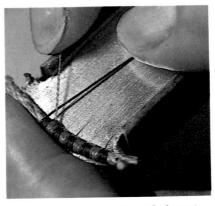

HEADBANDING *Its function is mainly decorative, but the headband also protects a book when it is taken from the shelf. Leather, catgut and other cores are bound in coloured silk.*

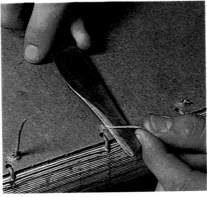

TRIMMING THE SLIPS *The slips of frayed-out cord which secure the body of the book to its cover boards are trimmed neatly. The book will flex incorrectly if they are not the right length.*

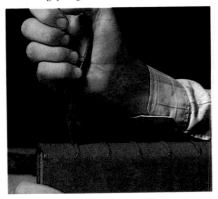

'NIPPING UP' THE BANDS *Plier-like 'band nippers' are used to shape and squeeze the spine's leather when it is covering raised cords or bands. They also enable the bands to be trued-up exactly.*

SETTING THE JOINT *The book is essentially finished when its endpapers are pasted down. Particular care is taken with the joint, because it forms the hinge for body, boards and spine.*

The binder has already toughened the hard 'millboards' selected for the binding by pasting linings of strong paper to each side. He now squares the boards, trims them to their exact size and pierces holes in them with an awl. Two holes are made for each of the cords which run across the spine of the book. The boards are fitted tightly into the backing joints of the book, and the cords, or 'slips', which have been lightly pasted, are threaded in and out of the adjacent holes, cut level with the surface of the board, hammered flat and pressed firmly.

The next operation is edge trimming. 'Incunabula' – that is, books that pre-date the invention of the printing press in the mid-15th century – must never be trimmed after sewing. Most modern bindings, however, are trimmed on all three edges and are often fully gilt. Books of the 17th to late 19th centuries vary: some are trimmed then gilt, coloured or marbled on all three edges; others are trimmed and gilt at the head only. What the binder needs, therefore, is a sensitive awareness of what is appropriate – something that is developed only with years of practical experience.

Traditionally, a 16th-century device called the 'press and plough' is used. It consists of a horizontal 'lying' press into which the book is lowered, this being fitted with runners along which the plough, carrying a very sharp knife, is moved briskly so that three or four leaves are trimmed off at each stroke. In expert hands, the smoothness of the edges that result cannot easily be rivalled. An alternative is to use a modern guillotine.

The edges are now gilded. A base colour, which dries quickly, is applied; albumen or vellum 'size', or adhesive, is brushed along the edges; and the gold leaf is skilfully 'laid on'. Then, at a carefully judged moment between being damp and fully dry, the gold is rubbed on to the edges with a bloodstone or agate 'burnisher'.

Putting on the headbands

Medieval bookbinders sewed around an extra cord at both head and tail of the spine, a practice pre-dating the kettle stitch. Modern 'headbanding', as an ornament and as a strengthener, is derived from this practice. Vellum, leather, hemp cord, catgut or even twisted paper can be used as the 'core' around which coloured silks are wound to form an attractive and a distinctive pattern. The silk is anchored to the kettle stitches at regular intervals.

When books are sewn on 'raised cords', the leather cover is stuck directly to the spine but has to be moulded over the sewing cords with 'band nippers'. The 'raised bands' which result stand out from the spine. Not all traditionally bound books, however, are sewn on raised cords. Since the late 18th century, the cords have often been recessed into saw-cuts across the spine – a practice that imposes less strain on modern papers and results in a smooth spine.

The 'hollow' spine-piece followed naturally the development of recessed sewing. It was designed to thrust the sections up so that the volume opened more easily for reading. Nowadays, the 'hollow' is a tube made of sturdy, unbleached paper, one side is stuck to the spine of the book, the other to the leather cover. To give the impression of raised cords, strips of leather, called 'false bands', are often glued to the side of the hollow that faces the cover material.

Various types of leather are used for the covers. The most commonly used is 'morocco' – a goatskin tanned and dyed with non-corrosive vegetable extracts. It is resilient, pliable, very durable and accepts gold-leaf 'finishing' well. Calfskin was very popular in the 18th and 19th centuries and is still extensively used, especially for rebinding and repair. Pigskin and hide are used for exceptionally large and heavy volumes. And vellum is also widely used, although it requires exceptional skill on the part of the bookbinder; it is

a rigid material with a will of its own that will only be tamed by the most expert hands.

The leather is cut to allow for the 'turn-in' over the boards and down the spine, and carefully 'pared'. With a razor-sharp knife the binder thins down the leather in selected places so that where it turns over the boards or in upon itself no double-thickness is noticeable. He coats the inner face of the leather with pure flour-paste – using this natural adhesive because it penetrates both boards and leather. Then he moulds the material over the board edges, spine, silk headbands and inside corners where it is carefully 'mitred' to form a neat 45 degree joint.

The book is then placed between wooden boards for about ten hours until everything has thoroughly dried out. Since books may be 'full', 'half', or 'quarter' bound, complementary cloth or marbled paper is needed for the parts not covered by leather. The insides of the boards are now rendered smooth and the board leaf of each endpaper is pasted down. When dry, the book is closed with thin protective 'tins' inside and is well pressed for at least two hours between spotlessly clean, smooth boards.

The skill needed to transform a binding into a work of art is learnt only through years of practice. Design and lettering are impressed, or 'blind tooled', on to the leather with heated brass tools. The surface of the leather must be clean and free from grease before the albumen size or 'glaire' is sponged over the areas to be tooled and allowed to set. A pure grease, such as olive oil, is then lightly applied over the glaire so that the gold leaf will stick temporarily.

Using considerable skill the binder lays the gold leaf on the surface. He then re-tools the design through the gold leaf. Only experience can tell the craftsman when his tools are at just the right heat for 'gold tooling' – they must be hot enough to activate the albumen size but not so hot as to scorch the surface or dull the gold impression.

Bookbinding can captivate those who practise it for a living and those who come to delight in it as a hobby. Over the past 20 years there have been many indications of a great surge of interest in the craft: the Designer Bookbinders' Association, the restoration by British craftsmen of many books damaged by the Florence floods of 1966, and the proliferation of craft bookbinding courses. All these suggest that future generations will continue, like Samuel Pepys, to buy books as much 'for the sake of the binding' as for the lure of what is inside.

SEWING ON RAISED CORDS

Genuine raised cords – as opposed to recessed cords – are one of the hallmarks of a traditional, hand-bound book. The technique goes back to the craft's early days and results in books of great strength and durability. Five is the most common number of cords, but exceptionally large volumes may have as many as 12. The cords are held in a sewing frame where they match up with markings made on the back of the book. Cords and sections are bound together with a sewing process involving kettle stitches. They form a series of knots which keep the thread firm and ensure the strength of the book's body. Figure-of-eight stitching is used when the book has sets of double raised cords.

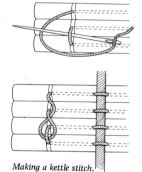

Making a kettle stitch.

THE
BOWYER
AND FLETCHER

THE LONGBOW'S ASTONISHING FIRE-POWER WAS
DECISIVE IN WINNING MANY A MEDIEVAL BATTLE –
OFTEN AGAINST FORMIDABLE ODDS

Eye-witness accounts of Crécy, Poitiers, Agincourt and many other medieval battles are vivid tributes to the terrible power of the longbow. English and Welsh archers capable of firing at least ten carefully aimed shots every minute made it the 'ultimate weapon' of the Middle Ages.

As French knights learned to their cost during the Hundred Years' War of 1337–1453, dense storms of arrows tipped with flesh-tearing 'broadheads' and armour-piercing 'bodkins' enabled great victories to be won in the face of seemingly impossible odds. Five-thousand archers, supported by 1,000 foot-soldiers, routed a 60,000-strong French army at Agincourt in 1415 during the battle immortalised by Shakespeare in *Henry V*.

Fearful slaughter was inevitable when both sides had large forces of skilled and disciplined archers. On March 29, 1461, during the Wars of the Roses, between 28,000 and 38,000 men were killed when the Yorkists defeated the Lancastrians at Towton, 10 miles south-west of York, in the bloodiest battle ever fought on British soil.

Nobody knows when the longbow was first used in Britain – its origins here and in many other lands are lost in the mists of prehistory – but examples nearly 5,000 years old have survived in Somerset. Longbows almost certainly

helped Duke William of Normandy to win the Battle of Hastings in 1066, but it was not until the 12th century that the weapon began to make a really significant impact on military thinking.

It was the fighting men of southern and central Wales who first made their Norman and Anglo-Saxon counterparts appreciate the longbow's immense potential. Some of their exploits were recorded by Giraldus Cambrensis, the cleric and chronicler who travelled throughout the principality in 1188. One of his accounts tells of an attack on Abergavenny Castle in which Welsh arrows 'actually penetrated the oak doorway of the tower, which was almost as thick as a man's palm'.

Giraldus also wrote, 'The bows they use are not made of horn, nor of sapwood, nor yet of yew. The Welsh carve their bows out of the dwarf elm trees in the forest. They are nothing much to look at, not even rubbed smooth, but left in a rough and unpolished state. Still, they are firm and strong. You could not shoot far with them, but they are powerful enough to inflict serious wounds in a close fight.'

The type of longbow that evolved over the next 100 years is still used by traditional archers. Fashioned from native or imported yew, a great deal of which came from northern Spain, it was a much more sophisticated weapon than the early Welsh bows described by Giraldus. It was used by yeomen whose obligations to own a longbow and practise with it regularly were laid down in such documents as the Assize of Arms and the Statute of Winchester.

Yew bows employed in the medieval wars were almost certainly more powerful than all but a few of their present-day counterparts. None has survived from that period, but there is every reason to believe that ranges of 300–350 yds could be achieved with bows of this type when shooting the lighter types of arrow.

Accuracy and fire-power
Modern tests with longbows that would doubtless have been considered puny by the archers who fought at Crécy and Agincourt have proved that bodkins can be shot almost 200 yds. As for accuracy, there is evidence that an archer was 'very lightly esteemed' if he could not shoot at least ten lighter arrows a minute, at a range of 240 yds, without hitting his target at each shot.

New types of protection were developed to ward off the deadly shafts, but even elaborate suits of plate armour – much stronger than chain-mail – could be penetrated by a heavy bodkin unleashed at a relatively short range. Deflected arrows often found a chink in the armour, such as one of the many places where it was jointed, or glanced off to claim a softer secondary target. Horses were always vulnerable, because it was impossible to provide them with complete protection against arrows, and the heavily armoured rider became a clumsy caricature of fighting efficiency the moment his mount was killed or crippled.

The heat generated by a man encased in steel and leather was another problem. The knight who opened his visor to gulp fresh air frequently attracted the lethal attention of a sharp-eyed archer.

Henry VIII, a great longbow enthusiast, was so delighted by *Toxophilus* – the oldest surviving book on archery – that he awarded an annual pension of £10 to its author, Roger Ascham. Although longbows and arrows were stockpiled in arsenals until the middle of the 17th century, the golden age of military archery had ended by the time Ascham's classic work was published in 1544.

As a result, the martial art became a sport, whose character did not change significantly until modern technology devised increasingly astonishing bows, many of which look like figments from a science-fiction artist's

THE IMMENSE POWER OF THE LONGBOW

Mighty bows with draw weights of 100 lb. or more were commonplace when archers formed the backbone of England's army during the Middle Ages. They shot arrows which could penetrate all but the best armour, and did not vanish from military inventories until the Civil War period. Extremely powerful bows with a draw weight of about 200 lb. can speed light arrows to a target almost a quarter of a mile away. Longbows made by Val Rawnsley normally have a 'weight' of up to 55 lb., but are still dramatically potent weapons. Here, he is testing an unfinished bow.

JOINING AND SHAPING THE BOW

Contrary to popular belief, churchyard yews were not cultivated for the benefit of medieval bowyers. They were relics of old, pagan religions whose followers regarded the trees as symbols of eternity and immortality. Six-foot lengths of good bow-wood are not easy to come by nowadays. The majority of traditional longbows are therefore made from paired, or 'sister', billets which are very carefully spliced and glued at the handle where the joint is concealed by the grip. The spokeshave is one of several tools used by the bowyer as he turns a rough stave into a traditional work of art. His other aids range from a small axe to fine sandpaper. A trained eye and a deep knowledge of the timber are essential. The bowyer must be able to gauge its strengths and weaknesses in order to extract the maximum power and durability.

Halves spliced together

imagination. They are very accurate, but there is still a demand for the traditional type of bow.

Osage orange, degame, greenheart, hickory, red cedar, snakewood and several other timbers make good longbows; but the yew, *Taxus baccata*, has long been acknowledged as the best raw material of all.

Suitable trees are now extremely rare in Britain and in Europe, and most traditional bows are made of wood imported from Oregon, in the north-west corner of the United States of America. Yew that has grown in a fairly hard climate makes the finest bow-wood, because the grain is close. By the same token, the wood should ideally be cut in winter when there is relatively little sap in the tree. Three or four years of seasoning are necessary before the craftsman can, with confidence, start shaping a bow from what until then looks no more beautiful or businesslike than a split log.

Some longbows are still made from a single billet of yew, but the majority are created from paired, or sister, billets

joined at the handle. This joining technique produces a bow whose upper and lower limbs are almost perfectly balanced. A true 'self' bow, so called because it is made from a single piece of wood, tends to be stronger at one end. Timber from either bough or trunk can be used.

Good yews make superb longbows because the sapwood and heartwood combine to form a natural laminate whose characteristics are ideally suited to an archer's needs. Sapwood is retained to form the back of the bow – the side facing the target – and performs extremely well under tension. Heartwood forms the belly – the side facing the archer – and reacts favourably when compressed.

A little whittling with a penknife can tell an experienced bowyer a great deal about the potential of his raw material. Timber that whittles smoothly, forming long and springy shavings, will almost certainly prove more satisfactory than wood which comes away in chips.

Rough shaping is done with a light hand-axe. At this

CHECKING FOR FLAWS

The moment of truth arrives when a bow is bent for the first time. The tiller of notched wood enables the bowyer to inspect his work at close quarters while subjecting it to varying amounts of stress. After hours of work, he can see if both 'limbs' are bending evenly, and is also able to check the wood for minute flaws. At a later stage, the draw weight of the bow is checked by drawing it with a spring-balance.

stage, when the billet's innermost secrets are being revealed for the first time, the bowyer starts watching for tell-tale signs. Years of growth may have sealed in wounds left by the claws of bears or the antlers of deer. They are obvious points of weakness which skill and experience – plus a measure of luck – may or may not be able to eliminate.

The bowyer's other enemies include compression fractures, known as chrysals, which may be no bigger than a minute length of fine hair. Fairy writing is a fungal infection that sometimes affects yew sapwood and does, indeed, resemble a mysterious script. Knots and other blemishes occasionally force the bowyer to reject a billet. However, some knots and chrysals can be removed, and replaced with patches or plugs called dutchmen.

Rough-cut billets become a genuine bow stave when they are double-spliced and glued together. Draw-knife, spokeshave and stock scraper are then used for hour after painstaking hour as the timber is gradually shaped into a graceful bow.

The bow stave that emerges from this long and careful process tapers from handle to tips, and has to be traditionally 'stacked' to comply with the British Long Bow Society's rules. In other words, it must have a D-shaped cross-section, with sapwood for the letter's vertical stroke and heartwood filling the curve.

The stave does not become a bow until it is tillered for the first time. The tiller is a stout length of timber which holds the bow securely by the handle while the string is eased down a series of notches. This process, always undertaken with heart in mouth, enables the bowyer to see just how his bow is bending.

Its draw weight can also be measured by pulling the string with a hook attached to a spring-balance.

The weight and the overall size of a bow depend on the weight, build and proportions of the archer. Most are as long as the archer is tall, but relatively short arms and other factors must be taken into account. A bow with a draw weight of 45–55 lb. is suitable for the average male, but 100 lb. and more was probably not uncommon in the Middle Ages, when bowmen practised constantly.

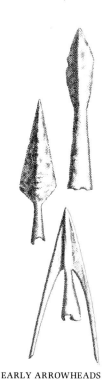

EARLY ARROWHEADS
Many different arrowheads were developed during the Middle Ages, as archer and armourer sought to outwit each other. The top arrowhead is a relatively heavy bodkin, whose use became widespread during the 13th century as armour became increasingly effective. Below it is a broader, flatter type from the early medieval period; it was able to penetrate chain-mail. Barbed heads were used for hunting.

STAGES OF AN ARROW *Ideally, every arrow in a set of eight should come from the same piece of wood so that each will match its counterparts as closely as possible. The timber is first cut into long rectangular staves (1) which are then planed or turned until they are circular (2). Some are perfectly cylindrical, while others – such as flight arrows used for long-range shooting – tend to be shaped like a very elongated barrel, with the thickest part in the middle. Footing an arrow with a different type of wood (3) increases its strength and is also an attractive cosmetic touch. The footing is then planed down (4) before the point, feathers and string-notch are added (5). Coloured bands, known as the crest, decorate the arrow and are an aid to identification.*

SKILLS OF THE FLETCHER

A longbow without its correct arrows is only marginally more useful than a rifle with bullets of the wrong calibre. Sets of competition arrows are matched for weight and 'spine', or flexibility. All arrows bend as they leave the bow, undergoing a phenomenon known as the Archer's Paradox. If they bend to different extents, the archer's performance cannot be consistent. The fletcher must therefore match his arrows to each other and to the bow from which they will be shot. 'The stronger the bow the stiffer the arrow' is the golden rule.

FOOTING THE STAVE

'Footing' an arrow increases its strength, and also makes it look more attractive. The stave is planed to a taper and then forced into a saw-cut footing of beefwood – so called because of its red colour – or another suitably hard timber. The arrow is then glued and bound before the footing is planed to match the rest of the shaft. Ash arrows were popular during the Middle Ages, but red deal and other woods are now used.

SECURING THE POINT

One of the tricks of the trade is to mix a pinch of fine brick-dust into the shellac which is used to glue the point, or 'pile', of the arrow to the shaft. The dust helps the heated adhesive to bond to both wood and steel. Today's arrowheads are made of turned steel. Their medieval counterparts were forged to high standards by arrowsmiths who were specialised craftsmen.

CUTTING THE FLETCHINGS

Making a top-quality set of eight competition arrows can involve just as much time as fashioning a yew bow. The feathers, or fletchings, are extremely important and must be matched as accurately as the arrows themselves. Fletchers rely on such birds as the grey goose, turkey and heron, all of which have strong, resilient wing feathers. The feathers are cut by hand or with a 'burning jig' of hot wire.

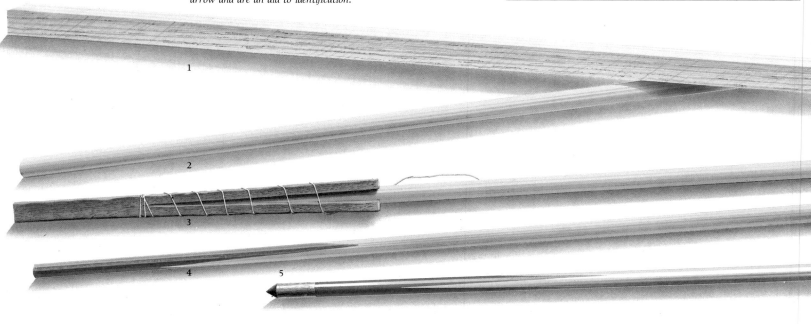

1

2

3

4   5

Val Rawnsley, perhaps the only full-time maker of traditional British longbows, has made bows of up to 180 lb. Even a weapon in the 50–60 lb. range can send a bodkin straight through a sturdy oil-drum or dustbin.

When the bowyer is satisfied that the bow is bending properly and is 'in tiller', he sets an arrow-plate into the upper limb, just above the handle, so that the departing shaft will not in any way damage the wood. Plates are generally mother-of-pearl, but ivory, tortoiseshell and similar materials may be used. Horn nocks with angled grooves for the string are glued to the bow's tips before it is ready to be finished with sandpaper, fine wire wool, French polish and a touch of linseed oil.

A block of cork or soft wood forms the handle block around which the grip is fashioned. It is bound with thread, fine cord or supple leather and, ideally, should be tailored to fit snugly into the archer's fist. When the finished bow is braced, the gap between the string and the belly side of the grip should be a fistmele – the span of a clenched fist and a raised thumb.

A leather bracer protects the forearm which holds the bow. The archer also needs a leather tab for the three fingers – one above the arrow, two below – that are used to draw the bow. Before the Battle of Agincourt, Henry V reminded his men that the French had vowed to cut these fingers from the right hand of every archer they captured.

Synthetic fibres, linen, hemp, and even such comparatively exotic materials as silk, are used to make the bowstring. One end is made into a permanent loop, while the other has an adjustable 'archer's knot' so that the string can be easily lengthened or shortened.

The world-wide shortage of suitable yew has made the laminated, or composite, longbow increasingly popular, although the limbs must be made of wood to satisfy the British Long Bow Society.

What could be termed a 'traditional-laminated' bow might be made from layers of degame, greenheart and white hickory. They are glued together, compressed in a former, and then worked very like staves of yew. Laminated bows are less expensive than self bows. They also tend to be slightly more robust, although a few exceptional yew longbows can still be shot when they are a century old.

The number of 'Fletchers' listed in any telephone directory is a reminder that arrow making was a trade in its own right during the great days of the longbow. It still demands a great deal of craftsmanship, because the competitive archer needs sets of arrows that are together perfectly balanced, otherwise his shooting will lack consistency. They must also complement the weight and draw of his bow.

FINISHING TOUCHES *Each arrow has three feathers; two stand parallel to the bowstring, while the 'cock' feather faces away from it. They must be strong, because the arrow spins as it flies. Feathers are glued to the shaft; modern adhesives are very strong, but medieval fletchers often used very fine thread as well as glue.*

Roger Ascham maintained that ash 'is much the best wood for shafts', but listed oak, birch, beech and brazil as acceptable alternatives. Port Orford cedar and red deal are now popular choices among traditionalists who resolutely eschew the high-technology shafts of tubular aluminium and other materials favoured by some modern archers. The size of the arrow depends on the draw of the bow, which in turn is dictated by the length of the archer's arms.

Sets of eight arrows should be made from the same piece of wood to achieve the closest possible match. The wood is sawn into staves, which are then rounded either by hand or on a lathe. Some arrows consist of a single piece of wood, but the best are footed – like the gripped end of a snooker cue – by splicing them into such strong and resilient timbers as beefwood and greenheart. Nocks for the bowstring are made of horn, secured with glue, and the piles, or points, are of turned steel.

Grey-goose feathers traditionally formed the fletchings, but turkey feathers are widely used nowadays and are glued to the shaft. Medieval fletchers often supplemented their glue with a binding of very fine thread, but modern adhesives are more trustworthy, and binding is no longer considered necessary.

After the arrows are fletched they are crested, or personalised, with bands of colour. This is partly for decoration, but the distinctive markings also help identification when a number of arrows shot by different competitors are in a target together.

The crafts of the bowyer and fletcher count for little if their products are not treated with care. Bows do not appreciate central heating, for example, and should be hung from the upper nock in a cool place with an even temperature. They should be polished with beeswax, particularly after being used in wet conditions. Beeswax also protects arrows and bowstrings.

If these and other basic precautions are taken, the archer with a traditional, craftsman-made longbow can enjoy the sport eulogised by Roger Ascham more than 400 years ago. 'Archery', he proclaimed, 'is a pastime fit for the mind, wholesome for the body ... fit for all ages, persons and places.'

WEIGHING AN ARROW

Val Rawnsley follows the traditional method of weighing each arrow against old silver coins, instead of more conventional weights. A typical arrow for a longbow with a 55 lb. draw weighs about 'five shillings' – equal to 436 grains or an ounce. A silver threepenny piece weighs 21.8 grains.

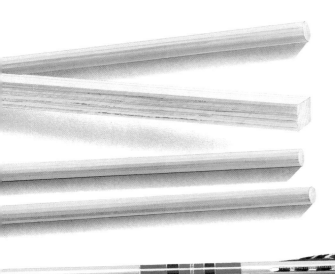

THE BRICKMAKER

THE SUBTLE COLOURS AND INDIVIDUAL PATTERNS OF
HAND-MADE BRICKS ENSURE A CONTINUING DEMAND, IN
SPITE OF THEIR RELATIVELY HIGH COST

The surprising discovery about hand-made bricks is that such seemingly mundane objects, so eminently suited to mass production by the million, are still being turned out one at a time by skilled men at a number of brickworks. There is a rewarding earthy satisfaction in the process – not unlike the deep-rooted delights of making bread – for the soft, tactile clay that forms bricks is mixed, folded and kneaded like super-heavy dough.

Like bread, bricks are baked in an oven – but at temperatures that would vaporise a loaf. For this oven is a kiln, in which temperatures around 2,200°F (1,200°C) bake the clay stone hard. Babylonians knew the secret of baking clay into bricks 6,000 years ago, and the Romans brought it to Britain. Roman bricks were so durable that they can sometimes be seen built into the walls of Saxon and Norman churches, though for 800 years after the Romans left the craft almost died, and very few bricks were made in this country.

They continued to be made on the Continent, however, and were brought to East Anglia as ballast in ships during medieval times. A few Flemish craftsmen also crossed the Channel and set up kilns, but generally houses were built of the cheapest materials available locally, such as stone, flint, timber or cob – a mixture of clay, straw and chalk.

Brickmaking began to revive in Britain around the start of the 15th century. The palaces of Hampton Court and St James in London, and houses such as Compton Wynyates in Warwickshire, are handsome testimonies to the burgeoning of the craft in the 16th century.

Later, a number of fires among old wooden buildings – and notably the Fire of London in 1666 – resulted in an urgent demand for bricks, as they were adopted widely for building town houses. For as well as being strong and weatherproof, they do not catch fire. Brickworks sprang up in many parts of the country, wherever there was clay of a suitable colour and consistency. Many survived until this century, when mechanisation and an ever-improving transport network enabled a few giants to force many smaller firms out of business.

The clay used in brickmaking is excavated with a mechanical digger after the covering of topsoil has been removed. It is then left to weather for up to six months: at one time the law demanded that it should be left all winter, so that unwanted salts could be washed away by rain, and frost could break it down to a satisfactory consistency. A white efflorescence seen sometimes on the surface of bricks can be caused by a failure to remove these salts, but it may also result from the bricks absorbing salts from the ground at the building site.

The weathered clay is made ready for moulding into brick-shape by being mixed with water, then passed between rollers and through a sort of mincing machine – a process once carried out by men who trod the clay with their bare feet. This removes any lumps or hard stones that could expand under heat and cause a brick to explode in the kiln. It also leaves the clay with just the right consistency for the brickmaker to handle.

Why bricks vary in colour

Clays vary in colour according to their chemical composition – in particular, the quantity of iron oxides they contain. Where a fair amount of natural pigment is present, the temperature of firing in the kiln will dictate the final appearance of the bricks. If the clay has little natural colour, stains have to be mixed with the moulding sand to give the required finish.

At the Colchester firm of Colliers – as also at the Bulmer Brickworks in Suffolk – brickmakers can still be found at their moulding benches. Beside each craftsman stands a mound of pug, or prepared clay, and before him lies the mould for the particular type of brick he is producing. This mould is a four-sided box made of wood or metal – but without a lid or bottom. Its dimensions vary in different districts, to suit the local clay. Some clays can shrink by as much as 12 per cent during drying and firing.

The mould fits over a base that is raised in the middle, so that the brick is formed with an indentation on one side called the 'frog'. This is the hollow that will be filled with mortar when the brick is eventually laid, to strengthen the bond. Often the initials of the brickworks are also impressed in the frog. In bricks with a decorative face, a decorative motif replaces the frog.

To fill the mould, the craftsman scoops from his mound of pug a lump slightly larger than is needed, then rolls and folds it into a short, fat sausage shape. He rolls it again, in sand to prevent it sticking, then throws the lump into the mould with just enough force to fill it completely and expel any pockets of air trapped in the clay. After removing the surplus pug from the top, he places a wooden board, or pallet, on top like a lid, and with a swift movement turns the mould upside down and lifts it, leaving the brick-to-be standing on the pallet.

Still on their pallets, the bricks are then put on a barrow and wheeled away to be dried in long rows. At older

ORNAMENTAL BRICKS

The National Trust is one of the main customers for ornamental bricks needed as matching replacements in ancient buildings. At the Bulmer brickworks, in Suffolk, the wooden moulds are made to order and scaled up in size to allow for shrinkage when the bricks dry out. The design or motif is raised in reverse on the base of the mould.

Wooden mould

STRIKING OFF *The brickmaker uses a taut wire bow, rather like a cheese cutter, to remove surplus clay from the top of the mould. It takes only a few seconds to mould each brick ready for drying and firing.*

brickworks, they were simply allowed to dry in open-sided sheds, but often frost would cause them to disintegrate in winter, or too much heat would warp them in summer. Nowadays, exhaust heat from the kiln does the job in a few days and without risk of damage.

Stacking bricks in the kiln calls for great experience. They must not be too near the heat source, but laid in such a way that the heat percolates through them gradually. For the first two or three days after the kiln is fired up at Colliers, a white smoke is given off, turning to a blue haze as any remaining traces of moisture are driven out and the clay begins to 'burn'. Then for two more days the bricks are given the full heat treatment and the kiln is sealed off with old bricks and clay. It is then left to cool for three or four more days before being opened up and unloaded.

Colliers fire their bricks in a tunnel kiln. The Bulmer kiln is circular, with the heat drawn down from the top and extracted through a series of flues.

One kiln load produces bricks in a variety of colours, ranging from light to dark. Dark bricks come from close to the source of heat and sometimes have black ends, which can be used to create the diamond-form patterns, owner's initials and dates seen on many old buildings. Terracotta – which means 'burnt earth' – is made by sifting and sieving the clay to give it a much finer texture.

Probably fewer than one in every hundred bricks produced in Britain are hand-made. An occasional new house is built with them – about 30,000 are needed for the job – and sometimes they are used for extensions to houses built originally with hand-made bricks. Architects may also specify them to enhance new buildings, and very special ones can be made to replace ornamental brickwork that has deteriorated in ancient buildings. The necessary moulds are still made at Bulmer.

Hand-made bricks cost about twice as much as those made by machine. But with their slightly rough texture and subtle variations in colouring, they are infinitely more pleasing to the eye.

LOADING THE KILN

After moulding, bricks at the Bulmer brickworks are carried first to the drying sheds and then to the circular kiln. The long, single-wheel barrow seen above is used for carrying freshly made bricks to the drying area. When they are dry, it takes a week to load the kiln, which holds 12,000 bricks, and a further week to fire them. Their final colour, which varies from orange to deep purple, depends on the bricks' position in the kiln.

THE
BROOM SQUIRE

NOTWITHSTANDING HIS ODD NAME – ORIGIN UNKNOWN –
THE MAKER OF BESOM BROOMS PERFORMS A THOROUGHLY
FUNCTIONAL TASK WHICH MEETS A STEADY DEMAND

A family named West has been making birch brooms in a small Hampshire village for at least four centuries. The craft has been passed on from father to son, and the latest of the line uses exactly the same sort of tools that his ancestors used when they first set up in business.

Business is still good. Finished brooms – or besoms, as they are also called – are sold in bundles of a dozen to all parts of the world. They have one or two surprising uses, apart from sweeping garden lawns and paths. Steel workers find them ideal for brushing away the coating of impurities from the surface of newly made steel plates. And in vinegar brewing, the bottoms of vats are lined with handle-less brooms known as swales to filter the vinegar. Moreover, the birch adds colour to the vinegar and also helps to create its acetic acid content.

Birch brooms have been made and used in Britain since Saxon times and possibly earlier. The tree grows profusely on the sandy heathlands of southern Britain, and the broom squire generally buys standing birch by the acre in the autumn. Cutting goes on through the winter months, and he prefers trees about seven years old, carefully selecting his twigs from the crown. Although many generations of craftsmen have drawn heavily on the region's birches, the hardy, fast-growing trees remain as prolific as ever.

In northern Hampshire there are workshops in villages such as Tadley and Baughurst where broom squires have carried on their craft since the 16th century. The West family business is, as it has always been, in Tadley.

There is a history of besom-making, too, in other parts of the south-east, including Surrey and Sussex. Surrey heathlands, in particular, have an abundance of birch, the basic raw material of the besom maker.

These craftsmen work at such tremendous speed that they need great quantities of twigs ready to hand when the broom-making season starts in spring. The cut bundles are piled in huge 14 ft high stacks in the workshop yards, where they must season for several months. This seasoning is of crucial importance: too little and the finished broom will be brittle and useless – pliancy is essential for it to do its job properly. So the stacks are built in a special way – open enough to let the wind penetrate and help the seasoning process, while still preventing rain and melting snow from reaching the centre of the pile and causing rot.

Stacking the birch brushwood

The bundles of brushwood are built up in layers, lengthways and crossways alternately, each bundle head to tail with the next. The layers must be perfectly level and square, so that the stack does not collapse in a high wind. When complete, the stack is thatched over with more bundles of brush, steeply pitched so that the rain runs off easily. The birch is ready for use when the twigs have become both hard and pliable.

Large numbers of handles are, of course, also needed. A variety of woods may be used, but they are usually hazel, ash, lime or chestnut. These too are selected, cut and stacked in thatched-over piles for months. When they are seasoned the broom squire holds them in a 'horse' similar to that used by many woodland craftsmen, and strips away the bark with a double-handled draw-knife. A semicircular draw-shave is used to smooth them, and their ends are chopped to a point with an axe. Finally they are piled up close to the workshop ready for use. As they need not be perfectly straight, wood not good enough for other craftsmen can often be bought cheaply.

Making the broom heads starts with opening up a seasoned stack, trimming the bundles with a short-handled billhook or axe, then sorting them for quality and length. This task is often done by women and children, who re-bundle unsuitable twigs for sale as firewood. Those selected for brooms are once more tied into separate bundles – longer, rougher brushwood for the core and the smoother, shorter twigs for the outside. Like the handles, the heads too are piled outside the workshop for instant use.

Once in action making the besom itself, the broom squire works at a formidable pace. He sits astride a low bench known as a broom horse – similar in many ways to the shaving horse but specially adapted to his particular needs.

SIXTY YEARS AT HIS CRAFT *Peter Burrows, who lives and works in Surrey, was only five years old when he began helping his father to make besoms. Today, more than a half a century later, he is still hard at work. Satisfied customers ensure a steady demand, as a besom used regularly is unlikely to last for more than a year. Mr Burrows, seen here binding the head of a besom with wire, cuts birch-tree crowns from an acre of woodland each winter to provide sufficient twigs for his annual output.*

Grabbing a handful of the longer, rougher twigs, he rolls them into a circular shape, then arranges another handful of shorter, smoother ones around them. Broom heads are made in two sizes, measuring 12 in. or 10 in. around the base of the head. The craftsman judges this entirely by hand and eye: when the tips of the fingers of both hands meet around the base, it is a 12 in. one; when they just overlap, it is the smaller size. Once he is satisfied with its size and shape, the head is ready for binding.

Willow twigs, thin strips of ash, oak and chestnut – even bramble – were once used for the binding. Later these were largely replaced by strips of imported cane, but supplies dried up with the outbreak of war in 1939 and craftsmen began using galvanised wire. Nowadays most of them still do, the wire lying in a coil by the broom horse and being led through its jaws via a small staple at the front. He is able to clamp or release it by simply pressing on a treadle with both feet.

When he is satisfied with the size and shape of the broom, he inserts the end of the wire about 4 in. from the top of the head. By rolling the whole bundle towards him he binds it with several strands, then clamps the wire. Heaving back, he pulls the binding really tight, and taking his pliers cuts it, twists the ends together and taps the twist flat. He repeats the process with another length of wire just below the first. Finally he chops the top of the head off square with a short-handled axe on a chopping block beside him. The head is then ready to be fitted with its handle.

This takes but moments: the pointed end of the handle is pushed into the exact centre of the broom head, then driven in about 9 in. with sharp blows, care being taken that it goes in absolutely square. It is held in place by a nail hammered through it between the two bindings. Sometimes the craftsman will fix it instead with a wooden peg. To do this he drills a hole in the handle with a small spiral auger, then taps the peg through.

He will complete a large number before tying them together in bundles of a dozen for sale. So swiftly does he work that he can turn out up to 12 dozen brooms a day. And happily the demand for them is still so great that he can seldom keep up with it.

Brooms are also made in the north of England and in Wales – but traditionally of heather rather than birch. The heather is cut during the spring and is used immediately, without first being seasoned. In some remote coastal districts, such as the west coast of Anglesey, marram grass has occasionally been used for making besoms, being about the only vegetation capable of surviving on the windswept dunes. Like heather, it forms a somewhat softer head than one made of birch twigs.

STRIPPING THE BARK *The craftsman clamps the handle in a horse while smoothing it with a knife.*

SECURING THE HEAD *As the bundle of twigs is rolled backwards, the galvanised wire binds them tightly.*

TRIMMING THE BUTT *After being bound in two places, the upper end is trimmed square with an axe.*

FIXING THE HANDLE *The pointed end is pushed into the head, then driven home with a series of sharp blows.*

BESOMS FROM NORTHERN AND SOUTHERN BRITAIN

In the south of England, most besoms have heads made from birch twigs and handles cut from hazel, ash, lime or chestnut. Birch is sometimes used, but chestnut is especially good because the bark peels off easily. In northern England and North Wales, heather is often used for the heads instead of birch twigs. Both sorts are made in much the same way, though with strips of ash (as here) sometimes replacing wire as the binding material.

Heather besom   Birch besom

THE
CALLIGRAPHER

USING HAND-MIXED INKS AND A GOOSE-QUILL
PEN, THE CALLIGRAPHER TRANSFORMS THE EVERYDAY
SKILL OF WRITING INTO AN EXQUISITE ART

Calligraphy has been described as writing elevated to an art form. A superb example is the 8th-century *Book of Kells*, now in Trinity College, Dublin. It was written by monks on vellum, with lavish illuminations and illustrations, and among the glowing colours that have remained fresh through 12 centuries is a deep clear blue that tells a story. This blue was made with the mineral lapis lazuli, brought thousands of miles from what was then its only known source, Afghanistan. Ground to powder it forms the pigment ultramarine. Although lapis lazuli has now become a fairly common gemstone, it was then more precious than gold. So was the vermilion red used – mercuric sulphide imported at enormous cost from Spain. At least 200 carefully selected calf-skins went to make the vellum for the book's 340 leaves, and originally it was bound in gold. The bill for materials alone would have been enormous, indicating the importance of the book.

But these were just the exotic trimmings. The rest was ink and inspiration – and years of patient work.

The calligrapher, or scribe, worked with tools of austere simplicity: quill pens and a sharp knife to cut them, a few brushes and perhaps a pair of compasses or dividers. The materials were provided. His style, his flourishes and his flashes of inspiration were all his own. So were any slips of his hand or other mistakes, which were eradicable at the cost of spoiling a page. His skills not only survive, but have enjoyed a resurgence of interest.

These skills go back thousands of years beyond the medieval masters – back to the invention of papyrus paper by the ancient Egyptians, which truly changed the world. Strong, light and relatively cheap, papyrus was easy to write on with a simple reed pen and ink, easy to handle, and easy to carry. It spread the art of writing.

The Egyptians themselves developed faster methods of handwriting from their hieroglyphic script, and many fine examples of their clear, flowing penmanship survive. Papyrus was supplanted gradually by the more durable animal-skin materials such as parchment and vellum, and by papers developed by other methods in the Far East – where calligraphy has long been considered a major art form, equal to painting.

The quill pen, made from the large flight feathers of various birds, began to replace the reed in western countries as parchment replaced papyrus, around AD 200. The English word pen is from the Latin *penna*, meaning 'feather'. Though both reed and quill remained in use through the Middle Ages, the quill became dominant until the metal pen was introduced in England in the 18th century.

Modern masters, with an armoury of sophisticated writing instruments available to them, still like to use a quill. They like also to write on vellum or parchment, to cut their own pens, and to mix their own inks and colours.

Donald Jackson is one such master. He gets very busy around the time of the Queen's birthday, 'doing the Honours' for life peers and such – producing magnificent scrolls gleaming with gold leaf, flourishingly inscribed, heavy with great red seals. His own inspired works of calligraphic art are much sought after. They all emanate from a tousled first-floor room of a tall, terraced house in Camberwell. A particularly fine example of his work may now be seen in the Victoria and Albert Museum.

Putting some finishing touches to it – and working on three presentation scrolls at the same time – provides a perfect demonstration of how vital to his art is a profound knowledge of the natural materials he uses, how necessary is a quite literal *feel* for them.

He starts by making a fresh goose-quill pen, which will have a nib of the exact size he needs for the particular script he has chosen. As he cuts it with short, firm strokes of his special knife, he explains how the slight judder of the blade tells him that the quill has been tempered to just the right degree of hardness.

Next he mixes some ink. The sort he uses comes in small rectangular sticks from China or Japan. 'They're just highly compressed soot, really,' he remarks. He puts a few drops of water into a hollowed dish, and gently rubs the end of the ink-stick against the bottom of the dish, grinding off the minute quantity needed to make, perhaps, two teaspoons of jet black liquid that will flow freely in a pen. He dips the end of the quill in it.

Then he writes on the vellum, swiftly and decisively, the quill moving in delicately graceful arcs, giving little squeaks under pressure ('Bob Cratchit would recognise that sound!') as the words flow. He explains that the quill must move quickly and naturally, or the spontaneity of line that gives the script character and individuality will be lost – it will look mechanical. In a remarkably short 20 minutes or so the lines are written – but as Mr Jackson says, it has taken many years to learn how.

His next task is to replace some raised and gilded words on another work-in-progress, with which he is not entirely satisfied. The words are simply scraped off the vellum with an ultra-sharp knife, leaving the surface unmarked visually, but subtly changed in texture – a condition which he will have to take into account.

The raised and gilded lettering is created by burnishing gold leaf on to work drawn or painted first with a mixture called gesso. This mixture contains sugar, white lead, fish

CUTTING A GOOSE-QUILL PEN

The feather for a goose-quill pen must first be tempered by soaking it in water, then dipping it in hot sand, to make the quill hard and springy. The nib is cut with a special knife – the blade is flat on one side and rounded on the other, and its wooden handle is shaped like an elongated teardrop. After stripping the feather from the shaft, Mr Jackson holds it in his left hand and, with the knife in his right, cuts towards himself. He keeps the thumb of his knife-hand under the tip of the quill to hold it steady, and the flat side of the blade uppermost, so that the rounded under-side hollows out the curve of the nib. When it is shaped to his satisfaction, he inserts the pointed tip of the knife handle into the hollow of the nib and gives a light push: a just audible click announces that the small vertical split which allows the ink to flow has been made. Finally he cuts the angled chisel tip of the nib to the width he needs. The whole job takes only about 30 seconds.

glue, slaked plaster and Armenian bole – an iron-oxide based gilder's clay. The calligrapher mixes it slowly with his forefinger in an egg-cup, using a few drops of water mixed with white of egg, trying not to make any bubbles of air. Some fine bubbles suddenly appear. He gives a grin, hooks his little finger into his ear for a little wax, and gently touches the surface of the mixture with it. 'A trick of the trade,' he says, as the bubbles disappear. When the mixture reaches the right consistency, somewhere between single and double cream, he dips a fresh quill in it and begins writing. The thickness of the creamy medium 'raises' the surface of the letters – but the consistency must be just right, or the gesso will craze or crumble later under the pressure of the burnishing tool. He sets it aside to dry.

The ultra-thin gold leaf is applied over this lettering by first blowing on the work through a thin tube to moisten the surface, then picking up a piece of gold leaf with the tip of a forefinger, and laying it over the raised letters. The gold is then pressed firmly down with the polished stone tip of a burnishing tool. It sticks only to the gesso – the remainder is removed gently with a soft eraser and knife-point, care being taken not to use too much pressure on a surface already slightly disturbed by the previous erasure.

Mr Jackson bemoans the increasing difficulty he encounters in obtaining basics like good hand-made paper (it must be made with long-staple cotton) and real fish glue, insisting that his materials *have* to be natural to achieve the standards he sets himself.

Donald Jackson went to art school at the age of 13 in Bolton, Lancashire, and at 20 he was lecturing at Camberwell School of Art. When pressure of work allows, he still lectures in Britain and America, passing on the message that there are no better or more personally satisfying methods than the old ones – even for the elegant and advanced styles of his private work. He is, in all senses, a modern traditionalist.

ELEGANT STYLE – AND A SWIFT TECHNIQUE

A superb example of Donald Jackson's formal style, this document records the creation of a life peerage. It was written with a goose-quill on vellum and decorated with gold leaf. The writing technique calls for swift, decisive strokes of the pen. For example, the 'f' below is made with three rapid strokes. The pen is held with the broad tip angled to the right.

THE CANDLEMAKER

ALTHOUGH THEIR HISTORY IS PRE-BIBLICAL, THE
METHOD OF MAKING THESE 'ICICLES OF WAX' HAS CHANGED
SURPRISINGLY LITTLE OVER THE CENTURIES

*M*ost candles are now mass produced in factories – mechanisation was introduced around the beginning of the 19th century – but some are still made by craftsmen whose techniques have changed only in detail since the Middle Ages. The medieval candle makers were themselves the heirs to a tradition that was old long before the birth of Christ.

Chapter 25 of the Book of Exodus relates how God instructed Moses to make an elaborate, multi-branched candlestick for the tabernacle when the Israelites were wandering in the wilderness. Its 'candles' consisted of wicks fuelled by containers of olive oil. Candles very like those used today were burned by the peoples of ancient Egypt, Crete, China, Japan and other countries where remarkably advanced civilisations evolved thousands of years ago.

Some were marked at regular intervals to record the passage of time. In more primitive parts of the world, wicks were pushed down the throats of dead fish and sea-birds whose natural fats and oils produced a smelly, spluttering flame that was anything but romantic. Fulmar oil was used on St Kilda, the most isolated of the Hebridean islands, until the entire population was evacuated to the mainland in 1930.

Candle making was firmly established as a trade in 13th-century Europe, but candles continued to be made domestically until Victorian times, particularly in the more remote

MAKING RUSHLIGHTS

Many humble homes, particularly those in rural areas, were lit by the feeble flicker of rushlights until as late as the present century, when mass-production techniques made candles available at prices which most people could afford. One of the oldest and simplest means of illumination, the rushlight was made by peeling the outer skin from a rush to reveal its thin, pith-retaining core. The slender strip was then soaked in tallow (animal fat) and had to be burned in a special holder. It was not sufficiently strong or stable to stand up on its own. Rushlights were smoky and smelly, but better than nothing during the long, dark nights of winter when firelight was often the only alternative.

Rushlight and holder

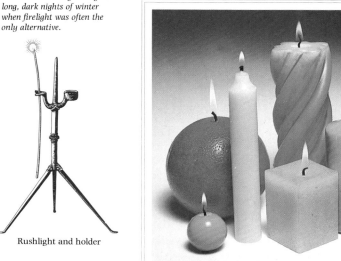

MOULDED CANDLES

Candles have been moulded in Europe since at least the 15th century, and the technique is still popular with both professional and amateur craftworkers. Its great advantage is that it enables candles to be made in a great variety of shapes and colours using simple household items as moulds.

rural areas. The most common raw material was tallow, an animal fat that gives off a good deal of smoke and burns with an acrid aroma. Availability was its great asset.

In direct contrast, beeswax has long been acknowledged as one of the finest 'fuels' for candles, but demand has always far exceeded supply. For that reason, beeswax candles were frequently reserved for religious purposes, such as symbolic altar lights, and beeswax was used to pay tithes to the church. In some areas special diets including ingredients such as lentil purée and white wine were devised for bees so that they produced the best possible wax for candles. The refined form, known as cerosin, has a higher melting point than ordinary beeswax and therefore is slower burning and longer lasting.

Other raw materials used in various parts of the world have included berries with waxy skins from the sumac tree of China and Japan, and the very hard carnauba wax from the Brazilian palm. Candles made from whale-derived spermaceti, which has a very low melting point, provided the standard by which artificial light is measured. One candlepower is the light produced by a pure spermaceti candle weighing 2 oz. and burning at a rate of 120 grains an hour.

All these substances are still used, to a certain extent, but paraffin wax is the most popular. It is a petroleum by-product whose suitability for candles was first exploited by a Scotsman, James Young, midway through the 19th century. It is often blended with stearin, or stearic acid, a pure form of animal fat that was also introduced during the 19th century.

The discovery of stearin is credited to a Frenchman, Michel Chevreul. It makes paraffin wax stronger, stiffer and slower burning.

Wicks of plaited cotton or linen, still used today, were introduced in 1825 by another French innovator, Henri Cambacérès. They are treated with such chemicals as nitrate of bismuth and boric acid, which produce a self-consuming effect.

Most traditional candle makers now buy machine-made wicks, but a few still produce their own. They are braided from three strings, the thickness of which depends on the thickness of the candle, and then soaked for about two hours in a solution of salt, borax and warm water. The wick is then hung up to dry and 'cure' for approximately 72 hours. Coloured flames are achieved by soaking wicks in a variety of chemicals, which can also be added to the wax.

The technique of dipping

Hand-dipping, the traditional way to make candles, was generally undertaken by the ladies of the household. They were at their busiest in the autumn, when stocks were prepared in readiness for winter. This method involves hanging wicks from a frame, or frames, then dipping them swiftly in a cauldron of molten wax.

Makers of Welsh 'water candles' still use a technique in which the wax floats on hot water. This avoids the problem that could otherwise be caused by the level of wax in the cauldron falling to a point where the candles could no longer be dipped along their entire length.

The first few dips leave an almost invisible coating on the wicks, but they soon start to take on a delicate, natural shape as the process continues. Dipped candles taper gracefully outwards from top to bottom, because the wax flows very gently and evenly downwards. They are generally dipped about 40 times to make a candle whose base is as thick as a man's thumb. Wax-based or oil-based colours and perfumes are often added. Gradations of colour are produced by slightly decreasing the depth to which the candles are dipped towards the end of the process.

Very few workshops are completely free from draughts, and even the most gentle breeze can bend hot candles very slightly. For this reason, the frames are turned two or three times to keep them straight.

Candles on the outside of each frame bend a little because they cool rather faster than those near the centre. They are carefully straightened by hand. 'Icicles' of wax accumulate at the base of each candle and are removed with a pair of scissors. This operation calls for considerable deftness and speed, because the wax is constantly hardening.

One of the main advantages of dipped candles is that minute pockets of air, trapped between the many layers of wax, help make the finished product burn with a strong, steady flame. A good, hand-dipped candle, thumb-thick at the base and 1 ft long, should burn for nine or ten hours.

Moulds, originally made of wood, have been used in Europe since at least the 15th century, when they were pioneered by a Parisian candle maker. Moulds used today are of virtually any material that will not melt when molten wax is poured in. Metal, glass, plastic, cardboard and sand are just five of the many possibilities.

A simple, cylindrical mould, suitable for making the most traditionally shaped candle, has the burning end of the wick suspended at the top while the other end is secured through a sealed hole in the base plate. Wax is then poured carefully into the mould, and the finished candle released either by opening the mould if it is hinged, or by breaking it.

Attractive results are achieved by using different-coloured waxes and tilting the mould this way and that as each layer is poured. Another variation involves pouring a relatively pale, semi-translucent wax into a mould containing numerous fragments of coloured wax.

Moulded candles are popular because they can be made in virtually any shape. Bottles, for instance, make very eye-catching candles that can be decorated to look like the original. Expert candle makers can replace the natural contents of an egg with wax carefully poured through a small hole. Decorative techniques include 'découpage' – the application of paper cut-outs – painting, adding colours derived from melted wax crayons, carving, texturing with heated tools and pinching with pliers or tweezers after the candle has been dipped in hot water to soften its surface.

Plain or fancy, dipped or moulded, candles reign supreme as the most romantic of all man-made lights. Their mellow magic, soft and golden, enhances the atmosphere of everything from an intimate dinner party to the majestic interior of a great cathedral.

MAKING CANDLES BY HAND-DIPPING

Strong arms and a resilient back are among the natural assets needed by the candle maker who uses the traditional hand-dipping method. Although not heavy in itself, the work involves a great deal of holding and bending as the wick-draped frames are moved constantly between the rack and the container of molten wax. It takes about 40 dips to create a candle whose base is roughly the same thickness as a man's thumb. The finished candles look like bunches of colourful, exotic fruits.

THE CHARCOAL BURNER

LIVING IN A TWILIGHT WORLD, DEEP IN THE WOODS,
THESE WANDERING CRAFTSMEN PLAYED A VITAL PART
IN THE DEVELOPMENT OF ART AND INDUSTRY

To those who still remember them, there was something a little uncanny, a touch gnomish, about the last of the traditional charcoal burners. Living rough for weeks on end in turf-covered wigwams in the depths of the woods where they tended their sullenly smouldering clamps of timber, they were glimpsed only occasionally. By day they might be shrouded in a swirl of blue-grey smoke, or by night, silhouetted against the red glow of a flare-up. Small wonder that they figured so frequently in the folklore and fairy tales of Europe.

Yet their craft was an entirely practical one, and one that was vital to the technological development of the world. For thousands of years, until the introduction of coke, charcoal was the only medium for smelting metals, since it was the only material that would both produce concentrated heat and, at the same time, form itself into a slow-burning cake strong enough to bear the weight of the ore piled on top. The glory of medieval glass would have been impossible without it, while less beneficially it was also an essential ingredient in gunpowder. Even today, though now largely made in kilns, charcoal has a variety of uses – in the manufacture of sugar, penicillin and fertilisers, as a deodorant, gas-absorbent and insulator. It is hard to say when the last charcoal burners using traditional methods fired their last wood-piles. Perhaps it was a quarter of a century ago, perhaps less, but until that time they practised skills whose roots went back to the beginning of the Iron Age.

Known as 'colliers' long before the first coal mine was sunk, they plied their craft in such ancient wooded areas as the Weald of Kent and Sussex, the Forest of Dean and the Furness Fells of the Lake District where there were also deposits of iron ore. But since it took 7 tons of wood to make 1 ton of charcoal, it was considerably easier to move the ore to the wood rather than the other way around. Until well into the 18th century, the distribution of iron foundries in Britain depended very much upon the distribution of woodlands and the consequent availability of charcoal.

Different grades of charcoal are produced from different kinds of wood. Artists, for example, prefer fine willow charcoal, but in the old days at least, the bulk of the supply for industry was obtained from coppiced oak. This wood-land harvest was grown by felling medium-sized trees from a point just above the ground and leaving the bole, or stool, to shoot. After about 15 years of struggling upwards towards the light, the shoots or poles had attained a height of a dozen feet or more, and a thickness at the base of several inches. When the poles were cut, usually in the early spring as the sap began to rise, the bark was removed and sent to the tanners – oak-bark tannin played an important part in the treatment of hides. The thicker parts of the poles were sold to the bobbin and cotton-reel makers. The top 3 ft or so, some 2 in. across, was the part used by the colliers.

The process of charcoal burning had probably changed

HOME FAR FROM HOME

Once the clamps of wood were lit, two charcoal burners had to stand watch and watch about, 24 hours a day, three or four months on end, to guard against a sudden flare-up that might destroy the season's work. During this time they took turns to rest in a hut built of turf on a triangular wooden frame. Meals were brought from the village by wives and children and, as a rule, the only cooking utensil in the camp was a battered iron kettle for making tea.

very little since man first began to make iron tools and weapons. It took place on a pitstead, a levelled-off area of earth or ashes about 20 ft across, in the centre of which was erected a post, or 'motty-peg', some 6 ft high. In the summer, after several months of drying, sticks and split logs were piled around the post, slanting up and outwards. Further wood was then added until the pile or clamp reached about 15 ft in diameter and 6 ft in height, when it was covered with a layer of turf, bracken and rushes cemented together with damp earth and ash. The centre post was then withdrawn, leaving a flue from top to bottom of the clamp.

With all prepared, a shovelful of red-hot charcoal and kindling wood was dropped down the chimney and topped up with cold charcoal. As soon as flames began to appear, a turf was slapped over the hole to check draught, the collier's unremitting enemy, against which he had to exercise constant vigilance. The whole point of the clamp was to heat the wood in such a way that all air was excluded, so

Making charcoal by the old, traditional means has now almost certainly ceased, though until the Second World War at least there were considerable numbers of charcoal burners or colliers practising their craft in such wooded areas of Britain as the Lake District, Shropshire, Kent and Sussex. It was tough work and seasonal; a rainy summer in the Lakes might curtail the productive period to a single month, though further south it was generally three months or more. Consequently, many colliers adopted additional skills, as a woodman perhaps, or as a bark-cutter for the tanning industry.

FIRING THE CLAMP

The clamp or stack was built of short lengths of timber piled around a stout central stake called a motty-peg. To ensure slow burning, the clamp was turfed, and a woven bracken screen – called a loo – erected to exclude draughts. The motty-peg was then withdrawn, leaving a chimney down which a shovelful of red-hot charcoal was dropped. When the wood began to burn, the chimney was sealed with hammered-in turfs.

LABOUR'S REWARD

It took 7 tons of wood, and days and nights of unremitting turfing, damping and trimming, to produce 1 ton of charcoal. Experience told the collier how his clamp was faring during the coaling process, and when it was completed. The turfs were then torn off, and water was thrown from flat 'saying-dishes' on to the glowing pile. The resulting steam extinguished the charcoal, which was raked over and left to cool before being shovelled into sacks. A clamp yielded about two sacks of charcoal which – at the turn of the century – netted the colliers a little under £4.

preventing complete combustion and in the end to produce pure carbon charcoal with only a few handfuls of ash.

A sudden change of wind could result in a flare-up and the destruction of weeks of patient work. To combat this, the charcoal burner erected a movable screen of canvas or wattled bracken and twigs called a 'loo', that was shifted around to stand always to windward of the clamp. Tending the loo and standing guard ready to smother any flare-ups with turf was a round-the-clock task, so colliers generally worked in pairs, one keeping watch while the other bedded down in the wigwam-like shanty. The work went on seven days a week all summer long, since once the first clamp was fired others were built and ignited in succession. There was little time to prepare meals. Bread, fatty bacon and cheese were generally brought by wives or children from home.

It took the best part of a week for a clamp to 'cook', the collier relying upon experience to tell him when the charcoal was ready. A few turfs were removed and dishes of water poured in to create the steam that began the cooling process. This was completed, after some hours, by pulling the clamp apart. Once cold, the charcoal was packed into sacks and sent off to the foundries by horse and cart.

It would be good to think that somewhere in Britain's forests there is still a charcoal burner munching his bread and cheese outside his hut and tending his clamp in the old way. But it seems unlikely. The last Devil's Chimney, as the clamps were called, is probably long extinguished, and all that remains, if you look closely in the fells and woodland clearings, are the odd levelled and hard-trodden areas where the pitsteads once were.

THE CHEESEWRIGHT

MARRYING TRADITIONAL SKILLS WITH SCIENTIFIC
KNOW-HOW, FARMHOUSE CHEESEMAKERS OFFER A RANGE
OF SUPERB AND DISTINCTIVELY FLAVOURED DELICACIES

*N*ames such as Caerphilly, Cheddar, Cheshire, Double Gloucester, Lancashire, Stilton and Wensleydale reflect the rich, regional traditions of small-scale cheesemaking in Britain. They also obscure the fact that production is now focused on large creameries, the first of which were established towards the end of the 19th century. Some can process more than 100,000 gallons of milk a day – each gallon makes about 1 lb. of cheese – and are as automated as any other type of factory.

But superb 'farmhouse' cheese is still made in rural dairies where, in many cases, only two or three people are employed. The methods used would not seem unduly strange to a medieval farmer, although techniques have been refined to ensure consistent quality and hygiene.

Contrary to popular belief, much of the cheese made in the 'good old days' was remarkably bad. Accurate means of checking acidity and temperature – two vital aspects of the cheesemaking process – did not evolve until Victorian times. Many dairies were infested with rats, mice, mites and other vermin.

Some cheeses, notably those from Suffolk, were notoriously hard and wrought havoc with all but the strongest teeth and most hardy digestive tracts. Softer types often became riddled with maggots or erupted into gaseous blisters and craters. Cheese that refused to 'work', or simply went bad, was blamed on anything and everything from the weather to witchcraft.

Today's makers of farmhouse cheese still have to contend with plenty of problems, but modern techniques, allied to years of experience, enable them to discover why this or that process is not progressing as it should. Armed with such knowledge they can take the appropriate action. It is an ideal marriage between scientific know-how and age-old traditional skills.

Cheese from the milk of cattle, sheep and goats is one of the oldest man-made foods. It is mentioned in the Old Testament and in the writings of Greek poets and philosophers, such as Homer and Aristotle, who lived long before the birth of Christ. Detailed accounts of the methods used in Roman times, when cheese first appears in Britain's recorded history, have survived for almost 2,000 years.

Until the advent of refrigeration, about the end of the last century, cheese was the only means by which milk could be preserved for long periods. It was made in the summer, when grass was abundant, and then stored away to be eaten during the long, hard months of winter. Peasant farmers made only enough for themselves and their families, but relatively large-scale production was undertaken by the great religious houses until they were closed by order of Henry VIII in the 16th century.

Dairymaids produced the monastic cheese – cheesemaking was long regarded as an essentially feminine task –

and at least one prior, presumably concerned about sins of the flesh, ruled that only 'old and ill-favoured' women were to be employed. Buxom lasses were appreciated elsewhere, however, because they could put more weight on a cheese before it went into the press. 'The bigger the dairymaid, the better the cheese,' was a favourite saying.

By the 17th century, improved dairy-farming methods, better communications and the steady growth of towns and cities encouraged cheesemakers in some areas, notably Somerset and Cheshire, to pool their resources. Milk from several neighbouring farms was taken to a single dairy. A lady who travelled through Cheshire in 1697 recorded in her journal that it was 'the custome of the country to joyn their milking together . . . and so make their great Cheeses'.

Despite communal enterprises, and the development of a marketing system run by merchants known as 'factors', the fundamental character of the craft in Britain did not change until the 19th century. The most fervent and enlightened advocate of improved methods and greatly enhanced overall quality was Joseph Harding, born early in the century, who came from a Somerset family that was locally renowned for its fine Cheddar.

Keenly aware of the fast-growing threat from imported cheese, Harding travelled the country, gleaning, analysing and spreading information and theories. He built his own model dairy to emphasise the importance of hygiene, pioneered chemical tests to check acidity, and proposed the establishment of dairy colleges where the ancient techniques could be mingled advantageously with new-fangled scientific refinements.

Turning theory into practice

Harding's bold reforms inevitably paved the way for the building of Britain's first cheesemaking factory, at Longford, Derbyshire, in 1870. Others were soon established to serve the major milk-producing regions, but the new ideas also enabled the more progressive makers of traditional farmhouse cheese to remain keenly competitive.

It was not until the 19th century that the now-familiar regional names – each indicating a distinctly different type of cheese – came into widespread use. Until then the only varieties whose characteristics were sufficiently well known to merit accurate identification were Stilton, Dorset's Blue Vinny, Cheshire, Gloucester, Devon Garland with its stripe of herbs, and Suffolk Bang, which, so it was said, was so hard that it could be used to replace a shot-away wheel on a Navy gun-carriage. Stilton, widely accepted as the most noble of all Britain's dairy products, has a particularly interesting history.

Tradition maintains that this rich, blue-veined delicacy was first made by a farmer's wife in the Melton Mowbray district of Leicestershire. She supplied it to her brother-in-law, Cooper Thornhill, who kept the Bell Inn at Stilton, on the Great North Road in what is now Cambridgeshire. In 1727, Daniel Defoe described Stilton as 'a town famous for cheese' in his 'Tour through England and Wales'.

Oddly enough, Stilton has never been made in the place whose name it has made famous. Nor may it be produced there without breaking the law. Understandably concerned about inferior imitations, the Stilton Cheese Makers' Association fought a long legal battle, in the 1960s, which resulted in their cheese being granted protection by a copyright. As a result, Stilton may be produced only in the counties of Leicestershire, Nottinghamshire and Derbyshire. Most of the dairies are in the Vale of Belvoir, between Melton Mowbray and Nottingham.

Cheesemaking techniques vary somewhat from type to type, and from dairy to dairy, but the basic processes are the same. Makers of traditional farmhouse cheese reckon that

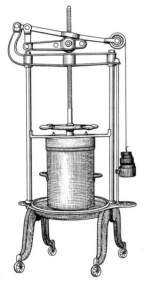

KEEPING UP THE PRESSURE

The earliest cheese presses were simply heavy stones laid on the lid of the mould. Centuries of adaptation and improvement led to this mid-Victorian cast-iron press, in which a wooden block, exactly fitting into the mould, is screwed down upon the cheese. Steady pressure is exerted by the weighted lever on top of the screw. Since the cheese is subjected to pressures of 15 cwt and more for the best part of a week, the steel or wooden moulds have to be of stout construction.

the superiority of their products stems from the fact that they can control their cows' diet. Kale is generally avoided, for instance, because it gives the cheese an unsatisfactory flavour. Large creameries, on the other hand, cannot exercise such tight control because they use milk from many different herds.

Milk from high-yielding cows, such as the Friesian, goes into a double-skinned tank of stainless steel and is heated to about 86°F (30°C) by letting steam into the space between the skins. The steam method was pioneered by Joseph Harding, and gradually ousted stoves and open fires. Annatto, a dye used since the 18th century, is added if a 'red' cheese is being made. The dye comes from a tree which grows mainly in the West Indies and South America.

Heat 'ripens' the milk before a 'starter' is added. The starter is a bacterial culture, often made on the farm, which converts lactose, or soluble sugar, into lactic acid and starts a type of fermentation.

The all-important rennet – about 1 oz. for every 40 gallons of milk – is stirred in after approximately two hours. It is an enzyme produced in a calf's stomach and makes the milk coagulate to form a kind of junket. This property can only have been discovered by accident, thousands of years ago, when nomads used the stomachs of calves and other ruminants as convenient containers for milk. Although they could not extract the precious enzyme, early cheese-makers realised that its miraculous ability to coagulate milk, thus forming curds, lasted long after the animal was slaughtered. For many hundreds of years, rennet was added simply by keeping portions of stomach in the dairy and dipping them in the milk.

Plants such as ladies' bedstraw, once known as the cheese-rennet herb, were also used in the past. Although easy to obtain, they produced bitter cheese of poor quality.

Rennet makes the milk coagulate in anything from 15 to 50 minutes. Differences of that magnitude underline the fact that cheesemaking conditions vary from day to day. The weather, the time of year and the state of the grass are three of several factors that must be taken into account.

The thick, smooth junket is eventually cut into countless small pieces, each about the size of a pea, with long, multi-bladed steel knives. This process starts to separate the curds and whey immortalised in the old nursery rhyme about Little Miss Muffet, the most famous of all dairymaids.

Cutting the curd by hand is hard, hot, steamy work which demands strong arm and back muscles. For that reason, most dairies now have machines with the blades suspended from overhead frames. At the other end of the scale, the earliest cheesemakers either left the curd to drain naturally or squeezed it with their hands. Separation is nowadays assisted by raising the temperature in the tank, again by letting steam into the cavity between the inner and outer skins. This process is known as 'scalding'.

Curd knife

Old-style dairymaids used buckets and scoops to remove the whey. It was a long and laborious task, because whey accounts for about three-quarters of the tank's original contents. The time taken could seriously affect the cheese if its natural acids were becoming stronger with every passing minute. Tanks fitted with drainage taps have been used for many years, and some dairies transfer the whey into a second tank with a special drainage channel running down the middle. Whey generally goes to feed the pigs, hence the old saying that 'the sow follows the cow'. Makers of farmhouse cheese make the point that their system is a perfect example of an ecological cycle. Cows feed on grass, which produces milk for cheese, and the whey by-product is fed to pigs whose manure is used to fertilise the pastures on which dairy cattle graze.

Despite natural drainage, a good deal of whey is obstinately retained by the porous curd. Its departure is hastened by cutting repeatedly into the mass with long, broad-bladed knives and turning the resultant chunks by hand. In the meantime, acidity levels are checked frequently by sucking whey into a slim, calibrated glass tube and carrying out a chemical test.

If the acid level is too high it is reduced by working the curds harder with knives and hands to speed up the draining process. It is called 'fast' curd. If the level is too low, the cheesemakers can work at a more sedate pace. Getting the level just right, day after day and year after year, is one of the craft's greatest challenges. Excessive acid results in a sharp, dry cheese of the wrong texture. At the other extreme, insufficient acid causes too much moisture to be

DELICIOUS CHEESES FROM THE REGIONS

CHEDDAR
A cheese that is now imported and exported round half the western world. Nevertheless, mature Farmhouse Cheddar from Somerset, which takes two years in the ageing, is still something of a rarity.

CHESHIRE
The recipe for this cheese may pre-date the Roman invasion. It is produced in the national colours of red, white and blue. The red – traditionally – is created by the addition of marigold or carrot juice, while the blue comes from penicillin spores. White or cream is the cheese's natural colour.

STILTON
It takes 17 gallons of milk and four months of loving attention to produce 14 lb. of this rich and revered cheese. The characteristic blue-mould veining is induced by airborne spores.

SAGE DERBY
Made for more than 300 years, this cheese gets its characteristic green veining from the chopped sage leaves that are spread among the curd. The inclusion of the leaves was originally intended as an aid to digestion.

RED WINDSOR
A relative newcomer to the cheeseboard, Red Windsor is a form of Cheddar made in the Vale of Belvoir. The red hue is derived from the addition of Sussex elderberry wine.

CAERPHILLY
A favourite with South Wales miners since about 1800, Caerphilly takes only two weeks to mature and provides a high return for the amount of milk used. Both these factors appealed to manufacturers of slow-maturing Cheddar, who also made Caerphilly as a profitable sideline.

CABOC
A rich, soft, double-cream cheese kept moist by a sealing of toasted oatmeal. Tradition says it has been made in the Western Isles and Highlands since the 15th century.

retained and makes the cheese 'soapy'. The importance of acidity was appreciated by Joseph Harding more than a century ago, but today's acidity tests were evolved in the 1890s.

The curds are cut and turned for as long as it takes to achieve the desired balance. Makers of some cheeses, notably Stilton, leave the curds overnight before moving on to the next stage. But most curds go straight into a mill, the first examples of which were introduced in the 18th century. It cuts and grinds the curds between spike-studded rollers and they fall back into the tank looking very like a mass of firm scrambled egg. The texture is porous and springy, and the taste is pleasant without having any of the richness of the mature cheese. Milled curds are sprinkled with fine salt, which improves the flavour, acts as a preservative and helps to balance the ever-present acids.

The moulds in which cheese is given its shape used to be made of wood – elm was widely considered to be the most suitable type, but aluminium is generally used today. Factories favour blocks of cheese, because they are easier to package and store, but Cheddar, Cheshire, Lancashire, Stilton and Wensleydale are traditionally cylindrical in shape. Caerphilly, Derby, Double Gloucester and Leicester look more like small, plump millstones.

All cheeses are moulded, but the extent to which they are pressed depends on the ultimate texture. Compact varieties, such as Cheddar and Double Gloucester, need more pressure than, for instance, Cheshire, which is squeezed to give it shape, rather than to force out moisture.

Blue Stilton is not pressed at all, but left to drain and mature naturally. Its weight falls from about 25 lb. to between 14 and 16 lb. while nature takes its course. When it is firm enough for the steel hoops – moulds – to be removed, the cheese is smoothed down by hand, wrapped in clean muslin and then put back in a hoop for another two days or so. The cloth is removed when the cheese goes to a room where carefully controlled temperature and humidity encourage the rich, golden-red coat to develop. It is turned by hand, day after day, and then goes to another room where it matures for at least three months.

The veins in Stilton, Blue Cheshire and other blue cheeses are caused by an airborne bacillus called *Penicillium roqueforti*. It cannot develop without sufficient oxygen and water, and is therefore found only in moist, open-textured cheeses. The growth is encouraged by piercing the cheese with long needles of stainless steel. As a result, the veins radiate out from the heart and are distributed evenly.

Most other cheeses are left in their cloth wrappers – dipped in a bath of very hot wax, which forms a thin, firm outer coat – and then left to mature in a store where temperature and humidity are of paramount importance. Moulds become over-exuberant if the atmosphere is too moist, but on the other hand, the cheese will crack if there is not sufficient humidity.

All cheese is graded before it goes on sale. Sight, touch, smell and taste – senses made acute by years of training – tell the grader all he needs to know. To get his sample he uses a long, specially shaped knife, known as a cheese iron, which resembles an apple corer and draws out a plug from the cheese.

Most cheeses are simply cut up and eaten, but Stilton in particular should be treated with considerable respect. In the Vale of Belvoir the traditional saying is 'cut high, cut low, cut level' to work round and down the cheese in a series of triangles. Makers of the 'king of English cheeses' throw up their hands in horror at talk of pouring port on to Stilton and using a scoop or spoon instead of a knife. They say it wastes a good drink and desecrates one of the world's greatest cheeses.

A SINGLE-MINDED CHEESE FROM GLOUCESTERSHIRE

At Laurel Farm, Dymock, Gloucestershire, Mr and Mrs Martell make Single (and some Double) Gloucester cheese from the milk of their pedigree herd of rare Gloucestershire cattle and feed the whey by-product to their Gloucestershire Old Spots pigs. The difference between Single and Double Gloucester is that the Double contains more cream and takes twice as long to mature as the Single. Consequently, the Double used to be kept for sale, while the Single was eaten by the farmworkers. At one time, the Single was known as Hay Cheese, since it was made in the spring to be ready in time for hay-making. But Single or Double, the cheese is a long day in the making, beginning at 6.30 a.m. when the Martells milk their cows. The Gloucestershire breed is one of the world's oldest, directly descended from the Stone Age wild ox.

2.10 p.m. *The milk has been warming in the tub since 8 a.m., and rennet was added at one o'clock. An hour later, the whey has separated from the solidified curds, which are cut into blocks with a curd knife.*

2.30–4.00. *Curds and whey are stirred together in a process known as scalding. In fact, though the heat of the mixture is increased by pouring very hot water into the tub's water jacket, it is never boiled.*

4.00. *The whey is drawn out of the tub through the whey tap, leaving the semi-solid curds behind. Rich in vitamins, lactose and minerals, the whey is poured into churns where it is kept until fed to the farm's pigs.*

4.30. *The curd is cut into square blocks and turned repeatedly to increase the acidity that creates flavour. The process continues for about half an hour when making a Single Gloucester, rather longer for a Double.*

5.00. *The blocks are fed into a peg mill which breaks the curd down again, before they are salted. The crumbled curd is then spread over the tub floor to ensure an even distribution of salt throughout.*

5.10. *Salt is scattered over the levelled curd. Salting is an important part of cheesemaking in that it preserves the cheese, helps to bring out the flavour, and slows down the development of acidity.*

5.20. *The curd is poured into a mould or vat lined with muslin cheesecloth. The mould, which contains and shapes the cheese, may be of wood or steel, but must be of great strength to withstand the press.*

5.30. *Feeding time for the farm's pedigree herd of Gloucestershire Old Spots pigs. It used to be said that Gloucester cheese would never mature properly unless the whey was fed to pigs of this ancient breed.*

Five days later. *The last muslin wrapping is removed – dry, since by now the last liquid has been squeezed from the cheese. A Double Gloucester cheese would be left in the press for only two or three days.*

The last touch. *A heavy bandage of cheesecloth is stuck on to the cheese with a flour and water paste. This prevents the cheese from spreading, drying or cracking, and gives protection in transit.*

5.45. *Pressing begins. The five Single Gloucester cheeses in the moulds are being subjected to a 15 cwt pressure which squeezes out liquid and compresses the cheese. During its five days in the press, the cheese is turned, and its muslin changed, daily.*

A matter of time. *Single Gloucesters, each pound of which represents a gallon of milk, mature on cool shelves. In the eight weeks before they are ready to eat, the cheeses must be turned daily to ensure that maturation is even throughout.*

THE CIDER MAKER

AT ONE TIME THE STAPLE DRINK OF
FARMING FOLK, CIDER HAS ATTRACTED ITS OWN RICH
FOLKLORE OF FACT AND FANTASY

'Cider is one of the most delicious and wholesome beverages in the world,' said John Evelyn, the 17th-century courtier and diarist who wrote a treatise on the subject. 'Generally, all strong and pleasant cider excites and cleanses the stomach, strengthens digestion, and infallibly frees the kidneys and bladder from breeding gravel and stone. Labouring people where it is drank affirm that they are more strengthened for hard work by such cider than by the very best beer.'

Cider is believed to have been made in Britain more than 2,000 years ago, before the Roman invasion, when the apple trees on which sacred mistletoe grew were venerated by Druids. Indeed, the tradition of spilling a few drops of cider on the ground, as a token offering to long-forgotten gods, was observed by old country folk until after the Second World War.

The first documentary evidence of cider making in England comes from Norfolk in 1205. A century later, cider is mentioned in the writings of Geoffrey Chaucer and William Langland. John Wyclif's 14th-century translation of the Bible uses 'cider' rather than 'strong drink' in some passages. Another cleric, writing during the same period, reminded his readers that water and not cider should be used for baptisms.

Although it now tends to be regarded as something of a West Country speciality, with Hereford and Taunton as the main centres, traditional 'farm' cider was made throughout the major apple-growing areas of England and the Welsh borderlands for many hundreds of years. A delightful jingle, penned early in the 19th century, pays tribute to the excellence of Sussex cider at that time:

> *'Some people give perry and call it champagne,*
> *Not so gives of Petworth the rector;*
> *'Tis cider he tells us his vessels contain,*
> *But on tasting it proves to be nectar.'*

Cider is still made commercially in Sussex, Kent, Norfolk and elsewhere, but the farm tradition tended to die out in eastern England as farmers switched from cider apples to dessert varieties. These were more profitable, and improved transport brought London and other centres of population within commercial reach of the orchards. Cider making also went into a temporary decline during the Napoleonic Wars, when soaring corn and meat prices encouraged many farmers to grub up their orchards.

Large-scale cider making dates from the end of the 19th century when such firms as Bulmers, Gaymers and White-ways were established. Percy Bulmer, the younger son of the rector of Credenhill, near Hereford, made his first cider on a nearby farm in 1887. Later that year he moved to a warehouse in Hereford, where he made and sold 4,000 gallons, founding what is now the biggest cider-making business in the world.

Farm cider was originally a domestic product rather than a cash crop. It was made and consumed by the farmer, his family and the people who worked for them. Although very little was sold, other than to friends and local pubs, some found its way to towns and cities after a particularly plentiful apple harvest. In the days when many water supplies were contaminated, cider's natural acidity made it an eminently safe drink.

Apples suitable for cider making are nowadays grouped into four main types. The sweet varieties, bland and with little flavour, are used mainly for blending. 'Pure sharp' apples, now fairly uncommon, have flavours similar to

culinary fruit. 'Bittersharps' have fairly high acid and tannin contents, but lack the full range of flavours found in the 'bittersweets'. Low in acid and high in tannin, 'bittersweets' are the most characteristic of all English cider apples.

Apples popular during the 19th century had such names as Slack-my-Girdle, Cherry Norman, Sam's Crab, Cider Lady's Finger and Dymock Red. A book published in 1876 describes the Foxwhelp as 'beyond all question the most valuable cider apple of Herefordshire', and says that its qualities had been appreciated by cider makers for more

than 200 years. Another favourite, grown throughout the West Country, was the Kingston Black.

The character and quality of 'farm' cider has always depended on three main factors – the apples, the weather and the cider maker. In the past, many farmers took a pride in their cider and would learn by experience, or know from local and family traditions, that a blend of fruit from various trees produced the best results.

The rough-and-ready method resulted in some horrifically 'rough' ciders, which did nothing for the drink's reputation. They may well have given birth to tales about

MILLING THE APPLES

Simple but effective, the old-style cider-mill has a circular stone trough, known as a chase, in which the apples are crushed by the runner – an upright millstone. Small versions, sometimes called perry mills, could be worked by a donkey or by farm labourers, but most were powered by a horse harnessed to the wooden framework. About 50 circuits were needed for each load.

the hair-raising strength and gruesome after-effects of 'scrumpy' – a term which tends to be regarded as 'touristy' by cider makers in general.

Most cider apples mature between mid-October and mid-December, although a few varieties are not at their best until January. Traditionally, apples were not picked but knocked from the trees when judged ripe, using a 'panking pole', or the branches were shaken with a hooked pole called a 'lugg'. Like the cider-making process in general, these and other terms vary from place to place.

Harvested apples should be allowed to mature for anything from a week to a month or more. In some areas they used to be simply left on the ground in heaps, or 'tumps', but this gave the cider an earthy taint if they were allowed to stand for too long. Other farmers put the crop in an open-sided barn, while the upper floor of a barn, known as a 'tallet', was favoured in Somerset. Apples may also be allowed to mature on hurdles covered with straw. No matter what method is used, the object is to let the apples 'sweat' a little to rid themselves of excess moisture.

When the apples are soft enough to give easily under thumb pressure, they are ready to be milled. Many traditional cider-mills have survived – perhaps 2,000 in Herefordshire alone during the late 1970s – but very few are still in use.

Some old cider-making buildings in Somerset and Devon are still known as the 'pound house'. The name recalls the days when apples were laboriously pounded with heavy wooden pestles. A slightly less primitive method involved a millstone being trundled up and down a hollowed-out log.

Eventually, the stone mill became synonymous with traditional cider making in the Herefordshire region. It consists of a circular stone trough, known as a 'chase', made from two or more pieces of stone held together by clamps. The typical chase is about 30 ft in circumference and 9–10 in. deep. Craftsmen from the Forest of Dean area produced many of the stone implements and utensils used by West Country cider makers.

The 'runner', an upright millstone, stands in the chase and has a wooden frame and yoke to which a horse is harnessed. Matured apples are placed on the flat stone 'pier' surrounded by the chase and tapped into the trough with a 'rowing-down stick' as the horse plods slowly round and round. Some cider makers add water at regular intervals

while milling. It lubricates the crushed fruit and helps the runner to roll rather than slide.

Water is also said to help prevent the cider going sour, but some cider makers – particularly in Worcestershire and Gloucestershire – maintain that water has no beneficial effects. It was certainly not appreciated by farmworkers!

Opinions about crushing also vary from place to place and from cider maker to cider maker. Some make a pulp, or 'must', with no piece bigger than a pea. Others keep milling until even the pips are crushed.

Although old-style cider making involved horsepower in the most literal sense of the word, 'scratter' or 'scratcher' mills driven by human muscle or machinery have been used extensively since Victorian times. They now account for virtually all farm cider.

The scratter was a rotary mill which could be moved from farm to farm. One advertised in the 1890s was designed to be belt-driven from a 4 hp engine and, it was claimed, enabled 108 gallons of juice to be produced in 39 minutes. Speedy and convenient, the scratter inevitably reduced the stone mill to the status of a rural relic, but the staunchest traditionalists maintain that it has always produced somewhat inferior results.

Some cider makers transfer the must to open vessels, where it is left for up to 48 hours. Others take it straight to the press. This is a very sturdy wooden frame with a stout upper beam through which a massive screw is threaded. The relatively modern double-screw press dates from the latter part of the 19th century and has screws on either side of the upper block, thus doing away with the need for a substantial frame. Like the scratter mill, this type of press is portable and was used by travelling cider makers.

Pressing the pulp

Milling is a straightforward process, but pressing demands a considerable degree of skill. A cloth known as a 'hair' is placed on the 'chuter' – the base of the press – and then covered with a layer of pulp about 3 in. thick. The sides of the hair are then folded over, before another hair and another layer of pulp are placed on top. This goes on until the cider maker has built up a 'cheese', or 'mock', some 3 ft square by 3–4 ft high.

Hairs in Herefordshire and the neighbouring counties were traditionally made of horse-hair, but Manila hemp and other fibres were in widespread use by the end of the 19th century. Fine reeds were used in some parts of the country. Cider makers in Somerset and Devon favoured layers of barley straw.

The weight of the cheese makes a certain amount of juice run out of its own accord, but the main work is done by forcing the screw down with poles. Juice flows out into a gutter, then runs down a spout to either a wooden tub, called a cooler, or to a stone basin on the floor.

The amount of juice produced by a given quantity of apples varies from year to year. If the weather has been dry there is relatively little juice, but it tends to be rich in sugars and flavour. Wet weather typically produces plenty of juice, but the cider it makes is 'thin'. The average farm cider maker gets 100–130 gallons from a ton of fruit. Mechanical presses date from 1909, when the first hydraulic type was used in the industry, and squeeze 170 or more gallons from a ton of apples.

In the old days, pressed must was sometimes returned to the chase, mixed with water, then milled and pressed a second time. This resulted in a much weaker brew known by such names as small cider, ciderkin and purr.

Some cider makers 'keeve' the juice for periods ranging from a day or two to more than a week. It is poured into open vats, or open-ended casks, and left to stand until debris

THE TRAVELLING CIDER-PRESS

The travelling cider maker became an increasingly familiar sight in the apple-growing areas of England towards the end of the Victorian era. Relatively compact machines, such as the scratter or scratcher mill, were hauled from farm to farm and gradually reduced the traditional mill to little more than a quaint rural relic. They were much more efficient, but connoisseurs of cider claim that the end product is not in quite the same class. The mill was accompanied by a press which resolutely defied mechanisation. Travelling cider makers saved the farmer's time, and often provided a much-needed dash of expertise.

which has found its way through the filtering hairs comes to the surface. This forms a crust, which can then be skimmed off. Keeving also removes pectins which make cider hazy. The length of time taken to keeve juice depends on its character and the temperature. The process has to be completed before active fermentation begins.

Most juice goes straight from the press to a cask. Fermentation, also called 'working' or 'fretting', generally starts after two or three days and can go on for anything from a week to several months if the weather is exceptionally chilly. There are sufficient wild yeasts present on the apples to start the process.

Modern additives may be used to assist certain aspects of the fermentation process. Their traditional counterparts ranged from raisins and parsnips to lumps of raw steak, rabbit skins and hunks of bacon. Additives provide extra sugar and additional nitrogen for the yeasts in the juice.

Air should not be allowed to reach the juice while it is fermenting. Today's cider makers use sophisticated airlock devices, but their predecessors had to rely on keeping casks filled to the brim of the bunghole. Air carries bacteria which will convert alcohol to acetic acid, or vinegar. Bacteria can also make the cider 'oily' – it feels like a thin lubricating oil – or 'ropy', like the raw white of an egg.

Natural fermentation is unstoppable and eats up all the sugars in the juice, which is why farm cider is characteristically very dry. But the fermentation can be checked by careful racking, which retains a modicum of unfermented sugar. Cider is drawn off from a tap near the bottom of the cask – leaving the 'lees' or sediment as undisturbed as possible – and poured into a clean cask.

When fermentation ends, the cask is tightly bunged. The bung itself may be sealed, traditionally with a mixture of lime and clay, to keep air out until the cider is ready for drinking. It may also be racked immediately after fermentation has ceased. This aids clarification, although the juice will sometimes 'drop bright' naturally if the conditions are just right.

Cask-maturing the cider

Preservatives familiar to do-it-yourself winemakers can be used to prevent cider going off before the cask is ready to be tapped, but many producers of farm cider decline to use them in case they spoil the taste. Cider is generally left in the cask for at least three months. It tends to deteriorate after 9–12 months, but has been known to taste excellent after four or five years. At the other end of the scale, 'summer' cider was drunk after only four or five weeks.

Farm cider is invariably still. Factory cider is made fizzy by having carbon dioxide gas pumped into it.

The slow but sure decline of farm cider making was brought about by several factors. For instance, the Truck Act of 1878 made it illegal for employers to provide alcoholic drinks in lieu of wages. The newly established factories started offering attractive prices for apples.

Old habits were also disrupted by the First World War. The steady spread of mechanisation reduced the number of people working on the land, and tractors replaced the horses which had so patiently powered the traditional stone mills. Free houses gave way to tied pubs, thereby shutting the door on many outlets for the small-scale cider maker.

But the old traditions were kept alive by a few farmers and others who regarded their cider-making heritage as something worthy of preservation. More recently, the major cider makers have been encouraged to revive traditional ciders, albeit using modern methods. Like the big brewers, who have reacted to the growing demand for 'real' ale, they are finding an enthusiastic market for latterday versions of the drink praised by John Evelyn more than 300 years ago.

Placing the pulp in a coarse filter, or hair, ready for pressing.

EXTRACTING THE JUICE FROM THE 'MUST'

The apple is a notably hard fruit which has to be pressed as well as milled before it yields its full store of juice. A few very old presses, made in the 17th and 18th centuries, still have a massive single screw made of hand-turned wood and traditionally lubricated with goose fat. The majority, dating from the 19th century, have two cast-iron screws which enable pressure to be adjusted. The crushed must is placed between filters, which are carefully folded in to form a 'cheese' ready for pressing. The typical farm cider maker extracts up to about 130 gallons from each ton of fruit.

IN THE DAYS WHEN WOODEN SHOES WERE
COMMONPLACE, MANY A FOREST GROVE RANG TO THE
CLOGGER'S AXE AS HE CUT AND SHAPED THE SOLES

*T*he great advantage of clogs, as a modern gene-ration has discovered, is that they are not only practical and hard-wearing, but also very comfortable.

They were even more comfortable, and certainly longer lasting, when a village clog maker was fashioning them to fit every bump, hollow and bunion of his individual customers. For clogs go back a long way – right back to the Middle Ages. Factory workers in towns and farming folk in the country were still wearing them at the turn of the present century, or even later – especially in the north of England and Wales, where hardly a town or village was without its clog maker.

Clogs were popular because they kept their wearers' feet warm and dry under most conditions, and were hard-wearing. Their iron-rimmed, thick, wooden soles raised the foot well above the level of soaking pavements and wet factory floors, while in muddy fields they were reckoned superior to rubber boots.

In the heyday of clog making there were two distinct types of craftsman involved: the clog maker and the clog-sole cutter. Clog makers worked in towns or villages, producing complete clogs to individual order with hand tools. This craft demanded considerable knowledge not only of woodwork, but of leatherwork, too.

The clog-sole cutter – or clogger – cut alder blocks and shaped them into rough soles for clogging factories. He was often an itinerant craftsman, travelling to where the best wood was to be found, and working on the spot. However, there were also clog-sole factories such as the one still in production at Hebden Bridge, in West Yorkshire, where the soles are cut by machine – often from imported timber.

Alder was once the wood most used, though village clog makers usually preferred sycamore, and beech is popular now, being easier to machine-shape. The alder is a quick-growing tree, coarse-grained and soft, and therefore easy to cut by hand. Its softness allows it to give to the shape of the foot, making the clog more comfortable to wear. It is also said to possess medicinal properties, and some people still wear alder-soled clogs as a remedy for foot troubles.

The village craftsman's preference for sycamore was carried even further by Welsh clog makers, who believed that sycamore cut from a hedgerow made better soles than that from a forest sycamore plantation.

Whatever wood was used, the felled tree was im-mediately – while still 'green' – split into what were called 'sole blocks', first with a beetle (a heavy wooden mallet) and wedge, then with an axe, and finally with a stock-knife.

This latter tool, used also by cloggers, is a one-piece steel implement about 30 in. long, bent at a shallow angle in the middle, with a handle at one end and a hook-ended knife-edge at the other. The knife-end was hooked into a ring on a bench or wooden post. Grasping the handle with one hand while holding the wood billet against the bench or post with the other, the craftsman would set to work, cutting a roughly shaped sole with swift, sure strokes of the blade, then carving a deep notch at the point where heel meets toe.

A tool called a hollowing knife was used for the next step, cutting the concave shape of the sole upper. This tool was worked in the same way as the stock-knife, but had a short, deep, concave blade. A third hook-ended tool, called a gripper, then came into action to cut a narrow channel all around the top of the sole, into which the leather upper would be fitted later.

The gripper had a slim V-shaped blade and was also known as a mortising knife. Finally, the sole was finished with rasps and short-bladed knives until it was smooth.

The leather uppers were cut to pattern with stiffeners sewn in at the heels, and eyelets inserted in the lace-holes. They were then strained over a wooden last, tacked into place on the last, then hammered into shape. The uppers remained in the last for several hours, to be moulded into the correct shape.

This achieved, they were removed from the last and nailed to the sole with short, flat-headed nails. A narrow strip of leather covered the join between sole and upper.

Replaceable grooved irons were nailed to the sole and heel, a bright copper or brass tip tacked to the toe, and the clogs were ready for wearing.

Until 1939, gangs of cloggers were commonplace in the alder groves of Wales and its border counties during the spring and summer. They were there to supply the clog-making factories of northern England, where there was little alder to be found. Often the cloggers lived and worked in roughly built temporary shelters.

They felled trees with a girth no greater than 24 in., then sawed them into short logs of four sizes – men's, women's, children's and 'middles'. The logs were split into blocks, which in turn were cut with a stock-knife into the rough size and shape of clog soles. These soles were then carefully stacked so that air could circulate between them, and left for weeks – sometimes months – to allow the green wood to dry out. Finally, they went to north-country clog-making factories, where they were 'finished'.

CLOGS FOR ALL OCCASIONS

Many patterns of clogs were made – most of them for farm or factory workers. Lighter ones, often decorated with patterned stitching, and shod with rubber rather than iron, were proudly worn as 'Sunday best'.

Industrial clog

Sunday clog

Agricultural clog

TAKING SHAPE

Two moments in the making of a clog ... Thomas James, working in 1972 in Solva village, Dyfed, uses a gripper, or mortising knife, to cut a channel in the sycamore sole before fitting the leather uppers (above). On the right he is seen tapping in the last tacks to fix the leather.

DRYING OUT *A stack of roughly shaped clog soles stands drying behind the two cloggers who cut them, Jonah Weaver and David Pugh. The year was 1930, and they were working in an alder grove near Talybont, in what is now north Dyfed.*

THE
Coachbuilder

ROYAL PATRONAGE AND A NEW BREED OF
SPORTSMEN HAVE BROUGHT RENEWED LIFE
TO THE CARRIAGE-BUILDING CRAFT

What few carriage-building craftsmen are now left in Britain have not been in such secure employment as at present for at least half a century. They owe their renewed prosperity to the tremendous and growing popularity of carriage-driving competitions. Since Prince Philip took up the sport with such great enthusiasm, the demand for suitable vehicles has outgrown the supply of restored or refurbished survivors from the days before the motor-car was invented. So orders are mounting steadily for new-built carriages from sportsmen undeterred by rising costs.

The origins of the horse-drawn carriage lie in medieval times, when new breeds of large, strong horses were evolved by crossing different strains of cavalry chargers. These 'new' horses began to replace the oxen pulling the crude, solid-wheeled, unsprung goods wagons of the day over the rutted tracks that passed for roads.

But carrying people rather than goods called for a very different style of wagon. Speed – and therefore lightness – was demanded, and comfort became paramount. So the coach was born. A far-sighted craftsman named Walter Rippon constructed the first purpose-built coach for the Earl of Rutland in 1555, and personal coaches soon became fashionable. But it was not until 1640 that the first stage-coach service began. However, journeys were slow and tiring; Exeter, for example, was a tough four-day slog from London over appalling roads.

Early carriages were built with a frame similar in layout to that of a wagon. But the timbers were thinner and lighter, and there was another big difference – the body, though still just a closed box with windows and a door, was slung from the frame on leather straps to give passengers a measure of comfort.

However, the improvement in roads triggered off some sophisticated developments. Ever thinner timbers were used to reduce the weight of the frame and bodywork. Wheels were 'dished' to make them stronger and lighter (see *The Wheelwright*, p. 212). New types of steel spring replaced the leather straps. Graceful C-springs – rather like the uncoiled mainspring of a watch – were followed by the more efficient and flatter leaf-spring, which also allowed bodies to be slung lower in the frame. In this way coaches became much safer, being more stable and, with their lower centre of gravity, less prone to overturning.

As a craft, coachbuilding was more complex than wagon-making. More than a dozen separate skills were involved. There were frame makers, upholsterers, coach-smiths – who made springs, axles, brackets, swivels and other items of metalwork – and coach painters, who produced a mirror finish that was also extremely durable.

Oak was used for the main frame, ash for shafts and wheel spokes, and elm for wheel hubs – 'naves'. As curves became ever more popular features of design, body frames were also made of ash. Its toughness and flexibility made it

ideal for steaming and bending to shape to form light structures that were still strong enough to absorb the punishment imposed by rough roads.

The first step in building a coach was to make the main frame – the 'perch' – from the timbers of young oaks carefully selected for their straight grain. The timbers would be joined by bolts and metal plates, then other metal parts would be fitted – stays and swivels, springs and axles. The body had seats and a floor of elm. The strong grain of this wood was ideal for parts not normally seen, but was liable to show through paintwork, making it unsuitable for outside panelling.

Outer panels had to be as thin as possible for lightness, and were usually of Honduras mahogany three-ply wood. This could be bent easily and took a first-class finish when painted. Panelling could also be done in a tough but less-easily finished wood such as cedar, which was covered with leather. The leather gave an attractive finish which was also weatherproof. Pine was often used for the carriage roof.

Today's coachbuilder can take advantage of modern materials and techniques. Marine grades of plywood are excellent for panelling and for making seats, floors and

COMFORT FOR THE TRAVELLER

The first carriage bodies were suspended by leather straps from extensions to the frame. This method provided a reasonably comfortable ride for the passengers, though the swinging motion could not have helped those prone to travel sickness. In time, metal springs replaced the leather straps, like the graceful C-spring shown below under construction in a 19th-century coachbuilding shop. The spring was formed from a series of laminations held together by iron box-section clamps. The picture shows one of the clamps being hammered into position.

Making a C-spring

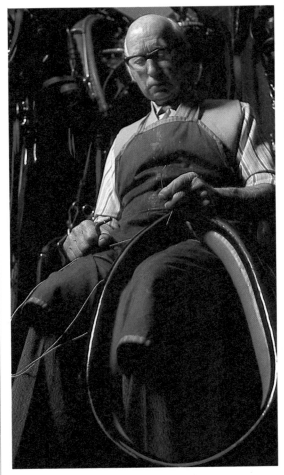

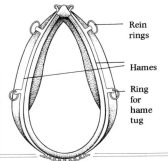

Rein rings

Hames

Ring for hame tug

ADDITIONAL SKILLS

At the Bath Carriage Museum workshops, a craftsman stitches a horse collar. The whole weight of the animal is thrust into the collar, so it must be snug and well padded. On to the collar fit the hames, to which are attached the hame tugs. These buckle on to the traces. The reins pass through the rings and buckle on to the bridle.

FITTING A NEW
LEATHER HEAD

*A superb example of a barouche
in Mr Brian Wicks' workshops
at Malmesbury, Wiltshire, has
its folding head restored by the
expert hands of Mr Lawrence
Roach. The barouche has seats
inside for two couples facing
each other, while the coachman
has a box seat in front. The
folding head is made of leather
stretched over and nailed to a
collapsible wooden frame.
Regular applications of oil and
wax polish keep the leather
supple and waterproof.*

other components. It is not only weather-resistant, but is also easily bent into curved shapes. Instead of being steam-bent, ash for shafts and body-framing can be laminated – thanks to modern glues developed for aircraft construction. The method is to cut lengths of ash to the required curves of the two shafts from a long, thick plank, using a bandsaw. These square-sectioned pieces are then sliced through lengthways again, each into four thinner pieces. Two pieces from each shaft are swapped over, so that when assembled, the laminates will be strengthened by the variation in grain of their component slices. They are then glued together and clamped in a jig until the bond sets. Finally they are given a rounded section with plane, draw-knife and spokeshave. Shafts made in this way are both pliable and strong – though sometimes their tips are protected by steel strapping bent lengthways over the end, and extended back a few inches on top and perhaps a couple of feet underneath.

Lionel Collins, who makes and restores wagons and carriages at Brockenhurst, in the New Forest, reckons the laminating technique superior to steam-bending. The old method, he says, weakens the timber by stretching and compressing its fibres.

Painting, too, is no longer the long, laborious process developed by the craftsmen of yesteryear. The objective, then as now, was to preserve, as well as decorate, the beautiful bodywork. Traditionally, a thick layer of paint was applied to the body panels, composed often of six coats of white lead and six of yellow ochre, in alternate coats. This was left to harden for about three weeks then rubbed down with pumice stone to remove all brush marks and leave a really smooth surface. On would go another two coats of white lead, which was again rubbed smooth, this time with sandpaper. Only then were the topcoats added – two or three of them, usually green or brown, sometimes maroon,

red or yellow. Often each panel would be picked out with thin gold 'coachlines', and a titled owner would have his crest in heraldic colours on the door. Metal fittings would be painted or plated black, and then the vehicle was given a smooth, gloss finish with six coats of copal varnish. The gloss could be preserved by regular polishing with a mixture of oil and rottenstone, a powdered sandy limestone.

Nowadays a good coat of primer-filler is followed by three or four undercoats – still sanding down between coats – and two or three of gloss. Lionel Collins gets good results with either yacht or coach enamel, taking care, of course, to damp down dust in his workshop before brushing it on. Like many modern paints, these enamels do not show brush marks.

Many styles of coach and carriage were built. Four-wheeled ones ranged from light phaetons and victorias up through landaus and berlins to heavy mail and stage-coaches pulled by up to eight horses. At the other end of the scale were two-wheelers so light that the power of a single horse was enough to make them the sports cars of their day – gigs, curricles and cabriolets. Sometimes speed was essential – the cocking cart, designed to rush fighting cocks to and from matches, was high-built with a box beneath the seat to carry birds. The Irish version was so fast and unstable it was called a suicide gig.

But two-wheelers were cheap to make and to run, and so were used for all kinds of workaday jobs. They ranged from butchers' carts and milk-floats to dog carts – for carrying the dogs to a shoot – and governess carts. In these the governess drove sitting sideways at the back so she could keep an eye on the children when taking them for a ride. They were very popular and remain high on the list of the many types that a modern coachbuilder must be able to construct or restore.

THE
COOPER

WORKING MAINLY BY EYE, THE COOPER FASHIONS
WATERTIGHT CONTAINERS OF IMMENSE STRENGTH
FROM CUNNINGLY SHAPED WOODEN STAVES

Making a barrel, like fashioning a wheel, calls for vastly more skill than its simple shape suggests. It is a sort of miracle that a bundle of wood strips can be shaped and secured to form a watertight container that will withstand all the rolling, dropping and other stresses of a busy working life.

For centuries, barrels were used everywhere as basic containers for all manner of goods – liquid and dry. Beer, brandy, flour, tobacco, gunpowder – all were transported and stored in wooden casks. As a result, the craft of barrel-making, or coopering, flourished in every market town and most villages, and was a stock in trade of every brewery and large ship. So sturdy were these containers that many found a further lease of life as chairs, bowls and water-butts when their main work was over.

Sadly, few crafts have dwindled so rapidly as that of the cooper. The vast increase in mass-produced containers – including the milk churns, pickling vats and other articles that were at one time part of his output – has cut the ground from beneath the craftsman's feet. Perhaps the biggest blow was the switch by most breweries to alloy casks. Now, coopers who are still practising the craft work mainly in distilleries, in independent cooperages, in the smaller, more traditional breweries, and in folk museums.

The roots of this demise may well lie in the very complexities of coopering, with its heavy demands on hand labour. To make a barrel, a cooper employs at least 20 different tools. He may use oak or beech, elm or poplar, chestnut, fir or spruce to make the staves for his casks and vats, and he uses hoops of wood and iron to strap them together. Most casks need to be watertight, but some, for holding wine, need to be porous as well to allow the

contents to breathe. Some have to hold 100 gallons or more of liquid, while others may contain only a couple of pints to wash down a farmworker's lunch.

Yet almost all the cooper's products share the great advantage of the barrel. Because they are made from thin staves of wood, stretched and strapped into a smooth curve, they have the taut strength of an arch or a bowstring girder. And because of their circular cross-section, together with the tapered ends, they can be rolled easily.

The history of the craft

Coopering goes back a long way: simple, untapered buckets made from staves appear in paintings on the walls of 4,500-year-old Egyptian tombs. Nearly 3,000 years later, the Romans switched from keeping wine in clay jars to wooden casks, and by Tudor times coopers were in great demand to make containers for shipping and commerce, vintners and brewers. So well established had the craft become that would-be recruits had to serve a seven-year apprenticeship before being able to join one of the guilds.

But the guilds in their turn had to fight long, and often underhand, legal battles to keep their monopoly against brewers recruiting and training their own employees to save the high charges levied by master coopers. In 1533 the Lord Chancellor was given half a butt (over 50 gallons) of malmsey to lend his support to the guilds.

In the end, their efforts were in vain. The brewers' prosperity grew, and along with it their need for coopers, so that they became the biggest and most powerful employers of all. Yet independent coopers still flourished; and at the turn of the century one London company employed 650 coopers. Other groups of coopers worked in the country, fulfilling the much more varied needs of their local communities, while another big branch of the craft involved coopering on board ship. Groups of craftsmen would form part of the crew of a merchantman, working through the whole of the outward voyage turning timber in the hold into casks and barrels to carry the cargo that would be loaded at their destination for the trip home.

The cooper's work, wherever he plied his trade or whatever the purpose of his barrels, began with selecting the wood. In making containers for food or commodities such as tobacco, he might use different kinds of timber, depending on price, strength and such characteristics as the absence of taste or smell. But for casks to hold beer, wines or spirits, the best wood to use was oak.

In the old days, this meant Memel oak, from the forests where Russia, Poland and East Prussia met. This wood was especially suitable for barrels because the young oaks grew among forests of faster-growing firs. As a consequence, they had to compete very hard indeed for life-giving sunlight, making them grow faster – and hence taller and straighter – than English oaks. This gave the wood a straight grain which was ideal for making the staves of barrels.

The tree would be felled, and the branches lopped off, before the trunk was sawn into lengths to suit the size of the finished barrels. Each length was then cleft down the grain into halves and quarters, and then into thinner wedge-shaped pieces like slices from a cake. Finally, each thin wedge was trimmed and planed to produce a single flat stave, with very little waste. Cut in this fashion, the medullary rays – layers of impervious wood which radiate from the centre of the trunk – ran across the stave, making the wood waterproof and resistant to warping. The bundles and staves were seasoned in the open for between three and five years, before the cooper set to work on them.

Although today's coopers do not use Memel oak, they go to considerable pains in picking the most suitable timber available.

A ONCE THRIVING
INDUSTRY

Until a century ago, every town and many villages had at least one cooperage. Barrels were needed for transporting a vast range of goods, wet and dry, both within the country and overseas. As this old print shows, methods have changed little over the years. Then, as now, staves were shaped by hand, and a small stove, or cresset (back, right), was used to set the wood into shape after bending.

The staves which make up the barrel start off as simple strips of wood (A), but they have to go through a series of shaping operations before they can be fitted together to make a watertight whole. First comes listing, or tapering the sides of the stave in towards the ends. Next, the stave is backed and the outside surface is tapered down towards the ends. The inside is curved or hollowed with a two-handed draw-knife (left) and then the stave is jointed – that is, the inside edges are bevelled to allow for the curvature of the barrel. Even then, the outside surfaces still have to be curved, and eventually the staves must be bent to the final shape in the course of assembling the barrel.

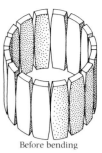

Before bending

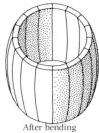

After bending

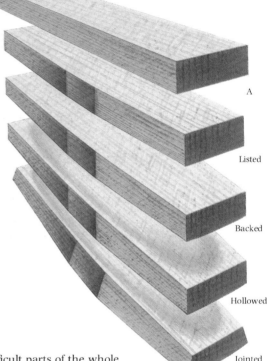

A

Listed

Backed

Hollowed

Jointed

When the staves finally reach the cooper's workshop they are straight and flat, so his first task is to inspect them to check for faults and blemishes and to decide which way each must be curved. Then he begins the long and complex process of cutting them to shape, or dressing them. Small staves, for casks holding less than 9 gallons, are cut on a horse, a small bench on which he sits astride and holds the workpiece with a pivoted clamp held down by foot pressure. Staves for larger casks are wedged on the working block with a metal hook, called a block hook.

The dressing begins with tapering each of the staves from the middle towards the ends, since a barrel is narrower at the top and bottom than it is in the middle. This is called listing. The cooper first cuts the stave roughly to shape with an axe, then finishes off with a two-handed draw-knife. Lastly, he hollows out the inside surface of each stave and smoothes the outside surface to an even curve, using a curved draw-knife for the inner surface and a long, straight-bladed knife for the outside.

Yet, even now, the staves are not finished. Because of the thickness of the barrel, the inner surface of each stave must be narrower than the outside, so the edges have to be jointed, or bevelled, with the aid of a long box plane, called a

jointer. This is one of the most difficult parts of the whole operation, since each stave must eventually be butted tightly enough against the next to prevent any liquid leaking out of the barrel, even under pressure. But as the staves have yet to be bent into their final shape, the cooper must rely on hand and eye to match the bevelled edges and ensure a perfect fit.

When all the staves are cut and smoothed to shape, he assembles them – as they will fit together in the finished barrel – inside a circular iron band called a raising hoop. This fits around the upper ends of the staves. Then he holds the staves in place by tapping a larger wooden hoop, called a truss hoop, down over the outside of the staves to hold their lower ends together. At this stage the barrel is still straight-sided; the narrow iron band at the top holds the staves together as tightly as they will fit at the end of the finished cask, but because they are still straight they splay outwards from the larger truss hoop at the lower end.

This same procedure is used for any size of cask, ranging from a pin of $4\frac{1}{2}$ gallon capacity to a 9 gallon firkin, a kilderkin of 18 gallons, a barrel of 36 gallons, a hogshead of 54 gallons, a puncheon of 72 gallons, right up to a butt, holding 108 gallons. In each case, the cooper must judge

RAISING THE BARREL

This is the first step in assembling the barrel. The cooper begins by fastening the staves together at one end with an iron band called a raising hoop (1), then he taps a larger wooden truss hoop (2) down over the barrel to hold the lower ends together. The intermediate booge hoop (3) reinforces the cask ready for bending.

TRUSSING THE BARREL

The conical barrel now has to have its wider end tapered. First, the cooper wets the wood and heats it by placing the barrel over a fire of shavings in an iron basket, called a cresset (4). As the wood softens, he bends the staves by hammering progressively smaller hoops over the barrel, until the lower ends of the staves are vertical (5). Now he up-ends the barrel and pinches the upper end by hammering just one side of each of a succession of smaller hoops (6 and 7) until, finally, the dingee – or end hoop – can be fitted (8).

FINISHING THE BARREL

The shaped barrel – called a gun – is still not finished. The end panels have to be fitted and a series of permanent metal hoops fastened in place after the temporary hoops are taken off and the outer surface smoothed. The inside may also be shaved smooth, depending on the proposed contents.

Chime

Quarter

Booge

Booge

Quarter

Chime

the radius and the curvature of the cask he is making so that it will hold the intended capacity of liquid when the work is finished. He also has to avoid putting very hard staves next to soft ones, and to watch out for any weaknesses which could eventually result in a stave snapping under pressure.

The most difficult stage is the trussing-up, when the straight staves are bent into their final curves to give the cask its familiar, double-ended shape. First the cooper hammers another hoop – called a booge, or bulge hoop – over the staves to just above the mid-point of the cask. This holds the staves tightly together for just over half their length, and provides reinforcement during bending.

But before bending, the wood of the staves themselves needs to be softened. In the case of 'slight' casks – those with timbers less than $1\frac{1}{2}$ in. thick, the staves are wetted and then warmed by standing them over a cresset, a small iron basket containing burning shavings. Bigger and stronger casks – 'stout' casks – are first put in boiling water or steam for up to half an hour, to soak and soften the wood fibres.

Bending, or trussing, the staves to shape

Once the wood has softened, the trussing begins, with the cooper and an apprentice hammering a smaller wooden truss hoop down over the staves from top to bottom, followed by a series of progressively smaller hoops until the splayed-out lower ends of the staves are pinched to the same dimensions as the middle of the cask. Then the cask is turned over, still over the burning shavings in the cresset, and the truss hoops are beaten back down towards the middle of the cask on one side only. This effectively tightens their grip on the ends of the staves, pinching them together still further until another iron hoop – called a dingee hoop, and equal in size to the truss hoop at the opposite end – can be hammered into position and the cask is finally formed into its finished shape.

By leaving the cask over the fire for another half-hour or so, the cooper can ensure that the staves are completely dried out and harden with a permanent 'set' into their curved shape, so that even if he were to remove all the hoops they would not spring back to their original straightness. At this stage, the cask is a hollow tube, called in the trade a 'gun', and the next step is to finish the ends, so that the 'heads', or end panels, can be fitted to close it off and seal it.

The cooper first hammers another hoop, called a chiming hoop, which is slightly larger than the end hoops of the cask, down over the staves beyond the end hoop, which is then taken off. He leans the barrel against his working block, and sets to work with a specially shaped adze to cut a bevel around the inside of the ends of the staves. He then squares off the end surfaces of the staves, using a curved topping plane, before switching to another curved cutting tool, called a chiv, to cut an evenly curved channel around the inside of the end of the cask. Finally, he uses a curved cutter, called a croze, to cut a deep groove in the centre of this channel, into which the head will be fitted.

The cooper then chimes the other end of the barrel in the same way, but only after checking its capacity by using a pair of metal pins, called diagonals, which are joined together at their upper ends like a large pair of dividers. In this way he ensures that the groove for the second head is cut at exactly the right level for the barrel to hold the required amount of liquid when full. He then knocks away the remaining truss hoops and shaves the outside of the cask to a smoothly curved surface. Sometimes, he finishes off the inside of the cask in the same way. If the casks are being made for wine, beer and certain types of spirits, where the contents continue maturing inside the cask, the inside is left as it is – rough and blistered from the heat of the fire.

The heads themselves are made from flat planks, set

'HEADING' THE BARREL

Fitting the ends, or 'heads', of the barrel calls for great skill. Not only does the cooper have to make them fit tightly and securely, but he has to position them so that the capacity of the finished barrel is accurate – with only his eye, and a pair of metal dividers, to guide him. Each head is made from a number of planks, pinned together with dowels and sealed with reeds, with a bevelled outer edge. The cooper then has to cut a groove inside the barrel (below) to hold the head.

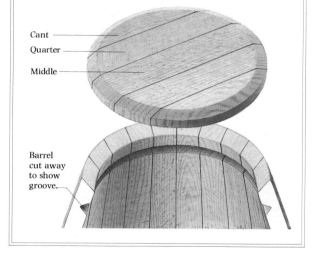

Cant
Quarter
Middle

Barrel cut away to show groove.

edge against edge and joined by pieces of dowelling fitted into holes drilled with an auger. The cooper plugs the gaps between the edges of adjacent planks with a layer of reed to make the head watertight, and then he cuts it to size. To do this, he first adjusts the setting of his compasses by trial and error until they can be 'walked' right round the open end of the cask in exactly six steps, which gives him the right radius for cutting the head. After marking the circle on the wood, he cuts the shape with a bow saw before shaving the surface smooth and bevelling the edges, inside and out, to produce a cross-section sharp enough to fit into the groove already cut inside the ends of the barrel.

Fitting the head at one end of the barrel is relatively easy. The cooper takes off the chime hoop and opens up the staves just enough to tap the head into position, with a layer of reed packed into the groove to seal the joint tightly. Then he closes up the staves and hammers the hoop back.

But fitting the second head is slightly more difficult, since the cooper now has no access to the inside of the barrel through the opposite end to help force the head into position

in its groove. There are different ways of solving the problem – one being to fit the head which contains the tap hole for the barrel last, so that a threaded handle, called a heading vice, can be screwed temporarily into the tap hole to give the grip needed to manoeuvre the head into place.

The barrel is now almost finished, but the cooper still has to fit the rest of the iron hoops which keep it in shape and help to resist the pressure of its contents. As well as the chime hoops at the ends and the booge hoops close to the middle, there are quarter hoops in between. Each of these metal bands has first to be riveted into a hoop of the right diameter by driving a rivet through the ends of the band.

Each hoop is driven home with a heavy hammer and an iron wedge called a driver, and when all are in place the cask is at last a solid whole – tight enough and strong enough to ring like a bell when struck a heavy blow. All that remains is to drill a hole for the bung in the middle of the barrel, which the cooper does with an auger and then smooths with a red-hot iron. The cask is then checked for capacity, and for leaks up to a pressure of 40 lb. to the square inch, before being stamped and passed for use.

MANY YEARS OF USE AHEAD

Making a barrel is a long and difficult job. But when the second head is fitted and branded with a working number, the end result is a tough and versatile container which is stable and easy to handle. In fact, if any damaged staves are carefully replaced, the working life of a renovated cask is almost limitless.

THE CORACLE MAKER

CUNNINGLY BUILT OF WILLOW AND CANVAS, FOR
THOUSANDS OF YEARS THE CORACLE WAS THE MAIN
WORKING BOAT ON SALMON RIVERS IN WEST WALES

*I*t would be hard to conceive a less promising fishing
boat than the coracle. Bowl shaped and without a
keel, it looks impossible to propel in a straight line. And
surely such a flimsy structure would capsize on the dark,
swirling waters of a fast-flowing river?

Yet coracles have been around for thousands of years.
Julius Caesar described their use in Iron Age Britain, and
during the long centuries between they have been the
mainstay of salmon and sea-trout fishers on many rivers in
Wales, and at one time in the Fens. In 1860 there were 300
coracles in use on the Teifi alone, with between 50 and 60
full-time fishermen on the tidal reaches near Cardigan. At
about the same time, 400 fishermen earned their living on
the Tywi.

So there must be more to the coracle than at first meets
the eye. Its current decline – and even disappearance on
some rivers – is due to official restrictions on fishing in non-
tidal waters rather than to competition from more sophisticated craft. Nowadays, a licence is needed for coracle
fishing, and new ones are issued sparingly.

The beauty of the coracle lies in its simplicity. The basket-
like framework is made from locally grown ash, willow,
hazel and even apple. Canvas, coated with pitch, serves for
the covering, though until the 17th century coracles were
clad with tanned animal hides. In those days the dimensions of a single ox or horse hide governed the size of the
finished boat.

Between the 17th and 19th centuries, waterproofed
flannel replaced hides as the covering material. The flannel
was immersed in a boiler containing a mixture of tar and
resin. When saturated, it was lifted out, laid on the
upturned coracle frame and tacked in place.

Lightness has always been one of the coracle's virtues.
Although the size and weight of these craft vary in different
parts of Wales, even the heaviest scales no more than about
40 lb. A strap fastened loosely to the seat, or thwart, enables
its owner to carry it on his shoulders from cottage to
estuary, then back home again after the day's fishing.

In use, a coracle proves a surprisingly handy craft and is
well suited to river fishing – once the user has gained
experience. It will float in only a few inches of water, and it

FRAMING A CORACLE

*Winter-felled pollard willow is
used to make the basic frame of
a Teifi coracle. The poles are
split lengthways with a
billhook, then, gripped firmly in
a 'horse' vice, they are trimmed
into laths with a draw-knife.
Cut to length and laid flat on
the ground, they are then
interwoven (1). The joints are
left unfastened to retain
flexibility and to avoid nails or
bindings chafing the tarred
canvas 'skin' later. Heavy
stones are used to hold the laths
in place while the ends are bent
up. Lengths of string are tied
between the bent-up ends (2) to
serve as a guide when the
builder shapes the gunwales
that will hold the craft together.*

FITTING THE SEAT AND GUNWALE

*The plain plank seat is supported
by a light framework at
gunwale height. The gunwale
itself is made of willow rods
woven together rather like a
basket edging. The bent-up ends
of the laths are simply tucked
into it. A carrying strap of rope
or leather is fixed to the seat –
then all that remains is to skin
the craft with tarred canvas,
nailed to the gunwale.*

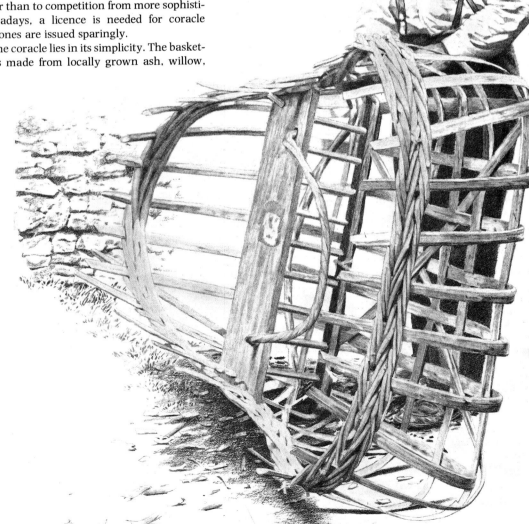

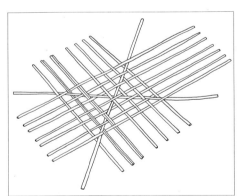

1. Laths laid out and interwoven – no fastenings used.

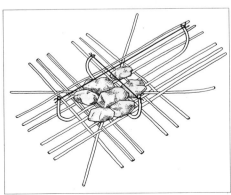

2. String between bent-up laths gives gunwale line.

64

A TIGHT COMMUNITY

The light construction of the Teifi coracle is revealed in the easy way two of these Cenarth fishermen are carrying them. A century ago, the village was the centre of salmon fishing in West Wales, and the men formed a tight community, regarding the river as their own territory. They would operate in pairs, the two coracles being allowed to drift gently downstream with a double-walled net slung between them. The nets themselves were made of hemp, and they were held by lines woven from horsehair.

is more manoeuvrable than boats of conventional shape. Propulsion is by a single paddle, which is worked in a figure-of-eight action over the prow – the blunt end of the coracle. In this way the craft is pulled rather than pushed through the water. Resting lightly on the surface, it can be propelled surprisingly fast, even against the current. An expert can maintain the boat's position with one hand while manipulating a net or rod with the other.

In spite of their lightweight construction, coracles are strong enough to give safe, reliable service for perhaps two years of regular use. Costing so little to make, they are considered disposable after this time.

Design has always varied in different areas of Wales, in part to suit the speed, depth and turbulence of local streams. Individual fishermen have their preferences, too, some favouring a light craft and others a heavy one. A Teifi coracle, for example, can weigh as little as 25 lb. or as much as 36 lb., with a length varying from 50 in. to 60 in. On the Dee, two-seater coracles weighing as much as 40 lb. were at one time commonplace around Llangollen.

Methods of construction, too, vary from river to river. Some coracles, such as those on the Teifi and the Tywi, have gunwales (sides) of plaited willow or hazel. In others, the gunwales are formed of either single or double laths or a curving branch cut from an apple tree. The framework is a sort of basket woven from laths of willow or ash.

For the most part, coracles were made by the fishermen themselves, following the traditional local pattern. But a few villages, such as Cenarth, had specialised coracle makers who were able to make superior boats.

The change from hide to flannel as a covering was triggered by the growth of the woollen industry in West Wales during the 18th and 19th centuries. The canvas used on present-day craft was originally looked down on as a cheap substitute for flannel. A writer in 1805 said that 'flannel is a more durable substance. It may be easier prepared and keeps out the water much longer than canvas.'

Whatever the truth of that, throughout the present century it has been the practice to cover all coracles with unbleached twill calico. After tacking the material to the frame, 6 lb. of pitch mixed with half a pint of linseed oil is boiled, allowed to cool and applied to the outside.

It is a far cry from the heyday of coracle fishing in the 17th and 18th centuries to its present diminished state. Until 100 years ago, the fishermen of the Teifi, for instance, formed what was virtually a closed community, resenting outside interference on what they regarded as their private territory. The main centre was the village of Cenarth.

Because of diminishing fish stocks, no new licences for the non-tidal section of the river have been issued since 1935. As a consequence, the use of coracles has declined year by year, and there are none now to be seen at Cenarth. Below Llechryd Bridge, which is regarded as tidal, there are no such restrictions and ten coracles are still licensed to fish in the picturesque Cilgerran Gorge.

On the Tywi, 12 nets are still licensed to fish for salmon in the tidal reaches of the river below the town of Carmarthen. On the Tâf, a short, swift river that flows into Carmarthen Bay near Dylan Thomas's village of Laugharne, only two licences are issued.

These are the only active survivors of a unique craft and a great tradition, although you can see the boats, and learn more about them, in the Welsh Folk Museum at St Fagans (see p. 255) and the Museum of English Rural Life at Reading (p. 240). Yet, even now, if you take a holiday in West Wales and have a good share of luck, there is just a chance that you may see a pair of these unique boats in action, with a net strung between them to catch the noble salmon on its upstream run.

EACH RIVER ITS OWN CORACLE

The shape and detailed construction of coracles varied from river to river. The round, bowl-shaped Severn coracle looked quite different from the squarish blunt-nosed Teifi craft – which was different again from the round-nosed, square-sterned Tywi version. Clues to the differences lay in the varying nature of the rivers – fast running or slow, deep or shallow, smooth or with rough water and rapids. Oars differed too, from the broad paddle of the Severn to the thin blade of the Teifi.

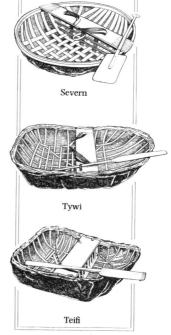

Severn

Tywi

Teifi

THE CORN DOLLY MAKER

THE ORIGINS OF CORN DOLLIES ARE FIRMLY
BASED IN PRE-CHRISTIAN RITUALS. SOME OF THE
BASIC SHAPES HAVE ENDURED FOR HUNDREDS, OR
EVEN THOUSANDS, OF YEARS

Corn dollies may seem little more than quaint and decorative by-products of the annual harvest, but their shapes derive from a rich and time-honoured folklore. They have been made for many thousands of years – the craft's European traditions may have originated in ancient Greece – and they are found in virtually every country where corn is grown.

Some designs are widespread, notably those symbolising the 'horn of plenty', or cornucopia. But British dollies also have strong regional characteristics. Traditional shapes include Cambridgeshire bells, Suffolk horseshoes, Welsh fans and Herefordshire lanterns.

Staffordshire's triple-looped knot recalls the story of four prisoners awaiting the gallows in the county gaol. The executioner is said to have struck a grisly bargain, whereby the man who devised a knot capable of hanging his three companions in a single 'drop' would be spared.

A few dollies are local to the point of being linked with individual communities. One is the 'kern baby' from the Northumberland village of Whalton. Made in the shape of a female figure, it used to preside as guest of honour at the annual harvest supper. A triangular dolly representing the Holy Trinity has become associated with Alwington, Devon. Dollies shaped like a chalice are typical of the Vale of Pickering, in Yorkshire.

There can be little doubt that dollies were originally made for religious reasons connected with the harvest. Old traditions and superstitions, strong enough to survive the advent of Christianity, varied greatly in different parts of the country. In many ways they formed the basis for the harvest-festival services, whose origins are as recent as the 19th century.

In some parts of Britain it was believed that the spirit who made the land fruitful gradually retreated before the reapers, finally taking refuge in the last of the uncut corn. The final sheaf was therefore made into a human effigy and kept in the farmhouse until the following spring, when the fields were ready to be sown again. The idea was to preserve the benevolent spirit throughout the winter. The dolly would sometimes be broken up and scattered over the fields as a charm to ensure another fruitful harvest.

Elsewhere, the dolly would be held aloft among farmworkers, who bared their heads and bowed three times as a mark of respect. Or it might be taken home, riding in a place of honour on the farmer's wagon.

Some makers, who were almost invariably men until the craft became popular, favoured dollies made from seven straws because they symbolised the seven years of plenty mentioned in the Old Testament. Their nimble fingers also fashioned decorative buttonholes and love tokens. Dollies in the form of a baby's rattle have long been associated with Anglesey.

Strength and pliability make wheat straw the most popular raw material, but changes in agriculture have made it increasingly difficult to obtain the most suitable types. Traditional wheat was long and willowy, and its hollow stalk supported a small head. But such varieties are of little value to the modern farmer interested in producing the greatest possible yield of grain. Scientists have therefore developed types of wheat with virtually solid stems – which make it either difficult or impossible to form satisfactory joins by pushing one piece into another. These varieties carry large, high-yielding heads which look out of proportion on a small dolly.

To counter these problems, today's dolly makers grow their own wheat, or rely on the few farmers prepared to cultivate such varieties as Maris Widgeon and Square-head Master. Rye, barley and oats, both wild and cultivated, are also used.

The introduction of the combine harvester was also bad news for the craft, because such machines strip heads and mangle stalks. Dolly straw must therefore be cut either by hand or by an old-fashioned cornbinder. It should be cut a week or two before the corn is fully ripe to avoid the grain dropping when the stalks are handled.

The weather is important, too. There must be sufficient rain to make the corn grow well, but with prolonged sunshine immediately before reaping to create a golden hue of deep richness and great beauty. Too much rain leaves ugly blemishes on the stalks. They range from light grey to black, and produce weaknesses where the straw will almost certainly split while it is being worked.

Preparing and storing the corn

The outer leaves are stripped off and the corn is graded – generally as fine, medium and thick – before being stored. It may also be trimmed at this stage, because only the length between the head and the stem's first leaf joint is used. Corn can be stored almost indefinitely in dry surroundings, but will certainly attract foraging mice if the storage place is not secure against them.

Other materials include strong, neutral-coloured thread, wire for the frames used in some of the bigger and more elaborate dollies, and decorative ribbons. There are five traditional ribbon colours, each with its own significance. White denotes purity, blue is for truth, red represents warmth, yellow honours the colour of the corn itself and green symbolises the eventual rebirth of the seeds in springtime.

Corn must be tempered, or soaked, before use to restore its natural flexibility. Wrapped in a towel, it is placed in water for about three hours, until the dolly-maker's experience indicates that it is ready. Some add a few drops of disinfectant or even bleach, but others prefer their dollies to remain as natural as possible. The corn is left in the damp towel while the dollies are being made, because it would otherwise tend to become dry and brittle as the water evaporates.

The old-time craftsmen had no such problems. They created their works of rustic art out in the fields, using corn that had only just been cut.

Making dollies is such an individualistic exercise that details vary considerably from craftsman to craftsman, as well as from region to region. Though some are quite complicated and ornate, it is the simple figures that best capture the spirit of yesterday's farmworkers making effigies to celebrate a successful harvest.

Spirals are the basis of many traditional designs. Their shape echoes that of the cornucopia, which is linked in mythology with Zeus, the greatest of the gods of ancient Greece. It is indeed remarkable that such forms should survive until nearly the end of the 20th century.

Cambridgeshire bell

Suffolk horseshoe

Staffordshire triple knot

Herefordshire lantern

Welsh fan

HOW A SPIRAL IS MADE

The simple Yorkshire spiral, demonstrated here by Maggie Evans, of Trefriw, Gwynedd, is made by binding five heads of corn together, very tightly, then opening out four of the stalks until they lie at right-angles to each other, like the main points of the compass. The work is held in the left hand, with the fifth, or 'active', stalk laid alongside the straw which points away from that hand. The active straw is passed under its immediate neighbour and bent back over it to form a right-angle. The work is then turned anti-clockwise, through one quarter of a circle, and the process is repeated using the straw alongside which the original active stem has come to rest.

The diameter of the spiral can be kept constant by placing the active straw on top of the one to which it is moved with each quarter-turn, or decreased by putting it on the inside. The cross-sectional shape created by using five straws is rectangular, but it can be made more circular by starting with a greater number. The spiral is eventually tapered right down and bound.

1. Binding the five heads together with thread.

2. Bending the active straw to start the spiral.

4. Like the cornucopia from which it derives, the top of the spiral is tapered.

3. The spiral grows as the process is repeated.

5. Remaining lengths of straw are plaited and tied.

6. The plaited ends, bedecked with ribbon, form a loop.

THE COUNTRY CHAIR MAKER

BODGERS, BOTTOMERS AND BENDERS WERE AMONG THE
HIGHLY SPECIALISED CRAFTSMEN WHO MADE WINDSOR
CHAIRS AND OTHER TRADITIONAL DESIGNS

There is no finer example of the country-chair maker's craft than the traditional Windsor or 'stick-back' chair. It was first made over 200 years ago in the beechwoods of England, at a time when the country was largely composed of villages – a rural society where the fashionable furniture of the day was either too expensive or insufficiently sturdy.

Why the Windsor chair is so called, no one knows for certain; but the name has been in use since early in the 18th century. The most likely reason is that since most of these chairs were first made in High Wycombe, they were often dispatched to London from the market at Windsor. Before they acquired the name, they were known, less attractively, as stickbacks.

The ancestor of the Windsor chair was the 'turned' stool – a commonplace piece of furniture from medieval times that was robust enough to survive rough handling.

The stool was made of oak and had three or four legs socketed into the seat. When this principle was extended – with back and arms socketed into the top of the seat – the Windsor chair was born: a cheap, strong and surprisingly comfortable piece of furniture.

At first the chair was confined to the cottage and servants' quarters. But by the 19th century it had spread to the tavern and club, and a century later was used in kitchens, nurseries, dining-rooms and schools. It was also a popular garden chair.

Although the principle of construction for a Windsor chair was always the same, there were many differences in design and style. These differences either reflected the latest fashions in town furniture, or were to satisfy special needs. For example, chairs with slightly shorter legs than normal – plus other features – were made for nursing mothers; low-backed chairs for men's smoking clubs and reading rooms; and chairs with an arm-rest that incorporated a flattened surface were made as writing chairs.

Various native woods were – and still are – used, with the seat made of elm, the legs of beech, and the back and arms of yew or ash. Beech is a strong timber, with a straight and close grain, that cuts smoothly and can be turned when green. Thus, beechwood was the life-blood of the 18th-century chair makers. And although the Windsor chair was ultimately made in many areas of England, including Norfolk, Lancashire, North Wales and the West Country, the craft was concentrated in the High Wycombe region of the Chiltern Hills in Buckinghamshire – where there is the largest acreage of beech forest in Britain.

Some craftsmen worked in the forest clearings, but most worked in village workshops. The man who made the whole of a chair himself was a rarity – usually many different people made the individual parts before a chair was assembled. Pit sawyers cut the felled trees into planks and logs; benchmen prepared sawn parts for the back, side rails

and arms; bottomers shaped the seats; bodgers turned the legs and the stretchers that formed the strengthening framework between them; benders made the curved backs and arms; framers assembled the chairs; and finishers and polishers completed them.

Tree-felling took place in autumn and winter months when the sap was down and was often done by the pit sawyers. Theirs was the hardest physical work. They worked in pairs, one man digging a pit – as deep as a man's height and up to 15 ft long – while the other, usually the senior, prepared the logs and the saw. This was a massive affair, more than 7 ft long and with a handle at each end, and tapering in width from 10 in. to 3 in.

With a log positioned over the pit, and resting on shorter logs laid across the pit, the planks were cut. The man above applied the cutting pressure and steered the saw, the man in the pit pushed the saw up again. From time to time the saw was lubricated with oil, the drips adding to the sawdust and sweat that coated the unfortunate man below.

The chair seats were cut from 2 in. thick planks with a frame saw. In the Wycombe district, this saw became

THE SAW-PIT

Cutting logs into planks was almost a craft in itself in the days before power saws were invented. The unfortunate pitman, often an apprentice, was showered with sawdust and had the strenuous task of pushing the saw back into the 'up' position. The top man steered the saw, which cut through the log on its down stroke.

ADZING A SEAT

The seats are shaped from lengths of 2 in. thick elm planks. Each length is cut on a band-saw to the shape of a seat template. With the seat on the ground, against a fixed stop, the craftsman – called a bottomer – carves the upper surface of the wood to resemble a saddle. In some cases this means reducing the thickness of the seat, in places, to $\frac{3}{4}$ in. The final shaping and smoothing to achieve subtle curves are done with various spokeshaves and stock scrapers.

TURNING LEGS

Beech logs that have been sawn into chair-leg lengths are split along the grain, with a mallet and wedge, into triangular-shaped pieces called 'billets'. When the billets have seasoned – about five or six weeks later – they are turned to give the design of the legs. The strengthening framework between them is made in the same way.

known as the Dancing Betty and, less commonly, the Jesus Christ Saw, since 'you did keep a-bowing to him'. The bottomer placed the seat on the floor, against a stop, and using a razor-sharp adze – similar to a curved axe – he carved the seat to the shape of a saddle. Swinging the adze with the rhythm of a pendulum, he reduced the seat to a mere $\frac{3}{4}$ in. thick. It was dangerous work, as evidenced by a 19th-century bottomer named Billy 'No-Toes' Neville.

How the bodger got his name is conjectural; but it was in no way related to the 18th-century derogatory term applied to a clumsy patcher, for the bodger was a highly skilled craftsman. Possibly it derives from badger, one-time name for a travelling salesman – which some bodgers were.

The bodger worked in a clearing in the woods, just inside the entrance of a small hut thatched with brushwood. A springy young larch tree provided the motive power for his lathe – a primitive but effective method used by the ancient Egyptians for turning wood. (See the Craft of the Wood-turner, p. 220.) With a selection of razor-sharp chisels, the bodger pared off the surplus wood and turned out legs with exquisite precision.

SHAPING A BACK-BOW

When the twine applied to secure the bent back-bow is no longer under tension, the wood is said to be cold – that is, it will retain its curved shape. Holes are drilled to receive the 'sticks' that form the back and sides of the chair – half depth for the back-bow, full depth for the arm-bows.

BENDING A BACK-BOW

The curved backs and arms are made from selected branches of yew or ash. The wood is put in a steamer for two hours, to make it pliable, and then bent round a block and cramped in place. The ends are tied with twine and the bow left to dry for about five or six weeks.

EDWIN SKULL.

SKULL'S PATENT PLECTANEUM CHAIR.
IN AMERICAN BIRCH.

EDWIN SKULL,
Manufacturer
OF EVERY DESCRIPTION OF CHAIRS,
HIGH WYCOMBE,
BUCKS.

During a five-and-a-half day week, working a 12 hour day, a pair of good bodgers in the early 1900s produced legs and frameworks for 360 chairs. For this each might share 76s. – poor money, even in those days.

Not all bodgers worked full-time or, indeed, for themselves. Often they were employed by a local farmer and only worked on the lathe in between other more important jobs, such as mowing, reaping or thatching.

Modern machine-turned legs are made with well-seasoned wood, and dry out circular in cross-section. But bodgers used green wood, which dried out oval shaped and so provided a clue when identifying a hand-made chair. If a chair has legs with three rings turned in them, this usually means it was made at Wycombe.

To make the bow – the eye-catching feature of a bow-back Windsor – lengths of timber were boiled, or steamed in a tank to make them pliable. They were then bent round a shaping-block and pegged until the wood was 'cold' – that is, dry enough to retain its shape. The wood was then transformed to the subtle shapes of a bow with a variety of draw-knives and spokeshaves.

In the workshops the chairs were assembled, stained and polished, and prepared for delivery. At the turn of the century, chairs bound for London from Wycombe were transported by road – the chairs wrapped in straw and piled five or six layers high on horse-drawn wagons. The 30 mile journey to London might be made by a train of 30 or 40 wagons, after a last drink at the King of Prussia, and take 36 hours in all.

A hundred years earlier, when country-chair making was still a cottage craft, both finished chairs and miniature sample versions were taken out on wagons for display to prospective customers. In the 1850s, hand-drawn and hand-painted catalogues were being produced, which by the 1860s were available in printed form for prospective buyers to keep and use. Sometimes these were in the shape of a broadsheet, as for the Edwin Skull advertisement shown opposite, while others were catalogues containing over 400 chair designs, all of which were available at short notice.

These catalogues, together with the mass-production methods introduced to the chair-making factories, changed the nature of the craft, and in many parts of the country large numbers of country chairs were made with little variation in design.

Another consequence of mass-production was that men were forced to abandon the woods and their village workshops. It was a time of change. Nevertheless, the craft of the hand-made chair maker lingers on even to this day, preserving a link with a centuries-old tradition.

Rush-seat chairs

Another type of chair that flourished for a while as a cottage industry was the rush-seat chair. During the late 19th century, many thousands of rush-seat chairs were made at High Wycombe for use in village halls and churches.

At first the chairs were made solely by men; but from about 1880 onwards, the work was shared by both sexes. Men made the wooden frame, generally of ash. Women – working in their homes – made the rush seats. The rush

'matters', as they were called, had a job that was both hard and unpleasant, since the rushes were full of dust and needed to be soaked in water in order to make them sufficiently pliable to weave. The rushes also smelled abominably, and it was a standing joke among locals to point out that you could 'smell a matter a mile off'. The rushes were harvested and stacked in barns to dry, until they were ready for use. A matter, who sat either on a low stool or on the floor, had to be able to judge how many rushes were needed, and know how to twist and weave them together in order to make a comfortable chair. The cushion-like seat was stuffed with broken rushes, pushed between the woven covering of rushes that formed the seat.

CANE SEATING – A COTTAGE INDUSTRY

Cane has been used for chair seats and chair backs since the early 17th century. When this photograph was taken, around 1910, caning was for the most part a cottage industry in the hands of women outworkers. The method they used has not changed to this day. The split canes are threaded through holes around the seat frame – some from front to back, some sideways and some woven diagonally. Temporary plugs used to keep the cane taut during threading are replaced, in the final stages, by plugs of thick cane tapped in flush with the surface of the wooden surround.

148 STYLES TO CHOOSE FROM *Edwin Skull's broadsheet of Wycombe chair designs includes folding (Plectaneum) and cane-backed types, as well as rocking chairs, reclining chairs, stools, high chairs for babies, and a remarkable assortment of dining and casual chairs. The firm was established during the 1830s and traded under its original name until taken over by Ercol Ltd, in 1932. The impressive range was designed with many interchangeable parts, so that orders were easily made up from stock. Some 2,000 rush-seated ladder-back chairs, supplied for St Paul's Cathedral during the 1860s, remained sound enough to fetch good prices when sold off during the 1960s. Many went to America.*

THE CRICKET BALL MAKER

HIS CUNNINGLY MADE SPHERES OF CORK AND LEATHER
MUST SATISFY BATSMAN, BOWLER AND FIELDER – NOT
TO MENTION THE GENTLEMEN AT MCC

A cricket ball has to be strong enough to withstand a blow that can propel it at over 100 miles an hour, yet soft enough to be hit all over the ground without losing its bounce or falling apart. It is this delicate balance that creates the sweet thud when bat meets ball.

At present the rules of Marylebone Cricket Club lay down that a full-size ball must weigh between $5\frac{1}{2}$ and $5\frac{3}{4}$ oz., must have a circumference of between $8\frac{13}{16}$ and 9 in., and must be red – a perfect choice of colour, since it is at the opposite end of the spectrum from the green of the cricket pitch.

Ever since cricket, as we know it, was first played in the south-east 200 years ago, West Kent has been the centre of the cricket-ball industry. Today there are only two manufacturers left – Alfred Reader and Co. and British Cricket Balls. Reader's, the larger of the two, have been making cricket balls for 170 years.

Until recently the firm's employees included generation after generation of the same families of cricket-ball craftsmen. Many of them are fanatical about the game they serve. During the lunch-break, improvised games of cricket in the yard are no unusual sight.

The white cow hides for cricket-ball covers are cut into strips and soaked for seven days in barrels of red chemical dye. They are then dried on a line and stacked in boxes so that any moisture that is left spreads itself evenly throughout the strip. To make the leather more supple, the strips are stretched on a small machine called a strake before being pared, or skived, to the correct thickness and cut into diamond-shaped quarters on a clicking press.

Several of the terms used in cricket-ball manufacture originated in other leather-working crafts. It is the closer – a name borrowed from the shoe-making trade – who makes the covers. He matches up the quarters for colour, thickness and texture and makes his own thread from six strands of hemp which he rubs down with a wax made from resin and lard. Then with a flurry of strong, darting fingers he sews up the two quarters into half covers. Since Alfred Reader and Co. first started manufacturing cricket balls they have used enough thread to stretch halfway to the Moon.

The turner stretches the halves and glues 'false quarters' of leather on the insides as reinforcements. He bangs out the ridge where the quarters were stitched together and stamps the halves to the right size and shape around moulds in a hydraulic press. Surplus leather is trimmed off under a turning press. About 20 years ago only knives and handpresses were used. The few machines that are used today, however, do little more than speed up what is still very much a hand craft.

By this stage the centres have already been made. Only a few years ago the 'quilts' – a term borrowed from the saddler's craft – were made by hand at Reader's, but today they are mostly machine-moulded. This is the only radical departure from traditional methods of manufacture. The quilt-maker used to take a 1 in. cube of cork and wind up to eight alternate layers of worsted and cork strips around it. Since the worsted was worked wet, it tightened around the cork as it dried out and shrank. It was this process that gave the ball its bounce. Occasionally he hammered the quilt in a mould to make it spherical, but the only other tools he had were a gauge and an experienced eye. With these, a skilled craftsman could transform the cube into a perfectly round ball in about a quarter of an hour.

Machine-moulds can now produce 60 identical centres in the same time. A tapered strip of material, consisting of a layer of cork and Terylene fibre and a layer of rubber, is wrapped around a rubber core. This is then moulded into a ball in a press.

After a fitter has weighed the centre and matched it up with the cover, a seamer places it inside the two halves which he then stitches up. The ball is held in a seamer's vice so that the seam stands proud; this stretches the leather to ensure a tight fit and makes the seam easier to sew. Depending on the quality of the ball, the seamer sews exactly 80, 70 or 60 stitches into the seam. He has nothing to guide him but his eye.

When he has finished, he places the ball in another vice which squeezes any proudness from the seam. A stitcher adds another two rows of stitches, thread flying and fingers dancing.

In the finishing department, the balls are stamped with gold leaf and moulded for up to 20 minutes in screw-presses until they are perfectly shaped. They are then tested by eye and feel, and also on gauges and scales. Finally, they are polished. Each craftsman – closer, turner, fitter, seamer and stitcher – has left his own mark on the ball in the form of a letter, a figure or a collection of dots. If anything is wrong, the ball can be sent back to the man responsible.

From the time the leather is first cut up until the ball is packaged, a Grade 'A' first-class ball has had two and a half hours of skilled craftsmanship put into it. There are three different sizes of ball – full-size, women's and youths' – each of which has several grades, depending on the quality of the leather and the number of stitches in the seam.

In 1950 there were seven factories producing hand-made cricket balls in West Kent; in all, they employed more than 200 craftsmen. Today, the two manufacturers employ a total of around 50. Cheaper imports from India and Australia have taken away much of the trade, but the balls are often made from inferior materials or machine-sewn. It is likely therefore that, as long as first-class cricket is played in England, there will be a demand for the balls that English craftsmen produce.

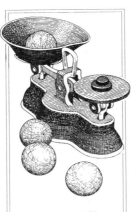

GETTING THE WEIGHT RIGHT

The weight of a full-size cricket ball, established in 1774 at between $5\frac{1}{2}$ and $5\frac{3}{4}$ oz., is one of three specifications that have to be met. The others are size and colour. Most of the standards in the craft of cricket-ball manufacture are maintained by the eye and expertise of the craftsman. However, scales are used for double-checking. The fitter uses them when he weighs the centre in order to match it up with a suitable cover. At a later stage they are used to check that the weight of the finished ball falls within the exacting tolerance of $\frac{1}{4}$ oz.

PARTS OF A CRICKET BALL

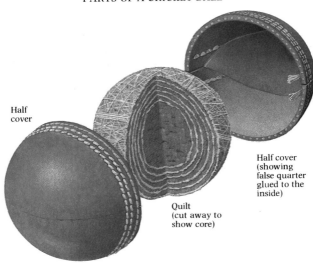

Half cover

Half cover
(showing false quarter glued to the inside)

Quilt
(cut away to show core)

JOINING THE QUARTERS *The closer holds the two quarters in position over a mould and stitches them together with a waxed hempen thread; he then turns the half cover inside out.*

DYEING *Only the very best leather is used in the making of cricket-ball covers. Strips of hide are left for a week in barrels of red chemical dye before being hung to dry in a Dutch barn.*

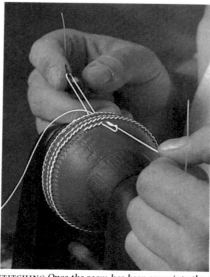

STITCHING *Once the seam has been sewn into the ball, two more rows of stitches are added. The job is very tiring on the eyes, and most craftsmen pay for their dexterity by having to wear glasses.*

POLISHING *Once the leather has been partially degreased over a Bunsen burner, the balls are polished. Three coats of lacquer, applied with a cotton-wool 'dolly' in the finishing department, transform the previously dull cover of the balls into a glowing, shiny red.*

THE CRICKET BAT MAKER

KING WILLOW'S GLORIOUS SUMMER REIGN DEPENDS
ON THE DEDICATED CRAFTSMEN WHO SHAPE BAT AND
HANDLE TO BOUNDARY-STRIKING PERFECTION

Down a green lane in deepest Sussex, in a well-weathered straggle of wooden huts, some of the best cricket bats in the world are made. The names of heroes who have wielded them read like a roll of honour from the court of King Willow. Headed by the legendary Dr W. G. Grace himself, who scored his 100th century and amassed 1,000 runs with one of these bats in the halcyon month of May 1895. Classical batsmen like W. R. 'Wally' Hammond and Sir Frank Worrell have swung them, and the incomparable Clive Lloyd heads a long list of today's smiters who swear by them.

The little 'factory' sits surrounded by trees just outside the village of Robertsbridge. The bats it now turns out look somewhat different from those used by the good Dr Grace, for they have cunningly sited hollows in the back of the blade to increase efficiency, and steel springs down the handle for added power. But the blade is still made of best English willow, and the handle of cane. And although machines take on preparatory work, the subtle shaping of both blade and handle is done as it was nearly a century ago, by craftsmen plying plane and draw-knife, chisel and spokeshave, working entirely by hand and eye.

THE CHANGING SHAPE OF THE CRICKET BAT

Although the cricket bat has evolved from a rough club to a sophisticated sporting 'weapon', its basic shape has remained familiar over the past 200 years or so. The bat of 1750, long-handled and carved from one piece of willow, has the meat extending down to its blunt toe, but is recognisably the ancestor of the 1980 version. Now the meat is tapered out towards the toe of the blade, into the top of which a sprung handle is spliced. The spliced handle, made from cane, arrived in the 1850s.

1750   1980

CLEAVING THE WILLOW *Cricket-bat willow is sawn into 26 in. logs, which are split down the grain into sections known as clefts. Here, one craftsman uses the back of his axe to hammer his partner's cleaving axe.*

The origins of cricket are ancient and obscure, but there are references to a game markedly similar to that played today dating from the late 16th century. Bats had evolved in shape from simple club-like sticks to the recognisable ancestor of the modern implement by the mid-18th century. They were, however, fashioned from solid wood, and the jar that resulted from hitting a ball hard was a palm-tingling experience. Then, in the 1850s, a Lord's cricket professional, Thomas Nixon, made a bat with a resilient, shock-absorbing cane handle spliced into the blade. His 'springy' handle set a pattern that has survived – developed and improved over the years by the insertion of other materials such as gutta percha, whalebone, cork and rubber for even greater comfort and resilience.

The blade had arrived at its present shape, straight-sided with a bulge known as the 'meat' about two-thirds of the way down the back, by around 1775. But subtle variations of that shape have been and still are the province of the bat-makers, each with his own theory of what constitutes perfection.

The maker has a free hand within maximum dimensions fixed as long ago as 1835: the bat must be no more than $4\frac{1}{4}$ in. wide and 38 in. long.

There are many varieties of willow, but few suitable for making cricket bats. Of these the best is *Salix alba caerulea*, which can grow up to 100 ft tall and 18 ft in girth. It is close-grained, resilient and when seasoned, resistant to splitting. The bat-maker quite often cultivates his own willow; otherwise he buys it from a willow plantation owner or timber merchant.

Bat willows are grown from cuttings known as 'setts'. They are selected for cultivation when they are 12 ft high, and must be perfectly free from knots and blemishes. They can be planted out either with their roots on or as cuttings.

The setts are planted 2 ft 6 in. deep in rows not less than 30 ft apart, as they need plenty of light and air. In their first years they may need to be protected from damage by cattle and wild animals, and the trunk is kept free from branches for its first 10 ft by rubbing off shoots and buds. They grow fast – one cut at Robertsbridge some time ago had a girth of 50 in. at a height of 5 ft from the ground after only nine years. This is the size considered large enough for bat-making, and usually takes 10–12 years to achieve. One giant willow felled at Boreham, Essex, in 1888, was 111 ft tall, weighed 11 tons and was 53 years old. It made 1,179 bats, each one 'sound as a bell'.

Cutting into blade-size sections

When the tree is felled, the trunk is sawn into short lengths. As soon as possible – preferably on the spot – these are then split by hand down the grain into sections known as 'clefts'. Great skill is required to make the most of each trunk section, with every cleft just the right size to make one bat blade.

The clefts are sawn into a rough blade shape – ending up looking like long, low, pitch-roofed huts in miniature. Both ends of each cleft are waxed to prevent the porous ends drying too quickly and perhaps splitting or warping. They are then stacked carefully for seasoning – in open-sided huts when possible. This process can take 9–12 months, the willow losing more than half its weight in moisture. At Robertsbridge, the final stages of seasoning are speeded by stacking the clefts in a kiln – an old Nissen hut heated by oil. They stay in the kiln for about five weeks.

Seasoned clefts are put through a couple of planing machines to smooth them to accurate size, and a precise 'V' is sawn in one end to take the handle.

Before going to the men who will finally shape the blade, the bat is put through a roller press which exerts a pressure of 2,000 lb. on the blade as it goes through – first forwards and then backwards. This compresses the fibres of the willow, 'tempering' the blade, reducing it in size by about $\frac{1}{16}$ in. Before the press was introduced, the willow was compressed by hand hammering.

Handles are made from best Sarawak cane at Gray-Nicholls, the Robertsbridge firm. The long canes, all between about $\frac{1}{2}$ in. and $\frac{5}{8}$ in. in diameter, lie stacked in an open-ended hut. When needed, they are cut into sections of varying sizes, according to the length of handles required. Then they are carefully sorted to ensure that only perfectly sound pieces are used. These are put through a cane-splitting machine, which also planes them into squared sections.

Each handle is made up of from 12 to 16 of these sections, with 'springs' of resilient, shock-absorbing material inserted. They are glued together, then turned to shape on a special lathe, which gives them a slightly oval, rather than round, section for a better grip. Finally, the bottom of the handle is sawn into a long wedge shape.

How the handle is fitted

Fitting it is another highly skilled exercise, done entirely by eye. After first tapping the handle in to gauge its rough fit, the handle-fitter removes it again, puts it in his vice, and planes minute shavings from it. Then, using a broad, razor-sharp chisel, he makes a vertical chop at the tip of the wedge to blunt it to a width of about $\frac{3}{16}$ in. He then tries it in the blade again – and often the fit is perfect.

If it is not, he repeats the process until it is, working all the time with great speed and accuracy. When perfection is achieved, the fit is so tight that a hefty downwards blow on the bat's shoulder is needed to remove the handle. Finally, he spreads a thin film of hot animal glue from a pot simmering at his elbow on to the mating edges, and bangs the handle in, giving it a finely calculated forward slant which makes all the difference between a well and a poorly balanced bat. Amazingly, the whole job takes only a few minutes.

Now comes the time when the still-unformed bat is shaped to final perfection. The craftsman who does this wears a heavy belt, buckled at the back and deepening to a short apron at the front. He puts the toe in his bench vice while the handle rests on the apron as he works the draw-knife towards him along the length of the blade. With rapid strokes he pares away the willow in long, thick shavings until the correct shape emerges, with the meat at its maximum thickness in just the right place.

Then he goes to work with a plane – drawing it towards him rather than using the more usual technique of pushing it forwards. Finer shavings fly as the marks of the draw-knife all but disappear. He pauses at intervals to wipe the shoe of the plane on a lightly oiled pad, to clean it and keep it

running smoothly. A spokeshave replaces the plane for the final, crucial strokes.

He also uses the draw-knife, then rasps and a file to smooth the handle to its correct final shape, taking special care where it meets the shoulders of the blade. He stops now and then to test the feel and balance of the bat by taking guard at an imaginary wicket, or making a few strokes at an invisible ball. Once satisfied, he gives the bat its first sanding, using a belt sander, and then a roller sander to work in the hollows of the shoulders.

The bat then goes for bleaching: coats of an ammonia-based bleach are sponged on to the blade at three 24 hour intervals – a process from which it emerges creamy-white. This bleaching is purely for cosmetic reasons – customers simply prefer their bats white. Once dry, the bat goes through a light roller press to compress any surface fibres raised by the bleaching, and is sanded once more, using fine-grit belts.

The blade is finally burnished with a white wax compound on a thick felt wheel, sealing the willow and giving it a most attractive, satin-smooth finish.

Women workers bind the handle with linen thread, after first giving it a light coat of hot animal glue. They mount the bat on a lathe, and with great dexterity run the thread on to the handle as it turns, finishing off with a special loop to avoid an unsightly knot. Finally, they fit the rubber grip.

All that remains is to brand the bat with its distinguishing marks and transfers, and it is ready for the customer – who is also given some written tips on how to look after it. Budding Gowers are advised to apply raw linseed oil sparingly to the blade (*not* the splice) with a soft rag before using it: and to 'play it in' with some gentle net practice, using an old ball, before going out to hit a 'ton'.

OK FOR SOUND

The sweet-sounding ring of leather meeting willow, evoking somnolent summer days of cricket on village greens, floats enticingly from a rural workshop window in Sussex. Inside, a craftsman is thoughtfully bonking the face of a new bat with a leather mallet. He listens intently to the sound, and feels the impact – muted by the thick willow meat of the bat and absorbed by the well-sprung handle. He is confirming that the blade has its heart in the right place to make the most of a well-timed stroke.

FITTING THE HANDLE

A few swift blows with the flat of a hammer wedge the handle firmly into the blade. Cane for handles is split, then planed into square-section strips, 16 to 20 of them going into each handle. They are glued together with strips of cork, rubber, or rubber-and-steel, inserted between to make a square-section cane batten which is then turned to shape. Finally, the bottom is sawn to its wedge shape.

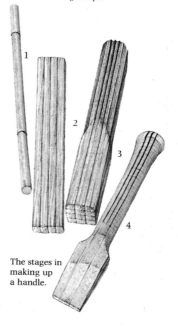

The stages in making up a handle.

THE DISTILLER

ANYONE CAN MAKE SCOTCH WHISKY – GIVEN AN
ADEQUATE SUPPLY OF SCOTTISH BARLEY, PEAT AND WATER.
OUT OF THESE, AND 150 YEARS OF EXPERIENCE, LAPHROAIG
CREATES ONE OF THE GREAT SINGLE MALTS

*I*n Scotland, there are only three things Scotch: terriers, broth and whisky, all else being Scots or Scottish. Of that noble three, it is the last – *uisgebaugh*, 'the water of life', whisky (without an 'e') – that is Scotland's greatest single contribution to the comfort and harmony of the world. It is utterly and inimitably Scots, being composed of Scottish air, earth, fire and water, and though other nations may put it to profound chemical analysis, produce such cunning substitutes as 'King Albert's Genuine Scottish Whisko', or even name a new distilling town after a famous Highland brand, no one who cares is fooled for a moment. Scotch whisky can be created nowhere but in Scotland. This does not in the least decry the many excellent whiskeys (with an 'e') that are produced elsewhere, notably in Ireland, the United States and Canada. It is simply that they are not Scotch, they do not taste like Scotch, and in many cases even the basic raw material is different.

So what is whisky? Or whiskey? Basically, it is a spirit distilled from grain, but then, so are vodka and gin, neither of which, so far as taste is concerned, are anything like any kind of whisky. Even in Britain, whisky means different things to different people, though in 1909 a Royal Commission, which had deliberated long on the subject, defined it as a potable spirit manufactured either from malted barley, or from a mixture of malted and unmalted barley and other cereals. Purists disagreed with the latter part of the definition, since it implied that a blended whisky containing a major proportion of patent-still grain spirit was the same thing as a single – that is, an unblended – malt whisky.

History, on the whole, is on their side. Whisky has been

SPRINGS OF THE WATERS OF LIFE

In its medieval beginnings, whisky distilling was a cottage industry and continued to be so – with varying degrees of legality – for many centuries. Scottish farmers used their surplus barley and water from their own streams to make a mash, which they distilled in pot stills over fires of peat cut from their own fields. Though on a much grander scale, modern distilleries like Laphroaig on the Hebridean island of Islay still follow exactly the same procedures, adding only the slight touch of magic that distinguishes their brand of single malt whisky.

A pot still of 1651.

made from malted, or fermented, barley in the Highlands since time out of mind, or at least, as seems likely, since the idea was brought from Ireland by missionary monks sometime in the Dark Ages. It was small wonder that the populace accorded far greater reverence to 'John Barleycorn' than they ever awarded to their kings. The grain is hardy, and grows easily in a chilly climate, and even the poorer hill-farmers usually had a small surplus they could turn into a brew at the end of harvest. The other necessaries, good water, and peat to stoke the still were also plentiful and ready to hand. The liquor they produced was no doubt of fiery potency, but in essence it was the same as the single malt whisky of today.

Some crofters made better whisky than others, and as their fame spread, they would barter their surplus with neighbours or sell it into the Lowlands as they would any other kind of farm produce. But such a happy state of affairs could not be allowed to continue, and in 1644, the Scots Parliament imposed the first excise tax on whisky.

To impose it was one thing, to collect it quite another, and for some years both Lowlands and Highlands shrugged their shoulders and continued in the same old ways. But in 1707, following the Union of Parliaments, the new British Government showed that they meant business by imposing the English malt tax on Scotland, and at the same time establishing a Board of Excise to enforce it. For the first time, the astonished clansmen beheld excise officers, who, braving the outrage they kindled, must have been courageous and dedicated men indeed.

The battle against illicit stills

The task they faced was a weary one. Before and after the Jacobite rising of 1745, smuggling and illicit stills throve in the land, the more so because no one could understand the morality of a tax upon what was, after all, a branch of agriculture. In 1777 it was reckoned that there were 408 distilleries in the city of Edinburgh alone, of which eight were legal, while in the Highlands, a reward of £5 was offered to anyone who betrayed the whereabouts of an illicit still. Since this was about the price of the copper worm or coiled tube essential in the production of distilled spirit, the stillmen, when their old worm was worn out, would claim the reward for reporting their own stills, buy a new worm and set up business again elsewhere.

After waves of ineffective legislation and bitter complaints from licensed distillers about the unfair competition from products that were often better than their own, it became apparent that there was no way to prevent Highlanders from making whisky.

In 1823, therefore, a more realistic act was passed which set a duty of 2s. 3d. on each gallon of spirit, and a licence fee of £10 on any still with a capacity of 40 gallons or more. This encouraged a number of farmers (and former bootleggers) to set up legal stills on a commercial footing. With centuries of experience of fermenting and distilling to draw upon, and a deep knowledge of the virtues of their local burns and peat cuttings, success was assured. In fact, in several cases it was already established, the names of the products being household words long before the makers took the path of legality. For example, a regular supply of Glenlivet was sent to George IV – who seemed to have small regard for the laws passed in his name – several years before its maker, a Mr Smith, applied for a licence.

Though greater production was now possible, the old painstaking leisurely processes of steeping the barley, allowing it to sprout, drying it in kilns, making a mash, fermenting and distilling in a pot still, were yet being carried out in the old way. But fierce competition was rearing its head, or rather heads, in the twin columns of the patent

still. This was invented by Aeneas Coffey in the late 1820s, and from a quantity-productive point of view, it had several undeniable advantages over the traditional pot still. Working upon a mixture of steam-cooked unmalted grain – mostly maize – and a little malted barley, it permitted continuous distillation which was impossible by the batch method employed in making pot-still whisky. Also, since neither peat nor mountain springs played any part in the operation, a patent still could be set up anywhere.

Scotch patent-still grain whisky is light in flavour and closer to 'neutral' spirit in character than malt whisky. Nowadays, however, it is very difficult to find since almost the entire production goes into blended whisky. This is, of course, the best known of all Scotch whisky types, but since each brand contains a small proportion of a large number of malt whiskies – as many as 30 or 40 – as well as grain spirit, they all differ considerably from one another. Maintaining the consistency of a blend from one year to the next is an immensely skilled job, depending almost entirely on the sensitivity of the blender's nose as he selects the ingredient whiskies.

It was the blends that really made the great Scotch whisky fortunes in the latter part of the 19th century, though their true founder was a small insect predator of the grape-vine called phylloxera. Until the 1870s, few English gentlemen had tasted whisky except perhaps in some dire emergency on a damp grouse moor or deer forest; brandy

and soda was their drink. But in the 1860s, the French vineyards were devastated by the attacks of phylloxera, which had been imported with new grafting stock from California. Cognac production fell steadily over the next three decades, and the road to the Englishman's decanter was open.

There is a saying that there is no sight more terrifying than a young Scotsman on the make, and it might well have been coined to describe the flamboyant and brilliant salesmanship of such future whisky barons as Dewar, Walker and Buchanan. Realising that single malt whiskies are destroyed by soda, they and others like them began to experiment with blends, though they might also have been inspired by the French, who in desperation were mixing grain spirit with cognac. At any event, within a few years they had ousted brandy and soda for ever as the

THE CHARACTER FORMERS

It takes about 5,000 gallons of wash – fermented barley brew – to make 10 gallons of proof spirit. The transformation, and the creation of the basic character of the whisky, takes place here in the still room. First, the wash is vaporised in the wash still, and the vapour condensed by running it through a tube or worm immersed in cold water. The result is a low-grade spirit called low wines, which is distilled again in the spirit still. What runs from here into the locked glass spirit safe is proof spirit, that in ten years will mature into the finest malt whisky.

Englishman's pre-dinner drink. Germans, Americans and even the French were swift to follow and also reached for the Scotch whisky at the hour of the aperitif.

Because there is a proportion of malt whiskies in every blended Scotch, their production too was boosted by the new demand. But as single malts, as drinks in their own right, they were to remain virtually unknown outside Scotland for many a long year, and even now few English bars carry anything like a representative range of the hundred or so to choose from. They are more expensive than blended whiskies, and to mix them with almost anything is considered sacrilege. Perhaps with a little water from the actual stream that gave them birth, or at a pinch, a touch of bottled spring water; but with city tap water, ice, soda or – horror of horrors – ginger ale, never.

Of course, whisky snobbery is as ridiculous as wine snobbery, but there is no doubt that single malt whiskies precisely reflect the places of their birth in just the same way that wines do, and for much the same reasons. With the malts, however, the regional differences are even more readily apparent.

Single malt whiskies are generally divided into four groups, Lowland, Highland, Campbeltown and Islay, and each group has its own very distinct flavour. The Islays have something of the bite of the Atlantic winds, the Campbeltowns are strong and full-bodied, the Highlands tend to be light, smooth and subtle, while the Lowlands are lightest of all. This is only the roughest of guides, since in fact no two malt whiskies are exactly alike. You can even have two distilleries standing side by side, drawing upon the same barley, peat and water, yet the variation between their two products is instantly obvious. The reasons for this may lie in the time of maturation and in the differing skills of the maltsters and stillmen. But there is also something else, a small mystery that seems forever to defy the most stringent analysis.

Take Laphroaig, for example, at once the most typical and the most individual of the Islay malts. It is strong, dry and distinctly peaty, and in its flavour some people say they can detect a far-off whiff of the sea. If so, there is good

reason, for the white fortress-like walls of the distillery rise straight from Islay's shores. From his office window, Murdoch Reid, the manager, looks out on a little cove containing a couple of small boats, beyond which there is nothing but America – unless he looks to the left where a small piece of Ireland is sometimes visible. Behind the distillery is all of Islay, southernmost of the Hebrides, some 25 miles long by 20 miles broad, and consisting mostly of low, treeless olive-brown hills inhabited by red deer and blackcock. But at the foot of the hills are the miles of peat that feed the furnaces not only of Laphroaig, but of the eight other distilleries on the island as well. This, and the water that flows off the granite and through the peat, is the reason for the distilleries' presence.

There has been a distillery at Laphroaig – 'the place in the hollow' – since 1823, the great year of distilling licences, and probably for some time before that. The scars of its ancient peat cuttings criss-cross the moors close by this year's, a 4 ft deep trench some 600 yds long. Rare among modern distilleries, Laphroaig still makes most of its own malt, and to do so, between September and the following July, will burn some 800 tons of peat hand-sliced out of the dark cuttings.

The barley to make the malt comes mainly from Angus, shipped over on the ferry from the mainland. The process of turning it into malt commences by soaking it in the local peaty water contained in large tanks called 'steeps' for anything up to 72 hours. The individualising of the final product has already begun. At the end of steeping, each grain shows a small white speck indicating that germination has begun and that the barley – or green malt as it is now called – is ready for the malting room, on whose vast floor it is spread out in a pale gold, sweet-smelling drift about a foot deep.

As germination proceeds, the green malt sprouts tiny hairs and generates considerable heat; during the next week it must be turned and raked two or three times daily to prevent the hairs matting together and to keep the temperature down. Maintaining the grain at a steady 60°F is the responsibility of the head maltman. So, too, is that of knowing the precise moment when it is ready for the next stage.

Further germination is stopped at about the time when the acrospire or sprouting stalk has reached almost the length of the grain. It is done by drying the malt in the kiln over a peat fire, whose eye-smarting smoke also imparts aroma and flavour to the grain. After 24 hours, the grain has absorbed as much of the peat scent as it will, and the drying is completed by a further day's heating over coal fires. Already by now, long before distillation, Islay's peat, soaked by a thousand years of sea-mist and salt spray, has put the island's stamp on the next batch of Laphroaig.

From the kiln, the green malt goes to the storage bins to

BARLEY TIDE

In many distilleries nowadays, the malted barley is bought in, but at Laphroaig, the grain is still steeped and then spread out to germinate on the hangar-like floors of the malting house in the old traditional way. The lines in the green malt – sprouting barley – are the marks of the ploughs operated by the maltmen, who must turn the grain over two or three times a day to prevent the temperature building up and to stop the sprouting hair-like roots from matting together. During germination, the starch in the seed is converted into maltose, a form of sugar that eventually produces alcohol.

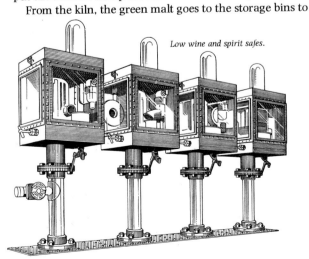

Low wine and spirit safes.

SCOTCH MIST

When the malt has fully sprouted, further growth is arrested by drying the grain on the steel-mesh floor of the kiln. The peat fire kindled beneath the floor has two purposes, the first to dry out the malt and the second to impart to it the flavour of the smoke. Working in the reek, a maltman turns the malt to make sure that each grain gets its share. To a large extent, the whisky's flavour is created by the smoke of the peat, which, in turn, is a reflection of the countryside where it formed. Laphroaig's peat is dug from the flat moorlands of Islay, constantly blown over by the Atlantic winds or shrouded in a sea mist. Small wonder, therefore, that those who know their whisky say that in Laphroaig they can detect a far-off tang of the sea. The pagoda-like towers (below), a feature of every malt whisky distillery, are the vents through which the smoke is finally dispersed from the kiln to the open air.

GROWING UP GRACEFULLY

All whisky emerges water-clear from the still; the colouring comes later. Blended whiskies are coloured with caramel just before bottling, but the malts take their hue from the oak of the casks in which they mature. It was discovered long ago that whisky matures very well in casks that once contained sherry – a dry sherry helps to make a pale whisky, while a sweet sherry imparts a darker hue. But Laphroaig, for its own reasons, prefers to use old bourbon casks, and in these it permits its product to mature for a full ten years. No one knows quite what happens in that period. Some evaporation certainly, and a slow mellowing caused by a whole range of factors – temperature, or the Atlantic breeze blowing through the warehouse. Some people even believe that the cobwebs in the corners have an effect.

cool – hot malt means bad fermentation – building up the 250 ton green malt 'bank' from which the malt mill draws about 90 tons a week. Here it is ground into grist, rather resembling coarse porridge oats. This is measured through a hopper to the mash tun, where it is mashed four times in waters of steadily increasing temperatures – 147°, 170° 174°, 196°F to release the different kinds of sugars required for fermentation. When the process is completed, the mixture of sugars and water, called worts, is drained off to cool while the draff, the remaining solids, is removed to make cattle feed.

From the cooler, the worts are pumped into the wash back, a huge vat of some 12,000 gallons capacity. Yeast is added, and for a time the surface seethes and churns alarmingly, and the carbon dioxide given off hits the nostrils as a cold shock. After about 40 hours, however, fermentation is complete and the wash, as it is now called, lies quiet. For the first time, the brew has an alcohol content – about 110° proof, like strong beer.

The wash goes to the wash charger, and from there to the wash still, the first of the onion-shaped copper vessels that make the difference between Laphroaig and mere whisky. Both wash stills and spirit stills are lovingly watched over throughout their long working lives, and when the time comes at last to replace them, all dents and bashes are carefully reproduced in the new vessels. That the dents make any difference to the whisky may be folklore, says Mr Reid; but no one as yet has had the nerve to omit them.

The wash still produces an intermediate spirit known as 'low wines', which in turn is fed into the spirit still. After vaporising and cooling, the spirit then runs into the spirit safe, a massive affair of plate glass and brass secured by a Customs and Excise lock. The first run is called 'foreshots', an oily liquid that gradually gives way to clear spirit. Knowing exactly when to switch the liquid into the spirit receiver is the responsibility of the stillman. So too is that of recognising the point when the run is dropping below an acceptable proof and is emerging instead as lower-grade spirit called 'feints'. These cut-off points vary by a degree or so of proof from one distillery to another, and are absolutely critical to the flavour of the particular whisky. Finally, the 'middle cut' is run off into casks and that is that.

Well, not quite. Until three years have been passed in cask, Scotch is not whisky at all, but by legal definition, Plain British Spirit. Laphroaig in fact keeps its whisky in cask for ten years; it is during this period that the colour and character of its whisky slowly and mysteriously develops. Some of it may come from the casks, which are second-hand, and once contained American bourbon; some of it from evaporation, which seeps hundreds of gallons into the Scottish skies – 'the angels' share', says Mr Reid.

But at the end of the day, there it is; Laphroaig, a whisky that is mispronounced and known the world over. Like the men and the island that made it, it is uncompromising, very much itself, and not to be trifled with. 'A drink for heroes,' it is said; but more perhaps, for those who enjoy life's good things, in the company of friends, in the quiet of the evening.

THE DRY-STONE WALLER

SETTING STONE UPON STONE, WITHOUT CEMENT OR
ANY OTHER BUILDING AID, HE CREATES FIELD BOUNDARIES
THAT WILL ENDURE FOR A CENTURY OR MORE

Graham Haslam lives on and by the eternal limestone and gritstone of his native Derbyshire. Like his father and grandfather and great-grandfather before him, he is a dry-stone waller, one of the few remaining of the tough breed of craftsmen. Over the last couple of centuries or so, they have overlaid the Peak District and much of the rest of the Pennines with a great open-work shawl of grey-white and dark brown walls.

Though accomplished at a leisurely pace – each waller builds at the rate of 6–7 yds a day – the task was and is nevertheless gargantuan. An average Pennine farm of 70–80 acres contains about 3 miles of walls, totalling literally thousands of miles within the region. The only disadvantage from the waller's point of view is that once built, barring county council edicts and careless lorry drivers, the wall is there to stay. Ever since the first land enclosures of the 1760s, the dry-stone wallers have gradually built themselves out of a job.

There is nothing makeshift or cheeseparing about a dry-stone wall. Quite apart from its aesthetic appeal in the stony bleak uplands, it is exactly right for its tasks, penning in the notoriously agile Blackface sheep and protecting them from the winter snows, or as a wind-break on arable land.

It is immensely adaptable, the result of a hundred tricks passed down from one waller to another. And it is also highly individualistic, according to the lie of the land and the particular needs of the farmer. Some walls, like the one-stone thick Galloway dykes, are left with large chinks in them that give a deceptively frail appearance but from which sheep will shy away. Some contain 'cripple holes' or 'sheep smooses' – apertures large enough to allow sheep to pass from one pasture to another while keeping cattle penned. Others, in hollows or along the contours of hillsides, have water 'smoots' or gates permitting the easy flow of flood debris through the wall after the thaw. Then there are steps and stiles like the slate steps of the Lake District for human traffic; and, most cunning, other smoots and passages that, constructed with a deep knowledge of the movements of local game, lead rabbits into snares.

But the one thing that all the walls have – or should have – in common, is that they are constructed without mortar. In some areas, particularly in the Cotswolds, the cope-stones, the upright stones surmounting the wall, are cemented together, but in Mr Haslam's opinion this quite defeats the point of the exercise. The strength of the dry-stone wall lies in its elasticity, in the fact that by their own weight, and over a period of several years, its rough stones settle and cling to one another.

The wall may settle by as much as 3 in., and of course should do so all of a piece. If the copestones are mortared, they will remain rigid and the remainder of the wall will gradually pull away from them.

The dry-stone wall too is the ideal construction to defeat the bitter Pennine winter. Water will find cracks in a mortared wall, and freezing, will prise the stones apart; but the dry-stone wall remains unscathed. The wind blows constantly through the many deliberately planned chinks and air spaces, drying the wall out and preventing snow and ice from settling. The first Pennine walls were built during the 18th century from the plentiful supply of stones yielded by the land as it was cleared for ploughing. Later, small quarries were dug. Transport was never much of a problem, since almost anywhere a rich harvest of the raw material can be found only a few inches below the topsoil.

How the stones are laid

A good Pennine wall consists of a double wall raised on a footing of a single course of large stones laid in a shallow trench. The space between the succeeding courses, staggered as in bricklaying and decreasing in size as the wall grows upwards, is blocked by 'fillings' or 'heartings' – small stones laid just as carefully as the large facing stones to facilitate the air flow. At each 2 ft or so of height, a 'through' is laid, a large, flattish stone lying upon, and supported by, the two face walls, so anchoring them together. The final row of coping stones serves the same purpose. Further throughs are laid on top of the wall as a base for the copestones. This, with a few regional exceptions such as the turf and stone 'hedges' of the West Country, and variations imposed by the prevalent rock of each district, is the general pattern in most dry-stone wall areas of Britain.

But the real art of the wall is in its 'batter', the gradual inward incline of the two faces from bottom to top, that adds strength to the wall and helps to shed water. The batter on a 4 ft high wall might be the difference between a 22 in. base and a 14 in. top along a length of 100 yds or more. Lesser wallers might use a simple template to achieve uniformity, but Mr Haslam generally does the whole thing by eye.

Curiously enough, the abandonment of tools seems to be a characteristic of the Pennine waller. Where Cotswold and Scottish fellow-craftsmen keep their hammers busy the whole time chipping, shaping and driving in the stones of their walls, the Pennine waller will simply pick the right stone for the right spot and maybe thump it home with a whack from his 'lump', or mason's hammer. Mr Haslam lays out the stones for the job, considers them awhile, then picks up one or two big ones and moves them a few yards along the course of the wall. He is not quite sure how he knows, but experience tells him that when he has built that far, those stones and no others will suit that place.

HOLE IN THE WALL

Small holes, called smoots, are built into dry-stone walls for all kinds of purposes, the chief of which is to run off flood water and to allow passage to wild animals that might otherwise dig beneath the wall. But to the countryman, the smoot's greatest appeal is that it makes the best of all places for setting rabbit snares.

BUILDING THE BATTER *A template can ensure the correct profile or batter of the wall, and the positioning of the 'through-stones' and courses as well. Many Pennine wallers, however, work almost entirely by eye.*

WALL AGAINST TIME

Graham Haslam builds a dry-stone wall in the Peak District National Park. The materials he uses are local gritstone and four generations of experience. Each yard of wall contains about 1½ tons of stone raised in a double row of 'facings' filled by a hearting of small stones anchored by slab throughs. The strength of the wall lies in the adhesion of the rough stones to one another as they settle, and in the ventilation provided by a myriad small gaps, keeping the wall dry and ice-free. How long such walls last is indicated by the pencilled names of wallers sometimes found in bottles beneath the ends of walls. Some of these messages date back 150 years and more.

Cross-section of a wall

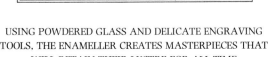

THE ENAMELLER

USING POWDERED GLASS AND DELICATE ENGRAVING
TOOLS, THE ENAMELLER CREATES MASTERPIECES THAT
WILL RETAIN THEIR LUSTRE FOR ALL TIME

*To create this intricate example
of* champlevé – *a girl's head in
the style of the art nouveau
artist and designer Alfonso
Mucha – an assortment of
almost 30 different enamels
were fused on to silver.*

*Orders of merit and insignia
form a large part of the
enameller's work. A leading
firm of jewellers commissioned
this enamelled and hand-painted
Order of St Michael and St
George.*

Enamelling is the art, over 2,000 years old, of fusing coloured glass on to metal. Originally, it may have been a substitute for the costly process of inlaying metal with precious stones, but later it became a craft in its own right. One of the beauties of enamel is that it does not fade – as do oils on canvas. Its brilliance is retained for ever. Even so, it has never been popular with pictorial artists, but has remained firmly in the hands of traditional craftsmen.

Charles Barnes is just such a practitioner. Now in his late 60's, he is the oldest working enameller in Britain. With two partners – his son Philip and Alan Mudd – he operates in the cluttered and friendly informality of a top-floor workshop in Islington. In 1971, at the age of 19, Philip was the first enameller to win the Craftsman of the Year Award. One other craftsman, Keith Seldon, makes up the team.

'Craftsmen never make any money,' Charles Barnes admits. 'It's the satisfaction that you get; the feeling that you have left your mark in the world long after you're dead and gone.' There are frustrations too, of course, in falling just short of the perfection attained by the early 20th-century Russian jeweller Carl Fabergé – in the opinion of Mr Barnes the greatest enameller ever.

They seldom get the credit, however, for the mark that they do leave. Like most craftsmen, they work behind the scenes. Most of their commissions come from West End jewellers. Occasionally, on television, they spot celebrities wearing pieces that they have enamelled; for people as varied as Paul McCartney, Prince Charles and Liberace possess examples of their work.

Enamelling done by Barnes and Co. can be found in surprising places, too: on the coats of arms on either side of the old London Bridge, now in Arizona, and on some of the coats of arms of the Knights of the Garter in St George's Chapel, Windsor. A fairly recent commission was to enamel a 20 in. high silver figure of the Sultan of Oman on horseback, resplendent in full military regalia. On a less opulent level, their stock in trade consists of enamelled boxes, miniatures, restoration work, insignia and orders of merit: GCMGs, KCMGs, and CBEs, for example.

Enamel is simply glass that has been coloured by the addition of a metallic oxide. The enameller buys it in lumps in a great variety of colours, some of which are transparent and others opaque. He grinds the lumps in water with a pestle and mortar until the grains are very fine, and mixes this powder with a little water before applying it to the metal. Once applied, the piece is placed in a kiln for the enamel to fuse on to the metal.

The enameller's art lies in the engraving and chiselling needed to create a design before the enamel is applied. There are several ways of doing this, the method most commonly used by Charles Barnes and his helpers being that of *champlevé* – literally, 'raised field'. In this, the enameller engraves cells, or channels, on the surface of the metal,

leaving thin ridges that form the outline of the design. This engraving is done with a 'scorper', one of a number of cutting and chiselling tools that come in up to 20 sizes.

To ensure a convenient working height, the craftsman places the object that is to be enamelled on a pile of little leather sandbags. Holding it with one hand, he begins to chisel away very delicately with the scorper to form the cells. When finished, all the cells must be of identical depth. Only when he is completely satisfied that this is so does the craftsman apply a thin layer of enamel to each cell. For this he uses a quill, and a totally steady hand is essential. He then fuses the enamel in a kiln, and repeats the process until the cells are filled.

After cooling, the enamel is rubbed down with a carborundum stone and water. Since this roughens the glaze, it is then cleaned and re-fired. Finally, it is polished with fine pumice powder and water, on felt wheels, until a mirror-like polish is attained.

The delicacy and precision needed for the engraving stage can hardly be overstated. Hundreds of times, Alan Mudd has cut the words '*Honi soit qui mal y pense*' around a regimental design with the help of only a pair of spectacles that magnify four and a half times. Some enamellers believe that years of such work keep their eyes unusually fit, for it is an odd fact that many jewellers and engravers can still do the most intricate work at the age of 70.

ENGRAVING THE DESIGN ON THE METAL

In the technique known as champlevé, *enamel is applied to recessed areas of the metal. Here, a 'scorper' is being used to engrave the cells which form the design. Scorpers come in a variety of shapes and sizes; the names – spit-stick, half-round and flat – describe the shape of the cutting edge.*

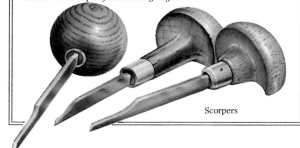

Scorpers

THE RAW MATERIAL *Enamel is a form of coloured glass. The enameller needs some 200 different colours, as they do not mix.*

In addition to basic enamelling, Keith Seldon does exquisite enamel paintings, an art which the Renaissance enamellers of Limoges, and the portrait miniaturists of the 17th century, excelled in. First he fuses a coat of coloured enamel on to the metal. Then, just as a painter would apply oil to a canvas, he applies the pigments; these are derived from metallic oxides but have not, as yet, been mixed with clear glass, or 'flux'. He uses the narrowest brushes available, but even these have sometimes to be thinned down so that only a few hairs are left. The painted enamels – floral designs, portraits and copies of great paintings – are then fired.

Basse-taille – literally, 'low relief' – is a refinement of the *champlevé* method. A picture is engraved on to the metal but, unlike *champlevé*, all the cuts are of different depths. The eye and feel of Alan Mudd are so acute that there may be as little as a fifteen-thousandth of an inch between the deepest and the shallowest cut, with as many as 15 gradations in between. The metal is then completely covered with a coat of enamel. After firing, the different depths give an impression of light and shade, for the colour is most intense where the cut is deep and the enamel thick. The image that results looks rather like a sepia print.

Cloisonné – literally, 'partitioned off' – was the favourite technique of enamellers during the Dark and Middle Ages – roughly, from the 5th to the 15th centuries. Beautiful work has also been done by the Chinese. But the method is little used today, for it needs a great deal of artistry and even more time. Whereas in *champlevé* the cells for the enamel are engraved into the surface of the metal, in *cloisonné* they are built up. Thin strips of metal, often gold, are curved to follow the decorative pattern. These are then soldered on to the surface to form miniature walls.

In the Ashmolean Museum, Oxford, there is a fine example of early English *cloisonné*. The so-called Alfred Jewel is thought to have belonged to Alfred the Great, who died in 899, for it bears the Anglo-Saxon inscription 'Alfred had me made'.

Plique-à-jour – literally, 'applied to let the daylight through' – is a technique similar to *cloisonné*, but using metal strips that are not soldered to the base. This allows them to be removed, leaving a network of channels filled with translucent enamel – rather like a stained-glass window. The technique, which is particularly suited to such delicate compositions as the wings of a dragonfly, was perfected by René Lalique, the leading art nouveau jeweller. Today, however, it is generally considered too time-consuming to be commercial.

All these techniques of preparing the metal in order to control the enamel have been evolved and perfected over the centuries by the artistry and ingenuity of individual craftsmen.

'We are traditionalists,' says Mr Barnes. 'The methods and techniques that we use are the same as they have been for generations. They won't change.'

GRINDING AND LAYING THE ENAMEL

For up to 20 minutes the craftsman grinds the enamel into a fine powder, using a pestle and mortar. The result is a tablespoonful of colour. Silt, or overground enamel, is washed away; the remaining powder, mixed with a little water, is transferred to pots or palettes and is then ready for application. Using a swan's feather quill, Charles Barnes lays the enamel in the engraved cells – the champlevé technique. On this occasion he is enamelling the centre section of an insignia cross. He holds a linen cloth to absorb the excess water, otherwise the mixture of enamel and water will boil when it is fired in the kiln.

THE ETCHER

DRAWING DIRECTLY ON TO A COPPER PLATE, THE
ETCHER'S DELICATE LINEWORK RECORDED EVERY ASPECT
OF LIFE DURING THE REGENCY ERA

*M*any people have an idea of how Britain looked in the late 18th and early 19th centuries, even though the camera was not invented until some decades later. A Palladian mansion set in a park of eternal summer; a black and primrose stagecoach plunging through a snowdrift; pink-coated, hat-waving horsemen following hounds into a mêlée of Waterloo-like proportions; frigates cannoning one another to pieces on a cold green sea. It is a world in which Derby winners pass the post with all four legs outstretched and soldiers fight battles in uniforms of incredible smartness.

All the same the images are extraordinarily tenacious, largely because they are forever being recalled in the etchings of the period that hang on the walls of every pub, club, country house and hotel of respectable age in the land.

A MINIATURE ETCHING IN THE MAKING

An etcher is both an artist and a technician. A wax-covered copper plate is his 'canvas'. He creates an image by drawing in the wax coating with a fine needle (right), so exposing the copper beneath it. When the plate is immersed in a dish of acid (below), the acid bites into the copper wherever the wax has been scratched away, leaving an etched image of the artist's design. After removing the rest of the wax, a print can be made by working ink into the etched lines and pressing dampened paper on to the plate.

They were printed from copper plates which had been etched, or 'bitten', with nitric acid.

The chief beauty of an etching is the delicate linework, in which the ink *stands out slightly from the paper*. In the earliest etchings, shadows and areas of flat tone had to be drawn as crosshatched lines. But in the mid-18th century a new etching process, called aquatint, was invented. This allowed etchers to print soft areas of flat colour or grey tone. Printed in colour, or hand-coloured with watercolour wash, aquatint etchings were particularly well suited to expressing the misty subtleties of the English landscape.

The use of aquatint in etching was introduced in England towards the end of the 18th century by Paul Sandby, best known as a watercolour painter, who used it to make prints of landscape subjects. William Blake made very original use of etching in his coloured book illustrations.

No one doubted the versatility of etching and aquatint, but it had its drawbacks. The processes of drawing on the plates and biting them with acid were lengthy, and the printing of the plates, particularly in colour, was a laborious task. Gradually, this and other engraving methods for producing prints and illustrations in books were in the main replaced by lithography – printing from an image drawn in greasy crayon upon a flat limestone block – and later by offset photolithography, in which the image is transferred photographically on to a sensitised zinc plate.

Nevertheless, the range and possibilities of etching and aquatint continued to interest a number of artists, particularly Picasso, who left an immense amount of work in the medium, and others such as Miro, Dali and Chagall. But still its appeal lies as ever in its soft effect, almost like watercolour, which can be used to depict natural subjects, particularly landscapes. And it is for this purpose that etching and aquatint are being used by a number of artist-craftsmen in Britain today.

One of them is Joseph Winkelman who, using exactly the same methods as his 18th-century predecessors, produces limited editions of 75 or so prints of Cotswold village scenes and landscapes, as well as a series of prints of circus life, worked up as etchings on copper from his own original drawings. Plates may deteriorate if more than about 75 are printed. Some of his most recent etchings are miniature in scale, the plates little more than 1 in. square.

The prints are made from plates of rigid, 18-gauge copper, whose surface, before he begins work, is polished to a mirror gleam. In preparation for drawing on the copper, Mr Winkelman warms the plate and spreads an even layer of wax across it with a roller. Into this dark wax ground the artist draws his image with a sharp needle, and, where he has drawn, the copper plate shines out through the lines.

When the linework is complete, the copper plate is put into a bath of nitric acid to be etched. The wax ground resists the acid, but the acid bites into the copper wherever lines have been drawn through the wax. The longer the plate is left in the acid, the deeper the acid bites; and the deepest lines print blackest when the plate is finally printed.

To measure progress at this stage, a proof print must be taken from the etched plate. Joseph Winkelman cleans off the remaining wax from the surface of the plate. He mixes the coloured ink that he will use for printing, usually a warm black, and dabs it on to the plate, taking special care to press the ink into the etched lines. He uses a stiff cotton gauze to wipe the surface clean, but the ink remains in the grooves where the acid has bitten.

The plate is overlaid with lightly damped printing paper, covered with layers of heavy felt and run through the press, a splendid machine with ponderous rollers and massive cast-iron wheels and gears.

The pressure forces the damp paper into every line in the

plate, and the ink is deposited on the surface of the paper. The printed proof is a mirror image of the plate; not only is the picture reversed, but where the lines were depressions in the plate they become ridges of ink on the paper.

It is difficult to produce a full range of tints and shadows by etched lines alone, and this is where the aquatint process comes into its own. Aquatint is a way of etching a copper plate to print flat areas of even tints, of varying degrees of darkness, to supplement the etched lines. To lay an aquatint on the plate, Joseph Winkelman uses the time-honoured method of sprinkling tiny particles of resin dust from a gauze-topped jar. The resin is scattered evenly over the surface of the plate, and then it is fused to the plate by heat from a gas burner.

Each particle will resist the acid when the plate is etched, but the acid will attack the copper plate around the particles, creating a network of tiny grooves. When inked and printed, this intricate network is too fine to be seen with the naked eye, and it appears as a flat area of coloured (or grey) tint. The term 'aquatint' derives from the Latin for nitric acid – *aqua fortis* – the means by which the half-tone is etched on to the copper plate.

Of course, an even aquatint is not needed all over the plate, and Joseph Winkelman uses a thick black varnish to paint out those areas of the plate where he does not wish the aquatint to be etched. To etch a very pale aquatint he leaves the plate in the acid for only a few seconds. Then he stops out the light areas with varnish before replacing the plate in the acid, so that the areas that are to print darker can be etched more deeply.

Many of Joseph Winkelman's etchings are printed in several colours, and this demands an elaborate preparation of a number of plates – usually one for each colour. The linework and aquatints have to be carefully located on the separate plates so that they print in register. When the plates are finally ready for printing – after several weeks of careful drawing and etching – Joseph Winkelman mixes his coloured inks and the printing of the edition begins.

All the plates are inked up and their surfaces wiped clean, as before. Sheets of fine, hand-made paper are dampened, ready for printing. Each sheet of paper is run through the press several times, once for each separate plate. The paper is held under the rollers so that it remains in the same place when the plates are exchanged.

With an elaborate coloured etching, Joseph Winkelman can spend a whole day perfecting a mere three or four proofs. The whole edition of 75 prints might take a month. No wonder the etcher breathes a sigh of relief when the time finally comes for him to sign and number his limited edition. The signature 'Joseph Winkelman' at the bottom of a print concludes a feat of endurance as well as an artistic achievement.

PRINTING AN AQUATINT ETCHING

Aquatint provides a means of producing areas of tone to supplement the etched lines on a plate. It is achieved by fusing particles of resin dust to the plate before immersing it in acid. Only the spaces between the particles, too small to be seen individually, are affected by the acid. This results in an overall tint, with a depth that depends on the length of immersion in the acid. Here, Joseph Winkelman is taking a proof by passing an etched plate, and dampened printing paper, through the heavy rollers of his press.

THE FISHING ROD MAKER

THE AIM IS TO COMBINE LIGHTNESS, PLIANCY AND
STRENGTH. TODAY'S FINEST RODS ARE STILL MADE BY
GLUING TOGETHER TAPERED STRIPS OF BAMBOO

GLUING THE STRIPS

*Before gluing, the strips forming
a rod section are assembled
together and their ends bound
with sticky tape. The tapes are
then cut across and unrolled on
the bench, leaving the strips
lying side by side, their ends
still held firm by the tape. Glue
is brushed along them and they
are re-assembled by re-rolling
the taped ends and running the
strips through bunched fingers.*

Split-cane rods are making a modest come-back in fly-fishing circles. Nothing spectacular as yet, but there are signs that the glass-fibre and carbon-fibre rods that have evolved through modern technology are perhaps losing a little of their appeal – if only on aesthetic grounds. Two of the very few craftsmen still making cane rods by hand can report a quite discernible surge of interest in their products – particularly from knowledgeable and demanding experts in America. The problem is that making a rod by hand takes a long time.

So what should you do when an order for six dozen arrives? Work day and night is what Marcus Warwick does, in his small loft workshop at Uppingham, Leicestershire.

Lying in long hessian sacks beneath the narrow stairs leading up to the loft are the thick poles of pale yellow bamboo that are his raw material. Out of 1,000 or so known species of bamboo, this is the only one suitable for rod-making, and it comes from the Kwangtung province of China, just opposite Hong Kong. Its advantage is that it grows up to 40 ft tall, and the first 26 ft or so are free of branches; only the characteristic bamboo rings, or nodes, mark the otherwise flawless stem. These nodes form diaphragms across the inside of the stem and Mr Warwick starts by knocking them out, banging a length of conduit straight through the cane.

Next, the poles are 'flame-baked' to remove any moisture remaining in them. For this he has what looks like a length of drain-pipe mounted on a trestle. Something resembling a gas poker is stuck in one end, so that its flame shoots down the pipe. As he inserts the pole, the flame curls round its length in a spiral, and wisps of steam emerge from the other end. He bakes half the pole at a time, giving each half about 20 minutes' heat treatment. After cooling down for a couple of hours the poles are ready to be split.

This is done with a sharp, stiff-bladed knife, a mallet and a 'splitting tool' – which looks like a thick screwdriver with the blade sharpened, rounded at the corners, and highly polished. He cleaves the pole in halves down its length by placing the edge of the knife across one end and hitting the back with the mallet. A split about 16 in. long is made.

Laying the pole on his bench, he then widens the split a fraction by twisting the knife – just enough to insert the splitting tool. Another tap with the mallet extends the split, making it wide enough for the knife to be removed and inserted again further down. The procedure is repeated until the split is complete. Each half is then split again – and again, until the pole is finally reduced to either 16 or 24 triangular-sectioned strips of almost equal size. Six strips will be used to make each hexagonal section of a rod.

The rod-maker resumes work, chiselling the remains of the inner nodes from the strips and filing off the outer ones. Sometimes the outer nodes are heated over a bunsen burner and carefully compressed flat in a vice to preserve the surface fibres intact. For it is the fibres in the outer $\frac{1}{8}$ in. of the cane that are the strongest – Mr Warwick calls them the 'power fibres'. This, of course, is why the rod is not just a simple, bamboo cane.

Each strip then goes on his steel 'planing board'. This is a length of large, square-section tubing, on two sides of which are welded strips of polished steel, each precision-cut along its length with three, 60 degree, V-shaped tapering grooves. These act as guides as, with the cane strip laid in a groove,

BINDING A SECTION *Once glued, the section is bound tightly with a double spiral of thread to hold the strips perfectly straight while the glue sets. This is done on an ingenious little home-made machine constructed with bobbins, brass hooks, nails and bits of wood. As one bobbin is turned the rod section revolves and is bound simultaneously in opposing spirals.*

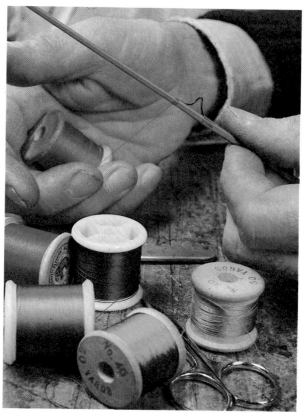

WHIPPING THE RINGS *The legs of the rings are filed thin at their ends so that when they are whipped on they merge imperceptibly into the body of the rod. Sticky tape holds them in position while the whipping of fine silk is hand-wound, and finished with an 'invisible' whipping knot.*

Mr Warwick carefully planes two sides of it, leaving the outer skin intact on the third. He reduces the strip to the exact size he has calculated for the rod he is making.

He uses a micrometer for frequent checks, and each strip takes four hours to plane. Each of the six strips that form the top section of the 6 ft rod will taper from 82 to 20 thousandths over its 39 in. length, giving overall dimensions of 164 to 40 thousandths when the section is assembled.

Even more incredibly, Mr Warwick confides that the taper is not constant, varying along its length according to calculations made over 30 years of rod-making, to ensure maximum efficiency over every inch of the rod. These measurements are his trade secret, hand written in a ledger.

While gluing the strips together, he reveals another subtlety of construction: the strips have been made so that the nodes do not lie next to each other on assembly. They appear on alternate faces of the hexagonal section; or, in top-quality rods, they are staggered along and around its length in a spiral. This is designed to prevent the nodes impairing in even the slightest way the progressive action of the rod, or creating any weak spots.

Once glued together, the sections – now called 'blanks' – are double-bound with thread and stood to dry for 72 hours in a dust-proof heated cupboard. However, two weeks will elapse before the glued bond attains full strength.

This achieved, the binding is cut away and the blank scrutinised closely for traces of warp or twist: even a couple of 'thou' deviation from the true line between butt and tip will affect the rod's ability to throw an accurate cast. Bends or twists are removed by heating the affected section over the bunsen flame and straightening it by hand and eye, using a groove cut in a length of hardwood as a guide. When cool again, the blank maintains its corrected shape.

All this has left the outer skin of the cane intact to form

each face of the six-sided blank. These faces are now cleaned up with the lightest of sandings, disturbing the vital outer fibres as little as possible. With the second – and, if necessary, third – blank that will form the complete rod made in similar fashion, the nickel-silver male and female ferrules that will join them are attached.

Cork for the handle comes in pierced discs about ⅝ in. thick, and as many as are required are 'threaded' on to the butt end and glued together. The handle-and-blank assembly is put into a lathe, and the handle turned to shape with a chisel. It is finished with fine sandpapers.

The mating ferrules that join each blank to form the rod go on next, the corners of the hexagon being carefully trimmed and the fittings chamfered with a file to ensure a smooth transition from cane to metal. They are glued on, great pains being taken to see that they are perfectly aligned so that the rod remains absolutely straight when assembled.

Then the rings through which the fishing line will pass are whipped on, and more whippings made over the ferrule-and-peg joints. With the reel-holding rings fitted, all that remains is for Mr Warwick to write his name, plus the rod number and type, on the cane near the handle. The rod is then ready for varnishing.

The heated varnish is applied in micro-thin coats, not with a brush, but by dipping finger and thumb in the pot, and running them along the rod. The cane gets four coats and the whippings six.

The finished product is a work of great beauty, the golden cane flashing in the sunlight as a few swishes – with a reel fitted – display the perfect balance and smooth action of a 6 ft two-piece just completed. And it weighs only 2 oz.

The final revelation comes as Mr Warwick produces his latest design – a three-piece rod that is 8 ft long when assembled, yet light as a feather. It is hollow! He reckons this his masterpiece – for the moment . . .

HOW THE SIX STRIPS FORM
A SECTION

A cross-section through a 'hollow' rod reveals its construction. The six cane strips that form it are each planed to triangular section, each angle being a precise 60 degrees. When glued together they make a perfect hexagon. The hollow core is created by planing the apex off the inner angle of each strip – but at 5 in. intervals the angle is left intact so that the rod remains 'solid' at these points, for added strength. This three-section rod is 8 ft long when assembled, yet it weighs only 4 oz.

Cross-section through split-cane rod.

THE Flint Knapper

BRITAIN'S OLDEST CRAFT HAS CHANGED LITTLE
SINCE STONE AGE KNAPPERS IN NORFOLK AND SUFFOLK
EXCAVATED FLINT MINES THAT ARE STILL IN USE TODAY

Remarkably, the era of the silicon chip has overlapped with that of the flint chipper, or knapper. At Brandon, near Grime's Graves, on the Norfolk-Suffolk border, where flint mines existed thousands of years ago, two British craftsmen still shape these brittle stones into saleable pieces.

In prehistoric times, men used stags' antlers to dig out chalk and flint in order to make flint adzes and chisels. They used these tools to produce arrowheads, scrapers, axe blades and saws. Today, the one or two remaining knappers shape flintstones with tools that are only a little more sophisticated – essentially a set of iron hammers. They produce building stones – or builders, as they are called – and flints for the muskets still used by sporting-gun clubs, both in Britain and the USA.

Flint occurs in horizontal bands of irregularly shaped nodules in chalkland, or scattered as flat or pebble-like pieces on the surface. In England, it is found in quantity in Norfolk, parts of Suffolk and in the south-eastern counties, particularly Kent and Sussex. The best flint, called floorstone, is the hard, black variety which lies between 30 and 45 ft down in the chalk. It is sharper and stronger than the greyer stone found near the surface.

The flint knappers of Grime's Graves operated a sort of flint factory. They and their fellow craftsmen in other parts of Britain played an essential role in late Stone Age society as makers of flint tools and weapons. They cleared areas of forest for cultivation, using axes made by hollowing out one end of a wooden stick and through it inserting a flint blade. The importance of flint knapping began to decline only when metal working was introduced into Britain, from about 2000 BC.

More than 2,000 years elapsed before flint came into its own again, this time as a building material for churches in later Anglo-Saxon times. The earliest churches were constructed with thick walls of uncut grey-and-white flints cemented together with mortar or with cob-clay or chalk mixed with gravel and straw.

The Normans built in stone on a much larger scale, erecting cathedrals, abbeys, castles, churches and homes throughout the country. When possible the stone was quarried locally, and in the flint areas they raised many structures with walls built mainly of flint but with cornerstones, lintels, arches and cills formed from limestone or sandstone.

During the Norman period, knappers began to cut random stones into more defined shapes. They split the stones to reveal the darker interior and, using simple templates, knapped one face to a square rectangular shape.

The three tools used by today's knappers are much the same tools as those of the medieval craftsmen. The quartering hammer is a 2–3 lb. club hammer of soft metal, made by

a blacksmith. With it, the knapper breaks large nodules of flintstone weighing perhaps 50 lb., to produce smaller pieces with 'workable' faces. The flaking hammer, also of soft metal, is a double-pointed hammer with a squared edge for rough-trimming the stone to shape. The knapping, or finishing, hammer, often made by a blacksmith from an old file, has flattened, drawn out ends and a centre handle.

If he is making a set of 'builders', perhaps for renovating an old flint cottage or church, the knapper uses a simple metal template, usually 2 in. or 3 in. square. He takes up a random stone, breaks it with the quartering hammer and selects the piece that he considers most suitable to be worked into a builder.

Putting the template on the exposed dark face, he draws round it with a pencil. Then, holding the stone between his knees, he strikes all round it with the flaking hammer until the shape is approximately right. This is the most difficult part, for it takes years of practice to learn exactly where to strike the face, and with what force. Although flint does not have a grain, a skilled knapper can judge exactly when to direct his blow in order to achieve the desired effect. A fraction out, and the stone flakes in a totally different direction.

In addition to making builders, knappers have for a long time fashioned minute flintstones which, when struck with steel, produce sparks to ignite tinder and make fire. The principle led to the introduction of the flintlock musket, early in the 17th century, in which the firing mechanism included a cock that gripped a flintstone. When the trigger was pulled, the flintstone struck a piece of steel and so produced a spark to ignite the powder.

Flintlocks were the dominant type of gun for many years, until the introduction of the percussion-cap principle of firing. Even today, in sporting-gun clubs in Britain and the United States, many people shoot with flintlock muskets and pistols – using original weapons carefully restored, or modern reproductions.

The flints are still hand-made by British flint knappers. They come in a variety of sizes, from about $\frac{3}{8}$ in. wide for a pocket pistol to $1\frac{1}{4}$ in. for a musket. Several hundred gun flints are produced every month at Brandon for the US market. Each is cross-cut from a long, double-ridged flake. This, strictly speaking, is 'knapping', and calls for somewhat less skill than 'flaking' – that is, striking off the double-ridged flakes from the flint core.

EARLY FLINT TOOLS AND WEAPONS

Flint nodules similar to the one shown above are often found on the surface in chalkland areas. They are the knapper's raw material. Below are some prehistoric weapons and tools. The Neolithic leaf-shaped spearhead (worked on both sides) was found at Mildenhall, in Suffolk. The rounded end would have been wedged in one end of a straight stick. Similarly, the central tang of the barbed arrowhead was slotted into the arrow shaft. It was found near Cambridge. The axe head, which dates from Neolithic times, was discovered in Wiltshire. It was probably fitted into a slot at one end of a wooden haft, making an axe suitable for felling trees and clearing vegetation.

Spear-head

Axe

Arrowhead

QUARTERING THE FLINT

Brandon flint knapper William Carter, who died in 1904, balances a heavy block of flint on one knee as he breaks it into manageable sizes with a quartering hammer. On the ground beside him are several flaking hammers. The barrels contain long flakes for cross-cutting into gun flints.

KNAPPING A GUN FLINT

*Flint knapping was a family craft at **Brandon**. Jack Carter, son of the William Carter pictured opposite, specialised in fashioning gun flints. With a knapping hammer, probably **made** for him by a local blacksmith from an **old file** drawn out to make it thinner, he cross-**cuts** a long flake into one or more gun flints. **The flints are trimmed into rectangular shapes.** The detailed drawings illustrate the separate stages: (1) A nodule of flint has had a number of parallel-sided flakes struck off its circumference. A second row has been struck to provide a set, each with two ridges which produce **bevelled** flakes for cross-cutting into sharp-edged rectangles. (2) A long bevelled flake. (3) A finished gun flint for the striker of a horse-pistol.*

HOW A FLINTLOCK WORKS

*Pulling the trigger causes the flint to **strike** the steel and knock it forwards. The impact **creates a** spark that ignites the powder in **the pan. This,** in turn, sets off the main charge through the **touch** hole. In the illustration, the steel is in the forward position as it would be before charging the pan with powder. A vice screw holds the flint between the jaws of the cock.*

THE FLY DRESSER

BLACK DOSE, HARE'S EAR, THUNDER AND LIGHTNING –
THE NAMES OF MANY FISHING LURES ARE AS BIZARRE
AS THE MATERIALS USED TO CREATE THEM

Like many other techniques for catching game, fly fishing is very ancient. The oldest English account of fly dressing – or fly tying – is in a work published in 1496 – the *Treatyse of Fysshynge wyth an Angle*, by Dame Juliana Berners. Among much sound advice she describes flies suitable for each season of the year. For instance: 'In the begynnynge of May a good flye, the body of roddyd (ruddy) wull and lappid abowte wyth blacke sylke; the wynges of the drake & of the red capons hakyll.' This fly is easily identified with a fly that is still in use today, called the Red Spinner.

Fly dressing seems to have made no great advance for a long period after Dame Juliana's pioneering book, although various authors stressed the importance of observing closely the habits of insects. The introduction of dry-fly fishing in the 1840s and of nymph fishing in the second decade of the present century were landmarks that demanded new approaches to fly dressing.

Fly fishing generally means angling for trout and salmon with an artificial fly as a lure. Catching trout is, if anything, the more complex pursuit, and depends a great deal on the careful study of the fish's feeding habits. The insects most attractive to trout belong to the family *Ephemeroptera*, which includes the mayflies. Each stage of the insect's life cycle is painstakingly copied by the fly dresser.

THE DEXTERITY OF THE FLY DRESSER

Fly dressing takes up little space but calls for careful observation and great delicacy of touch. A small vice holds the hook while the tiny pieces of feather and other materials are neatly tied on to the shank, transforming it into a lure irresistible to the fish. The hands belong to Jacqueline Wakeford, a skilled practitioner of the craft whose expertise lies behind many a successful day's fishing.

Salmon flies are another important class. They are not made to look like potential prey but rather as brightly coloured lures, since the salmon, intent only on spawning, is fasting when it comes up our rivers. Then there are somewhat similar, but less gawdy, flies for sea trout.

The food insects and their growth stages are represented by many different fly patterns, whose names are known to few outside the fishing fraternity. Some of the names, such as the March Brown and the Blue-winged Olive, refer to the appearance of the natural species; some, such as the Hare's Ear and the Grouse and Orange, refer to the materials of construction; others, such as Greenwell's Glory and Lunn's Particular, honour angling personalities. Salmon-fly names are somewhat easier to understand since they tend to refer to lethal qualities – the Black Dose, the Stuart's Killer, and the Thunder & Lightning, for example.

There are four main parts to an artificial fly: body, wings, hackle, and whisks or tails. Many materials are used for the bodies: fur from seal, mole, deer, and hare's ear; wool yarn, chenille and raffia; and the herls (or single strands) of peacocks' tail feathers. Among synthetics are latex sheet and polythene. Bodies are often ribbed with coloured tying silk, metallic wire or tinsel, and sometimes they end in a small 'tag' of coloured silk.

Wings are usually made of feathers from the neck, wing or tail of domestic poultry, or from ducks or other birds. Striking colours are produced by dyeing. Salmon flies need a much greater variety of feathers, including those from guinea fowl, pheasants, jay, heron, ostrich, and even from rarities such as the blue chatterer. In general, these flies are much more conspicuous than trout flies. Frequently, both bodies and wings are colourful, and sparkle like jewels.

How the 'legs' are made

Fly hackles represent the insect's legs and, in the case of the dry fly, support it on the water surface. Once again, feathers are used, the fibres trimmed and separated so that when they are wound round the body of the fly – usually at the neck – they open out like whiskers.

Not all flies are dressed with tails, but when present they consist of two or three whisks of feather. The tail end of a fly is always at the bend of the hook.

Fly dressing calls for very little in the way of equipment, but one thing is indispensable: a deft hand. In this respect, a craftswoman, such as Jacqueline Wakeford, has a distinct advantage. Her Southampton workshop is happily placed to serve anglers on two famous trout streams, the Test and the Itchen.

The largest item needed is a small-nosed vice, angled upwards so that it keeps the work clear of the bench. The fly dresser also requires two sizes of hackle pliers – small spring grips used for manipulating the hackles – fine scissors for trimming, tweezers, pen-knife, a dubbing needle for applying varnish and teasing-out materials, one or two tiny brushes, and perhaps some bobbin holders and a whip-finish tool.

The foundation of most flies is a winding of black tying silk which has first been beeswaxed to help it adhere. The winding is begun at the eye end and taken as far as the bend; on the return, it is used to secure the body, hackle, wings and tail.

A very simple fly, such as the Black Spider, has just a hackle, prepared from a black cock feather. The bare quill is secured with the tying silk and the hackle wound round the body with the aid of the hackle pliers. The tip is then tied in, the surplus ends cut off and the tying silk fastened at the eye and with a whip finish. A dab of black varnish ensures that it will not come adrift.

Fly bodies are usually made by winding materials and

EXOTIC MATERIALS *Typical fly-dressing materials are these feathers from (top to bottom) golden pheasant tippet, guinea fowl breast, golden pheasant breast, bustard and teal flank. Also in the picture: tying silks and tinsels, hackle pliers, and a tuft of Canadian red squirrel tail beside the lump of beeswax.*

absorbent materials can be used for wet flies, which will enter the water.

Wings are prepared from matching left and right wing feathers or from tail feathers. Small sections are removed and trimmed to shape and attached with the tying silk; the surplus is then cut off. On wet flies the wings lie flat along the back of the body and the hackle is brought below it. The wings of some dry flies are doubled and tied in upright so that they look like the wings of alighting insects. The wings of spent flies lie horizontally.

Many of these points apply to salmon flies, but they have a more complicated structure. The body may be in two or three differently coloured sections with different ribbings, and there may be a body hackle as well as a hackle at the throat. Just in front of the tag there is usually a small 'butt', often made from a black herl or else from a single strand of wool.

Wings may comprise as many as eight pieces of strikingly marked and coloured feather and usually include 'married' sections – made by stroking together single sections of contrasting feather. Over the wings lie 'sides' and 'cheeks' which often incorporate an eye-like marking. Carried above all this there may be a 'topping' of golden pheasant and perhaps 'horns' of blue macaw. The inclusion of 20 or 25 materials in one salmon fly perhaps not much more than an inch long is a remarkable tribute to the dexterity of the maker.

The whole business of fly dressing and fly fishing may seem to the layman to be heavily charged with mystique, and he cannot but wonder what the fish thinks about it all. If the fish survives, it will probably acquire a certain cunning, but it is debatable whether the precise dressing of a Blue Charm is really so critical as fishermen choose to believe.

any ribbings of silk or tinsel round the shank and securing them with tying silk. 'Dubbed' bodies are made by spinning small quantities of fur fibres round the tying silk after making it extra waxy. When wound on, this makes a fluffy body which can also be ribbed. The nature of the body depends, of course, on the way the fly is to be fished: dry flies must be made of light and buoyant materials; more

LIFE CYCLE OF THE MAYFLY

The mayfly (above) is particularly attractive to trout, and flies are tied to represent each stage of its life cycle. It hatches from the egg as a larva (nymph) and lives underwater for about two years – in the meantime, regularly splitting its outer skin – before rising to the surface as a hatching nymph. For about a day the insect remains in an imperfect sub-imago stage (called the dun) before a final split reveals the perfect fly, or spinner. After a brief existence for mating, the females lay their eggs on the water and sink down, exhausted, as spent spinners. Below: four flies based on the mayfly cycle.

A FAMOUS SALMON FLY – THE SILVER WILKINSON

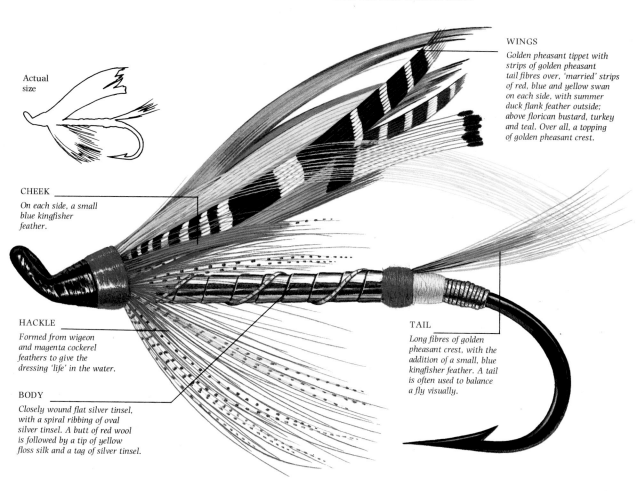

Actual size

WINGS

Golden pheasant tippet with strips of golden pheasant tail fibres over, 'married' strips of red, blue and yellow swan on each side, with summer duck flank feather outside; above florican bustard, turkey and teal. Over all, a topping of golden pheasant crest.

CHEEK

On each side, a small blue kingfisher feather.

HACKLE

Formed from wigeon and magenta cockerel feathers to give the dressing 'life' in the water.

BODY

Closely wound flat silver tinsel, with a spiral ribbing of oval silver tinsel. A butt of red wool is followed by a tip of yellow floss silk and a tag of silver tinsel.

TAIL

Long fibres of golden pheasant crest, with the addition of a small, blue kingfisher feather. A tail is often used to balance a fly visually.

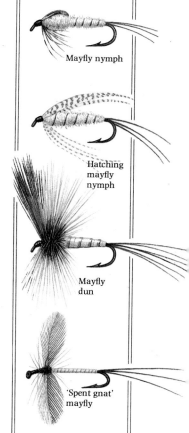

Mayfly nymph

Hatching mayfly nymph

Mayfly dun

'Spent gnat' mayfly

THE FURNITURE MAKER

NOTHING SO REFLECTS PEOPLE'S TASTE AS THEIR
FURNITURE. FOR MANY, IT REACHED PERFECTION WITH
THE CREATIONS OF THE GEORGIAN AND REGENCY
MASTERS, WHOSE TRADITIONS LIVE ON

Few things made by human hands reveal as much as furniture about those who use it – and about those who make it. The furniture maker must surely be numbered high among the craftsmen who have contributed most to the comfort of their race.

Modern furniture owes perhaps more to the skills of its designers and mechanised production techniques than to craftsmen; but a long tradition of fine workmanship persists in small pockets of resistance, and there are still patrons willing to meet the mounting costs of material and man-hours to enjoy the look, the feel, the indefinable 'rightness' of what will doubtless become tomorrow's antiques.

The English tradition in furniture making stretches back to the early Middle Ages, rooted in the ancient skills of the woodsman, carpenter and boatbuilder. The men who made it were limited to a rather basic tool-kit, in which the axe and adze played rather more part than the saw – hidden surfaces often show the slightly faceted marks of the adze blade. Smoothing was done with the plane and draw-knife, which was also used to cut chamfers – bevelled edges. There were moulding planes and scratch tools for cutting beadings and lines, and pole-lathes for turning legs and spindles. Joints were usually tenoned and pegged, a stout and simple method.

The wood used was mostly oak, which was easily cleft along a straight grain. Oak chests are among the medieval works that have survived – simple hollowed-out logs, or constructions of planks, with the end panels extended down to form legs, and the side panels nailed to them. Blacksmiths fashioned the hinges and hasps for the lid. However, shrinking and warping of the wood caused the planks to split, and the means devised to overcome this problem led to a revolution in the craft.

The new concept was framed-up construction: the chest was made as a framework, with thinner wooden panels slotted in between the frame members – but not fastened. The wood was thus left free to 'move' according to its needs. From then on furniture developed rapidly, and as tools improved craftsmen made great strides in the construction and finish of their work. Walnut, and later mahogany, came into favour, and increasingly furniture makers bowed to the dictates of fashionable designers.

Veneering – brought from Holland – and the arts of marquetry were used to create superbly decorated pieces, often enhanced also by quality fittings of brass and ormolu – fine castings of gilded bronze or other hard alloys. Many consider that elegance of design and perfection of craftsmanship in British furniture reached a peak in the 60 or so years from the middle of the 18th to the beginning of the 19th centuries, with the work of Thomas Chippendale, George Hepplewhite and Thomas Sheraton. This was the age of the master cabinet-makers, and their beautiful furniture is still reproduced widely – though not always very faithfully, accurately, or by genuine craftsmen. Not only are there few capable of the work: the very materials that go into it are becoming ever more scarce and expensive. Mahogany from the Caribbean islands and Honduras, in Central America, was once the favourite timber; supplies are now so short that craftsmen still making traditional Georgian and Regency-style furniture use African and South American varieties of mahogany. Sometimes, however, they will buy old but unimportant pieces of mahogany furniture and re-use the wood for special high-quality work of their own – though this practice is rapidly becoming uneconomical, due to the rise in prices paid for any solid, old furniture.

The importance of seasoning

Timber for furniture of the finest quality must be properly seasoned – or dried – before going into the workshop. The cells of a growing tree are full of water, which starts evaporating the moment the tree is felled, and is replaced by air. This process leaves the wood lighter, stronger and harder – but also causes it to shrink. And the shrinkage is often uneven, the outer wood from a log shrinking more than the inner, resulting in the cut planks warping or becoming distorted in other ways.

Eventually, however, the water remaining in the wood reaches a state of balance with the moisture in the surrounding atmosphere, and the timber becomes as stable as it ever will be. Fluctuations in humidity and temperature will continue to affect it to some degree by raising or lowering the moisture content: even in a centrally heated room, seasoned wood retains water equivalent to more than 10 per cent of its own weight when totally dry.

The simple way to season wood is to stack it out of doors – preferably in an open-sided hut – so that air can circulate freely around and between the planks. However, this method can take months, even years for certain woods, and kiln-drying has been developed to speed up the process. The planks are stacked inside a brick-built kiln and gently heat-dried, the temperature being carefully controlled to ensure that the wood does not dry, and therefore shrink, too quickly. This would cause it to warp seriously, and perhaps

THE ROBUST FORMS OF EARLY FURNITURE

Oak was the wood used most in early British furniture. It was plentiful, strong and easily cleft along a straight grain. Chests, tables and crude seats were made from planks fastened together by nails or simple joints. But the planks tended to warp and split as they were affected by heat and humidity. Chests were iron-bound not only for security, but also to hold them together. Frame-and-panel techniques – used in the chair below – solved this problem.

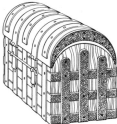

Oak chest with iron bands.

Oak chair – framed and carved.

A SCENE THAT CHANGES LITTLE

This engraving of a cabinet-maker's workshop was made in the 18th century, but much that is in it remains unchanged: the frame-saw one man is using, the try-plane at his feet and the rasp, chisel and tenon saws on the wall. And above all, perhaps, the craftsmen's total concentration on the job in hand.

A WORKSHOP OF TODAY WHERE THE BEST TRADITIONS OF QUALITY AND SKILL SURVIVE

Chisels, gouges and pliers are racked ready to hand in this corner of a workshop where traditions of quality and craftsmanship survive in the meticulous construction of furniture in the Georgian-Regency style. The lyre-shaped legs of a table, cut from solid mahogany planks, rest elegantly against off-cuts of timber and strips of beading. Intricately cut tenons and the housed mortise slot in the legs will fit perfectly into the top frame, stretcher and feet of the sofa table illustrated below. The bookcase, serpentine-fronted side-table and carver dining chair are also products of the village workshop of Redman and Hales in Hatfield Peverel, Essex. They are items from an extensive range of furniture made by this small firm, whose entire workforce is composed of only a dozen or so dedicated craftsmen.

Chippendale-style glazed bookcase with cupboard beneath.

Serpentine-fronted side-table in solid mahogany.

Lyre-shaped legs on this sofa table are cut from one plank of timber.

Inlaid splats and reeded arms on a Sheraton-style carver chair.

split. Kiln-drying seasons some timbers in about ten days, but even in a kiln, a massive 6 in. thick plank of mahogany can take months to reach a satisfactory condition.

Mahogany is, however, among the most stable of the hardwoods favoured by furniture makers, 'moving' very little once seasoned. The craftsman must be familiar with the properties of all of them, able to judge quality, condition and suitability for the work in hand.

Oak, elm and beech are plentiful and popular for work in both traditional and contemporary styles, as is the wide variety of more recently introduced hardwoods with un-familiar names, now being cultivated in tropical climes. Walnut, rosewood and other finely figured timbers once used in solid constructions appear now mostly as veneers, their scarcity having made them costly. However, from the time mahogany was introduced, it has remained a cabinet-maker's favourite – hard, but not too hard; close-grained for crisp carving and a fine finish; and ideal for the elegant and precise joints that demonstrate so eloquently the craftsman-ship of their maker.

In the workshop

Today's craftsman is aided by some excellent modern tools that would have brought a gleam to the eye of the great Chippendale himself. In a high-quality workshop they are used mostly to take the drudgery out of preparing timber – sanding and planing machines, bandsaws and circular saws, power drills and lathes. Some of these machines can produce work to rival that done by the most skilled hand – perfect mortise-and-tenon joints and delicate cuts for inlay work; rebates and intricate beadings that were once the province of special planes. However, the craftsman must still be the master of his hand-tools. The simple perfection of the dovetail joints in a Regency drawer-front is best accomplished with a fine saw, a sharp chisel and a lot of practice.

One of the very few workshops still producing Georgian and Regency-style furniture in solid mahogany by this blend of hand-tools and a few sophisticated machines is housed in a long, apple-green shed of timber and corrugated iron, standing behind a discreet showroom in the small Essex village of Hatfield Peverel. Ralph Rowlinson has worked there for more than 30 years, and like others among the dozen men who comprise the total workforce, can make by hand any item in the firm's considerable catalogue. He also makes special one-off pieces for connoisseur customers, working from his own drawings, carefully selecting wood from the firm's timber store, and carrying the whole project through until the finished article goes into the polishing shed.

The drawing itself requires great skill. Often it is made full-size, with each joint carefully detailed – many of them having to be set at compound angles to accommodate the curves of the design. The firm's timber store is an open-sided shed, with canvas curtains which can be lowered in very wet weather or when strong sunlight might affect the vulnerable ends of the boards stacked inside. To further protect these ends, they are often sealed with paint or varnish. Ralph explains that the wood needs constant watching if it is not to warp or develop 'shakes' – cracks or splits – in sudden changes of temperature and humidity.

One trick he uses for straightening out a board that has warped is to wet the concave side, which has shrunk, then lay it with that side downwards on dampened ground in strong sunlight. This replaces lost moisture in the shrunken side while the sun dries out the convex side, which pulls the board straight again.

The mahogany in the store is from Brazil, except for at least one massive plank from Africa, from which are cut and turned the solid pillars that support some of the larger tables. Also in the racks are sweet-smelling planks of superb, straight-grained and totally knotless Quebec yellow pine for certain frameworks, and sweet chestnut for drawer sides and bottoms.

The boards are cut and smoothed to approximate shape with accuracy and minimum waste as they are fed by experienced hands through the carefully set machines. Most curved components are cut from solid wood – and there are a lot of them; for serpentine-fronted and bow-fronted pieces; sabre legs; back-splats, top rails and arms for chairs; the lyre-shaped legs and sweeping tripod legs for pedestal tables, to name just a few. The boards and squared lengths from which they are cut must be carefully marked out to avoid waste and make maximum use of each board.

On the bench

It is when these components reach the craftsman's bench that the supremely satisfying aspect of the job begins. For this is Ralph's real domain: hanging neatly in racks or lying to hand on the scarred worktop among corkscrew shavings and chisel parings are his cherished hand-tools – chisels and gouges; spokeshaves for rounding curves and edges; routers for cutting grooves and housings; planes that smooth, or cut rebates or fancy beadings and edgings; marking gauges, saws, hammers, mallet and screwdrivers; drills and bits; spirit-level, ruler, try-square; pliers, files, rasps and punches . . . and always there are the oilstones to keep cutting edges keen.

At one of the benches a man is perhaps making a set of eight dining chairs – two of them carvers, with arms. The back and rear legs of the carver he is working on are formed from two long, curving pieces of mahogany, tapered subtly not only at each end, but also from front to back, because the front of the chair will be wider than the back. On the

Chippendale

Hepplewhite

Sheraton

SHERATON-STYLE CARVER CHAIR

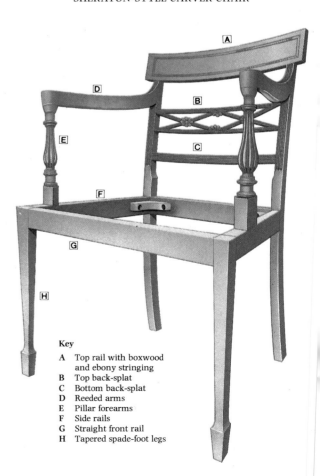

Key

A Top rail with boxwood and ebony stringing
B Top back-splat
C Bottom back-splat
D Reeded arms
E Pillar forearms
F Side rails
G Straight front rail
H Tapered spade-foot legs

inside face of each leg he chisels four mortise slots; three of them are at special, carefully calculated angles – for the back-splats that tenon into them are curved; the fourth is for the straight back rail of the seat. He chisels two more mortise slots on the front side of each leg – these too are angled, because the arms and side rails that will tenon into them angle outwards. Finally he cuts angled rebates at the top of each one, to take the curved top rail.

The front legs are tapered from front to back and from top to bottom, and a spokeshave is used to blend the taper into keystone-shaped 'spade' feet. Angled mortise slots are chiselled into the top to accommodate the side rails, and straight ones for the front seat rail. Each side rail has an angled tenon tongue to fit front and back legs, and near the front a housing is cut to accept the pillar that will support the arm. The arms will sweep downwards and outwards from just below the top rail, curving in again at their rounded front ends. A precisely angled housing is cut for each arm, which is angled to match the curve of the chair back, into which it is fitted.

Pillars supporting the front ends of the arms are turned on a lathe to a graceful, slim baluster shape, the bottom being left squared and a shoulder cut in it to fit the housing cut in the side rail. The top is turned as a thick dowel, which fits into a hole drilled into the underside of the arm.

All these joints are cut so accurately that they fit together tightly enough for the whole chair to be assembled without glue, for final squaring up and adjustments. They are made with infinite patience and minute parings by chisel and plane until each angle is perfect, each line marking a joint that is almost imperceptible.

Apart from this basic construction, the craftsman has also been responsible for the elegant, discreet decorations

REEDING AN ARM

Reeding became a popular form of decoration in the early Regency period, succeeding fluting – which was, however, still widely used. Reeding has convex 'strings', while fluted lines are concave. This chair arm is having its gentle double curves accentuated by six-string reeding. The craftsman is using a double-handed form of scraper, with a toothed blade, called a reeding tool. His control of it must be total as he follows the curves, working it forwards and back in short strokes. One slip and hours of patient toil will be wasted.

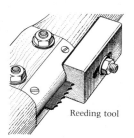

Reeding tool

CARVING A BACK-SPLAT *The curved splat has been cut from a solid piece of mahogany, with tenons at each end to fit into mortise slots in the back. The double-X design has been pierced through with a coping saw and the top and bottom triple-reeded. Now the craftsman is working on one of the rosette motifs, using mallet and carving chisel.*

that add so much to the attraction of the period style.

The curved, rectangular top rail is inlaid with narrow stringing – a thin strip of boxwood sandwiched between two even narrower strips of ebony – which follows its outline about an inch from the edge. The shallow groove into which it fits is cut with a small routing tool, and the stringing glued in. When the stringing is firmly fixed, the whole surface is planed and sanded to a fine finish, leaving the decoration perfectly flush with the surface.

There is reeding on the tops of the arms and on the turned pillars that support them; it also decorates the two horizontal back-splats, and the front of the vertical back components. This reeding is made by cutting a series of parallel, rounded grooves along the length of the component, the effect looking much as though a coarse comb has been run along the surface. The work can be done by a specially bladed tool when the width of the reeding is constant. However, on this chair it is not; and each strand of the reeding must be narrowed as the component narrows, and follow its curves. So the grooves are cut by hand with wood-carving chisels.

The top back-splat is pierced to form a wide, shallow 'XX', using a fine saw; and at the centre of each 'X' a flower motif

is hand-carved. In addition the top and bottom of the splat and the arms of the 'Xs' are decorated with reeding. The rounded front ends of the chair arms are cut with chopping strokes of a chisel, the parings becoming ever finer until a perfect radius is achieved, which is then hand-sanded. Finally, the vertical back pieces are rounded at the rear from just above seat level, with a spokeshave.

The chair is then glued together, with curved corner pieces glued and screwed at the corners of the seat frame for added strength.

The construction of this chair is given in some detail to indicate the quality of craftsmanship required for work of such high standard, and the amount of time a workshop must be prepared to devote to ensure that such standards are preserved.

But the carver chair is a relatively simple exercise for these men – one design among many in the catalogue. The skills and hours lavished on their major creations – sideboards, tables, bookcases, desks – are prodigious. From the workshop rafters hang sheets of beautifully figured rosewood veneer; bundles of ebony and boxwood stringings lie close to hand. The veneer will be knife-cut to make cross-banding on drawer-fronts and tops and edgings – often outlined by ultra-fine boxwood lines. Delicate marquetry designs – bought in by the workshop, for this is a separate craft – are lovingly inlaid to further enhance many of the pieces.

Furniture – new or old – made to these standards can be recognised at a glance. The drawers will be finely hand dovetailed rather than machine dovetailed, and their sides and bottoms will be made from solid wood. Carcases will be constructed with mortise-and-tenon joints and dovetails. The fittings – handles, hinges, castors and so on – will be of high-quality solid brass. They will be hand polished, not spray-finished.

The craftsmen work in absorbed, comfortable silence by the natural light streaming through windows that stretch almost the full length of the workshop. One man may be trimming the rosewood cross-banding around a drawer-front held in his vice. He uses the razor edge of a broad, bevelled chisel, cutting in small sideways sweeps in a sawing motion across the grain, so that he does not splinter the thin veneer. Scattered on the bench are the dozen or so small G-clamps he used to cramp the veneer down while the glue that fixed it dried. Among them stands an iron pot of good old-fashioned animal glue, rim thick with accumulations, small rivulets of it congealing down the sides. Inside the pot is the glue brush, its protruding handle darkened and polished with much use. And certainly with a lot more use ahead.

MAKING SURE OF A PERFECT FIT

The back-splat is finished and fitted; so is the top rail, its matching curve enhanced by boxwood and ebony stringing. Soon the complete chair will be assembled, its joints so snug that no glue is needed to hold it rock steady. During this process each component is fastidiously trimmed as it is fitted to ensure a flawless line when final glueing takes place. Here the craftsman is making a last guide-mark on one of the arms.

POLISHED AND UPHOLSTERED

Here in the showroom stands the end product of many hours' meticulous work of the chairmaker, the polisher and the upholsterer: a perfectly proportioned dining chair made to last for generations – an antique of the future. It is one of a set of eight, two of them being carver chairs, with arms. The colouring of the mahogany in each has been painstakingly matched with the others, and the deep glow of the polish is unblemished by those fake bump and stain 'distress' marks that are an immediate give-away on so much phoney reproduction-type furniture.

POLISHING TO BRING OUT ALL THE NATURAL BEAUTY OF THE WOOD

French polishing a piece of furniture to a professional standard takes almost as long as the time taken by the cabinet-maker or chair-maker to build it. That lustrous, unmistakable finish is achieved only by painstaking application of skills acquired through a long apprenticeship. For polishing is a craft in its own right. It calls for a deep understanding of the mostly natural materials used, and the timbers to which they are applied. Not to mention a fair amount of elbow-grease!

An item of furniture entering the polishing shop is first hand-sanded with glasspaper and flourpaper to an ultra-fine smoothness – this despite the maker having already sanded each individual component and the whole piece before it left him. It is then painted with a bichromate acid to bring up the colouring and grain of the wood. This is left to dry, when the surface is sanded down again and given a coat of raw linseed oil.

When the linseed, too, has dried, an oil-based stain of suitable colour is carefully brushed on. The craftsman needs an expert eye to ensure that variations in the shade of the mahogany used in the different components of the piece are compensated for. By the time the stain has dried – it takes about 24 hours – the colour will be uniform throughout. Except, that is, for any marquetry or other inlay work, which is masked off with special tape before polishing begins.

The stain will have raised the grain again, so this must be remedied if the final finish is to be perfect. A suitably coloured filler paste is used for the task: the polisher loads a soft rag generously with the soft paste, then works it into the surface with a brisk rubbing motion along and across the grain, so that every crevice is filled.

This too is allowed to dry for 24 hours before the surface is yet again sanded down to a smooth, matt finish. Now it is at last ready for the polish.

French polish – so-called because the formula was introduced from France – is shellac dissolved in industrial alcohol. The shellac itself is the secretion of an insect, and is found encrusted on the twigs of certain trees – mostly fig trees and mostly in India.

The polish is worked in with a special pad called a rubber, and as the shine begins to appear the polish is diluted slightly with spirit and the strokes become progressively lighter. In the final stages, light, sweeping passes are made along the grain with just a touch of spirit alone on the rubber, resulting in a dazzling, mirror-like gloss.

This is allowed to harden for 24 hours – then the gleaming perfection of the surface is seemingly destroyed by hard rubbing with a wire-wool pad, leaving it a dull grey. Then comes the almost miraculous finishing touch: a soft cheesecloth primed with wax polish is applied with a positive flourish, and the grey dissolves into a deep, glowing, grain-enhancing shine for which even modern technology has found no substitute.

STAINING

Varying shades of oil-based stain can be brushed into component parts cut from different pieces of timber to ensure a good colour match not only in, say, one chair, but throughout a complete dining suite.

FILLING THE GRAIN

The grain of the wood is raised as the stain dries out and must be filled in if the finished surface is to be perfectly smooth. This is done by rubbing it vigorously with a rag heavily loaded with a suitable filler paste.

MAKING A 'RUBBER'

French polish is applied with a rubber. This is made by placing a ball of cotton wool in a piece of soft, lint-free cloth. The cotton wool is then soaked with polish and the cloth twisted tight around it. Polish seeps through as the rubber is applied.

POLISHING

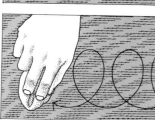

The polish is worked in with small, circular movements of the rubber along the length of the surface in overlapping 'strips'. After several progressively lighter applications, the shine starts to appear and the action changes to long strokes following the grain.

THE FURNITURE RESTORER

THE SKILLED RESTORER MUST BE A MAN
OF MANY CRAFTS AND MUCH KNOWLEDGE – FROM
CABINET-MAKER TO EXPERT IN ANTIQUES

Much speculation, not to say suspicion, attaches to the arcane arts of the furniture restorer. 'Woodworm holes' made by a judicious blast of shotgun pellets, and 'distress marks' inflicted by beating new work with chains, figure frequently in oft-told tales of their trade secrets. The only secret of the *real* restorer – as opposed to the back-street bodger – is soon revealed as simply painstaking, highly skilled work, resulting from years of hard-won experience in a variety of crafts.

Most important of these crafts is cabinet-making: any restorer hoping to gain a good reputation must have a cabinet-maker's intimate knowledge of the techniques and materials used in furniture construction. How else could he

take apart, repair and reassemble – frequently with several new components – items of great value from the workshops of past masters?

He must, indeed, be able to build (or rebuild) virtually any piece of furniture – and that is only the start. He should also have considerable experience in woodcarving, turning, veneering, marquetry, gilding, decorative paintwork, lacquer work and polishing. Not to mention an ability to recognise instantly a wide variety of woods – even different types of the same wood.

Finally he must possess an antique expert's knowledge of style and design, for often he will be called upon to replace components which have been totally lost. Many a beautiful table-top has been discovered standing on crude legs, banged together by some rustic carpenter totally indifferent to the quality of the three good legs he had chucked away because the fourth was broken and beyond his skills to reproduce or repair. A good restorer should know from the style, construction and material of the table-top just what the original legs must have looked like, how high they stood and what wood they were made of. Or at worst he should be capable of making an informed guess! Of course, he must also be able to reproduce them.

A good number of rough 'bodging' repairs were made before restoring became a craft in its own right early in the last century. Prior to that, a damaged piece of good furniture was returned to its maker for repair, or he was summoned to the owner's house to do the job there. The 18th-century cabinet-maker Thomas Chippendale once billed Sir Rowland Winn, of Nostell Priory, West Yorkshire, for four shillings – 20p – for 'planing over a kitchen table, mending a sash and putting a lock on a drawer'. But quite often the job was entrusted to the local carpenter, or even the blacksmith – hence all those pieces of antique furniture in museums and stately homes which are held together by iron strapping, bolts and screwed-on metal plates.

The specialist restorer is born

However, furniture-making expanded so swiftly in the 18th century that by the end it was a major industry. Chippendale, and other masters such as Hepplewhite and Sheraton, published books of designs for every conceivable type of furnishing – designs that were taken up or elaborated upon by craftsmen all over the country. Many works of outstanding beauty and quality were produced – but the makers found themselves with less and less time to undertake any repairs. As a result, certain craftsmen began to specialise in this type of work, and set up their own shops. The furniture restorer had arrived.

The demands made upon his skill and ingenuity have multiplied in the intervening years. A modern restorer is now dealing with British furniture spanning four or five centuries, plus pieces in the major European styles – notably French, Dutch and Italian. But the sights and sounds and smells of his busy workshop have changed little down the years. A bandsaw or two, electric power for the lathe and more refined basic hand tools are evident. But the pungent smell of old-fashioned animal glue simmering in its pot still tickles the nostrils, mingling with the heady aromas of French polish and fresh wood shavings.

Much of his work, now as always, is concerned with restoring chairs, tables and 'case furniture' – chests of drawers, cupboards, sideboards and so on. Sometimes the damage is accidental; often it is caused simply by wear and tear – joints tend to work loose in time, especially if the piece has been roughly handled or moved about frequently. The joints would have been secured with animal glue, which has the great advantage of giving way under stress before the wood itself splits, simplifying repairs. However, it is not

ASSEMBLING A COMPLEX VENEER

Boulle is a way of decorating furniture with elaborate brass and tortoiseshell inlays, often combined with ebony veneer – a method perfected by André Charles Boulle, cabinet-maker to the French King Louis XIV. The techniques used have not changed over three centuries, and there are restorers who not only repair boulle but reproduce it if necessary. Thin sheets of brass and tortoiseshell are glued together, and a drawing of the design is stuck on top of the sheets. The design is then cut out with a fine saw. When the brass and tortoiseshell are separated, the tortoiseshell from one layer and the brass from the other can be combined to make two distinct patterns. The one with the tortoiseshell-ground inlaid with brass is known as 'first part', and the other with the brass-ground inlaid with tortoiseshell is called 'counter-part'. The picture shows boulle held together with sticky tape, and being glued in place. The restorer is pressing it down with a veneer hammer to spread the glue evenly.

unusual to find that an ignorant owner or bodger has 'repaired' loose joints with nails or screws, which cause the wood to split, as they leave no margin for natural shrinkage or expansion of the wood due to changes in temperature and humidity. The drawers themselves may stick or may be loose, due to worn runners or in the case of some pieces, a worn front rail. Eventually, from whatever cause, the piece becomes so loose that even pulling out a drawer causes the whole carcase to lurch left or right, creaking in protest. It must be dismantled for repair.

The restorer begins by removing all nails, screws, knobs, hinges and any detachable decorations or mountings. Using his knowledge of construction, he then separates the components by placing a batten of wood against them, close to the points where they are jointed, and tapping it gently with a mallet until they come apart. If it is necessary to open a glued joint, he injects warm water into the back of the joint; this softens the glue enough to free its hold. During dismantling, he may number each part to make sure that it is reassembled correctly.

The next task is to clean up the separated joints by soaking and scraping away flakes of old glue. If there is damage, the restorer may cut away the affected part and replace it with sound wood, shaped to fit and glued in place.

Sometimes two components are glue-jointed on their longer sides – known as a rubbed joint. Should this glue have failed, the two surfaces are thoroughly cleaned and re-glued, the joints being rubbed lengthways to ensure an even spread, then held between clamps until the glue sets. As the carcase is put together again, each joint is fixed anew with hot glue and the components held firmly with cramps during the drying process. The cramps always bear on to battens or bits of scrap wood placed between them and the piece under restoration to avoid damaging surfaces.

However, the restoration may – and usually does – involve a good deal more than these relatively simple procedures. Chairs, in particular, are frequently in need of extensive work, being generally subjected to more misuse than any other piece of furniture. Heavy people seem to slump unerringly into the lightest chairs; loungers tilt them back at impossible angles; they are used as step-ladders and in children's games. Wear on the joints is the commonest damage, notably where the front legs meet the side rails and where these rails slot into the rear leg-cum-back members.

These joints can often be re-glued, and are usually reinforced with small blocks of wood glued into the angles where rails and legs meet. They are invisible when the seat is fitted. If the joints have been badly damaged, with split or broken tenons, these tenons are cut out and new ones made and glued into the rail. These joints are always reinforced with glue blocks – or maybe with a triangular wooden bracket glued in the corner. A strap cramp looped around the seat frame holds the joints fast while the glue dries. This type of cramp consists of a webbing strap and a device to tighten it. These are all fairly straightforward jobs.

It is when an elaborate major component – say an ornate back-splat or richly carved arm or leg – needs replacing that the restorer's real skills begin to count. Not only must the part be remade, but it must be remade in the correct wood, with the right colouring. Most restorers buy in job-lots of old furniture and wood at auctions, dismantle the furniture, and so build up a variety of timbers for just such occasions. But they must know exactly what they are buying! They must, for example, be able to recognise the various kinds of mahogany – notably Honduras, Cuban and African. They must be able to distinguish between British oak and American oak, which was not used in Britain before about 1750; between real rosewood and fake – which is usually

CRAMPING UP AN INLAID DESK-TABLE

The inlaid brass strips and ebony veneer on this elegant bureau-plat, *or desk-table, of about 1780 have both been restored. The new sections have been glued and are held in place with a flat plank of wood, a* caul, *held by G-cramps. This applies even pressure over the surface and protects it from damage by the cramps.*

stained beechwood; between ebony and black-dyed fruit-wood – often used as a substitute. There are dozens more, and the restorer must know where to lay hands on those he does not have in stock.

Having selected a piece of mahogany for, say, a replacement leg on a Chippendale chair, the restorer will set about making it in the same way as his 18th-century predecessor, cutting out the basic shape, then tackling the decorative work with woodcarving chisels and gouges. It will take considerable time and it will be expensive – there are no viable short-cuts. When it is completed, fitted to the chair, stained and polished to match, there will be no lashing it with chains to simulate the dents and scars of long usage. The farthest a good restorer will go in that direction is to gently round any sharp edges, in keeping with the wear on others on the chair. He will list the details of the restoration for the owner or any subsequent buyer. The name of a reputable restorer is sufficient testimony to the 'rightness' of the piece and the quality of the work done on it.

This is, however, rather drastic surgery, seldom undertaken except in a case of terminal woodworm damage or large bits missing after a breakage. If just part of a decorative carving has been lost, that section can be neatly cut out and a suitable piece of wood glued in, which is then carved to match the rest.

Repairing a broken leg

Sometimes a slim, tapered leg has simply snapped off – not all the most elegant furniture is also the most durable! If the break is some way down the leg it can be repaired by making a new bottom half and joining it to the top with a scarf joint. The broken top half is sawn off at a steep angle, then a new bottom half is made and given an acute diagonal cut to match that of the top. These two sloping surfaces are hot-glued together and cramped. Because of the relatively large surfaces involved, the glue dries to give a strong, durable joint which should not – contrary to some opinions – need any extra dowelling to strengthen it. Using this method, the grain of both pieces of wood is allowed to merge imperceptibly together on the outer surfaces, and the joint is hardly noticeable.

Similarly, replacement wood can be inserted into a broken leg – perhaps to preserve a well-carved foot – with two scarf joints.

However, chair backs present greater problems – and greater challenges. Early chairs had panelled backs inside frames which were held together by tapered pegs. The joints work loose but can be made secure, and even strengthened if necessary, by inserting larger pegs for a tighter fit. All fairly simple – but the highly decorated chair backs of the 18th century are another matter. These were made in a great number of styles, from the ornate ribband-back, with perhaps a Cupid's-bow top rail, to the intricate 'Chinese Chippendale' and the elegant but inherently weak shield-back and wheel-back.

Cutting, carving and fitting replacement sections for chair backs in these styles calls for craftsmanship of the highest order. Often special blocks of waste wood are cut to match the top of, say, a wheel-back so that the back can be cramped for gluing without damaging its finish. The block is placed on top and the long cramps are fitted over it and under the seat rail. The under surface of the block may even be covered with felt as a further precaution against marking the finish.

Cracked, blistered, raised or missing sections of veneer are also in frequent need of a restorer's skilled attention. Although found on some antique chairs, veneer was used more generally to enhance and decorate case furniture. Veneer can be up to $\frac{1}{8}$ in. thick, and the varieties of

surrounding original veneer, the 'patch' should be almost undetectable.

Veneer that has lifted at an edge can be re-glued fairly easily. Using cardboard to protect the surface, it is pressed with a hot iron to melt the old glue and lift the veneer a little more. The old glue is scraped out, fresh hot glue inserted with a broad, flexible knife-blade, and the veneer ironed flat again or pressed flat with the veneer hammer.

The technique for removing a bubble is much the same, but access for the glue is through a slit cut in the bubble with a thin, sharp knife. This slit is made at an angle through the veneer and along its grain, so that when the bubble is pressed flat again, the join is almost invisible.

Repairs to really intricate marquetry may well be entrusted to the handful of craftsmen who specialise in this work. But the simpler patterns on some English furniture, such as the half or quarter fan, can be restored in the same way as ordinary veneering, though small pieces of the pattern may be held down with sticky tape while the glue is drying.

The deep sheen polished into a piece of furniture by generations of loving hands will not lightly be disturbed by a restorer. To strip and repolish is unthinkable except for extreme cases of neglect or gross damage to the whole surface. So colouring and polishing renewed components to blend in with the old is given very special attention. A wide range of wood stains and dyes is kept. Some restorers add a small amount of thinned glue and a weak ammonia solution to the stain, and the mix is brushed on quickly then rubbed with a coarse cloth. When the colour is right the stain is allowed to dry and the surface is polished. If it was French polished originally – that is how it will be polished again. Or it may have been waxed over original coatings of boiled linseed oil, poppy oil or a mixture of beeswax and turpentine: it will be treated in the same way again. Regular application of furniture polish – which should *not* contain silicones – will eventually build up a patina fine enough to match the overall finish of the piece.

RESTORING A MARQUETRY CORNER CUPBOARD

Marquetry is a form of decorative veneer that has been used for over three centuries to embellish furniture surfaces – table-tops, doors and drawer-fronts. It is made in the form of a mosaic using shaped pieces of wood, bone, ivory or a metal such as copper or brass. If the pattern is geometrical it is called parquetry. Like other veneers, marquetry is subject to chips and blisters. Tiny pieces forming a floral pattern, like the top of the ornate corner cupboard above, are easily displaced but difficult to replace. A new piece has been cut to fit and glued in place. Using cardboard to protect the surface, the piece is pressed flat with a hot iron. Normally, ironing a blister will be sufficient, but if it is stubborn a block and cramp or a block and pins can be used while the glue dries.

wood used, the colours and grains, and the ways it is cut and laid are almost endless. The old craftsmen laid it with hot glue and a veneer hammer or pressed it down with a caul – a flat panel larger than the area being pressed – clamped tight with cramps around the edges. Over the years veneer may chip or crack due to mishandling; it may also lift or blister through movement in the wood – caused perhaps by dampness or over-long exposure to sunlight.

Chips on corners and missing sections are repaired by trimming the rough edges into straight lines, then gluing in a replacement piece of veneer. To ensure a good fit, paper is pressed over the area, its edges marked with pencil and a pattern cut from the paper. Veneer is then cut to the pattern, taking care that the grain matches the original as closely as possible. It is hot-glued and pressed down with a veneer hammer – a small, rectangular piece of wood with a polished brass strip inset on the bottom edge, and a handle at the back. The brass edge is pressed down on the veneer as the tool is moved backwards and forwards, spreading the glue beneath and eliminating bubbles.

The veneer should be slightly thicker than the original, so that it can be sanded down after gluing to make the edges perfectly flush. Expertly coloured and polished to match the

THE LUSTRE OF GOLD

Restoring the gilt on a piece like this 18th-century console table requires much care. Here, the restorer is using the oil-gilding method to patch a leg. The plaster of Paris moulding is first cleaned and then the damaged area is coated with gold size. This is left to dry until it is just tacky to the touch. Paper-backed gold leaf is then gently pressed against the surface, and the gold adheres to it. It can then be burnished with an agate burnishing tool. Another method of gilding is water gilding, in which the surface is wetted and individual gold leaves are applied with a gilder's tip – a wide camel-hair brush.

THE
GLASS ENGRAVER

'GLASS MAY LAST UNALTERED FOR A THOUSAND YEARS OR BE DESTROYED AT A TOUCH.' FROM THIS MEDIUM, LAURENCE WHISTLER CREATES IMAGES THAT SAY, 'I HAVE BEEN HERE BEFORE'

*L*aurence Whistler's craft is that of capturing the fleeting moment – the brooding silence that precedes a thunderstorm, perhaps, or the faint singing in the rails leading into the night from a country station, or an instant of starshine on the façade of a gracious house. And the medium he has chosen to encapsulate such moments, real or imaginary, is the contrast of light and darkness, locked into the fathomless depths of glass.

Glass is the very stuff of illusion – it is there, and yet it is not – and its possibilities have been explored by engravers down the years, reaching a climax in Holland between the 16th and 18th centuries. That was the time when Dutch artist-craftsmen, working with diamond-pointed pencils, drew and stippled exquisite pictures upon small drinking glasses. Perhaps because of the exacting nature of the craft, the numbers of those engaged upon it were never large, and each glass engraver was to some extent an innovator, picking up where his predecessors had left off. So it has been, too, with Laurence Whistler.

He is a poet and, aptly, his first work on glass was a charm of his own composing – 'No roving shadow of misfortune

GLASS FOR CANVAS

Mr Whistler prefers to work on goblets of lead glass which vary slightly in shape, but are generally about 9 in. high by 3½ in. in diameter. In most cases they have been specially made to his own designs and formulae, but the engraved goblet (right) is an exception, being originally a Victorian antique. The design, which shows Godmersham Park, Kent, enclosed in a cartouche and surrounded by rich decoration, was the work of Rex Whistler, the engraver's brother, who was killed in action in Normandy in 1944.

Godmersham Park, Kent, 1940.

stain/The shadows that across your windows pass ...' – that he engraved upon a window-pane in a friend's house in Northumberland in 1935. Within a few months, however, he was working with diamond point upon Victorian and Georgian goblets, creating splendid designs that combined calligraphy with rococo whorls of fruit, flowers and leaves. In 1940, following drawings made by his brother Rex, the theatrical designer and illustrator, he engraved upon a goblet what seems to have been his first portrait in glass of a country house, Godmersham Park in Kent.

His brother's baroque style continued to have an influence on his work, and it was not until some years after Rex Whistler's death that he allowed his own ideas to take root and flower. At the same time, he began to experiment with perspective and the illusions that could be coaxed out of rounded glass, beginning with a midwinter sunset on Salisbury Plain, glimpsed through a ghostly Stonehenge.

Later, and even bolder, experiments produced such dream-like works as *The Overflowing Landscape*. Here, a landscape painting hanging on the wall of a country bedroom engraved on the inside of the goblet overflows its frame, and apparently continues through the thickness of the glass to an eerie moonlit wood engraved on the outside. As the goblet is turned, the scene wanders from the bedroom to the wood and back again, drawing the viewer into a world of shadowed illusion.

Glass engraving is the reverse of all other art forms, in that its pictures are created out of white against black. The glass itself, of course, is clear, and the effect of the engraved image can be properly appreciated only when seen against a dark background, and when lit from below or from an angle. Dark forms – a tower, say, or a clump of trees or even a leafy twig – are left as unworked clear glass, apart from a

within and about this small compass that he engraves and records his view of the world. A good deal of his imagery is drawn from Wessex – its secret woods and unexpected valleys, its soaring cathedral and little churches, its high hills scarred with ancient fortifications and gigantic representations of gods forgotten. It is an elusive landscape, and a touch melancholy, exactly suiting Laurence Whistler's view that life is a matter of moments, which occur once only and are unrepeatable.

As the goblets turn, a shadowy Salisbury Cathedral rears up, to yield to moonlight filtering through trees, to a woodland pool, or a glimpse through a ruined tower of a distant valley through which a road runs to infinity. Then, as with a dream, when the goblet is lifted to the light, all distinction disappears, and it is simply glass once more.

A GLASS FOR A FRIEND

A leaded pane in the Church of St Mary's, Alton Barnes, Wiltshire, was engraved by Laurence Whistler in memory of a farmer friend, Mr A. G. Stratton. The pane summarises Mr Stratton's life by depicting his hilly fields covered with the corn stooks of his youth, while the foreground shows one of the rolled bales of modern farming.

STEADY HAND, SURE EYE *When engraving a goblet, Laurence Whistler first marks out the design on the glass with a wax crayon, then engraves it in a myriad tiny dots with a diamond point or – more usually – with a small electric drill armed with a point of steel or carborundum.*

few engraved highlights, and are given their shapes by the light, worked areas of cloud, water or sky.

A goblet or bowl so worked on both the inside and outside of the glass, stood against a dark backdrop and correctly lit, leaps to life as a sunlit, sombre, three-dimensional landscape, giving the impression to the observer that he might enter it and wander to its furthermost hills.

The effect is achieved on goblets by means of a myriad tiny dots and scratches, stippling and line engraving, inscribed by a steel point or, on larger work, by a small electric drill. The closer together the dots or lines, the whiter the area. Even a single misplaced dot will shine like a star when lit, so the engraver must have a sure and steady hand, for there is no way of obliterating mistakes.

Raising a picture out of thousands of dots is laborious and time-consuming, but, when working on a bowl or goblet meant to be viewed from a distance of no more than a foot or so, it is the only means of achieving the desired contrasts of light and shadow. On larger areas – a memorial window in a church, for example, which is meant to be viewed from a much greater distance – such fine engraving is unnecessary. On these, wider, more sweeping strokes are used to produce the same results.

For windows, Mr Whistler uses ordinary pane glass, fairly thick and hard. But his goblets and bowls demand the finest lead glass which he has had blown to his own designs by several famous companies.

The bowls of these goblets, standing upon delicate stems, measure about 9 in. high by about $3\frac{1}{2}$ in. across, and it is

THE EVENING PLANE

In contrast with the extravaganza opposite, the subject of this goblet is a tranquil evening in the cove of Rovinia on Corfu. You can almost feel the silence in the left-hand view, then, as the goblet is turned, the quiet sky over Paleokastritsa is pierced by the vapour trail of the late Athens flight. In this case, only the back of the glass is engraved, so increasing the extraordinary, three-dimensional effect.

THE GLASS MAKER

WORKING AS A TEAM, GLASS-BLOWERS USE AGE-
OLD METHODS TO PROVIDE ONE OF THE MOST ABSORBING
SPECTACLES IN THE CRAFT WORLD

The boundless beauty of glass was revealed by an unknown genius who lived in Babylon around the year 200 BC. Using a tube to force air into the molten material, he discovered that hollow objects could be formed, and so established the spectacular craft of glass-blowing.

Similar methods are used today. Naturally, there have been many technical developments, but the 5 ft blowing iron used 2,000 years ago might pass unnoticed in a modern glassworks.

The first glass was made some 3,000 years even before this – also in Babylonia. It took the form of a bluish glaze, which was used to embellish jewellery. We do not know how this early glass was produced, but the technique soon spread to Egypt and Crete. Then, in the 15th century BC, Egyptian craftsmen began to make hollow utensils entirely out of glass. These early vessels were made by winding threads of molten glass round a core of clay and sand. This core, or mould, corresponded to the desired inside shape of the vessel and was mounted on a rod for easy manipulation. Chemicals were added to the mixture to vary the colour of the glass. The Egyptians also made the first sheet glass, probably by making cylinders and then opening them out flat.

But it was glass-blowing that altogether transformed the craft. A 'gather', or gob, of molten glass, taken from the furnace on one end of a hollow metal tube, was transferred to a clay mould and then blown to fill it. As a result, hollow-ware became very much cheaper and more plentiful, and numerous glass factories opened up in the countries around the Mediterranean.

This early glass was coloured and barely translucent, but later Roman craftsmen discovered that a small quantity of manganese, added to a basic mix of silica (sand) and soda ash, helped to make the glass almost colourless and translucent. In Britain, they established glass-making enterprises in Lancashire and Norfolk. Their craftsmen also developed the art of glass cutting and engraving, and even made millefiori ('a thousand flowers') – a type of ornament still made today by embedding pieces of coloured glass rod in clear glass to create floral designs.

Millefiori paperweights

Roman traditions of glass making survived well into the AD 900s, by which time some glass makers had begun to use wood ash instead of soda ash in the mix, the purpose in both cases being to lower the melting point of the silica. Wood ash was not quite so effective for this purpose as soda ash, but it produced a harder glass.

The great centre of decorative glass making in the Middle Ages was Italy, predominantly in and around Venice. By about AD 1000, craftsmen were decorating glassware with fine engraving, gilding and painting, and Venetian craftsmen learned how to make glass with an almost water-like transparency.

In Britain, much of the glass for cathedrals, churches and palaces was imported from France and Germany. But there were a few isolated glassworks, such as those in the Sussex Weald, where a coarse glass was blown from the 14th century onwards. However, the prodigal use of timber for shipbuilding in the 17th century, and the resultant shortage, led to a royal ban on the use of wood for firing glass furnaces. Glass makers moved away from the rapidly thinning forests to go to the new coal-mining areas of Newcastle, Birmingham and Stourport. Coal remained the staple fuel until the present century, but gas is now the prime source of heat for glass-making furnaces.

The main constituent of glass is silica, a common mineral found in quartz, sandstone and other rocks – and in sand itself. This has to be melted, but the melting point of silica – over 3,000°F (1,700°C) – is too high for most furnaces. The problem is resolved by adding fluxes, so reducing the heat required down to a more manageable temperature.

Soda ash is the flux most commonly used, for it reduces the melting point dramatically to about 1,500°F (approx. 800°C). Unfortunately, glass made from a straight mix of silica and soda ash dissolves in water! To stabilise the mix, an extra flux has to be added – generally lime. Such glass is sometimes called soda-lime-silica glass. It is used for making windows, bottles and inexpensive tableware.

There are two other main types of glass – lead crystal and borosilicate. Lead crystal, invented by George Ravenscroft about 1675, has lead oxide as a flux in place of lime. It provides a glass of exceptional brilliance.

Borosilicate glass was the brainchild of Michael Faraday, the brilliant English scientist of the early 19th century, who discovered that a mixture of silica and boric acid gave a remarkably low expand-and-contract ratio. Such glass is ideal for household ovenware and scientific apparatus.

Whatever the basic mix, the process starts with heating the ingredients to a much higher temperature than their melting point so that the glass will stay in a fluid state long enough for the furnacemen to remove any air bubbles. The molten mass so formed is either mechanically moulded (in the case of inexpensive glassware) by complex automatic machines, or else hand-crafted into more delicate and desirable shapes. It is the latter process, so close to the

METHODS THAT HAVE SURVIVED FOR CENTURIES

Published about 1760, this print shows tools and methods similar to those still in use today. In the background, old glass is being broken for adding to the batch as cullet. On the left, craftsmen grouped around the furnace are blowing cylinders of glass which will later be opened up to form flat sheets. On the right, plate glass for mirrors is being cast.

ancient skills of Babylon, Rome and Venice, that produces glassware of the finest quality and provides such an exciting spectacle for visitors to glass-making establishments.

At the heart of a glassworks is the glasshouse, a hangar-like building where teams of craftsmen perform their rituals around a central furnace. The furnace heats a number of fireclay melting pots, which contain the molten glass.

Most visitors wince at the fiery blast that awaits them in the glasshouse. The pot openings appear as white-hot pits; the clay walls of the pots glow cherry-red. Around the perimeter are teams of sweating men who roll, blow and fashion the molten glass into satisfying and familiar shapes. The spectacle has changed little in hundreds of years. The tools used for handling and shaping the glass are identical to those of Tudor times.

As a forerunner to this exciting spectacle, the pots are loaded with precisely measured amounts of sand, lead, potash, soda, lime – the carefully formulated ingredients for a particular grade of glass. Only the finest silver sand is suitable, and even this has first to be washed, sifted and dried. The brilliance and clarity of the glass depends on the quality of the batch – the term used for the mixed ingredients. In addition to these ingredients, up to 30 per cent of cullet (waste glass) is added to help reduce the melting point of the batch.

The pots where these materials are melted, and then kept in a liquid state until used, are hand-made from fireclay. Each may hold up to a ton of molten glass and lasts for less than four months. This is because molten glass is corrosive and soon eats into the pot's lining. Before use, a pot has to mature for six months in a store where temperature and humidity are controlled. It is then preheated for five days before being placed in the furnace.

Fitting a new pot is no simple task. The furnace has to be kept at full blast, with the result that the workers' clothes often start to smoulder before the container is securely in place. This relentless heat is maintained day and night, 52 weeks a year, for as long as 20 years – the normal lifetime of a furnace.

The shimmering pool in each melting pot sets the scene for manufacture. The teams are grouped around, each consisting of a number of men who concentrate on producing a particular product at a given session.

In a typical operation, such as making a flask or a wine-glass, the first stage is performed by the footmaker, a craftsman who aims to gather exactly the right amount of molten glass on the end of his blowing iron for the work in hand. Having done so, he marvers (or rolls) the glowing gob on an iron slab to form a smooth, regular shape that is centred on the blowing iron. This process diminishes the thickness of the gob around the end of the iron and enlarges

THE INSTINCTIVE SKILL OF THE GLASS-BLOWER

Everything about glass-blowing calls for skills based on long experience. The tube itself – about 5 ft long and with a bore of ¼ in. – has to be warmed before its thicker end, or nose, is lowered on to the molten glass. The craftsman rotates it until he senses that he has collected just the right amount. From then on, the treacly gob can be kept on the nose only by constant rotation. Blowing needs unerring judgment of temperature and pressure in order to produce vessels of consistent size and thickness. It is an art at which not all craftsmen become truly expert, however long their apprenticeship.

the mass of glass beyond. While it proceeds, the glass starts to cool.

The footmaker then passes the iron to the next craftsman in line, the servitor, who swings the tube for a moment to a nearly upright position and blows a short puff of air into it to create an initial bubble inside the gob. At this point, in many glasshouses, the gob of molten glass acquires a new name and becomes the 'parison'.

If the vessel is to be moulded, the servitor swings the iron down again and lowers the gob into a hinged, wetted mould at floor level, which is opened and closed by foot pressure so as to leave his hands free. As the mould is closed, he blows steadily through the iron, while rotating it constantly. After about 15 seconds he opens the mould and withdraws the shaped glass – still attached to the blowing iron.

Now he passes the blowing iron and partly shaped vessel to the team leader, termed the gaffer. This is the master-craftsman who will complete the shaping process and maybe add a handle to a decanter, or the foot for a wineglass, with such accuracy that every item in a batch is identical. Watching a gaffer at work, displaying skills acquired over many exacting years, is to understand how this traditional term for 'boss' became part of our language.

An onlooker may ask why the process has to be so involved. Why cannot one craftsman make an object from start to finish? The answer is that in many cases he could, but that a team operation is generally more efficient. Each stage needs a different degree of skill, while the raw material being shaped – rapidly cooling molten glass – exacts its own discipline. It must be kept on the move the whole time, being twirled, rolled and shaped with tools to prevent the viscous substance becoming lop-sided or dropping off the blowing

Free-blowing

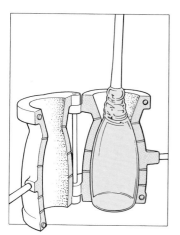
Blown and moulded glass

THE PERFECT CO-ORDINATION
OF A SKILLED TEAM

A group of three or four craftsmen is an average team for making such glassware as decanters or wine-glasses. To some extent they are graded according to skill, with a relatively inexperienced worker assisting the others with such tasks as carrying additional gobs of glass or heating the blowing irons, and the most critical tasks performed by the gaffer, seated in his wooden chair, with its arms specially extended for rolling the blowing iron. But, with the exception of the gaffer, they frequently exchange functions as they work – usually without a word spoken – in order to maintain a smooth, non-stop flow of finished glass-ware. It is hot, demanding work, which has to continue without a break during each session.

MARVERING *Twirling the iron to prevent the molten glass from dropping off, the footmaker carries the blowing iron to a flat metal slab. Here, he marvers, or rolls, the gob into an even shape centred exactly on the end of the iron. Subsequent stages cannot be carried out if the gob is uneven.*

BLOWING *After a preliminary brief puff to start an air bubble, the servitor inserts the gob into a hinged mould which he opens and closes by foot pressure. As the mould closes, he blows steadily through the iron while rotating it constantly. About 15 seconds later, he opens the mould and removes the shaped gob, which is still attached to the blowing iron.*

THE GAFFER (RIGHT)

Seated in his long-armed chair, the master craftsman of the team rolls the iron backwards and forwards to prevent the soft glass from sagging, meanwhile shaping it with a range of traditional tools which he holds in his other hand. Additional gobs of glass are brought to him as necessary for adding a handle, a stem or a foot. To ensure consistency, he frequently measures the length of a stem or the width of a foot with calipers.

GATHERING *The task of the footmaker, or gatherer, is to collect exactly the right amount of molten glass on the blowing iron to suit the job in hand. A notched bar supports the iron, giving his hands greater freedom of movement while he rotates the nose of the iron on the molten glass. It collects on the end rather like treacle on a spoon.*

iron. Meanwhile, additional gobs may have to be gathered and added to form a handle or a stem.

Free-blown glass – that is, when a mould is not used – follows a slightly different sequence of operations. After the gob has been given its brief, initial puff to create an embryo bubble, the gaffer takes the iron and 'necks' the bulb – that is, he reduces its thickness at the point where it will be 'cracked' (broken) off the iron. He does this by rolling the iron backwards and forwards on the arm of his chair while pinching the neck with a pair of wooden claws.

If the vessel is to be spherical, the next stage is to shape it by holding a beechwood cup, previously wetted, against the underside of the bulb while rotating it along the arms of the chair. Tapered shapes are formed by using cups with conical interiors.

The parison is now checked to see whether it carries an even amount of glass all round. This is because, when the main blowing takes place, the bulb will inflate in proportion to the thickness of its walls. Thin parts will expand more than thick parts. The thickness can be adjusted by marver-ing the bulb again, redirecting the glass to where it is needed.

When the parison is ready for the second blowing, the servitor takes the iron and holds it at about 45 degrees across one arm of a chair, or he may stand on a platform with the iron hanging downwards, the bulb beneath it. He blows down the iron, puffing at a pressure that he knows from experience will produce the internal shape he wants. Finally, the external surface is perfected either by further marvering or by shaping with wooden-clawed tongs.

Different vessels require different sequences, depending, for instance, on whether a stem, handle or feet have to be added. Teams of craftsmen develop their own variations, too, and in many cases the jobs they perform are interchangeable. The exception is the gaffer, who remains seated in his wooden chair, its arms extended for rolling the blowing iron. Footmakers and servitors – called gatherers and blowers in some establishments – remain standing.

The men work together as a closely knit team, the first two passing on their marvered or blown glass at the precise moment that it is needed. The gaffer completes the operation just before he is handed the next partly formed shape.

It is like a ballet performed to unhurried and unheard music. The smooth, purposeful movements may even

suggest that the process is simple, almost unthinking. Yet each craftsman is exercising constant skill and judgment – gauging the amount of glass to gather; deciding the moment when blowing is complete; knowing the stage when the fast-cooling glass needs re-heating in the glory hole (a small, independent furnace); determining the precise shape of a turned lip or spout; forming the exact curve and angle of a handle....

Different tools and methods are needed to shape the many products made in a glassworks. For instance, the traditional 'yard of ale', with its globular base and tapered stem, is formed by freehand blowing – a singularly difficult job, in this instance, which is generally performed by the most experienced gaffer.

For the great majority of glassware, however, the glass is blown into a mould. This is essential for any object which does not have the flowing lines needed for freehand blowing, but it may also be done for reasons of time or cost.

Even so, hand-blown moulded glass should not be confused with mass-produced factory glassware. The finished product is seamless, being rotated constantly while in the mould. When removed from the mould, such remaining stages as adding a handle or turning a lip are performed by a gaffer in the usual way.

Gradual cooling, known as annealing, is essential for newly made glassware. During a four hour period, it is subjected to ever-decreasing temperatures while passing through a lehr, or tunnel kiln. This slow cooling allows the stresses and tensions in the glass acquired during manufacture, to adjust gradually.

The glass-cutter at work

Most glasshouses produce lead crystal glass which will be decorated or engraved. At one time they employed skilled cutters and engravers, gilders and painters, who worked on crystal blanks made by the glass-blowers. Today, most glasshouses send these blanks to specialist firms who provide a comprehensive cutting service, using ancient techniques but modern tools. Blanks are also bought by specialist individual glass engravers.

At the cutters, blanks are first checked for flaws. Minor defects can be removed with pumice paste applied to an electrically driven wooden wheel. The blanks are marked with design guidelines, using another wooden wheel edged with pitch, which draws the pattern. The blank is then taken to a wheel of silicon carbide, which roughs in the design by breaking the 'skin' of the glass. This leaves it ready for the second, finer cutting.

For this, a bronze wheel with a diamond edge is used. It cuts much faster and more accurately than the carbide wheels used at one time. The shape of the cutting edge determines the type of cut: convex for a semicircular hollow cut, mitred for a V-cut, and flat for a flat cut. The mitred edge is the most widely used because it produces a cut whose facets refract light to give a sparkling effect.

When the main cutting is done, the blank is passed to another craftsman who completes the design. He may add such details as a star on the base of a tumbler, or groups of small lines on the base edge of a wineglass foot to stop it sliding off a polished table. In some patterns, an opaque surface is required, particularly with flowers or figures, and this is obtained by buffing with silicon-carbide paste, applied to a wooden or metal wheel, on the areas to be decorated. The designs are smoothed with a revolving felt or cork disc on which may be put a mixture of lead or tin oxide.

The glass is cleaned of all traces of pitch and put in an acid bath, generally a solution of hydrochloric and sulphuric acids. Immersion for about 15 minutes produces the brilliant effect that distinguishes the finest cut crystal.

THE BEAUTY OF CUT GLASS

The craft of glass-cutting demands as much skill, in its own way, as that of glass-blowing. Working to a pattern marked on the glass, the cutter presents the object to a power-driven, diamond-edged wheel. The depth and angle of each cut is critical in order to release the internal reflections and light. Afterwards, the glassware is dipped in acid to restore the brilliance of the cut surfaces.

800 MAN HOURS PER GUN

The workshop at A. A. Brown and Sons contains a bewildering array of tools – files, chisels, hammers and gouges, some of them familiar but many made to order for specialised jobs and handed down from father to son. Apart from boring the barrels, together with machining the action and other components from bar steel and drop forgings, all the work is done by hand, and each stage can take weeks of careful and painstaking work. Stock blanks (inset, top) can cost up to £500 for a specially fine piece, and come from similar walnut trees to those used for making Rolls-Royce dashboards. With increasing demand from foreign mass-producers, good walnut for gun stocks is becoming harder to find. The finished stock (lower picture) has to be a perfect fit for the barrels and the metal parts of the gun's action, and has also to be angled and weighted to suit the owner of the finished guns.

COSTING UPWARDS OF £12,000 A PAIR, TODAY'S HAND-MADE SPORTING GUNS ARE INDIVIDUALLY DESIGNED AND DECORATED TO THE ORDER OF DISCERNING CUSTOMERS

Gunmaking is one of the younger British crafts, being a mere 450 years old. The armies of Henry VIII were armed with weapons made in Belgium, Italy and Germany, since there were few British gunmakers able to undertake the work. Uneasy about this dependence on foreign suppliers, Henry encouraged European craftsmen to settle in London, so giving the home industry a sounder footing. The first substantial British gun workshops were set up in the Tower, where English apprentices learned the trade while equipping the king's soldiers with the arms they needed.

Henry's successors carried on this support for the gun trade, but when James VI of Scotland assumed also the title of James I of England, his morbid fear of assassination made him recoil at the idea of so many skilled gunmakers in his capital. With a stroke of the royal pen, he reduced their number to one.

The favoured craftsman was Edmund Nicholson, whom the king trusted well enough to award a complete monopoly of gunmaking in England.

Other craftsmen, now outlawed, presumably went underground – where their products might easily have proved far more dangerous to the monarchy. Before long, the hasty legislation was reversed.

By the time Charles I succeeded James, the gun trade was thriving again, and in 1637 the Worshipful Company of Gunmakers was founded as a London livery company.

A hazard which still sets gunmaking apart from other crafts is that faults in construction are apt to be lethal. The chief problem is that any weakness in the barrel may result in more damage to the marksman than to the target. For this reason, a duty laid upon the Worshipful Company was to test, or prove, all barrels made by its members, by firing them under carefully controlled conditions. Each barrel which passed this test was stamped with an official mark, and the absence of such a mark provided a clear warning to anyone who knew anything about weaponry.

Guns acquired a more formidable significance during the years of the Civil War, and there was an even bigger boom in gunmaking after the Scottish rebellions of the 18th century. Gun workshops sprang up in the provinces, centred mainly on Edinburgh and Birmingham. Gunmakers eventually established their own Proof House in Birmingham to carry out the same barrel-testing service as the London company.

As a trade, gunmaking varied enormously from craftsman to craftsman and from workshop to workshop. Many people specialised in a particular part of the operation, such as fitting the wooden stock or assembling the lock mechanism, and the gunmaker who stamped his name on the finished weapon might be little more than a skilled assembler of other people's work. Others preferred to carry out the whole business, from forging the barrels to the final blueing and engraving in their own workshops.

In the main, though, making the barrel was such a difficult and expensive job that most gunmakers went to specialised suppliers. This was one reason why, in the later years of the 18th century, Birmingham became established as a vital centre of gunmaking. Situated in the heart of the iron and steel industry, the city's metalworkers were able to work on a large enough scale, and with sufficient experience, to undercut most individual workshops in London.

In the old days, many gun barrels were made from melted down horseshoe nails, the idea being that the pounding the metal had endured in its previous role would ensure the strength and resilience needed to stand the stresses generated during the lifetime of a gun. But the forging process was very complicated. The nails had to be heated and beaten together into long strips of metal, which were then made up into a barrel by winding them round and round a long rod – rather like bandaging a leg – and hammering them together into a single tube.

This crude first stage of a barrel was then heated to a temperature where the adjoining strips could be welded together by hammering them over an anvil. Some specialists insisted that an essential part of the whole process was a barrel of beer for the forgers, to ensure that they swung the hammers with every ounce of their strength. When the welding was finished, the forgers had to get to work again, beating the cold barrel with hammers to harden the outside surface of the metal for extra strength.

The finished barrels had to be treated very carefully. The secret was to make the forged barrels as accurately as possible, so that the carefully created outer skin would not be filed away in bringing them down to the right size. Twin barrels were joined together by soft soldering rather than by using stronger methods, such as brazing, which were hot enough to run the risk of softening the welds which held the barrel bands together.

In time, all kinds of improvements were added to the basic method. Steel was added, usually melted down from old coach springs, and the fashion grew for elaborately patterned barrels based on the styles of Eastern gunmakers.

Barrel-making became more and more complex during the later 18th and early 19th centuries. One method involved twisting together six iron rods, between $\frac{1}{4}$ in. and $\frac{1}{2}$ in. across, and six steel rods to make a metal plait, and then using three of these plaits to make a thicker metal rope which was heated white hot and welded by hammering. After rolling out to the right thickness – varying from $\frac{1}{4}$ in. at the rear end of the barrel down to $\frac{1}{8}$ in. at the other end – the resulting ribbon was wound round a former and welded together in the same way as before.

Some of the best-quality barrels had up to 40 or more alternations of iron and steel in their making. The main purpose of mixing the metals was for decoration. After being bored and filed to the right size, up to 75 per cent of the original metal might have been cut away. Known as Damascus barrels, they were given a brown finish by heating in powdered charcoal, as opposed to the modern blue or black finish. They were called Damascus barrels because this city was one of the traditional markets for guns made by Eastern gunmakers, who used this style of barrel patterning.

But however elaborately made, every barrel had to be proved by licensed Proof Houses in London, Birmingham or Edinburgh, and the system was designed to reduce the danger of testing newly made barrels. They were tested in two ways: provisional proof, which was a test to assure the gunmaker that a barrel was sound enough to warrant all the work which would be done to turn it into a finished gun; and the definitive proof, which was the test of the almost complete gun. To prevent any suspicion of favouritism in

MAKING THE MECHANISM

The making of the action – the mechanism of the gun which locks it closed for firing, then allows it to be opened to eject the cartridges and load new ones – starts with the forged blank (1), supplied by an outside specialist.

The first stage is to machine the surfaces and reduce the thickness of the blank to fit the finished gun (2). Eventually, the front edge of the blank will carry the hinge which allows the stock and the barrels to be swung apart when the gun is opened. The flat face which will close off the rear ends of the barrels has two recesses hollowed out to form the end of the firing chambers, and the surrounding rim is shaped to provide an airtight seal when the gun is assembled ready for firing (3). Other holes and recesses are made for pins and components, and the whole assembly is carefully engraved.

MAKING A GUN TO FIT THE CUSTOMER

The chief difference between a hand-made gun and a top-quality mass-produced gun is the way in which the craftsman tailors his work to suit the owner. Each customer needs a particular angle and length of stock, depending on the length of his arms, the width of his shoulders and even how he was taught to shoot. All these are catered for by the gunmaker — sometimes by making a series of guns over the sportsman's lifetime.

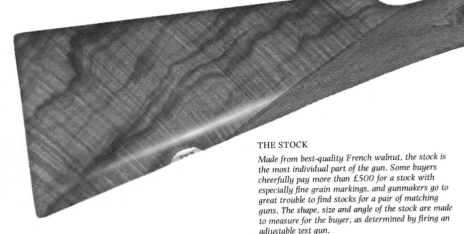

THE STOCK

Made from best-quality French walnut, the stock is the most individual part of the gun. Some buyers cheerfully pay more than £500 for a stock with especially fine grain markings, and gunmakers go to great trouble to find stocks for a pair of matching guns. The shape, size and angle of the stock are made to measure for the buyer, as determined by firing an adjustable test gun.

THE ACTION

The action is the heart of the gun. It ensures that the component halves are locked together before firing; connects the triggers to the firing mechanism; prevents the gun being fired without the safety catch being released; opens the gun after firing; and finally ejects the spent cartridges. Each action is made up of parts filed and fitted together individually, and the gunmaker can build in variations to order, such as the positioning, the angle and the pull on the triggers to suit a left-handed or right-handed shot.

ENGRAVING THE ACTION

One of the hallmarks of a craftsman-made gun is the fine engraving on the end of the barrel, on the side-plates, the trigger guard and the rest of the polished metal furniture. Elegant scrollwork, the names of maker and owner, and themes such as the commemoration of events like a Silver Jubilee or the Apollo moon landing add to the gun's beauty, its individuality and its value as a collector's item.

BALANCING THE GUN

Making the stock the right size and shape to suit the user is only part of the craft. For maximum comfort the gun must also be balanced, and this is done by drilling a series of holes in the end of the butt. To make the stock heavier, these cavities have weights inserted; to make it lighter, they are left empty. In either case, the ends are sealed off with plugs, with the grain chosen to match the rest of the butt.

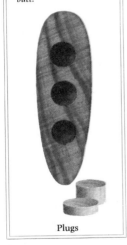

Plugs

---

the tests, instead of the maker's name the barrels carried a reference number and such details as the length of the chamber, the choke or internal taper of the barrel and the charge of the gun.

At the provisional proofing stage, the barrels were open tubes without a finished breech, or closed-off end, to the firing chamber, so they had to be fitted with screw-in plugs for the test firing. The barrels were loaded, and a number of them laid out on a grooved rack in the firing chamber. Here, they were set off by a train of gunpowder lit from outside the chamber and laid so as to pass below the vent hole of each barrel. The recoil from the firing blew the barrels back into a pile of sand, where they could be collected for checking and cleaning.

Each barrel was examined before and after firing for any signs of cracking or distortion, and any suspect barrels given a hydraulic check in which liquid was forced into the barrel under pressure to show up any hairline cracks. Proved barrels were stamped with a provisional proof mark on the rounded underside of the barrel, close to the breech.

Definitive proof – a test of the barrel with the action fitted – was a simpler process, since the gun could now be loaded in the ordinary way, but with special test cartridges. The gun was clamped into a firing block to avoid damage, and once again it was fired from outside the room by a cord attached to the trigger. The maximum stress on the gun from proof firing was about 5 tons per square inch, compared with $3\frac{1}{4}$ tons to the square inch in normal firing.

Barrels which passed their proof test had a further mark stamped on the underside, this time on the flat part of the barrels as well as on the action. These marks are an aid to dating and identifying old firearms.

This concentration of the business of barrel-making in the hands of specialists was just the beginning. It took the Americans to carry manufacture to its logical conclusion. Faced with the need for huge quantities of military rifles and muskets in the 18th century, and a chronic shortage of skilled craftsmen, they evolved the first mass-production assembly line in the world.

A series of machines was designed which could make all the parts of a military weapon to a standard pattern. They could then be finished and assembled by semi-skilled workers, with the added advantage that breakages in service could be repaired by replacing the broken part rather than the gun as a whole. In time, these methods became universal for military weapons, and nowadays

scarcely any military rifles are made by the old traditional methods.

But in the field of sporting guns – shotguns and sporting rifles – the priorities have always been different. Standardisation might certainly mean a cheaper gun, but in a world of wealthy sportsmen this has mattered little.

It has been considered more important to have a gun tailored to the individual owner, with the right size and shape of stock, the right balance, the right weight of charge, and the right kind of decoration and embellishments. It is still possible to buy guns made to measure by individual craftsmen, using many of the methods of a century ago but with the help of modern materials and ideas.

Such guns are costly. A family firm like A. A. Brown and Sons of Birmingham – less well known than Purdey's, or Holland and Holland, but a name to conjure with among connoisseurs of sporting guns – will charge anything from £5,000 upwards for a single gun. This is not surprising when you learn that the firm turns out only a dozen guns a year, each one taking some 700 to 800 man hours, spread over two years. Even at these prices there is a three-year waiting list on new orders.

Nowadays, barrels are made from steel, and so are lighter and stronger than their predecessors, but proving remains as important as ever. Chopper-lump barrels are forged with each barrel having half the 'lump' (the metal bar used to join the barrels together in a double-barrel gun) finished in one piece with it. The two barrels can then easily be joined by brazing the two halves of the lump together and soldering on the ribs and the loop which holds the forward end of the gun in place. The alternative type, known as dovetailed barrels, are joined together by brazing both barrels to a separate metal lump.

The most crucial joint, however, is between the ends of the barrels and the action, so that when the gun is closed the chambers are tightly sealed against the stresses of firing. The gunmaker usually blackens the two faces of the joint with the smoke from a paraffin lamp, then closes them together. Any proud spots on either of the faces show as bright patches against the soot, and he then carefully files these away until at each test the bright patches extend further and further. When they cover both faces of the joint completely, the fit is perfect.

Browns are unusual among present-day gunmakers in the amount of work they do themselves. The tubes for chopper-lump barrels are imported from Belgium, a country with an even longer record than our own in quality gunmaking. Tubes for dovetailed barrels are made by a specialist firm in Birmingham. But the only other parts bought from outside the workshops are the unshaped wooden blanks for the stocks, and a one-piece steel forging which forms the basis for the action of the gun. The blanks for the stocks are of French walnut, cut from the root of a mature tree and costing up to £500 apiece.

All the other parts, from boring the barrels onwards, are fashioned in the workshop. The process is painstaking and precise, for complex mechanisms have to be built up from blanks of metal by cutting and filing, often for weeks on end. The guns are side-lock ejectors made in sizes ranging from 12-bore down to 0.410 in. and can be fitted with a self-opening mechanism. There have to be parts which lock the gun closed before firing; to fire the cartridges when the triggers are pulled; to eject the spent cartridges after firing when the gun is opened; and to provide a safety mechanism to prevent the gun going off accidentally.

Once the barrels and the action have been assembled, they go through the definitive proof testing.

The next stage is the fitting of the stocks, and this is where the tailoring to the individual customer shows most clearly. Often a new buyer, when being measured for his guns, will be asked to fire an adjustable try gun to decide how much 'cast' and 'drop' to allow – to decide the precise angle at which the stock should be fitted to the gun. Guns can be made left-handed or right-handed to suit the user, with not only the stock but even the triggers angled for maximum comfort.

The stocks are carved from wood which grows quickly enough in the French climate to ensure a straight grain at the forward end of the stock, with attractive figuring at the butt end. But the most painstaking work of all is in the chiselling out of the part of the stock which is to be fitted to the gun's action: the wood surface has to be an exact counterpart, in three dimensions, of the outside of the metal mechanism.

The join between the action and the stock is eventually covered by the lock-plates of the finished gun. Here, too, the fit has to be so close as to be watertight, preventing the entry of moisture that might harm the mechanism.

Usually, all the metal parts on the outside of the gun, the gun's action and its furniture (the metal plates covering the gun's mechanism) are elaborately engraved with scroll-work. The traditional designs often featured game birds and animals, or even favourite gun-dogs, and owners might supply photographs to help the engraver to produce a good likeness.

Following engraving, there is still another vital stage in the gunmaking process which has to be carried out with the greatest care. All the metal components must be case-hardened, which involves packing the parts in a cast-iron pot and covering them with granulated bone-meal before heating them in a furnace for $2\frac{3}{4}$ hours. The carbon in the bone-meal is absorbed by the metal, and when the pot is taken out and tipped into cold water, the carbon coating forms a hard, mottled skin on the surface of the metal.

The case-hardening gives an attractive mottled finish to the metalwork of the gun, but some buyers prefer a brushed silver finish. At one time, some parts of the gun's metal furniture would be blued by heating in powdered charcoal, which eventually produced a hard, purple-blue sheen on the surface. Nowadays a similar effect can be produced by a chemical process.

Shooting for sport reached its peak in the closing years of the last century. Until then, stalking game was as important as shooting, but this gave way to massed shoots where the game was driven towards the guns by teams of beaters, and speed and sureness of loading and aiming became vital. When a sportsman such as Lord Walsingham could bring down 1,070 grouse on a single day (August 30, 1888), then clearly a high rate of fire was important. Buyers would order guns in matched pairs, with the weight, balance, accuracy and performance as identical as possible.

Even today, many buyers still specify matched pairs, fitted into a specially made leather gun case for which the waiting time may be longer even than that for the guns.

Today, a record like that of the 2nd Marquess of Ripon, whose total bag over 28 years amounted to a staggering 316,999 – including 47,468 grouse, 111,190 pheasant and 89,400 partridge – will probably never be equalled. He died in 1923 after shooting his 52nd bird on the morning of September 22. But the craft of the few surviving gunmakers is thriving, with their current lists of customers including doctors, farmers and builders, along with the landed gentry.

Another change is perhaps less surprising, given the rarity value of such superb skill in these days of mass-production. More and more guns are being bought as investments, just as much as for their sporting qualities.

THE BARRELS

The barrels are joined to one another in one of two ways: dovetailed barrels are each brazed to a separate metal joining bar, called the lump, which fits between them (above). In contrast, chopper-lump barrels are each made with half the lump forged in one piece with the barrel. All the gunmaker has to do is braze the two parts of the lump together to join the barrels into a solid whole. Other variations include the bore (or inside diameter of the barrel) and the choke (the constriction in the bore at the muzzle end of the barrels, which can be adjusted by the maker to vary the spread of shot).

IN MEMORY OF A FAVOURITE GUN-DOG *Among the most popular motifs for decorating gun furniture are one or more of the owner's dogs. A skilled engraver can work from a single photograph. Each line is cut into the metal by hand to produce an accurate likeness.*

THE HARPSICHORD MAKER

STRINGS PLUCKED BY A RAVEN'S QUILL CREATE
THE BRIGHT, WIRY TONE THAT HAS INSPIRED SO MANY
GREAT COMPOSERS AND MUSICIANS

For three centuries, from 1500 to 1800, the harpsichord was the undisputed queen of musical instruments. Its unique tone was just as suitable for the most brilliant solo work as for accompanying and holding together the orchestras of the day. Around 1700, the harpsichord was the chosen instrument for the descriptive pieces of François Couperin (1668–1733), for the mighty keyboard suites of Handel (1685–1759), and for the ebullient sonatas of Domenico Scarlatti (1685–1757). A hundred years earlier, a box-shaped harpsichord – the virginals – had inspired an English 'golden age' in the works of Orlando Gibbons, William Byrd and John Bull.

But the harpsichord's glory passed, or at least went into temporary eclipse, with the coming of the piano, whose full name – *piano e forte*, 'soft and loud' – shows the reason for the older instrument's decline. The harpsichord is a plucked instrument, with a single degree of loudness no matter how gently or firmly the player strikes the key. In contrast, the piano is a struck instrument, in which the force with which the hammer strikes the string is under the player's control.

New types of music demanded new instruments, and the emerging desire for expressiveness in music, typified by Mozart's piano concertos, spelled the doom of the harpsichord. It vanished almost overnight – though, to be fair, the tone of the earliest pianos was as close as possible to that of the familiar harpsichord.

The harpsichord's revival in the early years of this century is one of the great resurrection stories of musical history. Although even 30 years ago you might occasionally hear Bach's *St Matthew Passion* or Handel's *Messiah* accompanied on the piano, that would be an almost unthinkable anachronism today. And side by side with the revival of harpsichord music there has gone an ever-deepening study of the instrument's construction.

The earliest surviving harpsichords date from around 1500. But the instrument was certainly in existence a century or more before that, when it was known by the Latin term *clavicymbolum*, meaning a mechanised (keyboard-fitted) psaltery. The psaltery was one of those instruments often found in medieval Nativity paintings, played by angels above the heads of the Holy Family. Probably brought back from the East by returning Crusaders, it consists basically of a box strung with wires, which was held on the knees and plucked either with the fingers or a quill plectrum.

If you take the psaltery, add one quill per string and control each quill by an individual key on a keyboard, you have the ingredients of a harpsichord. Similarly, the harpsichord's great rival, the piano, derives from the medieval dulcimer, in which the strings were struck with small hammers or beaters instead of being plucked by quills.

How the mechanism works

From these simple beginnings the harpsichord's action grew into a marvel of mechanical ingenuity. At the heart of the instrument is the jack – a vertical slip of wood that carries the plectrum. This used to be a raven's quill, though synthetic materials are now a common substitute. When a key of the harpsichord is depressed by the player's finger, its inner end rises, lifting the jack past the string so as to pluck it with the quill. A rail above the jack limits the distance it can rise, and as soon as the string is plucked, the jack falls back to its original position. A cloth damper prevents the string from resonating further.

This almost instantaneous plucking, followed by damping, gives the harpsichord its crystal clarity from note to note, when compared with the fuzzier sound of the piano. It also means that the 'grace-notes' and other ornaments can be performed with immense speed and precision.

On all but the simplest harpsichords, there are up to three or four sets of strings, each with its own plucking mechanism. Each key is supplied with more than one jack, which may either pluck different strings, or pluck the strings at slightly different points, giving different sound qualities. In general terms, the nearer the plectrum is to the point where the strings are attached to the frame, the more muted and delicate is the note.

On many instruments there is a second complete set of strings tuned an octave higher than the main strings. The harpsichordist may either couple them with the main strings or play them separately.

In addition to the quilled jacks, there might be a set fitted with buffalo hide (*peau de buffle*), which gave a more rounded tone. The buffalo hide first used for jacks came from Poland. Nowadays, makers have to go further afield – to Java – for their *peau de buffle*. As to the jacks in general, modern technology has arrived on the scene in the form of plastic plectra, or even complete jacks made of plastic.

In October 1777, Mozart wrote a letter to his father, in praise of the pianos made by Johann Andreas Stein, of Augsburg. He emphasised the importance given to proper seasoning of the wood for the soundboard: 'When he has finished making one, he places it in the open air, exposing it to rain, snow, the heat of the sun and all the devils in order that it may crack. Then he inserts wedges and glues them in to make the instrument very strong and firm. He is delighted

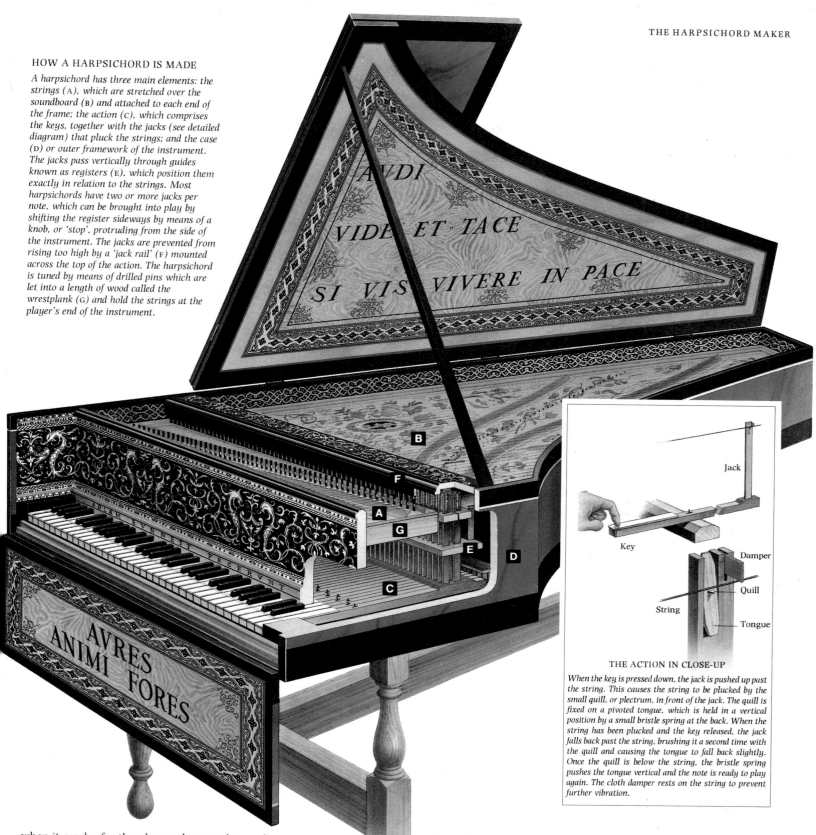

HOW A HARPSICHORD IS MADE

A harpsichord has three main elements: the strings (A), which are stretched over the soundboard (B) and attached to each end of the frame; the action (C), which comprises the keys, together with the jacks (see detailed diagram) that pluck the strings; and the case (D) or outer framework of the instrument. The jacks pass vertically through guides known as registers (E), which position them exactly in relation to the strings. Most harpsichords have two or more jacks per note, which can be brought into play by shifting the register sideways by means of a knob, or 'stop', protruding from the side of the instrument. The jacks are prevented from rising too high by a 'jack rail' (F) mounted across the top of the action. The harpsichord is tuned by means of drilled pins which are let into a length of wood called the wrestplank (G) and hold the strings at the player's end of the instrument.

AVDI

VIDE ET TACE

SI VIS VIVERE IN PACE

AVRES ANIMI FORES

Jack

Key

Damper

Quill

String

Tongue

THE ACTION IN CLOSE-UP

When the key is pressed down, the jack is pushed up past the string. This causes the string to be plucked by the small quill, or plectrum, in front of the jack. The quill is fixed on a pivoted tongue, which is held in a vertical position by a small bristle spring at the back. When the string has been plucked and the key released, the jack falls back past the string, brushing it a second time with the quill and causing the tongue to fall back slightly. Once the quill is below the string, the bristle spring pushes the tongue vertical and the note is ready to play again. The cloth damper rests on the string to prevent further vibration.

when it cracks, for then he can be sure that nothing more can happen to it.'

In his care for the basic materials of which his instruments were made, Stein was following the traditions of the harpsichord makers. And a visit to a modern workshop, such as the one run by Derek Adlam at Finchcocks, near Goudhurst in Kent, shows the same meticulous concern for the raw materials of the craft.

The instrument begins life as row upon row of planks in an open-sided shed, where they are left to dry and shrink for a year or more. The timbers from which the harpsichord is made have been tested down the centuries, and their various characteristics, and the proportions that go to make the whole, give each maker's instrument its individual

stamp – rather as all good port is made from a combination of Portuguese wine and brandy, yet each brand is subtly different from the rest.

The wood most commonly used by the great French and Flemish makers was poplar, which is strong and comparatively light and is still used for the baseboard, sides, internal frame and lid. The soundboard is made of Norway spruce, imported from central Europe. It is the most crucial part of the harpsichord from the point of view of tone quality. Strips of spruce are butted and glued along their edges, and the soundboard is carefully planed to shape so that it tapers from about $\frac{1}{8}$ in. at the centre to $\frac{1}{16}$ in. at the outer edges.

The total tension of the strings may be as much as half a ton, so English oak is used for the wrestplank – the heavy

Arnold Dolmetsch.

PIONEERS OF THE HARPSICHORD REVIVAL

Harpsichords had for many years been out of fashion when Arnold Dolmetsch made his first instrument, in 1896. Twenty years later, by the outbreak of the First World War, there had been a remarkable revival in its popularity – due in large measure to Dolmetsch's expertise as a designer and craftsman. Born in France, in 1858, he developed a passion for early instruments, including viols and lutes, while studying music in Britain. His talents were given full rein when, following an American tour, he established a harpsichord department at a leading piano makers in Boston. Many of the fine instruments from this workshop are still in use. Following a spell of similar work in France, he settled in Haslemere, in Surrey, where his family still live. What Arnold Dolmetsch did for harpsichord making was matched by Polish-born Wanda Landowska as a performer. Following her first public performance in 1903, her brilliant playing became the mainspring of the harpsichord's revival during the early years of the century. She visited Dolmetsch, and liked to play his instruments. Here, she is at the keyboard of a harpsichord with two manuals, a version of the instrument that provides a greater variety of tone.

piece of timber at the player's end of the instrument. Into this are screwed the wrestpins that hold the ends of the strings. When turned, these vary the string tension and thus tune the harpsichord.

Wild service wood, now becoming rare, is sometimes used for the bridge and the jacks. Other woods used for the jacks are beech, holly or hornbeam. Beech is also used for the registers (guides through which the jacks move up and down) for the nut (the narrow 'bridge' on the wrestplank, over which the strings pass on their way to the wrestpins), and for the soundboard bridge. Keys and keyframes are made from poplar or limewood. They are faced with a variety of materials, such as ivory, ebony, tortoiseshell, or even bog oak blackened in the peaty subsoil of the Fens.

The highest skills of craftsmanship go into cutting, planing, shaping and assembling the various sections. For example, every register has to have one hole per jack, so accurately cut that the jack can move smoothly up and down, yet is held firmly enough to stop any sideways movement, which would either cause the plectrum to miss the string or shift it so far towards the string that it might jam and not be able to pluck it at all.

Another important element is the keyboard – the intermediary between the player, the jacks and the strings. The keys are cut from a single panel of wood. In each of the octaves there are seven white keys evenly spaced, and five black keys, arranged in groups of two and three. Yet the strings for these keys have to be equally spaced where they are attached to the wrestplank, and the jacks, similarly, are an equal distance apart. This means that most of the keys are slightly angled where they pass out of sight under the wrestplank.

After the keys have been marked out on the panel, holes are drilled at the front and back of each, continuing down into the keyframe that will hold the completed keys. Balance pins are fitted into these keyframe holes, corresponding exactly with the holes in the keys and ensuring that the keys are positioned with total accuracy. The bone plates for the top of the white keys, and the bog oak or ebony for the black sharps, are glued on to the panel before it is cut up into individual keys.

The case of the harpsichord, which is dovetailed, pegged and glued together, consists of a straight side on the left of the player, the length dictated by that of the longest bass string; the bentside, gracefully curved to follow the harp-

Wanda Landowska.

like reduction in the length of the strings as their sound becomes higher (this curve gave the harpsichord its German name of *Flügel*, or bird's wing); the baseboard; and various strengthening members. To this assembly is added the soundboard – with its own ribs on the underside, and bridges on the upper side for the strings to pass over – and the wrestplank. The playing assembly of jacks, registers and keyboard slide in and out horizontally, like the action of a grand piano.

The strings, or rather wires, serve as the harpsichord's vocal cords. The lowest note of a large 18th-century harpsichord is usually the F two octaves below middle C, and the total compass is five octaves.

Wire of different gauges is used throughout the instrument – the higher the note, the thinner the wire. Usually, brass wire is used in the bass, and steel in the treble.

Unlike the modern piano, which has a cast-iron, warp-proof frame, and hence seldom goes out of tune, the wooden harpsichord is subject to the vagaries of humidity and temperature, and goes out of tune very easily. The player must be able to tune his own instrument – which might seem to present a problem, considering that a single-manual (keyboard) harpsichord may have 50 or more notes, with three sets of strings for each. But the great J. S. Bach is said to have been able to tune a harpsichord in a quarter of an hour; and about double that time is a good average for someone with a quick ear and sensitive touch when turning the wrestpins to raise or lower the pitch.

In the early days of the harpsichord revival, when the grand piano reigned supreme in the concert hall, makers tended to 're-invent' the harpsichord in terms of the piano, and their instruments owed a great deal to modern piano technology. But in recent years there has been a return to classical designs, such as those of Pascal Taskin, harpsichord maker to the French court in the 18th century, and to even earlier models – especially those made in Antwerp by the famous Ruckers dynasty. Their supremacy over all other makers lasted for a century, from 1580 to 1680, and the hundreds of harpsichords made by the four heads of the family (two named Hans and two named Andreas) were still being adapted and enlarged when the harpsichord era came to an end about 1800.

One curiosity about the Antwerp harpsichord makers is that, from about 1580 on, they all had to belong to the Guild of St Luke, which controlled the activities of painters – and hence of instrument makers, who painted their harpsichords both inside and out. This may give an indication of the relative importance attached to painting and music in the Low Countries at that time. But fortunately for us it means that the Ruckers harpsichords, such as the one used as a basis by the Finchcocks workshop, are covered with exquisite designs of flowers, fruit and animals, generally with some Latin tag praising the power of music to set the whole design off.

Not surprisingly, the skills that go towards making such an instrument do not come cheap in today's financial climate. A top-class harpsichord may well cost £8,000 or more, although there are kits by a number of makers for one-tenth or so of that price.

The harpsichord revival has now reached the stage where audiences and players can rediscover a treasure-house of early music, restored like a once-grimy painting to its original vibrant colour. As the great Couperin remarked: 'The harpsichord has in its way a brilliance that one scarcely finds in other instruments'; while the chatty Thomas Mace, a contemporary of Samuel Pepys, turned to the harpsichord 'when we would be most Ayrey, Jocond, Lively, and Spruce'. Without the harpsichord, the world of music would be a duller and far less exhilarating place.

FINAL STAGES IN PERFECTING A NEWLY MADE HARPSICHORD

TUNING A HARPSICHORD *Each string is attached at the keyboard end to a drilled pin, called the wrestpin. Turning the pin clockwise tightens the string and so raises the pitch of the note.*

TRIMMING THE QUILLS *Once the harpsichord is assembled, final adjustments can be made. Here, the craftsman is about to trim the quills with a scalpel – a task needing great precision.*

FINISHING TOUCHES *A fine harpsichord is a work of art as well as a musical instrument. Here, an artist-craftsman is painting a traditional design.*

THE
HEDGER

BRITAIN'S CHEQUERBOARD LANDSCAPE WAS CREATED
BY GENERATIONS OF SKILLED HEDGERS, A BREED OF
CRAFTSMEN NOW VANISHING FROM THE COUNTRYSIDE

A hedger does not need much in the way of tools – a billhook, an axe and perhaps a long-handled slasher blade. What he needs plenty of is time. For hedging is highly skilled, painstaking, strenuous work – but rather slow. Thirty yards a day is good progress and often 100 yds a week is a more realistic rate. And a modest-size field of 40 acres needs up to a mile of hedging. Time being – now more than ever – money, traditional hedging is giving way to mechanisation and wire fencing. Moreover, thousands of miles of hedges have been uprooted over recent years as arable farmers have expanded fields to maximise the efficiency of their combine harvesters and tractors.

But there are signs in areas such as East Anglia that farmers are beginning to worry about valuable topsoil being simply blown away from their vast, open fields, now that there are no hedges to shelter them and deflect the eroding winds. This may perhaps deter further uprooting – and of course stock farmers tend to favour hedges to protect their animals and stop them straying. There is little doubt that there will be work to be done on them for years to come.

The Enclosure Acts of the 18th century were responsible for most of today's hedged fields in Britain. They caused the huge strip-farming tracts of medieval times to be broken up into smaller units – a colossal programme of agricultural engineering which resulted finally in about 600,000 miles of hedge being planted. But there are many much earlier hedges to be found, some dating from Saxon times, when they were planted to mark boundaries. Whatever their age, they need constant cutting and re-laying.

Most hedges are of blackthorn or hawthorn. They are grown from seedlings and planted out after four years, taking a further 20 years to mature into effective wind-breaks and barriers against animals. Sometimes tree seeds will take root and grow to full size, giving welcome shade and shelter to men and animals, and beautifying the landscape.

The hedger's work is almost always done during the winter months – and usually at the same time that ditches are being cleared. After dead leaves and undergrowth have been removed, the hedger can get on with chopping away unwanted elder and bramble growths. The sides of the bushes are then trimmed to width, using upward strokes of the billhook to avoid tearing and splintering the wood.

Billhook

Axe

Slasher

The hedger begins by cutting stems (called 'layers', 'pleachers' or 'stowels' in different parts of the country) partway through at the base, and then bending them over to make a dense, compact barrier.

To support the layers, the hedger cuts a series of pointed stakes, which he drives vertically into the ground at regular intervals before interweaving the layers between them.

(RIGHT) *The final stage in building a tough, stockproof hedge is to make a tightly plaited binding from hazel saplings. This is tapped on to the stakes to hold the different parts of the hedge together.*

Now all is ready for the actual laying of the hedge – which may be scores, or even hundreds, of years old. Starting usually with the first major growth on his right, the hedger cuts the main stem partway through with his billhook, a few inches from the ground. He then bends it to the left at an angle of about 60 degrees – the trick being to cut through from one side enough to bend it, but leaving sufficient bark for sap to travel upwards and keep the layer alive. This process is repeated along the length of the hedge so that all the stems slope to the left and are parallel to each other at the same angle. To hold them in place, vertical stakes are driven in at intervals of about $1\frac{1}{2}$–2 ft.

The stems of the bushes, often as long as 10 ft, are then woven in and out of these vertical stakes, which are cut off at the height required for the hedge. It is then finished off with 'binders' – long rods of wych elm or hazel plaited together and twined in and out between the stakes.

If the hedge lies along a slope the stems will always be cut so that they slant uphill. They will also be laid so that they slope away from the ditch which runs alongside. The idea is to use the brush to keep the animals safely in the field, and so protect the new growth from the stumps, and to permit easy cleaning of the ditch. Thick growth at ground level is essential if the hedge is used to contain animals.

The only dead wood in 'live' hedges of this sort is in the vertical stakes and the binders. Hedgers sometimes leave tree saplings which, as the years go by, form a windbreak. They are trimmed to encourage growth and to prevent the branches becoming entangled in the hedge itself. Oak and ash are the saplings most often saved, together with elm, whose roots often form suckers, or secondary saplings, which can be woven into the hedge. If the mature tree grows tall enough, its spread of branches will not affect the hedge growing below. Unfortunately, thousands of these hedge elms have fallen victim the Dutch elm disease.

There are variations on these basic methods of hedging in parts of the country where climate or conditions impose special problems. Craftsmen may use tools of a slightly different shape, and use different terms when talking about their job. The hedger himself is called a 'plusher' in Pembrokeshire, where the fields can be swept by gales, and hedges are made on earth banks for extra shelter.

Here, stems are bent over at a particularly sharp angle and secured by 'crooks' or 'plugs' – dead saplings sharpened and driven deep into the ground, with hooked tops to hold down the hedge more firmly. The hedge itself is squat but strong, usually wider than it is tall – 2 ft tall and $2\frac{1}{2}$ ft wide is common – and angled towards the prevailing wind.

Another priority in areas with heavy snowfalls is to keep the top of the hedge fairly narrow to reduce the weight of snow that will lie on it.

Much depends also upon the availability of materials – in some areas hedgers will compromise with the traditions of their craft by using modern aids such as chainsaws. They may also, for example, put up a single strand of barbed wire as a guard fence to protect the hedge. Though a compromise, this is considered better than uprooting the hedge and replacing it with barbed wire or an electric fence.

PROTECTION FOR THE HANDS

Hedging is hard, rough work. Using axes, slashers and billhooks, cutting saplings, pulling them into shape and twisting them into plaits is so damaging to the hands that most hedgers wear thick, protective mittens. But the result of his labours is a combined boundary-marker, windbreak and stockproof barrier that will last for 20 years or more before needing major renovation.

THE HORN MAKER

THE SUBTLE, STIRRING TONES OF THE HORN –
FIRST HEARD ON THE HUNTING FIELD – STILL RELY IN
LARGE MEASURE ON THE SKILLS OF CRAFTSMEN

Three-hundred years ago a young Bohemian nobleman, the Graf von Sporck, went on the Grand Tour round Europe. In France he was so impressed with the horn playing of the royal huntsmen that on his return he sent two of his own huntsmen to Paris to learn the technique of the instrument. The horn's origin in France explains why the description 'French' is tacked on to it (though the French just call it *cor*). But it could equally well be called 'German' as, following Sporck's importation of it east of the Rhine, its development into a modern high-precision instrument took place mainly in Germany.

In the 17th century it was a simple coil of metal tubing, slung over the huntsman's shoulder and capable of producing only a few overtones of its fundamental note.

(Overtones are the higher notes produced when the player increases the air pressure by blowing harder. The first overtone is an octave above the fundamental; the second overtone is one-fifth above that; and so on at steadily decreasing intervals, until an approximation to a melodic scale of notes is produced.)

During the three centuries since, the horn has evolved into a sophisticated music maker, which, like a custom-built car, combines traditional handcraft and mechanised technology in about equal proportions. Yet its origins in the hunting field survive in its sound, which preserves a sense of distance and the outdoors, even in the confined conditions of a concert hall.

This combination of laborious craftsmanship and pre-fabricated working parts is evident in a horn-maker's workshop, such as Paxman's, in London's Long Acre. Here, the terminology is reminiscent of car manufacture, since the valve section, which alters the pitch of the notes by a complex system of rotary valves, tubes and slides, is referred to as the 'engine'. But though great engineering precision goes into the valve system – the valve rotors are turned to within one five-thousandth of an inch – the highest manual skills are applied to the body of the horn – or rather, to that section of it from the outer 'flare' to the valve system, that constitutes the 'bell' of the horn.

The bell is about 3 ft long and is in the form of an elongated cone, 1 ft across at the flare end, narrowing to about $\frac{3}{4}$ in. where it joins the rest of the pipework. It starts life as a flat piece of metal, looking like an elongated axe-head.

Many horns are made from yellow brass (70 per cent copper and 30 per cent zinc); however, some players prefer the other alloys – gold brass (85 per cent copper and 15 per cent zinc), or nickel silver (63 per cent copper, 27 per cent zinc and 10 per cent nickel). These are said to give different tone qualities corresponding to the alloy. Gold brass gives a more veiled and lyrical tone than yellow brass, and nickel silver is brighter and more strident in tone.

The first stage in making the tubular spout is to double the cut-out over on itself, bending it round a metal bar and clipping the edges together by little lugs cut along the edge of the join. This seam is then coated with spelter (a paste made of granulated brass, borax and water) and a blow-lamp is run along it, which fuses the spelter with the brass and makes the joint airtight. At this stage the metal along the seam is double in thickness where the join overlaps, so the join is planished (reduced from two thicknesses to one by beating it with a hammer round an iron bar). The spout is heat-softened and forced down over an iron mandrel – 'forced, beaten and generally punished' is how Richard Merewether, of Paxman's, puts it – into its final shape.

Next, the spout is brazed by the blowlamp to the flare, previously shaped from a disc of brass. The bell has begun to take on a definitely horn-like appearance. Now it is spun on a lathe, and the surplus metal removed by turning to give it an exactly uniform surface both inside and outside the bell.

The bell is now ready for the process that turns it from a straight tube into the graceful curve that makes a horn different from all other instruments. So that it will bend without splitting or excessive crinkling, it has to be transformed into a solid object. This is done by plugging it at the narrow end and filling it with a molten mixture of pitch and resin, with a metal rod protruding from its centre to give the craftsman something to grasp.

When the resin has solidified, the narrow end of the bell is clamped in a vice, and the craftsman bends it round a wooden bending block, using the rod to give him leverage. Inevitably, this process leaves some thickening on the inner side of the curve where the metal is compressed; this is beaten out with hammers and filed smooth. When all roughnesses have been removed, the bell is again heated with the blowlamp and the pitch runs out, beginning as a trickle and finally coming away in a large lump. The

THE BEGINNINGS OF A HORN

One of these flat pieces of metal will be shaped to form the part of a French horn known as the 'bell-tail', or 'spout', which is about 3 ft long. At its narrow end it is connected to the 'bell-branch' – and thence to the valve section – and at its wide end to the flare. Horns are made of various alloys, all with a basis of copper.

MAIN PARTS OF A DOUBLE HORN

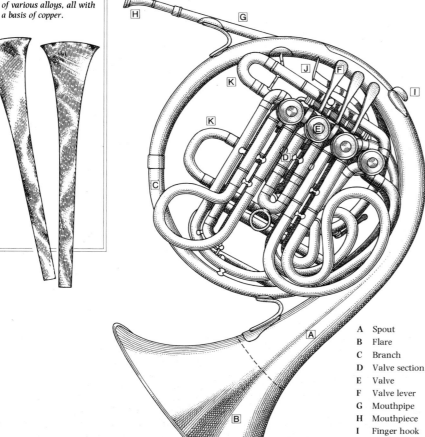

A	Spout
B	Flare
C	Branch
D	Valve section
E	Valve
F	Valve lever
G	Mouthpipe
H	Mouthpiece
I	Finger hook
J	Thumb lever
K	Tuning slides

Not surprisingly, in view of the horn's combination of craftsmanship and mechanical precision, a new double instrument sells for upwards of £1,000.

In the old hunting days the bell was painted black on the inside, as the horn was held pointing backwards, and a sudden glare from a polished bell might frighten the horse following behind. Today, the horn is still held pointing backwards and downwards, though for a very different reason. The player modifies the sound with his right hand inside the bell, while his left hand works the valve levers. This power of modification is unique to the horn, and makes it the most versatile of the brass instruments.

BENDING THE SPOUT *The tube is filled with a mixture of molten pitch and resin, which hardens. It can then be bent round the block.*

SMOOTHING THE SPOUT *During bending, ridges appear on the inner side of the curve. These have to be hammered flat.*

remaining pitch is removed with solvent, and the bell is ready for a final polish before assembly.

Adjoining the bell, the tubing that forms the complete instrument consists of the C-shaped bell-branch, the valve system, and ultimately the mouthpipe, which tapers down to the part which receives the funnel-shaped mouthpiece. These tubes are soft-soldered together, then checked for alignment to make sure that the various tuning slides and the rotary valves move accurately without sticking.

The most common horn nowadays is the 'double horn', which as its name indicates combines two horns in one. These are the F horn and the B flat horn, so called because a 12 ft tube gives low F as its fundamental note, while a 9 ft tube gives the B flat above. The advantage of this system is that the player has double the number of notes from which to choose, as simply pressing one of the four valves switches the horn from F to B flat, or vice versa. The other three valves have the effect of lengthening the horn tube, lowering the note by a semitone, a tone or a tone and a half, depending on the valve chosen. The valves may be used singly or in combination.

PUTTING THE FINISHING TOUCHES TO A HORN *The craftsman makes final adjustments to the lever system. This type of horn is known as a double descant. Its pitch is higher than the standard horn.*

THE
JEWELLER

THE EXQUISITELY BEAUTIFUL 'HIGH JEWELLERY'
DISPLAYED IN A BOND STREET WINDOW IS CREATED BY
A CLOSE-KNIT TEAM OF SPECIALIST CRAFTSMEN

A pretty American girl, stopping by Cartier's window in London's Bond Street, summed up her overall impression. 'That,' she said, 'is how point zero zero zero zero one of the other half live.' Her statistic might be challenged, since a few of the famous jewellers' products may be purchased for as little as £50, while perhaps as many others cost upwards of £500,000. However, the remainder lies somewhere between the two, so in spirit the young woman was perfectly correct. Cartier's window harbours an opulence and a splendour that has little to do with the ups and downs of recessions, and a great deal more with Scott Fitzgerald's dictum: 'The very rich are different from you and I.'

But if such envious thoughts are crushed awhile, then it becomes apparent that the window also contains considerable beauty and perfection of workmanship unexcelled by any other craft. Diamonds glitter from their fine-turned mounts with a cold fire that was lit thousands of millions of years ago, some set in bracelets, necklaces and ear-rings, others forming the numerals on a clock of gold, citrine,

mother-of-pearl and rock crystal. Rubies lend warmth to yellow gold, and emerald islets are protected by reefs of platinum. Within the shop, all pale wood and tailored fawn carpeting, the wonders multiply. A gleaming showcase of 'high jewellery' reveals a necklace of five identical emeralds that took five years to match. The backs are cut in faceted squares to admit light, and so enhance their colour, while tiny golden claws hold them in place and ensure that they will lie flat about the wearer's throat. The diamond clusters that separate them, on the other hand, are set in platinum. So too are the *pavé*-set diamonds (close-set like the cobbles on a street) that form the hide of the little hinged-pawed panthers that are a favourite conceit of Cartier; their spots are black onyx and their eyes faceted emeralds. But to anyone with a love for gems, or an interest in social history, perhaps the shop's greatest delight lies in its Estate Collection. In this you can see how much, and how little, fashions in jewellery have changed down the years, since it consists mainly of Cartier pieces going back to the beginning of the century. Massive chokers of pearls and diamonds, it seems, were in demand in 1917, and Art Déco bracelets and pins of diamonds and sapphires in the '20s; the '30s, however, apparently preferred to contrast its diamonds starkly with dark stones such as onyx.

'The finest jewellers in the world'

The firm's experience is considerable. They have been jewellers since 1847, or as they prefer to put it, '*Joailliers depuis 1847*', for that was the year when Louis François Cartier established the business in the Boulevard des Italiens in Paris. He could not have chosen a better moment, because by the dawning of the Second Empire five years later, his work was already well known, and the brilliance and originality of his designs assured him of many patrons among the glamorous court circle that orbited about Napoleon III and his empress, Eugénie. The House of Cartier flourished in those hothouse years, surviving even the Franco-Prussian war and its revolutionary aftermath to become, by the turn of the century, court jewellers not only to the royalty and aristocracy of Europe, but to the immensely rich railway and industrial dynasties of America as well. At this time the firm was controlled by Louis François' three grandsons, who were invited by King Edward VII to open the first of their overseas branches in London. Both Jacques and Pierre ran the London workshops at various times, but the presiding genius of the family was probably Louis, the inventor of the wrist-watch in 1904, and one of the first men to use platinum in jewellery. Though the firm has now passed out of the family's hands, it still owes much to the exacting and inventive spirit of Louis Cartier. From the beginning, each of the three main branches of Cartier International – Paris, London, New York – was to a large extent permitted to interpret national differences of taste in its own way and to train its own craftsmen as the best means of doing so. The London shop, like the others, prides itself on employing almost no outside labour. Designer, stone selector, mounters and polishers all work within the house, the one independent exception being the gem cutter. For the most part they came to the firm as apprentices and will probably stay there all their working lives. 'The reason is simple,' says Mr Joseph Allgood, the managing director, and himself a Cartier craftsman since his teens, 'Cartier are the finest jewellers in the world, and to a man who is Cartier trained, there is nowhere better to go.'

Creating a new line – or a one-off piece for a particular customer – is very much a matter of teamwork, and its innovator might have been any one member of a long-standing partnership of sales manager, designer, buyer,

FROM DOODLE TO DIAMOND NECKLACE

At Cartier, a new piece of jewellery very often begins with a doodle that combines the ideas of designer, workshop, sales manager and customer. This is translated by Dennis Gardner, the designer, into a full-scale watercolour that is the basic working drawing for the object. Mr Gardner's craft marries the skills of metal-worker and mechanic with a deep knowledge of precious stones. That he is also a brilliant draughtsman is apparent in his detailed representation of a diamond and gold necklace that is almost indistinguishable from the finished jewel that lies alongside it.

stone selector and works manager. The team is prepared to tackle anything from setting a pearl that once belonged to Cleopatra – so legend says – into a pendant for Elizabeth Taylor, to reproducing an aerial photograph of an oil terminal, complete with tiny, movable tankers, in gold, platinum and gems. Much depends on demand and opportunity, but perhaps a more usual, workaday kind of challenge might be that provided by, say, the arrival of a parcel of particularly fine rubies from India.

Until that moment there had been no particular intention of emphasising rubies in the following year's collection, but this seems too good an opportunity to miss. After discussion, the sales manager agrees that he has room in his stock for a number of sets – *parures* – consisting, in this case, of matching necklace, bracelet and ear-rings in rubies and diamonds. But a price ceiling is also fixed, and each *parure* must cost no more than £7,000 apiece.

PRECIOUS PANTHER

If Cartier had an emblem, it would be one of these panther brooches that the firm has been making for many years. Its spots are black onyx, standing against a hide of flat diamonds, and its eyes are faceted emeralds. Its paws move on tiny delicate hinges.

Bearing this in mind, the designer, Dennis Gardner, sets to work. His is an unusual craft, combining the skills of watercolourist, metal-worker and mechanic with a deep knowledge and understanding of precious stones. Like all the senior staff, he has been at Cartier for many years, and his room houses a splendid collection of designs, made by himself and his predecessors, reaching back to the beginning of the century. It is fascinating stuff. Album after album of bright, meticulous watercolours reflect the role of jewellery as fashion's accessory down the years. For example, since women stopped wearing suits, the demand for brooches is not what it was; but Mr Gardner still keeps the drawings of hundreds of Cartier brooches, most of them brilliant one-off designs. Diamond and jade insects and flowers, a coral flower-pot with blooms of emeralds, diamonds and sapphires – but most famous were the bird brooches that the firm made between 1945 and 1962.

Mr Gardner's job lies, as he says, between boardroom, workroom and drawing-board. He begins with a series of preliminary sketches that take in the conflicting factors of cost, both to the company and the customer, the best way of utilising the stones available, workshop time, the dictates of fashion and, of course, the attractiveness of the finished object. Out of these, in the case of the ruby and diamond *parures*, there emerge precise, life-size watercolour sketches that, when Paris has given its final stamp of approval, will be the blueprints of the new range.

Parallel with the design operation, Alec Clark, Cartier's

COLOUR, CLARITY, CUT AND CARAT

These are the great 'Four Cs' of the stone-selector's craft, the criteria by which Alec Clark chooses the diamonds that will bring Dennis Gardner's drawings to life. Obviously, the gems must be perfectly matched in shape and size, but the ability to select matching colour and clarity – so that the diamonds gleam at the wearer's throat with exactly the same glint of cold fire – calls for a skill that is based partly on science and partly on training. But a great deal more depends on an eye of rare discernment.

stone selector, is choosing the gems, whose worth must conform to the £7,000 ceiling, and at the same time be perfectly matched for size and colour. His workroom is an intriguing array of safes and sensitive laboratory scales. His table is piled with boxes of stones beside which lie little iridescent cascades of jewels. You cannot help but wonder just how many royal ransoms you are looking at, but like all Cartier craftsmen, Mr Clark looks faintly surprised when an awed layman mentions the financial aspect of his craft. It has long ceased to astonish him, if it ever did, and besides, his concern is not with a stone's worth, but with its standing in the great 'Four Cs' of the jewellery trade.

Colour, Clarity, Cut and Carat are the criteria by which gems are judged, and the ability to make the judgment is only partly based on science; the rest is a developed instinct and an eye of rare selectivity. Mr Clark was a cutter once, but the discovery of his unusual talent caused him to change naturally into a selector. His is no simple task. For example, colour grading is extremely complex and difficult to describe. Top-grade diamonds are purest white – apart from a few rare natural-coloured blues, pinks and jonquils – and the remainder are described in a descending scale of whites down to a yellow; however, a layman would be hard put to it to discern any difference at all between at least the top half-dozen in the scale.

Clarity too is scaled; the system varies from one country to another, but in the UK it runs from 'Flawless', through 'VVS' (very, very small piqué), 'VS', 'SI' (small inclusions or flaws), 'Piqué' (natural flaws visible to the naked eye), to 'Spotted' and 'Heavy spotted'. Grading for clarity may be carried out in artificial light, but colour grading requires daylight, and a clear north light at that. Mr Clark's task is made more complex by the canyons of London's West End that on days of heavy cloud bring darkness down early, while on bright days, as the sun moves round, it flings back a glare from the building opposite. Consequently, colour grading can only be carried out for a very few hours in the day. However, this does give Mr Clark a chance to replenish his stocks of gems within their various ranges.

As a general rule, stones are bought from traders in an already cut and polished state – the only operation that is not done in Cartier workshops – and by carat. The carat is a very ancient unit of weight; it comes from *keration*, the Greek name for the carob tree. The tree's fruits are black beans which, when dried, have an almost uniform weight, and so were used to balance the scales of the old Middle

Eastern pearl dealers. The unit is not often called upon to measure any very prodigious weight. One of the largest diamonds ever handled by the company was the perfectly pure 'Louis Cartier' weighing 107.7 carats, or $\frac{3}{4}$ oz. On the other hand, Mr Clark is often called upon to select the tiny stones used in clusters around larger gems; these may weigh no more than one three-hundredth of a carat.

Incidentally, and confusingly, the carat has nothing to do with 'karat', the unit used to define the amount of precious metal in an alloy. Gold, for example, is expressed in 24ths, 24-karat (24 K) gold being pure and unalloyed. Therefore, a gold alloy containing, say, six parts of copper or other base metal would be expressed, and stamped, as '18 K Gold'.

When Mr Clark has chosen the stones, they are parcelled up, together with the designs and a work-ticket, and sent to the workshop. This is the province of George Puddle, under whose general direction work three very distinct groups of craftsmen – mounters, polishers and setters – who, though their crafts are interdependent, have nevertheless served three different kinds of apprenticeship.

The differences in their callings are not immediately apparent, since each craftsman sits at a similar workbench with a semicircular bite taken out of the front, from whose centre juts a 3 in. wide wedge of worn, battered boxwood. This is the jeweller's peg or pin on which most of the work is done; beneath it is looped a wide apron, traditionally called a goatskin, but more likely nowadays to be rawhide.

Its purpose is to catch anything – tools, gems, fragments or filings of precious metal – that drops from the bench, a necessary precaution when working with such fantastically expensive raw materials. When Mr Puddle allocates a job to a particular mounter, he weighs out the metal required – gold or platinum in plate, sheet or round or rectangular wire – and when the mount is completed, weighs that too. The weight of the finished job, plus that of the filings and scraps raked out of the goatskin, should equal that of the metal issued, but as a rule, about 2 per cent has gone adrift. Some of it, in the form of fine dust, has stuck to the mounter's hands, and more still to his sandpaper. So the sandpaper is burned and analysed, and filters and baffles are fitted to the washbasins. Every so often, these are removed and analysed by precious-metal dealers, and the price of the dust regained is credited to Cartier, as is that of the 15 oz. of gold dust swept up from the floors during the course of the year and collected in a biscuit tin. One particularly satisfying act of thrift takes place every five years or so when the workshops are repainted. Then, enough gold and platinum is washed off the walls to entirely pay for their redecoration.

Each craftsman sits on a three-legged stool with the tools of his calling around him, the polisher with his bundle of linen threads and boxwood points, the setter with his tiny chisels bearing names like scorper and spitz-stick. The mounter's bench carries the widest range of all – an oxygen and gas torch with a blow-pipe to give extra heat when soldering platinum, a battery of needle files and fine-pointed pliers, piercing saws with blades of eight different thicknesses. Along the benches too are scattered Cartier creations at various stages of production, finishing at the end of the line with – for example – a necklace of 284 *baguette* diamonds. To make it involved 1,000 working hours of mount-building, 250 hours of polishing and two weeks of setting. Not all the value of the finished object is that of the gems alone.

The process of converting Mr Gardner's watercolours into three-dimensional jewels begins with the mounter who, armed with the designs and the gems, starts to make the collets – the tiny clawed metal cups that are tailored to fit each stone. Each collet is made by hand from precious metal – generally, platinum for diamonds and sapphires,

MOUNTS AND COLLETS

Once the diamonds have been selected, the process of turning them into a necklace begins with the creation of collets, tiny clawed cups of precious metal tailored by the mounter to fit each stone. These are soldered together in groups that in turn are joined by a flat-and-upright ring that will permit the finished necklace to conform to the wearer's movements. The mounter, using a battery of pliers, files, saws, and a blow-pipe gas torch, works on a worn jeweller's peg of boxwood. Each job presents a whole new range of problems; building the gold mounts for a diamond necklace – as here – might take 1,000 hours of painstaking work.

Collets – cups of bent gold wire – ready for soldering together.

and gold for rubies and emeralds – after which it is set in Plasticine in the position it will lie in the finished necklace. The collets are soldered together in sections of four, and a flat and upright ring, a hinge-like device that permits maximum flexibility around the wearer's neck, is fixed to each section.

When the mount is complete, it is sent for polishing. This is done with linen threads loaded with crocus or jeweller's rouge – both slightly abrasive derivatives of iron oxide – which are rubbed between claws and through crevices. Boxwood points dipped in crocus are used for the easier-to-get-at places. Then, because the mounter has finished off his part of the operation with fine emery paper, the marks of this too must be removed, a delicate task that proceeds in several stages. First, the emery marks are smoothed out with delicately abrasive Water-of-Ayr stone, and the stone marks in turn smoothed away with crocus. Finally, the faint traces of crocus are removed with a grease mop. Polishing is a highly important branch of the trade, since it makes or breaks the final appearance of the jewel. Careless polishing may round an angle in the soft metal, or flatten a curve, and everyone else's work is ruined.

Setting is the next stage, in which the mount and gems are finally and permanently married. First, the mount is

BEANS AND CARATS

Precious stones are measured in carats, a unit of weight that, far-off, is based upon the weight of the bean of the carob tree (Greek, keration), but is now standardised to 100 points to the carat (0.2 of a gram) and 5 carats to the gram. As can be seen from the drawings, a 5 carat diamond – which would have lost several more carats in the cutting – is not very large, but if it were a pure white stone, it would be worth many thousands of pounds. A pure white stone of this size, however, would be something of a rarity. One of the largest pure diamonds handled by Cartier weighed 107.7 carats, or ¾ oz.

 0.75 carat   1.50 carats

 3.00 carats   5.00 carats

fixed in plaster of Paris, or setting cement, to give a firm base, then, in the case of collet settings, the stones are pressed home and the claws turned over to grip them. But these are the simplest of settings; other designs call for different kinds of claws or for – among further examples – *pavé* or *calibré* settings. In *pavé* work, the stones are pressed into holes, then secured by closing the holes about them, and making sureness doubly sure with grains of metal raised from between the holes. *Calibré* setting, by contrast, is used only for straight-sided stones, when the metal is pushed up on either side of the gems, giving the impression that the rows of stones are divided by continuous lines of gold or platinum. In fact, no two jobs are exactly the same, which calls for considerable ingenuity on the part of the setters. Therefore, apart from the regulation scorpers and spitz-sticks that they use to raise grains and adjust *calibrés*, many of them also make up their own tools to work upon such out-of-the-way tasks as fitting the *baguette* diamonds or making an unusual form of claw.

When the necklace leaves the setter, the job is finished, apart from being given a bath in a tank of washing-up liquid, whose bubbles are activated and stirred by ultrasonic waves to ensure that they reach into the most minute crevices. It is dried by infra-red heat, given a final polish and at last is ready for the showroom or the Bond Street window, a jewel of exquisite beauty to tempt a passing prince or film-star.

BEDDING THE STONES

After a first polishing, the mount goes to the setter who marries it to the stones. The mount is fixed in plaster of Paris to give a solid footing then, in the case of collet settings, the stones are pressed into the cups and the claws turned over to grip them. Other settings are much more complex. Pavé setting, for example, involves raising tiny grains of metal to secure the stones.

THE LACE MAKER

THE GREAT DAYS OF LACE MAKING, AND THE EXPLOITATION THAT WENT WITH THEM, CAME TO AN END WITH THE INDUSTRIAL REVOLUTION. BUT NOW THE CRAFT IS REVIVING AS A HOBBY ...

Lace, in the form of sprang netting, macramé and cut work, has been in existence for a long time, but the lace we know today arrived in the early years of the 16th century.

The leap forward came during the reign of Elizabeth I, whose love of lace is plain to see from the enormous ruffs, edged and covered with the material, that she chose to wear when having her portrait painted. She is reputed to have spent as much as £3,000 on one ruff – a huge price even for today, but a reflection of the time, patience and skill needed to produce lace of supreme quality.

What the queen liked to wear was eagerly sought after by the nobility. By the time William and Mary were on the throne, lace had become commonplace, and it was the fashionable material in which to be christened, married and even buried. Highwaymen were known to face the gallows with their clothes trimmed with lace.

It was just as popular with men as with women. Lace was worn on ruffs, fell from elbow sleeves and was made into cravats and tuckers. Wives and mistresses, who in those days spent a lot of time entertaining from their beds, liked their night-wear and sheets to be covered with fine lace – a costly taste which often forced their men to sell part of their land in order to settle lace bills.

The early years of the 18th century saw an improvement in British lace making. This was due largely to the influx of refugees from Europe, who sought peace and safety on British shores from the turmoil and religious persecution in their own countries, and who brought their own traditions of lace making with them. Refugees from the Low Countries settled in Buckinghamshire; the Flemings round the coasts of Devon and Dorset. Huguenots, who came from France, were encouraged by Queen Anne's fondness for laces other than the popular Venetian. Many of them travelled around the country, adding a French touch to the English laceworker's craft.

Two main lace-making centres became established. One, where Honiton lace was made, was in South Devon, but it extended far beyond that small town. Lace making became very popular with West Country folk as a means of supplementing the uncertain income they derived from fishing.

The other main groupings of lace makers covered much of the Midlands, including Bedfordshire, Buckinghamshire, part of Northamptonshire, and extending to Oxfordshire, Huntingdonshire, Cambridgeshire and Hertfordshire.

Although there were many different influences on lace, there were, and still are, only two basic techniques – needlepoint lace and bobbin lace, the latter also called pillow or bone lace.

Making needlepoint lace

Needlepoint lace is constructed in much the same way as a spider builds a web. The lace maker first makes some anchoring stitches, following the basic guide lines of a drawn paper pattern – which also acts as a backing sheet. Alternatively, she tacks narrow braid in curves and lines, following a pattern, on to a backing sheet of paper or fabric. Using a needle and fine thread she then builds a web of stitches, from one anchoring thread to another, or from one piece of braid to another, but does not sew into the backing sheet. Buttonhole stitch is used throughout, and variations are built up by using the stitch in groups. These are attached to threads that link the anchoring stitches, or braid. The Italians call this form of lace *punto in aria*, which literally means 'stitches in the air'. When the work is finished, the anchoring threads or tacking threads are cut and the lace removed from the backing.

In those early days of lace making the threads were made of linen, which was imported mainly from Antwerp as none fine enough was made in England. It was expensive: the price of thread in the last years of the 18th century was £70–£100 per pound weight.

The thread was spun by hand, and the lace was made in dreadful conditions. Because the thread was so fine, the women would make their lace in damp cellars to reduce the risk of breakage. But though the damp made the threads more pliable, it was very unhealthy for the lace makers. As a result, lace became known as 'consumption lace'.

Without the aid of spectacles, a magnifying glass or proper lighting, women completed the most delicate work with the fine thread. It was not unusual for each inch of work to contain over 100 stitches. Nowadays, such fine thread is not available. From the end of the 18th century, machines took over, and cotton thread – which was thicker and did not produce such fine work – became readily available.

Bobbin lace is made with a number of bobbins, wound with fine thread, and a round, tightly stuffed cushion or bolster. The pattern is prepared on card or parchment and is perforated to hold pins that will shape and guide the lace during the work. The threads are anchored at one end and the bobbins moved in pairs to twist, weave or plait the threads. An experienced lace maker deftly throws her bobbins into position, producing a clicking sound as she works. A simple pattern will only need about three dozen bobbins, whereas an intricate design needs many more.

MAIN TYPES OF BOBBIN LACE

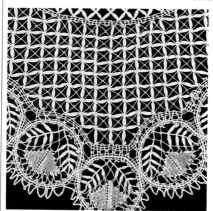

BEDFORDSHIRE

Running trails, sometimes called running rivers, are the main features of this lace. It also includes leaves or bars, plaits, and an edging called 'nine stick'. It has no set angles, as in bucks point and torchon laces. Many bobbins are needed, even for the narrow edgings. 110 pairs of bobbins were used to work the collar of which a part is shown here.

BUCKS POINT

This intricate lace may be recognised by its fine hexagonal and honeycomb stitches. The designs are very varied, ranging from simple shapes to elaborate floral patterns. Each mesh is made with four threads twisted in a diamond pattern. The angles of the lace vary between 55 and 72 degrees, which allow a much freer pattern; but considerable skill is needed to turn corners neatly. One of the chief centres for bucks point was Newport Pagnell.

HONITON LACE

The motifs of this popular lace are usually flower sprigs and sprays. These are made separately, then sewn together and appliquéd on to a backing of net – at one time hand-made, but later machine-made. The lace is worked on a circular pillow to allow the lace maker to turn the work in the direction in which the lace runs. It is similar to, but generally not considered as fine as, Brussels lace. In the old days the Honiton lace maker was often paid in shillings, receiving as many as were needed to cover the piece of lace worked.

TORCHON LACE

Easily recognised by its geometric design, this type of lace was not introduced into England until the second half of the 19th century. It is the easiest lace to make, and for this reason it became known as 'beggar's lace'. A small item could be completed in a few hours, and it was often used for trimmings. It is also the easiest lace to simulate with a machine.

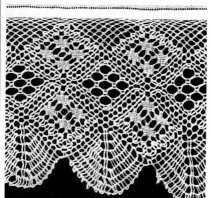

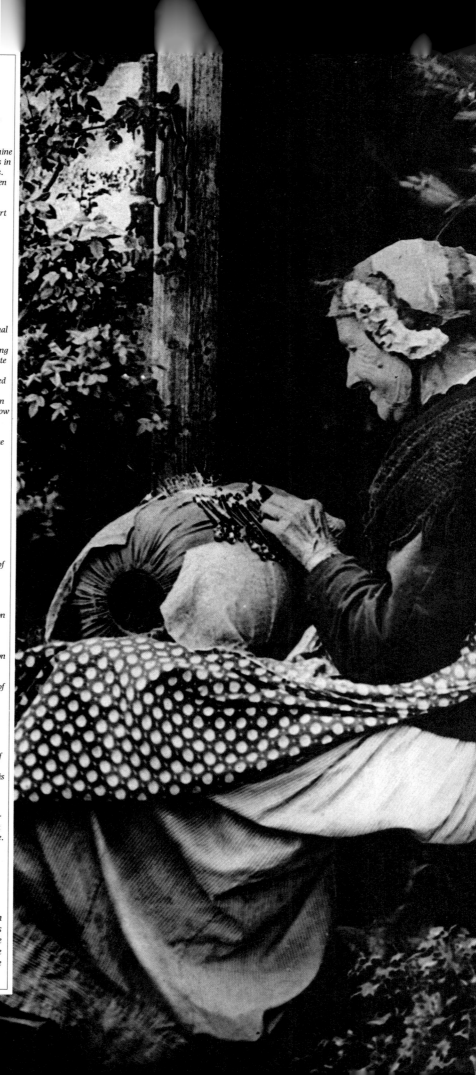

A REVOLUTION IN HER LIFETIME *As a girl, in the early years of the 19th century, this lace maker was probably paid at low piece-work rates for long hours of drudgery. Now, working at her cottage door in the 1880s, she is able to pursue her craft for pocket money and even for pleasure. During the years between, the demand for lace declined drastically and its manufacture was mechanised. The days of sweated labour came gradually to an end.*

TRADITIONAL LACE-MAKING EQUIPMENT

In the days before gas or electricity, lace makers had to manage with a candle placed behind a water-filled glass globe or flask, which concentrated the beam of light. Traditionally, the flask was filled with snow each winter to ensure that the water was clean and pure. A bobbin winder took some of the aggravation out of winding the threads on to individual bobbins. The beaded end of the bobbin was secured in a small tube, and the thread tied on to the other end. When the wheel was turned, the thread wound itself on to the bobbin. For bobbin lace, the pattern is fixed to a tightly stuffed pillow, which also holds the hundreds of pins that keep the stitches in place. About 200 are needed for most lace making, but up to 1,000 can be in use at one time. Holes in the pattern are made with a pricker (right foreground).

There are many different types of bobbin lace, as each lace-making centre tended to develop its own variety.

At first, a fine braid was worked, the women manipulating the threads with their fingers. It was generally considered more convenient to have the threads wound round a spool, and the small bones of pigs' or sheep's feet were found to be ideal.

It was from these crude bones that the bobbin developed. Bobbins enabled the lace maker to work much more rapidly, and, depending on the thickness of the thread, each could hold up to 8 yds. This was one reason why bobbin lace became more popular than needlepoint. Payments were often made on the amount of lace produced rather than its quality, and far more bobbin lace than needlepoint lace could be made in a given time.

It was common for lace makers to work desperately long hours for very little money. An accounts book from about the turn of the century records a payment of 3s. 6d. (17½p) for a 9 in. square of lace that took 72 hours to make.

During the 18th century, when lace making was at its height, lace-making schools sprang up all over the country. There were dozens set up in the Midlands, Buckinghamshire and Bedfordshire, and boys and girls from the age of four or five were sent to learn the craft. The schools also taught the rudiments of reading and writing, and it was not unusual for five-year-olds to put in a 12 hour working day.

A small fee was charged, and in return the children received part of the selling price of the lace they had made.

The schools were often overcrowded and the teachers very strict – in particular about the need for cleanliness. Lace had to be spotlessly clean, otherwise it did not fetch as good a price; so a bag of powdered starch was kept handy for the children to dip their hands in, to keep them clean and dry.

The regime got harder as the children got older. Each had to get through a certain amount of lace making every day, and many were obliged to stay on for even longer than their 12 hours. To help pass the time and keep themselves cheerful, they would sing songs called 'lace tells', a sort of lace-maker's equivalent of a sea shanty. No wonder they looked forward to the annual lace-makers' holiday in November – St Catherine's Day, known as 'Catterns Day'. Work was forgotten, games played, and cakes of dough and caraway seeds consumed.

Many adult lace makers – invariably women – made their lace while sitting in groups. Having no television or evening entertainment, they used to gather in each other's houses and, while working, would chat and gossip to help pass the long hours.

Lace making was very tiring on the eyes. In summer, the women sat outside so as to enjoy as much natural light as possible. During the winter months they used a candle lamp. This was made of glass in the shape of a round flask. When filled with water it provided a concentrated beam of light from a lighted candle placed behind it. Traditionally, the pure water from melted snow was used to fill these candle lamps.

Those creating the most intricate designs sat nearest to the light. Others, doing less-exacting work, had to be content to sit where the light was not so good. When it was cold, they kept themselves warm with a 'dicky pot', a small earthenware pot filled with hot cinders which they put

MOURNING LACE
During the reign of George II, both black and white laces were worn for limited mourning, but neither was considered suitable when individuals were in deep mourning. When Prince Albert died, Queen Victoria changed that custom by requesting that society wear black lace as a sign of mourning for her husband. As a consequence, lace makers were instructed to use black thread for whatever type of lace they made.

underneath their skirts. Smoke and dust from an ordinary fire would have made the lace dirty.

Many lace makers were cruelly exploited by agents who toured around collecting the finished articles. On the one hand the agents charged the workers for the hire of essential equipment for lace making, even bobbins. And on the other, they were fully aware of the value of the produce, and charged the fashion-conscious nobility vast amounts for small items.

Some women, in an effort to reduce hiring charges, cut hawthorn twigs which, because they were straight and strong, could be used as substitute bobbins.

In certain cases the agents were also small shopkeepers, who forced lace makers to accept payment in goods rather than cash. This was particularly difficult for the lace makers who lived in outlying villages and had to take their work to the agent to get paid.

Saturday was the usual day for this and the whole procedure proved quite exhausting. They had to stand in one queue to show their lace and in another queue to choose provisions, most of which had been artificially marked up for that day. Many of them returned home late at night with not much to show for their work and in fear of being attacked by footpads on the way.

The Industrial Revolution changed everything. Very soon many types of lace could be made far more speedily and cheaply by machine than by hand. As a result, many women were forced to give up their craft. Added to this, the import duty on foreign lace was removed in 1860, so that very beautiful French and Italian lace was available for

little more than the price of its somewhat inferior English equivalent.

Queen Victoria made determined efforts to keep the craft alive and gave vast orders for hand-made lace. She even ordered her wedding dress to be made in Honiton lace, in the coastal village of Beer, at a cost of £1,000. But lace was no longer very fashionable, and as skilled lace makers died in each area there was no one to replace them. Soon, all that was left were a few women who could afford to make lace just for the pleasure of doing so. Fortunately, this was sufficient to keep the old skills and traditions alive.

But as recently as ten years ago the story of lace making took another twist. Interest began to revive in the craft, and during the last decade women have again been taking up their bobbins and threads in craft schools and colleges round the country. In contrast to the bad old days of commercial lace making, there is every likelihood that more and more people will come to find in the craft a satisfying and rewarding hobby.

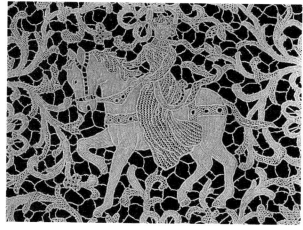

DELICATE NEEDLEPOINT *Needlepoint has always been known as the queen of laces, for it is the most beautiful to look at, the most difficult to make, and the most expensive to buy. Its beginnings go back to the late 15th century. Its place of origin has never been resolved, though it is thought to be either Italy or Flanders. Needlepoint is created with a needle and thread, and made by a series of buttonhole stitches and loops. In the heyday of lace making, women could sew about 100 stitches of fine thread to the inch. Because it was so difficult to make, it lost its appeal. In contrast, bobbin lace, which was quicker and easier to make and paid the lace makers better, became more popular. Needlepoint died out almost completely, and it is only in the last few years that it is enjoying a revival, along with bobbin lace making.*

LACE-MAKING BOBBINS – A CRAFT IN THEMSELVES

Like the tools of any craftsman, bobbins were greatly prized by lace makers. But, unlike most other tools, they have now become highly valued as artistic objects. Today, many are sought after as collectors' items.

Bobbins were made mainly of wood or bone, though occasionally of pewter or brass. Silver or gold bobbins were never actually used, although they were given as presents. Wood bobbins were often carved from fruit woods, such as cherry, plum and apple. Spindlewood was also popular. Wood bobbins were cheaper than bone, although not as long-lasting, and were used by workers. Bone bobbins were used by ladies. Bobbins of all types were often beautifully decorated, and their making became a craft in its own right.

Bobbins could often be decorated in many inventive ways. For instance, dark-coloured bobbins were often inlaid with light-coloured woods. Pewter was also popular as an inlay, and the bobbins were called 'tiger' bobbins if the pewter formed thin bands round the bobbin, or 'leopard' bobbins when little spots of pewter had been hammered in. There were 'mother in babe' and 'cow in calf' bobbins, in which the bobbin was made in two parts. The middle of the bobbin was hollowed out to allow a tiny bobbin to rest inside. There were also 'church window' bobbins, in which the main bobbin had pierced sides. The centre was hollowed out to allow a tiny bobbin to be inserted within the walls.

But perhaps the most fascinating of all are the 'message' bobbins. Inscriptions of all sorts were burned or carved into them. Sometimes they just stated the owner's name; or they might be coded secret messages, or puzzles, from a lover or husband. They might record an important event, such as the birth or death of a loved one; sometimes they were just fun – 'kiss me quick' being an example. Others – 'I love the Queen Victoria' – were determinedly patriotic.

An essential part of all bobbins, except those used for making Honiton lace, was the 'spangle' – a circle of beads attached to it. They made the bobbin heavier, and thus added extra tension to the thread. Having

square sides that gripped the pillow, they prevented the bobbins that were not being used, and were pushed to one side, from rolling back and getting in the way. The beads were square and made of glass. Clear glass and red were the most popular, although if a lace maker was in mourning she might have black beads.

Sometimes personal trinkets, such as small lockets, buttons or a crucifix, were attached to the bobbin. There was a lot of competition amongst the girls in the lace schools as to who would be given the most attractive bobbin. If a boy wanted to court a girl, he would often make her a bobbin and pass it to her across the church. If she accepted, an introduction was considered to have been made and the young man could feel free to speak to her after the service.

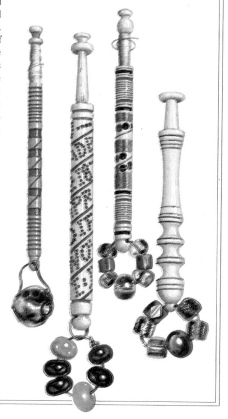

THE Leatherworker

LEATHER BOTTLES DO NOT BREAK... AND THE
CHAIN OF CRAFTSMEN WHO MAKE THEM HAS ALSO
SURVIVED INTACT SINCE ANCIENT TIMES

The craft of the leatherworker can be said to have reached its peak during the Middle Ages, with the invention of a revolutionary way of moulding the material. The method was called *cuir bouilli* – boiled leather – and it brought a dramatic increase in the range of products the craftsmen could make.

Bottles, helmets, fitted breastplates, 'black-jack' tankards and large jugs called bombards were among the many new wares the leatherworker began turning out. Some are still being made by these same methods in Britain today.

The *cuir bouilli* process seems deceptively simple. The leather is first thoroughly soaked, then moulded, pressed or stamped into shape over some suitable former. Once set it is dipped into scalding water, then withdrawn instantly and dried as quickly as possible. This drying must be carefully controlled, or the leather becomes brittle and cracks.

'It can break like a biscuit,' says Mr Anthony Mowles, a craftsman who uses the process at his workshop in Debenham, Ipswich. He makes black-jacks, bombards and other traditional vessels, and is not above drying out their bottoms in an oven if necessary. He reckons the quicker the drying, the harder the leather – and the bottoms need to be strong to hold their shape, which in turn governs that of the vessel he is turning out.

Today most leather is tanned, dried, curried, tawed and finished by mechanical means (see *The Tanner*, p. 194). But there are still many leatherworkers such as Mr Mowles using old skills, who want it prepared by hand for a variety of jobs. The material he prefers is cow hide which has been oak-bark tanned by traditional methods. This is still available from tanneries in Cornwall and Devon.

To make a bombard, for example, he first soaks the leather until it becomes really pliable. Then he rolls it into roughly cylindrical shape and packs it with wet sand, which enables him to mould it into the exact form he wants. Some craftsmen roll the leather around wooden moulds instead – the moulds being made in several sections which can be removed one at a time. Whatever the method, the leather will almost certainly have to be moistened again while the work is in progress, because it moulds best while actually drying out – a stage known as 'samming'.

The tubular shape that emerges is straight at the front, where the lip is moulded in, but narrowing from bottom to mouth at the back. The narrowing is done by pinching together a long, triangular fold of leather at the back, which will be used eventually to help make the handle.

The next step is to cut out two discs and two rings of hide, which will be used to make the bottom of the jug. This is done with a clicking knife, a basic tool of the leatherworker, which has a fine and extremely sharp blade with a rather long point – its name comes from the noise it makes when cutting around a template. The discs and rings are cut slightly larger than the bottom they will form, so that they

can be dished upwards. This ensures that the bottom is strong enough to support and maintain the rigidity of the vessel when it is in use. And to make doubly sure, the discs are treated by the *cuir bouilli* process.

They are then stitched into place with the rings forming a sort of welt between the bottom and sides of the jug, to make the joint as waterproof as possible.

Leather is normally stitched with waxed hemp thread, a job that is done by hand. The stitch holes are marked out with a multi-pronged punch which has its points evenly spaced. The holes are pierced with an awl, which has a thin, diamond-section blade with only two of its four corners sharpened, so that it makes a small slit rather than a round hole.

Two needles are used, one at each end of the thread, and both are passed through each hole from opposite sides and pulled tight. This is known as saddle stitching, and each stitch is independent; if one gives way the others will hold.

The inside of the jug is normally waterproofed by pouring in melted pitch, which is then flushed out, leaving a thin coat on the surface. This technique was used by medieval

PLAIN 'BOTTEL' AND
FANCY BLACK-JACK

Leather 'bottels' such as that above were commonplace vessels for many centuries in Britain. The earliest one surviving is about 600 years old, but this example is 17th century. However, its rather Gothic form points to a much earlier date for the design, and it is possible that this basic shape originated as long ago as the 11th century. Many versions of the black-jack beer tankard were made. The 18th-century one shown, ornately rimmed with silver, was made for a man of means: humble tavern tankards had no such frills.

MOULDING AND SEWING A BOMBARD

Two stages in making a bombard ... First the jug is filled with wet sand while the leather is still damp and pliable. The sand will help it to set in the shape to which it is being formed by the skilled fingers of Anthony Mowles. The lip has already been moulded and the rim is now given a slight flare. With the leather dried out and the bombard moulded, he grips it firmly between his knees in the traditional wooden clamp (below) while he stitches in the bottom. This is dished upwards for strength, and rings of thinner leather are sewn in with it to aid waterproofing.

craftsmen and works well, though its continued effectiveness depends upon the pitching, as it is called, being repeated from time to time.

In addition to being treated in various ways for particular uses, leather can also be decorated by a variety of methods. For example, its natural colour can be altered by staining or dyeing. Many craftsmen carry out this operation themselves and colour individual hides to meet their own needs rather than relying on the limited range of colours available through commercial suppliers. It is also cheaper for a craftsman to buy a hide in its pristine state and dye it himself. The heavy leathers used for caskets, cases, upholstery, pitchers and bombards are coloured by brushing several coats of weak dye solution on the grain side, or outer face, of the skin. Smaller pieces of leather can be dipped in trays of dye solution. Multi-coloured designs can also be painted on, using leather dyes or aniline dyes.

Leather can also be decorated by tooling and embossing.

Tooling consists of pressing or rubbing leather that has been moistened with metal tools of various shapes. The indentations formed remain after the leather has dried, and untouched areas stand out in relief. The technique can be combined with carving, in which the surface is gouged in much the same way as woodcarving. Embossing is done by hammering a stamping tool with a decorative design on its face on the moistened leather, so leaving an impression of the design on the surface.

Mr Mowles is carrying on a tradition of craftsmanship that goes back at least 4,000 years in Britain: evidence that leather was worked to make clothing was discovered in 1972 at Grimes Graves, the Neolithic flint mines near Thetford, Norfolk. And recent excavations at Catterick, Yorkshire, have revealed large-scale production of leather equipment for the Roman army. Since no substitute has been found for the jobs that leather does best, the tradition seems set to carry on for a few thousand years more.

TRADITIONAL LEATHER DECORATION

In his studio in Cupar, in Fife, Raymond Morris, one of Scotland's leading leather carvers, hand-tools the finishing touches on a leather casket. Hand-tooling is a method of producing indented designs by rubbing tools of various shapes against the wetted leather. The depressions so formed remain after the leather has dried, and the untouched areas stand out in relief. Morris of Eddergoll (to use his full title) also carves targes – Scottish battle-shields – one of which can be seen in the background.

129

THE
MASON
AND STONE CARVER

THE SOLID, ENDURING NATURE OF STONE HAS BRED
SIMILAR QUALITIES IN THE MEN WHO FASHION IT INTO
BUILDINGS THAT MAY STAND FOR A THOUSAND YEARS

A man shaping stone with hammer, square and plumb-bob is working in much the same way as the masons who built the pyramids and temples of ancient Egypt. These three tools are still the symbols of his craft. The Egyptians also used the chisel, though it was of bronze rather than today's steel; and their hammer was stone.

The range of tools used by masons has changed little since – except for the spirit-level, invented in the 17th century.

The skills of the men who wield them are in growing demand; for stone is back in favour. Many architects who feel that they have exhausted the possibilities of concrete and brick are returning to stone for both structural and decorative work on houses, public buildings, offices – and, of course, churches. Moreover, stone-built houses are no longer just for the wealthy: cubic foot for cubic foot, it now costs little more to build a stone bungalow than one of brick. Quarries are supplying more and more blocks to individual customers.

Although Neolithic Britons were constructing their huts and tombs of stone 5,000 years ago, it was the Roman invaders who first imported sophisticated techniques of stone cutting and building. But these skills were all but lost when they departed, and the great era of stone building in Britain dawned with the arrival of the Normans. For nearly 500 years, their castles, cathedrals and churches rose in mounting splendour as masons refined their tools and methods.

Many of these buildings survive as testimony to their genius. By the 14th century, indeed, the master mason stood high on the social ladder, in most cases being not only the builder but also the architect, designing and supervising the erection of buildings. Under him worked freemasons, allowed to display their skills in intricate carving and decoration, and served in turn by rough masons, who

SPLITTING BLOCKS AT THE QUARRY

These two quarrymen are splitting off a block of Portland stone from the side of a quarry. They started by drilling holes about 12 in. deep and 6 in. apart along a natural line in the rock. Plugs and feathers have already been inserted in the holes on the ledge and one man is hammering them home. His workmate below is meanwhile busy inserting more in the face of the rock. When they, too, are hammered in, their combined splitting action will part the block from the bedrock. A row of holes left by previous work can be seen along the top edge.

Newly quarried rock, showing drill holes and the near-smooth surface where it has been split.

hewed and dressed the stone. Finally came the labourers, who did the heaving and carrying.

The techniques employed depended largely on the properties of the particular stone being used. A profound knowledge of these properties was, and is, vital to the mason. He must, for example, know whether the stone he is using for a building is strong enough to bear the loads and stresses that will be imposed on it. Colour and texture, weathering qualities, hardness or softness, and heat resistance in case of fire are all essential considerations.

But before the 19th-century revolution in transport, local availability was usually a decisive factor in the choice of material: the mason often had to make do with what was near to hand – though in Norman times some was shipped from France.

To the layman, the durability of a stone may seem related to its hardness. But stone is a material with almost the characteristics of a living thing. It is all more or less porous, which makes it vulnerable to the weather. It can disintegrate internally through chemical change or by the action of alternate freezing and thawing, or simply by absorbing water over long periods. It can be seriously eroded by air pollution – smoke and industrial gases – and by salt air.

Paint, boiled linseed oil and sodium silicate solution can be applied to offset these effects. But stone also grows its own protective 'skin'. Natural moisture present in all stone fresh from the quarry – called quarry sap – combines with the atmosphere to produce a gradual hardening of the surface over the early years. This is the weathering process, and it is encouraged by masons, who 'comb' the surfaces that will be exposed with drags – semi-circular shaped tools with the straight edge toothed.

The tool is drawn across the surface in all directions, which leaves an attractive criss-cross pattern and opens up the pores of the stone, increasing the area that can weather.

Evidence of an ancient skill

Medieval masons understood this weathering process and used drags – fine examples of their work were revealed during excavation of an earth-covered 12th-century castle at Sandal, in Yorkshire, between 1964–73. And they certainly knew about the chiselling and carving characteristics of many different kinds of stone.

The three main kinds used in building are:
Igneous rocks such as granite, which were once molten and then cooled and hardened deep below the surface.
Sedimentary rocks, including limestone and sandstone, mostly formed by the gathering together of minute particles.
Metamorphic rocks – notably slate and marble – which began as igneous or sedimentary but were changed later by heat and pressure.

Granite is hard to cut but has few flaws, and it can be ground and polished. It is found mostly in Scotland, Cornwall and Devon. Today, masons use tungsten-tipped chisels on it, but in medieval times they also needed the blacksmith's skills, because their tools would wear out or break and they had to make new ones on the spot.

Slate can be split into thin sheets, and roofs have been made of it for centuries. Cut thicker, it makes door and window lintels, fence-posts, gravestones – and even ornaments. The major source in Britain is North Wales. Very little marble is found in Britain, but some hard limestones – especially one from Purbeck, in Dorset – can be cut and polished to good effect.

Limestones and sandstones are the most familiar types used in building. Many can be worked easily in any direction and are often called freestones. Limestones are quarried largely from a great S-shaped belt of rocks

stretching from Dorset through the Cotswolds to Lincolnshire and Yorkshire. They vary in shade from near-white to brown. Sandstones vary much more in colour, the commonest being brown, pink, red and cream. Yorkshire sandstones – often seen in paving slabs – are brown and blue. A fine red one comes from Herefordshire.

Both limestones and sandstones also vary considerably in hardness and durability. Some are almost as hard as granite; others can be cut with a simple handsaw.

The physical work of stonemasonry starts in the quarry. These are mostly open-cast in Britain, though a few stones such as flint and slate are also obtained by mining. The usual method of prising stone from its bed is to drill holes at intervals along a clearly visible natural line in the bed, using a compressed air drill fitted with a 3 ft long bit.

Into these holes are inserted plugs and feathers: the plug is a wedge-shaped iron pin; the feathers are two half-round sections of steel, flanged at the top, which fit in the hole on each side of the plug. The plugs are then sledge-hammered down between their feathers until the rock fractures along the natural line. Ancient Egyptians used to hammer in wooden plugs, then soak them with water so that they split the rock as they expanded.

The large blocks quarried are then taken to the stonesawyer to be cut into more manageable sizes. Before the advent of mechanical saws, single or double-handled saws were used. They cut soft stone quite easily, but the task of cutting harder stone was long and boring, relieved only by breaks for sharpening or re-cutting the teeth of the saw.

CUTTING TO A DESIGN *This is soft Bath stone, allowing the banker mason to cut it with a wooden-handled chisel, which he strikes with a metal-headed mallet called a dummy. One of many skilled craftsmen at the Cambridge firm of Rattee and Kett, he is finishing a pair of blind tracery battlements for a church.*

Here the mason has paused to check that he has carved a section correctly, using a template to ensure that the curve is precisely as planned.

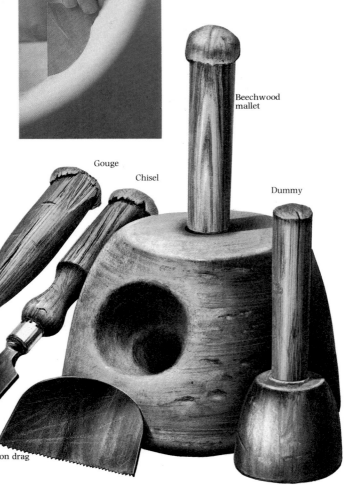

TOOLS IN A MASON'S WORKSHOP

The saws are for cutting soft stone. Some allow the blade angle to be varied for making awkward cuts. The heavy metal chisel is a claw boaster for dressing hard stone, and below it is a waster, for fine shaving. The wooden-handled gouge and chisel are for intricate work in soft stone, and the drag smooths flat surfaces. Beside the beech mallet is a 2 lb. lead-and-zinc-headed dummy, used with wooden-handled tools.

Mason's saw

Saw with adjustable blade

Claw boaster

Waster

Half-moon drag

Beechwood mallet

Gouge

Chisel

Dummy

However, one ingenious device, the frame saw, was used to reduce the labour. It had a long, 4 in. deep blade and was suspended from a pulley system, which took the weight, but allowed enough vertical movement for the blade to cut. The cutting action was aided by sand and water. It was so efficient that it could be worked by one man. Now, many quarries and firms of stonemasons have at least one large and one medium-sized mechanical saw, with tungsten or carborundum-toughened blades. Running water is directed on to the teeth at the cutting point for cooling and lubrication.

Stone blocks for building are cut in several basic shapes to produce roughly rectangular faces. Some are cut more carefully so they can be set in tidy, horizontal courses. They are cut with true angles and the faces that will show are smoothed. These are called ashlar blocks, expensive to make now, but widely used in medieval days when labour was cheap.

The craftsmen who dress the smooth outer surfaces are the 'banker masons' – a name taken from the benches at which they work. They also turn blocks into carved shapes – work requiring great skill. It can encompass a series of sections for a pierced parapet on a new church or repair work on the delicate traceries of a cathedral window.

The banker mason begins by checking the dimensions and angles of the block with a set-square. Then a design template – either of cardboard or zinc – is placed on the surface and the shape traced out in pencil. A pitching tool –

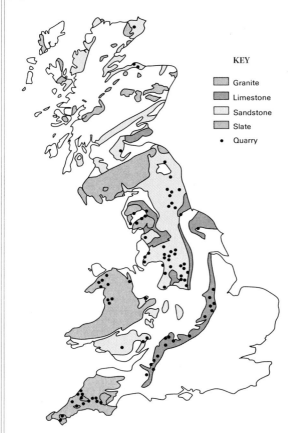

WHERE OUR STONE COMES FROM

A simplified geological map of Britain shows where the three main types of stone used in building are found. By far the most widely used – and readily available – are the limestones and sandstones in the great belts of sedimentary rocks sweeping from the south-west to central and eastern areas, and across the Scottish Lowlands and border country. Easily worked and usually simple to quarry, they contrast with the tool-blunting granites of Devon, Cornwall and Scotland, and the slates of Wales.

KEY

Granite
Limestone
Sandstone
Slate
• Quarry

YEARS OF EXPERIENCE *Skills accumulated over years of specialising in architectural sculpture are employed as this mason works on a huge Corinthian capital. It is built up from three great slabs of stone, each carved with acanthus leaves so that they integrate into one whole. The slabs were first cut into rough shape by banker masons at their yard. They are supported at working height by piles of stone slabs.*

a kind of cold chisel with a blunt, broad edge – is used with a mason's mallet to chip the stone down towards the template lines.

The process is then carried on with another chisel called a waster, which removes thinner shavings of stone. The mallet is unusual in shape and made of dense beechwood, not easily split. Its cylindrical head is about 6 in. across, tapering slightly towards the handle. A wooden mallet used on a metal tool produces little recoil when the blows are struck, so a cleaner cut is made.

The banker now starts the actual finishing of the block. Where lines and surfaces are straight, he uses a boaster – rather like a sharpened pitching tool – and chisels along them. With the tool held at just the correct angle, accurate slices are pared away. For rounded hollows and surfaces he uses a gouge similar to the woodworking tool. Awkward pieces are cut off with a handsaw and the final finish is with a set of drags – those with large teeth leaving a coarse surface, and fine teeth producing that handsome criss-cross pattern.

There are, of course, several other finishes available for the outer surfaces of building blocks. One, applied with a heavy, pointed hammer, is called 'scabbling': quite large flakes are knocked off the surface, leaving a rough-hewn effect rather like coarse adze marks on timber. To ensure accurate fitting, blocks finished in this way are often given a 'chisel draughted margin' – a smooth border about an inch wide chiselled around the edges. If a really smooth finish is required, the surface is rubbed with a piece of harder stone, using sand and water between the faces. Granite and marble can be polished with turpentine, beeswax or putty applied with a soft flannel.

In 'droved work' parallel marks are cut across the surface with a boaster – though not in continuous lines. If the lines are kept continuous and parallel, it is known as 'tooled work'. When deeper and broader parallel grooves are cut, the finish is called 'furrowed work'. Yet another finish is obtained by working over the entire face with a pointed punch, to leave a grainy near-smooth effect. These are but a few of the many techniques in a mason's repertoire.

Usually the banker mason numbers each block as he completes it, so that 'fixer masons' at the building site know exactly where to place it. They mortar and trim it into position – and sometimes carry out additional carving once the block is in place. It is, however, more usual to employ sculptural masons for this work – men skilled in carving figures, animals, foliage, heraldic designs and so on. At one time the banker mason also did the fixing, and would cut his individual mark on each block – usually on an inner surface, to be revealed only if the building was repaired or demolished.

Although there is now a shortage of skilled masons, there are plenty of school-leavers wishing to learn the craft. Some technical colleges offer training, and a number of large contracting firms have special stonemasonry divisions which allow craftsmen to practise their skills to the full, using wholly traditional methods. And in the village of Orton, near Kettering, Northants, a unique scheme founded by a quarry owner has been operating since 1969: the Orton Trust, which provides intensive training and refresher courses for masons.

The trust took over the old Norman village church, saving it from demolition after the Church Commissioners had made it redundant. There, stonemasons can work and learn in a truly practical way, restoring and replacing parts of the building under the guidance of skilled instructors.

CARVING A NEW PIECE TO MATCH THE OLD

Masons who are architectural sculptors can carve exact copies of earlier works that have been damaged or lost. On the left is a severely cracked stiff-leaf capital in Early English style from St Albans Cathedral; beside it is a fine copy cut in Ancaster stone – one of a set cut for a cluster of pillars on the west front. The damaged carving has delicate claw-cut lines on the leaf stems, which catch the light and emphasise their direction of growth. They must be faithfully reproduced in the copy. The mason's callipers (below) help him to make exact measurements.

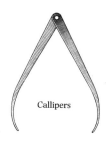

Callipers

133

THE MASTER BREWER

OUR BEER IS AS BRITISH AS THE BULLDOG BREED,
AND CENTURIES OF KNOWLEDGE AND EXPERTISE ARE
EMBODIED IN OUR 1,200 BREWS

There is much talk about liquor among brewers. They mean water, which is treated, rather surprisingly, with near reverence by the men to whom good brewing is something more than a craft, almost an art. They hold that there is no good beer without good liquor – and that is why breweries can still be found where beer has been brewed since ancient times. In these places the water has a certain something that makes all the difference to a drinker of taste and discernment.

All beers are brewed by the same basic method: crushed malted barley is steeped in hot water, and the extract is boiled with hops and fermented with yeast. The brewery may be an ancient outbuilding of the only pub it serves, or it may loom startlingly from the landscape looking more like a nuclear power station than a source of sparkling pints. The method remains the same.

The ways in which the method is applied, and the subtle differences between the waters, malt and yeast used, are what separate one brew from another – the light from the dark, the bitter from the mild, the weak from the strong.

There is, contrary to some opinion, no such thing as 'chemical beer'. All British beer is made from natural ingredients and brewed to meet the requirements of the pure-food laws and those of the Customs and Excise. An excise officer can enter any part of any brewery at any time.

Beer was certainly flowing at Belshazzar's feast in Babylon 2,500 years ago, when the mysterious 'writing on the wall' foretold the fall of the city. Indeed, its history can be traced back at least twice as far as that, and to Egypt and many other parts of the world as well as Babylonia. Barley was not the only grain used in its manufacture, but most of the alcoholic beverages made from cereals over the centuries would be recognised now as beers.

The British were drinking Celtic beer long before the Romans arrived; Flemish settlers introduced hops into beer, and most of the common English terms used in brewing today are north European or Anglo-Saxon in origin, including malt, mash, wort, ale – and the word beer itself. Methods were improved in medieval monasteries, while home brewing by housewives was common from the 12th to about the 18th centuries.

As towns grew in size, small commercial breweries were set up, selling on the spot. Later they began distributing their beer to inns. But it was not until the Industrial Revolution began in the 18th century that large breweries were set up, and national distribution of beers is mainly a 20th-century development.

However, smaller regional breweries continue to thrive, each brewing beer with its own taste and character. There are about 80 of them, together with a growing number of pubs that brew their own beer and are currently enjoying a resurgence of popularity.

Each head brewer has his secrets, but whatever the brew

it gets its strength, colour and underlying flavour from the malt, and its bitterness and other subtle flavours from the hops. More than 900,000 tons of barley are bought each year by maltsters who supply breweries, yielding about 700,000 tons of malt.

At the maltings, the grain is first steeped in water then spread on a malting floor. There the temperature and humidity are carefully controlled as germination takes place, resulting in natural changes in the grain – including the formation of enzymes which allow the starch it contains to be converted into sugars during the brewing process.

After about five days the grains grow tiny roots, at which

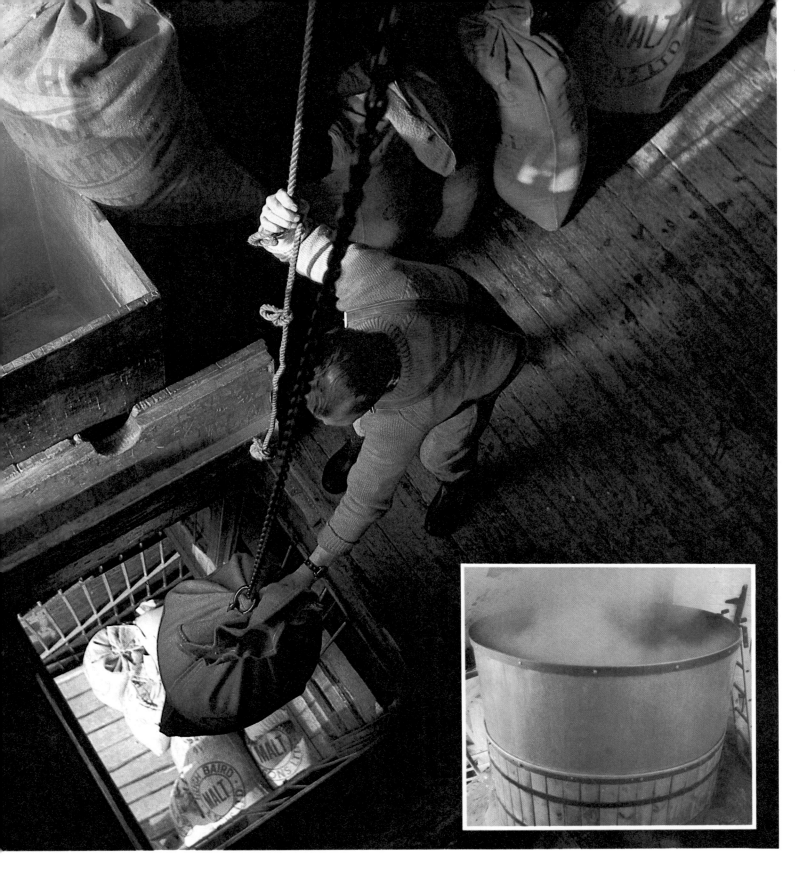

stage they are kilned – that is, dried and heated. Kilning halts germination, brings out the flavour and, according to the time it takes and the degree of heat that is applied, changes the colour and nature of the malt. The skill of the maltster produces the precise malt his customer needs for a particular brew.

Nowadays, nearly all brewers buy their malt from outside maltsters, and it is with this that the process begins. The malted barley is crushed lightly, and the rather coarse meal of grains and husks that results is called the grist. The grist is mixed with the correct quantity of hot water as it goes into a large circular vessel called a mash tun. This mixture varies from between two to four parts of water to one of grist, and the process is called mashing-in.

Mashing converts the starch in the grist into a number of different sugars, which together with other carbohydrates and protein material form a sweet liquid called the wort – pronounced 'wert'. The mashing temperature is also vitally important. The different malts for a variety of beers call for slightly differing temperatures, but all are in the region of 150°F (66°C). After a period ranging between one and three hours – depending on the type of malt being used – the wort is slowly drained from the mash tun and passes into a boiling copper. More hot water is sprayed on to the mash

MALT FOR THE GRIST

Sacks of malted barley are hoisted up for milling. The grains are crushed between carefully set rollers that separate the husk from kernel, and also crack the kernel itself. The mealy mixture that emerges is called the grist, which goes into the mash tun to be mixed with hot water. Brewers call the sweet liquid that is formed the wort – which is steaming in the copper pictured above.

135

while the wort is draining, to wash out any remaining sugars – a process known as sparging.

It is when the wort reaches the copper that the hops are added, and the fragrant, unmistakable, malty and hoppy odour of brewing-in-progress drifts on the air.

The hop plant from which they come is a vigorous, vine-like climber, but the cultivated strains used by brewers are difficult to grow. They need constant attention from early spring until late September, when the ripe cones – mature female flowers – are picked, and dried immediately in an oast-house. They are spread on the floor of a kiln, covered with a fine-mesh net, and hot air is passed through them from below.

Old oast-houses, with their steep, cowled roofs, used open fires for kilning, burning only smokeless fuel such as charcoal or best anthracite, because smoke spoils the hops. Modern kilns have closed furnaces, with smoke escaping through a chimney and fans driving hot air through the hops. The hop-drier's task calls for great skill, experience and nice judgment: the hops must emerge just dry enough to be stored, but with their brewing properties still intact.

They are by weight the most expensive of the brewer's ingredients, and are grown principally in the Weald districts of the south-east, and in the Hereford and Worcester area.

After the hops are added, the wort bubbles and boils for about two hours – this is the time during which beer acquires its bitterness. Boiling has another important function: it sterilises and concentrates the wort.

After boiling, the wort is drained off into another tank called a hop-back, the bottom of which forms a sort of giant sieve, trapping the hops but allowing the wort to filter through them and then through a cooler into a fermenting tank.

The brewer has made the unfermented wort in about 12 hours, but much more time will elapse before the wort becomes beer. It needs to ferment for around five days, and to start this off the yeast is now added – or pitched, as the brewer would say. Before this is done the wort must have

COOLING IT *This small cooler at the Donnington Brewery reduces the temperature of the wort as it flows from the hop-back into the fermentation tank, ready for the yeast to be added.*

cooled to about 60°F (16°C), which allows the yeast to multiply. The tank is kept cool afterwards, usually by internal cold-water pipes, to control the rise in temperature that results from fermentation.

As fermentation proceeds, the living yeast feeds on the nutrients in the wort, using up sugars as it does so and producing alcohol, carbon dioxide gas and other compounds. As the yeast grows, it collects on the surface of the wort and is carefully skimmed off from time to time.

The brewer ends up with about five times as much yeast as he started with, and after storing some to use again he sells the surplus for food and tonic preparations. Different beers call for different yeasts, and care is taken to keep individual strains free from infection by wild yeasts.

When fermentation is complete and the surface yeast has been skimmed off, the beer is allowed to rest so that any yeast remaining can settle out. Then the beer is run off into storage, or racking, tanks. However, this so-called 'green beer' is still not ready for drinking – it needs to mature, or 'come into condition'.

Cask-conditioned beer is run out of the racking tank into casks of up to 36 gallons, and may have a handful of dry hops added for extra aroma. Finings, usually isinglass, and a little sugar are also added, and the beer is allowed to come into condition in the pub cellar. There, once the cask is at rest, the finings sink to the bottom, at the same time precipitating any remaining solids left suspended in the beer, and leaving it bright and clear.

This takes about 24 hours, and beer finished in this way continues to ferment in the cask and is 'live'. Once tapped, it must be drunk within a week or so, after which it begins to deteriorate.

An alternative method is to condition the beer and add finings in brewery storage tanks. It can then be sent directly

HOP-PICKERS A CENTURY AGO

Shades of a long-lost Victorian summer ... workmen fasten up a bale – or surplice – of hops, fresh-picked by the men and women in the background. The time is 1880, and the place is Amery Farm, Alton, in Hampshire. During brewing, hops are added as the wort steams and bubbles in the copper, and give beer its bitterness and heady aroma. Their secret ingredient is the golden dust at the base of the 'petals' in the female hop cone. It contains oils and resins not normally soluble, but which will dissolve in the wort as it boils. From the resins comes the bitter tang, and from the oils, the aroma.

PALE FOR INDIA

India pale ale was brewed originally for export to India – hence labels like that on the left. The story goes that 300 hogs-heads of it, saved from a shipwreck in the Irish Sea, proved so popular when sold by the underwriters in Liverpool in 1827 that the fame of 'India beer' spread rapidly throughout Britain.

to pubs for immediate consumption. Other beers, also matured in storage tanks, may be filtered instead of fined, removing any solid matter completely instead of letting it collect at the bottom of the container. These are 'bright' or 'keg' beers, and keep longer than cask-conditioned brews, as fermentation is halted completely.

Most canned and bottled beers are bright, and are usually pasteurised as a guard against deterioration by microbiotic infections. Some keg beer is pasteurised for the same reason.

There are well over 1,200 different beers available in Britain, a richer variety than in any other country. These variations on a main theme are achieved by cleverly manipulating the basic recipe – that is, by blending malts and perhaps adding other cereals to the mash tun, according to whether the brew is to be mild or bitter, pale or brown.

Advantage is taken, too, of the unique characteristics of the brewery's particular water supply – its liquor. This is where the head brewer's expertise comes into its own. He is the man who sees that the customers in the pubs his brewery serves get the flavour they prefer – and that they continue to get it.

His craft began to take on new dimensions in the 17th and 18th centuries. Before then, travellers in certain areas had noted that the ale seemed particularly good there, but nobody could fathom out why. Gradually, however, it was realised that the water used was in some way responsible and, as science advanced, that certain waters were good for some beers but poor for others.

The secret of London stout

Investigations confirmed marked differences in their chemical make-up. The water at Burton upon Trent, for example, was found to be strong in gypsum – calcium sulphate – which accounted for the excellence of the pale ale for which the district was, and is, renowned. London, on the other hand, was famed for its rich, dark beers and heavy stouts, due to calcium carbonate and some sodium chloride in the water. Other areas, notably in the south, brewed delicious mild ales, because the water contained plenty of calcium chloride and some gypsum.

Armed with this information brewers could, of course, 'doctor' their water to suit the sort of beer they wanted to make, by adding or removing appropriate salts. Nowadays most brewing liquor is treated in this way, but even so, the best – and cheapest – method is to use natural water for the type of brew to which it is best suited.

Water apart, the different types of beer are produced, broadly speaking, by varying the content of the grist and mash. Malts for pale ales are cured more lightly than those for dark beers, and often small but critical quantities of other cereals are added. Among these extra cereals are wheat, rice, maize and even unmalted barley. Sugar, too, may be added at the boiling stage, often for greater strength.

The proportion of hops that goes in is relatively small – much smaller, indeed, than was used before the Second World War. Pre-war beer would be too bitter for today's drinkers, say the brewers.

In modern times, too, the terms 'ale' and 'beer' have come to mean the same drink. However, ale was once relatively weak, made without hops and drunk in large quantities; beer was altogether stronger stuff, made with hops. Today's beers usually have an alcoholic content of 3.5 per cent by weight, but strong ales may contain 11–12 per cent.

Stout is brewed like beer, but a proportion of roasted barley or malt and other ingredients are added to the normal malt before mashing, which gives it that characteristic dark colour.

Lager is brewed with a yeast different from that used in other types of beer. The yeast sinks to the bottom during fermentation, which takes place at between 43–54°F (6–12°C), compared to 57–68°F (14–20°C) for other beers. Fermentation and conditioning usually take longer: the name of the brew derives from the extended period of cold storage known as 'lagering'. Commercial lagers, though light in colour, can contain some highly alcoholic beers.

Head brewers are understandably reticent about discussing exactly how they juggle the various elements of their beers. However, Claude Arkell, owner and brewer of the small Donnington Brewery, in the Cotswolds, says that he uses 10 cwt of straight barley malt, without added cereals, for each 650 gallon brew of bitter. He adds just 14 lb. of hops, and drinkers at his 17 pubs testify to its quality.

FILLING UP
Some breweries still use wooden casks, though metal ones are now more common – brewers claim that metal casks make no difference to the beer. The word barrel, often misused, refers to a cask of a specific size, holding 36 gallons. A kilderkin is a cask holding 18 gallons, a firkin takes 9 gallons and a pin 4½ gallons.

THE
MILLWRIGHT

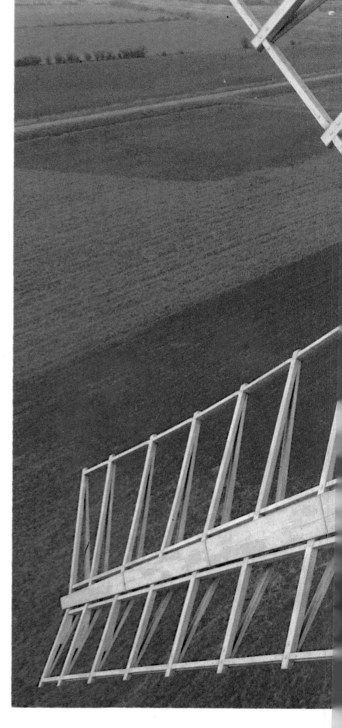

ONLY 70 YEARS AGO, THERE WERE THOUSANDS
OF WORKING MILLS IN BRITAIN. LIKE SAILING SHIPS,
THEIR DECLINE CAME WITH THE DEVELOPMENT OF
STEAM AND DIESEL ENGINES

Windmills and water-mills are like old ships: the same demands made on human ingenuity and the elements, the same massive use of timber and iron, the same sense of personality. Even in decrepitude they are alike, for perhaps the only fragment of industrial archaeology to equal an old, neglected ship in pathos is an abandoned mill. Its tattered arms reach out to touch the hearts of the most prosaic county council, and send preservation societies into a flurry of jumble sales. And it is this urge to rebuild and restore that keeps the few remaining millwrights in business.

In their heyday, mills represented some of the most remarkable achievements in man's technical development. Who was it that first harnessed the insubstantial air to grind corn or, centuries earlier, set a water-wheel to turn millstones through a pair of gears? They are long forgotten, but they were men of genius.

Water-wheels, the ancestors of turbines, were known to the Greeks as long ago as 65 BC, and may have come to Britain with the Romans. Windmills, on the other hand, were probably brought to Europe by Crusaders returning from Middle Eastern lands where streams of sufficient size to power water-mills were rare. In both cases, it seems quite possible that the Chinese invented them first and that their ideas penetrated slowly westwards along the ancient caravan routes.

But once armed with the principles, Europe was swift to make its own adaptations, the most far-reaching of which was to turn the motive power – sails or water-wheel – from the horizontal to the vertical. Horizontal power simply turned a pair of stones, but vertical wheels or sails, working through gears, could perform all manner of tasks.

In Tudor England, and for centuries after, water-wheels not only ground corn, but also operated bellows for furnaces, drove fulling mills and forge trip-hammers, and powered irrigation systems and mine pumps. A whole range of overshot and undershot wheels was designed. There were wheels rimmed with buckets, wheels with blades angled to get the utmost velocity from the water supply – whether it struck from the top, the middle, or ran underneath – while leats (man-made channels), mill-ponds and sluices controlled the flow. By one means or another, almost any water source could be utilised, from mountain stream to estuary.

Windmills, due to the inconstancy of the element that drove them, were less versatile. Iron foundries, for example, could not wait for a calm to pass, though from the 17th century onwards some ingenious windmill adaptations produced materials as diverse as snuff, bone-meal, porridge oats, linseed oil and sawn timber. But for the most part British windmills were used for grinding cereals, and peas and beans for animal feed.

In the waterless Downs and the East Anglian plains, where the rivers were too sluggish to turn water-wheels effectively, wind-driven mills provided the only reliable source of power. And it was largely in such places that they reached their peak of usefulness.

A far cry from the little medieval post-mills that had to be dragged round into the wind by hand, the great wooden octagonal smock-mills and the majestic 80 ft multi-sailed tower-mills of Lincolnshire were marvels of engineering.

With the exception of the brickwork, every part of the mill, from the finial, or ornamental spike on top of the cap, to the front door, was built by the millwright. With saw, adze and chisels he converted massive baulks of timber into sails, drive-shafts, wind-shafts, cog-wheels and all the complexity of machinery that has to be contained within the body of the mill.

SAILS TO THE WIND

Windmills can work only when the sails are turned into the wind. The most primitive mills (1) are hauled round bodily by means of a tailpole, operated by man, beast or windlass. Since the late 18th century, however, British milling problems have been eased by the fantail – a small, secondary windmill set at right-angles to the main sails. This turns the entire post-mill (2) or the cap in the case of the smock-mill (3).

1

2

3

Because millwrights are by nature innovators, no two mills are exactly the same, and this is reflected especially in the cunning arrangement of ancillary machinery, such as sack hoists, sifters, bolters and wire machines for dressing flour, that all worked by a system of gear wheels off the main drive.

In Britain there are three main types of windmill: the post-mill, and the smock and tower-mills. The first and oldest type is so called because the entire mill is mounted on a heavy post on which it can be swivelled round into the wind. But with the others – and notably the smock-mill, whose eight or ten-sided walls may or may not resemble an old-time labourer's smock – only the caps bearing the sails revolve.

In most British mills, the sails are kept constantly facing into the wind by means of a brilliant 18th-century in-

vention called the fantail. In effect, this is a small windmill set behind the building at a right-angle to the main sails; when the wind veers, it catches the fantail and turns the cap – or the entire mill in the case of post-mills – to face into it.

This is not just a matter of working the mill. In a gale, a mill turned away from the wind can have its sails torn out. Building the ponderous and complicated turning mechanism was part of the old millwright's job, just as maintaining or replacing falls to his present-day successors.

When the millwright finished building Sibsey Mill in Lincolnshire in 1870, he signed his work by embedding his beer mug high up in the interior wall. Exactly a century later, the mill's restorer followed suit and embedded his beer mug alongside. This salute by one craftsman to another across the years gently underlines the sense of continuity that permeates the trade; modern millwrights may some-

WIND INSTRUMENT

Eighty-odd feet up Sibsey Mill, Mr Davies and his son make final adjustments to the windshaft, the axle of the sails. Running through the cap, it is set a few degrees off the horizontal in order to transfer some of the enormous weight of the sails to a bearing at its far end. White-leaded canvas shutters (inset) are then fitted to the sails. These can be opened and closed by cranks connected to a rod running through the windshaft to a chain-operated wheel at the rear of the cap.

times use modern tools, but the old ways are never forgotten.

For example, when Jim Davies, of Alford, Lincolnshire, was restoring one East Anglian mill, for once he forbore to use a crane to haul the 32–36 ft sails into place. Because the work had been commissioned by a local restoration society, he felt it more fitting to use the traditional method of ropes, blocks and tackle. Like yards being hauled up the mainmast of some man-o'-war, the great spars soared up the tower, with no more machinery involved than a small hand-operated windlass.

Like the other, and very few, full-time working mill-wrights in Britain, Mr Davies and his son are engaged entirely in restoration work, though some of the buildings are in so ruinous a state that the job is tantamount almost to building from scratch. They will rebuild any kind of mill, from ancient hand-mills to the puffing, steam-driven monsters that used to be taken out into the fields at the beginning of the century; from water-mills to the gallant little post-mills. But because they are Lincolnshire based, the main part of their work is on the great brick tower-mills of the area.

The degree of restoration depends on funds available. Some customers simply wish to refurbish a beloved landmark, in which case sails, cap and fantail are replaced, but the machinery is omitted. Others, wishing to taste again the delights of stone-ground flour, demand that their mill should be restored to full working condition, down to the last cog.

Although much of the work is done on site, a great deal also takes place in the workshop – a splendid, dim-windowed place smelling of rope, sawn timber, paint and oiled steel. It has been a millwright's shop since 1800, vouched for by a glacier of white lead on the wall by the door. This is the patch where, over 180 years, workmen rubbed their paintbrushes clean.

Among the earlier dabs were those applied by the men who built Alford Mill in 1813; later ones by Mr Davies's crew when they restored the mill in 1978.

Bench big enough for a sail

In the yard there is a 60 ft saw table. Though unused these 20-odd years since it became more practical to have timbers cut in a sawmill, it still makes a convenient bench when working on a whip, the backbone of a sail, consisting of up to 36 ft and three-quarters of a ton of pitch pine.

Leaning against the wall are a pair of millstones waiting to be dressed, and one or two more lie in the shed.

These are the very point of the mill; the reason for the great spread of sails, or the machinery of the water-mill. Each stone is about 4 ft across and weighs approximately a ton. They are constructed either from Derbyshire grit, generally used to grind cattle feed, or French burr, an immensely hard stone from the Paris Basin, that is better suited to the production of flour.

Within the mill they are arranged in pairs. The lower one, the bedstone, lies stationary while the runner stone rotates above it, driven by the drive-beam from the sails or the water-wheel. They are set at an infinitesimally tiny distance apart – close enough to grind the grain, yet they must never touch. If they do, they may suffer serious damage, or the friction beneath the stones may start a fire.

Maintaining or dressing the stones used to be the millwrights' winter bread and butter, and specialist stone-dressers also wandered from mill to mill after the harvest, renewing the worn and pitted surfaces of the stones and re-cutting the furrows that guide the milled grain out to the sacks waiting below.

Though no longer seasonal, it is still a highly skilled job,

requiring a steady hand and an unerring eye. Having levered the stones up and over, the work surfaces are smeared with raddle, a mixture of red oxide and water that highlights any unevenness. The dresser then chips at the surface with a mill-bille, an oddly primitive-looking implement consisting of a steel pick set into a handle called a thrift. An expert millwright makes 16 cuts to the inch in the furrows, the cuts becoming progressively more shallow from the skirt, or edge of the stone, to the centre.

Mr Davies's workshop casually records the story of millwrighting over the last century or so. There are bundles of patterns from which the cranks were cast for the sail shutters on mills long defunct, representing what was probably the last major development in windmill technology.

Until the mid-18th century, British mills were powered literally by sails – more or less jibsails that had to be reefed or furled like sails on a ship to conform to the wind. Then, in 1772, Andrew Meikle, a Scottish millwright who had already invented the threshing machine, produced the spring sail, in which the framework attached to the whip was covered by canvas shutters. Working rather on the principle of the Venetian blind, the system had the great advantage that the sails could be opened or closed to gain or spill wind without stopping work.

Various improvements followed, the most important of which was an arrangement allowing the miller to adjust the shutters without touching the sails at all. The shutters were mounted on cranks geared to a rod running through the

STREAMS IN HARNESS

The water-wheel represents one of man's earliest and most successful attempts at harnessing nature to his own purposes. Two of the most common types are shown. The overshot wheel (top) is used where there is a high velocity of water but little volume, while the undershot wheel is more successful in slower-flowing streams with a good volume of water.

RIVER POWER TO GRIND THE GRAIN

A late-18th-century engraving of how a simple water-mill works. The horizontal drive of the undershot wheel (1) is converted via the pit wheel and lantern gear to the vertically turning main beam (2). This works the great spur wheel (3) that through another gear, called a stone nut, operates the runner stone; this, with the stationary bedstone, is concealed within the stone case or vat (4). Grain is fed to the stones through the hopper (5), and the ground meal is discharged into sacks through a sieve.

STONE AND STEEL

Good flour is a matter of the clean cutting of the wheat grain. As the grain moves between the millstones from the centre to the edge, it is sliced by a myriad sharp-edged cracks – about 16 to the inch – cut into the working surfaces of the stones. But after some two weeks' steady work, even the immensely hard French burr facings of the runner stones – like the one on the left – become worn, and the cracks have to be re-cut. Nowadays, this is done by the millwright, but at one time it was carried out by stone-dressers who travelled from mill to mill. It takes several days to re-crack a pair of stones. First, the surfaces are brushed with a feather dipped in raddle, a red-ochre mixture, to highlight any unevenness. These are the places where the cracks have become dulled, and have to be re-cut by steady chipping with a mill-bille, making the deeper and closer cracks at the circumference and fading towards the centre. An occasional job is to re-cut the furrows that convey the meal out of the stones. This is done with a sharp-pointed mill-pick.

central windshaft to a chain-wheel at the back of the mill, and, by hauling on a chain, the miller could move the shutters. Installation and repair, however, could be a hazardous business, and there are many stories of old-time millwrights being seized upon by a wandering gust and whirled up into the air – trapped by hand or foot between a shutter and the whip.

Apart from the crank patterns, which differ in angle for each part of the sail's length, and differ again between mill and mill, Mr Davies also hangs on to large quantities of enormous nuts, bolts and pulley wheels, 'just in case'. Lengths of coarse green canvas lie waiting to be stretched over the shutter frames and daubed with white lead, and there is usually some massive piece of carpentry under way – a ball-topped finial for example, like a newel post of some gigantic balustrade, or the solid oak barrel for a sack hoist being shaped on the lathe. This is powered by an elegant cast-iron engine that looks as though it did former service on an African riverboat; it has run sweet and true since 1936.

But most impressive is a 9 ft diameter, 71-cog brake wheel which, like many of the working wheels in a mill, is made almost entirely from wood – elm for the rims, oak for the cogs. These are rough-cut and hammered into the rim before being shaped by a chisel from the enviable row that hangs above the work-bench.

Installed in a mill, the brake wheel turns on the windshaft just behind the hub of the sails; it is named from the brake on the rim that can normally stop the sails turning, though a sudden high wind can defeat it. Meshing with the brake wheel, and turning the power from the vertical to the horizontal, is the cast-iron wallower, a cog-wheel that operates the main drive to the stones and powers much of the ancillary machinery as well.

The advantages of marrying wooden with cast-iron cogs were discovered long ago. Worn wooden cogs can be replaced fairly easily; there is less risk of sparks and fire; and, above all, compared with the deafening hullaballoo of iron upon iron, there is a blessed, relative silence. A deep knowledge of wood is part of the millwright's craft, from the installation of ponderous, weight-bearing oak beams to the last covering of springy spruce planks curving over the cap.

Looking at the tower-mills, standing smart as sentinels in their black-and-white livery and punctuating the flat Lincolnshire landscape, it is easy to forget what hard taskmasters they were, both to the men who built and maintained them, and to those who worked them. The wind does not conform to regular working hours and, despite the aid of sack hoists, many millers' men spent their days in heaving 20 stone sacks of flour or meal.

Then, too, the nobility of craftsmanship must have been far from the minds of the millwright's crew as they struggled 80 ft off the ground with frozen sails.

It might be argued that mills have had their day, and that their preservation is a reminder of times best forgotten. Yet at the same time they do represent something rather splendid. There is the cunning of men's minds set to overcome the apparently ungovernable elements, and there is the harmony of simple things – of wood, iron and stone – playing in perfect orchestra. As with the last clipper ships, the beauty of mills is a happy accident, the result of using natural materials with a practical purpose in mind.

MILLWRIGHT'S TOOLS

Pointed picks and chisel-ended billes are wedged into handles called thrifts. Since millstones are extremely hard, both types of blade are of high-carbon steel. Even so, tiny splinters fly off and embed themselves in the dresser's hands. Once it was customary for the man to 'show his metal' – that is his hands – to prove his experience.

THE
MODEL MAKER

FOR A LUCKY FEW, A BOYHOOD HOBBY BECOMES
A PROFESSION IN WHICH ART AND CRAFTSMANSHIP
COMBINE TO PROMOTE TOTAL JOB SATISFACTION

*S*mall is truly beautiful to the model maker. His miniature world of trains and planes, cars and castles, ships and soldiers represents in many cases the fruitful maturity of a talent that blossomed in boyhood. The 'toys' he made then – perhaps from construction kits – have given way to works that demand the highest levels of craftsmanship. Some would call them works of art. For a fortunate few of these men, an obsessive hobby has become a most satisfying profession.

Classic cars in meticulous detail

Such a man is Gerald Wingrove, who makes models of classic cars. So accurate, so detailed and so finely finished are they that, unless they are photographed alongside something that reveals their one-fifteenth scale, they could be taken for the Bentleys, Bugattis, Alfa Romeos and Ferraris that inspired them. And it is with photographs of the real thing that he commences work.

He takes pictures from at least nine different angles, then makes precise measurements. From these pictures and measurements he is able to make accurate scale drawings. Ensuring that just one front wing is the correct shape can call for half-a-dozen separate measurements, backed by several clear photos. Equal care is taken with all the bodywork, a three-dimensional amalgam of curves and angles which, given the slightest error at the drawing stage, will look hopelessly wrong on the finished model.

Again working from accurate drawings, the chassis frame components are cut out of sheet brass with a fine saw and silver-soldered together, using a gas flame rather than a soldering iron to generate the high temperatures needed. A leaf spring is built up, leaf by small leaf, from shaped strips of brass. A single component, such as the supercharger for a 'blower' Bentley, can entail a daunting amount of work. It is assembled from four pieces of metal, each machined from a solid block, plus smaller details ranging from carburettor to fuel pipes – all carefully fixed together with tiny bolts and metal dowels.

Even a handbrake lever mounted outside is a complex affair calling for nine metal components. The handle itself is turned and tapered on a lathe, and the minute release trigger is bent into shape from sheet brass.

The main bodywork panels are made the way real ones were made before machinery supplanted craftsmen: by beating them into shape over wooden patterns. The patterns must be carved from a wood such as pearwood that is tough enough to withstand the hammering. Mr Wingrove uses aluminium for his panels. First he anneals it by heating it then allowing it to cool, to release all the internal stresses in the metal. This is delicate work, for too much heat will buckle or melt the aluminium in an instant.

He beats a panel into shape with a soft-faced hammer – one face rubber and the other plastic – to avoid damaging

the metal. However, this beating hardens up the metal, which must be annealed again before final shaping is carried out with a light jeweller's hammer.

Whenever possible, materials similar to those in the real car are used – but not always. Leather, for example, has a texture too coarse for one-fifteenth scale models, so Mr Wingrove uses pearwood instead. In fact the interiors of his open cars are made in part from the wooden patterns used to shape the panels, but they are hollowed out and carved to represent the contours and textures needed. The seats are carved with the correct number of pleats and buttons, with a thick paint mixture sprayed on at low pressure to simulate the look of leather. Hoods and tonneau covers of canvas are much too crude, so Mr Wingrove makes his from satin, welding the pieces together with a soldering iron rather than stitching them. The bodywork is given five thin coats of paint before being polished to a rich, deep shine.

No mechanical component is overlooked, from spark-plugs to shock absorbers. All are painstakingly made by hand. However, Mr Wingrove feels that adding working features – apart from doors that open and bonnets that lift to

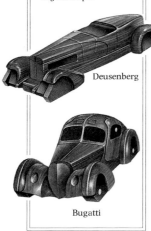

CARVED PATTERNS

Two of the beautifully carved wooden patterns made by Gerald Wingrove. He uses them to beat out the metal bodywork panels for his finished models, shaping small sheets of aluminium with soft-faced hammers and smoothing them finally with a jeweller's hammer. The top pattern is for an American Deusenberg and the bottom one for a rare Bugatti coupé.

Deusenberg

Bugatti

reveal mechanical detail – would be counter-productive. He reckons that no practical model can be built on this scale and be truly accurate: handling bodywork made in metal of scale thickness would be like grabbing a full-sized car in a mechanical crusher. To build steering gear and suspension that worked would demand oversize components or parts too fragile to be practical.

However, some idea of the lengths to which he will go to achieve an authentic look may be judged from the way he makes the wheels and tyres.

The tyres are cast from cold-cure silicone rubber, which can faithfully reproduce the subtle details of tread patterns and trade marks. First he makes a master pattern in Perspex, turned on a lathe, from which two half-moulds are cast in rubber. The half-moulds are then used to cast another master in silicone rubber, on which any final details can be carved. This second master is used to cast a pair of much harder half-moulds in resin – from which the actual tyres for the model are finally cast.

Most of the wheels are turned on a lathe from brass or aluminium, with slots and other details pierced or milled to

the correct profile later. But the wire-spoke wheels so characteristic of classic sports and racing cars are built in a quite different way. The rims and hubs are turned on the lathe, then fixed in a Perspex jig. This holds them in position while the spokes – made from stainless-steel wire – are threaded into place through precisely spaced holes in the jig. When the tyre is put on the rim, the result is nothing less than perfection in miniature – and anything less is not acceptable to Mr Wingrove.

The beauty of sail

Some of Mr Wingrove's exquisite carving in miniature can be found in a quite different context at the small but fascinating Maritime Museum in the village of Bucklers Hard in Hampshire. It decorates the elaborate stern of one of the many superb ship models built by Pat Curtis, an ex-submariner who has worked at the museum since leaving the Royal Navy 19 years ago. He made model ships as a boy; he made them on patrol beneath enemy waters; and now he makes them for the museum. They are a world and two centuries apart from Gerald Wingrove's jewel-like cars, but

MASTERPIECE IN MINIATURE

Lifting the bonnet of a model Bentley adds a new dimension to the extraordinary illusion of reality created by its maker, with its finely detailed engine and other mechanical components. Only the scale drawing on which it stands gives the game away ... while a second glance at the maestro at work in the smaller picture reveals that the bonnet strap he is adjusting is on that same model Bentley. The outside handbrake lever alone is made up of nine separate components.

TAKING SHAPE *The curved frames of a new model of the* Agamemnon *are assembled in place. Even before the planking is fixed over them, the eventual lines of the hull are already easily discernible.*

his dedication to accuracy and authenticity are no less obsessive.

The models he constructs with meticulous craftsmanship are of the wooden merchantmen and fighting ships built in this small village on the Beaulieu River from oaks of the New Forest. Ships like the 74-gun *Illustrious*, launched in 1789, and the 64-gun *Agamemnon* – a favourite of Nelson, who took command of her in 1793. Mr Curtis builds to a scale of $\frac{1}{4}$ in. to 1 ft, and the *Illustrious* model needed 840 ft of $\frac{1}{16}$ by $\frac{1}{4}$ in. planking for its decks and hull. The guns were turned on a lathe from 28 ft of brass rod, and the woods used included birch, box, apple, lime, pear, obechi and raimin. The rigging required 2,240 knots.

He works in a small wooden shed behind the museum, using very few tools – fine cabinet-making saws and fretsaws, sharp knives, the odd chisel or two and a small electrically driven universal machine tool of a type popular with many serious model makers. He cannot, of course, photograph the long-vanished ships – but he can and does obtain detailed plans of them ready-drawn. The National Maritime Museum at Greenwich preserves the original

THOUSANDS OF KNOTS

Rigging a model with total authenticity is a major task in itself, calling for thousands of knots. Mr Curtis has the good fortune to possess two magnificent reference books: Steel's Elements of Mastmaking, Sailmaking and Rigging, *published in 1794, and* The Young Sea Officer's Sheet Anchor, *dated 1808. He also has miniature rope-making equipment to ensure that every piece of cordage and cable is to scale.*

builders' draft of them, and can supply photostat copies.

These plans show the details of hull construction in plan, profile and section – the frames are even numbered from stem to stern. For Mr Curtis, the reproduction of the component parts in miniature is simply a matter of working out the scale, cutting them out – mostly with a fretsaw – and assembling them 'like Meccano', as he puts it. The keel, stem, sternpost and deadwood are assembled on a wooden base, and the floors – cross-pieces set at right-angles across the keel – fixed in place. The curved frames are then cut and jointed to the floors, so that together they form U-sections of differing widths along the keel, narrow at the bows, widening amidships and narrowing again at the stern.

He explained his methods as he worked on a new model of *Agamemnon*, using elm for the main timbers because he had some to hand and thinks the wood entirely suitable. But he added that if he was building a model to be exhibited with the frames and other timbers exposed to show methods of ship construction, he would use oak for authenticity.

Planking is fixed on with brass pins, and detailed work such as the ship's wheel, deck-housings, stern galleries and other features are carved from boxwood or fruitwoods. However, when masts, sails and rigging are to be made, Mr Curtis augments his own wide knowledge by consulting a splendid pair of old books: *The Young Sea Officer's Sheet Anchor* by Darcy Lever, and *Steel's Elements of Mastmaking, Sailmaking and Rigging*. The first is concerned with sails and rigging, and with all aspects of ship-handling in those days. Both are lavishly illustrated with highly detailed, diagrammatic engravings, and Mr Curtis uses them not only for planning the rigging of models, but also for calculating the height of masts, width of yards, length of booms – even the weight of rope and cordage.

Steel's, for example, tells him that for ships of the Royal Navy, the height of the mainmast is obtained by adding together the 'length of the lower deck and the extreme breadth' of the hull, then dividing the total by two. The foremast is eight-ninths the height of the mainmast and the mizen-mast three-fifths. To ensure that ropes and hawsers look right and are in scale, Mr Curtis has a small rope-maker's jack and top (see *The Rope Maker*, p. 162), and he lays them up in hemp and cotton. All the blocks and tackle, dead-eyes, chain-plates – even cleats and belaying pins are faithfully reproduced.

But he is not keen on sails, believing that they seldom really look right on models, as they cannot be filled with wind and tend to spoil the symmetry of the bare masts and rigging. 'If I have to make them, I get my daughter to do the sewing,' he says. His models are either painted in their authentic colours, or finished with a fine, clear varnish that enhances the beauty of the timber he uses, and allows many details of construction to remain visible.

Armies in miniature

Toy soldiers were the boyhood passion of Len Taylor. They still are, though nowadays he makes them by the hundred in a tiny workshop at the end of his garden in Penarth, near Cardiff. He turns out more than 400 different variations on soldiers from individual regiments, all accurately uniformed and decorated according to the campaigns in which those regiments fought.

His armies in miniature are in demand all over the world, and among his latest creations are the men and animals of every unit which served with Kitchener in the Sudan – not to mention the white-clad Dervishes and mailed horsemen of Britain's adversary there, the Mahdi.

But every soldier, no matter what his eventual role is to be, starts off as one of a small set of basic figures cast in tin, which serve as masters. They have no uniforms, headgear

two or three minutes is usually enough for a perfect reproduction – ready for painting.

His 'mass production' figures, though accurate, wear the glossy paints of the Victorian nursery. But his pride and joy are his 'connoisseur' figures, for the collector who wants a convincing miniature rather than a toy soldier. These are cast in a harder alloy that allows much sharper detail.

The paint is different, too, being matt-surfaced with muted tones and subtle shading to create a far greater illusion of reality. A grey-bearded standard bearer of the Mahdi's army has a hawk nose, tanned and weatherbeaten skin, and patched homespun clothes; Samurai warriors wear highly detailed costumes and equipment – carefully researched over months, and even years in some cases.

Such accuracy is not only satisfying and desirable – it is almost vital in what has become a most demanding craft. Some military model makers paint in the irises, pupils and whites of the eyes; they even add the tiny pink spots in the corners. And a medium-sized figure of an Imperial Guardsman in Napoleon's army must be detailed down to the eagles embossed on his buttons. Small worlds can, it seems, be just as competitive as the real one.

CENTRIFUGAL CASTING *Figures of men and animals are duplicated, with their fine detail preserved, by means of centrifugal casting. Moulds made from the master model are pressure-filled with molten metal, poured into the central hole of the circular casting machine as it revolves at high speed.*

or weapons, and are not detailed in any way. All their individual items of clothing, from a Highlander's kilt to a solar topee, must be shaped and added by hand.

Sometimes Mr Taylor will build up these details with solder, cutting and filing it to shape after it has cooled and hardened. However, mostly he uses an epoxy putty compound called Milliput, which is mixed in two parts to start its hardening process. By pacing his work carefully, he can cut the basic shape of, say, a back-pack or water bottle with a scalpel, while the compound is still soft. Then, when hardening is complete, he works on the detail with fine files. The skill involved is akin to that of a sculptor in miniature. Careful cutting and filing can even reproduce the hang and texture of chain mail, or the folds of a Hussar's cape.

When the figure is complete it is put in a small drop mould and a solution of cold-cure silicone rubber poured over it, to make a detailed mould from which a new tin master figure can be cast. Extra details are added at this stage, then a final rubber production mould is made – usually from a number of master figures at the same time, by centrifugal casting.

The production figures turned out from this final mould are also made by centrifugal casting. A molten tin-lead mixture is poured into the central hole of the casting machine as it revolves at several hundred revolutions per minute, forcing the mixture into every crevice of the moulds, which radiate from the hole like the spokes of a wheel. The speed of the centrifuge and the time taken to cast the figures vary with the proportions of the mixture, but

ANGEL OF DEATH

Labour of love . . . Mr Taylor at work on his personal favourite, a Polish winged Hussar – a fearsome 17th-century cavalryman who wore a 4 ft high feathered head-dress through which the wind would whistle as he charged. His terrified enemies called him the Angel of Death. Mr Taylor had to go to the National Army Museum in Warsaw to get full information about the Hussar, but the result is a wealth of detail over which the connoisseur can enthuse.

THE NET MAKER

MACHINES CAN TURN OUT NETS BY THE ACRE
IF NECESSARY ... BUT ONLY NIMBLE FINGERS
CAN SHAPE AND MEND THEM

*T*he sight of fishermen absorbed in mending their nets has aroused pangs of envy among generations of town-dwelling summer visitors to little harbours all around the coastline of Britain. And it will continue to do so, for while machines can now turn out netting at high speed, almost every other task in the industry is done by hand – mending included.

Machines cannot shape a net. Neither can they finish its edges nor fix on the floats, ropes and other fittings needed for whatever job it may be designed to do in fishing, sporting, industrial or domestic use. These tasks are reserved for nimble fingers, which is why there are hundreds of men and women still engaged in the work – especially in and around Bridport. This small Dorset town is probably the largest net-making centre in England, as it has been for three centuries and more.

Hand-made netting is still produced, but usually only for specialised and awkwardly shaped items such as aircraft cargo slings, billiard-table pockets and heavy climbing nets. These are made mostly with natural materials – hemp, cotton or flax twine of varying thickness – as opposed to the man-made fibres used in netting produced by machine.

But while machines have grown ever more complex since their introduction 160 years ago, little in the way of equipment is needed to make netting by hand – known in the craft as 'braiding'. The most important tool is the braiding or netting needle, which is illustrated on the opposite page. This tool is nothing like a needle. It is flat, about 6 in. long as a rule, pointed at one end and deeply grooved at the other; the front half is cut out, leaving a toothpick-like tongue pointing forwards. The needle can be loaded with twine, which is looped over the tongue, taken back around the groove at the rear, then forwards to loop around the tongue again – and so on until a suitable length of twine is wound on.

The width and length of the needle depends on the size of netting and the thickness of twine employed.

The other essential tool is the mesh-pin, also called a measuring-stick or lace. This can be either a round or flat piece of wood, around which the twine is passed before being knotted – ensuring that each 'hole' in the net is the same size.

Finally a firm bench is needed, equipped with a ring or post to which the first loop of the net is tied. From then on the process is rather like that involved in knitting: the meshes are made by tying a series of sheet-bend knots in successive loops of twine. The net maker does this by passing the braiding needle through the meshes and manipulating it to tie the knots.

The sheet bend was used originally to attach a rope – or 'sheet' – to a small loop, or eye, at the corner of a sail. The rope is passed up through the eye from behind, looped around the back of it, then tucked under itself at the front, so that it is nipped tight by any pull on the rope. The greater the pull, the tighter the knot holds.

Net makers have two different ways of tying this knot – the fisherman's method and the Bridport method – according to how they loop the twine and manipulate the braiding needle. There are still arguments about which is the faster, but either way a skilled worker operates at very high speed. When making something small, such as a billiard-table pocket, he can tie about 40 knots a minute. The mesh-pin ensures that all the meshes are the same size, but tying all the knots at an even tension calls for nice judgment.

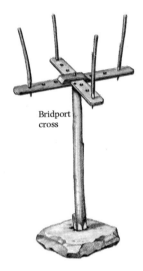

Bridport cross

BRIDPORT – NET-MAKING CENTRE OF BRITAIN

For three centuries and more, Bridport and the villages around have formed the largest net-making centre in Britain. Women have always played a large part in the industry and this picture, taken in 1913, shows a typical scene from that era in the small village of Eype, about 1½ miles from the town. Mrs Prunella Hodder is working outside her home, Balloon Cottage, making a net with the aid of a twine swifter, known also as a 'Bridport cross'. The twine is wound around the upright sticks of the cross, which revolves as the braiding proceeds and the twine is used up. Nets are still braided by hand in Bridport, but usually only for such specialised items as billiard-table pockets, heavy climbing nets, cargo slings and so on. Much of the hand-work done now is concerned with shaping and finishing nets for specific uses in industry, sport, agriculture and fishing – and even in the home.

When synthetic twine such as nylon is being used, the net maker puts an extra loop in the knot, which is then called a double sheet bend. This is for extra security, because knots in twine or rope made with synthetic fibres are more prone to slip than those in natural-fibre cordage.

As the twine on the braiding needle runs out, a new piece is joined on with a reef knot – also called a weaver's knot. By careful planning, the knot can be placed unobtrusively at the side of the net. The reef knot was also used for the braiding process in Roman times, and is still employed by net makers in the Far East.

Some meshes are square and others diamond-shaped. They are all one to the net maker, who can also shape a net. He – or she – can widen it, narrow it or taper it simply by casting on extra meshes or reducing the number. Net-making machines are not designed to do this, being concerned with turning out large sheets which are then cut and fitted out for their specific tasks. The first of these machines was called a jumper loom, because the operator had to jump smartly on to a large pedal to compress the 200 or so wire springs that worked the knot-tying mechanism. Around the turn of the century the jumper was superseded by a far more efficient power-operated machine invented by a Parisian named Zang. Others followed, but recently the market has been dominated by Japanese-made machines.

Machine-made nets are always diamond-meshed: if a square mesh is needed, the sheet of netting is cut diagonally across. The side edges are always loops, and extra width is

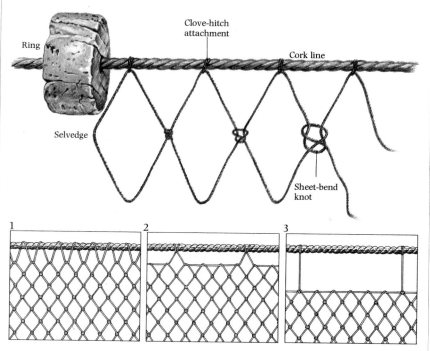

HOW A TYPICAL NET IS MADE BY HAND

A rope known as a cork line, stretched between posts or hung by rings, is used to start the first row of half meshes, made with a series of clove hitches from right to left. The second row is then tied on to the first in a series of sheet-bend knots, from left to right. The process is repeated, working from alternate ends and using a mesh-pin – or lace – to ensure that the meshes are of equal size. The sides of the net are called the selvedges.

Ring

Selvedge

Clove-hitch attachment

Cork line

Sheet-bend knot

VERTICAL NET SETTINGS *Three ways of narrowing the top and/or bottom, to make a net bag in the middle: 1. Reeving – passing a line shorter than the net's width through the top meshes. 2. Stapling – hitching every third mesh to the head-rope at intervals less than their total width. 3. Norselling – suspending every sixth mesh by a short line, again at intervals less than their total width.*

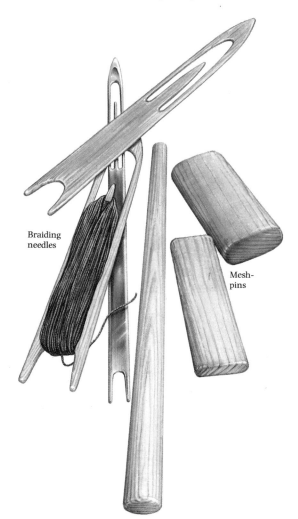

Braiding needles

Mesh-pins

SIMPLE TOOLS, DEXTROUS HANDS *Simple tools serve the net maker; dextrous hands do the rest. Braiding needles vary for different types of net – the wire one is for shrimp nets – and the mesh-pins are used to gauge the size of the meshes.*

obtained by joining more on with a half-mesh between the two pieces, the joint being undetectable. This is known as a 'shut' or 'cross join'. Meshes at the top and bottom of machine netting end in 'cut knots' – they are cut off below the last row of knots. An extra length can be tied on by what is called a 'scun' or 'long join'.

These are the more straightforward jobs in the often complex business of net-fitting – a part of the craft which has been likened to tailoring. The net maker may be called upon to shape, for example, a football net, which must fit the form of the goalposts and supporting poles, while having the correct slope at the back to prevent the ball from rebounding out of the goal. Some fishing nets, too, are subtly shaped to keep the strain even and spread the load. The shaping is done by altering the meshes by hand – as in braiding.

Many of these jobs are done by outworkers at home – several hundred in and around Bridport. They are paid reasonable piecework rates far removed from the sweated-labour conditions of earlier times. Towards the end of the 19th century, Bridport folk braiding nets at home were paid according to how much twine they used. A tennis net, for example, consumed nearly 800 yds of twine and required around 8,000 knots. This represented about eight hours' work, for which the net maker got 15 old pennies – 6½p.

Some large and awkwardly shaped net-fitting jobs need a lot of space and may be done at the net factory or in old sail lofts in the case of fishermen's nets. Trawler owners can save money by doing the work themselves, and of course inshore fishermen are continually repairing tears and holes worn in their own nets – as many holidaymakers know!

A SIGHT THAT HAS ALMOST VANISHED

Fishermen with cottages on gale-swept coasts would often secure their thatched roofs against the elements with sheets of stout netting stretched right over them, and lashed firmly to pegs built into the walls. Few are to be seen now; this is one of several preserved at the Manx Open-Air Folk Museum in the village of Cregneish.

THE
Organ Builder

'THE KING OF ALL INSTRUMENTS' OWES ITS BEING
TO CRAFTSMEN WHO COMBINE THE SKILLS OF METAL-
WORKING, WOOD-WORKING AND INSTRUMENTATION

Over 1,000 years ago a Saxon monk called Wulstan wrote a poem in which he praised the great organ in Winchester Cathedral. Though it may not have been as tuneful as the giant instruments found in Victorian town halls, it must certainly have been as loud. 'To such an amount does it reverberate, echoing in every direction, that everyone stops with his hands to his ears.' The wind was supplied by 26 bellows, 'worked by 70 strong men, labouring with their arms, covered with perspiration, each inciting his companions to drive the wind up with all his strength, that the full-bosomed box may speak with its 400 pipes that the hand of the organist governs'.

So, in the 10th century, the organ existed very much in the form we know today. And 1,000 years before Wulstan, Roman amphitheatres had echoed to the strident notes of the water-organ, or hydraulos, played as interlude music during gladiatorial shows, like cinema organs during the heyday of the cinema.

Reduced to its simplest terms, the organ consists of a set of pipes or whistles, each giving out a different note; a wind chest supplying air to the pipes at a constant pressure; and a keyboard which determines the notes to be sounded. The advent of electronics has not changed the basic concept of pipe organs, though in many modern instruments the connections between keyboard and pipes are made with electric circuits instead of mechanical levers. But in electric organs even the pipes have vanished, and the sound is produced electronically and amplified by loudspeakers.

Not that any organ purist would consider the electric organ to be a proper organ at all! The trend among today's organ builders is to confine the electrics to the bellows, dispensing with the need for the 'strong men', and in all other ways getting back to organs of the type familiar to J. S. Bach in the first half of the 18th century.

Anyone looking at even a modest-sized organ in a parish church must be struck by the enormous number of pipes, and must wonder whether they are all necessary. Their number is due to the fact that each 'stop' on the organ needs one pipe per key, and even the smallest chamber organ will have a dozen stops and 56 keys, making a total of 336 pipes. By contrast, the organ in Canterbury Cathedral has three keyboards, each with 58 keys, and a pedal-board with 30 keys, making 204 keys altogether. When these are multiplied by the number of stops controlled by each keyboard, you get a total of 4,343 pipes, which gives some idea of the size of the organ-builder's task. Each pipe is hand-made, then tuned before being fitted into the instrument, so it is little wonder that the organ-builder's craft demands a commitment and dedication without parallel among the makers of musical instruments.

Organ pipes are of two main types. Flues are the commoner, and they act on the principle of the tin whistle or recorder, with the sound produced when air is forced

SMALL BEGINNINGS

The medieval positive organ was so called because it was fixed in one place – as opposed to the portative organ, which could be carried about by the player. In the Middle Ages the organ was used to accompany secular songs, in the same way as other keyboard instruments. Its exclusive use as a church instrument came later.

The small chamber organ is a descendant of the positive organ. Such organs were often built for private chapels in great houses, and were also used for secular music, such as the organ concertos of Handel.

under pressure past a slot cut in its front. The other sort are 'reeds', in which the air is forced past a vibrating metal tongue into a conical pipe. Variations on these two basic types give the organ its unrivalled contrasts of tone colour, and enable the organist to have a complete orchestral palette at his fingertips.

When he sits down to play, he first decides what stop or combination of stops will give him the tone he requires. Each stop controls a rank, or 'register', of pipes, and the action of pulling out the stop brings the register into action by moving a slider, drilled with one hole per pipe, into a position where the holes coincide with the bottom ends of the pipes. This means that the pipes are now in potential contact with the air under pressure in the wind chest.

However, the air cannot enter any pipe until its individual key is depressed. The key is connected by a system of levers or 'trackers' to a 'pallet', which allows air into that particular pipe. So the principle is: each register is brought into play by a slider controlled by a stop; each pipe is sounded by depressing a key and releasing a pallet. This type of mechanical connection is known as 'tracker action'. It is the traditional action of the finest period of organ building, which lasted from the 14th century to the 19th century, and is becoming increasingly popular with both builders and organists today.

Working on the old and the new

Among the enthusiasts for the revival of the old-style organ is Noel Mander, whose organ workshops in London's East End tackle the complete job, from casting metal for the pipes to the final assembly in churches all round the world.

Apart from building new organs, his firm has been responsible for the restoration of many of the country's most famous instruments, such as the organs in Canterbury Cathedral and St Paul's. On a visit to the works you may find craftsmen carefully reconstructing a 17th-century chamber organ, far gone in woodworm and general decay; rebuilding the console of a large organ from a school chapel; or completing a brand-new instrument for a church in Nigeria, with a case made of wood chemically treated against termites.

The pipes of an organ begin life as ingots of metal. The first stage is to melt the ingots in the furnace of the casting shop, a process which takes place twice a year and involves melting down about 3 tons of metal on each occasion. The molten metal is poured on to a stone 'casting bench' – a slab about 15 ft long by 3 ft wide – where it solidifies into flat sheets of metal. Three main alloys of tin and lead are used, with names indicating the proportions of each. Commonest is 'plain metal' (15 per cent tin and 85 per cent lead), which has a silvery matt finish. Spotted metal (45 per cent tin and 55 per cent lead) is so called because, on cooling, the metals separate out to some extent, looking rather like a giraffe's coat in two shades of silver. It is used for the conical-shaped reed pipes. Finally, there is high-percentage tin (about 70 per cent tin and 30 per cent lead), which has a bright finish and is used for the front pipes, the public face of the completed organ. Other metals such as brass, are occasionally used for specialised pipework such as the 'Trompette Militaire' pipes in St Paul's Cathedral.

The pipes are made in the metal shop, according to specifications laid down in the drawing office, where every detail of the organ has been determined before construction begins. The metal sheets are planed into various thicknesses, depending on the eventual size of the pipes, which range from giants 16 ft long down to pygmies of less than half an inch.

Flue pipes are beaten into a cylindrical shape round wooden mandrels and then soldered along their length.

They consist of three parts; the 'body', or main tube, whose length determines the pitch of the note; the 'languid', or bar across the bottom of the slope or 'cut-up', which directs the wind upwards; and the conical 'foot' at the base of the pipe which connects it to the wind chest. The name languid comes from an old French word *languette*, meaning 'little tongue', and is a reminder of the international origins of the organ. The cut-up usually has 'ears' on either side to steady the note and prevent the force of the wind from being dissipated sideways.

Reed pipes are a good deal more complicated. As the body is conical, it has to be cut to an exact triangular shape before being beaten round the mandrel. The base of a reed pipe is in three distinct units, which together are known as the 'boot'. Central to the reed-pipe boot is the 'block', a small lead cylinder drilled to take the body at the upper end and the reed unit, or 'shallot', at the lower end. The second unit, the shallot – presumably so called because it looks a little like a small onion – consists of a brass tube with a metal tongue fixed to it at one end and free to vibrate at the other, on the principle of the reed of a mouth organ. The third unit of the base is an outer casing, with the block plus shallot inserted

THE MAIN ELEMENTS OF AN ORGAN

On this moderate-sized organ, the player operates two manuals or keyboards, and a pedal-board, each of which controls the air supply to a different set of pipes, giving in effect three different instruments. These are the great organ, the smaller positive organ, named after the medieval positive or fixed organ, and the pedal organ. The pipes are divided into different registers, which give different tone qualities and are brought into operation by pulling out the stop knobs ranged above the keyboard on either side. Air is supplied to the pipes by means of bellows, powered by a motor and blower. When the organist presses down a key, a complex system of levers or 'trackers' allows air to all the pipes for that particular note. Which pipe actually sounds is determined by the stop, which allows air to only one rank of pipes. Organs have both flue pipes and reed pipes. The foot of each pipe is set in the sound-board, which forms the upper side of the pallet box, so called from the hinged flaps or 'pallets' that allow air to enter the pipes.

KEY

A Keyboard
B Pedal-board
C Great organ
D Positive organ
E Pedal organ
F Stop knobs
G Bellows
H Motor and blower
I Trackers
J Flue pipes
K Reed pipes
L Sound-board
M Pallet box

THE TWO TYPES OF ORGAN PIPE

FLUE PIPE *This works on the principle of a flute or recorder. The foot or base of the pipe (A) is fixed into the body of the organ. Wind under pressure is forced from the foot across the upper lip of the mouth, or slot (B), and vortices of air in the upper part of the pipe (C) cause it to resonate. The pitch of the note is determined by the length of the pipe – the longer the pipe, the lower the note.*

REED PIPE *Its principle is the same as that of a clarinet, in which a single reed is held at one end and vibrates when air is forced past it. The central section that holds the reed (actually a metal tongue, B) is called the block; at its lower end it is connected to the air supply in the wind chest (A), and at its upper end to the resonating pipe (C). The tongue is held in place by a wire tuning spring (D), which alters the pitch of the note slightly when it is raised or lowered.*

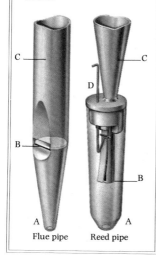

Flue pipe   Reed pipe

at the top, and connected at the base to the wind chest.

From the metal shop the roughly finished pipes are transferred to the voicing shop, where they receive the adjustments that turn them from crude noise-makers into finely tuned parts of a musical instrument. Voicing is a specialist's art, and the expert who carries it out has to bear in mind not only the actual pitch of the pipe, but also its position on the organ as regards the other registers, and even the musical requirements of the building where the organ will finally be installed. Each register of pipes then is placed in a 'voicing machine', a kind of skeletal organ which can provide a supply of wind while the necessary alterations are made.

Much of the voicing consists of removing metal from the pipe, especially from the mouth or cut-up of a flue pipe; in addition, the rough pipes will have been made deliberately too long in the metal shop, and now have to be cut to the exact length to give the correct pitch. Another aspect of voicing is the regulation of air pressure; this is done by means of a water gauge, which can measure the extremely light pressure needed to make an organ pipe 'speak', or sound in a musical way.

While the pipes are being made and voiced, the organ

casework and all the other wooden parts of the instrument are being cut out and assembled in the wood shop. These include a certain number of flue pipes, as some stops on the organ require the mellow tone of wood rather than the brighter sound of metal. Wooden pipes are square in section, consisting of four separate sides, not drilled like an oboe or other woodwind instrument. At Mander's, the keys are the only wooden parts not made in the workshop.

The casework is the frame that holds the pipes, keyboards, pedal-board, and action, whether mechanical or electronic. Probably the most complicated of all the wooden parts is the sound-board, which is carved with air channels to bring the air from the wind chest to the pipes. The sound-board also carries the pallets, which release the air to the individual pipes, and the sliders, which bring each rank or register of pipes into play. So it will be seen that the sound-board, which is built up in layers like a giant wooden sandwich, needs the greatest ingenuity both in its planning at the drawing stage and during its construction in the wood shop.

The final piece of the organ jigsaw is the console – the assembly of keys, pedals and stops at which the organist sits, corresponding to the instrument panel of a car. This is put

CASTING THE METAL FOR THE PIPES

Organ pipes are made of various alloys of tin and lead, of which the most common is called 'plain metal' (15 per cent tin and 85 per cent lead). The molten metal is poured from a large pivoted ladle or 'skillet' into a wooden box or 'gauge', which runs along the top of a slab of stone called a 'casting bench'. As the box has no bottom, the metal spreads on to the stone, and a narrow gap at the bottom of the box keeps it to a constant thickness. The box is held on either side by craftsmen, who run with the box from the ladle end of the bench to the far end, trailing a thin sheet of metal behind it. When the molten metal has set, it is planed smooth and is ready for shaping into pipes.

TUNING AN ORGAN *At the top of each pipe is a steel collar, which can be raised or lowered by tapping with a metal bar, thus altering the pitch of the pipe. Here the craftsman is actually inside the organ, working in a closely confined space.*

together in the console shop, which to the outside eye is a bewildering confusion of half-assembled keyboards, stop knobs and levers, and assorted electronic gadgetry. The electronics nowadays include printed circuits for the computerised major organs. These have memories which the organist can programme, so that stops come into action in certain orders or combinations, without the organist having to go through the frantic tugging of stops familiar in the old-fashioned organ loft. The ivory knob of each stop is carefully hand-engraved using a reducing machine, which reduces the larger scale lettering drawn on paper.

The names of the stops are a marvellous blend of the poetic and the practical. There are the various kinds of 'diapason', the fundamental stop which forms the groundwork of the organ's sonority. There are instrumental stops, some self-explanatory, like 'trumpet', 'trombone', 'viola' and 'French horn', and others not found elsewhere in music, like 'salicional' (a reedy-sounding stop whose name comes from *salix*, the Latin for 'willow') or 'larigot' (the old name for flageolet). There are stops which approximate to the voice, either of mankind ('vox humana') or of the heavenly hosts ('vox angelica'). Then there are 'mixture stops', which operate not only the register of pipes at the pitch of the note played, but pipes tuned to various harmonics above the note. This procedure strengthens certain overtones of the basic note, thereby altering the tone quality. Other stops couple together various major subdivisions of the organ, such as two of the manuals, or the pedal-board and one of the manuals.

Since most organs are tailor-made for an individual space in a particular building, the craftsmen who make them often have to travel halfway round the world to set them up and make sure they are working properly. Mander's have

made organs for Nigeria, Taiwan and Oman, as well as the more expected places such as the United States and South America. Prices vary enormously; but as a rough guide a small portable organ, of the type carried by angels in medieval paintings, costs something under £1,000, while a modest two-manual instrument with tracker action and electric bellows is in the region of £30,000.

The great 14th-century composer Guillaume de Machaut called the organ 'the king of all instruments'. In his day it was a comparatively crude affair, with a primitive keyboard which needed considerable strength to operate, and a limited number of stops. In the 600 years that have passed, the organ has mirrored every change in both music and the technology of wood and metal. By the time of Bach in the early 18th century, the French and German traditions had separated to some extent, the French preferring gentler, more subtle tones, while the Germans went in for robustness. In this country we relied on foreign makers, such as Bernhardt Schmidt, known as 'Father Smith', Renatus Harris and Johann Snetzler, who between them covered the period from about 1660 to 1790.

But all the music of Bach and the other masters of the organ requires great clarity in the interweaving lines of sound if it is not to become an indefinable mixture of sounds. The 19th-century cult of size and grandeur at all costs extended to the organ builder, who constructed massive instruments with multiple manuals and actions worked first by wind (pneumatic action) and later by electricity. Organ music followed suit and became ponderously slow and grandiose; even Bach's music suffered, becoming inflated out of all proportion, like an athlete pumped full of steroids. Detail and definition were lost, and the delicate structure of sound turned into a kind of porridge.

Today, organ builders have reacted against the worship of sheer size, and are producing instruments that Bach would have recognised as true successors to the organs of his own time. And even large modern organs, like the one in London's Royal Festival Hall, are far brighter than instruments of the fairly recent past, reminding us of the 'merry organs' that we sing about each Christmas but so seldom have the opportunity to hear.

ADJUSTING THE KEY ACTION

Each organ key is connected to the valve that lets wind into the pipes by a complex series of rods and levers called trackers. Careful adjustment of this part of the mechanism is needed to make sure that the touch on the keyboard is light and even.

THE PAPER MAKER

MEN HAVE MADE PAPER FOR NEARLY 2,000 YEARS.
A FEW STILL DO IT BY HAND – AND BY METHODS THEIR
ANCIENT PREDECESSORS WOULD RECOGNISE INSTANTLY

There is an almost sensual satisfaction in simply holding a great, creamy sheet of hand-made paper between finger and thumb, feeling its weight and texture, experiencing the urge to put pen or brush to an inviting surface – an urge that has been with man since he drew on cave walls. Which is just as it should be, since a lot of hand-made paper is produced for artists and lovers of penmanship, as well as for high-quality books, documents and other fine printing work.

The processes by which paper is made look astonishingly simple. They turn out on closer examination to be astonishingly complex, almost wholly dependent on the sensitive judgment and varied skills of the craftsmen involved. Seven years are needed for an apprentice to master these skills – the accumulated knowledge of nearly 2,000 years of paper making.

However, it was not until 1150 that these skills reached Europe, where cotton – or 'rag' as the paper maker calls it – was the material used up to about 1800. It is still used exclusively in one of the only two English mills remaining that make paper by hand on a commercial scale. This mill is at Wookey Hole, in Somerset, and production began there around 1610. Electricity now drives the still-simple machinery, replacing steam power which had in turn replaced the original water-wheel – just restored by the mill's owners.

The rag used there, like that of all European mills, was once literally composed of rags – cotton or linen waste. It arrived in cart-loads which went into the mill's rag room, where a team of women sat at a bench removing buttons and other non-cotton bits, then cutting up the pieces into rough squares about 5 in. × 5 in. This cut waste went into a huge, spherical boiler, where it was boiled in caustic soda to remove impurities.

The next stage was called 'breaking', in which the material was crushed and ground in constantly running water to destroy any remaining thread or weave pattern, separate the fibres, and remove all traces of caustic and dirt. The resultant thick cotton-and-water pulp – called 'half-stuff' – was then 'beaten' by hand or powered crushers again. This further crushed the fibres themselves, to make them absorb more water and increase the area of contact among them for better bonding later.

The prevalence today of cotton and man-made fibre mixtures, together with stiffening additives, has seriously reduced the availability of pure, clean cotton rag, and the mill now buys semi-processed raw cotton in sheet or flock form. This does not need cutting up, so the women have gone from the rag room and the great copper boiler stands idle. Neither does it need breaking, so the breaker – a Dutch-invented machine – is also unused. The process now starts with the beater, which is similar to the breaker in action. These two machines – called Hollanders and bought as a pair more than a century ago – both work by grinding the cotton-water mixture under a heavy roller in the beater.

The man who operates this machine – the beaterman – needs careful judgment, for his mixture may be in the machine for anything up to eight hours. It must contain the correct proportion of cotton to water for the type of paper being made, and the cotton fibres must be ground to the correct consistency and 'wetness'. The latter term applies to the amount of water actually beaten into the cellular structure of the fibres by the process. The 'wetter' the fibres become, the stronger and more compact will be the paper. Conversely, when the fibres are less heavily impregnated, the mixture is easier and quicker to drain, making a bulky, opaque paper. In the final stages of beating, a small amount of sizing mixture – usually a resin and alum mix, or an acid-free chemical size – is added to make the finished paper less absorbent – otherwise it would act like blotting paper.

During the whole process, the beaterman must watch that his mixture – or half-stuff – does not generate any lumps or knots. When he is finally satisfied with it, the beaten stock, looking something like thick porridge, is fed into a large, circular tank called a 'stuff chest'. There, a rotary stirrer keeps it agitated while it waits to go into the heated rectangular vat from which it will be sieved into sheets.

This vat also has an agitator, and is heated to keep the mixture warm enough to be handled in comfort.

Operating it is the 'vatman', whose first task is to transfer the pulp into the vat by means of a mixing pump, which adds a carefully controlled amount of water to the mixture, to bring it to the correct proportion of cotton and water for the type of paper being produced. For a thin paper, the cotton pulp content is as little as 1 per cent, increasing to 3 per cent for heavier qualities. The thick porridge becomes a thinner gruel.

The sieve on which the sheets are made is called a 'mould'. The vatman has two identical moulds and a single, lighter frame, the 'deckle', which fits closely around the

IT ALL STARTED IN CHINA . . .

So far as is known, the Chinese invented paper making around AD 105. It took another 1,000 years to reach Europe, via the rest of Asia and the Middle East. The first European paper-mill was set up in Spain in 1150, and Britain did not have one until 1494. All paper was made by hand until as late as the 19th century, when a paper-making machine was invented. The basic raw material has always been vegetable fibre, because of its composition and chemical properties. Cotton is generally thought to be the best, because its fibres are both long and strong. But many other plants and grasses have been used – notably rice in the East. And whole forests have been razed to provide the wood-pulp that feeds modern paper factories. The basic method of paper making is to beat and crush the fibres to a pulp in water, remove 'sheets' of mixture on a suitably shaped fine sieve, then bond together the fibres forming each sheet by pressure and heat.

SIEVING THE STUFF *The vatman lifts a sheet of stuff from his vat on a mould – a frame supporting a fine copper-wire mesh which acts as a sieve. As the water drains out, he gives the mould a double shake, backward-forward then left-and-right, to spread the fibres evenly.*

craftsman can turn out hundreds exactly the same in weight, colour and texture. So finely honed are the paper-maker's skills that they can be temporarily impaired by illness or personal stress problems. Sometimes, tragically, these skills never return.

The coucher – pronounced 'coocher' and deriving from the French verb *coucher*, meaning to lie down – works equally fast, synchronising his movements to the vatman's. He has before him a thick sheet of wool felt lying on a board. Beside him is a stack of similar felts. He quickly turns the mould face down on the felt, then lifts it, leaving the sheet of paper lying on the felt. Returning the empty mould to his partner, he takes another felt from the stack, covers the newly deposited sheet with it, and repeats the process with the next mould, which by now is ready for him. Their rate is about ten sheets per minute.

The work continues until there is a sizeable stack of felts interleaved with sheets of stuff, which is then slid under a hydraulic press. This applies 2,500 lb. per sq. in. of pressure on the stack, forcing out water until it emerges about one-third of the size it went in. Peeling off the top felt, the coucher uncovers a still-damp sheet of paper, but which is strong enough to be handled. The sheets are stacked, lightly pressed again, then dried.

There are several ways of drying them at the mill. In one of the large drying lofts they are simply draped like washing over rope lines. In another they are laid flat on large squares of hessian stretched between posts. Either way, drying takes several days. Another – and quicker – method is to feed the sheets around heated, revolving rollers.

As they dry the sheets shrink – but this has already been allowed for by the paper maker. However, they tend to shrink unevenly, generating a slightly undulating – or 'cockled' – surface. The surface, too, will be quite grainy, having conformed to that of the felts during pressing. This textured surface suits many of the artists and printers using the paper, and is often left undisturbed. But both character-istics can be removed in the final pressing given to the dried sheets. And if a really smooth surface is required, they are interleaved between thin metal plates in batches of about 30, called 'books', and passed under heavy rollers. Finally, the edges may be trimmed dead straight on a guillotine or left untouched – when they are known as 'deckle-edged'.

STACKING THE SHEETS *The coucher rests the edge of his mould on the felt, then flips it face down and lifts it off, depositing a sheet of stuff cleanly on the felt (inset picture). After pressing, the sheets are stacked again into what is called a pack, which is usually given a second, lighter pressing before the sheets are dried.*

mould so that together they form a shallow tray. The size of the mould-deckle combination varies according to the size of sheet required. He dips it into the vat, lifts it out, and as the water drains away, the sheet of paper begins to form. He lifts off the deckle and pushes the mould across to his assistant, the 'coucher', who pulls it against a curved stay to drain further.

Even as the coucher takes one mould, the vatman is reaching for the second and dipping it into the stuff. The work is continuous, demanding and very heavy – especially when the stuff is at its thickest and the sheets are big.

Yet during this rapid process the vatman's judgment of the amount of stuff on the mould must be immaculate, because the final weight of the paper depends on it. Paper is sold in terms of the dry weight of 500 sheets – 70 lb. paper, say, is 500 sheets weighing 70 lb. The range produced by the mill goes from 18 lb. to 140 lb., and the size of page from 6 in. × 9 in. 'note-paper' (eight sheets to a mould) through 25 in. × 20 in. 'royal' to the larger sizes.

Anyone, it is said, can make a sheet of paper – only a true

HOW A WATERMARK IS MADE

Many papers carry their maker's distinctive watermark – visible when the paper is held up against a light. This is produced by lettering or illustration 'embroidered' with thin phosphor-bronze wire on the copper-mesh sieve of the mould. The indentations they make in the wet sheet of stuff during moulding are flattened out completely by the press, but the texture of the mix has been altered where they were. It is this change of texture that shows up against the light.

THE
POTTER

WITH A LINEAGE THAT STEMS FROM THE REMOTE REACHES
OF PREHISTORY, POTTERS REMAIN THE MOST NUMEROUS
AND PROLIFIC OF CRAFTSMEN IN BRITAIN TODAY

About 8,000 years ago, groups of people living in isolation in various parts of the world made the discovery that clay, when baked at high temperatures, changes its nature and becomes a hard substance relatively impervious to both fire and water. And if, before baking, the clay is shaped and hollowed, then the result is a utensil that can be used for either cooking or storage. Necessity no doubt triggered the discovery, for it was between 12,000 and 8,000 years ago that the hunter-gatherers of the Middle and Far East, of the plains of Europe, and of the New World, too, began to lead more settled lives as farmers and stock-breeders. Means to cook and store their produce had to be found, and as mankind has always done, they made the best use of what was to hand. Their ingenuity gave rise to one of the first technologies, and one of the most enduring. In some cases, indeed, the pottery has long outlived any other record of the people who made it. The so-called Beaker Folk of Wessex, for example, are known mainly by their pots, yet from these sturdy artefacts, archaeologists are able to infer a great deal about the lives of the makers.

Most early pottery was made by the coil method, in which rolled 'snakes' of clay were placed ring upon ring to build up the shape before being smoothed and fired. Then, between 3000 and 4000 BC, some unknown genius – probably in the Middle East – invented the potter's wheel on which clay

was thrown, then hollowed and raised up into smooth, symmetrical forms that the potter decorated with lines, whorls or coloured liquid clay called 'slip', as his fancy took him. From these simple beginnings there evolved the coloured amphorae and vases of classical Greece and Etruria, the lead-glazed pots of the Roman world, and the splendours of Chinese porcelain, translucent and delicate as jade. Later, medieval Europe and Islam decorated their robust pots and vessels with glazes – whose primary purpose is to make the clay non-porous – and coloured them with oxides of metals such as manganese and copper.

From the first cooking vessel to the latest Wedgwood tea service, all ceramics have one thing in common, the clay from which they are made. It is an old saying among potters that the Earth was created for them, and it is certainly true that a large part of the planet's crust is made up of the raw material of their craft. Clay derives from decomposed igneous rock, and in this pure state occurs in pockets around the globe – the white china clay of St Austell in Cornwall is a good example. However, over aeons, such 'mother clays' – called primary or residual clays – are often eroded, and then transported, across the face of the globe by winds, glaciers, rivers and seas, collecting on the journey all kinds of minerals and organic substances, until, when they are finally deposited, they have totally changed their character. These secondary, or sedimentary, clays are more malleable than the original material, and are consequently of greater use to the potter. In early times, it was the mineral content of local clay deposits that determined the most suitable firing temperatures, and therefore the character, of local pottery, while naturally occurring pigments dictated its colour. However, modern potters do not necessarily simply dig a lump of clay out of the ground and begin work, since this may not provide exactly what they want. Instead, they mix together clays of known composition and blend with them such materials as feldspar, quartz, sand and grog – clay that has already been fired and then ground up. The resulting mixture – called a clay body – is a substance that will meet the requirements of texture and firing temperature of the particular job in hand.

The three main types of pottery
Most pottery falls under the heading of one of three major groups – earthenware, stoneware and porcelain – depending on the clay body used and the firing temperature. Earthenware is the most ancient form and is fired at low temperatures, ranging from between 1,382 and 2,012°F (750–1,100°C), the highest temperatures available to the old-time craftsmen. The material is porous, and if non-porosity is required, it must be glazed. Earthenware does have the advantage, however, of being able to take a wider range of brilliant colours, derived from oxides, than may be used if higher temperatures are involved. But during the last century the ceramics industry has rather confused the issue by making a non-porous, vitrified earthenware. This is done by giving the clay a first, or biscuit, firing at a high temperature and a glaze, or second, firing at a lower one. Most earthenware 'china' is made in this way, though flower-pots and tin-glazed and lead-glazed slipware are all still created in the traditional manner.

Stoneware, on the other hand, does not require glazing at all, though glaze is often added to provide an easier-to-clean surface in casseroles, or to enhance the clay with a subtle range of earthy hues derived from iron. Fired between 2,192 and 2,372°F (1,200–1,300°C), the clay particles fuse together and vitrify, giving a non-porous surface. The process was widely employed in China as long ago as 1000 BC, but was not successfully copied in Europe until more than 2,000 years had passed. In the 18th century, how-

MULTI-FLUE FOR MASS PRODUCTION

By the 17th century, the growing demand for pottery led to the construction of kilns like this one, whose remains have been excavated at Pule Hill, West Yorkshire. Large numbers of pots were stacked within the 9 ft diameter firing chamber, whose heat was provided by five fire-mouths, each with its own flue leading to a central vent. The fuel could be either coal or peat, and high temperatures were achieved, though careful stacking was required to ensure that the outer pots did not 'bloat' through overheating, while the centre remained relatively cold. The massive outer wall and heavy roof were built to protect the potter from the Pennine gales as he stoked the fires and – more important – prevented draughts from reaching the fire-mouths, so causing them to burn unevenly.

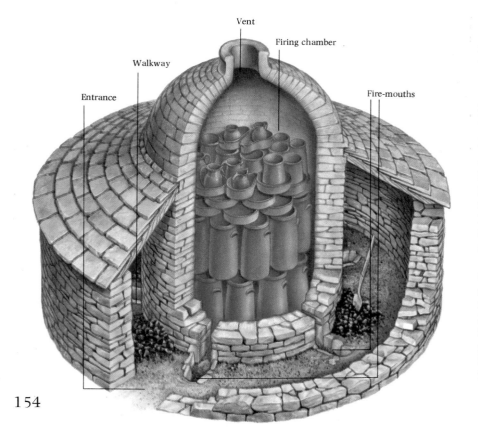

Vent

Firing chamber

Walkway

Entrance

Fire-mouths

SPUN FROM THE EARTH

Consciously or not, the hand movements of this modern potter are mirroring those made by her predecessors 5,000 years ago when the potter's wheel was first invented. From the spinning clay lump, adroit fingers open up a hollow in the material and raise the sides to create a fine jug or massive plant pots (inset) with magical speed and apparent ease.

THREE KINDS OF POTTERY

The three types of pottery result from using different mixtures of clays and other substances fired at different temperatures. Porous earthenware is fired at around 1,382–2,012°F (750–1,100°C); non-porous stoneware 2,192–2,372°F (1,200–1,300°C); and hard porcelain, with its high feldspar and quartz content, above 2,372°F (1,300°C).

Earthenware – English Prattware jug c. 1790–5.

Stoneware – Candlestick c. 1880.

Porcelain – Coalport cup and saucer c. 1810.

but they must have come to some swift and amicable agreement, since two years later Böttger was working for the Elector in his newly founded Meissen ceramic works. During the same century, English attempts to discover the secret of porcelain, carried out chiefly by Josiah Spode, led to the invention of bone china, in which bone ash and ground glass were added to the clay. In time, bone china became the standard English porcelain.

Whatever the type of pottery, the preparation and blending of clays and other minerals that make up the body from which the pot is made is a skilled business. All potters tell of the joy of handling clay, of wedging and kneading it, of twisting, turning and compressing the material to drive out the air bubbles that might cause the vessel to explode when fired. Washing, grinding and blending, the craftsman nurses the body along until it reaches the right state of plasticity and is ready for use. Often, the method of building the pot and the scale of the work is suggested by the feel of the body; a good potter always responds to the dictates of his materials.

There are several ways of constructing a pottery vessel. The simplest and most primitive is to make a hollow in a ball of clay with the thumb, then following through with a rhythmic pinching between thumb and fingers to raise and thin the walls. The coil method of our far-off ancestors is still employed by many potters, who knit and squeeze the clay coils together to make sturdy pots, often of considerable size and complex shape. Slabbing is more limited in scope, since it consists merely of rolling the clay into a flat slab and cutting it into regular shapes with a wire. The pieces are then joined together with liquid clay slip to form hard-edged shapes. Press-moulding and casting are mass-production techniques, more often employed in factories than by studio potters. In the first, clay sheets of suitable plasticity are pressed into or over a mould of biscuited clay or plaster of Paris. Casting takes mass production a step further, since by this method dozens of vessels can be made at once by pouring liquid clay into moulds.

But the most satisfying technique, and the one most widely used by craftsmen-potters is 'throwing' – the term is used in its ancient sense of twisting or turning, rather than in its modern one. The chief tools involved are the potter's wheel, a flat turntable operated by a kick-wheel or an electric motor, and the potter's hands. All other tools are of the simplest, and mostly home-made – 'ribs', for example, pieces of curved wood, metal or slate that help to shape the

Cow-horn slip trailer

Turning tools

Ribs

Roulette

TOOLS FOR DECORATING

Potters' hand tools are of the simplest and usually home-made from scraps of wood, slate or metal.

ever, Josiah Wedgwood made use of the medium to create his starkly elegant black basaltes and coloured Jasperwares, while the rich possibilities of glazing stoneware have attracted artist-potters ever since.

Porcelain, the princess of pottery, is a relative latecomer, having been invented by the Chinese as recently as the T'ang Dynasty – that is, between AD 618 and 907. Like stoneware, it is non-porous, while its firing temperature of between 2,372 and 2,552°F (1,300–1,400°C) – higher in the case of some industrial porcelains – makes it extremely hard. Whenever specimens appeared in Europe, they were highly prized and excited deep envy among potters. Middle Eastern and European craftsmen all strove to copy the material, but it was not until 1708 that a Saxon, von Tschirnhaus, and his partner, an alchemist named Böttger, managed to achieve the right mixture of china clay, feldspar and quartz. Their patron, the Elector of Saxony, promptly incarcerated the alchemist in order to preserve the secret,

PAINTING POTTERY *The patterns on a Spode bone-china plate are hand-painted by an artist. Painted decoration can be added to pottery before or after glazing. However, overglaze colours do not have the durability of underglaze ones, and can fade after repeated washing.*

walls, turning tools of bent mild steel for gouging and cutting, a sponge to carry water, callipers and a cheese-wire-like device for cutting the pot from the turntable.

But the hands are everything. When the clay has been thumped firmly on to the turntable, and the wheel set in motion – anti-clockwise in the Western world – the potter's hands take command with deftness and authority. Locked on and into the clay they perform a series of almost balletic movements, centering the material, opening it up, creating a hollow in the middle that spreads higher or wider as the thrower desires. An amazing variety of shapes appears as if by magic as the clay spins. Small and delicate, or large and robust, there is seemingly no limit to the forms that can be raised by a skilled potter.

Once the piece has been made, by whatever means, it must be allowed to dry, in order to drive out the water that helps give the clay its plasticity. Other water, chemically combined with the clay when it was formed, must also be driven out, but this can only be done in the kiln. In both cases, slow drying is essential, otherwise the clay may crack or even explode.

It is firing in the kiln that gives pottery its permanence, not merely by drying and baking, but because at about 1,112°F (600°C), clay goes through irreversible chemical changes and becomes pottery. When this fact was discovered, or by whom, is lost in antiquity, but it seems likely that the first firings were accomplished by lighting fires under and upon sun-dried clay bodies; some primitive peoples still make their pottery in this way. Later, the fires were lit at the bottom of right-angled sections cut into earth banks. From there, it was but a small step to the bottle-shaped updraught kiln, which served the requirements of Western potters from Roman times almost to the present day. Kilns have been fired with wood, charcoal, peat, coal and camel-dung, each fuel in its own way exercising some effect upon the finished pots. Most modern potters, however, use gas, oil or electricity which, expensive though they may be, enable the

A POTTER'S DICTIONARY

Ash glaze A glaze that includes a proportion of vegetable or wood ash. Different ashes impart different colours and textures to the glaze.

Biscuit The first firing that changes clay into pottery. The pot is then ready for glazing and some forms of decoration.

Body The mixture of clays, feldspar, quartz, sand and other additives, from which a particular piece of pottery is made.

Bone china An English form of porcelain first made by Josiah Spode (1754–1827). It derives its hardness and translucency from a 50 per cent admixture of bone ash to the clay body.

Casting A largely industrial process in which liquid clay is poured into moulds.

Celadon The name given to a wide range of glazes whose colours range from light green to deep olive.

Delft Dutch and English earthenware, whose main feature is the addition of tin to whiten the glaze and make it opaline. This gives a ground for decoration with paints. Also known as majolica and faience.

Earthenware One of the three main types of pottery, the others being stoneware and porcelain. Fired at relatively low temperatures, 1,382–2,012°F (750–1,100°C), the material is porous unless a glaze is applied.

Enamels Coloured pigments applied on top of the main glaze and fired at low temperatures.

Fettling Finishing off the surface and edges of dried vessels – especially the seams of cast pottery – before firing.

Glaze The impervious, glass-like coating on a pot. Basically it is a mixture of silica, alumina and flux, which is fused during firing.

Grog Fired, ground clay sometimes added to a body.

Hand-building Making a pot by any method other than on a wheel – for example, slabbing, coiling and pinching.

Jiggering and jolleying Using a former, which spreads the clay into a rotating plaster mould, to make repeated shapes on the wheel – usually cups, plates and saucers.

Leather-hard A stage in drying when the clay has hardened, but is still sufficiently plastic to have other pieces – handles and so on – joined to it.

Lustre An additional glaze of metallic oxide applied on top of the main glaze and fused to it at about 1,472–1,652°F (800–900°C).

Oxidation A firing process in which sufficient air is admitted to the kiln to give a clear atmosphere, permitting metal oxides in clays and glazes to impart their colours – such as copper-green, manganese-mauve and cobalt-blue.

Porcelain A white, hard and translucent material made from a mixture of china clay, feldspar and silica (quartz or flint), and fired at 2,372–2,552°F (1,300–1,400°C), or higher in the case of some industrial porcelains. It originated in China, probably between AD 600 and 900.

Press-moulding To make shapes by pressing sheets of clay on to moulds of plaster or biscuited clay.

Pulled handles Handles made by pulling them into shape by hand. Throughout the process, the hand is constantly dipped in water to lubricate the clay.

Raku Low-fired earthenware that is taken straight from the hot kiln and either reduced by rolling in combustible material, such as sawdust or leaves, or oxidised by immersion in water. The different colour values can be controlled by a combination of these processes.

Raw glazing Raw-glazed pottery is fired once only, after the glaze has been applied to the unfired clay. Glaze mixtures must be very carefully balanced to obtain the best results from this method.

Reduction Reducing the amount of air in a kiln to the point where unburned carbon particles remain suspended, giving a smoky atmosphere within the kiln. In these circumstances, copper oxide turns red, iron pyrites in the clay produce a finely speckled appearance, and many other changes of colour and texture take place.

Refractory Resistant to heat; a refractory body is one that is capable of withstanding high temperatures, in the range of 2,372°F (1,300°C) plus.

Salt glazing A glazing method, not often used today in the UK, in which damp salt is thrown into the kiln at about 2,282°F (1,250°C). The salt volatilises to form a pitted, orange-peel-like glaze over the pottery.

Sgraffito A decorating method in which a layer of slip is scratched through to reveal a differently coloured clay beneath.

Slabbing Cutting sheets of clay into slabs which may be joined at the edges, in the manner of woodwork, to form boxes or other shapes.

Slip Liquid clay, containing metal oxides when changes of colour are desired. The pot may be *dipped* or immersed in the slip; otherwise the liquid is *trailed* or *dribbled* across the pot's surface.

Sprig Usually – as in Wedgwood's Jasperware – a finely modelled 'relief' taken from a plastic mould and added to the clay vessel.

Stoneware Hard, opaque pottery whose non-porosity is in part due to its being fired at temperatures in excess of 2,192°F (1,200°C).

Tenmoku Japanese name for a brown-black, orange-edged glaze that originated in China. The effect is produced by adding iron oxide.

Terracotta An unglazed form of red earthenware; of ancient origin.

Turning Upending the pot on the wheel to remove excess clay and at the same time forming a foot-ring on the base.

Wax-resisting Applying wax in patterns to the surface of a pot to prevent slip or glaze adhering. Similar, though not identical, results may be obtained by blocking out the slip with wet paper.

desired temperatures to be reached and controlled much more easily than with the old fuels.

Once the pots are thoroughly dried, they are ready for their first, or biscuit, firing. They are packed into the kiln – a skilled job in itself – and the temperature is taken up to around 1,832°F (1,000°C) of good red heat. When the pots emerge, some 24 hours later, they have the porosity of flower-pots and so must be glazed. This is done by dipping the biscuited ware into a liquid mixture containing silica, alumina (the clay substance that permits the glaze to adhere) and flux to melt them. Often a metal oxide such as iron, copper, chrome or cobalt is added to give colour. The porous pot soaks up the liquid, but the ingredients of the glaze are left on the surface in the form of a fine powder; this is fixed to the pot by a second, and usually higher, firing. The variety of glazes is almost infinite; matt, shiny, opaque, translucent, crystalline, richly or subtly coloured, and all these qualities are controlled by the way in which the potter fires his kiln. The temperature, the atmosphere inside the kiln, smoky or clear, must be judged just right each time if the desired effect is to be achieved.

This often means long hours of working far into the night, watching anxiously over the kiln, balancing fuel against draught. Few modern potters are quite so obsessive as Bernard Palissy, the 16th-century French craftsman who burned all his furniture and then his floorboards to drag his kiln up to the right temperature; but they might easily sympathise with him.

Decorating pottery

Methods of decoration are equally varied, and can be added at almost any time during the making of the pot. In fact, enamel and lustre decorated pots actually require a third firing, since in this case the metallic oxides are painted on to the glaze and then fixed at a low heat of between 1,112 and 1,652°F (600–900°C). The earliest form of decoration, of course, and still a firm favourite, is to make incisions in the clay during throwing or building. This is done with various implements ranging from fingernails to strips of metal or wood, to knotted string, pastry cutters, or, so it is said, false teeth. Alternatively, once the clay body has stiffened slightly, further rolls or pads of clay can be added as relief decoration. When the body is firmer still, liquid clay slip in a choice of colours may be added by dipping or pouring. All kinds of effects can be achieved by stopping-out the slip in patterns with wax or paper, or by sgraffito, a method in which a layer of slip is scratched through to reveal a different colour beneath.

It is told of Josiah Wedgwood that when he set up his factories in the 18th century, he 'found a craft and left an industry'. In the short term there may have been some truth in this, but it can hardly be said that there is any shortage of craftsmen-potters in Britain today. Some of the revival is due to William Morris and the Arts and Crafts Movement of the late 19th century, whose devotees wished to dissociate themselves from a world of mass production and return to the values of a hand-made Golden Age.

More still is due to Bernard Leach who, after studying ceramics in the Far East for many years, settled at St Ives in Cornwall in 1920. He devoted the rest of his life to showing how the ideas that inspired the stoneware and earthenware of China, Korea and Japan might be combined with those of medieval and 18th-century England to create a form of pottery that was both functional and an art form in its own right. His ideas have travelled round the world, but are reflected especially in the hundreds of small potteries up and down the country, in each of which one or two craftsmen work to produce practical kitchen and tableware that at the same time add grace and colour to the household.

MIGHTY MEN OF LITTLETHORPE

When the people below were photographed in 1913, Littlethorpe Pottery near Ripon was famed as the finest maker of 'bigware' – bread-crocks, drainpipes and huge horticultural pots – in the country. The firm's reputation owed much to the work of Albert Kitson (the man with the dog), who for years was renowned as the best of all bigware throwers; however, some credit is also due to the alluvial clays of the nearby River Ure, which are particularly suited to this branch of the potter's craft. The 'clayboy', or apprentice (bottom), is George Curtis, who took over the firm in 1922. Mr Curtis still works the pottery, and still produces horticultural wares as his predecessors have done since Littlethorpe was founded in the 1830s.

Albert Kitson

George Curtis

FROM CLAY TO KITCHEN SHELF

Philippa Lee works at the Towy Pottery at Rhandirmwyn, in Dyfed, which specialises in the production of sturdy kitchenware – mugs, jugs, platters and casseroles. Like her partner, Will Marno, she carries through the whole pottery operation from start to finish; in this case, the making of a stoneware mug. First, she blends the clay and minerals that make up the body, which she kneads over and over to make sure that all air bubbles – which might cause an explosion in the kiln – are excluded. The mug is then raised on the wheel, and when it is half-dried, the 'pulled' handle is attached. When the mug is thoroughly dry, it is ready for its first, or 'biscuit', firing, which shrinks it considerably. When it has cooled, it is glazed inside and out with a mixture of silicates and feldspar, together with a metallic oxide which at the second firing will fuse to the clay as a glassy, colourful surface.

1. A pug-mill combines clay and minerals.

2. The potter kneads the body to condition the clay.

3. Mug-sized balls of clay stand ready as the wheel is prepared for action.

4. Work begins with hands locked in the classic potter's grip.

5. Skilled fingers coax the hollowed mug shape up from the rotating wheel.

6. The curved rim is delicately smoothed into the fully raised mug.

7. A handle is pulled from a roll of clay and attached.

8. The shaped handle is pressed on to the half-dried vessel.

9. Glaze is poured into the mug.

10. The exterior is glazed by dipping.

WITH ITS CONSTRUCTION VARYING FROM REGION
TO REGION, THE HAY RAKE IS A STRIKING EXAMPLE OF
HOW DESIGN CAN EVOLVE TO SUIT LOCAL NEEDS

*D*uring yesterday's tranquil summers, before tractors and pick-up balers intruded on the scene, wooden rakes reigned supreme in the hayfield. Faced with a freshly mown meadow, you could ask for no better tool for turning and gathering the grass. Its rounded teeth were designed to slip easily over the sun-baked sward, and long hours of manual labour were eased by the tool's light weight.

Today, only a few rakes are made by two or three surviving craftsmen in Hampshire. Yet in many a dimly lit barn and hay loft you may still find these mute reminders of a more strenuous age.

Picture, for a moment, the contrast .... A century ago, gangs of itinerant workers, each wielding a scythe, cut the grass and helped resident farmworkers gather the crop into thatched stacks. There were cider flagons under the hedge, and the final wagon-load, drawn in by weary horses, was a cause for celebration. Now, a lone tractor driver can cut, turn and bale a meadow of hay in a fraction of the time. It is all vastly more efficient, yet one can still regret the passing of these long-ago hay harvests.

A rake's design has always depended on where it is made. Haymakers on the sloping fields of Wales, for instance, favoured rakes with heads a mere 15 in. wide and mounted at 45 degrees to the handle. A dozen teeth, or tines, were set closely together to gather the short grass on mountain slopes. Elsewhere, they mostly had broader heads – up to 30 in. wide – with maybe 15 well-spaced tines set at right-angles to the handle.

In Wales and the Pennines, rakes were strongly made, with a life expectancy of several years. In southern England, where tradition dictated a simpler construction, they were reckoned disposable after a single season. As a consequence, they were virtually mass-produced, and sold at low prices, by craftsmen such as those at Pamber End, near Basingstoke, in Hampshire, which was one of the principal centres for rake making.

There was, too, much variation in the type of wood used for the head and tines. Though ash was preferred in Wales and the West Country, and willow in southern England, birch, pine and alder were widely used elsewhere for heads and tines. But ash was generally the favourite material for handles.

Wherever it was made, a rake was required to combine strength with lightness. The handle had to pass smoothly through the worker's hands, with the teeth set in such a manner that hay could be gathered efficiently. Too gentle an angle and the rake would not collect it; too sharp an angle and the tines might break off.

Without pattern or measurement, template or working drawing, each craftsman's products had to satisfy critical customers, whose long days in the hayfield were sure to reveal any defects in design or workmanship.

It has been said that in making a rake the wood has to pass through a craftsman's hands at least 50 times – from cutting the timber to the final smoothing with draw-knife and sandpaper. It is the ease of providing a smooth finish that has always made ash the preferred wood for handles. After cutting, the sticks and branches are seasoned in the open for about a year until ready for shaping. Though the aim is to secure wood that is naturally straight, many handles have first to be steamed, and are then straightened in a 'straightening brake'.

Shaping the handle

The straightening brake consists simply of a pair of wooden pegs inserted in an upright post. By placing the steamed handle between the pegs, the ash stick can be levered straight. The lower 20 in. of each handle is chamfered with an axe and then clamped in the jaws of a primitive vice. The bark is removed with a two-handled draw-knife and a strangely shaped plane, known in Hampshire as a stail engine, is used to shape the handle.

This tool consists of a pair of connected wooden blocks, with a central hole large enough to admit the rake handle, or stail. Adjustable blades in each block pare the handle to a smooth, rounded shape when the tool is turned. The lower 20 in. of the handle is then split or sawn, and a strip of metal nailed round the end of the cut to prevent further splitting.

The rake head, generally of willow or ash, is shaped with axe, draw-knife and spokeshave, and the position of the teeth marked. The holes are then bored with a brace and bit, together with larger holes for the handle and stays.

The wooden pegs for the teeth are shaped in a driving stool, a work-horse on which the craftsman sits astride and drives each wooden peg through a tube-shaped knife in front of him. The work proceeds rapidly, for, as each billet is hammered almost flush with the cutting edge, another is placed on top of it, so pushing the first through to the waiting basket below.

The head of the rake is clamped in the jaws of a tining horse – a table equipped with a wooden vice. The teeth are dipped in water for a few minutes, which acts as a lubricant, before being hammered into the head.

Finally, the head is clamped in the vice again and each tooth shaped with a draw-knife. After smoothing with sandpaper, the rakes are tied in bundles ready for sale.

Design varied with the region. For instance, compared

THE HAYMAKERS

George Stubbs could have had no conception of how hay-making would change when he painted this pastoral scene in 1785. Everything had to be done by hand, from mowing the grass with scythes to turning and gathering the cut sward with the ubiquitous hay rake. It is debatable whether most farmworkers really wore such cumbersome clothes, but the design and balance of their tools was certainly crucial in helping them through the long hours of strenuous work.
(A detail from 'Haymakers', at the Tate Gallery.)

with the simple tools mass-produced in Hampshire workshops, those in Wales were always more elaborate. Instead of a split handle, the joint between handle and head was strengthened with a pair of ash bows.

In the past, many rake makers were equally skilled at fashioning wooden parts for other agricultural tools, from basic handles for shovels to the complex curves of scythe handles. As with rakes, the work generally involved steaming, bending and smoothing – but always with the aim of providing light, well-balanced hand-tools to ease the endless hours of manual work in the days before mechanisation.

HAMPSHIRE RAKES

The tines, or teeth, are of tough willow and generally vary between 11 and 15 in number. The rakes have ash handles, which are split and divided at the bottom before being fixed to the heads. The handles have to be smooth enough to slip easily through the hands when gathering hay.

CUTTING THE TINES

Sitting astride a driving stool, the craftsman taps a billet of willow through the cutting tube to trim it to a circular shape. The process is continuous, for the next billet is placed on top of the first just as it becomes flush with the cutting edge.

FINISHING THE HEAD

The rake head is shaped with a broad axe, followed by smoothing with a two-handled draw-knife. Two holes, into which the split ends of the handle will be inserted, are bored with a brace and bit.

STAIL ENGINE

This circular plane, peculiar to Hampshire, is used for smoothing rake handles, or stails. After the handle has been inserted in the hole, the tool is worked with a circular movement to give a smooth, rounded finish.

161

THE
ROPE MAKER

THOUSANDS TOILED TO MAKE THE ROPES
THAT RIGGED NELSON'S FIGHTING SHIPS . . . A FEW
STILL MAKE THEM IN JUST THE SAME WAY

The massive hemp anchor cable of Nelson's flagship *Victory* measured 24 in. in circumference, and its 100 fathoms weighed about 12½ tons. It was just one of seven carried in the ship at the Battle of Trafalgar, at a time when every seaport and many towns inland had rope makers by the hundred labouring to satisfy the demands of Britain's huge fleets. Just one ship like *Victory* consumed nearly 15 miles of rope in its complex rigging.

Best known of the naval ropewalks during the 17th and 18th centuries – up to around Nelson's time – was in Bridport, Dorset. The finest hemp available was grown in the area, and the Navy Board – forerunners of the Admiralty – issued instructions that all anchor cables for British warships should be made in the town, of local hemp.

The wide pavements and long, straight alleyways still to be seen in Bridport were once used as ropewalks. Whole families would be engaged – father and son making light ropes and twine outside their home, while mother and daughter made nets in the kitchen. Rope and nets are still made in the town, though the last ropewalk closed down in 1970. Nearly all rope is now turned out by machines, often in man-made materials such as nylon or polythene.

Before the advent of machines and man-made fibres, rope was produced by twisting the fibres of certain plants with the aid of a few simple implements. Apart from hemp (*Cannabis sativa*), jute, sisal, cotton, coir, manila and flax were commonly used.

Hemp was – and still is, in some cases – the favoured material. It was cultivated around Bridport until the mid-19th century, when cheaper imports – mainly from Italy and the Baltic countries – displaced it. The plant grows up to 15 ft tall, and it is the supporting fibre under the skin of the stalk – known as the bast – that is used. The stalks are soaked in water until the pithy core rots away, then beaten to separate out the bast. The rope it makes is hard, smooth and straw-coloured, tough and long-lasting.

Manila rope is made from the leaf fibres of the abaca, a

Throw hook

STRAW AND YARN

The throw hook, like a brace with a hooked bit, was used to make rope out of straw. This particular one was carved from a single piece of apple wood on a farm in Anglesey. Straw rope was usually laid on a wet day in the barn. One worker sat on a milking stool beside a pile of straw, and the hook was held by an assistant. The first man looped a bundle of straw over the hook, then the hook was twisted, the worker feeding in more straw as he walked backwards. In the engraving below, a worker is spinning yarn from hemp fibre wound around his waist. The hemp is fastened to one of the revolving hooks on a jack, which is again turned by an assistant. As the spun yarn lengthens, it is supported by a wooden T-piece.

species of wild banana, and is notably strong and quite resilient. Sisal is from the spiky, fibrous leaves of the *Henniquin* plant, which grows widely in central Africa and Latin America; hairy-looking and not as strong as the first two it is, however, cheaper. Coir rope – made from the coconut palm and known to seamen as 'grass line' – is the weakest of the natural-fibre ropes. But it floats on water, is light and springy, and is still widely used as mooring rope.

Rope making by hand is the same for all these materials. It starts with the preparation of the fibres by pulling them through a bed of pointed nails or rods. This is called 'hackling', and gets the fibres all running the same way. A little oil can be applied to them to make the work easier. Next they must be spun into yarn. A method that has now died out, but was used within living memory, was for the spinner to wind about 40 lb. of fibre around his waist and spin by hand in a ropewalk. He fastened the free end of fibre to a revolving hook turned by an assistant, then walked backwards, feeding in the fibres – each about 5 ft long – with enough overlap to form a continuous yarn as they were spun together. Nowadays, yarn is made by machine.

The third stage of production is to twist a number of yarns together to form a strand. In hand-made rope this is again done by the revolving hook, the number of yarns used depending on the thickness of strand required.

Three – and sometimes four – strands are twisted, or 'laid', together to form the rope itself, which is made in standard lengths of 120 fathoms – or 240 yds. Ropes of this length are seldom made by hand now, but to do so requires a ropewalk about 440 yds long. This is because the yarns must start very much longer than the strand into which they are twisted: they lose about one-third of their length in the process. Then of course the strands are also shortened as they in turn are laid into rope, so a quarter of a mile was once the normal length of a ropewalk.

To make the usual three-stranded rope, the ends of three lengths of twine are fixed to three revolving hooks on a simple mechanical device called a jack, at one end of the walk. The hooks revolve together, driven by gearing or a pulley-belt from a large wheel turned by hand. At the other end of the walk, all three strands are fixed to a single hook on another simple contrivance called a traveller. This hook is free to revolve, and the traveller – usually mounted on a weighted trolley – can move forward as the strands are shortened by twisting.

When the rope maker judges the tension to be exactly right, he inserts a hardwood 'top' between the strands near the traveller. This top – usually of apple wood – is rounded, pointed at the tail end, and cut with three deep grooves. With one strand slotted into each groove, the rope maker walks slowly towards the jack, pushing the top before him – and the rope simply forms itself behind the top. This is due to the twist imposed on the strands causing the traveller hook to revolve – and since all three strands are fixed to it, they in turn are twisted into rope.

Ropes made by these methods are called 'hawser laid'. For a really thick rope – such as the anchor cable of the *Victory* – three lengths of hawser-laid rope are twisted together to form one large 'cable-laid' rope.

It has been calculated that during a working lifetime in a ropewalk, a rope maker walked a distance equivalent to the circumference of the earth – about 36,000 miles. However, there are few still working by hand – perhaps half a dozen. They are usually engaged on special orders for bell-ropes, show-ring animal leads and such like. Many church bell-ropes are hand-made for two reasons: they all differ in length according to the distance between belfry and ringing chamber; and they have to be laid more softly at the ringer's end to make them flexible and easy to hold.

FROM FINE CODLINES
TO MIGHTY HAWSERS

Rope is made in many forms, from light codline – which is laid up with 18 threads – to massive cable-laid towing lines, thicker than a man's arm. The craftsman on the right is making a three-stranded inch-thick rope, using a top while his unseen assistant turns the wheel of a jack, revolving the three hooks to which the strands are attached. A cable-laid rope is made by twisting together three three-stranded ropes. Four-stranded ropes are also produced, but as they are prone to kink, this tendency is offset by running a core of twine down the centre. The top used to make them has an extra groove, and a hole in the centre through which the twine core is passed. However, steps to prevent ropes kinking and unwinding are taken throughout manufacture, by twisting in a different direction at each stage. For a right-hand-laid rope the yarn is spun right-handed, the twine strands twisted left-handed, and the final rope twisted right-handed. For the same reason the final twist of a cable-laid rope is left-handed. Codline was made originally for cod fishing, but it also has many uses on board ships for purposes where even a small rope would be too thick and clumsy.

HOW ROPE IS MADE UP

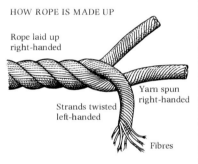

Rope laid up
right-handed

Yarn spun
right-handed

Strands twisted
left-handed

Fibres

TWO TYPES OF ROPE

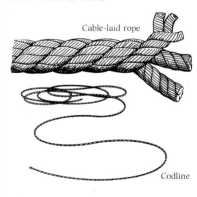

Cable-laid rope

Codline

THE
SADDLER

DECEPTIVELY SIMPLE IN APPEARANCE, SADDLES
ARE SOPHISTICATED RIDING AIDS THAT HAVE TAKEN
MORE THAN 2,000 YEARS TO PERFECT

*T*here is no quick way to make a riding saddle; no machine that will mass-produce them. A master craftsman takes between 30 and 35 hours to complete an ordinary general-purpose saddle, and even a simple light-weight racing type takes at least a couple of eight-hour days. This is because much of the work is hand-stitching leather with immaculate needlework – which cannot be hurried. One Newmarket saddler reckons to work a 12 hour day at least three times a week. Patience is as essential as a strong, skilled hand. Five years are needed for an apprentice to learn it all.

The first crude saddles were invented a little over 2,000 years ago in Central Asia by the Steppe tribes, who practically lived on horseback. They invented the stirrup, too, in the 4th century AD. Their saddle was a simple framework of two horizontal wooden bars joined at each end by cross-pieces. A padded leather seat was slung across this frame – or saddle tree, as it came to be called. It was designed not only for the comfort of the rider, but to ease the burden on his mount. The rider's weight was distributed over the flesh-padded areas of the horse's back rather than its spine. It did wonders for the endurance capabilities of both man and animal, and to this day all saddles use the same principle.

The scene in a saddler's workshop has changed little over

WHEN EVERY VILLAGE
AND TOWN HAD ITS
SADDLER

Small saddler's shops such as this were a familiar sight in the towns and villages of Britain at the turn of the century – when horse-power still meant just what it said. The workshop window had become the 'shop window' and the saddler and his apprentice packed it with small items. But they proudly displayed their saddles, collars, harness and whips outside. Most of their products were made to measure and to order, but some would be turned out as 'off the peg' wares that could be adjusted to fit a customer's horse later.

the past century – and the opulent aroma of high-quality leather that pervades it has changed not at all. The saddler sits on a tall stool at a high bench. Tools in immediate use lie close to hand; others are slotted neatly into leather strapping tacked around the raised back and sides of the bench. They make a fascinating and formidable array: awls, punches, pincers and pliers, mallets, knives – including curious half-moon shaped ones – and needles both straight and curved. Not to mention tools with such earthy names as belly-stuffers, mashers, rolling sticks, pricking wheels and creasers. And special pliers called bulldogs, a hammer magnetised to pick up stray tacks from awkward crevices, and the extraordinary clam – like a large pair of wooden forceps with springy blades that curve in to meet at the tips.

Their varied uses become apparent as the work of making a general-purpose saddle proceeds.

The materials needed apart from the saddle tree are: unbleached saddle linen, webbing, $2\frac{1}{2}$ in. and 3 in. wide, white saddle serge for the seat and prime pigskin for covering it, panel hide, lining hide, chrome leather – named after a method of tanning with chromium salts – for girth straps, bridle leather for the forepiece and skirt welts, and flock fibre (man-made these days, rather than the traditional wool) for stuffing the seat and panels.

Clams, mashers and stuffing sticks

The clam is not only the largest of the tools used – it is, perhaps, the one used most. Gripped between the saddler's knees, it acts like a portable vice, holding the work fast as various components are stitched together. The masher is employed for shaping and smoothing the seat and panel leather, both parts being stuffed with the aid of long curved tools called stuffing sticks.

The half-moon is a utility knife, used by the saddler mainly for cutting out flaps, skirts, panels and seats. And because its crescent blade is sharpened all round it can make almost any cut required in leatherwork – so workers in other branches of the leather industry also find it invaluable. Girth straps are cut, however, with a plough-gauge – a tool reminiscent of an adjustable plane, with a vertical blade which can be set to the desired width of the strap, then simply run along the straight edge of a sheet of leather. Along with the pricking wheel for making lines of stitch marks is the pricking iron – like a broad chisel with a sharp-toothed edge. Both tools usually make between six and 12 marks to the inch. Stitching is done with the aid of a palm iron, the cupped handle of which fits into the hollow of the hand and is used to push the needle through holes pierced by an awl.

Construction of the saddle starts with the saddle tree, usually bought in from specialised workshops in the Midlands, and the first job is to fix the webbing to it. The initial piece is tacked to the cantle slightly left of centre, stretched forward to the head and tacked again there, then taken back to the cantle and tacked in place slightly right of centre, so that it forms a very narrow 'V' along the length of the tree. The next piece, of slightly wider webbing, goes across the first and is tacked to both sides of the tree, just forward of the middle, leaving an extra 4 in. or so hanging down on each side. Later, the girth straps will be stitched to these pieces. A final length of webbing also goes across the tree, tacked into place a few inches behind the second.

The webbed tree is then covered with saddle linen, which is stretched over and tacked on. This in turn is covered with the 'saddle serge' – a thick woollen cloth. Using a long, curved stuffing stick the saddler forces a layer of flock fibre between linen and serge, spreading it evenly to form the padding of the seat. The stuffing is flattened and smoothed with a rolling stick and finally the masher is used to smooth

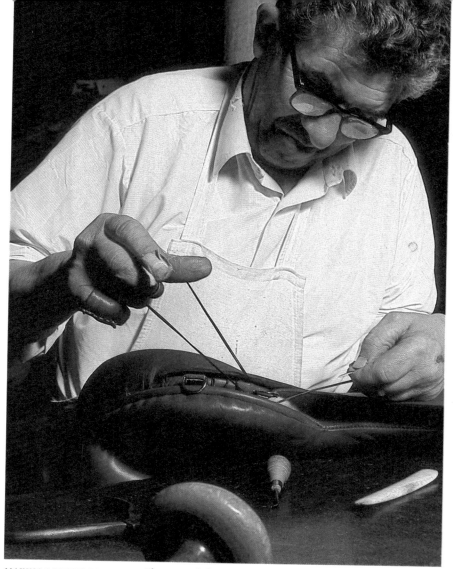

it into a firm, even shape. At this point a paper pattern for the saddle-flaps is held against the serged tree and guide marks made on it and the tree when the alignment is correct. The marks will be used when the flaps are tacked into place under the skirts later.

The next job is to tack the 'bellies' on each side of the cantle. These are crescent-shaped leather pads, tightly stuffed, that cushion the rider's buttocks. To a great extent they govern the 'size' of the saddle, their length and thickness being varied to suit the build and preferences of the rider.

The seat is now ready for 'blocking' – covering with the pigskin upon which the rider actually sits. This must be of the highest quality, with a perfectly even texture. Usually only two seats can be cut from each complete skin, and the saddler, thoroughly familiar with tanning processes, can immediately spot a skin that is less than perfect. Once cut to pattern with a razor-sharp knife, the seat is soaked in water, stretched tightly over the tree and tacked in place on the underside. As the water dries out, the seat contracts to give a taut, creaseless covering.

The skirts are then pinned to the seat to mark the exact position into which they will be stitched. They may be of pigskin or hide – again cut from patterns – and their top edges are thinned down where they will join the seat. But between seat and skirt runs a welt, a fine line of piping, made by thinning a $\frac{1}{2}$ in. wide strip of leather to almost paper thickness, folding it in half along its length, then tacking it into place between skirt and seat. Stitch holes are then pierced through skirt, welt and seat with a pricking tool and awl. The seat is then removed from the tree by

MAKING A SADDLE TO MEASURE *The owner of a first-rate – and probably expensive – horse is likely to have a saddle made specially for it. The tree will be modified to ensure a good, comfortable fit over the animal's back. All subsequent stages of the job will be geared to seeing that as close a contact as possible is made between horse and rider when the saddle is finally used. Here, a craftsman at Jabez Cliff and Co. Ltd, of Walsall, is busy stitching the panel to the saddle through the forepiece at the front and the cantle at the rear.*

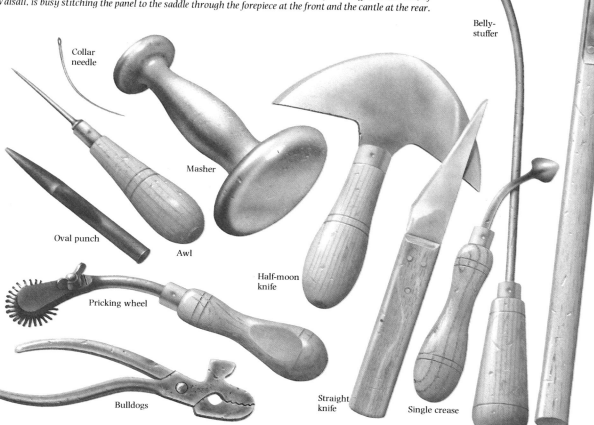

Collar needle

Tack hammer

Belly-stuffer

Masher

Oval punch

Awl

Half-moon knife

Pricking wheel

Bulldogs

Straight knife

Single crease

THE BASIC TOOLS OF THE SADDLER

These are just a few of an imposing array of tools used by saddlers. The tack hammer is for tacking the webbing, linen, serge and leather components to the tree. Flock stuffing is forced into padded sections with a belly-stuffer – among other tools – and the single crease marks lines for cutting and stitching. The half-moon knife is in constant use for general leather cutting, and particularly for irregular shapes. Trimming in confined spaces is done with a straight knife. The pricking wheel marks stitching holes and there are numerous awls for piercing stitch holes through tougher hides. Bigger holes and slots are made with a variety of round or oval hollow punches. Both curved and straight needles of many sizes are used for different stitching tasks. Special pliers called bulldogs have a block sticking out on one jaw that acts as a fulcrum when the tool is used to grip material and stretch it over a sharp edge. The masher is for smoothing and compacting stuffed components.

levering out the tacks, and the skirt and welt stitched to it, the saddler picking up the stitch holes he has made and using a fine, waxed cotton thread. When the stitching is complete, the thread is invisible, and the welt is only about $\frac{1}{8}$ in. wide. Finally the seat, now complete with its skirts, is re-tacked to the tree.

The flaps are cut with a half-moon knife from cow-hide, and have a lining of serge or thinner leather stitched on. They can be flat, or given a knee-roll at the front edges by stuffing with flock, according to the rider's preference. They are tacked on to the tree underneath the skirts, using the guide marks made earlier. Then the girth straps, three on each side, are stitched to the webbing tabs – though in some saddles one of them on each side may be nailed directly to the tree.

The saddle itself is completed by stitching in the forepiece and the two D-shaped metal rings for carrying sandwich cases or other gear. The forepiece is a short, curved strop that fits under the head as a reinforcement and bridge between the panels. It is made from two pieces of leather with a third, tougher piece sewn in between them. Sometimes, for a horse with narrow withers, the whole head of the saddle is made in a cut-back U-shape so that it fits the animal more comfortably. Finally the panel – the softer 'under-saddle' – is made and fitted, and the job is complete.

Of course, not all saddlers work in the same way, and there are also a number of specialised saddles calling for different methods. The modern jumping saddle, for example, is built on a spring tree, in which the wooden side bars are reduced in width and spring steel is inserted to provide

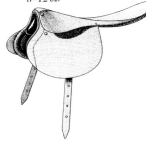

LIGHTNESS FOR THE JOCKEY

Racing saddles must be as light as possible. The tree shape is trimmed drastically and metal parts are aluminium. Fittings, too, are pared to the minimum, the triple girth straps being cut down to one. Light pigskin only is used for the covering and the whole saddle weighs as little as 8–12 oz.

CUTTING TO A PRECISE PATTERN *The saddler uses templates of thick paper or cardboard as patterns when cutting out parts of the saddle. Standard templates are used for off-the-peg saddles, but a saddler will make special patterns to measure for 'bespoke' saddles. Here he is cutting out a skirt – later he will thin the top edge with a half-moon knife.*

greater resilience and comfort. This makes for a thinner seat and gives the rider closer contact with the horse. The beauty of the spring tree is that its resilience can be varied by making the steel strips thicker or thinner. Saddlers can order them from the manufacturers to meet their customers' individual 'springing' demands.

The jumping saddle is designed to allow the rider to sit well forward, with his weight over his knees so that he is better balanced for the jump. This can be seen clearly at the great international horse shows, which are frequently televised.

Also popular at horse shows are the dressage events, in which horse and rider are required to perform a series of manoeuvres with great precision. This, too, calls for a specially made saddle, which has straight flaps and a short seat built on a straight tree. It gives riders total freedom to use their legs from the knee downwards to give them absolute control of the horse.

Then there is the racing saddle, weighing as little as 8 oz., which uses an ultra-light development of the spring tree. The side strips are of thin-gauge aluminium rather than steel, and the saddle is fitted with pockets into which small lead weights can be inserted if necessary, to bring the weight carried by the horse up to what is required under handicap rules.

In total contrast, there are still nomad horsemen in Central Asia using wooden saddles bolstered with fur padding, just as their ancestors did 2,000 years ago.

Much of a modern saddler's time is devoted to repairing worn or damaged saddles and other items of harness. This often accounts for the long hours he tends to work, for a man whose livelihood may depend on keeping horses at work or in training must have damage or wear to

THE SIMPLE DESIGN OF A MILITARY SADDLE

The military – or trooper – saddle is quite different from the standard type. The tree is very basic – two lengths of wood shaped roughly to fit a horse's back and bridged by steel hoops at head and cantle. The seat is one piece of thick hide, soaked in water for three days to soften it. Two men stretch it tight over a wooden former and tack it down. That job done, the craftsman is wiping the surface dry with a cloth pad. When dry, after about three more days, the seat is removed from the former, but retains its new shape and has once more become tough and hard. It is slung hammock style between the hoops, and stitched over them at head and cantle. The skirts and double girth straps are tacked to the tree. Normally there is a felt panel, $\frac{1}{2}$ in. thick, attached by pockets and buckles.

equipment rectified as soon as possible – or sooner. And some of the work inevitably involves putting right sloppy or 'bodged' mending done by unskilled hands, perhaps as a temporary measure until it can be done properly. Typical is a girth strap which has been torn in a fall and repaired not by carefully cutting the ends and stitching them together, but by clumsily riveting them.

Stitching plays such an important part in the craft that it is the first technique an apprentice must master. There were, indeed, times when craftsmen specialised only in hand-stitching, and even that took three years to learn. Although the pricking iron or pricking wheel mark out the stitch holes, they must be pierced individually for each stitch. The awl must go through the leather at just the right angle – about 60 degrees – and the stitches must be made with just the right tension on the thread. Stitches pulled in too tightly on the top side spoil the look of the work. They are called 'dead men' and are spotted instantly by expert eyes. Deductions in pay used to be made for any found in a finished job.

The London Saddlers received a charter from Edward I in the late 13th century, and the Association of Master Saddlers is today a flourishing organisation which sponsors courses for master saddlers, promotes apprenticeships and holds examinations for them. Saddlers tend to group particularly in or around areas with racing associations, such as Newmarket, Cheltenham, Chepstow, Newbury, Thirsk and York. Most of them run apprenticeship schemes.

THE SADDLE

The saddle is made in two parts – the seat and the panel. First the tree is webbed, then covered with linen. The bellies – shaped leather or felt pads – are tacked either side of the cantle, after which the whole seat is serged. This means covering it over the top and round the edges, and tacking it under the tree. A small slit is made in the serge, and flock padding is pushed through and spread between serge and linen. The hole is stitched up and the pigskin covering is first stretched over and tacked down wet for a tight fit, then removed when dry for the skirts to be stitched on. With seat-skirt combination re-tacked to the tree, the flaps are fitted beneath the skirts and the forepiece is stitched into the head to form a bridge between the flaps. Girth straps and D-pieces complete it.

THE PANEL (OR LINING)

The panel acts as a form of cushion between saddle and horse. This example is a full panel – probably the type most widely used. It is fitted to the underside of the seat and stretches from head to cantle. It is made of hide and lined with felt or softer leather, often with flock stuffed between for extra cushioning. A point pocket is stitched on at each side to receive the tree points when the panel is joined to the saddle. Rolls of extra padding for the rider's knees run up the front edges, curving backwards at the top. In some panels these knee rolls join up with thigh pads down the rear edges.

HOW A TYPICAL RIDING SADDLE IS CONSTRUCTED

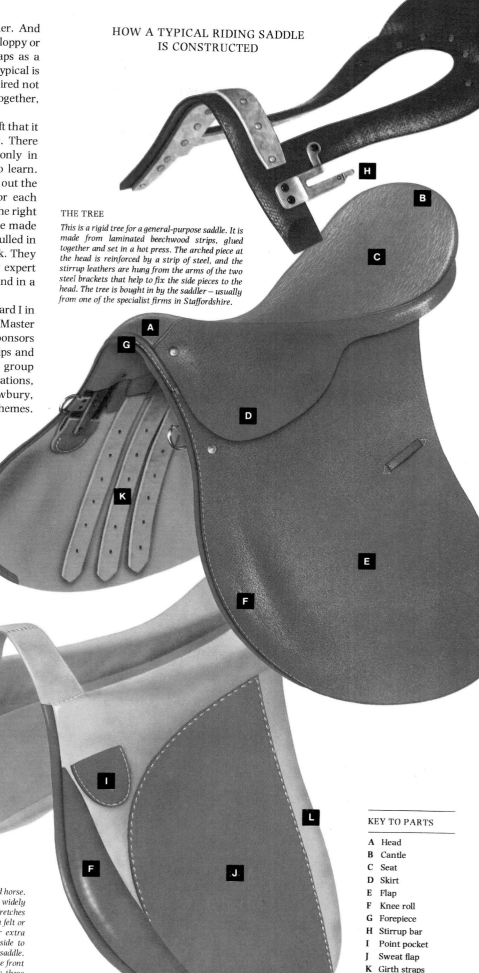

THE TREE

This is a rigid tree for a general-purpose saddle. It is made from laminated beechwood strips, glued together and set in a hot press. The arched piece at the head is reinforced by a strip of steel, and the stirrup leathers are hung from the arms of the two steel brackets that help to fix the side pieces to the head. The tree is bought in by the saddler – usually from one of the specialist firms in Staffordshire.

KEY TO PARTS

A Head
B Cantle
C Seat
D Skirt
E Flap
F Knee roll
G Forepiece
H Stirrup bar
I Point pocket
J Sweat flap
K Girth straps
L Thigh pad

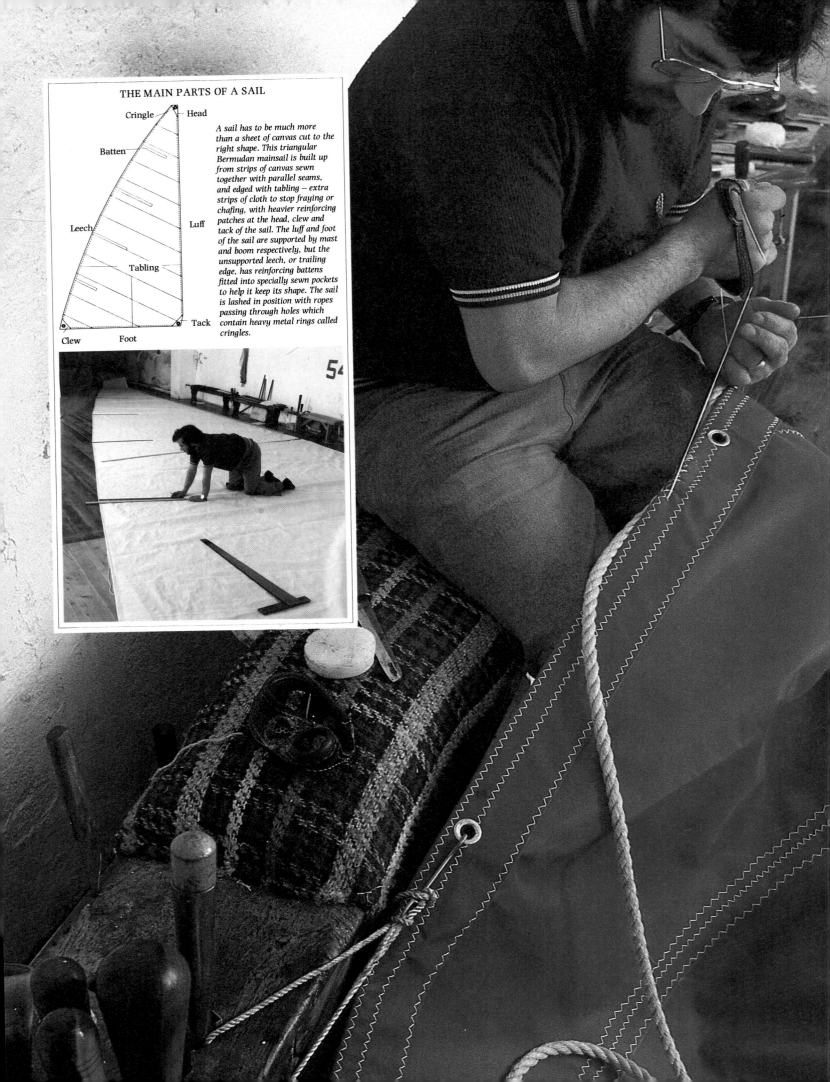

THE MAIN PARTS OF A SAIL

Cringle • Head

Batten

Leech

Luff

Tabling

Tack

Clew • Foot

A sail has to be much more than a sheet of canvas cut to the right shape. This triangular Bermudan mainsail is built up from strips of canvas sewn together with parallel seams, and edged with tabling – extra strips of cloth to stop fraying or chafing, with heavier reinforcing patches at the head, clew and tack of the sail. The luff and foot of the sail are supported by mast and boom respectively, but the unsupported leech, or trailing edge, has reinforcing battens fitted into specially sewn pockets to help it keep its shape. The sail is lashed in position with ropes passing through holes which contain heavy metal rings called cringles.

THE
SAILMAKER

HIS SUBTLE SKILLS CREATED THE BROAD ACRES
OF CANVAS NEEDED TO DRIVE CLIPPERS AND OTHER
TALL SHIPS ACROSS THE WORLD'S GREAT OCEANS

For centuries, the energy that moved cargoes from one end of the world to the other was literally as free as air. But harnessing this energy was made possible only by the skill and craftsmanship of one man: the sailmaker. The largest and fastest of the sailing ships – grain, wool and tea clippers, such as the *Cutty Sark* – might easily carry an acre of canvas. They needed the best part of a gale to drive them at their top speed of perhaps 18 knots, for days, weeks or even months on end. Under these conditions, it was small wonder that each ship's sailmaker, and his mates and apprentices, spent so many hours in making repairs and replacements against the endless process of wear that in time would reduce even the toughest canvas to tatters.

Compared with this last great commercial use of wind power, the earliest sailing ships were very inefficient. The first sails were secondary to the muscle power of oarsmen – and consisted only of a large rectangular cloth that could drive the vessel in roughly the same direction that the wind was blowing. The sail needed to be strong, and shaped so that it would belly out to trap as much of the wind as possible. But beyond that there was no great skill required in cutting and shaping. In any case, if the course were in any direction other than downwind, the sail was completely useless, and the only practical motive power was that provided by the oarsmen.

Before the sailing ship could really develop, it was necessary to discover a way of sailing against the wind. One of the earliest means of doing so was provided by the triangular lateen sail of the Middle East, which, rather than being set across the beam of the ship, was rigged fore and aft along its length instead. When the ship was steered close to the wind, the sail was set so that it tended to form a slight curve. This meant that the air passing around the convex side of the sail's surface had further to travel than that round the concave side, so causing a speeding up of the airflow and a reduction in pressure. The effect was similar to that of the aerofoil section of an aeroplane's wing, which induces lift through this speeding up of the air stream over the curved upper surface. However, in the case of the sail the 'lift' is a force acting to push the boat sideways and forwards. The sideways force is resisted by the boat's keel and rudder, and the net result is that the boat moves forward, even though the wind is coming from an angle to the bows of the boat rather than from the stern.

Even with this new rig, no boat could actually sail straight into the wind, though it was possible for them to sail at angles approaching 50 degrees or so to the wind's direction. This meant that if the boat's course was directly

upwind, it had to sail in a series of zigzags to port and starboard, at an angle to the wind. Progress was slow, but it was possible, and over the years rigs grew more efficient and more sophisticated. Seamen found for example that if a sail were set in front of the mast on a fore-and-aft rigged ship (one in which the mainsail is aligned with the hull, as opposed to being set at right-angles to it) it channelled and accelerated the airflow on its way to the bigger mainsail set behind the mast, and so produced much more power. The size and shape of the curve of each sail and the gap between them grew ever more crucial in deciding a vessel's performance.

In consequence, the sailmaker's craft became increasingly complex, and though sailmaking continued to be a seagoing trade, new suits of sails were generally made in a sail loft ashore. It was vital that the sails took up the right curve when hoisted – no easy thing to ensure since both ropes and canvas tended to stretch with use. In theory, every variation in the wind's strength and direction called for a different degree of curvature, which in practice meant that the sails had to be as good a compromise as possible. Sails for use in light winds had to be made of light materials, so that they could assume their proper shape in the lightest of breezes, while at the other end of the scale storm sails had to be thick and tough enough to stand up to the fiercest winds the ship was likely to meet in her working life.

In the old days, sails were usually made from cotton or flax. Egyptian cotton was the best for light-weather gear, but it had its drawbacks: it tended to rot, and when it was wet the fibres absorbed moisture so that the sail became stiff and difficult to handle. Most naval and merchant vessels used a fairly coarsely woven flax instead, despite its greater tendency to stretch.

Most sailcloth was woven in 36 in. widths, so that every sail had to be built up from a series of strips carefully stitched together with overlapping seams. But since the canvas stretched more across the bias of the weave than it did along the length of the threads, the sailmaker had to pay special attention to the way the strips were matched and joined to make sure that the sail kept the same smooth curve as it stretched. Very often a mainsail would be built up from a simple series of parallel strips, though the amount of overlap was often increased at the points of greatest stress. Jibs and other headsails, however, were frequently built up in a herringbone pattern, with the spine running from the rearmost lower corner of the sail forward to a point part-way up the leading edge.

AN ACRE OF SPREADING CANVAS

The aristocrats of sail, like this Glasgow-built tea clipper of 1869, were designed for high speed with a following wind, the power being supplied by the big square sails set on booms slung from the fore, main and mizzen masts. When the ship had to sail as close as possible into headwinds, she depended on the fore-and-aft sails; the headsails set on the stays joining the foremast to the bowsprit, the staysails set between the masts and the spanker at the stern, which helped balance the ship and gave easier control. When the wind dropped, light-weather sails like the royals and the gallants would be set. With a moderate side wind, all would play their part. In really light breezes, studding-sails would be set alongside the square sails on special booms, to give an even greater area of sail.

   Square sails

   Fore-and-aft sails

   Royals and gallants

STITCHING A BOLT ROPE TO A SAIL *One of the hardest jobs for a sailmaker is stitching a rope reinforcement, called a bolt rope, along the edge of a sail. The needle has to be pushed through the multiple layers of canvas and between the strands of the rope, using the metal-reinforced rope palm in his right hand. The craftsman at work here is in the Falmouth sail loft of Penrose Sailmakers Ltd.*

Wind
direction

Sailing
direction

The first step in making any sail was to mark out the full-size shape on the floor of the sail loft. This was done either in chalk lines on the polished wooden floor, or by tapes fixed to wood-handled pins called prickers. On the pattern the sailmaker laid out the strips of cloth that would make up the finished sail – each strip cut oversize with a sharp knife.

The really hard work was in sewing the cloth strips together, and here again it was essential to keep the tension even to avoid the wrinkles that might interrupt the airflow and reduce the efficiency of the rig. Therefore, when the strips were matched up on the floor plan the sailmaker made pencil marks on the edges of adjacent strips at intervals of 9 in. or so. By matching the marks as the seam was sewn, he ensured that the tension was equalised.

Sailmakers wore soft canvas shoes to prevent damage to the sail-loft floor, and a pair of canvas overtrousers to protect the sailcloth. Each man worked at a bench fashioned like a long, rectangular stool with a lip along the edges to prevent tools and needles dropping off. At one end was a rack for tools and reels of thread, protected by canvas to save the sailcloth from catching on any points or projections. Hanging from the side of the bench were bags containing spare thread, food, snuff or even chewing tobacco. Because of the high fire risk, smoking in a sail loft was strictly forbidden.

The sailmaker sat on the bench with the length of sailcloth stretched across his knees. His sailmaker's needle was threaded with a doubled yard of beeswax-rubbed twine, and pushed through the thickness of strong canvas with the aid of a seaming palm, a broad leather band fitting round the hand and held in place by a thumb-hole. Set into the palm was a metal plate with a series of indentations which the sailmaker pressed against the end of the needle to force it through the cloth; some 180 stitches to the yard required more than mere callouses.

Lengths of twine were never knotted together; instead, the sailmaker would tuck the ends in between the layers of cloth and stitch them firmly into place. This prevented any breakage in the twine from running the full length of the sail. Since each yard of twine stitches rather less than a foot of seam, if a break did occur, it would be limited, and fairly easy to spot, since most sailmakers made their stitches in a colour that contrasted with that of the canvas. When the stitches had been pulled taut, they were bedded into the cloth with a steel tool known as a rubber.

Once the strips had been stitched together, the final shape of the sail was fixed. The cloth was laid out against the marked-out shape on the sail-loft floor, and the edges cut to the required curvature, or roach. This ensured that when the sail was hoisted and the edges pulled straight under tension, the spare material would belly out into the right shape to provide power from the speeding up of the airflow.

The skill lay in judging the correct amount of curvature and allowance for stretch. Usually the curve would deviate from the straight edge of the floor plan by an inch or two for every 5 or 6 ft along the edge, and was outlined by prickers and thread. The line was established by eye, or sometimes by means of a flexible batten called a spleen stick which, held in place between sets of prickers, guaranteed a smooth curve. Once the roach was determined, the sailmaker drew the shape in pencil on the sail for final trimming.

After trimming, edges had to be reinforced with extra strips of canvas called tablings, to prevent fraying and wear, and the corners of the sails patched with extra layers of canvas at the points of greatest strain. Mainsails were often fitted with battens – thin strips of wood inserted into specially sewn pockets – to help the unsupported trailing edge of the sail to keep its shape.

Some sails required extra strengthening. This was provided by stitching a bolt rope into the edge of the sail, even tougher work than making the sail itself. Best-quality hemp was used, and considerable effort was needed to force the needle through the combined thicknesses of rope and sailcloth. The needles were less sharply pointed than the sailmaking needles, so that the thread went between the strands of the rope rather than penetrated them. Each stitch on the largest sails took a minute or more to complete, as the needle was tapped through with a stitch mallet.

Other stitched-in ropes were used to limit the stretch of a sail, but the ends of these ropes were tapered down by cutting away some of the fibres from each strand.

Sails were reefed in heavy weather. That is, the area of sail presented to the wind was reduced by rolling it up partly or wholly and lashing it to the boom. Reefs were taken in by means of lengths of rope stitched and knotted into the canvas, at regular intervals in straight lines, one line for each reef or reduction in area that was required. Some sailmakers preferred another method by which a small hole was cut in the sail where each reef point was needed. Then a metal ring was placed in the hole and stitched around, and a further, smaller turnover eye hammered in to protect thread and canvas. These sewn eyelets, as they were called,

THIMBLES AND EYELETS *Holes have to be cut in the sail to pass ropes through it, for holding it to spars or to reduce its area – reef it – in heavy weather. The holes are lined with metal rings, called eyelets or thimbles, to prevent the rope from chafing the canvas, and the sailmaker hammers the ring tight with a special mallet.*

threaded with lines, served both as reef points and as a means of lashing up the sail when in harbour.

The heaviest of all such fastenings was the cringle, the ring that secured the corner of the sail to the ropes that held it in tension. It was made by threading a ring of spliced rope through two sewn eyelets near the corner of the sail, and lining it with a thimble or metal ring that took the wear of the rope when the sail was hoisted. A tight fit was ensured by hammering the rope ring or grommet down a wooden cone called a fid. The sailmaker then pulled the grommet off the fid and hammered in the thimble, which was held in place by the subsequent contraction of the rope.

When the sails were finished they had to be proofed, and each sailmaker had his own recipe for doing this. Sails and ropes were steeped in troughs containing a horrid broth whose ingredients might include red ochre, pilchard oil and crushed stones. The sails were said to be properly proofed when they had absorbed enough of the paste to stand up on their own.

Making sails for even a small merchant vessel involved a lot of work. A suit comprising mainsail, topsail, mizzen, foresail and three jibs for a Thames spritsail barge, for example, took four months of skilled and strenuous labour. There were 650 sq. yds of thick flax canvas to be sewn, with some of the sails requiring as many as 14 layers of cloth at the stress points. Some 800 ft of bolt rope was involved. The head rope of the mainsail alone was fully 8 in. in circumference, and weighed the best part of 100 lb.

Modern materials, such as Terylene, have made the sailmaker's job easier, since they are far less prone to stretching and far more resistant to rot than the old sailcloth. On the other hand, the virtual disappearance of working boats under sail, and the production of mass-produced classes of yachts with identical sailplans, has led to a huge contraction in the trade. Falmouth, for instance, still a thriving yachting centre, was able to provide work for

more than a dozen sail lofts at the turn of the century. Now there are only two.

The sailmaker is still a craftsman, even in a world where Terylene is cut with scissors or a heated knife and the traditional tools have been abandoned. Since the modern materials last much longer than either canvas or cotton, the threads and bolt ropes are usually synthetic, too.

Yet some of the old skills are just as much in demand as ever. The tough competition of ocean racing creates a demand for new sails in which the control of tensions and shapes is vital. Cutting and sewing a big tri-radial spinnaker, for example, requires more than a nodding acquaintance with three-dimensional geometry.

And fortunately for the survival of the craft, there is still a small remnant of the business that was once its staple trade. There are sailing oyster dredgers farming the oyster beds in the sheltered waters of the Fal estuary for example, and the growing interest in the restoration and maintenance of old ships or modern replicas by the Maritime Trust, the Sea Cadets or the Sail Training Association keeps the old ways alive. The materials may be new, but the sailmaker's skills are every bit as vital as those of his predecessors who made the sails that carried the *Victory* into Trafalgar.

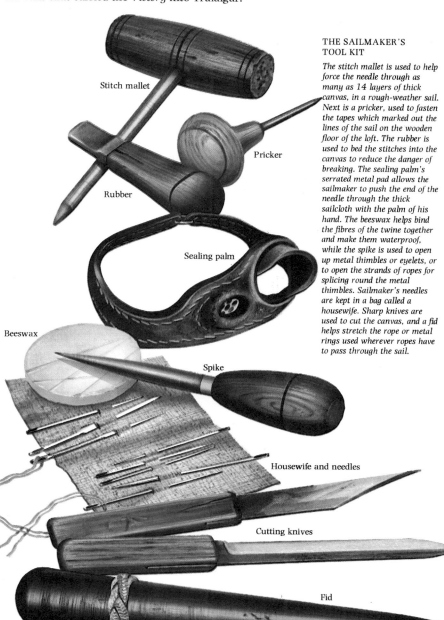

THE SAILMAKER'S TOOL KIT

The stitch mallet is used to help force the needle through as many as 14 layers of thick canvas, in a rough-weather sail. Next is a pricker, used to fasten the tapes which marked out the lines of the sail on the wooden floor of the loft. The rubber is used to bed the stitches into the canvas to reduce the danger of breaking. The sealing palm's serrated metal pad allows the sailmaker to push the end of the needle through the thick sailcloth with the palm of his hand. The beeswax helps bind the fibres of the twine together and make them waterproof, while the spike is used to open up metal thimbles or eyelets, or to open the strands of ropes for splicing round the metal thimbles. Sailmaker's needles are kept in a bag called a housewife. Sharp knives are used to cut the canvas, and a fid helps stretch the rope or metal rings used wherever ropes have to pass through the sail.

Stitch mallet

Pricker

Rubber

Sealing palm

Beeswax

Spike

Housewife and needles

Cutting knives

Fid

THE
SILVERSMITH &
GOLDSMITH

WORKING EITHER METAL CALLS FOR SIMILAR
TOOLS AND TECHNIQUES. AS MANY AS 40 DIFFERENT
HAMMERS ARE NEEDED, AND A PRECISION FOSTERED
BY LONG APPRENTICESHIP

*M*en go mad for gold. They kill for it, die for it, and endure hardship and privation to win it. And the world revolves around thousands of glittering tons of it, hidden in silent caverns of steel and concrete guarded by every means man can devise: the everlasting, untarnishing security for currency dealings between men and between nations.

For the very few, it is fashioned into precious objects that are treasured and passed on through generations.

Silver, once used in common coinage, is now deemed too precious for the pockets of the people – modern coins are of base metal alloys – but it is still within the reach of many in the form of knives, forks and spoons; bowls and dishes; pots and jugs, and many other ornamental and useful wares.

Both gold and silver are mined in an almost pure state – often together – and easily worked by similar methods that have changed little down the ages. They can be beaten, bent, cast and cut with sharp tools into almost any shape. The men who do it are goldsmiths and silversmiths – the craft is the same, but they tend to work with one metal or the other.

Craftsmen who work in gold are deeply conscious that what they make – like the metal – can last for ever; and that it will have to stand comparison with the beautiful artefacts of their predecessors back through the centuries. For, astonishingly, almost all the gold mined since the Stone Age – about 100,000 tons of it – can be accounted for, and about half that quantity has been mined since 1850. All the gold that has ever been mined could be cast into a cube measuring only about 19 yds on all sides. But if the gold were to be spread rather than compressed, an ounce of gold could be beaten into a microscopically thin sheet covering 100 sq. ft, or drawn into an ultra-fine wire 50 miles long.

It is normally cast into ingots with a minimum purity of 995 parts of pure gold per 1,000. Goldsmiths buy it from bullion dealers in sheets and wires of varying thicknesses, and beadings and castings of varying patterns. There are, too, a selection of colours available, from almost red to silver-like 'white gold', according to the other metals with which it is alloyed.

Both gold and silver in their pure state are too soft for practical use, and are usually strengthened with a copper alloy: 18-carat gold, for instance, is 18 parts gold to 6 parts copper alloy, 24-carat being pure gold. Silver, also delivered by bullion dealers in sheets, wires, tubes and castings, is usually of a quality known as 'standard' or 'Sterling' silver, which is 925 parts pure silver to 75 parts copper alloy. A finer quality, used less frequently nowadays, is 'Britannia standard', 958 parts silver to 42 parts copper alloy.

Before working on either sheet silver or gold, the craftsman usually cleans and 'anneals' it. The metal is 'pickled' in a bath of warm, diluted sulphuric acid to remove

MARKS OF QUALITY

LONDON

EDINBURGH

BIRMINGHAM

SHEFFIELD

Everything made of gold or silver in Britain is stamped with symbols and letters indicating its purity, where it was assayed (valued), who made it and when it was made. This is known as hallmarking. There are four British assay offices – their emblems are shown above. Sterling silver is marked with a lion, and Britannia with a seated figure of Britannia. Gold is marked with a crown, and numerals showing how many parts per 1,000 are pure gold. Single letters in various scripts on differently shaped shields denote the year of manufacture. The maker's mark is the firm's symbol, or often simply initials.

grease and dirt from the surface. It is then heated up to a dull red – not more than about 1,100–1,300°F (590–700°C) generally – allowed to cool for a moment or two, and finally quenched, again in diluted sulphuric acid. This burns off any remaining dirt and evens out stresses and strains in the metal, leaving it soft and more easily worked.

To work the metal, the craftsman uses a bewildering array of tools, implements, equipment and materials – and he will have spent up to five years as an apprentice, learning to handle them. He will also have accumulated many of the hand-tools he will need throughout his working life – including probably 40 hammers of varying kinds, pincers, pliers and other gripping tools, incredibly fine saws, files, chisels, scoring tools, punches, measuring instruments and

RAISING THE SILVER

The grey piece of metal that silversmith George Oliver is working on here will become, eventually, a graceful, octagonal cream jug. Below are two of the many 'stakes' on which he raises the original flat disc of silver. In the first of the small pictures, he is using a doming hammer to curl over a lip on the saucer shape he has already made. He forms the lip by beating the silver against an indentation hollowed in a stump of wood – one of several cut in the stump for this kind of work. Other pictures show how different stakes and hammers are brought into play at earlier and later stages of the raising. On the left, against the background of his busy workshop, George shows how a 'flat' of the octagon shape is formed.

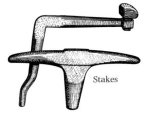

Stakes

shaped pieces of metal and wood upon which the work is formed.

Broadly speaking, domed or dished articles are made by being beaten to shape; boxes are made by scoring sheet metal, folding it into box shape, and soldering the joints together; other items are cast from wooden or base-metal patterns – often in hollow halves, to save weight, which are soldered together later.

This casting technique is used also for decorative designs that are soldered again on to other work; and in silverware for such parts as spouts, handles and feet, though complete pieces such as candlesticks and candelabra can also be made in this way. Castings are worked on with files and chisels to sharpen the design details.

To watch a master craftsman make something even as mundane – in terms of silversmithing – as a humble cream jug, is a most rewarding experience. George Oliver works still for the London firm to which he was apprenticed in 1937 – Nayler Bros, of Clerkenwell Road. He still has the two craft manuals and the family Bible presented to him at Goldsmiths Hall, in the City, when he was accepted for training.

When he completed his apprenticeship and was admitted to the 'freedom of the Mystery of Goldsmiths of the City of London' he became entitled to apply to become a Freeman of the City. He did so, and walked from Goldsmiths Hall after receiving one freedom, to the Guildhall, to receive the other.

To make the jug, which as an added complication is

octagonal rather than round, George starts with a simple, flat disc of sheet silver. Having cleaned and annealed it, he begins 'raising' it by placing the edge against a suitably shaped steel stake and beating it with a 'raising hammer' until it assumes a shape something like a tea plate.

Other smiths might start by 'doming' the disc – beating it with a 'doming hammer' into a shape hollowed out in a block of wood. He demonstrates by hammering the raised rim of his 'plate' into a curled-up lip, beating it against one of several small, rounded indentations hollowed in the top of a wooden stump.

'Whichever method you use,' he says, 'you always start at the edge – never the middle.'

He resumes his raising process, turning the silver round so that he beats it in overlapping concentric circles, first one way, then the reverse, to keep the metal at an even thickness. This beating hardens the silver again, so he anneals it, to soften the metal and relieve the new stresses imposed by the hammering. Annealing takes place at frequent intervals – as many as 20 times – in the course of the work, for the same reasons.

Gradually, by doming and raising, the 'plate' takes on a bowl-like shape, and as the bowl deepens and the mouth becomes too narrow for a normal hammer, he selects one with a long, curved head that reaches inside the vessel.

As he works he reveals the secret of the 'snarling iron', with which a vessel may still be beaten when the neck opening has become too narrow even for a curved-head hammer. The snarling iron is a stake with a long shank curved up and shaped at the end, which can reach inside the vessel. The other end of the iron is gripped in a vice, and it is at this end that the stake is struck, the sympathetic vibrations causing the end inside the vessel to continue hammering until the required shape is achieved.

'For this part of the job,' says George, 'we have X-ray eyes!'

Now the jug is beginning to take on its basic form, and he

checks the accuracy of his work by placing it in a plaster-of-Paris mould or passing it through a cut-out template to ensure that its lines and proportions are absolutely correct. A few careful taps are usually enough to make good any deficiencies.

Then comes the task of turning the shape of the vessel from round to octagonal. This is begun by dividing the circumference into eight segments, marked vertically from base to lip with a pointed scriber. George then begins to flatten each segment, beating it over a shaped stake, hitting the rounded surface – never the corners. As if by magic, the octagonal lines begin to emerge as all eight segments are flattened, until the body of the jug is complete.

At this stage the hammer marks of the raising and doming processes must be removed. This is accomplished by beating the surface lightly with a highly polished 'planishing hammer' in overlapping strokes. As George taps away, the matt-grey surface of the silver begins to shine as the old hammer marks are smoothed out. Finally, the 'lines' of the octagon are made perfect, usually by the most delicate hammering.

The base of the jug is raised and made octagonal in much the same way, then soldered on to the body, along with the spout and elegant handle, which are both castings and which have been filed and chased to perfection. Finally, the edges of the base and rim are stiffened with soldered-on 'wire' of the required shape, and the jug is ready for the polishers.

SIGN OF A GOLDBEATER

*This brawny arm wielding a
huge mallet was a sign mounted
outside the workshop of a
London goldbeater in the late
18th century. It is made of
gilded wood, and heavy mallets
of the same type are used still to
beat gold into micro-thin sheets
of gold leaf.*

How the soldering is done

Soldering silver, like many other aspects of the silversmith's art, is simple enough in itself, but requires great skill, precise judgment – and a steady hand. The solder used is a silver alloy with a melting point only slightly lower than that of the silver used in the parts to be joined, and is made mostly in rods and strips of varying thickness. As in ordinary 'tin' soldering, a chemical 'flux' is needed to ensure a proper joint, dissolving the oxides in both silver and solder and preventing oxides from forming when heat is applied.

The flux in this instance is made by grinding up a lump of borax and mixing the powder with water until it forms a light, creamy paste. This is painted on to the parts where the solder must run, the solder strip laid between the parts, and just enough heat applied with a blow-lamp to make the solder run, without melting the silver.

Gold is soldered in the same way, again using borax for the flux and, of course, gold solder.

The art of decoration

Many and wondrous are the ways of the artist-craftsman given the freedom to stretch his skill and imagination on an artefact in gold or silver. Some of the most beautiful pieces ever made grew under the hands of men working at the dawn of history – Egyptians, Greeks and Cretans. Rome and Byzantium added to the treasure, with early Celtic masters whose delicate and convoluted designs and decorations are still copied.

The Middle Ages saw great advances in techniques, flowering into the superb Renaissance masterpieces of such artists as Benvenuto Cellini. Florid 18th-century rococo, with its ornate scroll-work, gave way to Regency elegance, and the heavy extravagance of the Victorian era to the flowing, natural lines of *art nouveau* and the cerebral simplicity of the modern masters.

But design and inspiration apart, their decorative effects were mostly achieved by a few established basic methods:
Repoussé, in which the design is raised in relief from the surface by being punched out from behind with special punches and hammers.
Chasing, in which the design is cut into the metal with sharp chisels and other tools.
Engraving, by which the design is first drawn or traced on to the surface with a sharp-pointed tool, then deepened with a hardened-steel tool called a graver, making the work glitter attractively as light falls on it from different angles. Designs in low relief can also be made by this method, using another tool, a scorper, to pare away thin, broad shavings – rather like super-delicate wood-chiselling.
Filigree work, done by applying a design to the surface in thin wire.
Inlaying, in which different metals are cut out into mating shapes that are then fitted together to form a design which can be soldered on to the work. Sometimes the article itself is cut and inlaid with a different metal, and 'Damascening' is the art of inlaying gold and silver on steel or iron.

Another form of inlay is called Niello: a black alloy made of silver, copper, lead and sulphur, which melts easily, is run into a design cut into the silver or gold. The technique was used by the Romans, and can be seen decorating the ring of King Aethelwulf (839–58) in the British Museum, showing that it was established in England at an early date.
Silver gilt, a process by which a thin film of gold is applied to silver. The modern method is by electro-plating, but the older way was to apply a mixture of gold and mercury to the surface, then heat it to burn away the mercury.
Cut card, in which sheet silver or gold is pierced with cut-out designs, then soldered on to other work to form a design in relief.

The special skill of the polisher

The flawless polish on a new piece of silver is the product of craftsmen whose skills take five years of apprenticeship to master. The piece, matt-grey from its final clean-up in the pickling bath, is polished first with a special sand and a leather buff mounted on a powered spindle.

Holding the silver against the revolving buff, the polisher feeds fistfuls of sand between them, manipulating the piece until the surface is smooth and bright. Next, a calico mop primed with a mixture of wax and mild abrasive is used to give the work a second, finer polish, followed by a third, using a softer mop and a rouge-based proprietary polish. Small rotary brushes – sometimes on a flexible-drive spindle – polish inside crevices and take care of detail work. Sticks of a special stone are also used for detail polishing. This ultra-fine grindstone is found only in the Water of Ae river, in Dumfries and Galloway, and is always used wet. Final polishing is usually with a mixture of paraffin and rouge powder on a very soft mop. Occasionally, swansdown mops are also used when a super-fine finish is required.

SPINNING THE SILVER TO SHAPE

A quicker method of producing bowls, cups and similar round, dished vessels is known as 'spinning'. It is particularly useful if a number of similar pieces have to be turned out. For instance, a bowl can be made by first turning a piece of hardwood to the required shape on a lathe, then remounting it on the lathe with a disc of sheet silver held at the base of the wooden 'pattern', so that both turn together. As they turn, a spinning tool – which looks like a long-handled chisel with a rounded, highly polished tip – is used to force the metal against the pattern, so that gradually it, too, assumes the shape of the wooden 'bowl' around which it is formed.

This sounds easier than it is, for it demands great skill and a fairly strong arm. The silversmith above has almost completed a spinning: the spinning tool, held steady against a 'stop', is forcing the metal into the shape of the base. Some of the wooden patterns used are illustrated here.

Wooden patterns

THE SKILL OF THE SPLITTER

A skilled splitter opens up a gap between adjacent layers of slate in a single block with a sharp-edged, broad-bladed chisel. First he taps the handle of the chisel gently with a mallet to start the split and then, by working the handle of the chisel to and fro, he widens the crack until the whole block splits into two pieces. For roofing, he repeats the process to split the block into layers $\frac{1}{6}$ in. thick. A good splitter can cut slates considerably thinner than this, though much depends on the quality of the block.

THE
Slate Worker

FROM THE MIST-SHROUDED VALLEYS OF NORTH WALES
CAME THE DURABLE ROOF OF MANY A SUBURBAN HOME
– AND MORE DELICATE CREATIONS BESIDES

For centuries, slate roofs have been as familiar a part of the British landscape as roofs covered in thatch or tiles – and with good reason, for top-quality slates are practically everlasting.

When restoration work on St Asaph Cathedral, in North Wales, reached the re-roofing stage, the plans had to be changed. As the existing slates were removed, the experts were astonished to find that after 250 years of rugged Welsh weather they were still as good as new – so good that, instead of being thrown away, they were replaced to serve for another two or three centuries.

Why is slate such a good roofing material? Few things are harder or tougher than rock, and true slates are made from thin layers of sedimentary rock. These formed originally from sand and mud at the bottom of ancient seas, and then dried, hardened and became compressed over millions of years. Because this process was gradual, compared with the violent spasms that created volcanic rocks, the rock strata tends to be formed in flat sheets. This enables the slate to be split into very thin layers along the grain of the rock, assuring both lightness and economy.

Slates of one kind or another occur in many parts of Britain. Elland flags and Rochdale flags, which are used in West Yorkshire, East Lancashire and Derbyshire, are quarried from coal-bearing rock, as also are the Rough Rim flags of Halifax and Huddersfield and the Alton rock of North Staffordshire.

Collyweston slates in Northamptonshire and Rutland, and also in Oxfordshire and Lincolnshire to a lesser extent, are not true slates at all but are split from blocks of limestone. The same is true of the Stonefield slates of Gloucester and Dorset.

Northern slaters often use sandstone slates, quarried in the Yorkshire Dales, while their opposite numbers in the south-east use the same material in the form of Horsham stone slates.

But the best slates of all, having no rivals for strength, lightness and resistance to fire or water, are found mainly in Westmorland and Cornwall and, above all, in the dark, brooding valleys of North Wales.

The North Wales slate industry dates back to the middle of the 18th century when the first groups of quarrymen, working on the Pennant estate in the wilds of Snowdonia, brought their slates on pack-ponies down the precarious mountainside paths to the creeks and harbours of the Menai Strait. The Pennants had made their fortune in the West Indian sugar trade, and Richard Pennant was quick to recognise the potential of the slate business in an otherwise totally unproductive part of his lands.

He bought out all the local men, took them on as workers when he opened up the vast quarry at Bethesda, and set about building roads, tramways and a big new harbour at

Port Penrhyn. Within 40 years, slate production had gone up from 2,000 tons a year to 40,000, and Richard's descendants were the Barons of Penrhyn, living in a new mock-medieval castle built at a cost of half a million pounds when the working wage was less than a pound a week.

By then, quarries had been opened up at nearby Dinorwic, at Blaenau Ffestiniog, which was destined to become the slate capital of the world, and as far away as Llangollen.

Experts can tell where slate comes from by its colour. Slate from Nantlle tends to be greenish-grey, while Corris slate has rusty hues in the basic grey. In some parts of Caernarfonshire, slates vary from blue to a reddish-purple tint, while most Ffestiniog slates are blue-grey. Slates from Penmachno and Dolwyddelan, like Cornish slates, tend to be almost black.

Like mining for gold or drilling for oil, the financial and physical risks in quarrying were enormous, but the profits were correspondingly vast. It used to be said that a successful quarry needed three companies to develop it, the first two going bankrupt in the process while the third would survive to reap the benefits.

These benefits could be generous indeed, as in the Llechwedd Old Vein above Blaenau Ffestiniog, which was found after 15 years of searching and which produced slate by the thousands of tons for a century and a half. Even now, it is the main source of slate for one of the few surviving working slate quarries in North Wales.

Working the slate was a hard and often crippling life, the chief hazards being the penetrating slate dust which collected in the lungs, and the danger of broken bones resulting from a missed step high on the working face. But compared with coal-mining, the hazards were fewer and less lethal: there was no risk of gas, and the roofs in the underground galleries were self-supporting provided huge pillars of slate were left in between the working chambers. Also, most seams of slate were so thick that there was no need to work in the kind of cramped conditions so common at the coal-face.

Yet the operations were on an epic scale. The Llechwedd quarry, which was not the largest in Ffestiniog, had at one time more than 100 working chambers at 24 different levels, burrowing deep into the mountain and fed by almost 60 miles of tramways and cable hoists.

The first step was actually to reach the slate, and clearing the site of a quarry could easily account for one-third of the

WELSH SLATE

To the uninitiated, all slates are grey, but a closer look shows tones varying from purple to green or blue, or even red – depending on the quarries from which they came. Slate is fireproof, rotproof and waterproof, as well as light in weight. A roof covered with top-quality slates is lighter than thatch and only half the weight of a tiled roof. Most slate is still used for roofing, but other uses include tombstones, fence-posts, billiard tables, blackboards and electrical switchboards. Even the powdered waste can be used in making paint and toothpaste.

Roofing slates (see drawing) are nailed through drilled holes to horizontal battens, which, in turn, are fastened to rafters. Each row overlaps the one below, and the vertical joins are staggered.

company's costs. Sometimes the seams of slate reached the surface in a cliff-face, so that they could be worked on a series of open-air terraces like giant steps in the hillside, as they were at Dinorwic.

More usually, the seam was buried under the surface, as in the Llechwedd Old Vein, which slopes down into the mountain at an angle of 30 degrees, so that the workings have to follow it deeper and deeper into the earth.

These underground workings followed strict rules: a working chamber could be up to 45 ft wide, but it had to be separated from the next chamber by a pillar of slate at least 40 ft wide to support the levels above.

Once the slate was reached, it was the job of the rockmen to bring it out. Splitting, or cleaving, the slate along the grain was easy enough, but 'pillaring' it – splitting it across the grain to produce roughly rectangular blocks with as little waste as possible – was much more difficult.

Sometimes the rockmen were lucky enough to find a joint in about the right place and at the correct angle, a natural crack across the cleavage planes of the slate caused by stress or shrinkage while the slate was being formed. They would then have to set to work with hand drills, called jumpers, to bore a hole large enough to place explosive charges within the joint.

If all went well, a block of slate as nearly rectangular as possible and large enough to be economic was blasted out of its place in the quarry face. But if the charge was too big, or too small, or in the wrong place, then much of the slate would be smashed into slivers and unusable fragments.

If there was no convenient joint in the rock, then the rockmen would have to make their own by boring a series of holes in a long line, and then joining the holes together in an operation called channelling, using a special broaching tool in a sawing action.

Each block of slate produced by the rockmen weighed several tons, and had to be split, with a hammer and chisel, along the grain to produce blocks of around 2 tons in weight. These were loaded on to trucks and taken to the splitters and dressers.

Each underground chamber was let to a team of four men – two working underground extracting the blocks, and two working in the mill splitting slate from those blocks. The men in the mill worked only on blocks from their own chambers. When unloaded from the trucks, the blocks were roughly split again, into layers 4 in. or 8 in. thick, and then they would be sawn across the grain into something like the size of the finished slates. Only then did the splitter start work on them.

There were many different sizes of slate, and different qualities to denote thickness, toughness and uniformity of grain. In Cheshire, slates had picturesque and complicated names such as 'Haughattles' and 'Widetts', while in North Wales they were usually classified by degrees of female nobility, ranging from Narrow Ladies at 16 in. × 8 in., up to Viscountesses, Duchesses and Princesses, the latter measuring 24 in. × 14 in.

The final splitting and dressing was a highly skilled business, since any mistake could ruin a top-quality slate and even spoil a whole block. This was disastrous, for men were paid by results.

The splitter would take the block and stand it on end with its face resting against the outside of his leg. Then he would take a small mallet and a broad-bladed chisel and carefully tap a straight cut across the end face of the slate block. Once the cut had been made right across the end of the block, he could use harder taps of the mallet to drive the chisel deeper. By working the blade of the chisel to and fro by hand, he could widen the cut to the point where the slate block would suddenly pull apart into two separate pieces, splitting along the cleavage plane opened up by the original cut.

He would then repeat the operation, splitting and re-splitting each section into halves, until the original block had been cut into a pile of thin, even slates.

For roofing slates, the ideal thickness is around $\frac{1}{6}$ in. – that is, 24 slates from a 4 in. block – but a skilled splitter can split the slate into much thinner layers if needed. At one competition in 1872, a champion splitter cleaved a $2\frac{1}{2}$ in. block into 45 separate and even-sized layers – each of them just over $\frac{1}{20}$ in. thick.

PILLARING THE SLATE

The first step in quarrying the slate is to split the vein into blocks which can be taken to the splitters and dressers, to be cleaved and trimmed to the required size and shape. High on the working face, the rockman is anchored by a safety chain as he uses a rock drill and explosive charges to break the slate seam along transverse cracks and water channels called joints. This produces blocks weighing many tons, which then have to be split into blocks small enough to be moved.

SLATE FAN

The best-quality slate is soft enough for its regular grain to be cut with a knife into paper-thin slivers – hence the fashion for delicately decorated ornaments like the traditional fans, with scores of identical slats, each one carved from the same block of slate and held together by a central pin. This one bears the name of the Oakeley quarries, largest of the slate-quarrying companies of Blaenau Ffestiniog, together with the crest of the Prince of Wales. It was made in 1913, one of the last of the relatively good years in the slate industry. Most fans were made in spare moments, snatched from a busy working day.

Using top-quality slate like that from the Old Vein at Llechwedd, today's splitters can coax as many as 35 sheets to the inch for delicate ornamental work.

But splitting is only half the job. Although the split slates are now of the required thickness, their shape is still that of the rough block from which they have been cleaved. They still have to be dressed, or cut to final size and shape, and given the right kind of chamfered edge needed for roofing slates.

In the old days this was done by hand with a knife, and great care was needed to avoid spoiling a set of beautifully split slates through clumsy dressing.

In the end, the problem was solved by developing a powered dressing machine. A set of blades arranged like those of a lawn-mower in a rotating cylinder, and driven slowly by water, steam or electric power, allowed the dresser to hold the slate at the correct place and angle for the blades to trim each edge in turn to the right dimensions.

Splitting and dressing, like all the other operations connected with producing the slates, was done on the spot, in the heart of the quarry itself. Often, the men had to spend an hour or more at each end of the day walking to and from their work high on the mountainside or deep below the surface. Thus, visitors to the remote upper lake of the Electricity Board's Ffestiniog pumped-storage scheme high above the town can see no sign of human handiwork at that height other than the waste tips of old quarries on the crest of the ridge several hundred feet higher still.

Shelters that became meeting places

All breaks, for rest or meals, had to be taken on the working face, usually in the rough stone shelter, or caban, where the men would take refuge from blasting. As a result, the caban became a social centre, a political club, a debating society and a general meeting hall.

In a trade and a society so remote from the outside world, education was highly prized and most of the men's savings went on buying books, setting up libraries, and helping to found the University College of North Wales at Bangor. Even in Victorian times, there were quarrymen who could read Latin and Greek, as well as English and their own native Welsh.

Eventually the slate reached its final user, the slater whose job it was to use the sheets to cover a roof – and here methods varied from area to area. In the Cotswolds, for example, a 'slatter' would be prepared to work with quite rough material, plugging holes in broken slates and using smaller pieces of slate, called gallets, to fill gaps between badly dressed slates. In the Pennines, in Wales or in Cornwall, slaters expected their slates to be properly trimmed and sized, and they worked to definite local patterns in the way they used different sizes of slates to cope with gables and dormers and other features of a roof.

In North Wales, too, slates were hung on the walls as well as on the roofs, overlapping in elaborate patterns.

Not all the slate left the quarry villages though. The very best slate was so soft that it could be carved by hand, using a sharp knife and a steady hand, and there is a long-established tradition of making delicate slate ornaments.

Slate fans, for example, are made of as many as 50 wafer-thin slats. Each one is elaborately carved, and all are pivoted at one end to open up into a curve as smooth and regular as that of any Japanese paper fan. They are so light and delicate that it is difficult to remember that the basic raw material is rock.

There are other uses for slate too: from doorsteps and window-sills to tombstones and fences, made from narrow slabs of slate set upright in the ground and joined together by wire.

MOVING THE SLATES TO MARKET

One-third of the cost of producing a roofing slate went into carrying it to wherever it was needed. For the Ffestiniog quarry owners, this at first meant shipping it down-river by boat to the sea at Portmadoc. Losses, breakages and high costs led to the building, in 1836, of a narrow-gauge railway, linking the different quarries at Blaenau Ffestiniog to the Portmadoc wharves. Empty wagons were hauled up the 13 mile line by horses. Because of the continuously falling gradient, loaded trains could freewheel all the way downhill, with the horse riding in its own wagon ready for the next uphill journey. In time, steam locomotives took over the work, including the pioneer Fairlies – in effect, two engines joined together back-to-back, with a cab in the centre, to provide adequate power within the confines of a narrow-gauge line. In its time, the railway carried quarrymen to work, children to school and on holiday trips to the seaside, and corpses to the graveyard in a special hearse wagon. Closed after the war with the decline in the slate trade, it has now been restored.

Unfortunately, not all the slate blasted from the terraces and galleries of the quarries could be used. It takes between 10 and 20 tons of slate to produce 1 ton of good-quality roofing slates. The waste – blocks which are broken or splintered by blasting, or which have faults in the grain, or cracks of one kind or another – is piled into mountains all over North Wales, giving an idea of the scale of the industry at its peak.

The last 70 years have seen a decline caused by several different factors, including a sharp increase in cheaper roofing tiles and even slate imports from highly mechanised quarries in France.

Yet slate remains probably the toughest and longest-lasting of all building materials. Though slate roofs are expensive, there are signs that enough people are becoming aware of their virtues to produce a turning of the commercial tide. Several areas of Britain have bye-laws which make slate roofs compulsory on all new buildings.

The nature of Ffestiniog slate is such that it is doubtful whether it could ever be produced as a totally mechanised operation. For the time being at least, the jobs of the craftsmen seem safe enough, whether producing roofing slates in the methods of their fathers or grandfathers or fashioning plaques and ashtrays, fans and paperweights, to satisfy growing public appreciation of the intrinsic beauty of the slate itself.

THE
SPINNER
AND WEAVER

THOUGH THE WOOL TRADE, SOURCE OF SO MUCH PAST PROSPERITY, HAS DECLINED, THE AGE-OLD CRAFTS OF SPINNING AND WEAVING HAVE CHANGED HARDLY AT ALL

As his soldiers mounted the breach in Harfleur's defences, Henry V led them on with the words 'Cry God for Harry, England and St George!' Perhaps into his helmet he added, 'And for the wool trade, too', and if he did not, he should have, since without the support of the English wool and cloth merchants he would not have grounded a single keel on the beaches of France.

Not that their motives had much to do with King Harry's dreams of empire, and fame in battle. Like their ancestors before them, for 200 years and more, their chief concern was to ensure that the markets of the Continent remained open to them, and the best means of doing so was to provide the monarch with an army sufficiently well-equipped to hold and expand England's possessions in France. Considering the profits involved, it seemed a reasonable price to pay.

Throughout the Middle Ages, and for centuries after, wool was 'the flower and strength, the revenue and blood, of England'. Many reminders of its importance are with us to this day – the sumptuous churches of East Anglia and Wessex, the legend that London Bridge was built on sacks of wool (actually from the proceeds of a wool tax), the woolsack seat of the Lord Chancellor, and the 150 'lost' villages of the Lincolnshire Wolds whose medieval inhabitants had been evicted to make way for sheep runs. For centuries, to encourage the wool trade, the English were legally bound to be buried in woollen shrouds; and half the artisans of Europe were clad in tough cloth from Kersey, now a sleepy but elegant Suffolk village. Even English

surnames bear witness to the large numbers of people involved in the wool trade. Weaver, for example, and Dyer, Mercer, Fuller and Walker – a walker was a labourer who trod cloth to shrink and compact it.

English cloth, or rather, British, since the cloths of Scotland and Wales have achieved equal fame, has retained its reputation down the years. Much of the credit is due to Robert Bakewell and his fellow stock-breeding pioneers of the 18th and early 19th centuries; it was their efforts that led to the breeding of sheep whose wool was intended to match a variety of purposes. The Cheviot, for example, whose crisp fleece makes fine tweeds; the Dalesbred, whose tough wool is better suited to making carpets; and the Dorset Horn, with its close, white fleece ideal for sheepskin coats.

But though sheep may have changed, the basic principles of spinning and weaving have hardly changed at all. Present-day wool fabrics go through essentially the same set of processes as they did in the Middle Ages, even if those processes have been progressively mechanised and automated over the intervening years.

Spinning and weaving – farm crafts

For hundreds of years, weaving was carried out on the farm. It was a useful occupation for the winter months, and in parts of Wales, for example, farm workers were expected to know as much about spinning and weaving as they did about ploughing or tending animals. Sometimes, when the farm did not produce sufficient wool to keep the weavers busy, a farmer would buy further supplies from neighbours. Of course, since he would be able to buy only at shearing time, he would have to purchase enough to last him through the winter.

But gradually, as machines took over more and more work from local craftsmen, output increased and the producers had to look for markets farther and farther afield. Increased competition and mechanisation led to industrialisation, and to concentrating the trade in the urban areas of places such as west Wales and mid-Wales, and later in Yorkshire and in south-west England. It was only in the more remote parts of Britain that individual craftsmen continued to serve the needs of their own communities. In such places, the old craft has survived almost unchanged to the present day. Curiously, despite regional variations in weaves and patterns, the processes that transform wool into cloth differ very little from area to area and from workshop to workshop.

Newly sheared wool is heavy with grease, so the first step is to clean it. In the Middle Ages, weavers used lye, an alkaline mixture of water and vegetable ashes, but this was replaced by a formula of one part of urine to three parts of water. The wool was then washed and rinsed in baskets at the bottom of a fast-flowing stream, after which it was spread on a hurdle to dry.

Unravelling the tangled fibres was a matter of feeding the wool into a machine called, in different parts of the country, a devil, a tucker, a willey or a wool mill. It consisted of a large drum studded with rows of iron spikes inside a wooden box. When the drum was turned, by hand or by water power, the rows of spikes acted as a rough comb, which pulled the matted fibres apart. The willey could also be used to mix wools of different colours or grades. The famous Welsh grey blankets, for example, were given their colour by feeding equal amounts of black wool and white wool into the machine.

Of course, many other colours could be produced by dyeing the wool, either before or after it was passed through the willey. Natural dyeing agents included elderberries, indigo or woad to give different kinds of blue; gallnut or oak

CARDING THE WASHED FLEECE

Wool fibres grow in all directions on the sheep's back. They must be combed to make them all lie the same way before they can be spun, so yielding longer and tougher strands. Before machines took over, workers used hand cards to do the job. (The word 'card' comes from carduus, *the Latin for thistle. Teasels, thistle-like plants, were at one time used for combing.) Hand cards were, in fact, wooden bats studded with metal spikes, and the wool was combed backwards and forwards between them until all the fibres had been separated.*

bark to turn white or grey wool black; gorse, broom, birch or iris to turn it different tones of green; bramble to produce orange; blackberries for purple; hazel or bracken for yellow; foxgloves for red; and dandelion for a rich magenta hue.

But the willey was only the beginning of the separating process. Before spinning can begin, the fibres must be thoroughly and finely combed, or carded. Traditionally, this was done with teasels, the fruit of a thistle-like plant whose hooked spines were ideal for combing wool, and in some weaving areas the plants were grown specially for this purpose. Later, teasels were replaced by hand cards whose wooden or leather faces were studded with rows of metal teeth. They were always used in pairs, the wool being combed backwards and forwards between the two cards until all the fibres had been separated.

This was a laborious business, and eventually the job was taken over by machinery. The hand-held cards were replaced by a large toothed drum called a swift, driven by water power – or later, by steam – and with a set of smaller rollers called workers. The wool was combed in between the swift and the workers, while any wool which remained on the workers was combed off by strippers, a set of still smaller rollers.

There was another advantage to machine carding: when wool was carded by hand, the fibres were still too short for spinning, so they had to be joined together by workers called pieceners. Often, these were children, whose nimble fingers were particularly suited to the task. But eventually, carding machines came to incorporate a comb that separated the wool off the final roller and which rolled it into a soft continuous thread.

Even at this stage, the filaments of wool are far too weak for weaving, and must first be spun. Twisting wool fibres makes them thinner but stronger, and also at the same time joins individual fibres together into a tough continuous thread that holds together in the loom and gives strength to the finished cloth. At first, the only tools used were a distaff to hold the bundles of carded wool fibres, and a spindle on to which the wool was stretched and twisted. The task was made a great deal easier by the invention of the treadle-

SPINNING ON A WHEEL

Even after carding, wool fibres remain too short and too weak for satisfactory weaving. They have to be twisted round one another to build up a longer, stronger thread. Traditionally, this was done on a spindle, usually driven by a wheel and treadle to speed the process.

SPINNING ON A HAND SPINDLE

Before the invention of the spinning-wheel, the thread had to be spun on a hand spindle, a much more laborious business but one that needed little concentration. It was usually done at the same time as other routine tasks, such as watching over cooking pots.

powered spinning-wheel. In this, the rotary movement of the wheel is transferred by a driving belt to the spindle which pulls the raw wool off the distaff, stretching and twisting the fibres as it spins. But, efficient as it is, this spinning-wheel can only create one thread at a time – perfectly adequate for a cottage industry, but hardly suited to the demands of the textile boom that began in the late 18th century.

The answer lay in the development of more and more complex machines such as the spinning-jenny, the spinning-mule and the spinning-jack, in which, using the same principle as the spinning-wheel, whole rows of spindles and bobbins were powered first by water and later by steam. In other words, it was not the basic methods that changed, but the power sources and the production figures. So it was, too, with the loom, the main tool of the craft, the principle of which has changed little since it was invented at some time in prehistory. Any woven fabric has two sets of threads: the longitudinal warp threads, and the transverse weft threads which are passed between them, over some warp threads and under others, according to the pattern of the weave.

The warp threads are generally stronger than the weft; in the old days they were coated with size, produced from boiled rabbit skins. Now, as then, warping, the business of fitting the 800-odd warp threads to a full-width loom in the right sequence and at the right tension is a lengthy one, involving at least half a day's work by a highly skilled weaver. As a rule, he begins by assembling the bobbins of warp threads in a long, narrow, wooden box called a creel, containing as many as 30 bobbins of variously coloured yarns.

Great care must be taken to ensure that each thread is arranged in exactly the place it will occupy in the finished pattern. In a simple weave, with alternate warp threads going over and under each crossing of the weft, this is not too difficult, and in fact the whole method was designed to

Cheviot

Dorset Horn

Exmoor Horn

SELECTIVE WOOL BREEDING

The various breeds of sheep kept in different parts of the country – to suit local conditions – produce fleeces with distinctive qualities. For instance, sheep kept in the warmer, southern areas tend to grow finer wool. Two examples are the Dorset Horn, whose short fleece is ideal for sheepskin coats, and the Exmoor Horn, whose superb wool is fine enough for weaving into cloth for dress uniforms or for covering billiard tables. In contrast, the Cheviot, bred in cold, damp areas, grows a long, tough coat.

DYEING THE YARN *Apart from shades produced by mixing wools of different natural colours, wool can be dyed by boiling it in solutions such as elderberry for blue, bracken for yellow, or foxgloves for red. Here, wool is being dyed by Vanessa Robertson, who is in partnership with Norman Young (opposite page) at Dartington, in Devon.*

help the weaver keep track of how the threads were arranged. The bobbins in the creel are placed in two rows, depending on which threads will be above or below the weft thread at any given point in the pattern.

The threads are led one by one from their bobbins to a warping bat which the weaver holds in his right hand, and from there to the pegs on the wall-mounted warping frame. At each step, there is a check that the pattern is being followed. For example, each thread from a front-row bobbin comes out of the creel through its own individual hole in the lower of two rows of holes at the top of the creel, while threads from back-row bobbins, that will appear on the opposite side of the weft thread in the pattern, come out of the upper row of holes on the creel.

Operating the loom

When sufficient threads have been warped, the weaver begins the process of looming or beaming – that is, putting the threads on to the loom. It is absolutely vital that each thread is given exactly the same tension as all the others, or the finished article will never lie flat. However, if they are fastened to the loom between the same points and in the same way then the load on each thread should be the same.

Modern hand looms are almost indistinguishable from their 18th-century forbears, and even power looms have changed little, though sometimes they are more versatile, and certainly they are speedier in operation than their predecessors. Most looms are constructed rather like the framework for a four-poster bed: at the head (or the back, as the end farthest away from the weaver is called), the warp threads are tied to a horizontal beam called the warp beam. From this, the warp threads run along the length of the loom to another beam – the cloth beam – at the front of the machine. On the way, the threads pass through rings or eyelets, called healds or heddles, carried on sets of upright wires. Each set is stretched in a wooden frame, which can be raised or lowered by operating a foot pedal or hand lever.

The simplest loom needs only two frames, or shafts, as they are called on hand looms – one for all the odd threads in the warp and the other for the even threads. By raising one of the shafts and lowering the other, the weaver creates a shed, or opening, between alternate threads. If he passes a weft thread through this opening, right across the width of the loom, it will automatically go over and under alternate threads. As soon as the pedal is released, the gap closes up and the weft thread becomes an integral part of the weave. By pressing the other pedal, the warp threads are opened up again, but this time the threads which were at the bottom are now at the top and vice versa, and the weft thread can now be passed back in the reverse direction.

Of course, not all weaves are as simple as this: a loom with its warp threads split up between four shafts gives the weaver the opportunity of bypassing part of the warp with some of the weft threads, thereby creating more complex patterns. In the same way, each weft thread can be chosen from a range of different colours to build up different effects over a series of weft crossings.

Over the years, several improvements were made to the basic hand loom to make it more efficient. The weaver has to put most of his effort into passing the weft threads backwards and forwards, and anything that makes this easier is bound to speed the whole operation.

The first improvement was the development of the fly shuttle, a wooden block with pointed ends which contains the bobbin of weft thread that unrolls from inside the shuttle as it shoots from one side of the loom to the other. Then a track was provided for the shuttle to run in: actually, a movable batten called a sley which stretches right across the warp and has a comb attached for the warp threads to pass through. The sley is suspended from the beams at the top of the loom, and has a box for the shuttle at either end. Inside each shuttle box is a leather 'picker' which is attached to a spindle, while a length of string links the two pickers at opposite ends of the sley.

As he works, the weaver builds up a fast, jerky rhythm – he presses the foot pedals to set the shafts and then jerks the string attached to the pickers. This tugs the picker along its spindle to strike the shuttle and shoot it across to the other side. As soon as it arrives in the other shuttle box, the weaver pulls the sley towards him to push the thread firmly against the other weft threads, then tramps the pedals to reset the shafts before tugging the string to shoot the shuttle back again. To change colours, all he has to do is lift the shuttle out of the box, and drop another shuttle with the new weft thread into its place.

Gradually, thread by thread, the weave is built up until the article is finished. To reduce the work of warping and looming for each job, most warp and cloth beams are made in the form of rollers. This permits the weaver to roll extra long warp threads around the beams to make, say, half a dozen blankets in succession. As each one is finished, all he has to do is cut the warp threads and then tie the threads still remaining on the warp beam to the ends tied around the cloth beam, though of course, he must first thread them through the healds in the right sequence to suit the pattern he is making.

Once the woven cloth has been taken from the loom, it has to be cleaned and textured. Long ago, this was done by laying the cloth on the bed of a stream and walking over it, treading it back and forth; this caused the fibres to swell and bind together. Though correct in principle, the method was hardly efficient, and fulling was actually the very first part of the whole spinning and weaving process to be mechanised. From around 1300 onwards, the work was taken over by the fulling mill. This consisted of a pair of huge wooden mallets driven by a water-wheel. As each mallet

THE PRINCIPAL PARTS OF A FOUR-SHAFT LOOM

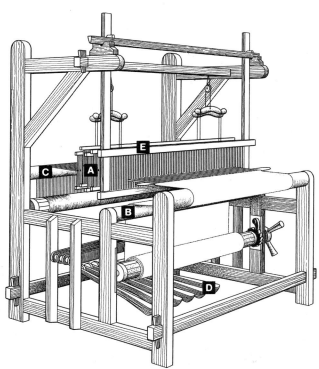

BASIC OPERATION *The heddles (A) hold sets of warp threads, stretched between the cloth beam (B) and the warp beam (C). They can be raised individually by treadles (D), so that the shuttle can pass between different groups of warp threads along a track called a sley (E).*

was raised in turn by the wheel, the other fell back to pound the cloth spread on the bed of the stream below.

Having gone through this punishing process, the cloth was pounded again in a mixture of urine and water, then in fuller's earth – an absorbent clay that collected any remaining grease – then in hot, soapy water, before the final rinsing. Finally, it was stretched over a vertical wooden framework, where the nap was raised with teasels or hand cards, and any outstanding fibres were cropped with shears.

This, at least, was the treatment meted out to fine cloth, but rougher materials, such as those destined to be made into shawls and blankets, did not require such careful finishing. They were simply washed in soda, then in hot, soapy water, after which they were rinsed and mangled. The material was then hung out to dry on tenter frames – and suspended, incidentally, from tenterhooks. Once dry, the cloth was trimmed to shape, the edges hemmed, and given a press between metal plates, heated over a coal, wood or peat fire.

It is astonishing that this entire process of spinning, weaving and dyeing was carried out in small mills, serving small localities up and down the country until quite recent times. In a single month, one such mill might produce more than a quarter of a mile of cloth, ranging from blankets and broadcloth to flannel for shirts and underwear for local farmers, made from the wool grown on the backs of their own sheep. Today, happily, the beautiful traditional patterns and colour combinations of hand-woven cloth produced by the old methods are still in sufficient demand to keep hand-loom weavers hard at work from the Western Isles to the valleys of South Wales.

PASSING THE WEFT

Raising and lowering different groups of warp threads opens up a gap called a shed, through which the weft thread can be passed by shooting a shuttle from one side of the loom to the other. The shuttle carries the weft thread, either wrapped round it (stick shuttle), or wound round a bobbin (boat shuttle), so that it can unroll inside it. In a complex pattern, a weaver uses a different shuttle for each colour of weft thread.

Stick shuttle

Boat shuttle

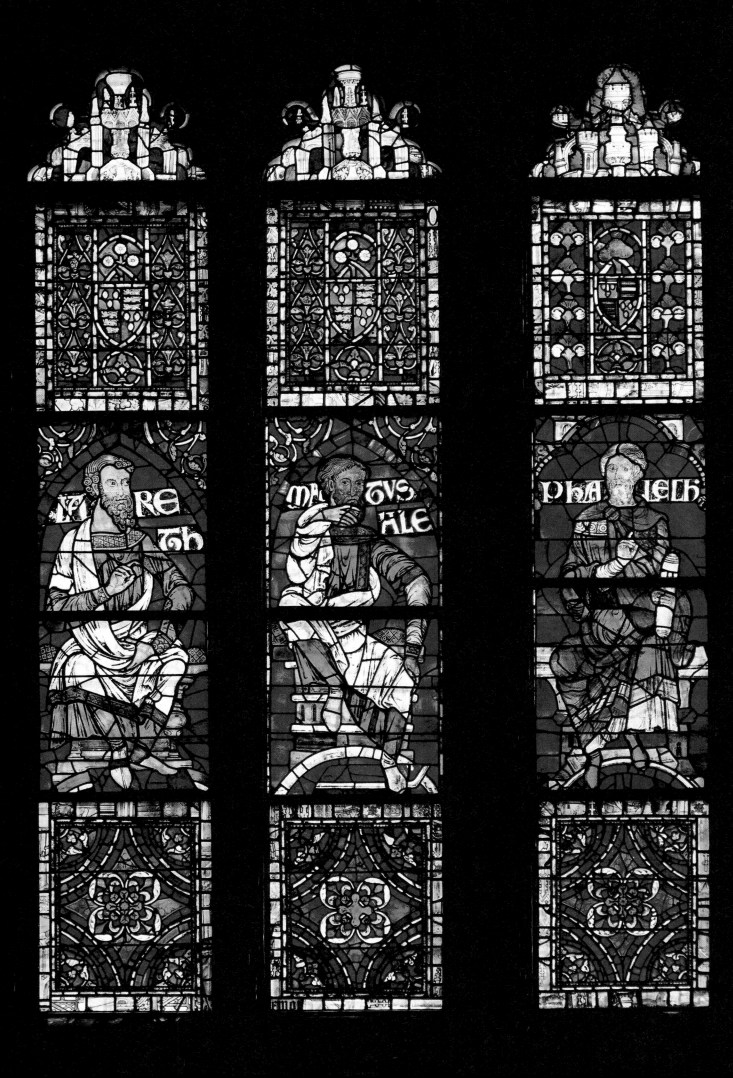

THE
Stained Glass
MAKER

UNIQUELY AMONG ARTIST-CRAFTSMEN, THE MAKER
OF STAINED-GLASS WINDOWS KNOWS THAT HIS PICTURES
WILL REMAIN UNCHANGED FOR CENTURIES TO COME

Of the many ways of making pictures, there is surely none more difficult or laborious than to fashion them out of stained glass. Each patch of colour must be cut from a different sheet, then fixed into place with a lining of lead and secured by carefully soldered joints and a layer of cement along each of its edges. Every tone, every texture, every detail must be painted with enamel, which has no colour value and only renders more or less opaquely the desired pattern. When fired at the correct temperature in a kiln, it fuses with the surface of the coloured glass.

Yet the finished composition will have a life and an endurance denied to most other pictures. Stained glass made 600 years ago remains as vivid as the day it was first installed in church or cathedral. All the centuries can do is to crown the picture with a patina of age and weathering which actually enhances the quality of the colours; for, unlike paintings, stained glass is seen by direct light rather than reflected light. And stained glass made today shines with the same fresh and unwearying brilliance, being made with the same materials and essentially the same methods as in the days when the Plantagenets ruled England.

The raw material – glass – is still formed by hand blowing. This produces a balloon of glass which has then to be turned into a flat sheet. The glass-blower puts his thumb over the end of the blowpipe to seal the air inside the glass bubble, then heats the end of the bubble over a flame. This causes the air to expand, eventually blowing a hole in the base.

When the craftsman rotates the pipe, this hole spreads over the whole of the bottom of the bubble, so that when he breaks the glass away from the blowpipe he is left with a cylinder with open ends. Running a glass-cutting tool along the side of the cylinder, and tapping it several times, produces a break along the line of the cut. When the cylinder is placed in a furnace and heated to a temperature high enough to soften the glass, the cylinder can be opened out and rolled into a slightly rippled, but otherwise flat, sheet of glass.

The mixture of ingredients used in making the glass is critical. For one thing, the glass needs to be more elastic and less brittle than normal glass, as the craftsmen must be able to cut it into intricate and elaborate shapes without accidental cracking or breaking. It also needs to have a clear and vivid colour, which is achieved by adding different metallic oxides to the mixture. Some of these oxides, such as the purple-blue of cobalt or the pale yellow of lead, give definite colours, but in other cases the colour may vary with the type of glass being made. Oxides of nickel can produce browns or violets, and ferrous oxides can be pale blue or

THE SPLENDOUR OF MEDIEVAL CRAFTSMANSHIP *These three panels form part of the Great South Window in the south-western transept of Canterbury Cathedral, once part of a set of 84 portraits of the ancestors of Christ. The colours remain as brilliant and visual as on the day of its completion in the 12th century.*

dark green, depending on the proportions of the mixture making up the glass. Adding copper oxide to the glass produces a rich peacock blue, but increasing the proportion of copper turns the colour progressively into green. Again, if copper oxide is reheated the glass turns to a rich, ruby-red – the powerful red so apparent in many of the great medieval windows. The choice of colours is staggering, for a stained-glass window maker can choose from hundreds of different hues and tones of red alone.

But the glass is only the means; the inspiration for the finished window must begin with the craftsman's original design. This first appears as a detailed small-scale drawing, usually made at $1-1\frac{1}{2}$ in. to 1 ft, showing how the window will be composed of individual panes of glass. The lead channels which will hold them together, and the iron bars which will support the finished window, are all drawn accurately to scale. Each piece of glass is coloured in on the drawing, and areas of tone and fine detail added, to give as true a rendering as possible of the finished window. It is usually this sketch which earns the craftsman a commission.

A costly raw material

In the Middle Ages, the colours used in a particular window were very much a matter of chance. Glass makers worked by instinct and experience rather than by using precise formulae, and one consignment of glass of a particular colour could differ from the next quite considerably. But good glass was expensive – a single sheet just 1 ft square would cost the equivalent of hundreds of pounds – so a place had to be found for it even if the colour was not exactly as ordered. Even now, a designer may have to make compromises, since every different shade means a sizeable order of expensive glass.

Next, the designer expands the small-scale drawing to full size. This is the cartoon, or working drawing, for the window, and it must be correct down to the smallest detail. The exact space allocated to each of the lead strips which hold the glass pieces in place has to be included, and the shapes of the glass fragments chosen to allow the leading to be bent into the curves and corners demanded by the design. Once again, the areas of texture, tone and extra detail – like the features of a face or the folds of a robe, for example – have to be drawn in to the last brush-stroke.

In the Middle Ages, paper, like glass, was scarce and expensive, and it was especially difficult to find sheets large enough to use for full-scale cartoons. Instead, the medieval stained-glass makers used paint or charcoal to draw the plans directly on to the smooth surfaces of their work-benches, and to save time and trouble they would often re-use as many parts of the drawing as possible. Thus, the same template for a human figure would often appear in a whole series of panels making up a large and complex window. The use of differently coloured glass, changed in details and shading, or the addition of such features as a beard on a face, or a different set to the hands, were surprisingly effective in disguising this repetition.

From the cartoon, the craftsman then traces a simpler drawing, called the cutline, which is his only means of transforming the cartoon into stained glass. The lead-line – of which the black line on the cutline represents the heart of the lead – is drawn where the colour changes occur in the cartoon, and a new piece of glass is required. The cutline is used for cutting and shaping the glass, and every fragment on the drawing is given some sort of identification, such as a code number or letter to identify the precise shade and hue of glass – and in most cases the individual sheet – from which it will be cut. This also enables the position of each fragment to be accurately located in the jigsaw puzzle

A MUSSEL KNIFE
MADE UNIQUE

The most versatile of all the stained-glass maker's tools starts off life as an oyster knife or mussel knife. First, he bends the blade to an angle suitable for prising out the farrier's horseshoe nails which hold the glass and the leads in position on the bench as the window is built up. Then he weights and strengthens the handle so that it can be used to drive the nails home. He drills a longitudinal hole in the handle, followed by several transverse holes. Then he fastens a paper collar around it and pours a molten alloy of tin and lead into the cavities. When the soft white metal hardens, he sands the handle smooth. As a result, he has two tools in one – a hammer to drive the nails into the bench, and a knife to pull them out.

Window-maker's knife

of the composition throughout the various stages of production and acts as a guide in the final assembly of the stained glass.

Cutting the glass is another part of the process which is much easier for a present-day craftsman. In the Middle Ages, this was done by running a red-hot iron along the surface of the glass on the line of the cut. This softened the hard surface of the glass and created a weakness so that the glass would then split along this line when given a sharp blow. But the method had two drawbacks: it was all too easy for a split to run along some other line of weakness; and even when this did not happen the cuts could only be made along straight lines or very gentle curves. Any more complex shapes had to be produced with a tool called a grozing iron – a shaft with a slot in it which enabled the craftsman to nibble away at the edge of the pane and so achieve the desired shape.

Today's tungsten carbide or special alloy steel-wheel glass cutter is much more reliable than the old red-hot iron. It uses the hardness and sharpness of the steel wheel to start a break along the outside face of the glass. A steel-wheel cutter can make curved cuts, whereas a diamond cutter tends to slip when cutting curves. For intricate shapes, the craftsman still has to nibble the glass to the outline he wants, though instead of a grozing iron he uses a special pair of pliers which have the jaws set so that the edges stay parallel as they open and close.

One by one, the pieces of the window are cut out. The craftsman then fixes them in place on a sheet of plain glass laid over the working drawing. In the past, glass makers used spots of beeswax to stick each piece of coloured glass to the clear glass sheet, but some present-day craftsmen favour Plasticine. Others like to make up an elaborate mixture of beeswax, resin, olive oil, corn-starch and turpentine to give the right combination of cleanliness and stickiness.

When all the pieces are stuck firmly in place, the craftsman can see the window as it will appear, either by setting the pane vertically and letting daylight shine through the window or by setting the glass over a light-box. But the window still consists only of basic coloured shapes – flat blocks without the tones and the details which will bring it to life. So he now shades in these details by brushing pigment on to the glass and then firing the individual pieces in a kiln. In some places he may add a network of fine lines, in others a smooth area of shading.

Sometimes he may use a badger-hair brush to stipple the painted surface to produce a different texture or a mottled shading effect, and sometimes he may scrape the pigment with a wire brush to take out the highlights and produce a darker, matt texture.

The pieces of glass must now be fired to fuse the paint into them. This means dismantling the picture and setting the pieces on to flat ceramic trays, laying them on a bed of sieved powder, called whiting, which stops the glass from fusing to the surface of the tray. The trays are loaded into a kiln and heated to a temperature of just over 1,100°F (about 600°C), at which stage the glass is just on the point of melting. As the surface softens, the painted surfaces take on a glossy sheen where the paint fuses into the glass. When the trays are taken out of the kiln and allowed to cool, the shading and details have become a permanent part of the fragment on which they were painted.

Pieces of glass needing shading, detail and extra texture may require two or three firings to build up enough layers of pigment. Eventually, all are ready to be assembled in the finished window, which is done on a flat wooden bench over the full-scale drawing.

ASSEMBLING THE FINISHED WINDOW

The window is built up against two strips of wood nailed to the bench along the bottom and one side of the finished panel. The pieces of glass are put in place with channels of lead in between them, and hammered in towards the strips to keep the assembly tight. As each row is assembled, it is held in place by hammering a set of nails along the outside edges. When the next row is fitted, these nails are pulled out and new ones hammered in along the new outside edge. When all the pieces are in place, the window is bound together firmly by soldering the joints between the lead channels.

The craftsman begins by tacking the drawing down on the bench, nailing two pieces of wood, called furring strips, at right-angles to one another. One runs along the base of the window, the other down one side, and the picture is built up from the corner where they meet.

Stained glass is held together by specially shaped strips of lead, just like ordinary domestic leaded-light windows. These strips of lead, sometimes called 'cames', come in different sizes and types, but they all have a cross-section rather like a letter 'H' lying on its side. The pieces of glass fit between the flanges, with the cross-piece, or heart, of the came separating the two panes.

Lead is soft and relatively easy to work; but, fixed properly, it is surprisingly strong. Many 800-year-old windows, such as those at Canterbury, still survive, with the original leading holding the original glass in place. But great care has to be taken to fix the glass and lead as tightly as possible, and the whole process is slow and painstaking.

First, the craftsman has to straighten out two strips of lead – called binder leads – each one long enough to act as the base or side of the window. These are stretched and straightened by pulling the lead through a pair of jaws fixed to the workbench, after which the flanges which will hold the glass have to be opened up by pressing them apart with a blunt-bladed tool called a lathykin. The two binder leads are placed in position against the furring strips, and are held firmly by hammering glazing nails or horseshoe nails at intervals along their length into the wood of the bench.

Assembling the picture begins with the piece of glass which fits in the corner where the two furring strips and binding leads meet. The craftsman taps the glass into position, with its two right-angled edges fitting inside the channels of the binding strips. He uses a wooden mallet to drive it firmly home, then fixes it in position by hammering glazing nails against its other edges.

Planning the lead strips

Before fitting any more pieces of glass, the craftsman cuts and fits the strips of lead which will line the as-yet-uncovered edges of the first piece, and which will separate it from the neighbouring panes. He has to decide which strips can form a continuous line right across the window, curving past a whole succession of different pieces of glass, and which should be fitted in between these long strips. Measuring and cutting the strips to length is more complex than it sounds, for each strip not only has to fit the glass but must be long enough to fit into the channels of the strips against which it is butted.

As the lead strips are fitted to the uncovered edges of the first piece of glass, the glazing nails are pulled out and the next panes are tapped home in the same way as the first. In this way the whole composition is built up, piece by piece, working upwards and sideways from the original corner. Because the successive panes of glass are hammered into

place back towards that corner, the whole picture is held together securely.

There are other steps the craftsman takes to build strength into the window. For instance, he takes care to press the edges of the channels down as tightly as possible against the surface of each pane, using the blade of a special knife called a 'stopping knife'. When the assembly is finished, the two remaining binder leads (for a square or rectangular window) are hammered into place on the two outer edges. Then the whole network of strips is fastened together into a strong latticework by soldering every joint where two or more strips meet. A large iron and plenty of solder are used, ensuring a strong joint and helping to fill any slight gaps between the strips of lead.

But the craftsman's job is not yet over, for he still has to make the finished window waterproof. To do this, he seals any gaps between glass and lead by packing with putty or, for a larger window panel, a specially mixed cement. He opens up the flanges of the leads with the stopping knife, brushes in the cement and closes down the flanges to seal the gaps tightly.

The final step comes when the finished window is fitted into its appointed place. Small panels can be held in position in the same way as an ordinary window, using pins or wedges and a layer of putty, but larger ones need iron or aluminium reinforcing bars to support the whole length and breadth of the window.

One method of fixing the window to these bars is for the craftsman to solder lengths of copper wire to the leads where each one crosses the line of a reinforcing bar. The bars are cemented in place across the window opening, and when the window itself is placed in position the lengths of copper wire can be bound tightly around the bars to provide extra support.

For the modern craftsman the work is still reasonably plentiful and varied. Apart from new churches, chapels and public buildings there are commissions from private patrons, or for memorial windows to be added to existing buildings. And the styles requested vary, too, from careful re-creations of traditional patterns and themes to entirely new subjects and treatments. But the skill, the care and the basic methods and materials still endure across the centuries, linking today's stained-glass makers to the men who built the great windows of York and Canterbury, Salisbury and Westminster Abbey.

STAINED GLASS FROM VICTORIAN DAYS

Not all stained glass dates back to the Middle Ages; nor was it limited to churches. In Victorian times, many houses and public buildings made use of the richness and variety of stained-glass designs. This panel from a window of the Queen's Hotel, Crouch End, London, shows the extravagant art nouveau decoration popular in the 1890s. It was made by Cakebread, Robey and Co., whose neatly conceived telegraph address was 'Splendour', London.

THE SWORDSMITH

ONCE, THE 'QUEEN OF BATTLES', NOW THE TRAPPING OF CEREMONY ... YET MODERN CRAFTSMEN CREATE SWORDS MORE TECHNICALLY PERFECT THAN AT ANY TIME IN THE WEAPON'S AGES-LONG HISTORY

Ancient though its place is in the annals of war, the sword is actually the latest of the edged weapons devised by man. Spears, axes and daggers of stone or bronze long preceded it, and though the bayonet was not invented until the beginning of the 18th century it was, strictly speaking, no more than a development of the spear, a weapon that enabled the foot soldier to defend himself when he had discharged his firearm and the enemy was too close to give him time to reload.

The reason for the sword's comparatively late arrival is that it really belongs to the age of iron. True, the Egyptians and the Greeks both possessed swords of bronze, but the metal was inflexible and lacked the ability to hold a cutting edge. Opposed to the *gladius*, the sharp iron stabbing sword of the Roman legions, the wielders of bronze weapons stood no chance.

Like the ancient bronze swords, it was short – no more than 2 ft overall – and designed for close in-fighting in the hands of densely packed bodies of highly disciplined infantry. Conversely, the swords that were eventually to overwhelm Rome and its empire – those of the Saxons, Gauls, Vikings and other warrior peoples – were 4 ft long or more, and were an equally effective arm for cavalry or foot soldiers who swung them in a vicious, slashing arc, rather than stabbing with the point. Viking and Saxon blades were especially fine, being made of strips of iron twisted, welded

and hammered together, giving them great strength and resilience. When the blade was forged, the hard cutting edges were also added by hammer-welding.

With modifications and adaptations, it was the long sword that ruled the battlefield for many centuries to come. To the medieval knight, it gave rise to all kinds of conflicting problems. How to make his armour strong enough to deflect his opponent's weapon, yet light enough to retain mobility? And at the same time, how to find a sword that would batter through, slide under, or find the chinks in the enemy's carapace, but sufficiently wieldy to be manageable in the thick of the throng? Some of the answers were provided by the terrible 6 ft long two-handed sword, whose operation must have called for considerable physical strength; the falchion, with its wide, flat point designed to slip under plate armour; and the long, rigid, narrow-bladed swords that were intended to seek out the enemy's armpit or other unarmoured crevice.

When gunpowder made the armoured knight obsolete, it also considerably reduced the weight of the sword which, from the beginning of the 16th century onwards, developed along two diverging lines, the slashing sabre of the cavalryman and the cut-and-thrust weapon of the fighter on foot. It was in making cut-and-thrust swords that European swordsmiths rose to their greatest height, first with the long, slender rapier, whose blade might be double edged, triangular or square in section and was so finely tempered – especially the blades made by the craftsmen of Toledo in Spain – that the tip could be bowed back to touch the hilt.

The small sword was almost entirely a civilian weapon, carried by every gentleman as a matter of course, just as he learned fencing as a basic part of his education. However, by the end of the 18th century, as ever-more stringent laws against duelling were enacted, the civilian sword went out of fashion, and from then until its surprisingly late demise as a fighting tool in the Second World War, the sword was an entirely military weapon.

Though now obsolete in war, the sword retains its importance, as it always has, in ceremony and symbolism. No dress uniform is complete without one, whether the uniform is military or that of the *Corps Diplomatique*. Swords, symbolising justice, are much in demand in court-rooms in many parts of the world, while governments local and national require them for processional occasions.

All in all, there is still plenty of work for firms like Wilkinson Sword, who have been making swords since the 19th century, and to a large extent still follow the old, time-honoured methods. The blade is born from a 1 ft bar of high-quality steel. In the old days, the bar was heated to red heat and beaten out to the right length and shape by a bladesmith's hammer, but for more than a century the job of stretching the steel has been taken over by a series of belt-driven pistons called Ryder hammers, each one matched to a specially shaped anvil. The swordmaker then reheats the bar and passes it through a set of profiled rollers that squeeze the metal out to the final proportions of the finished blade.

At one time, at this point, the butt end of the blade was opened with a chisel and a soft-iron tang – the metal spine of the hilt – hammered in while the blade was still hot. Since the beginning of this century, though, it has been the practice to ensure greater strength by making the tang from the metal of the blade. This is done by heating the metal for a third time and passing the butt under the Ryder hammers to draw it out to the right shape.

The final shape and cross-section are ground into the blade by the swordmaker, who sits astride a saddle, facing a large grinding wheel. As it revolves, he holds the steel

DEDICATED TO SERVE

When the blade has been polished, the swordmaker adds a final touch – the insignia of the sword's future owner, or that of his country or service. In this case, a British Guards' sword is being etched with the royal coat of arms and cipher. First the blade is coated with an acid-resistant resinous wax into which the pattern is drawn with a fine point. Next, nitric acid is smeared over the wax and left to bite into the steel through the lines left by the point. Finally, the acid is washed away and the blade is wiped clean, leaving the coat of arms and cipher as a pale grey pattern upon the polished metal.

A SWORD IS BORN *A sword blade begins life as a steel bar, 1 ft long, an inch across and half an inch thick. It is beaten and stretched into its final length and thickness by a series of pistons called Ryder hammers.*

against the rough surface, upon which jets of water constantly play to keep the metal cool.

A sword must be hard along its edge, yet flexible within its body. Hardness is induced by heating the blade then cooling it rapidly – quenching it by plunging it into a tank of oil which conducts the heat away from the metal at the right rate. The quenched blade is now hard but extremely brittle, which could cause it to shatter like glass if it were struck against a hard object. Flexibility is restored by tempering, in which the sword is heated again, this time in a bath of molten lead. This heats the blade through and removes the internal stresses that were set up during the rapid cooling of the quenching process.

After tempering, the blade is checked by eye for straightness. If required, straightening is carried out with hammer and anvil, after which the blade is subjected to the proofing test. This is done by a machine which bends the sword under a series of increasing loads, measures deflection, and checks that the blade springs back. It is then checked to ensure that it has been tempered correctly by repeatedly striking the edge and back of the blade by hand against a metal block. Blades that pass these tests are stamped with a proof mark, a guarantee of perfection that releases them to the complexities of the finishing processes.

First, the blade is polished, then etched – say, with a royal emblem – with nitric acid blocked by wax. Next, the hand grip of beech or walnut is turned roughly to shape and then finished smoothly with file and sandpaper. Generally, it is then covered with shark skin, cut to shape, soaked in water and then wrapped tightly round the wooden grip and bound in place with cord. When the skin has dried and shrunk around the grip the cord is cut away, and the swordmaker glues the layer of skin over the grip, decorating it with a binding of finely twisted brass or gilt wire. The design of the remainder of the hilt depends on the style of the sword – in some cases the hand is protected by an elaborate metal 'basket', in others by the much simpler single-banded knuckle bow. In either event, the metalwork may be cast from an alloy called gilding metal or stamped from brass or steel sheet which the swordmaker files to shape. He then chases it with elaborate patterns and designs such as royal ciphers or regimental crests, and plates it with gold, silver or nickel before fitting it to the finished weapon.

Ironically, the craft of swordmaking reached its peak

STONE AND STEEL *The swordmaker uses a 5 ft diameter carborundum wheel to grind the profile of the blade – that is, its final shape and size in cross-section.*

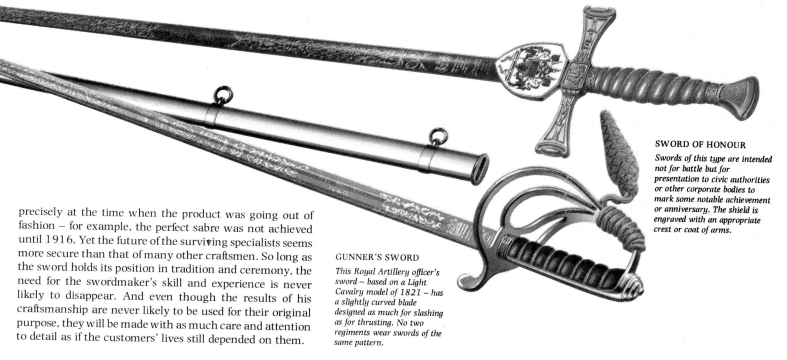

SWORD OF HONOUR

Swords of this type are intended not for battle but for presentation to civic authorities or other corporate bodies to mark some notable achievement or anniversary. The shield is engraved with an appropriate crest or coat of arms.

GUNNER'S SWORD

This Royal Artillery officer's sword – based on a Light Cavalry model of 1821 – has a slightly curved blade designed as much for slashing as for thrusting. No two regiments wear swords of the same pattern.

precisely at the time when the product was going out of fashion – for example, the perfect sabre was not achieved until 1916. Yet the future of the surviving specialists seems more secure than that of many other craftsmen. So long as the sword holds its position in tradition and ceremony, the need for the swordmaker's skill and experience is never likely to disappear. And even though the results of his craftsmanship are never likely to be used for their original purpose, they will be made with as much care and attention to detail as if the customers' lives still depended on them.

THE TAILOR

THE QUIET AUTHORITY OF SAVILE ROW TAILORING
IS RESPECTED THROUGHOUT THE WORLD. 'HAND-MADE
IN LONDON' IS THE CACHET THAT SAYS IT ALL

*I*n the Great Room at No. 1, Savile Row, there hangs a *Punch* drawing of September 1943. It depicts the landings at Salerno. Shot and shell scream overhead; landing-craft crash on to the beaches; grim-faced soldiers storm forward to the battle. In their midst stands a single imperturbable figure, immaculately hatted and clad, inquiringly smiling and with pencil and order-book poised. Beside him, a shot-torn notice proclaims, 'Gieves: Naval and Military Tailors'.

This is only a slight exaggeration, since for the last 200 years, wherever His or Her Majesty's Forces – and especially the Royal Navy – have gone, there Gieves have gone too. Lord Nelson paced the quarterdeck of the *Victory* in a Gieves uniform. Captain Bligh faced the mutineers in a Gieves coat. Admirals all, from Collingwood to Lord Louis Mountbatten, have defied the enemies of the realm, dressed from head to foot by Gieves. The company was in the Crimea, operating from a yacht fitted out as a floating tailor's shop; and in both World Wars its representatives went into action with the battle-fleets.

Not so long ago, its intelligence service was such that a boy who passed the examination and interview to win a coveted place in Dartmouth Naval College would learn of his good fortune from Gieves: their telegram of congratulation would arrive ahead of the official communication sent by the Admiralty. With luck, one of the boys might one day become First Sea Lord and, throughout his career, would remain a loyal customer of Gieves.

For generations, the company has been the Navy's friend and mentor. In the First World War it produced thousands of life-saving waistcoats and, on one occasion at least, one of its branches paid off the entire crew of a warship which had the misfortune to dock at a weekend after the banks were closed.

Officers, tailors and cutters grow together as old friends, keeping a proprietorial eye on each other's careers.

This makes Gieves's present amalgamation with the equally famous firm of Hawkes a particularly happy one, since what Gieves is to the Navy, so Hawkes is to the Army. Founded within a few years of Gieves as a firm of military helmet makers, Hawkes dressed many of the British officers who fought at Waterloo and counted the Duke of Wellington among its more distinguished customers.

Gieves and Hawkes's air of assured but unassuming elegance, and the firm's association with far-away places are matched by its Savile Row premises. In the 17th century the building was the town house of Lord Fairfax, and in the

MATHEMATICS OF STYLE *Creating a suit is a matter of balancing vanity with reality, current fashion with the customer's wishes, image with bank account, the customer's opinions with his wife's certain knowledge. All these are translated first into choice of cloth and then into a web of measurements by the cutter, which begin, as always, with centre of collar to natural waist, to length of coat, to ground . . .*

19th century it housed the Royal Geographical Society. The Great Room, with its domed glass ceiling, was the Society's library, and here, in 1874, the body of David Livingstone lay in state before burial in Westminster Abbey. A drawing by Edward Whymper, the 19th-century mountaineer, shows how the room looked in its library days. It is not so very different despite the scarlet, blue and gold of uniforms and the hanging rows of civilian suits whose cut murmurs, rather than proclaims, 'Hand-made in London'.

Just what makes a Savile Row suit different is hard to define. Even the men and women who make them find it difficult, though they can spot each other's handiwork at 50 paces. Nevertheless, the street and several of the tailoring establishments within it grew up together, and it was here – and in neighbouring St James's and Bond Street – that there occurred at the end of the 18th century, a revolution in male costume that to a large extent has remained with us ever since.

It has been suggested that it was part of a much larger revolution, the one that had taken place in France a few years earlier. As the French court was swept away, the silks and satins, the powdered wigs, the buckles and bows and bright colours that characterised it were swept away too. The courtier was no longer a figure to emulate, and in his place there arose a very different and more democratic model – the country gentleman, whose archetype was the English sporting squire. Not for him the skirted satin coats and periwigs; his no-nonsense life-style was centred on the horse, and his clothes were cut accordingly – riding boots and breeches, close-fitting with tails that could be swept up when he was mounted; and hats that would protect the skull in the event of a fall. The squirearchy of Leicestershire and Somerset must have been astonished indeed to discover that its everyday wear – though considerably streamlined – had suddenly become the attire of men of fashion.

Chief among the dandies of the new style, but by no means its innovator, was George Brummel (1778–1840). Though he was nicknamed 'Beau', his dress had nothing to do with the extravagances of the beaux, fops and macaronis of earlier eras. Rather, his impact was one of superb understatement, whose point was made by good cloth well cut, the studied carelessness of the cravat and the fathomless gloss of his boots.

'No perfumes,' he said, 'but very fine linen, plenty of it, and country washing. If John Bull turns round to look at you, you are not well dressed, but either too stiff, too tight or too fashionable.' A dab of aftershave apart, it is a dictum that might have been engraved on every well-dressed Englishman's wardrobe ever since.

The restraint of Brummel and his disciples made the bright silks and satins look tawdry. In the daytime, their fine leather breeches fitted with never a wrinkle; their pastel coats lay on their backs as though sculpted; while their black-and-white formal evening wear created such an impression that its style has remained virtually unaltered to this day. Cut and fit were everything, and the subtlety of line demanded could only be achieved in woollen cloth, a much more pliable fabric than silk, and one that could be moulded, stretched and shrunk into shape by the tailor's iron.

Long used to making plain cloth country coats, London tailors adapted their skills to the new high fashion, which advanced some of them at least to fame and fortune. Brummel employed one firm of tailors to make his coats, a second his breeches, a third his waistcoats and a fourth and fifth the thumbs and the remainder of his gloves respectively. Not all of them had been paid by the time he fled, bankrupted, to France where he died, slovenly and mad, 14 years later.

RIDERS OF GHOSTS
About the 1790s, Western man abandoned silks and satins and took for his model the English country gentleman, who elevated the horse from a means of transport into a passion. He thought horse, talked horse and dressed horse, from crash-proof hat to cutaway coat that divided over the saddle, to streamlined boots and breeches. In aeroplanes and office blocks we dress still to please his phantom steed. Lapels roll up into a tunic collar in modern suits; pockets slant to facilitate reaching for change in the saddle; cuffs button back – or look as if they do – to give better rein control over the long-departed quadruped. Even the coat is divided by one or two vents to give a more elegant line when hacking up to town in bus or train.

191

Tools of the tailor and cutter

CHALK AND SHEARS

Having worked out the details on a paper pattern, Gordon Jones, head cutter at Gieves and Hawkes, begins to mark up the cloth for cutting. His skills lie in accuracy of hand and eye developed through 30 years of experience. But his tools are simple – shears and tape measure, chalk, measuring stick and pincushion. There is also a square marked with graduations that he uses to work out the flow of the line of the suit between two measuring points – say, the outward curve of the trouser seat between waist and thigh.

He is supposed to have remarked in a moment of clarity that at least he had taught his countrymen to wash and to wear clean linen. But some of the lesser trends established by his friends and himself were hardly less epoch-making. Only slightly modified, the country gentleman image they popularised is still inherent in every well-tailored suit, in its hacking vents, lapels that roll up into tunic collars, and cuffs that button back.

In fact, as Gordon Jones, head cutter at Gieves, points out, male fashion (in which he does not include jeans and T-shirts) has changed almost not at all in this century, but has simply gone through a series of ten-year cycles. In these, trousers and lapels are sometimes wide and sometimes narrow; coats are single-breasted, waisted and three-button, or double-breasted, two-button and looser fitting.

The disappearing hat apart, the greatest revolution in man's garb since the Second World War, or at least since the British adapted themselves to central heating, has been in the weights of materials. Cloth comes in 56 in. widths, and its weight is estimated in ounces per yard of length. At the beginning of the century, a 23 oz. serge for a formal suit was quite usual, and from it were constructed a coat, trousers and waistcoat designed to reinforce the protection of flannel shirt and woolly underwear. Nowadays, except from the inhabitants of baronial halls, it is rare to receive a demand for anything more than 16 oz. The normal business

suit is made from 12–14 oz. worsted flannel; some younger trendsetters, however, prefer mohair – a goat's-hair mixture weighing no more than 9 oz.

Cloths may have decreased in weight, but in texture, quality and pattern they have changed not one whit since Bertie Wooster and Savile Row had their first historic encounter. West of England flannel, blue or grey, striped or plain, is still the most popular choice for town wear, as are tweeds for the shires. Then, by way of compromise for the countryman coming to town and for the townsman visiting the country, there are still the faintly striped Cheviots, and the Prince of Wales and hound's-tooth checks whose character can be altered by a change of hat and shoes.

The point is, what aspect of your life will the suit reflect, and which cloth will do it most justice? At Gieves and Hawkes such questions, and those of style, are settled in the elegant, high-windowed Adam Room by assistants like Edward Cripps. Mr Cripps has been with the firm for 50 years, and can estimate a customer's height and build to within half an inch at a glance. If you are a regular customer, there may be nothing more to do than to settle style and cloth and re-order to your pattern. On the other hand, if your waist has increased since the last visit, he will murmur kindly. 'Your present suit seems to have grown a little young for you, sir,' and suggest a re-measuring.

At this point, or if you are a new customer, Mr Jones or

one of his assistant cutters is summoned. There is a preliminary chat about the state of the world, or gardening, or cricket, to put you at your ease, and at the same time to yield a glimpse of your personality; for the suit must fit your life-style as elegantly as it fits your shoulders.

Then the measuring ceremony begins. It is always done the same way – length of centre collar to natural waist, to length of coat, to ground, then, with the arm bent at a right-angle, the tape is run from the centre back to the base of the hand to obtain sleeve length. Chest, waist, seat, outside leg and inside leg follow, the cutter intoning the measurements in swift dictation to the assistant – '17½, 30½, 62, 8½, 20½, 32' – and so on. Sometimes the litany is interrupted by mysterious initials such as 'DRS', 'FS' or 'SRB'. It is as well that they should remain mysterious, since 'Dropped right shoulder', 'Forward stomach' or 'Slightly round back' might have a depressing effect on the customer. Most wounding perhaps would be 'BL', either 1, 2 or 3, indicating bow legs to the first, second or third degree.

All this information is carried up by Mr Jones to his eyrie on the balcony that surrounds the Great Room, where the figures and initials are translated into paper patterns. These are the blueprints of the suit, incorporating the ideas of both the customer and the cutter.

The paper patterns take twice as long as the actual cutting to execute. They may even take longer in the

case of a dress uniform, the details of which might call for a careful sifting of regimental tradition.

Style, the customer's stance and about 40 years of experience are reflected in the patterns from which the pieces of cloth that make up the suit are cut. When the cutting is completed, papers and cloth are rolled together with the work ticket into a neat, blue-ribboned parcel and sent upstairs to the tailor's shop. There, the pieces of cloth are tacked together, and the canvas bastings – interlinings – that give the suit shape and help to conceal the odd DRS, are added. The customer is then summoned to the first fitting.

At this stage there is only the tacked-together ghost of a suit – no lapels, no buttonholes and no pockets – and the customer has to be pinned into it. Adjustments, the position of buttons and pockets, and the slant of trouser bottoms fore to aft are marked in chalk, before the parts of the suit are successively ripped off the customer.

By the second fitting, a week or so later, pockets, lining, lapels and buttonholes have all been added. Only interior seams are machined, all other stitching being done by hand, including the buttonholes which alone take a skilled tailoress about four hours to complete. However, the suit is still only held together by tacking.

By now, the suit is almost complete and the cutter and customer have reached a state of mutual congratulation. A third fitting is seldom necessary; usually, when the customer calls for the third time it is to take away his suit, exquisitely folded and wrapped, in its discreet box marked with the coats of arms of H.M. the Queen and H.R.H. Prince Philip. Mr Jones and Mr Reeve, master cutter and master tailor respectively, agree that the creation of a bespoke suit or uniform is a team job, and the fact that the customer is part of the team makes their craft all the more satisfying.

How the third member of the team pays for the garment is one of the craft's subtler aspects, and in Savile Row there is generally an air of slight surprise and delight if anyone actually offers to pay cash. At No. 1, many of their customers are officers whose accounts accompany them throughout their service lives. Long ago a Mr Hawkes said to a Mr Gieves, 'Everyone knows how much the nation owes to the Royal Navy, but no one knows how much the Royal Navy owes to Gieves'.

TRAPPINGS OF GLORY

Though their civilian suits have excited admiration for more than a century, Gieves and Hawkes have been famed as naval and military outfitters ever since they made uniforms for Lord Nelson, the Duke of Wellington – and Captain Bligh. The measurements of these and many other famous soldiers and sailors can still be seen in their order-books, and the company's knowledge of tradition in matters of formal military dress is encyclopaedic. Here, gold-rose pattern lace is added as a finishing touch to the mess jacket of an officer in the Royal Tank Regiment.

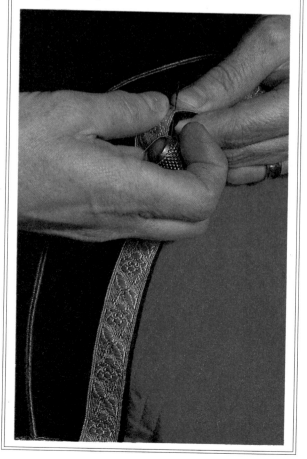

FIRST FITTING

When the suit has been cut, the pieces and the interlinings are roughly tacked together and the customer is invited to the first fitting. It is at this point that the style of lapels, the slant of pockets and trouser bottoms and the position of buttonholes are finally determined.

IRON AND PLONKER

The shaping and final pressing of the suit is done with a heavy iron, each of whose strokes is followed up with dabs from a wooden block known as a 'plonker'. This sharpens the creases and helps to prevent stretching after pressing.

THE
TANNER

THOUGH SLOWER THAN MODERN FACTORY METHODS,
OAK-BARK TANNING REMAINS SUPREME WHERE LEATHER
OF THE VERY HIGHEST QUALITY IS REQUIRED

VALONIA AND OAK BARK, THE SOURCES OF TANNIN

Hemlock, willow, larch, spruce, elm and birch all produce tannin – as do many other trees and plants – but oak bark has been favoured by traditional British tanners for many hundreds of years. The great forests which once covered much of the country provided a seemingly inexhaustible supply, but the precious raw material is becoming increasingly difficult to obtain. Valonia, the acorn cups of an oak grown in Turkey, has a very high tannin content and has been used by British tanners for almost 200 years.

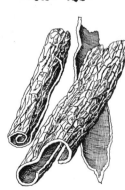

The world would have been a very different place without the leather made by generation after generation of tanners. For centuries it was indispensable for boots and clothing, shields and armour, tents, bottles, buckets and fire hoses. Without leather there would have been no drive belts for the machinery that powered the Industrial Revolution. Today, despite synthetic substitutes, it is still in great demand for shoes, saddles and harnesses, suitcases, handbags, wallets, upholstery and many other high-quality products.

Tanners can trace their craft back for over 500,000 years. Primitive cave dwellers, battling to survive the Ice Age, fashioned crude garments and footwear from the skins of animals killed to provide food. The last traces of flesh were laboriously removed with flint scrapers, many of which have been found by archaeologists.

The skins must soon have rotted and fallen apart, but at some stage it was realised that they would last much longer if they were either stretched out to dry or smoked. But longer life had to be balanced against the fact that such skins were stiff and uncomfortable to wear. That problem was solved by rubbing in fats and brains to replace the original oils. Despite the prehistoric nature of such methods, a leather-processing patent involving both smoke and brains was registered as recently as 1914.

Many thousands of years passed before it was discovered that the bark of certain trees, when soaked in water, produced a dark solution that miraculously transformed rough-and-ready skins into what we now call leather. This is the liquid now known as tannin. The discovery can only have been made by accident, almost certainly after a skin had been left for a considerable length of time in a puddle filled with bark, twigs and other debris from a tree. The 'invention' of leather defies accurate dating, but pieces about 7,000 years old have been found in the Middle East.

Oak bark became firmly established as the main source of tannin in Britain, and tanners gradually developed means of making a wide variety of leathers suitable for many different applications. Only towards the end of the 19th century did much faster tanning methods, involving mineral solutions, bring about radical changes in the ancient craft.

Among the most important innovators were two Americans, Augustus Schultz and Robert Foerderer. Schultz was a chemist who developed 'chrome' tanning – so called because it involves chromium salts – while his compatriot was a Philadelphia tanner who devised ways of making such leather acceptably supple.

Although the use of mineral and chemical solutions saves much time – for leather can be produced in two or three weeks instead of a year or more – one or two English tanneries have remained faithful to the age-old method involving tannin extracted from oak bark. The tanneries, many of whom have deep-rooted family traditions in the craft, believe that their techniques are the only ones capable of producing leather of the very highest quality. Their opinion is endorsed by the Department of Health, which insists that only leather tanned by the oak-bark process may be used to make orthopaedic and other medical appliances. Apart from being a completely 'natural' material, it is easy to shape and can stand up to a great deal of hard use.

Suitable bark is becoming increasingly difficult to obtain, however, because few timber yards can be bothered to strip their felled oaks. Another problem is that the best tannin comes from young trees, but there is an understandable reluctance to cut down anything other than mature specimens.

Ideally, trees are felled and the bark stripped off in April or May, when they are full of sap, and then stored under cover for about two years until perfectly dry. A tannery handling 100 or more large hides every week needs about 25 tons of bark each year.

Machinery is used to shred each batch of bark before the tannin can be extracted. At J. and F. J. Baker's tannery in Colyton, Devon, where leather has been produced for hundreds of years, the bark mill is powered by a 19th-century water-wheel which complements the traditional character of the business. Experience alone tells the tanner just how much the bark should be ground. 'The finer the better' is the basic rule, but too much grinding results in a soggy, sponge-like mass that can block drainage channels and pipes.

'Valonia', the name given to the acorn cups of an oak grown in Turkey, is added to provide additional hardness if the leather is to be used as soles for shoes. Valonia contains three or four times as much tannin as oak bark. It gives the leather 'weight' and solidity, and also increases its resistance to moisture. Valonia has been imported by British tanners since the end of the 18th century.

The tanning liquor produced by oak bark works very slowly, but is nothing if not thorough. It creates leather with the strength, pliability and hard-wearing qualities needed, in particular, by saddlers and harness makers.

Ground bark and valonia are taken from the mill to one of a series of leaching pits – known in Devon as leaches – into which water and tannin-rich liquor is added from another pit. Typical pits – anything from 5 ft to 7 ft deep – are lined with wooden boards set in clay and are set into the floor of an open-sided building. It takes from six to eight weeks for the crushed bark and acorn cups to leach out their full quota of dark brown tannin.

The tanner divides the source of his leather into two categories. Cattle and other large animals provide hides, while skins come from smaller animals, such as sheep and goats. Both types are carefully checked for defects before being accepted. Trained eyes look for flay cuts – marks made when the beast was skinned – and for scratches caused by such everyday hazards as barbed wire and broken branches. The ox or steer hides used by hide tanners are examined for holes made by the warble fly, an insect that

TEN MONTHS IN THE
LAYER PITS

Modern techniques enable leather to be produced in two or three weeks, but oak-bark tanning takes a year or more. Pelts often spend as long as three months making their way through the open-sided tan-yard before being taken to the layer pits, where they remain for up to ten months. They are stacked in pits of tannin liquor and have oak bark spread between them to form a huge, multi-decked sandwich. Time alone enables the entire pelt to be thoroughly and evenly tanned. Mixtures of tepid water and animal dung were also used until the end of the 19th century.

195

lays its eggs under the skin. A hide ravaged by warbles looks as if it has been blasted with a shotgun fired at close range.

All hides and skins are divided into three layers. The epidermis on the outside and the flesh layer on the inside are separated by the corium, or dermis, that provides the tanner with his raw material. The true nature of the corium could not be appreciated until the advent of powerful microscopes. It consists of millions of extremely fine fibrils, each about a five-thousandth of an inch thick, which cluster together to form fibres. Bundles of intricately interwoven fibres are created in such a way that minute air passages enable the finished leather to 'breathe'.

Pelt rounded for harness leather

Belly
Whole back
Half back
Belly
Half back
Shoulder
Butt
Belly
Belly
Bend
Bend

Rounding knife

Butt knife

Pelt rounded for sole leather

STRIPPING OAK BARK FOR TANNING

At the turn of the century, when this photograph was taken at Brimpton, in Berkshire, large quantities of bark were still needed to supply the tanning industry. For the most part it came from oak trees felled in the spring, when the rising sap makes stripping much easier. The bark was levered off in semi-cylindrical plates, each about 2 ft long, and then stacked in the dry before being ground and mixed with water to make the tanning liquid. Barking was by no means always a man's task, for women and children often worked in the woods to supply local tanneries.

That is why leather makes the best footwear, for perspiration can escape through the maze of tiny channels and evaporate on reaching the shoe's outer surface. At the other end of the temperature scale, the air trapped between the bundled fibres acts as an insulator.

The layers on either side of the corium have to be removed before tanning can start. They can be loosened in several ways, but the traditional tanner relies on the time-honoured method of soaking hides and skins for about two weeks in pits filled with a mixture of water and lime. Bacteria in the solution destroy the roots of the hairs, making them easy to remove with either a machine or a long, two-handled knife known as a scudder. Liming also makes it easier to remove the fleshy layer.

At this stage the hides and skins become 'pelts', and the tanner's experience tells him for what purpose they are best suited. One critical factor is thickness – or 'substance', as it is termed in the trade. Hides with plenty of substance tend to be used for sole leather, while thinner ones are earmarked for harness leather, and so on.

Markings derived from dialect

All pelts are also marked in the most literal sense, so that their progress through the tannery can be checked and recorded. In the old days, when many tannery workers were illiterate, specialised markings were often used. For instance, some Devon tanners based their marks on the rich local accent. A five became a V while a seven was a Z and an eight was denoted by an A minus the horizontal stroke.

Unlikely though it may seem, some pelts used to be taken from the lime-yard to vats containing a nauseous brew of tepid water and the dung of hens, pigeons and dogs. Excrement from hunting kennels was widely regarded as the ideal material for this process, which was known as bating. It neutralised the lime, softened the pelt and resulted in a fine, pliable leather suitable for such purposes as glovemaking. Fortunately for those living close to tanneries, artificial bating agents were introduced around the end of the 19th century.

The pelts are rounded – that is, cut into sections – after being removed from the lime pits. The largest piece, known as the butt, is flanked by two belly sections, while above it are the shoulder and the cheeks. The butt from large animals generally provides sole leather, with the other sections going for other relatively heavy products. Each half of the butt is called a bend.

Pelts spend a few hours being de-limed in a solution of ammonia, and are then taken to the tan-yard. Here, everything depends on the tanner's ability to judge such vital factors as liquor strengths and the way in which the process is being affected by the weather. He knows, for instance, that the liquor tans better during a warm spell.

The traditional tan-yard is an open-sided building with a series of large pits in which the pelts are suspended from wooden poles and immersed in oak-bark liquor. The pelts are moved from pit to pit at regular intervals as they make their way through solutions in which the tannin content becomes stronger and stronger. Liquor strength is accurately measured with a barkometer – a special type of hydrometer – but most tanners can gauge it by instinct. The old method was simply to dip a finger into the solution and taste it.

If the pelts were dropped straight into a top-strength liquor they would be thoroughly tanned on the outsides, but underdone in the middle. Oak-bark tanning is therefore a lengthy and painstaking process, because the tannin solution is relatively weak, and time alone enables it to work its way right through the corium's myriad bundles of tightly packed fibres.

Tannin is really a preservative. The whole object of the exercise is to drive out the water that accounts for as much as 70 per cent of the pelt's weight, then to combine with and coat the fibres. The process increases the corium's ability to resist heat, decomposition caused by water and attacks by all manner of organisms.

Pelts take as long as three months to make their way through the first series of pits and are handled about once every week. It is hard, heavy work, but regular movements promote even tanning. The pelts then spend up to ten months in layer pits, where they are stacked with oak bark spread between them to form huge, multi-layered sand-wiches swimming in a sea of dark liquor. Stout cords, attached to boards on the edge of each pit, enable the saturated butts, bellies, shoulders and cheeks to be hauled out when the tanner is finally satisfied.

Cleaning by centrifugal force

The pelts are then taken to a large tanning drum in which they are spun for three or four hours. Nothing is added at this stage, not even water, but the drum acts like a giant washing machine and cleans the leather by centrifugal action.

Drums are generally lined with wood, because some metals – notably iron – are liable to make marks on the leather. Before machines were introduced in the 19th century, this scouring process involved hours of tedious labour with scrubbing brushes.

Bends of sole leather are stacked and allowed to drain before being treated with cod oil. Applied by hand, using a thick wad of sheepskin, the oil keeps the leather supple and also acts as a barrier against the atmosphere. Hanging the leather in a half-lit room helps to prevent it becoming dark and brittle. These steps, known as samming, prepare the bends for the next stage of their long journey to the shoemaker.

This involves a machine with a heavy brass roller whose ancestor was a hand-operated roller weighed down by a heavy iron box. Guided by years of experience, and working in perfect harmony with his machine, the operator first treats the grain side of the leather – the side from which hair once sprouted. The roller's relentless action smooths out any irregularities and starts 'putting the leather together', or firming it up.

The bend is stacked, given another application of cod oil, and finally damped with water before being 'rolled off' on both sides. After hanging up to air, the leather is at last ready to be taken to the warehouse and sold.

Unlike sole leather, harness leather generally has to be shaved down to an even substance. Sometimes it is split, using machines that were first introduced in 1809 and which at once gave this aspect of the craft unprecedented standards of efficiency and accuracy. One puzzling fact about harness leather is that its substance was measured in millimetres long before the metric system was introduced to Britain. In contrast, the thickness of sole leather is tradi-tionally measured in 'irons', with a millimetre equalling approximately two irons.

The curriers who prepare harness leather use a two-handed, square-edged blade called a slicker, which stretches and 'sets' the leather. It is then rubbed with cod oil before being set once again. After it has dried, the leather is stained – generally black or brown – and the flesh side is 'boshed' with a mixture of boiled tapioca to make it good and tight.

In addition, harness leather is often put into baths of a solution made from the ground leaves and roots of the sumac, a bush which grows in Mediterranean countries and elsewhere. Rich in tannin, the solution enhances the

SETTING A BELLY *The currier's skill and patience puts the finishing touches to harness leather. Slickers with blunt blades of steel or glass are used to stretch and set the material before it is rubbed with cod oil and then set once again. This process improves pliability and also replaces natural oils lost during the tanning process.*

colour of the leather as well as helping to increase its strength.

Finally, the leather is greased with a blend of mutton tallow and cod oil – a mixture that gives it something to 'feed' on and also acts as a preservative. Many tanners give stirrup leather a particularly generous treatment with the mixture to compensate for any neglect on the part of the harness-buying customer.

In general, however, leather tends to improve if it is treated with the care it so richly deserves. In this age of mechanisation, mass production and advanced technology, the leather made by traditional craftsmen stands out as a product whose many qualities have yet to be rivalled.

Glass slicker

Steel slicker

THE
TAXIDERMIST

ONCE PROVIDING SHOWPIECE TROPHIES FOR
HUNTERS AND COLLECTORS, THE TAXIDERMIST TODAY USES
HIS SKILLS TO BENEFIT SCIENCE AND EDUCATION

A taxidermist tends to spend a lot of time outdoors, watching birds and animals moving about in their natural environment. His observation of them must be acute, and he will take a special interest in how they walk, stand or fly; in their characteristic actions and behaviour; and in their seasonal changes of coat or plumage.

The knowledge he accumulates is put to practical use when he comes to present a stuffed specimen in just the right attitude – and frequently in just the right natural setting. This may be as simple as a couple of rocks arranged as a base, or as complicated as building a diorama in which a number of birds and animals are placed.

Authenticity and attention to detail have been a priority ever since the craft underwent rapid development in the mid-18th century. That was when the great voyages of

scientific discovery created an urgent need to find means of preserving the many creatures that were collected for study. The breakthrough came when chemical means of preserving their skins were found: earlier attempts had been far from satisfactory because no methods other than actual tanning had been discovered.

Scientists began bringing home large collections for study and display, some of which later formed the nuclei of natural-history museums. More than half Britain's taxidermists now work in museums, preparing study collections and exhibits. They have a strong professional guild which fosters high standards of work.

Apart from a general interest in wildlife, a taxidermist needs a good working knowledge of anatomy – and a fairly strong stomach. He is, after all, going to be dealing with very dead animals, and most workshops have a large deep-freeze. There are three distinct phases in preparing a specimen for mounting: removing its coat or plumage as intact as possible; making up an artificial body to fit into the skin later; and – the ultimate test – finishing and posing it to look totally natural.

Skinning – the first step

Skinning is done with a variety of sharp knives and scalpels, making as few incisions as possible. For a bird, an opening is made from breastbone to vent and the skin gradually turned inside out, rather like a glove, as it is separated from the body. The wing and leg bones are cleaned off and kept, along with the skull, complete with beak. The rest of the skeleton is discarded.

As soon as possible preservative is applied, the most common being borax, which also dries the skin so that the feathers are held secure. If the plumage is dirty, it is washed in detergent, rinsed, then cleaned with acetone. Liberal quantities of magnesium carbonate are used to dry it, the fine white powder being shaken off afterwards, or blown away with a hair dryer.

For all birds, a 'soft body' is made up from a bundle of wood-wool bound with hemp thread. So far as is possible, the exact size and proportions of the original are copied – the craftsman may even keep it alongside him for guidance. The skull is packed with tow, and glass eyes are set in the sockets with modelling clay. The skull is then fixed on to a wire inserted in the neck. More sharpened wires are passed up beside the leg and wing bones, and bound with tow to replace the flesh. When the soft body is slipped into the skin, these wires can also be manipulated to position the legs and wings. The leg wires are left long enough to stick out of the feet, so they can be passed through a perch or baseboard. Finally, the original incision is carefully sewn up.

At this stage the bird may still look far from realistic, and all the taxidermist's skill is called for as he adjusts it to a lifelike stance while the skin is still flexible. He also spends considerable time preening the feathers to ensure that each one lies as it should. When he is at last satisfied, he binds the body and wings lightly with thread to keep everything in place while the skin dries and sets.

Small mammals are prepared in much the same way as birds, but anything larger than a fox calls for a different treatment of the skin and a different filling for the body.

The skin is pickled for 24 hours in a solution of salt and sulphuric acid, which kills off any bacteria present and fixes the hair permanently. Afterwards it goes into a solution of weak ammonia and borax to neutralise the acid before it is dried.

Something more substantial than a soft body is needed to support a large animal skin, so a strong but light structure called a manikin is made up. This starts with a body profile cut from plywood, slightly smaller than life size. Steel rods

---

PRODUCING A LIFELIKE IMAGE

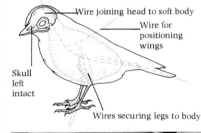

Wire joining head to soft body
Wire for positioning wings
Skull left intact
Wires securing legs to body

The taxidermist's craft is directed not only towards preserving the remains of animals but, more importantly, towards producing a lifelike image. In the case of a bird, the natural outline of the body is modelled from wood-wool with particular attention to the exact proportions of the original. Wires inside the body can be manipulated to give the correct stance. The final touch is to preen the feathers and bind them in place until the skin has dried.

which will go through the legs are attached to it, then bent to the posture required. The ends of the rods are threaded so that they can be bolted through the baseboard. Wads of wood-wool are attached to the profile panel by threads which are wound around nails tapped into the edges. When both sides have been built up, a neck rod is fixed in place, to which the skull – or a cast of it – is attached. This, too, is built up and the glass eyes fitted.

A layer of scrim stiffened by plaster of Paris goes over the wood-wool body, and when that is set final modelling can be completed with papier mâché. The whole manikin is then sealed with two or three coats of shellac. For really large animals, the manikin can be made with glass fibre, resin or polyurethane.

Fitting the skin is made easier by pasting both the manikin and the inside of the skin itself before it is manipulated into place. Then the incisions are sewn up and the fur groomed. When it has thoroughly dried, any hairless areas such as the nose, lips or palate are painted in lifelike colours. Powder colours are preferred for mammals, as they do not hold down fine hairs; oil paints are used on birds.

Although most of the taxidermist's work is on birds and mammals, there is a steady demand from proud anglers who want to preserve their prize catches. However, the scaly skin of fish does not respond well to the basic methods described, as it shrinks and loses colour. So fish are rarely stuffed; instead an accurate cast of the specimen is taken, and it is then moulded in glass fibre or some other suitable material. Each scale is painted individually with oil colours, and varnished. Needless to say, this is time-consuming work, and an angler must consider seriously whether his catch is worth the expense of immortality. Reptiles and amphibians are usually made from painted casts, too.

In striving for ever more realistic settings for his specimens, the taxidermist picks up a number of minor skills. He can cast fake rocks from real ones, or model them in papier

MOUNTING 'FROM THE FLAT'

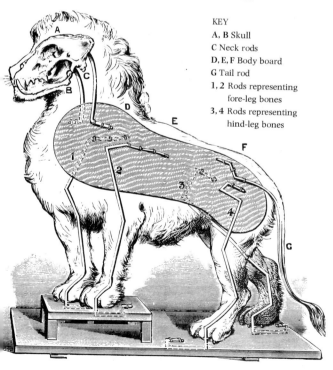

KEY
A, B Skull
C Neck rods
D, E, F Body board
G Tail rod
1, 2 Rods representing fore-leg bones
3, 4 Rods representing hind-leg bones

HUNTING TROPHY *In Victorian times, skins of large game animals were sent from abroad for mounting 'from the flat'. As there was no body, the taxidermist drew an outline of the folded skin. From this he cut out a plywood oval, or body board, slightly smaller than the body outline, to which were attached the supporting leg and head rods.*

mâché; twiggy plants have to be dried properly and painted; and flowers are modelled in wax-coated paper.

Today hunting folk, television studios and heart-broken pet owners whose animals have died create a certain demand for his skills. But his study collections and museum exhibits represent a major contribution to science and education.

It was not always so, and there is no denying that two less worthy developments provided powerful stimulants to the craft. They were the growth of big-game hunting and an extraordinary obsession with wildlife decorations that flourished throughout the 19th century and into the 20th century. Countless beautiful creatures were doomed to become ornaments in homes great and small.

Happily, society is now generally enlightened, and conservation measures are giving birds, animals – and fish – a measure of protection against such excesses.

RESTORING NATURAL COLOURS

No amount of careful work on a skin can prevent some natural colours being lost. In the case of a small mammal, like the fox above, there will be bare areas of skin – such as nose, lips, eyelids or palate – to which the sparkle of the natural colours of life must be restored. An expert knowledge of living animals is therefore all-important for the taxidermist.

SENSITIVE SKILLS AND A DEEP UNDERSTANDING
OF NATURAL MATERIALS GO INTO THATCHING A ROOF
– TOGETHER WITH ARDUOUS, BACKBREAKING TOIL

Up to and even after the First World War, almost any farm labourer in England's wheat-growing shires could plough a field, hedge and ditch around it – and thatch the roof of his cottage or make a waterproof covering for a stack. Thatching was just one among many rural skills he would acquire quite naturally in the course of a working life. Learning it was a simple necessity – thatching was a cheap and, to him, easy way of keeping a warm, dry roof over his head, quickly made and quickly renewed when necessary.

It had been so for 2,500 years and more: thatching is the oldest of all the building crafts used in Britain. Long before cultivated wheat and barley provided the straw to roof their huts, men were using the wild reeds and rushes of the marshlands, heather and even bracken.

Reeds and heather are still used, along with straw, in a craft that reached a pinnacle in the Middle Ages and has changed little since. Also little changed are the few simple hand tools employed. And though tiles, slate, stone and other materials have almost totally replaced thatch for roofing, it is enjoying a modest return to favour in the countryside. This is due not only to its handsome appearance and the rediscovery of its excellent insulating properties, but to a recent dramatic improvement in supplies of suitable straw and reeds. Paradoxically, it is modern machinery which has brought about this improvement – machinery for gathering reeds and for processing wheat stalks into what is called combed wheat reed.

Norfolk reed and combed wheat reed – sometimes called Devon reed – are two of the three principal thatching materials used in England now. The third, and most difficult to obtain, is long straw. All three are used wherever houses are thatched, which is roughly south of a line drawn between the Humber and Mersey rivers. But Norfolk reed tends to be concentrated in East Anglia and combed wheat in the south-west – hence its other name. Heather is still used occasionally in Scotland.

Norfolk reed

Generally acknowledged to be the best and longest-lasting, Norfolk reed has been called the prince of thatch. It has a more distinctive profile than the others, and the ridge along the rooftop is made from sedge – another marsh plant, with a three-sided, saw-edged leaf – which turns golden-brown as it matures, contrasting with the darker brown of the reed. These roofs last 60 years or more, and have been known to last a century.

The reed, *Phragmites communis*, grows between 3 ft and 8 ft tall, and is found in marshlands, waterways and tidal estuaries. It is recognisable instantly by its brown, feathery seed head on a single stem. Besides growing in quantity across vast tracts of Norfolk, it is found also in other counties – notably Suffolk, Kent, Essex, Dorset, Hampshire and Glamorgan. The reeds must be harvested only after hard frosts have stripped the long leaves from the stems, which usually means the depths of winter, starting around December. Until recently, they were all cut by hand, with a scythe or a sickle-like tool called a hook. Some still are, though the backbreaking work in bitter cold weather has reduced the number of men willing to undertake it to just a few. They bundle the reeds under one arm as they cut with the other.

When a good armful – known as a bunch – has been gathered, it is tied 12 in. or so from the butt-end with string or with a reed bond, made by twisting a few reeds together. The bunch is then bumped up and down on a spot-board – also called a butting-board – to level off the butt-ends. The spot-board is usually a large wooden disc, but other shapes can be used, so long as their surfaces are flat.

Thigh-length waders are worn, and some reed-gatherers work alongside broad-beamed, punt-like boats. The bunches are loaded into the boat, or stacked at the nearest roadside, to be picked up later by truck and transported to the site where they are needed.

However, in the 1950s mechanical cutters began to ease the toil of harvesting considerably, and by 1970 a sophisticated machine had arrived in Norfolk that both cut the reeds and bound them. This large, tractor-like device came from Denmark, where thatching has also had a long history. It has revolutionised reed-gathering – cutting and binding 40 bunches a minute.

Many thatchers believe that a Norfolk reed roof lasts longer if the reeds are mixed with 10–15 per cent of two other reed-like plants that grow with them in certain marshes and waterways. They are the reed mace (*Typha latifolia*), known locally as 'boulder'; and the wild iris (*Iris pseudacorus*), known as 'gladden'.

Combed wheat reed

At first sight, combed wheat reed can be mistaken for Norfolk reed in a thatched roof. Both are laid with the butt-ends of the reeds exposed, but wheat reed has a finer stalk and so tends to look more closely butted. Gables and eaves of roofs are also cut to shape in a quite distinctive way.

The wheat reed is gathered at harvest time with a binder, then fed through a machine called a reed comber, fitted to the top of the threshing drum, which removes the grain and

THATCHING THE BARN AT TISBURY

The largest area of thatch in Britain was renewed in 1971, on the Tithe Barn at Place Farm, Tisbury, in Wiltshire. The roof covers 1,450 sq. yds, and a team of five Norfolk reed thatchers took four months to complete the job. They used 130,000 bundles of reed weighing around 270 tons. Like most Norfolk reed roofs, it should last at least 60 years, and could last a century if given the necessary maintenance.

HOW NORFOLK REED THATCH IS LAID

Norfolk reed thatch is laid in courses – bunches of reed fixed side by side in overlapping layers. The eaves course (A) is stitched on, but subsequent ones are secured by hazel rods called 'sways' (B), fixed horizontally over the reeds to trap them and hold them firm. These sways are held down in turn by iron thatching hooks driven into the rafters beneath. Each succeeding course covers the fastenings of the previous one up to the roof ridge, which is laid with sedge (C), again secured by hazel spars. The butt-ends of the reeds are beaten to the correct slope with a leggett, which also drives them up even more tightly under the sways.

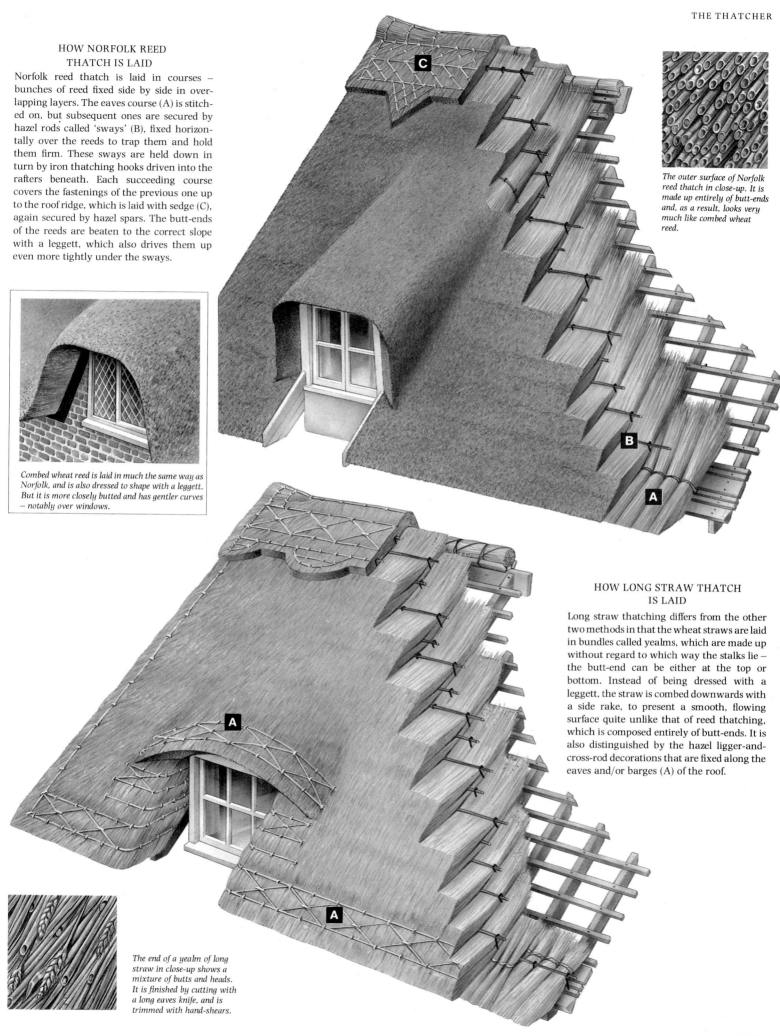

The outer surface of Norfolk reed thatch in close-up. It is made up entirely of butt-ends and, as a result, looks very much like combed wheat reed.

Combed wheat reed is laid in much the same way as Norfolk, and is also dressed to shape with a leggett. But it is more closely butted and has gentler curves – notably over windows.

HOW LONG STRAW THATCH IS LAID

Long straw thatching differs from the other two methods in that the wheat straws are laid in bundles called yealms, which are made up without regard to which way the stalks lie – the butt-end can be either at the top or bottom. Instead of being dressed with a leggett, the straw is combed downwards with a side rake, to present a smooth, flowing surface quite unlike that of reed thatching, which is composed entirely of butt-ends. It is also distinguished by the hazel ligger-and-cross-rod decorations that are fixed along the eaves and/or barges (A) of the roof.

The end of a yealm of long straw in close-up shows a mixture of butts and heads. It is finished by cutting with a long eaves knife, and is trimmed with hand-shears.

leaves from the wheat. The stalks do not go through the drum, and so remain undamaged, emerging with their butt-ends all laid in the same direction. They then pass down conveyors to a platform, where they are bunched. As with Norfolk reed, the bunches are butted level on a spot-board and then stacked. A combed wheat reed bunch is called a 'nitch' and usually weighs about 28 lb. A roof thatched with it can be expected to last from 30 to 40 years, and should cost about three-quarters the price of a Norfolk reed roof – though there may be variations between areas.

Long straw

A roof thatched with long straw is unmistakable; the thatch flows over window and roof angles as though poured, while eaves and gables are decorated with quite intricate patterns of hazel rods.

Long straw, like combed wheat reed, depends on a supply of straw that has been cut with a binder and not with a combine harvester. There are still some farmers willing to set aside a few acres by arrangement, and part of the

bargain may be that the thatcher will harvest it, keeping the stalks for his own use and passing the grain back to the farmer.

The straw is prepared for thatching in quite a different way from that used for reeds, in bundles called 'yealms'. It is taken to the site either in tied bundles or loose loads, according to how it was harvested. It is then placed flat in layers, each layer being damped with a bucket of water, to make the stalks more pliable when the thatcher comes to use them. When the straw has been standing a couple of hours to absorb the water thoroughly, the worker uses a two-tined hay fork to rake any crossed straws roughly straight, and generally tidies up the stack. The prepared stack is then called a 'bed' and is ready for 'yealming'.

The worker makes a yealm by standing sideways-on at one end of the bed and taking double handfuls of straw, which he arranges flat at his feet with the ends as level as possible. He pulls the straw back against his insteps to compact it as he works slowly backwards. A yealm is complete when he has a firm layer 14 in. to 18 in. wide and 4 in. to 6 in. deep – a handy size for picking up. Six to eight yealms are wedged into a 'yoke' – a large forked hazel branch – for carrying up to the roof.

Tools and methods

Methods of thatching vary from county to county, and according to the materials being used. But basically all thatch is laid in 'courses' – overlapping layers of reed or straw running the length of the roof. The thatcher starts at the eaves and works his way up to the roof ridge. The courses are fixed to the roof battens by trapping them under hazel rods 4 ft to 5 ft long, which are held in turn by stout iron hooks driven into the rafters. The fastenings on one course are covered by the next course as it is laid, resulting in an unbroken surface of thatch up to the roof ridge, which gets special treatment – as do windows, chimney-breasts and gables. Another method used to secure thatch to roof battens is to stitch it down with tarred twine. This is done with the aid of a large iron needle threaded with the twine, which is passed through the thatch by one man and out again by an assistant inside the roof.

The more noticeable variations in thatching techniques are governed largely by the materials used, each having its traditional methods.

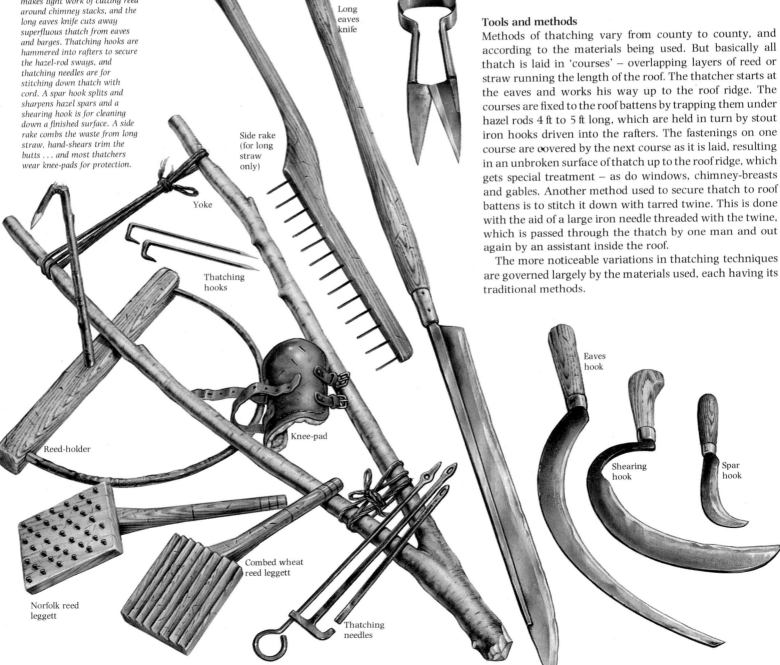

Long eaves knife

Hand-shears

Side rake (for long straw only)

Yoke

Thatching hooks

Knee-pad

Reed-holder

Eaves hook

Shearing hook

Spar hook

Norfolk reed leggett

Combed wheat reed leggett

Thatching needles

DRESSING THE BUTTS *Working with combed wheat reed, this thatcher has laced the bunches down to the roof battens with tarred twine, using the large thatching needle on the left. Now he is dressing the butts into shape with his leggett, which also tightens them into the lacing.*

Norfolk reed comes in bundles of five or six bunches known as fathoms – a length of string passed around the bundle at butt level should measure 6 ft, or a fathom.

Courses of Norfolk reed are laid with the thicker, butt-ends at the bottom, so that when all the courses are complete the entire surface of the thatch is made up of butt-ends. The butts are 'dressed' to the rather steep slope required with a tool called a leggett – nobody knows when this tool was invented, but a sketch of one appears in a document dated 1364 relating to the manor of Crowle, in Lincolnshire. The leggett is a piece of wood about 12 in. square and $1\frac{1}{2}$ in. thick, faced with iron studs and with a handle fixed to the back at an angle of around 40 degrees. As he lays each course the thatcher gently beats the reed butts in an upward direction, and at an angle, with the face of the leggett, so that the topmost reeds are forced further back than the bottom ones. This gives the surface its smooth, even slope.

When all the courses are complete, the thatch is about 13 in. thick over the whole roof. It is beaten with the leggett to a neat, cropped finish above windows and at the gable-ends. The apex of the roof – before it gets its sedge capping – is finished by tying a thick, bound roll of reed along the ridge timbers, then cutting off the final courses where they meet above it from each side.

The capping is made by fastening yealms of sedge along each side of the ridge and over it, finishing with a smaller roll of sedge along the top of the ridge, and final yealms bent over the roll. The sedge is pinned to the thick reed beneath it by 'spars' – split hazel sticks twisted in the middle and bent double, like hairpins. The side 'skirts' of sedge are made quite thick, and usually deep enough to allow for some ornamental cutting along the bottom. The whole ridge capping is fastened down finally with long and short lengths of split hazel called 'liggers' and 'cross-rods', again pegged into position by spars. These liggers and cross-rods are formed into attractive patterns – herringbone and cross-hatching are the most common – and are a distinctive mark

of Norfolk reed thatching. Another distinguishing mark is the pronounced upturn worked into the sedge at the peak of each gable-end of the roof, said to represent the last vestiges of the dragon long-boat figureheads used by the Vikings to decorate their houses when they colonised the area.

Combed wheat reed is laid in a similar way to Norfolk reed, but the eaves and gables – or 'barges' – are cut to shape in more flowing, rather less severe lines. The roof ridging is of wheat reed, instead of sedge, and is less thick and deep-skirted – often it is 'plain finished', flush with the roof surface. However, it is still fastened with liggers and cross-rods sparred on in patterns, and the skirts are frequently trimmed into ornamental points and scallops.

The butt-ends of wheat reed are dressed with a leggett that has a ridged face, rather than a studded one, and the eaves and gables are cut to shape with a curved knife called an eaves hook.

The special patterns along eaves and gables of long-straw thatch are also formed with liggers and cross-rods. Along with the 'poured-over' look of the roof they make long-straw thatch easily distinguished at a distance. Closer inspection reveals that the straw is fixed in a different way, too. The yealms are laid so that a much greater length of stalk is visible – the surface looks more like combed hair than the brush-bristle appearance of reed. This is not surprising, as it is dressed with a tool rather like a large comb, instead of a leggett. This wooden tool, called a side-rake, is about 3 ft long, half its length being the handle and the other half set with a dozen large, nail-like teeth. The thatcher uses it with a combined combing-beating action, bedding the yealms firmly down while also removing any loose straws. The result is a most pleasing, natural-looking surface.

Long straw is also used for the ridging, which again is fastened and decorated with liggers and cross-rods. The fairly deep skirts are often trimmed into complex patterns of points and scallops. Eaves and gables are cut with large knives similar to those used for cutting off Norfolk reed tops; hand-shears are used for trimming. This form of thatching is prone to damage by birds, so is almost always covered by galvanised wire netting with a mesh fine enough to keep them out – $\frac{3}{4}$ in. is usual. Reed-thatched roofs are often treated in this way too – especially the ridging, if not the whole roof.

Inevitably a good deal of a thatcher's work is concerned with repairs, and re-thatching existing roofs. A process carried out on wheat reed or long straw roofs is known as top coating. The thatcher first pulls away the top layer of thatch to make sure that damp has not penetrated and rotted the under-thatch and battens. If all is well, a new top layer is fastened on with hazel spars, leaving the roof slightly thicker than before. If the battens are found to have rotted they must be replaced and the whole thatch renewed. Finally, the roof ridge will always need replacing at some stage before the roof itself.

Thatchers tend to be tough and individualistic, specialising in just one – or perhaps two – of the three methods involved in the craft. Reed thatchers may also on occasion use each other's materials – either Norfolk or wheat reed – adapting them to their own styles, leading to even more confusion when trying to differentiate between the two! They labour often under the most arduous conditions, carrying large loads up high ladders upon which they perch for most of their working day. With both hands in continual use and body twisted one way or the other as the job proceeds, they support themselves with feet and knees. Thick leather knee-pads are essential equipment, as are thick leather boot soles. Only high winds, freezing snow or the heaviest of rains will deter them – indeed a hardy breed.

THE FINISHING TOUCHES

No two thatchers work in exactly the same way, and within a region they can tell immediately who has thatched any particular roof. Many have their own styles of ornamental finish, and some like to perch a straw peacock or pheasant on a ridge or gable. These are usually covered with a fine wire mesh as a protection against real birds. Thatchers also have individual patterns for decorative sparring along ridges and under windows.

THE TRUGGER

MR SMITH'S 'LITTLE MASTERPIECE', SO
PLEASING TO QUEEN VICTORIA, REMAINS ONE OF THE
MOST PRACTICAL OF GARDENING AIDS

There is an elegant simplicity about a Sussex trug basket. It is a perfect example of the old adage that 'what looks right, *is* right'. Queen Victoria thought so, anyway. She took an immediate fancy to the first one she saw, placed an order, and soon they were in use in the royal gardens at Buckingham Palace. Almost overnight, the unknown country craftsman who had made them found himself famous – and prosperous.

His name was Thomas Smith, and he lived in the village of Herstmonceux, in Sussex. His basket was a little masterpiece in sweet chestnut and creamy willow: light but sturdy, and fashioned with both art and skill. So proud of it was he, and sure of its excellence, that he took some samples up to London and entered them in the Great Exhibition of 1851.

That was where they caught Victoria's eye . . . and Mr Smith was awarded a prize medallion and a diploma.

Not trusting the deliverymen of the day – and not unmindful of his debt to the Queen and his new-found reputation – he determined that the trugs she had ordered should reach her in mint condition. So he walked the 60 miles or so from Herstmonceux to London, carrying them.

In the 130 years since he did so, his Sussex trugs have changed not a whit; and the way they are made has changed but little. Indeed, until recent times his descendants ran the village workshop where they are still produced, and even now he would recognise some of the original tools and jigs that he used.

Even the curious name he found for his basket was inspired. 'Trug' derives from the Old English word *trog*,

meaning tub or boat, acknowledging the resemblance in shape. The rim and handle are made from sweet chestnut, with the bark cunningly preserved as a protective covering and decoration. The bowl is made of thin slats of willow, and the whole basket is fastened together with perfectly placed copper nails. Normally, no surface finishes are applied. A trug not only looks right, it *feels* right, because it has the warm, comfortable feel of natural wood.

Kept reasonably dry, a trug can last a lifetime and more. Many have, not only in Britain but as far afield as Australia and New Zealand, America and Canada, to which countries they are exported in a steady stream. All are hand-made by half-a-dozen craftsmen and women – sometimes more if there are people available, for the work demands dedication as well as skill, and persuading modern youngsters to take it up is not easy.

The trugs start life as willow logs and sweet-chestnut saplings stacked in the yard beside the main workshop. This workshop is, perhaps fittingly, also made of wood – being an army barrack hut dating from the First World War. At one end, facing the road, is the showroom and small office. Behind this section is the long main workroom, with another equally ancient hut of timber and corrugated iron joined to it at right-angles at the other end.

In a third hut across the yard is the only machinery used. A couple of table saws cut the willow logs into short lengths, then divide them into thin slats – or 'planks', as the truggers call them – and a small planing machine finishes them to their final thickness of about $\frac{1}{8}$ in. This seems a sensible concession to the times – and is, indeed, the only phase of production that *can* be mechanised.

Bending the timber to shape

The planks are carried across the yard to the timber-and-corrugated-iron hut that is possibly the most fascinating part of the whole factory. This is where they are steamed to make them pliable and bent to shape, and where the sweet-chestnut saplings are split and trimmed by hand, then steamed and formed into rims and handles.

There are two steam ovens: one, a marvellous Heath Robinson contraption, is made from an old ship's boiler and fired from the outside with shavings and off-cuts of wood; the other is, more prosaically, heated by electricity.

Before going into the steamer, the planks have their ends thinned and narrowed slightly to ensure a snug fit. This is done by a craftsman sitting astride a wooden 'horse' – a primitive form of vice – and using a draw-knife. Splitting and trimming saplings for the rims and handles is an equally fascinating process. The trugger uses a cleaving tool to divide them lengthways, first into halves, then into quarters. Then they are wedged firmly into a horse and the centre sapwood is cut out down the whole length with a draw-knife. This leaves a thin 'strap', with the bark intact down the outside, that will become the rim or handle of a trug. This job is usually done by a tall, spare man named Tony Ransome. He has spent a lifetime at Smith's, starting as a lad under his father, who was a trugger before him.

The planks and handle-rim assemblies then go into the long main workroom to be made up into finished trugs. The men and women who complete them sit astride more horses, using nothing more than hammers, sharp trimming knives and copper nails. When the planks have been nailed into place the protruding ends are swiftly trimmed off level with the rims – and, amazingly, the basket is complete.

So deft are these men and women that they can complete four trugs an hour.

The last of the Smith family to own the business retired some years ago, but still lives in the village and is often consulted by the new owner, Roy Firman Ltd.

VICTORIA'S MEDALLION
This is the magnificent bronze medallion awarded to Thomas Smith after his country-crafted little garden basket caught the appreciative eye of young Queen Victoria as she walked around the Great Exhibition of 1851 in the Crystal Palace. The large medallion is all of 3 in. in diameter, and bears relief portraits of Victoria and Albert, superbly cast in fine detail. It is kept in the firm's office, along with an original small trug from the exhibition and a Napoleon III bronze medallion won at a Paris exhibition of 1855.

ALL SHAPES AND SIZES
Trugs are made in many different shapes and sizes, depending on the uses to which they will be put. There are deep garden trugs and shallow flower trugs, square baskets and round bowls – even fire-side trugs to hold logs. Some are stained and, for special orders, handles can be decorated with pokerwork.

1 *Willow logs and saplings of sweet chestnut stand in the open outside the workshop. From the saplings, a craftsman selects one ready to be split and trimmed by hand, to form rims and handles. After splitting, the sapwood is removed with a draw-knife, leaving the bark intact. This work is done while the wood is still green, otherwise the bark peels off as the wood dries and shrinks.*

2 *The straps of split and trimmed sweet chestnut have been softening for five minutes in a steam oven. Here the trugger is bending one into shape around a wooden former. Once bent, the ends are fastened together with copper nails – and the rim of the trug is complete. Handles are made in the same way, on another former.*

3 *This is the moment when handle and rim come together. The trugger slides the longer rim 'hoop' inside the loop formed by the handle. He judges by eye the depth of the trug to be made, then fastens handle to rim where they cross, using more copper nails. He works with speed, certainty and total accuracy, years of practice making the highly skilled job seem simple and uncomplicated. And like all the truggers in the small workshop, he can bring equal skill to bear on every other process involved.*

THE WOODEN HORSE

The wooden horse astride which this trugger sits to work is more than a century old, as are several others still used at the workshop. The willow plank he is shaping is held firm by the pressure of his foot on the frame, as he plies the draw-knife with swift, sure strokes towards his chest. He is tapering the width and reducing the thickness of the wood at each end. Again, his eye is the only gauge as the different shapes of centre, seconds and sideboards are cut. Afterwards they go into the steam oven for softening and bending to shape before they are nailed into place.

4 *Here a trug is nearing completion as the shaped willow planks that form the main body are fixed to the rim-handle assembly. Six – or sometimes seven – planks are used for each trug, and the centre one is the first to be fitted. It is copper-nailed in the middle to the lower half of the handle loop, and at each end to the rim. The 'seconds' are nailed each side of this centre plank, and finally the 'sideboards' are fixed.*

205

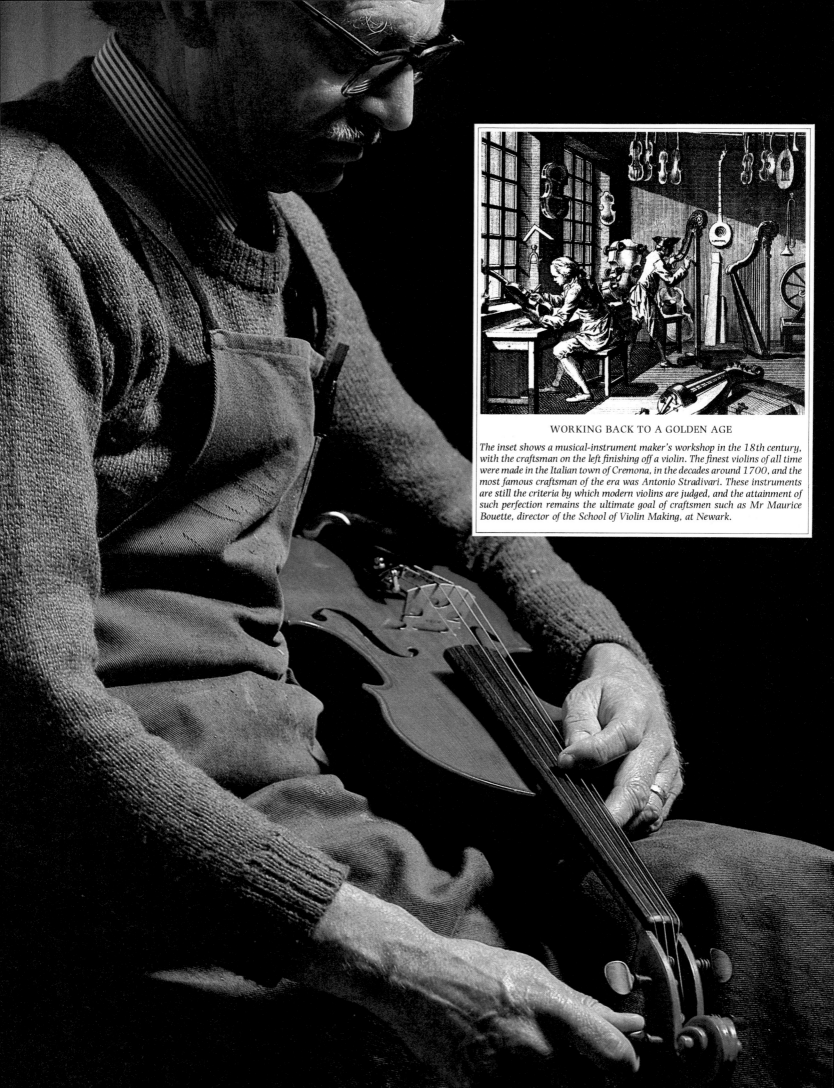

WORKING BACK TO A GOLDEN AGE

The inset shows a musical-instrument maker's workshop in the 18th century, with the craftsman on the left finishing off a violin. The finest violins of all time were made in the Italian town of Cremona, in the decades around 1700, and the most famous craftsman of the era was Antonio Stradivari. These instruments are still the criteria by which modern violins are judged, and the attainment of such perfection remains the ultimate goal of craftsmen such as Mr Maurice Bouette, director of the School of Violin Making, at Newark.

THE VIOLIN MAKER

THE AMBITION OF TODAY'S CRAFTSMEN – NEVER
QUITE REALISED – IS TO ACHIEVE THE PERFECTION OF
INSTRUMENTS MADE 300 OR MORE YEARS AGO

Like all the greatest inventions, from the steam-engine to the bicycle, the violin reached perfection quite early in its career; in essentials, it has hardly altered since. It first appeared in recognisable form in Italy about 1550. A century later, the North Italian town of Cremona had become the world centre of violin making, and has remained so to this day.

Why this happened is something of a mystery. Perhaps it was just a combination of the right time and the right place. As the 17th century progressed, composers, players and audiences looked for ever increasing brilliance in their music. The violin was the perfect medium, and Italy was the centre of the musical world.

Another reason must have been the long lives and enormous output of the two greatest makers, Nicolo Amati (1596-1684), and his pupil Antonio Stradivari (1644-1737). Their creative lives spanned 120 years, and the products of their workshops have never been equalled. To own a Stradivarius ('Strad' for short) is the ambition of every violinist, even though the demands of more recent music have led to considerable alteration in the inner workings of the violin.

This means that making a violin in the 1980s entails a constant backward-looking effort in order to re-enter the world of the 1680s. Whereas the maker of a wind instrument has endless scope for individual trial and error, and may even make his own improvements, the violin maker has no such opportunity. He must work backwards towards a vanished golden age. So, inevitably, much of the time and energy of violin craftsmen go into the repair of old instruments. Most of them are restorers first and makers second, but they are all obsessional about their craft.

One of the few workshops where construction rather than repair is the norm is the School of Violin Making, at Newark in Nottinghamshire. Even here, however, the emphasis is on the great Cremona makers. 'All we're trying to do is progress backwards,' says Maurice Bouette, the school's director. 'Nothing is as good as the original.'

What is this original, and how was it achieved? Reduced to its simplest essentials, a violin is a wooden box, about 14 in. long, over which are stretched four strings, each tuned to a different note. When a string is plucked with the fingernail, or, more usually, set in motion by the friction of horsehair stretched between the ends of a bow, it vibrates at a certain frequency, or pitch. This vibration is carried down from the strings, through the bridge, to the violin body, which enormously magnifies the initial tiny vibration, turning it into the characteristic tone of the violin.

What distinguishes one violin from another is the quality of wood that goes into it, the glue that fastens the pieces together, the varnish that gives it its marvellous sheen, and above all, the experience of the craftsman, working with no mechanical aids apart from simple hand tools.

The violin is a combination of hard and soft woods, in proportions found by trial and error to have the best effect. The most visible parts of the violin, which give it its beautiful outline, are the top, or 'belly', which lies directly below the strings, and the back. The belly is made of soft spruce, which vibrates readily when the strings are set in motion; the back is hard maple, which gives rigidity to the whole 'box'. Belly and back are joined by six curved ribs, convex at either end and concave in the middle, or 'waist', of the violin. These are also of maple, as is the neck of the instrument, which is carved at its far end with a graceful scroll. The best wood comes from the mountains of Germany. Ebony – a hard, heavy, black wood from the tropics – is used for the fingerboard, which runs between the neck and the strings, and for the tailpiece, which carries the strings at the tail end of the violin.

Most crucial of all to the tone of the violin is the spruce that forms the belly. The spruce trees are about 300 years old – planted when Stradivarius himself was working – and should have an even, straight grain. Ideally, they should be on the leeward side of a mountain range, protected from the worst of the wind. They should be high up, just below the snowline, where they grow at an even rate each year, unaffected by the fluctuations in climate that vary the growth rings of trees nearer the valley floor. If the rings are close and even, then the wood is better in both appearance and musical quality. After being sawn into planks, it should be left to season for seven to ten years before use.

A violin has about 70 different parts, so it is not surprising that it takes about 150 hours to make – even though some small parts, such as bridges, pegs and tailpieces, are brought in from outside already partly formed. At the Newark school, a flow chart lists over 20 main processes in the construction sequence, each with several subsidiary processes attached.

The first stage is to make a 'form', or mould, which will dictate the shape of the ribs and hence the outline of the violin. The form consists of a piece of thick plywood cut to a

THE MAIN PARTS OF A
VIOLIN

A violin is basically a wooden box, which amplifies the sound of four strings stretched over it. It consists of about 70 different pieces, made of several kinds of wood, every piece hand-carved and made without any mechanical aids except simple hand tools. The sounding part of the strings runs from the bridge, along the fingerboard, to the nut on the neck. When a string is sounded by passing the hair of the bow over it, the sound is transmitted down through the bridge to the belly (upper surface of the box). The sound-post, placed under the bridge, carries the vibrations through to the back of the violin. The bass bar adds strength to the belly, and also spreads the vibrations throughout the body of the violin.

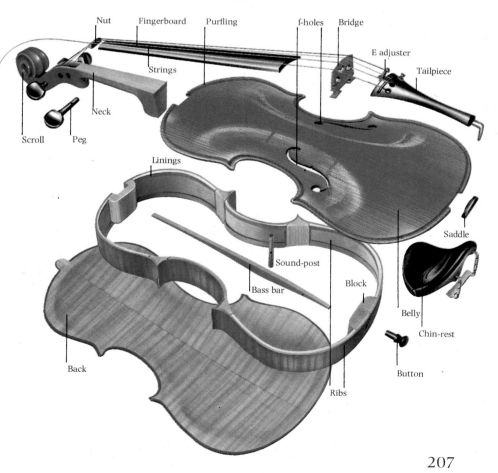

zinc template, which may itself follow the outline of a famous violin, such as the well-known 'Messiah' Stradivarius. Stradivari himself left several such forms, so his outlines can be followed exactly.

Now six willow 'blocks', which act as anchor-points for the ribs, are carved to shape, one for each end of the violin, and four for the corners where the ribs meet. Next, the maple ribs are planed to a uniform thickness of about $\frac{1}{32}$ in., bent to the curves of the form round an electrically heated bending iron, clamped to the exact outer shape of the form and glued to the blocks.

When the form is removed, ribs and blocks make the skeletal outline of a violin, like the sides of a box without lid or bottom. As a final preparation, ribs are strengthened at top and bottom with narrow strips of wood called 'linings', which also provide a larger surface for gluing the belly and back to the ribs.

The back is made from a wedge-shaped block of maple, cut in two and glued edge to edge so that the grain is symmetrical. At this stage it is an oblong, flat on one side and rising to a ridge in the centre. A template is placed on the flat side, and the back is cut to shape. As the back will overhang the ribs all the way round, this template is slightly larger than the form on which the ribs are shaped. The back is now ready for 'arching' – that is, carving to the gently swelling curve that characterises the back and belly of the instrument. This is done by a combination of gouges, planes and scrapers.

At Newark, some of the small planes, called 'thumbplanes', are minute – just an inch or so long – and are made by the craftsmen themselves in the metal-working shop at the Technical College of which the violin school forms part. Sandpaper is forbidden, as even the finest glasspaper tears the fibres of the wood rather than cutting them cleanly. However, Stradivari himself cheated in this respect, as he used rough dog-fish skin to smooth his wood, followed by horsetail grass for a perfect finish.

Putting in the purfling

Next, 'purfling' is inserted all round the back, about $\frac{11}{64}$ in. from the outer edge. This is a narrow sandwich, consisting of a strip of white wood between two strips of black fibre (in earlier times it was all of wood). Purfling is both decorative and functional, for it follows the graceful outline of the violin and emphasises its shape, while giving greater strength nearer the edge and preventing any small cracks from extending into the main body of the violin.

The groove for the purfling is cut about halfway through the thickness of the back. The exact position is indicated by a 'purfling marker', which scratches a double line. The groove is cut with a knife and a 'purfling pick' – a kind of miniature plane which looks like a bent-ended screwdriver and is pushed along the groove after the sides have been cut with a knife.

The purfling is glued into place. Some craftsmen use a doctor's hypodermic syringe to inject the minute amount of glue needed into the groove.

Once the arching is completed and the purfling is in place, the back is hollowed out to the correct thickness. The craftsman uses a kind of contour map taken from a classic Cremona violin and constantly checks the thickness with calipers. The back is now glued to the ribs.

The belly is made in the same way as the back, with two important differences. First, it has to have the two 'f-holes' cut in it – gracefully curved slots, one on either side of the bridge, which enable the belly to vibrate freely and also allow the sound to escape. These are marked out with templates, cut with a fretsaw and finished off with a razor-sharp knife. The second difference between belly and back is the 'bass bar', which is shaped and glued inside the belly. This is a strip of spruce which runs the length of the belly, in a position directly below the left-hand foot of the bridge; its function is to give added strength at the point where the strings are exerting the greatest pressure, and also to spread the vibrations as widely as possible throughout the violin.

The belly is now ready to be glued to the upper edge of the ribs; but before this is done and the box is completed, the craftsman glues in a label giving his name and the date – the only authentication any violin can have, apart from the quality of the work.

The glue comes in granular form, looking rather like

MAKING THE BODY

The first stage is to assemble the six ribs that form the sides of the violin (above) and the wooden blocks that join them. The ribs are usually shaped to a wooden mould based on a famous violin; the one shown here is the 'Messie' or 'Messiah' Stradivarius, kept in the Ashmolean Museum, Oxford. When the ribs are completed, the back and belly (below) are cut out and carved to shape, using calipers to get the correct thickness, and gouges (left) and small thumb-planes (right) to remove surplus wood. Finally, the back and then the belly are glued to the ribs.

brown sugar, and is made from animal hide. It is heated with water to a tacky consistency – the less water used, the stronger the glue. The belly is glued to the ribs with a weaker mix than is used for the rest of the instrument, because, when a violin needs major repair or alteration, the belly may have to be removed.

The remaining major section is the maple neck and pegbox, terminating in the fluted scroll. To carve the spiral scroll two templates are used: a zinc side template which gives the overall outline, and a flexible plastic template which gives the varying thicknesses of the scroll.

The completed neck is fitted into a mitre slot cut for it in the upper block, and is glued into position. Stradivari himself used nails to fasten the neck to the body, but the angle of the neck has altered since his day. There is now insufficient wood at the base of the neck for nailing.

At last the violin is ready for varnishing, a stage as crucial to the instrument's tone as any of the phases of actual construction. At one time it was thought that Stradivari's secret lay in his varnish.

Basically, varnish is a means of spreading resin and colouring evenly over the whole surface, and there are two main types: spirit varnish, in which the resin is dissolved in alcohol; and oil-based varnish. Spirit has the advantage of drying almost instantaneously whatever the weather, and the ten or 12 coats needed can be applied at intervals of a day or so. Oil takes longer to dry and is thus far easier to spread and so achieve an even finish. However, it needs sunlight to dry properly, and in damp weather a coat may take weeks to dry.

All that remains is to add the pegs and other pieces – the stage known as 'fitting up'. One piece, the sound-post, is vital to the violin's sound-producing capability, as it carries the vibrations from the belly through to the back. This short length of spruce dowelling runs vertically from a position directly below the bridge, on the opposite side to the bass bar, to the back of the instrument. Inserting it is tricky, as it has to be threaded through the f-hole on the point of an S-shaped blade called a 'sound-post setter'. Its fit has to be perfect, for it is not glued into place, but is held by the inward pressure of the back and the belly.

The other pieces – pegs, fingerboard, tailpiece, bridge and chin-rest – are bought in the rough. Though the craftsman

FITTING THE NECK

Made of maple, this is one of the most important parts of the violin. It is drilled with holes to take the four pegs, and carries the fingerboard glued to its upper surface. Its inner end is glued to the rib and block assembly; its outer end is carved into an intricate scroll (above). The scroll is carefully fluted into a spiral, using chisels and gouges and working from templates. After the neck has been attached, the violin is ready for its many coats of varnish.

has to finish them off and make them fit the violin exactly, they are the trimmings on a completed work of art.

Since Stradivari's day, the violin has undergone various modifications, in line with changing musical taste. The chief demand has been for a fuller tone, which has meant stronger strings, subjected to greater tension, requiring an increase in the size of the bass bar. The strings have also been lengthened somewhat, which has entailed a longer neck, set at a slight angle to the body instead of being in the same plane. This alteration to the angle has made it necessary for the bridge to be higher and more arched.

How the bow is made

Without the bow the violin remains a box, capable of giving out the sound of plucked strings but nothing more. As the name implies, the bow is probably derived from the hunter's bow; medieval paintings show the fiddles of the day being played with convex bows, like miniature versions of the longbows used at Agincourt. The bow reached its final form a good deal later than the violin itself, in the hands of the great French maker François Tourte (1747-1835).

The bow consists of strands of white horsehair held in tension between the two ends of a stick. If the bow in this state is passed across the strings of a violin, no sound is produced, except perhaps for a high-pitched squeak; so friction is provided by rubbing resin on the horsehair, which catches on the string as the bow passes across it and causes it to vibrate. The overall length of the bow is about 29 in., with a playing horsehair length of about $25\frac{1}{2}$ in. The wood used is pernambuco, from South America; to give the bow its graceful, slightly concave shape, the wood is heat-bent. It is then given four to six coats of polish.

At the end furthest from the player's hand the bowstick is carved to a hatchet shape, which provides a secure attachment for the horsehair. At the other end the hair is held in an oblong block called the 'nut', or 'frog'. Set in the end of the stick is a screw cap connected to the nut; when the player turns this, the nut moves back along the stick, thus tightening the horsehair ready for playing. The invention of the adjustable nut was Tourte's main contribution to the bow's evolution. The nut, made of tortoiseshell or ebony, is often beautifully decorated.

CUTTING THE F-HOLES *The two f-holes, marked out with templates on the belly of the violin and cut to shape with razor-sharp knives, allow the belly to vibrate freely and also permit the sound to escape. The triple strip right round the belly is the purfling, set in a shallow groove.*

VIOLIN BOW

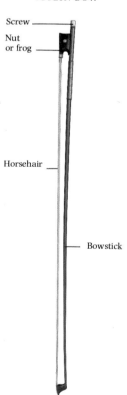

Screw

Nut or frog

Horsehair

Bowstick

A ONCE-FLOURISHING CRAFT

The workshop of this famous walking-stick firm – Lintott's, in Sussex – was typical of a number of large country stick makers. From humble beginnings in the middle of the last century, it grew into a small factory employing 30 or 40 workers. Lintott's made sticks for many different uses, their products being in great demand for wounded servicemen during the two World Wars. Sadly, the firm is now closed.

At Lintott's, a stick was given its curved handle by heating the thicker end in hot, damp sand, then bending it to shape.

Placing the handle end in a bending jig.

Bending the handle, which was then tied and left to set.

THE Walking Stick MAKER

THE COUNTRYMAN'S COMPANION, THE HIKER'S FRIEND,
THE SHEPHERD'S TOOL — WALKING STICKS ARE CRAFTED
TO SUIT MANY DIFFERENT LIFE STYLES

*T*here are two kinds of walking-stick maker — the craftsman who makes them as much for pleasure as for profit, who may produce a hundred or so in a year; and the craftsman in a more serious way of business, who grows saplings specially for the job and turns out several hundred.

There are probably more of the first kind, and they have to gather their raw material many months before they start working on it. Actually finding the right sort of sticks is probably their most difficult task. First, the wood must be of the correct type — hazel, ash, holly or blackthorn. Then it must be in straight lengths, with a block from a branch or root at one end, from which the handle will be formed. Or, if a thumb-stick is to be made, it must be forked at one end, with the fork branches of roughly equal thickness.

In the days before farmers ruthlessly cut down or ripped up the hedges beside their fields, suitable sticks were fairly easy to find. But now the craftsman must scour woodland for supplies — often doing a deal with the owner for permission to do so. The most fruitful source is usually a wood that slopes sharply down to a river or lake: the angle of growth imparts a natural tilt to the handle.

The sticks are gathered in winter, when the sap is down — usually before the end of the year — otherwise the wood is liable to split when it is worked on later. When the craftsman has gathered sufficient, he takes them back to his workshop and immediately sets about straightening any bends there may be in them. He does this by clamping the stick tightly to a straight, rigid pole, then wiring both together. They are then hung vertically from the ceiling of the workshop for several months, during which the sticks set straight in the dry, moisture-free atmosphere. A label is tied to each stick, with the date of hanging.

Some time in the following October, the sticks are taken down — probably just one or two a day — and clamped in a bench vice to be worked into shape. A popular one is the simple knobstick, for which chestnut is sometimes used. It is about 3 ft long and has a rounded knob at the top which is shaped by rasp and file, with some of the bark removed to reveal the grain. The stick is then polished, sealed with a quick-dry sealant, and given six coats of varnish. Finally a brass or rubber ferrule is fitted to the end.

More complex shapes exercise the craftsman's talents to the full. Among these are the 'goat's-foot top' and the 'trigger grip' — both names coming from the shapes of the handles, and both made of hazel, which becomes speckled when roughed down. Then there is the 'cleeve grip' handled stick, an invention of the Devonshire stick maker Eric Blake. This is about 3 ft 9 in. long, made of holly or hazel, with a special ridge on top of the handle for the thumb and indents along the sloping edge of the handle for the fingers: it provides an excellent grip for rough country walking.

There is also a great demand for the thumb-stick, a tall walking stick at least 4 ft long; the handle is Y-shaped and is formed from a fork of two branches of roughly equal thickness. A much rarer sight is an ash stick entwined with honeysuckle. This starts off as a sapling or branch of woodland ash along which a creeper of honeysuckle has coiled itself. When the ash is cut it must be hung for at least a year, to ensure that the honeysuckle is entwined very firmly around it. For extra decoration, some craftsmen remove a segment or two of honeysuckle to expose the deep indentations it has made in the shank of the ash.

A shepherd's crook takes about twice as long to make as a walking stick — eight to ten hours, against four or five. Although shaping is a relatively complex process, the job is done by hand and eye alone. Instead of conventional measurements, the craftsman's fingers serve as a gauge for determining the width of the handle and the gap between shaft and hook.

Commercially minded stick makers, growing their own saplings, use rather more sophisticated methods. They favour ash and sweet chestnut, and ash saplings are even trained to grow at an angle, to make cross-head sticks. Young trees are lifted when about two years old, then pruned back to one side shoot or bud low down. The tree is then replanted, with the main stem below ground and the side shoot or bud pointing vertically upwards. The shoot is allowed to grow to walking-stick length — about three or four more years — during which time shoots or buds are removed from it to retain a single, upright stem. When uprooted again, the old underground main stem of the original sapling forms the knobbly handle that is the special feature of the cross-head stick.

Any further forming needed is done in a sand bed. This is really a simple way of steam-bending: the sticks are placed in a bed of damp sand, which is heated by a boiler underneath, leaving the sticks pliant so that handles can be easily formed. Any unwanted bends in the shaft are straightened out at the same time.

In the north, and particularly in Scotland, the handle of the stick is often fashioned from a suitably shaped section of deer antler or from ram's horn. Ram's horn can be easily sawn to size, then straightened as necessary by boiling it in water for a few hours. It is then formed to shape with rasp, file and sandpaper. Lastly it may be boned to give a smooth and polished finish. The shaft of the stick is glued into a hole drilled in the horn.

Today, the whole craft of stick making is perhaps taken rather more seriously in the north, with competitions between stick makers at country fairs and agricultural shows in places like the Lake District and the Fell Country; there is even an association of stick makers in Scotland. Possibly the more rugged terrain there still fosters the craft more than in the south.

MAKING A SHEPHERD'S CROOK

A stick between 4 ft and 5 ft long is needed, with a substantial block at the end which is to form the crook. To start shaping the crook, the centre of the block is removed by drilling a circle of holes with a handbrace and bit, then sawing between them with a fretsaw. The shaping is completed with saw, rasp and file — though a quicker method is to use a cylindrical plane. The crook and shaft are rubbed smooth with sandpaper, and the whole stick sealed and varnished. It may also be fitted with a ferrule.

THE RAW MATERIAL

Some walking sticks are made from ash saplings (above) specially seeded and grown for several years. Others are made from suitable lengths individually cut from holly, hazel or blackthorn. Walking sticks for 'men about town' are often made from Malacca palm or Rattan palm, whose stems are slim and straight.

THE Wheelwright

MAKING A SPOKED WHEEL CALLS FOR A
SORT OF GENIUS, FOR ITS STRUCTURE IS A GREAT DEAL
MORE COMPLEX THAN MIGHT BE IMAGINED

*N*early 6,000 years ago, a scribe in Mesopotamia (present-day Iraq) drew a picture of a wheeled cart. It is the earliest surviving evidence of the use of the wheel, the transport breakthrough that helped man to advance into civilisation. The wheels of this cart were not the crude, unevenly rounded slices of tree trunk that might be imagined. They were made from three planks, joined by cross struts to form a circle, the middle (and largest) piece being bored centrally to hold the axle end.

Clearly, a wheelwright had been at work and a new craft had been born.

Wagon wheels continued to be made solid for the next 1,000 years, and there was only one significant improvement. This was to allow the wheels to turn freely on a fixed axle, instead of the former method of fixing the wheels to an axle that revolved through two hoops slung under the wagon.

Then, around 1750 BC, a light battle-chariot appeared. It was fitted with a pair of quite different wheels – with spokes. The chariot was probably introduced by the Hyksos, a Semitic people who overran Egypt in the 18th century BC. It was a fast-moving vehicle from which warriors could dash into the battle and fire bolts or hurl spears. The chariot was also used for hunting lions and other wild animals.

A casket found in Tutankhamun's tomb, dating from the 15th or 14th century BC, bears a marvellous painting of several chariots, each carrying two men and driven by pairs of horses. Interestingly, the wheels have only six spokes. They look fragile for the weight they carried. Since the Middle Ages, at least, it has been customary to fit 12 spokes

to heavier wheels and 14, sometimes 16, to lighter ones.

Perhaps 200 years after the invention of spokes, around 1500 BC, the rims of wheels began to be fitted with metal bands, or tyres. This was a great improvement upon the earlier practice of binding them with leather, which must have had a very short life on the uneven tracks and roads of the time.

The introduction of the spoke enabled wheelwrights to improve the strength and durability of wheels. Wagons travelling along uneven roads move from side to side – alarmingly, if you study the movement closely. This is compounded by the swaying movement of the horse. So, the wheelwright designed wheels to be 'dished' to counterbalance the continual outward thrusts, and also to prevent the hub being smashed out of the wheel as a result of a violent blow against a boulder or the side of a rut.

Exactly when, or in what land, this improvement was introduced is not known, but remains of a lightweight chariot of the 1st century BC, complete with dished wheels, were found in Anglesey in 1947. A replica can be seen at the Welsh Folk Museum at St Fagans, near Cardiff.

There were two methods of dishing a wheel. One was to set the spokes at a slight angle. Another was to fit the iron tyre on the rim while it was red hot, so that the contraction caused by cooling made the wheel concave. In most cases, wheelwrights coupled the two processes, and this is still the case today.

Although dishing a wheel adds to its strength, it is essential to mount it on an axle whose ends are angled downwards to compensate for the angle of the spokes. This ensures that each spoke turns to a vertical position at the moment when it is carrying maximum weight – that is, when it is upright between ground and hub.

Methods that have lasted centuries

The techniques of making wheels in a wheelwright's workshop have remained much the same for more than 2,000 years. The only significant benefits from modern technology are mechanical saws in place of hand saws, electric drills for forming spoke and dowel holes, planes to replace adzes, and powered lathes for woodturning. Before the mechanical saw, wheelwrights used huge, two-handled saws which were worked up and down by two men, one of them standing at the bottom of a saw-pit some 6 ft below the other (see p. 68). Most present-day wheelwrights can show visitors a defunct saw-pit somewhere on their premises.

The strength of the wheel for a cart or wagon depends to a large measure on the hub, or naff – called the nave in some workshops. The naff is almost always made of elm, because the grain of this wood runs in every direction, giving it uniform strength. Since a wheel is jolted at every point along its circumference when out on the road, the timber must not be weaker in some positions than in others. Equally important, an elmwood naff does not split when the spoke holes are cut into it.

Wheelwrights order trunks of elm, saw them off in short, chunky sections and stack them in the yard for seasoning. At least five years is needed for this, but many wheelwrights leave them to season for even longer, at the rate of a year for every inch of thickness. During this time the end-grain is brushed frequently to remove the sap and shift any mould. Some wheelwrights help the seasoning process by boring a hole through the middle of the trunk, accelerating the sap dispersal.

When the wood is seasoned, the wheelwright cuts off the length he needs for the particular wheel and turns it on the lathe, cutting a recess at each end for the naff hoops. These iron bands, which help hold the naff together, are made by a blacksmith and pulled on to the naff ends when red hot.

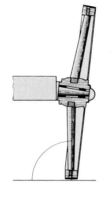

THE COMPLEX GEOMETRY OF A WHEEL

Viewed from front or rear, a cart wheel is saucer-shaped, with its concave face on the outside. This angling of the spokes adds greatly to its strength. The ends of the axle slope downwards, so that each spoke turns into a vertical position as it passes beneath the hub and is under maximum load. The metal tyre is cone-shaped to match the contour of the rim.

PARTS OF A WHEEL

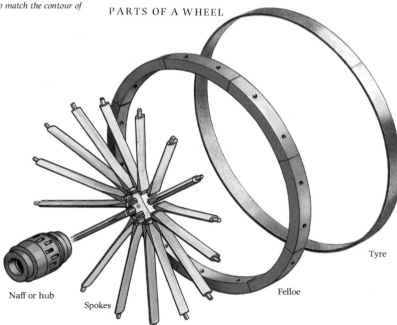

Naff or hub

Spokes

Felloe

Tyre

Many of the wheelwright's methods have changed little over the centuries. For instance, to make it easier to cut mortises for the spokes, generations of wheelwrights have secured the naff in a holding frame (left) so as to drill it with a brace and bit at equidistant intervals. One job that has altered is the method of making the felloes – at one time shaped with an adze from a block of wood, but nowadays cut to pattern with a band saw and trimmed with a plane (top). When the wheel has been assembled, the naff is bored with a boxing engine (centre) to take the iron bearing. Then, before fitting the tyre, the evenness of the wheel rim is checked with a traverse (bottom) and any proud points removed with a plane.

Shaping a felloe with a plane.

Boring the axle hole in the naff.

Checking the evenness of the rim.

213

The wheelwright uses a pair of compasses to mark the spoke-hole positions round the naff. The holes, or mortises, are then cut with a chisel ready to receive the spokes. These are cut vertically in the naff, the dished contour of the wheel being created by angled tenons at each end of the spokes.

Spokes are nearly always made from oak, whose great strength will withstand the tremendous strain exerted by the wheel as it is driven forwards. Wheelwrights generally use the centre of the tree, where the grain is straightest.

Spoke shapes vary with the type of cart. Wagon-wheel spokes, for instance, have an oval cross-section, with the narrower ends facing inwards and outwards. This, like the overall dished shape, provides maximum strength to withstand sideways thrusts.

Each spoke is cut to the right length, chiselled to provide a rectangular or a round tenon at each end, and the shoulder squared off to take up the stress when the weight of the wagon compresses the rim towards the naff. Spokes are shaped with a spokeshave, and those for a given wheel must all be exactly the same shape and size. Ideally, too, they should all weigh the same – something which the wheelwright gauges by feel rather than with a pair of scales.

When the spokes are ready, each is driven by mallet into its mortise to give the tightest fit possible. No glue is used. The wheelwright then takes the naff and its radiating spokes to a special four-legged wheel stoll, or stand. This is where the felloes are fitted.

Felloes are the curved sections of timber which, placed together in a circle, form the rim of the wheel. They are usually made of ash, which is springy and resilient and is able to withstand the uneven surfaces which a wagon may have to encounter. The heaviest wheels sometimes have felloes made of elm. Whatever the timber, they are cut from planks to the required size and curve.

Once the naff and spoke assembly is on the stoll, the wheelwright takes up a traverse. This is a wooden rod, with a pin through one end, which is put into the centre of the naff. At the opposite end there is another point which is used to mark the exact place on each spoke where the tenon is to be cut for insertion in the felloe. The traverse is in fact a sort of giant compass.

Usually, two spokes are fitted into each felloe. The slots for the spokes are cut with a chisel, and a special process is followed for knocking the felloes on to the spoke ends. A spoke cramp is placed across the rim ends of two spokes and drawn tight, pulling the ends closer together until the wheelwright gauges that the felloe can be tapped and slid on to the spoke ends, lining up correctly. When the cramp is released, the spoke will be an extremely tight fit. Additional strength is provided by a dowel fitted between each pair of felloes.

The basic structure of the wheel is now complete. The wheelwright trims any excess wood off the felloes and prepares the resulting rim round the circumference to receive the iron strakes or tyre. Normally, these are fixed by a blacksmith who visits the wheelwright's yard, and many wheelwrights have the necessary tools and equipment on their premises.

Strakes are, in effect, a tyre divided into segments – one for each felloe. For maximum strength, a strake spans the joint between a pair of felloes, to which it is fastened at each end by several nails.

Strakes, like tyres, are secured to the wheel while hot from the blacksmith's fire. Cooling – hastened by douching with water – has the effect of tightening the joints more surely than any amount of hammering. A tyre does this

SPECIAL TOOLS FOR MAKING WHEELS

Among the wheelwright's more distinctive tools are: calipers, for ensuring that the second of a pair of naffs (hubs) exactly matches the first; adze, a sharp-edged tool formerly used for shaping felloes; boxing engine, worked by hand, for boring the axle hole through the naff; samson, a clamp for drawing adjacent felloes together while fitting a strake; auger, a drilling tool, used like a brace and bit; spoke dog, used to draw two spoke ends together when fitting a felloe on to the spoke tenons; jarvis, a type of spokeshave; felloe pattern, an arc-shaped length of wood which serves as a guide when cutting felloes; traveller, a calibrated wheel, mounted on a rod, for measuring the circumference of the wheel.

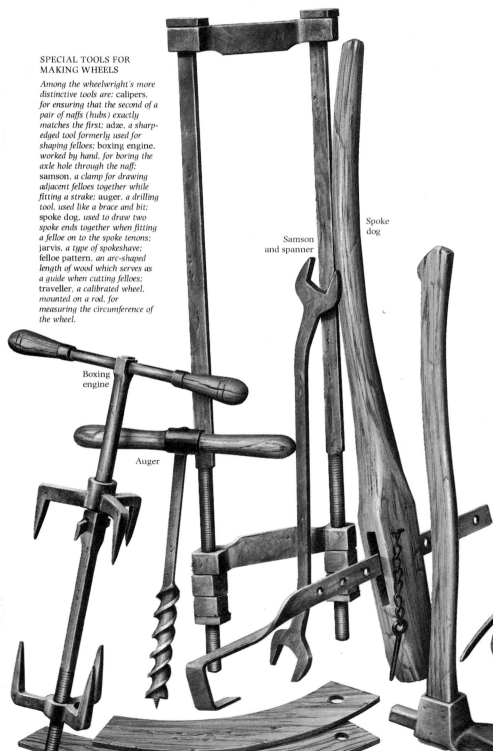

Spoke dog

Samson and spanner

Boxing engine

Auger

Calipers

Traveller

Adze

Felloe pattern

Jarvis

more efficiently than strakes, for it exerts even pressure all around the rim.

Except on the narrowest wheels, both strakes and hoops have to be angled, or coned, to compensate for the angle of dish. That is, the inner edge of the hoop has a slightly greater circumference than the outer edge.

The wheelwright's final task is to make a large hole through the middle of the naff to hold the iron box which turns on the axle. The hole used to be bored out with a large auger and widened with gouges, but a relatively new tool now does the job. This is the boxing engine, a long, threaded rod with a handle at one end and a tripod grip at the other. There is a cutting tool which travels along the shank when the handle is turned, boring through the naff with great accuracy.

For centuries there was a wheelwright in almost every British town and village. He was by training a carpenter and joiner, and when business was slack he turned to making gates, ladders and beehives – or even acted as an undertaker. In rural areas the wheelwright usually made carts and wagons as well as wheels – a craft that in cities was the responsibility of cartwrights or coachbuilders. Country wagons differed from one part of Britain to another, resulting in a remarkable range of regional carts.

The wheelwright's skill takes years to master. In the days of formal apprenticeship, wheelwrights expected the assistants to serve for at least seven years: a few would not give them a free hand for ten. Once the apprenticeship was served, the young wheelwright was often sent from village to village to extend his experience by working in other workshops as an 'improver'.

Many wheelwright firms are old family businesses, with two, sometimes three, generations of men working together. Today, there is still a demand for wheelwrights' services, but the number of craftsmen has declined rapidly since the end of the First World War – faster than the need for their skills. Those who are still in business – and most of them are thriving – make new wagons and carts, and new wheels for old vehicles.

In recent years there has been an increasing demand for restoration work on old railway rolling stock. George Stephenson's *Rocket* had oak spokes for its driving wheels, and so did most of its contemporaries. The National Railway Museum at York, and several others, are continually acquiring Victorian engines, coaches and goods wagons, often in derelict condition, and most wheelwrights' yards today have a repair job or two of this kind on their order books.

In addition, several brewing firms, particularly in the north of England, require traditional brewing drays, which have to be made from scratch. Ceremonial gun-carriages still have wheels made by craftsmen, while pony carts are beginning to take the place of second cars in some farming families. It is restoration work and new jobs like these that have helped to keep the wheelwright's craft alive.

Wagons and carts

Until about a century ago, you could generally tell from its design where a wagon (four wheels) or cart (two wheels) originated. From medieval times, regional and county differences in shape, and often in colour scheme, were very pronounced. The shapes were dictated as much by the nature of the countryside in which they were expected to be used as by their particular purpose. Then, factories began to turn out more uniform styles of wagons and carts, and the range of shapes diminished.

Farmers' wagons in the flat plains of East Anglia were more heavily built than those in the hilly parts of the West Country. Wheelwrights in Lancashire supplied the valley

THE DRAMA OF FITTING A TYRE

A local blacksmith is generally called in to help with this job, though some wheelwrights used to do the work themselves. The wheel is clamped to a stand, called a tyring platform, close to the fire. Here, a red-hot iron hoop – previously forged to the correct size – is waiting. The blacksmith lifts the hoop with tongs and places it over the outside of the rim, hammering it down as he does so, amidst a great deal of steam, hissing and even flames from the scorching timber. One of the wheelwrights drenches the tyre with cold water as soon as it is in position, so preventing damage from burning and speeding contraction of the tyre. A clamp placed on the naff, and screwed down tightly, keeps the spokes at a constant angle as the red-hot tyre cools and contracts. The greatest care has to be taken with this operation, for if the tyre is too tight it may cause the spokes to bend and so damage the wheel. After a few minutes the hissing subsides as the wood begins to cool. This may be accompanied by a period of creaking and groaning, as pressure from the contracting tyre tightens the joints at each end of the spokes and forms a vice-like grip that will endure for the life of the wheel.

farmers with wagons of light construction, but with broad wheels so that they would not sink into the mud. For those who farmed the hilly sides of the valleys they made vehicles with narrower wheels that would grip more surely on the slanting tracks.

Two-wheeled haycarts made in Essex were recognisable by their detachable back and front extensions, known locally as 'ladders' because they were slatted to cut down the weight. These enabled such carts to carry large loads and still turn in narrow or confined spaces that would not admit four-wheeled vehicles. Hop wagons in Kent, which are still in use today, have detachable sides so that the base of the body can be used directly for carrying wide loads, which may be tied down.

One particular vehicle used in Midland counties, especially Leicestershire and Nottinghamshire, is the hermaphrodite, or 'mophrey' in local parlance. It consists of a two-wheeled cart which is converted into a four-wheeled vehicle by removing the shafts and fixing the pole of a two-wheeled extension under the cart. Boards are laid across to form a floor. It is called hermaphrodite 'because it's neither one thing nor the other' – as a Midland farmer put it.

The four-wheeled wagon articulates on its smaller two front wheels, and the lock varies with the type of wagon. If the design of the body is such that it is slung below the tops of both pairs of wheels, the front wheels can turn only a few degrees to left or right. The turning arc will be greater if the shaft between the wheels is lengthened, but there is a limit to the width of a front-wheel assembly. The body can also be waisted towards the front to permit a greater arc, while the wagon can be turned through an almost 180 degree lock if the front wheels are made much smaller so that they clear the bottom of the body.

Wheelwrights chose the timber for building wagons and carts with the same meticulous care lavished on the component parts of the wheels. They knew, and many still know today, almost every mature tree in their neighbourhood – its shape, condition, approximate age and its owner. Sometimes they kept an eye on a tree because it had branches in shapes that would do nicely for making curved parts of a wagon. Oak trees are more prone to produce curved branches than are ash trees. If a wheelwright needed ash components for a special wagon, he had to be exceptionally vigilant to ensure that when a suitable tree was felled it was not carted away for other uses.

The wagon frame is basically in three parts: the body, supported by a sub-frame of strong cross-members called

bolsters; the forecarriage, which carries the front axle and its articulating parts; and the hindcarriage, which incorporates the rear axle. The body is generally one of two kinds: either a box body, which is deep and rectilinear; or a bow body, which is shallower and has gentle curves at the sides and ends. The two undercarriages are linked by a strong, centrally placed pole running from front to rear, bolted through a bolster to the bottom of the body.

Wagons are not fitted with brakes, but a skid is put under one or more wheels on an incline. This is an iron pan, shaped like a kitchen coal shovel, which is attached to the wagon frame by a chain. Extra wheel-locking is provided by winding a chain round two spokes and the hub of the axle.

Some wagons are drawn by a single horse, others by a pair and occasionally even by three. The East Yorkshire two-horse wagon was often pulled by two Clydesdales, harnessed side by side with a single pole between them. The Hereford wagon, a much smaller vehicle, is drawn by one horse between a pair of shafts. The Sussex wagon usually has two pairs of shafts.

The construction of a wagon or cart requires great skill and attention to detail. While being drawn along a road or track, the vehicle sustains tremendous stresses – from side to side, upwards and downwards – due to the combination of road surface, the weight of the load and the movements of the horse or horses pulling it. For this reason, the component parts have to be shaped individually before being fitted together.

The casual observer might think that it was a waste of time to produce so many components that are so attractively chamfered and tapered. Yet chamfering reduces the weight of a frame member without weakening it. Tapering strengthens a joint. Together, this delicate shaping of the wooden members can reduce the weight of a wagon by up to one-eighth. Curved parts bend more easily with the direction of stress than do straight members.

It is a tradition of wheelwrights not to hand over their vehicles until they have put all the parts together once, tested the joints and the moving parts, dismantled them and then reassembled everything again after making the necessary adjustments. Painting and decoration are then put in hand. Vehicles could be recognised not only by their regional characteristics but also, in many cases, by decorative features added by individual craftsmen.

Thus, wagons in the south-east tended to have very simple colour schemes – often an overall buff or blue. Yellow was the predominant colour in Oxfordshire; orange in Northamptonshire; blue in Dorset.

A more individual style of decoration, sometimes of fairground brilliance, was often to be found in Somerset and Northamptonshire – as in other counties where it took a particular craftsman's fancy. From Scotland came the custom of painting eyes, or circular designs resembling eyes, on the fronts of wagons.

Wagons are the more glamorous of the wheelwright's vehicles, but during his lifetime the craftsman probably made more carts than wagons. Most farms had at least one or two carts for carrying out a variety of jobs, the dung cart being perhaps the most widely used. This has a hinged end that lets the manure slide to the ground when the cart is tipped backwards. Until the 1930s most farmers used to drive themselves about the farm, or to and from market, in a low cart drawn by a pony.

Carts may well come into their own again as farmers weigh up the costs of keeping a pony, and the consequent slower rate of travel, against the ever-rising costs of motor fuel for a tractor or car. One collector of old carts in Suffolk has received numerous enquiries in recent years from farmers interested in buying his carts.

A COMBINATION OF SKILLS

Although some wagons were built entirely by wheelwrights, general carpenters were responsible for the bodies of many carts and other horse-drawn vehicles. Below, a group of carpenters is seen making a farm cart. Such craftsmen formed part of a team, for the wheels still demanded the special skills of the wheel-wright, and a blacksmith was responsible for the ironwork. Carpenters who specialised in vehicle construction were called wainwrights.

Oxfordshire bow wagon

Essex cart

East Yorkshire wagon

Kentish dung cart

Midlands hermaphrodite

Lincolnshire wagon

Sussex wagon

WAGONS AND CARTS FROM THE REGIONS – AS VARIED AS BRITAIN'S COUNTRYSIDE

Oxfordshire bow wagon *The curved top-edge boards are designed to support an overhanging load of hay or straw.* **Essex cart** *Fore-and-aft ladders increase its carrying capacity without widening the vehicle.* **East Yorkshire wagon** *Distinctive features include the gracefully curved plank sides and the panel decoration of the tailboard.*

Kentish dung cart *The body tips, allowing the load to slide out under a hinged tailboard.* **Midlands hermaphrodite** *Basically a two-wheel cart, the front wheels are added as an extension when a four-wheel wagon is needed. It weighs less than a true wagon, making it easier for a single horse to pull.* **Sussex wagon** *Unlike many built in the county, this*

one has shafts for only one horse. **Lincolnshire wagon** *Spindle sides and a pronounced wheel dish are distinctive features of this elegant vehicle.*

Particularly fine displays of wagons and carts may be seen at the Welsh Folk Museum, Cardiff, and at the Reading Museum of English Rural Life.

THE
WINE-GROWER

THE WINES OF BRITAIN ARE REARED
LIKE DELICATE CHILDREN – WITH LOVE, FAITH AND
CONSTANT, WATCHFUL CARE...

*G*iven Britain's notoriously unstable climate, wine growing as a business demands a more-than-average commitment – and a degree of the gambling spirit. Uncertain summers, prolonged, unpredictable rains and freak frosts are among the cards stacked against anyone attempting it. What is also required is an ability to study the subject in depth, practical flair, a tough constitution, resources against a (literally!) rainy day – and a love of wine.

If the vineyard is to pay it must also cover at least 3 acres – preferably on a sheltered slope facing south-east. Such a slope just outside the Hampshire village of Hambledon supports and nourishes in its chalky soil 5¼ acres of the very same vines from which the renowned Pol Roger champagne is made. At Hambledon their grapes are pressed into a delicate, still white wine.

Major-General Sir Guy Salisbury-Jones planted the vineyard in 1951. It was the first commercial vineyard to be planted after Castle Coch, near Cardiff, where the last vintage was in 1915. Perhaps fittingly, Sir Guy grows two varieties of a grape introduced to Britain by the Romans – the Pinot. These are the black Pinot Noir and Pinot Meunier. He also cultivates the green Chardonnay, and Seyve-Villard 5-276. These four varieties were chosen because they are able to thrive in the chalky Hampshire soil – almost identical to that in the Champagne region of France, where the Pinot Noir is widely used in making the region's famous sparkling wine. The vines are bought in France ready-grafted on to phylloxera-resistant American root-stock. Phylloxera, a parasitic root louse, came to Europe on some American vines and devastated vineyards over a 30 year period between 1870 and 1900. It was finally defeated – and European grape varieties saved – by grafting cut shoots from European vines on to American roots that had built up a natural resistance to the parasite. The practice has continued ever since.

The infant vine arrives with its root dip-coated in paraffin wax to prevent it from drying out during shipment between the plant nursery and the vineyard. It is planted with the graft at least 2 in. above the ground – otherwise the graft can put out its own roots and leaf. The plants are set 3 ft apart with 4 ft between the rows – about 3,500 to an acre. They may yield a light crop in their third year, but are not adult vines until they are from five to seven years old. From the moment of planting, however, they need constant attention – pruning and trimming, tying up, spraying, fertilising and hoeing to keep weeds at bay. They are usually replaced after about 25 years.

The vine is planted against a stake, and as it grows it is pruned and disbudded so that only two branches are allowed to flourish. These are trained to spread in opposite directions along the horizontal wires of a low trellis, in what is called the Double Guyot system.

Kept down to about waist height, the two branches are less vulnerable to chilling winds, and can get maximum benefit from soil-reflected heat on sunny days. Offshoots of these main branches are trained to grow vertically, and tied to a second, higher wire on the trellis. This allows the leaves and setting fruit plenty of sunshine, and ensures good coverage when spraying. It also allows a special tractor to straddle the trellis and trim back both top and sides of the vines in one process as it is driven along the row.

Between May and September, the vines are sprayed on average eight times, depending on weather conditions, to guard against mildew and fungus infections. A sulphur spray is used on young leaves at the start of the season, and later a stronger proprietary one. It is important that the spray reaches the underside – the 'breathing' side – of the leaf, because that is where mildew can kill the plant by literally choking it. A nitrogen-based fertiliser is used in April, and potash or phosphate fertilisers in December.

The vines flower in July – three weeks later than in France – and normally 100 days elapse before the fruit is harvested. Barring disasters, the grapes should be well set by September, their condition dictated largely by the weather of the preceding months.

Their growth cycle begins in spring temperatures of about 60°F, and they need a good proportion of higher temperatures from then on. The amount they need is called the 'heat summation'. This is worked out by adding up the number of degrees *over* ten they receive per day over the growing season. Three days at, say, 20 would add 30 to the total, which should reach 1,800 for successful growth. Anything less and the grapes will end up low in sugar content and high in acid. However, this can be countered by adding sugar during the wine making.

By mid-October there is little that can be done to the vines themselves until they are ready for harvesting. But they must – at Hambledon, anyway – be protected from hungry wildlife. Rabbit-proof fences have been put up around the vineyard, and it is covered with large nets to keep off a persistent local marauder – the blackbird. But the size and quality of the harvest is finally dependent on the weather. In a good season like that of 1976 this vineyard produced 26,000 bottles of wine. Two years later, in the disastrous summer of 1978, production was down to just 846 bottles. An average year yields about 10,000 bottles – quite close to the annual average in Britain of 2,000 bottles per acre.

When picking time arrives, about 16 people – family and villagers – assemble to gather the grapes at Hambledon. Good harvest or poor, it is, as in vineyards the world over, a joyous occasion. The bunches are piled into large trug baskets, from which the contents are transferred to tubs at the end of each row. As the tubs are filled, they are towed off

CRISP AND FRUITY

There are at least 100 vineyards in Britain, producing around half a million bottles a year. The wines are white, with the exception of one rosé, and many are made with the same varieties of grapes as those used for German wines, which they resemble closely. Hambledon wine, however, is made from French varieties, and has a crisp distinctive tang of its own. The gold-topped bottle is Magdalen Rivaner '76, made in the old village of Pulham St Mary, Norfolk. This is a more fruity and fragrant wine, based on Mueller-Thurgau grapes – and is one of the better-known German-style vintages. Most of the vineyards are in East Anglia, Sussex, Kent, Hampshire and the Isle of Wight, where they stand the best chance of suitable weather.

THE DECLINE AND RISE OF THE BRITISH VINEYARD

It was the Roman Emperor Probus who first authorised wine making in Britain, in AD 280, and the vine was cultivated in many places roughly south of a line between The Wash and Anglesey. Production continued on fluctuating levels until the 18th century. It rose dramatically in AD 579, when the arrival of St Augustine sparked off a sharp rise in the demand for communion wine. Monasteries responded enthusiastically by planting new vines, but the marriage of Henry II to Eleanor of Aquitaine in 1152 set back the progress of English wines, for the union brought with it large cheap imports of good wines from Bordeaux. Black dots show the sites of modern vineyards; red dots mark medieval vineyards.

. Medieval sites   . Modern vineyards

tested for sugar content with a hydrometer, and for acid using litmus paper. When the must is transferred to a fermentation tank, enough sugar is added to bring the hydrometer reading up to 82 degrees, and to ensure that the alcoholic content of the wine will be 11 per cent.

Fermentation is started by adding live yeast. At Hambledon 5 gallons of yeast 'starter' is poured into each 100 gallon batch of wine. The starter is made a week before harvesting, when enough grapes are picked to make 5 gallons of must, using a small wooden hand-press. To this is added 3 fl. oz. of a liquid yeast culture. Fermentation of the wine can take anything from eight days in warm temperatures to ten weeks in cold. Six to eight weeks seem to give the best results. Fermentation is complete when tests show that only 3 per cent of sugar remains in the wine.

Once fermented, the wine is transferred to a maturing tank where it spends a week settling down again and clarifying. Finings are sometimes added to help the process along – usually bentonite, a type of clay that removes unstable proteins in the wine. Cleared and settled, the wine then goes into a refrigeration tank where it remains for five days at a temperature of 28°F. Finally, it passes to another settling tank where it is allowed to return to room temperature before being bottled.

Small bottling and corking machines perform this task, and the bottles then go into a cellar for at least three months, to be kept at a temperature between 40°F and 50°F. This allows the wine to recover from the shock of all it has been through. Now at last it can be drunk – although it is best left to mature in the bottle for three years to achieve its full flavour.

by tractor to the winery. There the fruit goes straight into the hopper of a powered grape-mill, the serrated rollers of which are set $\frac{1}{4}$ in. apart, to break the skin and lightly squash the grapes without damaging the pips. The pulp passes straight into a large glass tank beneath, where it stays for three hours to allow enzymes – chemicals present in the grapes – to break down as much cell tissue as possible, so that the maximum amount of free-flowing juice is obtained. Pulp and juice then go into a cylindrical horizontal wine-press, which squeezes out just the juice, leaving skins, stalks and pips behind.

This juice is called 'must', and it is pumped into a settling vat. There it sits for at least 12 hours to allow any unwanted solids remaining to settle to the bottom. At this stage it is

THE FRUITS OF THE VINE

Gathering in the grape harvest is a time for rejoicing in vineyards wherever wine is made – and no less so in Britain. But choosing the moment to begin is tricky. By late October an extra week could possibly increase the sugar content of the grapes – or a violent hailstorm could ruin the whole crop. So at this stage constant checks are made on the sugar content with a refractometer, which measures the amount present in the juice squeezed from a single grape. This period of waiting has been likened by a French writer to that of an anxious husband pacing the corridors of a maternity home.

219

WOODCARVER

MANY CRAFTSMEN COMBINE THE TWO SKILLS,
HAVING AN INTUITIVE SENSE OF HOW TO REVEAL THE
FULL BEAUTY OF THE WOOD THEY ARE SHAPING

The woodcarver and the woodturner share not only one natural medium, but a mutual delight in revealing its hidden beauties and in using its endless varieties of colour, grain and texture to enhance their work. When masters of both crafts are given full freedom to exercise both talent and imagination, remarkable similarities of outlook emerge.

Oddly enough, it was the army that made a woodcarver out of Ron Butterfield. Before the war, in his native Sheffield, he was a junior designer-modeller at a leading firm of silversmiths and goldsmiths, modelling in hard wax items to be cast in one of these precious metals. Sculpting, his main passion, he pursued four nights a week at evening classes. However, when his call-up papers arrived, he came to the reluctant decision that a sculptor's hammer and heavy chisels had no place on campaign, and that he would have to explore some more portable form of art. Instead, therefore, he packed a few woodcarver's gouges into his haversack and set off to war.

As the Eighth Army moved up Italy, he utilised the odd spare hour and the odd spare piece of timber in carving portraits – 'whittling in 3-D', he calls it – of his friends, and it was in Italy, too, in its churches, that his sense of kinship with the craftsmen of the Middle Ages first began to grow upon him. It is a sense that has never deserted him, as his sketch books show. There, interspersed with meticulous drawings of animals and birds – 'drawing is the basis of good carving' – are little details from British churches that took his fancy; a bench end, a fragment of interlacing strapwork, a misericord. It is not just the craftsmanship of the medieval carvers that touches him across the centuries,

GRINLING GIBBONS – MASTER OF THE CRAFT

So lifelike are the fruits, flowers, musical instruments and scrolls of this supreme craftsman that it seems impossible they could have been carved from a single block of wood. So cunningly are grain and natural shape worked into the carving that they appear to have aided rather than restricted the design. Born in 1648, Gibbons was appointed Master Carver to the Crown in 1693. Though he worked also in stone and bronze, his lasting fame derives from woodcarving. Among places where the public can see examples of his work are St Paul's Cathedral and Hampton Court. The illustration shows part of the reredos carved for the chapel of Trinity College, Oxford, in about 1694.

but their humanity and warm humour. To him, these forgotten men are far more sympathetic than Grinling Gibbons (1648–1720). Though he acknowledges that the artist was the greatest of all woodcarvers, he feels that his work – his exquisite foliage, his near-edible fruits, his musical instruments that look almost capable of being played – seizes more upon the intellect than the heart. But if you come across a little carving in a neglected corner of a church, perhaps a pair of grinning lop-eared dogs fighting, then you smile too, sharing the joke with the craftsman who whiled away an afternoon carving them so long ago.

After the war, and a brief return to the silversmith's, Mr Butterfield began a liaison with C. H. Gillam and Sons, of Sheffield, a four-generations-old firm of church builders and restorers. It is their boast that they will do anything from carving a wafer box to rebuilding an entire church interior, and for some years Mr Butterfield took his turn at swinging an adze, balanced on roof beams high above nave floors. Nowadays, however, like the medieval master-craftsmen, he concentrates on the finer details, such as crucifixes, altars and eagle lecterns, working in a studio on the firm's premises. By way of contrast, he also carves highly individualistic pub signs, heraldic shields and emblems, and lively representations of birds and animals for private commissions.

The first step – detailed sketches

Whatever the job, he always approaches it in the same way. First, he makes careful drawings that not only indicate the angles and planes of the carving, but also sum up the details of the finished work. For instance, though lectern eagles are to a large extent stylised, he makes certain that the feathers and bone structure of the outstretched wings are correct by making sketches at the zoo, while human faces and expressions are often borrowed from friends and acquaintances. Next, he makes a Plasticine model, probably no more than 3–4 in. high. This gives him an idea of how the carving will look in the round; and, by scaling up, it tells him how much wood he will need, and where to allow for mortise and tenon joints.

Wood, he feels, is a friendly material to work with, a living material that has much to say in the creation of the carving. In fact, wood, hands and tools all have something to say; he himself is simply the guide in the background, watching the shape gradually emerge from the block. He has no particular preferences in woods. Some are good for one thing, and some for another, though he enjoys contrasting grains and colours. On one plaque, a rosewood otter sinuously chases a fish through a limewood pool in which water-weeds wave, carved in low relief. In a life-size crucifix, on the other hand, the figure of Christ is carved in oak, and the cross is made from the same wood.

The old aristocrats of the craft like Gibbons and, earlier, John Ripley, who worked for Henry VIII at Whitehall and Hampton Court, used anything up to 300 tools, mostly gouges, with glorious names such as flutaroni, bacaroni, veiners and pod spades, and their apprentices learned their trade by reducing blocks of wood to piles of shavings of uniform thickness, using each tool in turn. Modern carvers, however, are generally content with no more than 30 or 40 tools, including of course, a round mallet, advisedly made from beech, elm or *lignum vitae* (guaiacum, a West Indian tree). Mr Butterfield's in fact, is made of a bit of old beech table leg; it has served him well for many years, as has his collection of chisels and gouges. One of them, a spoon gouge now half its original length, is at least 125 years old. As well as spoon gouges for shaping, there are also grounding tools for creating a textured background to a relief, skew chisels for getting into corners, fish-tail gouges for lettering, and smallest of all, a tiny 4-gauge fish-tail that he uses to carve the eyes of his animals and birds.

The problem is, the work does not pay well. Churches are poor, wood is expensive, few people want ships' figureheads any more – though, surprisingly, there are still two or three craftsmen who carve them – and for large repeat orders, perhaps fibreglass is more practical than wooden sculptures, each of which involves many hours of painstaking work. Mr Butterfield makes ends meet by teaching adult classes to carve – including a number of blind people – and the pleasure he derives from developing their skills helps to offset his own up-and-down existence. Occasionally, too, there is the really satisfying one-off job – a coat of arms for the Buttery at Trinity College, Cambridge, for instance, or an inn sign in high relief that allows him to exercise his particular talent for foreshortened perspective.

Despite the financial drawbacks of his craft, he would not choose any other way of making a living. Carving is intensely personal, always with a touch of wonder. His great crucifix was commissioned by the parents of a boy killed in an accident, and before beginning work he talked to them for a long time. As Christ's face grew out of the wood, he realised that this was not at all the image that he had conceived. On the other hand, it reflected his own sorrow, which in turn reflected theirs.

When Gwyndaf Breese, master woodturner, talks about his craft, his first words almost echo those of Ron Butterfield. He is holding up on extended fingers a small, deepish bowl with exotic graining, a wavy, uneven rim and small holes in it here and there, where burrs or knots have come out while he was turning it. The effect is stunning – a wholly practical little work of art.

'The wood seems to decide what it is to be made into,' he

THE LECTERN EMERGES
Using chisels and gouges that are well over 100 years old, Ron Butterfield fashions his eagle lecterns and animal carvings from drawings made at a zoo. This ensures that bone and muscle structure, as well as feathers, are true to life. To date, ten lecterns have been completed for churches as far apart as Wales and Canada.

To breathe life into carved wood calls for the sensitivity of an artist rather than mere manual dexterity, believes Ron Butterfield.

WOODLAND CRAFTSMEN

Working in simple shelters deep in the woods, bodgers were specialised woodturners who made the legs, stretchers and back spindles for Windsor chairs. Their principal aid was a pole lathe – the pole being a springy sapling of ash or beech. A cord tied from the tip of the pole to a treadle was passed round the work, causing it to spin backwards and forwards as the downward movement of the treadle was followed by the upward pull of the pole. To prepare the wood for turning, a craftsman sitting astride a shave-horse trimmed the legs and other pieces roughly to shape with a hand axe and a draw-knife.

says, 'rather than me deciding to make something out of a particular piece of wood.'

He made the bowl from the crutch of a small lilac tree that came down in the ample grounds of the Welsh Folk Museum at St Fagans Castle, 4 miles west of Cardiff. There Gwyndaf demonstrates, teaches and practises his craft at the museum in two workshops. One is plain, whitewashed and full of traditional equipment such as pole and bow lathes, old chisels and gouges, draw-knives and axes. The other has an array of modern woodturning tools and machinery. With this broad range to hand, he can indulge a passion for developing new techniques while ensuring that the old ways survive and are passed on to others. And the old ways are old indeed.

Wooden platters and bowls turned on a pole lathe have been unearthed on the sites of prehistoric lake villages in Somerset, and lathes have been found in the ruins of ancient Glastonbury. Britain bristled with forest up to late medieval times, so wood was plentiful. Wood was also durable – and there for the taking, to be made into dishes, spoons, scoops, ladles and hundreds of other household articles now mass produced in metal, clay and plastic.

Woodturners worked almost everywhere, but there were places where the right kind of timber was especially plentiful, and they evolved into centres for the craft that flourished up to quite recent times. One was at Abercych near Cardigan, on the Pembroke peninsula in Wales, where a group of turners kept the whole Principality supplied. Another was at Bucklebury Common, in Berkshire, where the last working woodturner in the locality, George William Lailey, died in 1958. He had worked for nearly 80 years at a craft which his family had followed for more than two centuries – so long, indeed, that the small hamlet where they lived and laboured was known as Turners' Green.

TURNING A BOWL *Having secured the base of the bowl to the face-plate of the lathe, the turner uses specially shaped gouges to fashion the concave interior. The central column is later cut away by hand.*

There are two basic kinds of turning. For spindle turning a long piece of wood is clamped between the headstock and tailstock of the lathe for shaping into anything from a ladder rung to a chair leg. For bowl turning the wood is mounted on the face-plate of the lathe, so that the turner can bring his cutting tools to bear on as much of the surface as possible.

Gwyndaf Breese demonstrates in his 'old' workshop how the pole lathe is unable to cope with a squared-off length of wood, lacking the power to turn it against the edge of the cutting tool. He removes the wood, clamps it in a draw horse – a primitive form of vice which he sits astride – and taking a draw-knife, rapidly removes the long edges, leaving it roughly round in section. The pole lathe is then able to deal with it quite easily.

In both workshops, he has to hand a wide variety of chisels and gouges. They are longer than the carver's, both in blade and handle, to allow very precise control of the tool in use. The end of the handle is tucked under the arm, and both hands are used to guide and steady the blade as it is held against the work rotating on the lathe. They are used with a sort of rubbing action above the centre-line of the work to avoid digging into the wood and causing a jam; or they are worked by a scraping action below the centre-line, to hollow out awkward contours such as the insides of bowls and dishes.

Turning a wooden bowl

To make a bowl on the pole lathe, Gwyndaf chooses a section of log slightly deeper than the finished article will eventually be – say $3\frac{3}{4}$ in. for a 3 in. deep bowl. This he fixes in the lathe. He shapes the outside of the bowl with deep, U-shaped gouges, which give a smooth, even finish. He leaves a small central shaft of wood attached to the face-plate to retain the piece, while he hollows out the inside with a different set of gouges. These have blades which curve back on themselves to follow the concave surface. Finally the bowl is removed, its supporting shaft is cut off, the bottom is cleaned up and the wood sanded and polished.

Gwyndaf has a part-finished demonstration of turning that shows how four bowls can be cut, one from inside the other, using a single piece of wood. His more artistic creations are turned from many different types of wood, but the one commonly used for domestic utensils in his part of the world is sycamore. The tree is plentiful in west Wales, and can be turned and carved while still 'green'. It dries out to a lovely creamy-white, does not crack in water and has neither taste nor smell, so does not affect the flavour of food.

Berkshire woodturners, on the other hand, always used elm for their bowls, a common tree in the locality until Dutch elm disease struck. Elm has its own advantages, being extremely strong and resistant to cracking while being turned. This makes it especially suitable for the 'four-bowls-in-one' technique.

However, by no means all the turner's products are made on a lathe. And, in times past, distinctions between the turner, carver, furniture maker and even cooper could become very blurred – especially in dairy-farming country, where the turner would make churns and milking pails, chairs, stools and butter prints. The latter were used for stamping butter with the individual mark of the farmer producing it. The turner would carve designs such as hearts and flowers, anchors and animals on a circular or oval plate, surrounding them with an elaborately carved border. The design would appear in relief when the butter was stamped with them. Gwyndaf still makes them, and he can also demonstrate perhaps the most difficult of the turner's tasks – spoon carving.

He begins by taking a sycamore log about a foot long and

splitting it into three segments, using a small axe on a chopping block. Each segment will make one spoon, and still using the axe, he chops out its rough shape – a flattened bowl tapering into a long handle. He does a surprising amount of quite delicate work with the axe, explaining how he uses the curving grain to help in hollowing out the bowl. He explains also that the more work that can be done with the axe, the more time is saved in later stages – important when turners made spoons by the dozen. However the axe has its drawbacks – one false blow can ruin the job.

To finish the bowl he uses a long-handled gouge with a blade that curves back on itself, called a bent knife. The handle is clamped under his arm, and his elbow and forearm apply strong leverage to the blade while his hand steadies the cutting edge at the awkward angle necessary to scoop out the wood. The back of the spoon is shaped to an even thickness with a spokeshave, but this is not held in both hands in the conventional way. Instead, the spoon is held in one hand and the tool in the palm of the other. As work proceeds, he alters the angle of the blade as necessary with a couple of smart blows against the chopping block.

A bigger ladle is made in much the same way, but the bowl is hollowed out with a short-handled adze, followed up by a larger version of the bent knife.

Gwyndaf's 'old' workshop is bursting with such traditional products of the craft. But his modern one looks to the future, as he experiments with many different woods – and also with timber that is beginning to decay. This is called spalted wood and it produces bold grain markings and vivid colour combinations. From it he has made some amazing bowls and handsome boxes. The craft's future, he is sure, can be as long as its past.

CARVING A SPOON

The carver first splits a log into segments (1), each the size of a single spoon. He does this with an axe, and uses the same tool for trimming each segment roughly to shape (2). To fashion the inside of the bowl, he uses a long-handled gouge with a blade that curves back on itself. He shapes the back of the bowl with a spokeshave and trims the final shape (3) with a knife.

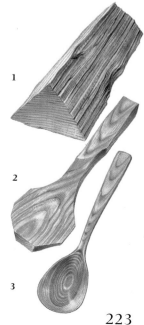

1

2

3

223

CRAFTSMEN AT WORK

A VISITOR'S GUIDE TO THE CRAFT WORKSHOPS AND MUSEUMS OF BRITAIN

In more than 800 craft workshops and museums the length and breadth of the nation, the treasures of British workmanship past and present await the discerning visitor. Some are intangible treasures, in the form of skills honed over the centuries and still practised by Cornish potters, Kentish ironworkers, East Anglian stained-glass makers, Welsh weavers and Orkney furniture makers. Others are tangible treasures, that can be seen, and often handled and bought – from heirlooms of a national culture, such as the 18th-century schooner in the Isle of Man's Castletown Museum, to the fine silver artefacts of a jeweller and the delicately fashioned harpsichord of a musical-instrument maker.

The entries in the guide tell of each worker's speciality and working methods. Often, they reveal how the business came to be set up, and the philosophy behind the craftsman's work. Where the setting of a workshop or museum is of special interest or beauty – perhaps in a historic house, or up a hidden lane in an ancient market town, or tucked away in a green valley far from the traffic's roar – the entry describes it. More detailed information about the techniques of particular crafts may be found between pp. 8–223.

Special illustrated panels are devoted to regional crafts such as bagpipe-making, and to museums that are unusually rich in the craft products of past generations.

VISITING A WORKSHOP

All the workshops and museums are open to visitors during the opening hours given at the end of each entry, or else by appointment. Opening hours may change, and wherever possible it is advisable to telephone first before making a special journey that may be wasted.

Craftsmen can usually be watched at work. Their handiwork can always be seen and, when it has not been specially made to order, it can usually be bought. But remember that the craftsmen are busy making a living – do not call outside the opening hours given, and do not distract them by chatting about their work unless they encourage you to do so.

Many of the museums described are devoted entirely to the products and techniques of crafts past and present; all the rest have strong craft collections that are well worth a visit. Some include 'live' displays by craftsmen at work on traditional crafts.

FINDING THE WAY

On the outline map on the facing page, Britain's craft workshops and museums are divided between 11 areas covering the whole country, from the far South-West to the Scottish Highlands and Islands. Before the entries on each individual area is another, more detailed, map showing the counties or regions, and the places within them where workshops and museums are situated. Each place is identified with a special symbol:

□ Craft workshop ■ Museum ◨ Craft workshop and museum

Within each area the entries are arranged by county or Scottish region – first the workshops, then the museums, in alphabetical order. Each entry begins with the name of the  city, town or village in which it is located, or to which it is closest. In Greater London (South-East area), the name of the borough is given. In some places there is more than one workshop or museum.

A map reference then enables the intending visitor to locate the place on the area map. When he has arrived there, the full name and address and – where necessary – detailed local directions guide him to the workshop or museum, and its nearest car-parking area.

Further directions, and any other information, can be obtained by using the telephone number that accompanies most entries.

COUNTY GUIDE TO CRAFTSMEN AND MUSEUMS

THE SOUTH-WEST

KEY TO SYMBOLS
- □ Craft workshop
- ■ Museum
- ◧ Craft workshop and museum

MILES
0   5   10   15   20

No part of Britain is richer in crafts than the West Country. Nowhere else can you see so many craftsmen at work, or find such an array of goods for sale. Doubtless the holiday trade has something to do with this; but so has the region's rural character. Until recently, the farming community could hardly have survived without such skills as those of the blacksmith, the thatcher, and the wheelwright. These, and many other traditional crafts are still widely practised; though now they serve a wider public.

In the past, craftsmen used the materials that lay near to hand – which accounts for the large number of 'reed-thatched' cottages in Devon, for instance; and for the numerous potteries, supplied by the clay deposits of

the West Country. The new breed of thriving artist-craftsman that has grown up often still depend on local resources – for example the furniture maker with his table tops of Cornish slate; the potter with his glazes made from ground-up Somerset rock; the walking-stick maker with his holly, hazel and blackthorn from Devon woodland; and the spinners and weavers with their wool from Dorset or Wiltshire sheep.

History has left its mark, too, on the region's crafts. The reputation of the Honiton lace makers owes much to Flemish settlers in the 16th century. The craft was exploited as an additional source of income to supplement meagre farm wages.

Opening times and other details may change. Check by telephone before making a special journey.

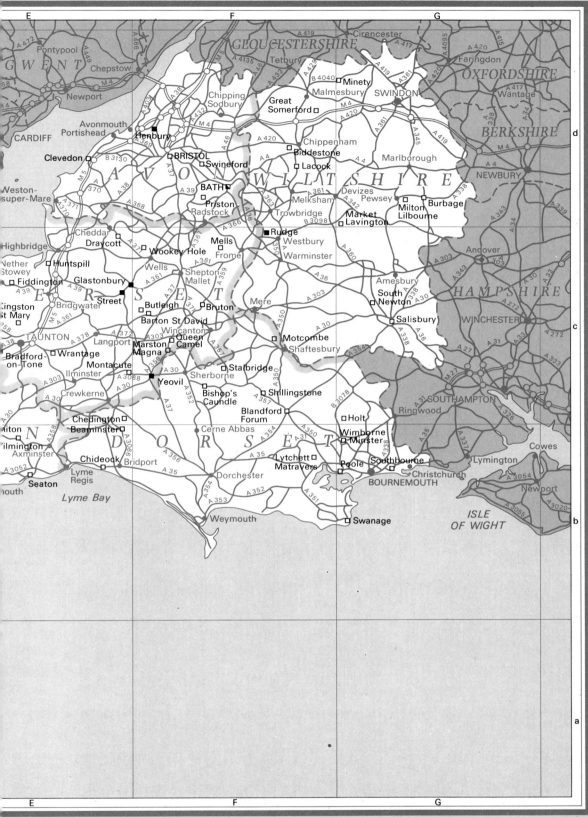

designs. Jewellery can be designed to suit a customer's own tastes and the studio will also re-mount, re-model and, if necessary, repair jewellery and silverware. The gold and silver pieces on display are often combined with enamel, resin, wood and the metal titanium, which can produce clear, electric colours.

Studio open all year: Tues.–Fri., 9.30–5; Sat., 9.30–4.30. Workshop may be seen by appointment only.

BATH   Map ref: Fd
Wellow Crafts, Kingsmead Square, Bath.
Tel. Bath 64358

In the upper room of a converted coach house there is a display covering some 30 local cottage industries. These include tatting and smocking, chair caning, fence hurdle making, basket and rush work, Dorset button making, corn dollies, pottery, patchwork, spinning and weaving. At weekends there is usually someone practising a craft, and visitors are encouraged to ask questions.

Open Easter until Christmas, Mon.–Sat., 9.30–5.30. Sun. and Bank Holidays, 2–5.30.

BRISTOL   Map ref: Fd
Bristol Craft Centre, 6 Leonard Lane, Bristol.
Tel. Bristol 297890
(In centre of Bristol, down an alley off Corn Street. Several public car parks in Bristol.)

At the top of a spiral staircase on two floors of a Victorian building, this craft centre consists of about 20 workshops and an exhibition area. Visitors are likely to see jewellery, pottery, leather goods, textiles, furniture, stained glass and musical instruments being made. Textile conservation is also practised. Craft and art exhibitions change each month.

Open all year, Mon.–Fri., 10–6; Sat., 10–5.

BRISTOL   Map ref: Fd
Mrs Cherry Jelfs (Rush and cane-work), Goose Grout, Wraxall Road, Warmley, Bristol.
Tel. Bristol 673849
(Wraxall Road is situated between Kingswood, Warmley and Cadbury Heath. The cottage stands on its own near bottom of hill. Parking on premises.)

With rush from the dykes in Holland and cane imported from the Far East, Mrs Jelfs can make an old chair look like new. In her garden workshop she works on chairs and stools of all periods, from Elizabethan up to the present day. Rush and cane stools are for sale.

Appointment necessary.

CLEVEDON   Map ref: Ed
Clevedon Craft Centre. Moor Lane, off Court Lane, Clevedon.
Tel. Clevedon 872867
(From Clevedon, take B3130 Bristol road. After ¾ mile turn right up Court Lane. Moor Lane is just beyond Clevedon Pottery.)

Newhouse Farm was originally part of the Clevedon Court estate. It is no longer a working farm, and the long, low outbuildings have been transformed into workshops and studios for a great number of crafts, including glass blowing and engraving, hand-weaving, leatherwork, quilting, silversmithing, wood-carving and woodturning. Wax flowers are made for the Natural History Museum in London. A museum of rural life, showing farm implements, craftsmen's tools and an unusual collection of remedial horseshoes can be seen in the old wagon house.

Open all year, 10–5, though most studios are closed on Mon. (except Bank Holiday Monday).

CLEVEDON   Map ref: Ed
Craft Workshops and Clevedon Pottery, Court Lane, Clevedon.
Tel. Clevedon 872952
(Directions as for previous entry. Parking: no coaches.)

AVON

BATH   Map ref: Fd
Bath Crafts and Bath Pottery, Broad Street Place, off Broad Street, Bath.
Tel. Bath 62192
(In walkway between Broad Street and Walcot Street, by YMCA. Public car park in Walcot Street.)

A number of craftsmen and craftswomen have started their careers at this co-operative workshop. Overheads and other expenses are shared, and once a craftsman has become established he often – but not always – moves on to premises of his own. Mr Stephen Mills, who started the co-operative, is a potter producing domestic and decorative stoneware and slipware. Also on display are examples of titanium and silver jewellery, woodwork, and a range of other crafts from Bath and the surrounding district. The workshop sells kilns, wheels, clay and a variety of other potters' supplies.

Open daily except Sun., 10–6 approx.

BATH   Map ref: Fd
Gold and Silver Studio, 11A Queen Street, Bath.
Tel. Bath 62300
(Queen Street is reached from Quiet Street, situated off Queen Square. Public car park in Walcot Street.)

The studio is housed in a picturesque Georgian street and displays work by outside craftsmen, as well as jewellery made on the premises. The jewellery extends from traditional bangles, ear-rings, wedding, engagement and signet rings to more adventurous pieces in contemporary

Opening times and other details may change. Check by telephone before making a special journey.

227

The wood-burning kilns that Norman Darby uses to fire domestic stoneware in his cottage workshop creates an attractive 'toasted' effect. As the pots are fired, the flames and the ash from the wood react on the unglazed parts, producing a beautiful reddish hue. The converted outbuildings of the cottage are used as workshops by other craftsmen. Typical crafts on view are woodcarving, furniture making, spinning and weaving, and glass work; but from time to time new craftsmen join the group and others leave. Exhibitions are staged, and there is an art gallery.

Open all year, including Bank Holidays. Tues.–Thur., 10–5; Fri.–Sat., 10–4; Sun., 12–5. Closed 1–2.

CLEVEDON Map ref: Ed
'Yeo' Pottery, Moor Lane, Clevedon.
Tel. Clevedon 871421
(Directions as for Clevedon Craft Centre – Pottery is 50 yds beyond it. Parking outside.)

Mr Janes and his partner, Mr Gooding, make thrown slipware, hand-decorated with designs that include birds, dragonflies and cockerels. They specialise in privately commissioned commemoration plates, but jugs, coffee sets, tankards, bowls and plates are also on display in the pottery – which is 350 years old.

Open weekdays, 9–5; Sun., 2–5.30.

PRISTON Map ref: Fd
Priston Mill, Priston, nr Bath.
Tel. Bath 23894
(Half a mile north of the village. Parking outside mill.)

The mill stands on or very near the site of one recorded in the Domesday Book. Visitors can watch the water-wheel turning, and inspect the mill where stone-ground wholewheat flour is produced. The farm shop at the mill stocks a wide range of farm produce and craft goods, most of which are locally made. Items include hand-carved butter moulds, beeswax candles, thatched bird houses and feeders, domestic pottery and leather belts.

Open Easter to end of Oct., by appointment only. Weekdays (milling), 2.15–5. Weekends and Bank Holidays (no milling), 11–12.45 and 2.15–5. Closed on Mon., except Bank Holiday Mon. Children under 15 must be accompanied by an adult to see the mill. Small charge.

SWINEFORD Map ref: Fd
R. & R. Starling (Furniture). The Mill, Bath Road, Swineford, Bristol.
Tel. Bitton 3603
(In Swineford, opposite Swan Inn, Swineford is 5 miles from Bath on the A431. Parking in lay-by opposite pub.)

The Starling brothers, working mainly to commission, specialise in reproductions of mahogany furniture of the late 18th and early 19th centuries. They make leather-topped desks, dining tables – with rosewood crossbanding and satinwood inlays – chairs, sideboards and glass cabinets.

The showroom is open to visitors Mon.–Fri., 8–5, and Sat. from 8–1. Workshop by appointment only.

MUSEUMS

BATH Map ref: Fd
Holburne of Menstrie Museum, Great Pulteney Street, Bath.
Tel. Bath 66669

A Crafts Study Centre, featuring the work of the finest British artist-craftsmen of this century, has been established in the museum. The nucleus of the collection consists of exquisite examples of textiles, pottery, calligraphy and furniture. There are also constantly changing exhibitions.

Open Mon.–Sat. 11–5; Sun. 2.30–6. Charge for admission.

HENBURY Map ref: Fd
Blaise Castle House Museum, Henbury, Bristol.
Tel. Bristol 506789

Intricate watches – a reminder of Bristol's clockmaking industry of the 18th and 19th centuries – 18th and 19th-century costume, and old agricultural implements form three of the collections that illustrate aspects of West Country life over the last 500 years. The museum is housed in Blaise Castle, a handsome, late-18th-century building set in a landscaped park.

Open Wed.–Sat., 2–5. Admission free.

CORNWALL

BOSCASTLE Map ref: Cb
Camelot Pottery, The Old Bakery, Boscastle.
Tel. Boscastle 291
(In main street close to harbour, opposite large car park.)

A traditional form of pottery known as mochaware has been revived here by Roger Irving Little. Its distinguishing feature, a delicate frond-like pattern, is obtained in the final stages of decoration. After the pot has been coated with slip (liquid clay containing colouring oxides), a drop of herbal essence is painted on. (The name of the herb is a trade secret.) This immediately spreads and, as if by magic, mimics the vein pattern of the original plant. This unique decoration adorns coffee and tea sets, goblets and vases, as well as decorative items such as bells.

Open daily, 9 to dusk.

BOSSINEY Map ref: Cb
Fenterleigh Woodcraft, nr Bossiney, Tintagel.
Tel. Tintagel 293
(Half a mile out of Bossiney on road signposted to Launceston. Limited parking on forecourt and in lane.)

Coffee tables (some with tops of local slate), spinning stools and small rocking horses are among items displayed on two floors of a small showroom. They are all designed and made in English hardwoods, such as elm, ash, sycamore and chestnut. Special commissions, including dining tables and large rocking horses, can be made to order. The doors of the workshop are left open in fine weather.

Open daily from Easter–Oct., 9.30–6. During rest of year, Mon.–Fri., and weekends by appointment.

DOWNHILL Map ref: Bb
St Eval Leather Crafts, Downhill, St Eval, Wadebridge.
Tel. St Mawgan 357
(Three-quarters of a mile west of St Eval parish church. Parking for about eight cars.)

In Shakespeare's day, ale and sack were drunk from blackjacks and bombards, and reproductions of these leather vessels are among the items visitors will see being made by Tony and Dawn Dennis. Other leather goods include fire bellows, bags, belts and key cases. There is also a selection of framed wildlife prints, produced from paintings by two local artists.

Open Apr.–Sept., Mon.–Fri., 9–4.30. Between Oct. and Mar. it is advisable to telephone first.

EAST LOOE Map ref: Ca
Looe Glass, Higher Market Street, East Looe.
Tel. Looe 3526
(In town centre near the Old Guildhall. Public car park at approach to town centre.)

Barley sets (ears of barley with a field mouse climbing one of the stems) and small animals are fashioned from glass in a small workshop next to the display area. Visitors can watch the

fascinating process of heating and drawing strands of glass to form the sculptures. Ships in bottles and paperweights are also sold on the premises.

Open every day during Easter, and July–Sept., 10 to dusk. During rest of year, open Mon.–Fri., 10–12 and 1–4.

GUNNISLAKE Map ref: Cb
David Plagerson (Toymaker), 5 Cliff View Terrace, Gunnislake.
Tel. Tavistock 833035
(Directions will be given on telephoning for an appointment.)

Noah's Arks and sets of animals to fill them, ranging from giraffes to ladybirds, and Nativity sets are the speciality of David Plagerson, who works from his home – mainly to commission. They are made in pine and either left with a natural finish or brightly painted and then varnished. He will also make farm sets, circuses, model villages, shops and similar items to order.

Open by appointment only. Mon.–Fri., 10–5.

HAYLE Map ref: Ba
Prykernow Pottery, Penpol Avenue, Hayle.
Tel. Hayle 752738
(Turn left immediately after taking the B3302 out of Hayle, then left again opposite school. Car park outside.)

The pottery is housed in a long, low building of slate and granite which used to be the stable block of the local brewery in the days when beer was delivered in horse-drawn drays. A small team of craftsmen, led by the family Herschel, can be seen throwing pots made from Cornish clays, which are decorated with a corn pattern. Of special interest to the visitor are tall vases, hand-painted with oriental designs, model figures, circular barometer cases and lanterns.

Open Mon.–Sat. 9–6 in summer. Mon.–Fri. in winter.

HAYLE Map ref: Ba
Duchy Folk Originals, Foundry Lane, Hayle.
Tel. Hayle 753134

In Hayle's old foundry, a number of craftsmen can be seen practising their skills in a series of stalls grouped together under one roof. The stalls are rented by the year, so the goods made will vary as time goes by. But visitors are likely to see bronze figurines, Cornish characters made of clay, glass sculptures, tooled leatherwork, jewellery and soft toys – such as hobby horses and rag dolls – being made by the resident craft workers.

Open all year, 9–5.

KILKHAMPTON Map ref: Cc
Cornish Ironcraft Co., Brentspool, Kilkhampton, Bude.
Tel. Kilkhampton 350
(On A39 to Kilkhampton from Bude, opposite Penstowe Manor. Car park behind workshop.)

Visitors from places as far away as Canada and Germany have bought items forged by Richard Scaife at this small smithy. He designs and makes ornamental ironwork, often to commission. His work covers traditional hearthware, lanterns and gates.

Open all year, Mon.–Sat., 10–4.

LAMORNA Map ref: Aa
Lamorna Pottery, Lamorna, nr Penzance.
Tel. St Buryan 330
(Signposted from B3315. Car park outside.)

For many visitors, the highlight of a visit to Lamorna Pottery is the chance to try their hand at throwing a pot on a simple kick-wheel. Those who are happy with the result may have it fired. The pottery made by the craftsmen, mostly by casting liquid clay in moulds, includes lamp bases, coffee sets, wine sets and vases, some decorated in a sea-blue glaze.

Open daily in June, July and Aug., 9–9; during rest of year, 9–5.30. A small charge is made for throwing a pot.

LOWERTOWN Map ref: Ba
Tweenstream Weavers, Lowertown, nr Helston.
Tel. Helston 2411
(Signposted from B3297 just outside Helston. Space for two or three cars outside workshop.)

The equipment that Mrs Madden and her assistant use to prepare and weave their cloth dates back to the turn of the century. The yarn is wound on to a large cast-iron and wooden-slatted warping mill before it is threaded on to a magnificent cast-iron treadle loom. It is then woven into lengths of medium-weight Cheviot tweed.

Open all year, by appointment.

MORWENSTOW Map ref: Cc
Gus Ravine (Woodturner), Yeolmouth. Morwenstow, Bude.
Tel. Morwenstow 473
(On a branch of the North Cornwall Coast Path, ½ mile north of Morwenstow. Accessible by car, signposted off the Morwenstow–Marsland road. Parking for two or three cars.)

In the upper storey of a former granary and byre, which lies only yards from Cornwall's rugged coastal cliff path, Mr Ravine and his son make many small turned articles in English hardwoods such as yew, the fruit woods and beech. Their products include lace bobbins, needlework accessories, spice jars, pestles and mortars, and ornaments.

Open most days, but it is advisable to telephone first.

NEWLYN Map ref: Aa
Alan Brough Pottery Workshop, Duke Street, Newlyn.
Tel. Penzance 66605
(By car park next to Lloyds Bank in town centre.)

No two pieces of decorative porcelain made by Alan Brough are the same. Using metal oxides, including cobalt which produces shades of blue, he applies different motifs to each item. He also produces a range of kitchenware, such as casseroles and coffee sets. His studio is at the back of the shop, but as he is very busy he usually admits only people who are commissioning work.

Shop open all year, Mon.–Sat., 9.30–7. Studio open by appointment only.

NEWLYN Map ref: Aa
Joan Godfrey, 'The Studio at Kiln Cottage', 38 Boase Street, Newlyn.
(In narrow side street – Boase Street – off harbour front. Public car park at southern end of harbour.)

Richly coloured ceramic tiles are made by Joan Godfrey in her studio. She adds small pieces of coloured glass to the glazes before firing, and these melt and fuse together in the kiln, creating interesting 'crackled' surfaces. Joan Godfrey models terracotta mythical creatures such as dragons and unicorns, and produces stained-glass panels and batik wall hangings.

Open Mon.–Fri., 11–5 (often later in summer). Maximum of five people.

NEWLYN Map ref: Aa
Tremaen Pottery Ltd, Newlyn Coombe, Newlyn.
Tel. Penzance 4364

The busy comings and goings of Newlyn's fishing harbour are to be seen close by this pottery, which occupies a converted barn. Sculptured lamp bases in stoneware are the main product, their texture and shape based on weathered pebbles and rocks found along the Cornish coastline. The potter can usually be seen hand-building, wheel-throwing or decorating in the studio, which is beside the display area.

Open all year, Mon.–Fri., 9–5.

NEWQUAY Map ref: Bb
Lorna Wiles Designs, Wesley Yard, Jubilee Street, Newquay.
Tel. Newquay 6840
(Between Tower Road and Manor Road. Limited parking outside shop.)

Floral and abstract patterns, designed by Lorna Wiles, are silk-screen printed on to lengths of cotton and wool materials in this workshop. The printed cloth is then made up into a range of clothes, toys, table and kitchen linen.

Open Apr.–Sept., Mon.–Sat., 10–5.
Mon.–Fri. during rest of year.

PENRYN Map ref: Ba
Bakehouse Pottery, St Thomas Street, Penryn.
(At bottom of St Thomas Street in town, close to clock-tower. Parking near top of street.)

Displayed on shelves inside this former bakery are hand-thrown candle holders, night-lights and plant holders in porcelain, all with an enamelled or gold-lustre finish. There is also a selection of domestic stoneware. Visitors can usually see some of these goods being made.

Open Tues.–Fri., 10–4.30, and on Sat. mornings, all year.

POLZEATH Map ref: Bb
Original Leatherwork, 'Chy-an-Mor', Polzeath, nr Wadebridge.
Tel. Trebetherick 2567
(Signposted from Tristram Field car park, overlooking beach.)

In addition to his skills as a leather worker, Steve Walton has become adept at metal work. For not only does he make the brass buckles which adorn his high-quality, saddle-stitched or thonged leather goods, he also designs and makes the patterning tools. He can be seen at work in a section of his garden workshop, where items for sale include shoulder and clutch bags, belts, purses and leather-inlaid wooden boxes.

Open daily in summer, 9–6; Mon.–Sat. in winter.

PORTHALLOW Map ref: Ba
Fogou Crafts and Camphor-Craft, Withy Cottage, Porthallow, St Keverne, Helston.
Tel. St Keverne 0567
(Signposted from beach, where there is a car park.)

Miniature Cornish fishing luggers, Norfolk wherries and models of the clipper ship Cutty Sark are made on the premises by Kenneth Smith with meticulous attention to detail. The models can be camphor-propelled. His wife, Patricia, makes knitted clothes. These are sold alongside locally made craft goods ranging from woodcarvings to small baskets, woven with pine needles.

Open Easter to Oct., Mon.–Fri., 9.30–6; during rest of year, Wed. and Thur., 10–5.30.

PORTHLEVEN Map ref: Ba
Tony Bird Jewellery. The Harbourside, Porthleven.
Tel. Helston 3120 (Home)
(Ample parking space for cars around harbour area.)

Many of the pieces of silver jewellery fashioned by Tony Bird incorporate ivory, tortoise-shell and ebony, and are inset with precious stones. Although he works mainly in silver, he also makes a limited amount of gold jewellery. Items for sale include bracelets, pendants, rings and ear-rings.

Open from Easter until end of Sept., 10 to dusk, except Sat. afternoons. Also most days in winter.

St Ives Museum

ST IVES, CORNWALL

From the upstairs window of the museum, visitors overlook the sea and the bustling quayside of St Ives. In the days when huge seine nets, a quarter of a mile long, trapped pilchards in the sandy coves around St Ives, fishing was the town's main source of wealth.

The exhibits include a screw fish-press, nets and a 'gurry' – a wooden carrier that held 700 fish. St Ives was the last place in Britain where in the late 1920s fish were still sold by numbers and not by weight. Other relics include shipwrights' caulking tools, coopers' tools and a cork cutter for making the corks used on fishing nets.

The sea played a dominant role in the history of St Ives, but local industries and agriculture are also covered in the museum. There are models and photographs of the mines and their machines, including a Newcomen steam engine that was used to pump water out of the tin mines. The large collection of rural implements includes a portable blacksmith's forge, complete with hand-operated blower, and a rare foot-operated hammer.

Wheal Dream, St Ives, Cornwall. Tel. Penzance 795575.

Open Easter weekend, then mid-May to Sept., 10.30–12 and 2.30–5, Mon.–Sat., and on Sun. afternoons. Also evenings 7.30–9.30 during high season. Small charge for admission.

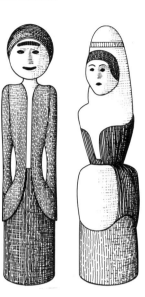

CARVED DOLLS *'Joanies' – crude dolls that were carved from broken oars – were carved by St Ives fishermen when work was slack.*

ONE-MAN HAMMER *Worked by a treadle, this unusual hammer left the craftsman's hands free to manipulate the metal.*

REDRUTH Map ref: Ba
The Foster Pottery Company, Tolgus Hill, Redruth.
Tel. Redruth 215754
(Leave A30 at Redruth interchange and travel ½ mile south towards Camborne. Pottery is on left. Large car park available on site.)

During conducted tours around this large pottery, visitors can see all the processes involved in making pottery of many different types. The finished pieces, displayed in a spacious showroom, include dinner, tea and coffee sets, casseroles and gift items, most of which are decorated in a dappled crystal-green or rustic-brown glaze.

Showroom open Apr.–Sept., Mon.–Fri., 9–5; Sat., 10–12. Tours (small admission fee) Apr.–Sept., Mon.–Fri., 10–3.45. Oct.–Mar., showroom open on weekdays only, 10–12 and 1.30–3.45. Closed Bank Holidays.

ST AGNES Map ref: Ba
St Agnes Pottery, Beaconsfield Place, St Agnes.
Tel. St Agnes 2842
(Just off main street behind St Agnes Hotel. Public car park where B3277 enters village.)

This former mine building, now the property of the National Trust, contains an array of stoneware pottery ranging from cheese dishes to coffee pots. They are made on the premises by John Sneddon, mainly from local clays. He decorates the pots with two distinctive glazes – a grey-green celadon, and tenmoku, giving a lustrous black, breaking to rust.

Individuals and small groups with a genuine interest may see the workshop by appointment. Open Mon.–Sat., 9–6.

Opening times and other details may change. Check by telephone before making a special journey.

229

ST IVES Map ref: Ba
Sloop Craft Market, St Ives.
Tel. Penzance 796051
(Signposted just off harbour front. Restricted parking in summer. Large car park above town, then walk or bus.)

St Ives was once a busy fishing port, where catches of pilchards were stored in large fish cellars by the harbour. One such building, which stood empty for many years after the industry declined, has been renovated and transformed into a craft centre. Visitors may wander round the dozen or so stalls and watch craftsmen making such things as enamel-painted copper jewellery, leather bags and belts, pottery, glass engravings, and paintings on wood. The centre also contains an aquarium of local marine life.

Open Mon.–Sat., 10–10, in summer; 10–5 in winter.

MUSEUMS

CAMELFORD Map ref: Cb
North Cornwall Museum and Gallery, The Clease, Camelford.
Tel. Camelford 3242

Single-handed, Sally Holden assembled the North Cornwall Museum and Gallery in a building that was originally a coach and wagon-building establishment. The museum, which in 1978 won the Pilgrim Trust Award for the best small museum in England, contains wagons and the tools of the farrier, blacksmith and cobbler. There are also small displays depicting two nearby quarries that are still being worked – the Delabole slate quarry and the St Breward granite quarry.

Open Apr.–Sept., Mon.–Sat., 10.30–5. Charge for admission.

HELSTON Map ref: Ba
Helston Folk Museum, Old Butter Market, Helston.
Tel. Camborne 714766

A cider press, 14 ft tall and with massive screws made of apple wood, dominates the 19th-century market hall – now the museum – where local farmers used to sell butter and eggs. The museum contains the tools of craftsmen, such as the cobbler, saddler, thatcher and wheelwright, who served the extensive farming region of which Helston was the centre.

Open Mon.–Sat., 10.30–12.30 and 2–4.30. Early closing at noon on Wed. Admission free.

MEVAGISSEY Map ref: Ca
Mevagissey Museum, Frazier House, East Quay, Mevagissey.
Tel. Mevagissey 843568

On the quay beneath the colour-washed houses that clamber up the sides of the harbour stands the Mevagissey Museum. Built in 1745, it was once the workshop and yard for Mevagissey's first firm of boatbuilders. Today, visitors can wander round a boatbuilding yard that has been reconstructed upstairs. Other exhibits include an apple crusher and cider press carved by hand from granite, and the screw presses that once crushed pilchards to provide oil for lamps.

Open Easter–Oct., from 10–6 on weekdays and from 2–6 on Sun. Small charge for admission.

ST IVES Map ref: Ba
St Ives Museum.
(See panel on p. 229)

ZENNOR Map ref: Aa
Wayside Museum, Zennor, St Ives.
Tel. Penzance 796945

Atlantic winds blow fiercely across the small garden that contains the Wayside Museum. The exhibits, which illustrate the prehistory and former industries of this part of Cornwall, include quarrying tools, domestic and agricultural implements, a reconstruction of a Cornish kitchen, and models of mines and cottages. They all evoke the rigours of life a century or more ago.

Open daily May–Oct., 9.30 to dusk. Admission free.

DEVON

BABBACOMBE Map ref: Db
Babbacombe Pottery Ltd, Babbacombe Road, Babbacombe, Torquay.
Tel. Torquay 38757
(From Torquay take road north-east towards Babbacombe. Pottery on right. Car park on site.)

Craft shops in many parts of Britain, and even overseas, are supplied from the Babbacombe Pottery. Visitors can follow all the processes of pottery making, from slip-casting to decorating and glazing. Firing is done at night, and while the kilns are cooling during the day, hand-pushed trucks are loaded for the following night's firing. The tour ends in a large display area where visitors can buy pottery, including seconds at reduced prices.

Open daily, 9–5.

BARNSTAPLE Map ref: Dc
Newport Pottery, 72 Newport Road, Barnstaple.
Tel. Barnstaple 72103
(One mile from town centre on A361 to Taunton. Parking in Congram's Close.)

Commemorative plates, bowls, tankards and lidded pots are decorated and inscribed, using the ancient method known as 'sgraffito', in which a stained slip is applied to the base of buff earthenware clay and then scratched away to form the lettering and designs. Other methods of decoration include the use of wax emulsion, brushed on to a base glaze and then oversprayed. The wax resists the darker overspray, thus forming an abstract pattern. The clay comes from South Devon.

Open all year, Mon.–Sat., 10–8.

BEAFORD Map ref: Dc
Beaford Pottery, Old Parsonage, Beaford, nr Winkleigh.
Tel. Beaford 306
(From Beaford take B3220 towards Great Torrington. Turn right ½ mile out of village by bungalow. Pottery on left. Parking on site.)

Since this is a one-man pottery, visitors should telephone for an appointment if they wish to see pots being thrown on the wheel. Many of Bernard Jones's glazes contain wood ash, which produces an attractive greeny-blue finish on his stoneware. The most popular glaze is an oatmeal colour, with painted decoration. Items for sale include casseroles, goblets, biscuit barrels, salt pigs, cider jars, lamp bases, vases and plant holders.

Open all year: Mon.–Fri., 9–1 and 2–5.30; Sat. 9–1. Other times by appointment.

BICKLEIGH Map ref: Dc
Bickleigh Mill Craft Centre and Farm, Bickleigh, nr Tiverton.
Tel. Bickleigh 419
(Four miles south of Tiverton on A396 to Exeter. Free car park.)

A 300-year-old stone bridge spans the River Exe, 100 yds upstream from where an old water-mill has been converted into a craft centre. The mill's machinery has been restored to full working order, and grouped around it on three floors are a number of self-contained 'log cabins' for local craftsmen. Crafts such as pottery, ceramic art, glass engraving, corn-dolly making, spinning and weaving, and lace making can be seen. The farm next to the mill is a living museum of Devon rural life, showing machinery and farm implements used at the turn of the century. Further crafts are practised here, including leatherwork, ironwork and woodturning, and visitors can see shire horses, longhorn cattle, hand milking and cream separating.

Open daily: Apr.–Dec., 10–6; Jan.–Mar., 2–5. Admission charges for both mill and farm.

BOVEY TRACEY Map ref: Db
The Bovey Handloom Weavers, 1 Station Road, Bovey Tracey.
Tel. Bovey Tracey 833424
(Opposite car park and information centre in village.)

Weaving remains a cottage industry in some distant parts of the British Isles, but is fast disappearing elsewhere. The Bovey Handloom Weavers, an outpost of weaving in Devon, use Hattersley domestic looms, which are pedal-driven and the kind which in the 1920s revitalised the Harris tweed industry. Hand-looms are used as well. Mr and Mrs Litster make up their own designs, simply changing the weft colours to give them hundreds of permutations. A weaver may be seen at work during the summer months.

Shop open all year on weekdays, 9–1 and 2–5.30; early closing at 1 on Wed. Weaving shed open on weekdays. Whitsun–Oct., 10.30–12.30 and 2–5; early closing, 12.30 on Wed.

BRAUNTON Map ref: Cc
Studio Ceramics, East Street, Braunton.
Tel. Braunton 812714
(Just off main crossroads in centre of town. Car park in Caen Street.)

Two disciplines are combined to produce lustreware at Studio Ceramics. Cecil Hodkinson was a metallurgist before he became a potter, and he uses his knowledge of metals to give a unique finish to his pottery. Helped by his wife, he blends white Devon and Cornish clays, at the start of a process that includes four firings and takes six weeks to complete. Many of the pieces are brightened with flower transfers and decorated with 22 carat gold. Among examples of this fine lustreware for sale in the showroom are lamp bases, posy troughs, butter dishes, powder bowls, biscuit barrels and vases coated entirely in gold or platinum.

Open daily except Mon., winter 10–4; summer 10–5. Appointment necessary for parties.

CHUDLEIGH Map ref: Db
The Wheel Crafts Centre, Chudleigh.
Tel. Chudleigh 853255
(Down Clifford Street from Memorial in main street. Car park on site.)

Flour is no longer produced at this finely restored water-mill, but throughout the three-storey building the machinery has been left intact and the wheel is still working. Visitors can watch local artists and craftsmen at work, the crafts including weaving, needlework and pottery. Stainless-steel wall sculptures are on display.

Open daily, 10–6. Charge for admission.

COMBE MARTIN Map ref: Dc
Potters Wheel Gallery, 31 High Street, Combe Martin.
Tel. Combe Martin 3788
(Near top of High Street. Car park within 100 yds of pottery.)

A potter's skill is best displayed in the age-old task of throwing pots on a wheel. In a corner of her gallery, Diana Roberts demonstrates this technique, together with all the other processes involved in making pots, up to kiln firing. She specialises in commemoration plates and mugs and will take commissions. A large selection of paintings by North Devon artists lines the walls, and stoneware pottery from Ilfracombe and other locally made crafts are displayed.

Open all year, Oct.–May, 10.30–5.30, closed Wed. and Sun.; June–Sept., 10–9, closed Sun.

DARTMOUTH Map ref: Da
H. G. Middleton & Sons (Blacksmiths), 3 Broadstone, Dartmouth.
Tel. Dartmouth 2346
(Broadstone is a small street at the northern end of Dartmouth. Parking available near by at harbour front.)

In 1960 this family business was asked to take part with five other West Country blacksmiths in the task of forging the gates and railings at the entrance of Falls Church National Memorial Park, Virginia, USA. Other examples of the Middleton's craftsmanship such as hearth furniture, lamps and candlesticks can be seen in their shop. A large picture window allows visitors to watch the shower of golden sparks as work is carried out at the forge.

Open all year; Mon.–Fri., 8–5; Sat., 9–12.

EXETER Map ref: Db
Quayside Pottery, City Basin, Exeter.
Tel. Exeter 35898
(From Exeter follow signs to Maritime Museum. Pottery is opposite museum on quayside. Parking near by.)

Mr Stuart produces very finely thrown stoneware and porcelain-type pottery, decorated with oriental-style brushwork and glazed in olive, blue and white, satin matt oatmeal, and classic celadon. Most of the work is domestic ware, and there are also planters, goblets, vases and bonsai pots. Much of the work is commissioned.

Open most days, 10–5, but advisable to telephone if making special journey.

GREAT TORRINGTON Map ref: Cc
Dartington Glass Limited, Great Torrington.
Tel. Torrington 3797
(Signposted from main street opposite church. Free parking on site.)

The highlight of a tour of Dartington glassworks is a visit to the Furnace Hall, where teams of seven or eight men, under a master blower, give shape and lasting beauty to gobs or 'gathers' of molten glass. From the moment the first gather comes out of the furnace, it is blown, moulded, shaped and sheared with tools little changed from those used hundreds of years ago. Visitors are taken through all the processes of making lead-crystal glass, from the careful gathering of the molten glass to the final inspection, in which each piece is graded into 'A' or 'B' quality. The 'A' quality glass is sent out to stockists, but visitors can buy 'B' quality glassware from the glassworks shop.

Shop open Mon.–Fri., 9–5; Sat., 10–4. Factory tours Mon.–Fri., 9.30–10.30 and 12–3. Advance booking necessary for parties of ten or more. No factory tours at weekends or Bank Holidays. Only limited tours available during factory holidays, so visitors are advised to telephone first to confirm opening times.

HARTLAND Map ref: Cc
T. H. Conibear & Sons (Blacksmiths), Ford Hill Forge, Hartland, Bideford.
Tel. Hartland 208
(Just south of village, on B3248. Restricted parking in yard.)

The farming revolution since the last war has seen horses give way to tractors in their thousands. Village blacksmiths have had to turn from shoeing to producing weather-vanes, sign brackets, sun-dials, hearth furniture and similar items. T. H. Conibear's have kept up with the times in this way, but there is also a racing stable near by and they are based in hunting country. So they still make horseshoes – the elegant sort needed for racehorses, as well as more workaday shoes for hunters. Small items of ironwork are for sale.

Open all year, Mon.–Fri., 9–5.

HONITON Map ref: Eb
Honiton Pottery, 30–34 High Street, Honiton.
Tel. Honiton 2106

Map ref: Db

Finch Foundry Trust and Sticklepath Museum of Rural Industry

STICKLEPATH, DEVON

For nearly 150 years, from 1814 to 1960, the Finch Foundry produced edge-tools such as hooks, hoes, scythes and shovels for West Country farmers, quarrymen and miners. But then the Finch family business closed down and the buildings fell rapidly into decay. Today, however, they have been restored as a museum and the foundry is alive and its machinery working again.

Water from the River Taw powers the three wheels. The stream is diverted into a 'launder' – a small wooden aqueduct, from where the water plunges through hatches to activate the wheels below. Visitors can walk along a series of cat-walks beneath the launder in order to see exactly how the foundry worked. One wheel drove the fan that produced air for each of the furnaces; another operated the trip-hammer and shears; the third powered a band-saw, a grindstone for sharpening the tools and an emery wheel for polishing them.

One gallery is devoted to an exhibition of water power and its applications. There are drawings of machinery at various mills, 18th-century water-power designs by John Smeaton, examples of different types of wheel and a geological map of the area. In another room the visitors can see examples of the sort of work that the foundry would have produced in its heyday – not only agricultural machinery and hand tools, but also surgical appliances to meet the demand created by an outbreak of polio after the Second World War.

Sticklepath, Okehampton, Devon. Tel. Sticklepath 352

Open daily 11–5 or dusk. Charge for admission.

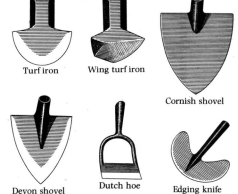

Turf iron   Wing turf iron

Cornish shovel

Devon shovel   Dutch hoe   Edging knife

TOOLS OF EVERY SHAPE *Among the multitude of tools made at the foundry, many were mainly for use on the land.*

HAMMER ROOM *Two mighty hammers and a pair of mechanical shears are powered by the 12 ft water-wheel that turns on the far side of the brick wall. The shears, on the left of the picture, were used to cut shovels to shape. In the centre, the steeling hammer was for drawing out bars to make hooks. The plating hammer, on the right, was for flattening shovels and other tools.*

(Situated in main street. Car parks in Market Place and New Street.)

A highlight of any tour of the Honiton Pottery is that, for a small fee, visitors are allowed to try their hand at decorating their own pottery. If they like the effect, they can have the piece fired and glazed, and sent on to them, for a further small charge. The tour takes in all aspects of pottery-making, from slip-casting and hand fettling to glazing and painting. The pottery has been here since the 1880s, and the original clay seam is behind the factory.

Open all year (except potters' holidays). Mon.–Sat., 9–5.30.

ILFRACOMBE Map ref: Dc
Watermouth Castle (Craft centre), nr Ilfracombe.
Tel. Ilfracombe 63879
(Off A399 between Combe Martin and Ilfracombe. Car park on site.)

The 'Castle', standing like a sentinel above Watermouth Harbour, is not as old as it looks, for it was built in Victorian times, as a folly. A potter, a coppersmith, a leather worker, a blacksmith and other craftsmen can be seen at work in the 'dungeons'. An ironfounder finishes off his pieces in another 'cell', and answers questions about his craft. The dungeons also house antique shops and galleries of paintings,

and in the main rooms of the castle visitors may see mechanical music-making machines, a kitchen from the last century, a model railway and cider-making apparatus.

Open Easter to Whitsun and mid-Sept. to end Oct., Tues., Thur. and Sun., 2.30–4 (last admission). Whitsun to mid-Sept., Mon.–Fri., 11–4; Sun., 2.30–4. Also open Bank Holiday afternoons. Closed Sat.

KINGSTEIGNTON Map ref: Db
Westward Pottery, 96 Exeter Road, Kingsteignton, Newton Abbot.
Tel. Newton Abbot 61011
(On A380 in Kingsteignton.)

Most outsized pots are thrown by building up the clay, section by section. From the outside they look as if they were produced from a single slab, but rings on the inside reveal their method of construction. At the Westward Pottery, Robert Tinnyunt has revived a tradition dating back thousands of years and throws giant-sized vases – up to 2 ft high – from a single piece of clay. He specialises in stoneware pottery, and many of his pieces are decorated with oriental brushwork designs. Some are specially commissioned. In the showroom above the pottery are coffee and tea sets, lamp bases, vases, plant pots, bowls, dishes and jugs.

Open Mon.–Sat., 10–5.

Opening times and other details may change. Check by telephone before making a special journey.

231

Map ref: Dc

Tiverton Museum

TIVERTON, DEVON

A mass of fascinating relics from the past jostle for position in the 19th-century school building that is now the Tiverton Museum. The agricultural gallery houses an early cider press, a Norwegian harrow – probably the only one of its kind in England – a salmon-poacher's brazier to lure salmon at night and the 'humane' man-trap which merely broke the leg of a trespasser rather than tearing it. Another gallery is devoted to exhibitions of local industries, such as weaving and brewing.

On one side of a little courtyard stands a forge full of tools and equipment amassed over two centuries. They belonged to the blacksmith who ran the forge in the nearby village of Silverton from 1918 to 1973 – a man said to have the uncanny gift of being able to make warts disappear simply by looking at them.

There is a large collection of wagons and carts, ranging in size and purpose from an elegant little children's donkey cart to a handsome and robust Devon farm wagon. One of them has an interesting history – the extraordinary tale of the horsemanship of Alf Wyatt who, in 1914, won a wager for driving the wagon 7 miles from Netherexe to Exeter, with three horses in tandem, without reins. He relied solely on his word of command and on a perfect understanding with his horses.

In 1977 the museum won a much-coveted 'Museum of the Year Award'.

St Andrew Street, Tiverton, Devon. Tel. Tiverton 56295
Open Mon.–Sat., 10.30–4.30, except Bank Holidays. Admission free.

One of the first attempts (early 19th century) to mechanise clothes washing.

A 'long' trap, with teeth that caused profuse bleeding.

A 'square' man-trap – termed 'humane' because it only broke the poacher's leg.

ANCIENT FORGE *In an inner courtyard, once the headmaster's garden, are the tools and equipment of a 200-year-old smithy.*

MODBURY Map ref: Da
Robert Stubbings of Modbury (Furniture maker), Overmeadows, Back Street Lane, Modbury.
Tel. Modbury 830493
(Turn up Brownston Street from Main Street. First turning on left. House and workshop on right. Free car park in centre of town.)

Some people never forget a face. Robert Stubbings is a craftsman who never forgets a piece of wood once it has been through his hands. Even if he comes across a table or a Welsh dresser he made for a customer ten years ago, he instantly recognises a particular joint that may have caused him a problem, or even a particular grain in the wood. A wide range of pine furniture is on view in his combined workshop and showroom – kitchen and dining tables, dressing tables, desks, cupboards, shelves, stools and coffee tables.

Open Mon.–Sat., 9–6; Sun. by appointment.

MODBURY Map ref: Da
Woodturners (South Devon) Craft Centre, New Road, Modbury.
Tel. Modbury 830405
(On outskirts of town on A379 to Kingsbridge. Car park by health centre in town.)

Until 1927 this building was an old coaching stable, hiring out an assortment of horse-drawn coaches and carriages to the local gentry. Old photographs inside the entrance are a reminder of those bygone days. The hay loft above the stable houses a display of locally made crafts, including pottery, basketware, weaving, leatherwork and woodwork. But the main attractions are furniture making, woodturning and carving. The craftsmen can be watched at work through a window, and samples of their products are on display in the showroom.

Open Mon.–Sat., 10–6.

OTTERTON Map ref: Eb
Otterton Mill, Otterton, nr Budleigh Salterton.
Tel. Colaton Raleigh 68521
(The village lies off the A376, 2½ miles north of Budleigh Salterton. Mill is on right entering village. Car park beside mill.)

Flour-millers have used water power to drive their machinery since Saxon times. And this economical method of milling is still carried on today at this meticulously restored medieval mill. A small permanent exhibition of lace is housed in the storage area at the top of the mill. In a gallery on the grinding floor, changing exhibitions, some of arts and crafts, are held during the year. A local lace maker gives demonstrations of her intricate craft several days a week. The outbuildings of the mill have been converted into workshops for glass blowing, pottery, furniture making and woodturning. Examples of the craftsmen's work are for sale in the mill shop, along with other hand-made articles and stone-ground flour.

Open daily, Nov.–Easter, 2–5.30; Easter to end Oct., 11–5.30.

OTTERY ST MARY Map ref: Eb
Anthony Miller (Furniture maker), Daisymount Mews Workshop, Daisymount Cross, Ottery St Mary.
Tel. Whimple 822758
(Two miles west of Ottery St Mary on B3180 between B3174 and A30. Car park.)

Anthony Miller is a craftsman who makes furniture in the traditional manner, with traditional skill and care. Examples of his work – small tables, longcase clocks, tea trolleys, book cases, desks, dressers and dining suites, as well as smaller turned items such as bread boards and fruit dishes – may be seen in the small showroom in his house. Almost all of his work is made to order.

Showroom open Mon.–Sat., 10–4.30. Workshop not suitable for visitors.

PAIGNTON Map ref: Db
Wellhouse Pottery Ltd, Well Street,
Paignton.
Tel. Paignton 558865
(Well Street is situated between Church
Street and Cecil Road, off the A379
Paignton–Torquay road. Restricted parking
outside pottery.)

*Since being founded in the mid-1960s,
Wellhouse Pottery has become known all over
the country for the special pale blue glaze,
known as Portals glaze, given to its
earthenware. More recently a new colour,
oatmeal, was introduced. This takes its place
alongside Portals as a glaze used on coffee sets,
teapots, soup bowls, celery jars, vases and
preserve jars. Visitors are welcome to wander
around the attractive old three-storey building
and watch hand-throwing and other processes
in the manufacture of earthenware pottery. In
the display room, pieces are for sale.*

Open all year, Mon.–Fri., 9–4.30.

PETROCKSTOWE Map ref: Dc
W. H. Moulsley (Blacksmith), Petrockstowe
Forge, Petrockstowe, Okehampton.
Tel. Hatherleigh 358
(Situated at the southern end of village.
Parking available outside forge.)

*Mr Moulsley, having been at his craft for over
40 years, still considers himself an apprentice.
As he works on pieces of ironwork, or
machinery for local industries, he keeps up a
non-stop commentary, explaining to visitors
exactly what he is doing every step of the way.
His fine pieces of ornamental work go on
display at the Royal Bath and West Show, and
at the County Show.*

Open all year: Mon.–Fri., 8–5; Sat.
mornings in summer. Other times by
appointment.

PLYMOUTH Map ref: Cb
Barbican Craft Workshops, 1 White Lane,
Barbican, Plymouth.
Tel. Plymouth 66338
(Follow signs to Barbican. White Lane
connects Southside Street and New Street.
Parking available at harbourside.)

*The workshop has been converted from an old
warehouse. It houses a potter, a weaver and a
furniture maker. John Pollex, the potter, makes
large commemorative dishes decorated in a
vigorous 'peasant' style that harks back to the
work of the 17th-century Staffordshire potter
Thomas Toft. Fergus Parsons weaves pure wool
rugs, following traditional designs and some he
has created himself. The third member of the
group, furniture maker Trevor Pate, can be seen
working only by request. Examples of their
work and that of other West Country
craftsmen are on display.*

Open Mon.–Sat., 9–6. Sun. by appointment
only.

SEATON Map ref: Eb
Edwin Spencer (Jewellery), 36 Fore Street,
Seaton.
Tel. Seaton 22482
(Fore Street is the main street on the one-
way system running south towards the sea.
The Edwin Spencer shop is the first on right
at top of street. Parking in town.)

*Visitors are immediately struck by the
colourful effects Edwin Spencer achieves with
his wood jewellery. When they ask what paints
he uses they are surprised by the answer –
none. The glowing colours come from the
natural colours of the woods themselves. He
uses woods from all over the world ... dark
golden-yellow opepe from West Africa,
lavender-grey to purple rosewood from India,
salmon-pink paduak from the Far East. The
pieces are cut into thin slices, glued together to
form laminated blocks and then cut again in
various ways to produce unusual patterns and
grain effects. The pieces are finally sanded and
polished by burnishing. In his shop are hair
slides, ear-rings, bracelets, necklaces, rings,
pendants, cuff links and jewel boxes.*

Shop is open all year: Mon.–Sat., 9–6; Sun.
in July and Aug., 9–6. Workshop open by
appointment.

SHEBBEAR Map ref: Cc
Shebbear Pottery, Shebbear, Beaworthy.
Tel. Shebbear 271
(Two miles north-west of Shebbear village.
From Bideford take A388 towards
Holsworthy. At Stibb Cross take Shebbear
road for 2 miles. Bear right ¼ mile beyond
Rowden Chapel. Pottery is 1 mile down
lane. Car parking available.)

*The Shebbear Pottery is buried in the heart of
rural Devon; and the work of Clive Bowen and
his assistant is rooted just as deeply in the
traditions of English pottery. They use a rich
red earthenware clay from Fremington, near
Barnstaple, and decorate their domestic and
garden pots with slip, or liquid clay, in
contrasting colours. Firing takes place about
eight times a year, in a bottle-shaped kiln that
can take up to 2,000 pots. The kiln is wood-
fired, and smoke and flames travel between the
pots, introducing a random element that can
produce some highly interesting glazes.*

Open all year, Mon.–Sat., 10–6.

SOUTH MOLTON Map ref: Dc
The Potter's Arms, 16 Station Road, South
Molton.
Tel. South Molton 2829

*The design traditions followed in this pottery
come from a distant age and a distant part of
the world. For Takeshi Yasuda, as his name
suggests, is Japanese. And his partner, Sandy
Brown, served her apprenticeship in the village
of Mashiko, famed throughout Japan as the
'village of a thousand potters'.
Mr Yasuda uses a Japanese kick-wheel, and
the influence of the Japanese masters is clearly
to be seen in his work. His pots and stoneware
for cooking, eating and drinking are notable for
their simplicity. Sandy Brown's work is based
on Motto ware from the late 19th-century
potteries in Torquay.*

Open all year at most times.

SOUTH TAWTON Map ref: Db
Andrew Holden, The Pottery, South
Tawton, nr Okehampton.
Tel. Sticklepath 609
(From South Tawton take road north of the
church signposted 'Wood'. Pottery 1 mile
down road on left. Parking available.)

*Andrew Holden's reputation as a potter has
spread far from his rural base. Visitors come
from places as distant as Germany and Holland
to buy his high-fired stoneware and tableware –
baking dishes, wine and cider jars, porringers,
casseroles, and pestles and mortars. He runs
summer courses for hobbyist potters.*

Open Mon.–Sat., 9.30–5.30.

WILMINGTON Map ref: Eb
Mr E. C. Blake (Walking sticks), Higher
Cleave, Wilmington, nr Honiton.
Tel. Wilmington 277
(Take the Axminster Road from Honiton.
After Windmill Garage continue for 1½
miles, then take second on left. House is 1
mile down lane over crossroads. Bear to the
right at fork. Parking space in drive.)

*In the winter months, when the sap is down,
Mr Blake cuts sticks of holly, hazel or
blackthorn to make into walking sticks,
shepherds' crooks and riding canes. For a year
the wood is left to season, then each stick is
carefully fashioned into shape and varnished
several times. Some still bear spiral grooves left
by the honeysuckle that once entwined the
branches of the living tree.*

Visitors are welcome at any time, except
Sun.

WINKLEIGH Map ref: Dc
Michael Hatfield, Seckington Pottery
Models, Winkleigh.
Tel. Winkleigh 478
(Off B3220, 1 mile to north-west of village,

down lane near Oaktree restaurant. Parking
available outside house.)

*More of a ceramic sculptor than a potter,
Michael Hatfield makes miniature models – a
tiny mouse on a wedge of cheese, a pair of
wellington boots, a hedgehog, a frog or a rabbit,
some of them less than ¼ in. high. He finds the
fine Devon clay excellent for reproducing detail.
His models are on display in his showroom.*

Open all year, Mon.–Fri., 9–1 and 2–5.
Also open most weekends, but telephone to
avoid disappointment.

MUSEUMS

ASHLEY Map ref: Dc
The Ashley Countryside Collection, Ashley
House, Wembworthy, Chulmleigh.
Tel. Ashreigney 226
(At Ashley, 1½ miles north-west of
Wembworthy. Signposted from the B3220
and A377.)

*Deep in the heart of rural Devon, this
fascinating assembly of old agricultural
implements and tools has been amassed by a
local farmer, who used to plough with horses
on the nearby farm where he grew up. There
are over 1,000 items of agricultural
machinery, including numerous horse-drawn
ploughs, seed drills, cultivators, wagons and a
threshing drum. There are also coopers' tools, a
collection of weights and measures, a
blacksmith's forge, a wheelwright's shop and a
unique collection of 28 British sheep breeds.*

Open Easter to first weekend in Oct., Mon.,
Wed., Sat., Sun., 10–1, 2–6. Also daily in
Aug. except Thur. Charge for admission.

EXETER Map ref: Db
Royal Albert Memorial Museum, Queen
Street, Exeter.
Tel. Exeter 56724

*The museum's fine collection of over 30,000
pieces of lace includes samples of the local
Honiton lace. In the late 1600s, Flemish
Huguenots, fleeing from religious persecution
by the Catholics, settled in the small villages
along the south coast of Devon. They taught the
locals, who were already skilled lace makers,
new designs and techniques. The lace was then
dispatched to Honiton for sale. Other displays
of local crafts and industries illustrate the
making of butter and clotted cream, the fishing
industry and cider making.*

Open Tues.–Sat., 10–5.30.

KINGSBRIDGE Map ref: Da
Cookworthy Museum, Old Grammar School,
108 Fore Street, Kingsbridge.
Tel. Kingsbridge 3235

*One room in the museum commemorates
William Cookworthy, the first man to
recognise that the white clay found in the West
Country was the 'Kaolin' used by the Chinese
in the manufacture of porcelain. Included in the
local history collection are tools for
wheelwrighting, basket making, thatching,
shipwrighting and sand-moulding. The farm
gallery contains a large collection of
agricultural machines and implements.*

Open Easter to Oct., Mon.–Sat., 10–5 (last
entry 4.30). Small charge for admission.

STICKLEPATH Map ref: Db
Finch Foundry Trust and Sticklepath
Museum of Rural Industry.
(See panel on p. 231)

TIVERTON Map ref: Dc
Tiverton Museum.
(See panel on facing page)

DORSET

BEAMINSTER Map ref: Eb
The John Makepeace Furniture Workshops,
Parnham House, Beaminster.

Tel. Beaminster 862204
(Half a mile south of town on A3066 to
Bridport. Car parks within the grounds.)

*Parts of this lovely old house are Elizabethan.
Surrounded by landscaped gardens, it makes an
ideal setting for the workshops. Visitors can see
craftsmen at work on unique commissioned
pieces, and a steward will answer questions on
their work. Makepeace furniture is on display
in the Great Hall; the Drawing Room contains
exhibitions by living artists and craftsmen, and
the Library houses a collection of craftsmen's
tools, timber samples and examples of the
woodcraftsman's art from many parts of the
world.*

Open Apr.–Oct., Wed., Sun. and Bank
Holidays, 10–5. Charge for admission.

BISHOP'S CAUNDLE Map ref: Fc
Blackmore Vale Forge, Bishop's Caundle,
Sherborne.
Tel. Bishop's Caundle 404
(Situated in the main street opposite the
White Hart Inn. Parking outside forge.)

*The day-to-day work of a 20th-century rural
smithy usually involves a good deal of farm
repair work. Michael Malleson intersperses this
work by designing and making traditional iron
work. He uses special blacksmith's coal which
produces a soft white heat, and for his craft
work he prefers to use traditional joining
methods such as riveting or collaring, and fire
welding instead of welding with an
oxyacetylene torch or electric arc welding. His
pieces include hearth furniture, lighting units
and gates made to order.*

Open all year, Mon.–Fri., 9–4.30.

BLANDFORD FORUM Map ref: Fc
David A. Law (Silversmith), Charnwood,
Milldown Road, Blandford Forum.
Tel. Blandford 52813
(Take A350 Shaftesbury road from
Blandford. Just past hospital on right, turn
down long driveway on left.)

*A simple elegance is the 'hallmark' of David
Law's silverware. Most of his work is done on
commission, and his gift sets – coffee and tea
sets and table centre pieces – come complete in
presentation boxes. Examples of his work can
normally be seen at the Dorset Craft Guild
Annual Exhibition and the Dorset Arts and
Crafts Exhibition, which are held in August
each year.*

Open Mon.–Sat., 9.30–4.30. Appointment
necessary.

CHEDINGTON Map ref: Ec
Beresford Pealing (Pottery), Manor
Farmhouse, Chedington, Beaminster.
Tel. Corscombe 482
(In village, which is situated ½ mile south of
A356 Dorchester–Crewkerne road. Turn off
at Winyards Gap Inn.)

*In the stable block of his Elizabethan
farmhouse, Beresford Pealing makes a wide
range of domestic stoneware, exhibition pieces,
and unusual items such as alarm, carriage and
pendulum quartz pottery clocks. He will make
pieces to order.*

Open daily May–Sept., 10.30–7.30. At
times when it is inconvenient to admit
visitors they can watch work in progress
from the showroom next door.

CHIDEOCK Map ref: Eb
The Old Bakery Pottery, Main Street,
Chideock, Bridport.
Tel. Chideock 298
(Situated on south side of A35
Bridport–Lyme Regis road. Parking along
Main Street.)

*Dorset-type model cottages and even entire
streets of cottages, together with small animals
such as owls, tortoises and mice, are hand-
made by Mrs Godwin. Her husband makes
hand-thrown decorated stoneware, which
includes bowls, candlesticks, lamp bases,
ashtrays and cheese and butter dishes.*

Opening times and other details may change. Check by telephone before making a special journey.

233

Showroom open in summer Mon.–Fri., 9.30–1 and 2.15–6. In winter, Tues.–Fri., 9.30–1, 2.15–5. Open Sat., 9.30–1. Workshop by appointment only.

HOLT Map ref: Gc
Parnell's (Woodcraft), Holt Green Farm Cottage, Holt, Wimborne Minster.
Tel. Wimborne 887211
(Holt is signposted ½ mile from Wimborne Minster on B3078. At the Old Inn, take bridle path opposite pub. Parking at the workshops.)

In converted 300-year-old farm buildings, craftsmen can be seen making anything in wood, ranging from garden furniture, oak casks and house signs to clocks, cradles, door knobs and vanity boxes. They even make a four-poster bed to order. Other crafts on view include pottery, glass blowing, spinning and corn-dolly making. A small stable near by has chickens, ducks, geese, goats and rabbits to occupy visitors' small children while their parents watch the craftsmen at work.

Open Easter to Oct., Mon.–Sat., 9–4.30.

LYTCHETT MATRAVERS Map ref: Fb
Adrian Lewis-Evans, Stoney Down Pottery, Lytchett Matravers.
Tel. Lytchett Minster 622392
(On A350 Blandford Forum–Poole road at Stoney Down Cross.)

Up to the turn of the century, Dorset farmers took cider out to the fields at harvest time in a globular pot, called a 'Dorset Owl', slung beneath the farm cart by leather thongs. Reproductions of these cider flagons of yesteryear are among the items of special interest at the Stoney Down Pottery. Adrian Lewis-Evans also produces oriental-design vases with rich glazes, pitchers, planters, wine and water sets and tankards.

Visitors are welcome to go round the pottery on most days. Usually open from 9 to dusk, all year.

MOTCOMBE Map ref: Fc
Wing and Staples (Blacksmiths), The Forge, Motcombe, nr Shaftesbury.
Tel. Shaftesbury 3104
(Situated in village. Parking in street.)

There is a showroom at the forge, where visitors can see examples of both practical and decorative forged ironwork. Mostly made to order, items include traditional hearthware, weather-vanes, trivets (kettle stands), wall lights, gates and grilles. Horse-shoeing is also done occasionally.

Normally open Mon.–Fri., 9–5. Appointment necessary.

POOLE Map ref: Gb
Poole Aquarium and Crafts Centre, The Quay, Poole.
Tel. Poole 86712
(Parking at quayside, or in car parks in town.)

The greater part of this old four-storey mill overlooking bustling Poole Harbour is taken up by an aquarium and serpentarium, with fossil and shell exhibitions. The craft centre, on the ground floor, displays the work of several resident craftsmen, including pottery, leather work and woodcarving as well as other Dorset crafts. Visitors may wander round at their leisure, watch artists and craftsmen at work, and see a collection of traditional tools displayed around the centre.

Open daily except Christmas Day, 10.30–10 in summer; 10.30–5.30 in winter. Charge for admission.

POOLE Map ref: Gb
Poole Pottery Ltd, The Quay, Poole.
Tel. Poole 2866
(Parking at quayside, or in car parks in town.)

On a tour of the factory, occupying three-quarters of an hour, visitors can watch the mass-production of hollow-ware, including cups, jugs and casseroles. A miniature museum at the pottery shows pieces made in the past, and visitors can browse around the showroom. This is also open to visitors who are unable to do the tours.

Factory tour: all year, Mon.–Thur., 10.15–11.30 and 1.15–3.30; Fri. in morning only. Closed Bank Holidays and some works holidays. Advisable to book in advance. Admission charge for tours.

SHILLINGSTONE Map ref: Fc
Cecil Colyer, MA, FSDC (Designer craftsman), Orchardene, Candys Lane, Shillingstone, Blandford Forum.
Tel. Child Okeford 860252
(In centre of village, down lane opposite Methodist Chapel.)

Cecil Colyer combines the skills of furniture maker, woodturner and silversmith. He works mainly in hardwoods, such as yew, rosewood and rippled ash. His pieces range from bureaux, sideboards, tables and chairs, to turned mirrors and bowls in the rarer woods. Silverware items include sherry goblets, mazers, salt and pepper sets and church silver. He has a small display room in his house, but examples of his work can be seen at his workshop and at annual exhibitions of the Dorset County Arts and Crafts Association and the Dorset Craft Guild, which are held at Puddleton and at Bridport in August.

Appointment necessary.

SOUTHBOURNE Map ref: Gb
Dorset Craft Galleries, 93 Belle Vue Road, Southbourne Crossroads, Bournemouth.
Tel. Bournemouth 429644
(On south side of B3059 at Southbourne Crossroads, to the east of central Bournemouth and 1 mile from Christchurch. Parking in street or at large car park near by.)

Demonstrations of pottery, spinning and making corn dollies are given throughout most of the year. Craft goods made elsewhere in the locality are on sale, including woodcraft and soft toys, together with objects made on the premises.

Open Feb.–Dec., Tues.–Sat., 10–1 and 2.15–5.

STALBRIDGE Map ref: Fc
John Dike (Violin maker), Nottingham House, Ring Street, Stalbridge, Sturminster Newton.
Tel. Stalbridge 62285
(Situated in main street behind village stores. Public car park near by.)

As well as making violins, John Dike produces violas and cellos. He uses hardwoods such as maple or sycamore for the back of the instrument, and softwoods such as spruce or pine for the front. The instruments are fitted with ebony pegs, then varnished. John Dike also repairs and restores stringed instruments.

Open most weekdays, 9.30–6. Appointment necessary.

SWANAGE Map ref: Gb
Leslie Gibbons, ATD, The Owl Pottery, 108 High Street, Swanage.
Tel. Swanage 5850
(Approached from main shopping centre, The Owl Pottery is on right-hand side of High Street, past Town Hall and near the Millpond.)

A large display of hand-thrown and moulded earthenware pottery can be seen – all decorated by hand. There are small dishes and bowls, vases and plant pots, plates with owl designs, small animals and ceramic jewellery. The workshop is at the back of the pottery shop, where visitors may watch work in progress.

Open all year on weekdays during normal shop hours, and on summer evenings. Closed Sun. and Thur. afternoon.

WIMBORNE MINSTER Map ref: Gb
Wimborne Pottery, 6 West Borough, Wimborne Minster.
Tel. Wimborne 887613
(Off the main square in Wimborne Minster. Parking in town car park.)

Visitors can see potters at their wheels, and artists decorating the finished pottery, on the ground floor of this three-storey craft centre. Craft goods on sale range from pottery and woodcraft to basketware, hand-printed clothing, corn dollies and toys. The first floor has a selection of home-spun fabrics and clothes. Spinning and weaving are often demonstrated on the floor above, where patchwork and appliqué work are also carried on.

Mon.–Sat., 9.30–5, from first Mon. in Jan. until Christmas Eve.

SOMERSET

BARTON ST DAVID Map ref: Fc
Jaquie Baker, Weaver's Dream, Mill Road, Barton St David, Somerton.
Tel. Baltonsborough 50584
(Second house on right up a no-through-road beyond post office. Limited parking outside.)

Trained as an artist, Jaquie Baker has become a skilled woodturner, spinner and tapestry weaver. Her chief interest is in producing lace bobbins, which she paints with detailed flower, bird or animal motifs. The bobbins are made from hardwoods, including holly, and are bought by lace makers in all parts of the world. She keeps Dorset Horn sheep and uses their fleece for spinning yarn, which she weaves into commissioned rugs, cushion covers and wall hangings.

Open all year, Mon.–Fri., 9–5, by appointment only.

BRADFORD-ON-TONE Map ref: Ec
R. J. Sheppy & Son (Cider makers), Three Bridges, Bradford-on-Tone, Taunton.
Tel. Bradford-on-Tone 233
(On A38 between Taunton and Wellington. Car park available.)

In the autumn and winter months, after the apples have been harvested, visitors who have made an appointment can watch cider being made. At other times of the year they may wander from the apple bay to the press room and see the machinery used to make the cider. There is also a small museum, containing cider-making equipment dating back to the 18th century, and a number of farm implements and craftsmen's tools. Cider and dairy products are for sale.

Open Apr.–Dec., Mon.–Sat., 8.30 to dusk; Easter to Christmas, Sun., 12–2. Shop open all year, 8.30 to dusk; also on Sun., 12–2.

BRUTON Map ref: Fc
Bruton Pottery, Patwell Lane, Bruton.
Tel. Bruton 3328
(On bank of River Brue, opposite parish church. Parking space.)

The peaceful setting of this small pottery near the church and river befits the quiet but purposeful activity of John Crisp and his son, Bruce. They produce hand-thrown ovenproof stoneware in glazes which give white, blue, green and brown colours. They make coffee pots, tea sets, jugs, mugs, casseroles, bowls, vases and ornaments.

Open all year, Mon.–Sat., 9–5.30.

BUTLEIGH Map ref: Fc
Dove Workshops (Craft centre), Barton Road, Butleigh, nr Glastonbury.
Tel. Baltonsborough 50682/50385
(South-west of village on road to Barton St David, ½ mile from Rose and Portcullis pub. Parking on premises.)

A group of craftsmen live and work in converted and extended farm buildings. Paul

Stubbs, a potter, has given his name to the pottery oil lamps he throws, in addition to his range of oven and table stoneware. Modern furniture is designed and made to order by Roger Frood, who works in a variety of hard and soft woods. His wife, Bronwen, is an etcher. She produces limited editions, mainly of local landscapes. From time to time other crafts may be represented at the workshops.

Open all year, Mon.–Sat., 9.30–5.30.

DRAYCOTT Map ref: Ec
W. E. S. Garrett (Saddler), South View, Back Lane, Draycott, nr Cheddar.
Tel. Cheddar 742367
(Off A371 at bottom of lane. Parking on premises outside stables.)

Besides making and repairing all types of saddlery and harness for horses, Mr Garrett – a master saddler – equips circus animals, such as elephants, with their fancy harnesses. He uses high-quality leather that has been tanned with oak bark, and most items are hand-stitched. His workshop, which can be viewed on request, is above a well-stocked display area of goods for sale.

Open all year, Mon.–Sat., except Bank Holidays, 9–1 and 2–5.

DRAYCOTT Map ref: Ec
Westfield Barn (Furniture makers), Wells Road, Draycott, nr Cheddar.
Tel. Cheddar 742845
(On A371 at northern end of village. Parking space available.)

Ray Holloway turns and hand-carves solid Tudor-style oak furniture with richly carved panels, ranging from four-poster beds to dining tables, chairs and rocking-horses. These are made to order, but he applies the same skills to making many everyday, smaller items – butter pats, shortbread moulds and lamp bases – which visitors may buy.

Open most days throughout the year, from 9.30–1 and 2–5.30. Advisable to check by telephone.

DUNSTER Map ref: Dc
Dunster Water Mill, Mill Lane, Dunster.
Tel. Dunster 759
(In the grounds of Dunster Castle. Car park in castle grounds.)

This beautiful 18th-century building has been restored to full working order, returning to a tradition that reaches back to the Domesday survey when two mills were recorded on the estate. Flour is milled once or twice a day, but if visitors miss this they may still wander round the mill and see not only the cast-iron machinery but also a collection of old agricultural implements.

Open Easter to end Sept., Sun.–Thur., 11–5. Also Tues., Wed. and Sun., 2–4, in Oct. Small charge for admission.

FIDDINGTON Map ref: Ec
Whitnell Pottery, Fiddington, Bridgwater.
Tel. Nether Stowey 732663
(Signposted off A39 between Cannington and Nether Stowey, about 1 mile from main road. Parking for a few cars outside pottery.)

John Harlow grinds local rocks into a fine powder to form the basis of his glazes. He uses limestone, volcanic rock and, in particular, a sandstone with a high silica content known as hangman's grit which gives the pottery a hard, durable finish and an attractive green colour. A brushwork pattern, based on the reeds found in the low-lying land around Somerset's north coast, decorates many of the pots – including casseroles, dishes, mugs and teapots.

Open daily, 9–6; closed some Fridays and Saturdays in winter.

HUNTSPILL Map ref: Ec
The Haven Pottery, West Huntspill, nr Highbridge.
Tel. Burnham-on-Sea 783173

(On A38, just south of the village of Huntspill, before river. Parking space.)

A small team of potters can be seen hand-throwing, slip-casting, glazing and decorating pots in a spacious workshop, and visitors are welcome to ask questions about their work. Goblets, coffee sets, candle holders and lamp bases are some of the goods for sale in the nearby showroom.

Workshop open Mon.–Fri., except Bank Holidays, from 10–1 and 2–5. Showroom open Mon.–Sat., 9.30–1 and 2–5.30.

KINGSTON ST MARY   Map ref: Ec
Church Farm Weavers, Kingston St Mary, Taunton.
Tel. Kingston St Mary 267
(Next to church. Car park outside.)

Nearly all the craft processes that go into

making a length of cloth, including combing and carding, are practised here by Talbot Potter and John Lennon. After hand-spinning wool, they dye it with extracts from plants such as heather, weld, privet and yew which grow in their garden. The yarn is then woven on large floor looms into lengths of tweed, rugs, stoles and church furnishings, examples of which are in the parish church. The fabric is finally washed, then wound tautly on to rollers to dry for several days, to give the 'finished' cloth.

Open all year, Tues.–Sat., 2–6, and at other times by appointment.

MARSTON MAGNA   Map ref: Fc
Michael Illingworth Workshop (Pottery), The Manor House, Marston Magna, Yeovil.
Tel. Marston Magna 850447/850895
(On A359 in centre of village, next to church. Parking to right of manor.)

The craft of silk-screen printing and that of the potter are practised by Michael Illingworth in his workshop – the manor's former coaching house. Working largely to commission, he makes a range of white earthenware china including tiles, tankards and plates, which he decorates with colourful illustrations or lettering to celebrate such occasions as wedding anniversaries and regimental reunions. He usually has a small stock for sale in his workshop, where he holds twice-yearly exhibitions.

Open daily, 9–6. Appointment necessary.

MELLS   Map ref: Fc
'Iron', Laurel Cottage, Little Green, Mells, Frome.
Tel. Mells 812640
(Half a mile south-west of post office. Limited parking in drive or lane.)

Landscapes and wildlife provide the inspiration for much of Alan Gwyllt's ironwork. He works to commission, designing and forging such items as fire baskets, screens and fenders, which he decorates with reliefs of birds, trees and hills. The result is refreshingly different from traditional hearthware. He also makes ornamental wall brackets and sculptures.

Open by appointment.

MINEHEAD   Map ref: Dc
Greenaleigh Glass, Greenaleigh Farm, Minehead.
Tel. Minehead 4945
(Parking in Burgundy Road, west of shopping centre. Farm is ¾ mile along cliff walk.)

Greenaleigh Farm is situated high on wooded cliffs, with views across to Wales. At the farm,

---

Map ref: Ec

Somerset Rural Life Museum

GLASTONBURY, SOMERSET

The roof of the 14th-century Abbey Barn, which houses many of the exhibits of the Somerset Rural Life Museum, is a splendid testimony to medieval carpentry – a fitting shelter for a collection that commemorates the skills of past generations of craftsmen.

Since the aim of the museum is to illustrate rural life in the 18th and 19th centuries, the exhibits naturally include cider presses, for cider has been brewed in Somerset for 700 years. In the 17th century the writer John Evelyn described the local cider as 'generous, strong and sufficiently heady'. Farm labourers often received as much as one-fifth of their income in the form of cider.

There is a small display of withies – grown in Somerset for basket making since the Iron Age. There are also various agricultural implements, such as a winnowing machine, harrows, a binder made in 1910, and a peat barrow and boat – the latter used to carry peat on the Somerset moors.

Specialised displays are clustered around the old farmyard. There is a wagon shed, a reconstructed wheelwright's shop, a forge, and the tools of craftsmen such as the thatcher and the millwright. The Abbey farmhouse itself is devoted to the reconstruction of a Victorian farmhouse and displays of the crafts of smocking, lace making and embroidery. The museum also arranges events and demonstrations of traditional crafts.

MOORLAND BOAT *The flat-bottomed boat and the broad-wheeled barrow were used to carry cut peat across the streams and wet moorlands of central Somerset.*

Abbey Farm, Chilkwell Street, Glastonbury, Somerset.
Tel. Glastonbury 32903

Open Mon.–Fri., 10–5. Weekends: 2–6.30 from Apr.–Oct.; 2.30–5, from Nov. to Easter.

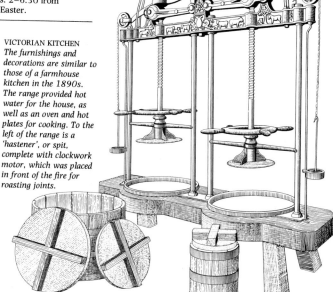

VICTORIAN KITCHEN
The furnishings and decorations are similar to those of a farmhouse kitchen in the 1890s. The range provided hot water for the house, as well as an oven and hot plates for cooking. To the left of the range is a 'hastener', or spit, complete with clockwork motor, which was placed in front of the fire for roasting joints.

Cheese press made in 1869.

Opening times and other details may change. Check by telephone before making a special journey.

235

Map ref: Ec

Street Shoe Museum

STREET, SOMERSET

From Roman shoes to the most recent fashions and from Red Indian moccasins to miniature shoes for dolls, the Street Shoe Museum charts the development of shoes and shoemaking techniques. In particular it celebrates a century and a half of business by the firm of Clarks in Street.

In the mid-1850s, C. and J. Clark employed 600 people, most of whom worked at their homes in local villages. Each week these outworkers brought in their completed work, were paid and collected ready-cut uppers and soles. One of the exhibits is a page of rules from an outworker's tally book, complete with a list of fines for such transgressions as 'tying odd shoes together'.

An outworker's shop has been reconstructed with all the hand-tools and with a pictorial display of shoemaking by hand. In the late 1850s, however, machinery was introduced and the factory became the centre of manufacture. One gallery contains the sorts of machine that were used – the sole-cutting press, for example, the heel attacher and the sewing machines.

High Street, Street, Somerset. Tel. Street 43131

Open Easter to Oct., Mon.–Sat., 10–4.45.

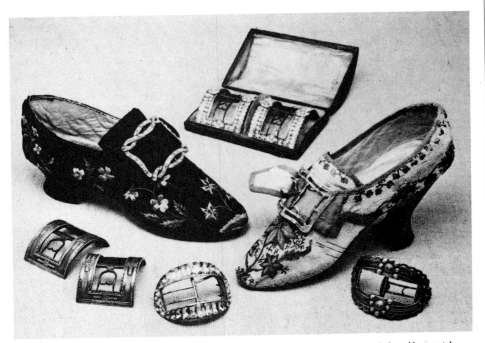

LADIES' SHOES OF YESTERDAY *Decorated with embroidery (left) and beadwork (right), satin was a fashionable material during the 1760s. The buckles, made about 20 years later, are finished with gilt, gold inlay and paste.*

Satin-and-lace boudoir bootee, made for royalty in about 1870.

Embroidered satin bar shoe, about 1895.

Girl's glacé-kid button boots, made about 1898.

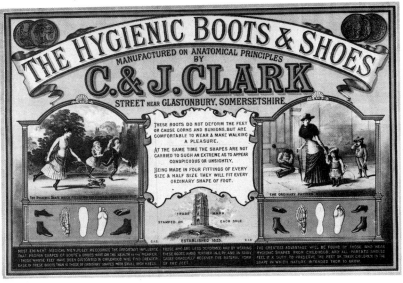

A Clark's poster sent to retailers in 1883.

Norman Wallace makes glass teapots, coffee sets, vases and animals, as well as unusual tree-shaped candelabra and bells which can be inscribed to order. Visitors are welcome to watch him blowing and shaping the glass in his workshop.

Open most days, 10.30–5.30, but telephone to check. Workshop closed Sat.

MINEHEAD   Map ref: Dc
Minehead Pottery, 98 Periton Lane, Minehead.
Tel. Minehead 5748
(Off A39, south-west of town centre, near the parks. Small car park at side of pottery.)

Visitors to this small family pottery will see punch bowls, cider jars, plates and posy bowls and general domestic ware being hand-thrown and painted. Chris Holman, who throws the

pots, likes to work with a variety of clays, producing such contrasting finishes as highly glazed and patterned earthenware, and fine, translucent porcelain.

Open summer months, Mon.–Fri., 9–1 and 2–5.

MINEHEAD   Map ref: Dc
The Workshop (Jewellery), 51 The Avenue, Minehead.
Tel. Minehead 3148
(In town centre, near sea front. There are several car parks in Minehead.)

Celia West designs and makes silver and gold jewellery. Visitors can watch her at work in the front of her shop, where items for sale include silver pendants inlaid with gold, mosaic brooches, flower lockets and enamelled silver or copper pendants.

Open daily in summer, 10–6; in spring and autumn, Mon.–Fri., 10.30–5. Closed between Christmas and Mar.

MONTACUTE   Map ref: Ec
Taunton and Thorne (Glovemakers), Townsend, Montacute.
Tel. Martock 3606/7
(In main street, close to car park, at southern end of village.)

In a former Elizabethan bakery, visitors can see a glove cutter at work, then move to a workshop behind the bakery to see gloves being stitched. You can order a pair of best quality cape leather gloves, and return to find them made up ready for collection a few hours later.

Open all year, Mon.–Wed., 9–5.30; Thur. and Fri., 9–4.

OLD CLEEVE   Map ref: Ec
John Wood (Tanner), Linton, Old Cleeve, Minehead.
Tel. Washford 291
(Take turning to Old Cleeve off A39, 5¼ miles from Minehead. Follow Linton sign.)

This tannery was established more than 100 years ago by the present owner's great-grandfather. On guided tours round the premises visitors will see the stages involved in transforming sheepskins through processes such as scouring, curing and softening to produce rugs, moccasins, coats and gloves.

Tours from Apr.–Oct., Mon.–Fri. at 11; also at 3 on Thur. Rest of year by appointment. Shop open all year, Mon.–Fri., 9–4.30. Also on Sat., 10–4 from Mar.–Dec. Large parties by appointment only.

QUEEN CAMEL Map ref: Fc
Robinsons (Furniture maker), High Street, Queen Camel, nr Yeovil.
Tel. Marston Magna 850609
(In main street. Space for about four cars outside.)

Using old timbers collected from auctions, Mr Robinson makes traditional furniture in oak, walnut, mahogany, satinwood and rosewood. He works mainly to order, making such items as desks, tables, dressers and corner cupboards. Some of the pieces are decorated with attractive inlaying, or with unusual 'oyster' patterns created by arranging cross-cuts of wood side by side.

Open all year, Mon.–Fri., 9–6. Sat. by appointment.

SIMONSBATH Map ref: Dc
Simonsbath Pottery, Pound Cottage, Simonsbath.
Tel. Exford 443
(Situated on main road. Space for parking.)

Replicas of wild flowers, birds, animals and butterflies of the Quantock Hills decorate Rod Billington's pottery. Robust casserole dishes, made to hold up to 6 pints, have game animals and birds in relief on their lids. Wild flowers and butterfly designs are used on lamp bases and vases. Rod Billington can be watched at the Simonsbath Pottery on Tuesdays, Wednesdays and Fridays. On Mondays and Thursdays he can be seen working at his other pottery, Quantock Design, at West Bagborough, near Taunton, in Somerset.

Open Mon.–Fri., 10–5; Sat., 9–1. Other times by appointment.

STOGUMBER Map ref: Ec
Vellow Pottery, Lower Vellow, Williton, Taunton.
Tel. Stogumber 458
(Two miles south-east of Williton, on road to Stogumber. Parking outside pottery.)

During the past 300 years, farriers and a cider maker worked in the building of mellow stone which now houses the pottery. Surrounded by reminders of these crafts, David Winkley can be seen throwing pots in stoneware and hard porcelain. His work includes large bread crocks, pitchers, cooking pots and tableware which he glazes in soft, muted colours and then decorates.

Open all year, Mon.–Sat., 8.30–6.

WOOKEY HOLE Map ref: Fc
Wookey Hole, Wells.
Tel. Wells 72243
(Two miles north-west of Wells, off A371. Large car park.)

An immense Victorian paper-mill is one of the unlikely attractions nestling in the Mendip Hills at Wookey Hole. It was once the largest paper-mill in Europe, and today's visitors can still watch paper of the highest quality being made by hand. The mill is part of a more extensive tourist attraction, which includes a caves museum, a colourful fairground collection and a water-wheel. Together, they occupy a tour lasting 1½ hours.

Open every day, Apr.–Sept., 10–6; Oct.–Mar., 10–4.30. Charge for admission.

WOOTTON COURTENAY Map ref: Dc
Mill Pottery, Wootton Courtenay, Minehead.
Tel. Timberscombe 297
(1¾ miles along signposted turning off A396, just outside Dunster. Car park outside pottery.)

A water-wheel turns in an old threshing shed, attracting the attention of visitors on their way to the pottery showroom. It was installed by Michael Gaitskell, the resident potter, to power his clay-mixing equipment. He can be seen at work, throwing and glazing fine stoneware in muted blues and greens, cream, grey and black.

Open all year, 9–5.

WRANTAGE Map ref: Ec
R. B. Higgs (Woodworker), 4 Barcroft Crescent, Wrantage, Taunton.
Tel. Hatch Beauchamp 480201
(Barcroft Crescent is off A378 near Wrantage post office. Parking for several cars.)

Cabinets for displaying collections of thimbles and lace bobbins, coin display boxes, church fitments, and complex puzzles are among the varied commissions designed and made by Mr Higgs. Each piece is shaped to enhance the grain of the wood – which may be yew, rosewood or other beautiful woods – and is polished with beeswax. Apart from special orders, Mr Higgs makes marquetry pictures, decorative boxes and small sculptures, which are for sale in his home.

Visitors are welcome at most times, by appointment.

MUSEUMS

GLASTONBURY Map ref: Ec
Somerset Rural Life Museum.
(See panel on p. 235)

STREET Map ref: Ec
Street Shoe Museum.
(See panel on facing page)

YEOVIL Map ref: Fc
Brympton d'Evercy, Yeovil.
Tel. West Coker 2528
(Two miles west of Yeovil off A3088. Parking on site.)

There is no place that summarises English country life so perfectly as Brympton d'Evercy and its estate. Next to a handsome 17th-century mansion stands the Priest House, a 14th-century building that was originally the manor house but which is now a Country Life Museum. There are displays devoted to rural interests and to the history of the Clive-Ponsonby-Fane family and the estate. There is also an exhibition of traditional coopering (barrel-making) and cider-making.

Open daily (except Thur. and Fri.), May–Sept., 2.30–6. Charge for admission.

WILTSHIRE

BIDDESTONE Map ref: Fd
Gordon and Dorothy Whittle, Starfall Pottery, Sheldon, Chippenham.
Tel. Corsham 713292
(About 1 mile east of Biddestone on Biddestone–Allington road. Parking by farm.)

Little disturbs the tranquillity of this pottery, housed in the stable block of a 17th-century farm and surrounded by a labyrinth of country lanes. Gordon Whittle specialises in commemorative pottery, traditional kitchenware and cooking pots made in stoneware. One unusual item is a serving dish that allows water to drain from rice and pasta. His wife, Dorothy, has a spinning-wheel and hand loom for knitting and weaving the wool that she spins from fleeces bought from local farmers.

Open daily.

BURBAGE Map ref: Gd
Impi (Miniature furniture), North Wing, Wolf Hall Manor, Burbage, nr Marlborough.
Tel. Marlborough 810519
(Directions will be given when an appointment is arranged.)

Regency dining tables and chairs gleaming with French polish, mahogany corner cupboards with rosewood inlays. Victorian cabinet water closets with hinged lids . . . all of these are produced by Major Holgate at his small workshop near Burbage. Every piece is to the scale of 1 in. to 1 ft. This retired army officer makes miniature furniture perfect in every detail. His Queen Anne bureau, for instance, is complete with lopers that pull out to support the writing flap. Bow-fronted mahogany sideboards and kitchen dressers in pine, sanded and French-polished or waxed to a fine finish, are among the items produced for collectors.

Open all year, Mon.–Fri., 9–5. Appointment necessary.

GREAT SOMERFORD Map ref: Fd
Hector Cole (Ironworker), The Mead, Great Somerford, Chippenham.
Tel. Seagry 720485
(Situated north of crossroads in centre of village. Parking outside house.)

This craftsman is one of the few remaining ironworkers still doing traditional work with a forge in which the bellows are pumped by hand. Most work is done on a commission basis to customers' designs, and Mr Cole has undertaken commissions for the Royal Family. He forges such pieces as fire grates, screens, chestnut roasters, candlesticks and pokers, as well as reproducing antique ironwork.

Open daily, July–Sept. Weekends only rest of year. Appointment necessary.

LACOCK Map ref: Fd
G. & J. M. Watling (Gold and silversmiths), Lacock Gallery, 15 East Street, Lacock.
Tel. Lacock 422
(East Street lies behind the main street in centre of village. Parking in East Street.)

A narrow street in the heart of this quiet village owned by the National Trust leads to an old butcher's premises, set back from the road in a tiny courtyard. Here, in the unlikely setting of the former slaughterhouse, and in the Lacock Gallery next door, visitors will see one of the largest collections of modern gold and silverware in the country. Mr Watling specialises in presentation pieces as well as church silver and jewellery. The work of other craftsmen is also displayed; visitors will see glassware, and a fine collection of scales and balances.

Open daily except Christmas Day. Workshop by appointment only.

MARKET LAVINGTON Map ref: Gd
Peter Pullan (Glass engraver), Crispian Cottage, Drove Lane, Market Lavington, Devizes.
Tel. Lavington 3525
(Drove Lane is near school off B3098, towards Easterton. Restricted parking.)

Hold a decanter engraved by Peter Pullan against a dark background, turn it a couple of degrees into the light, and as if from nowhere there will emerge unicorns, griffons and other heraldic beasts, incised with diamond-point brilliance on the fragile surface. Mr Pullan developed his interest in military badges when he was serving with the RAF. He also makes use of birds, dogs and houses as decorative subjects for engraving on his goblets, plates and decanters.

Open most days, by appointment.

MILTON LILBOURNE Map ref: Gd
John Jones (Fire bellows), 35 Milton Lilbourne, nr Pewsey.
Tel. Pewsey 2696
(The cottage is up a narrow alley opposite the village hall. Parking in lay-by in front of hall.)

Leading off a narrow pathway called 'The Drunge' (a dialect word meaning 'way between high banks') is the cottage workshop where John Jones makes the kind of bellows that have been used for centuries to make fires burn more fiercely. He makes the frames and handles out of elm (French-polished or oiled), and the concertina-like working part from cowhide. The nails are brass headed and the nozzles of solid brass.

Open most days, except when at shows, but not on Tues. between Sept. and Apr. Appointment necessary.

MINETY Map ref: Gd
Triscombe Pottery, Silver Street, Minety, nr Malmesbury.
Tel. Minety 513
(Just off the B4040 in the village. Restricted car parking, but additional space opposite school and in Oakleaze Road.)

Visitors to the Triscombe Pottery can see the two basic methods of pottery making in operation – throwing pots on a wheel and building them up by hand. Tony Fursman uses the wheel to make bowls, mugs, jugs, wine sets and casseroles which he then decorates and glazes. His daughter, Jackie, builds up pieces such as vases or ornamental domino sets from slabs of clay. She also paints decorative wall tiles and makes batik scarves.

Open daily, 10 until dusk. Up to six visitors at a time can watch work in progress.

SALISBURY Map ref: Gc
Winstanley (Salisbury bookbinders), 213 Devizes Road, Salisbury.
Tel. Salisbury 4998
(From Salisbury follow the signs for Devizes – A360. Winstanley's is on left near the top of Devizes road.)

Mr Winstanley can turn his hand to almost anything in bookbinding, from repairing a chewed-up library book to designing and binding a rare printed edition; from calligraphy to binding miniature books. He works in pigskin, Morocco goatskin, and other fine leathers. With his collection of over 2,000 traditional tools, he can re-create bookbinding designs similar to those of the days of Elizabeth I.

Open all year, Mon.–Fri., during normal working hours. Appointment necessary.

SOUTH NEWTON Map ref: Gc
M. & S. Cumper Ltd, Furniture Workshop, Warminster Road, South Newton, Salisbury.
Tel. Salisbury 742166
(On A36 Salisbury road, 5 miles north-west of Salisbury. In centre of village, 100 yds from post office. Parking on site.)

In the heart of the Wiltshire countryside, traditional English furniture is hand-made in solid oak, mahogany and all the traditional hardwoods by this small family firm, which claims to be one of the country's leading cabinet workshops. The standard range includes desks, bookcases and corner cupboards. It is worth noting the careful construction of the drawers, with their hand-cut dovetails. Private commissions and restoration work are undertaken. A small range of gift items are on sale.

An associated firm, T. M. Wright Instruments Ltd, works with Cumpers to produce a fine range of barometers, together with a restoration service for any type of barometer.

To see the workshop, visitors must make an appointment.

MUSEUM

RUDGE Map ref: Fc
The High and Hazel Woods Woodland Park, Brokerswood, Westbury.
Tel. Westbury 822238
(Four miles south of Trowbridge. Turn off A361 at Southwick. Museum is on the road to Rudge.)

Tony Phillips smudged some of the accepted rules of forestry when he set up this woodland park as a unique mixture of commercial woodland, leisure centre and conservation area. Occasionally a young craftsman can be seen making thatching spars or other products of this working forest. There is also a museum and a collection of woodland and forestry-workers' tools.

Open all year, 10 to dusk. Charge for admission.

THE SOUTH-EAST

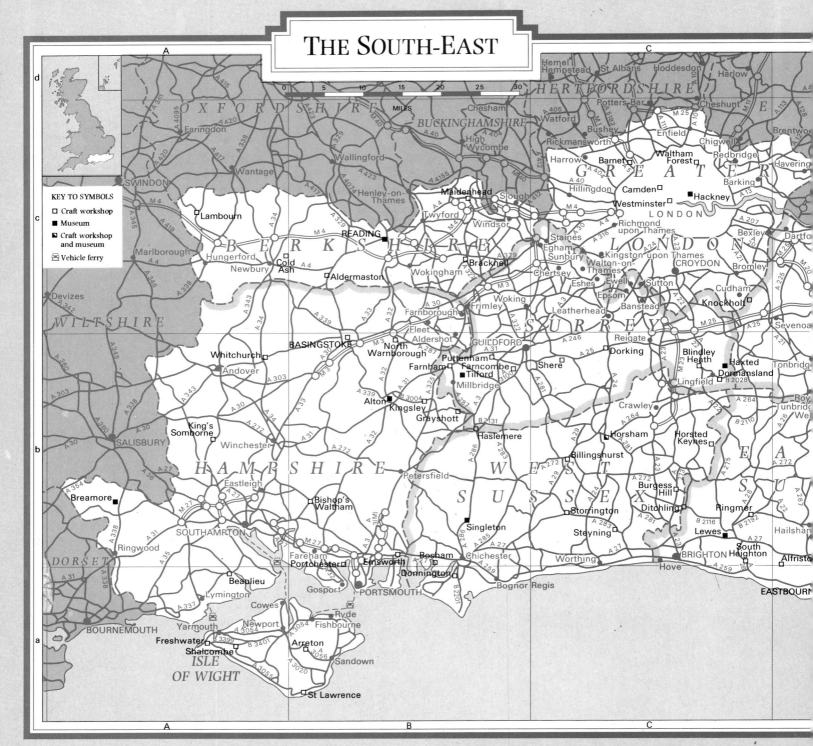

The varying landscapes of the South-east, and the region's position as 'Gateway to England', have nurtured a wide range of craftsmanship. In the muddy creeks of the Thames Estuary, barge-building and the old skills of sailmaking and spar-making are still remembered. Iron ore was mined, smelted and cast in the water-powered forges and furnaces of the Weald, while charcoal burners practised their craft in the Weald's wooded valleys until the 1950s or thereabouts. On the open downs, such ancient skills as those of the blacksmith and wheelwright were needed to make tools and wagons for the men who made lime by quarrying and burning chalk.

There are many workshops in the region, where craftsmen may still be seen at work. Skills less in evidence today, including those of the millwright and the charcoal burner, are featured in several museums.

BERKSHIRE

ALDERMASTON   Map ref: Bc
Aldermaston Pottery, Aldermaston, nr Reading.
Tel. Woolhampton 3359

(In centre of village, in main street. Parking outside.)

An 18th-century building of mellow red brick with low, beamed ceilings forms the central part of the pottery workshops. Craftsmen can be seen at work throwing on the wheel,

turning, handling, glazing and painting tin-glaze earthenware, and sometimes preparing a firing or unloading one of the kilns. Their work includes tall, hand-built vases, large dishes for festive occasions, and a selection of tableware. Some of the vessels are decorated with brushwork in a 'smoked lustre' technique, which gives a sheen of red-gold, orange or silvery iridescence. Others are painted with bold, abstract designs. The character of the work is distinctive and not often seen elsewhere.

Open daily except Sun., 8–5. By appointment only. Maximum of six people.

BRACKNELL   Map ref: Bc
South Hill Park Arts Centre, Bracknell.
Tel. Bracknell 27272
(1½ miles south of Bracknell, signposted from the A322. Large car park.)

An imposing Italianate mansion surrounded by 15 acres of parkland provides a splendid setting for the arts centre. A wide, sweeping staircase

leads to a number of craft workshops where relief and screen prints, silver jewellery, ceramic sculptures, and musical instruments such as lutes and harpsichords are made. Demonstrations of other crafts are organised, and regular exhibitions held. A craft shop has an attractive selection of goods.

Open Mon.–Fri., 9 a.m.–10.30 p.m.; Sat., 10 a.m.–10.30 p.m.; Sun., 12–10.30 p.m. Advisable to telephone to check when craftsmen are working. Shop open Mon.–Fri., 11–4, 7–10.30 p.m.; Sat. 12.30–2.30 and 7–10.30 p.m.

COLD ASH   Map ref: Ac
Alec McCurdy (Furniture maker), 'Woodland Leaves', Cold Ash, nr Newbury.
Tel. Thatcham 63258
(Towards north end of the hill leading through the main village street. Parking outside.)

Alec McCurdy trained as a furniture maker, and has had his own workshop since 1954.

events. Twice a week, a farrier comes from Hampshire to renew their quickly worn shoes – a daunting task, as these magnificent beasts stand up to 18 hands high and weigh around a ton. Visitors can watch them being shod during a tour of the stables.

Open daily (except Mon., unless this is a Bank Holiday), Mar.–Oct., 11–5. (Last admission at 4.) Charge for admission.

MUSEUM

READING   Map ref: Bc
Museum of English Rural Life.
(See panel on p. 240)

EAST SUSSEX

ALFRISTON   Map ref: Db
J. C. J. Pottery, Drusillas, nr Alfriston.
Tel. Alfriston 870234
(Signposted from A27 at roundabout junction with road to Alfriston.)

Cider jars, decanters, teapots and parsley pots are among the items visitors can see being hand-thrown by Jonathan Chiswell Jones. His work, which covers all kinds of domestic ware, is decorated in predominantly pale green and sandy-brown glazes. Next door to his studio is a leather workshop where customers can have their names tooled on to belts, bags, hats and purses, all of which are made and dyed on the premises. Also at Drusillas are a small zoo park with bears, monkeys and rare breeds of cattle, a miniature railway and a garden centre.

Pottery open Apr.–Oct., Mon.–Fri., 9–5.30; also Sun. afternoon between Apr. and Oct. Leather shop open 10–5.30.

DITCHLING   Map ref: Cb
The Craftsman Gallery, 8 High Street, Ditchling.
Tel. Hassocks 5246
(Car park beside village hall, east of High Street, on B2116.)

Besides displaying goods made by Sussex craftsmen, the gallery houses a small pottery workshop. The potter, Jill Pryke, makes earthenware pottery in a soft green glaze decorated with incised patterns which reveal two contrasting underglazes. Her work includes lanterns, vases, jugs, a variety of tableware, and commemorative plates and mugs. The other craft goods for sale include jewellery, corn dollies, copperwork, woodturnery, batik, weaving, and pottery from other Sussex potters. Craft exhibitions are held at the gallery several times a year.

Open Mon.–Sat., 10–1 and 2–5, but closed Wed. afternoon.

DITCHLING   Map ref: Cb
Veronica Prindl (Weaver), Wings Place, Ditchling.
Tel. Hassocks 2117
(Opposite the church. Parking in street or around green by the church.)

While living for several years in Japan, Veronica Prindl learned an ancient weaving technique known as 'ikat'. It involves immersing yarn in dye after it has been tied off at carefully calculated points, so that the undyed parts form the desired pattern as the cloth is woven. She uses this method to create delicate motifs in finely woven silk and woollen cloth. She weaves rugs, wall hangings, cloth for men's and women's suits, and mohair stoles. Her studio is in her home, a fine old timber-framed house, where she has assembled a small museum of old textiles and weaving equipment that she has collected from all over the world.

Individuals or small groups may visit, by appointment only.

EASTBOURNE   Map ref: Da
Isobel Kennett (Lacemaker), 34 Rise Park Gardens, Eastbourne.
Tel. Eastbourne 764717

(Off Langney Rise – B2104 – 2½ miles north-east of Eastbourne. Parking outside.)

Over the years, Isobel Kennett has built up a large collection of antique lace bobbins, some of which are carved of bone and decorated with brass or inscribed with verses. With these she can work fine linen or cotton thread into delicate and intricately patterned lace of all kinds, including the exceptionally fine Honiton. Lace edging, collars, bordered handkerchiefs, miniature lace pictures, and bridal crowns are among the items visitors can buy or order.

Open Mon.–Sat., 9–6, by appointment only. Maximum of ten people.

FAIRLIGHT   Map ref: Db
Olive Heaton Clarke, 'Junipers', Farley Way, Fairlight, nr Hastings.
Tel. Pett 3659
(From the Ore-Fairlight road turn right down Waites Lane, which is by the Fairlight Cove Hotel. Farley Way is first on the right.)

Peaceful Sussex landscapes and flower studies are captured on canvas by Mrs Heaton Clarke, who makes miniature embroidered collage pictures. She portrays the scenes by sewing together very fine materials such as silk, cotton and lace, and creates depth and texture by embroidering them with silk. From a distance, the completed pictures resemble water-colours. She works from her home, where the pictures are for sale.

Open most days. Advisable to make an appointment.

HASTINGS   Map ref: Db
J. C. L. Glasscraft, 23 Mount Pleasant Road, Hastings.
Tel. Hastings 434049
(Half mile north of town centre, near Ore Station. Parking in side street close by.)

Molten glass rods are drawn and manipulated into lively ornamental sculptures by a team of craftsmen. Visitors can watch the process through a window of the showroom and see graceful dancing figures, 'ring' trees, and bird cages with imprisoned, brightly coloured birds taking shape. There is also a display of glass ornaments by other craftsmen.

Open Mon.–Sat., 9–5.

HASTINGS   Map ref: Db
The Rushbrooke Studio-Gallery (Ceramics), 10 High Street, Hastings.
Tel. Hastings 428518
(Follow signs to the Old Town at eastern end of Hastings. Several car parks close by.)

In contrast to the modern method of producing large quantities of identical ceramic figures from moulds, every piece made at this studio is individually designed and modelled by hand. After being fired once, the details are painted on in vivid colours, then the figures are glazed before a final firing. The figures, which include witches, clowns, owls, cats and Old Town characters, all have different expressions and stances.

Open Mon.–Sat., 10–12.30 and 2.30–5.30, but closed Wed. afternoon.

RINGMER   Map ref: Cb
Elizabeth Clifford, 'Chapters', Bishops Lane, Ringmer, Lewes.
Tel. Ringmer 812588
(Approaching Ringmer from the north-east on the B2192, Bishops Lane is first turning on right after Green Man pub.)

An unusual feature of Mrs Clifford's hand-weaving is the use of dried grasses and seeds, which are interwoven with jute and flax to make lampshades. Working from home on a large loom of Columbian pine, she also weaves woollen skirt lengths with decorative borders, and wool, cotton or linen cloth which is made into dresses, skirts and waistcoats, or sold by the yard.

Open Mon.–Fri., 11–4, by appointment only. Maximum of four people.

His furniture is made from solid English timbers which he seasons himself, and he specialises in chests of drawers and cabinets in well-figured walnut and cherry. But when his daughter asked for a cello he decided to make one for her. He was so successful that he now makes these beautiful instruments on commission. He uses spruce and sycamore for the body and scroll, and coco bolo (a Central American hardwood) for the pegs and tailpiece. As almost everything is crafted by hand, each cello can take up to 750 hours to complete.

People who wish to see Mr McCurdy at work should telephone for an appointment.

LAMBOURN   Map ref: Ac
E. J. Wicks (Saddlers), 1 Newbury Street, Lambourn.
Tel. Lambourn 71766
(Next to George Inn at crossroads in town centre. Parking by church.)

Lambourn is an important racehorse-training centre, with around 2,000 thoroughbreds stabled near by. It is not surprising that this small family firm specialises in light race saddles, many of which have been ordered by such champion jockeys as Lester Piggott, Pat Eddery and John Francome. Made from top-quality pigskin and cowhide, some weigh as little as 10 oz. The saddlery, which has been in business since the turn of the century, makes riding tack of all kinds.

Open Mon.–Fri., 8–5.30, Sat., 8.30–12.30.

MAIDENHEAD   Map ref: Bc
Courage Shire Horse Centre, Cherry Garden Lane, Maidenhead Thicket, Maidenhead.
Tel. Littlewick Green 3917
(On A4, 2½ miles west of Maidenhead. Large car park.)

A collection of old photographs at the centre recalls the days when heavy horses pulling brewery drays were a familiar sight. Courage stopped using shires for their deliveries in the early 1950s, and those stabled here compete at major horse shows and take part in publicity

Map ref: Bc

Museum of English Rural Life

READING, BERKSHIRE

The main purpose of this superb museum is to keep alive the history of hundreds of years of farming experience. The displays of tools, photographs and models which lead visitors through the farming year – from hedging and ditching, ploughing, cultivating and seeding through to harvesting, threshing and milling – could hardly provide a better introduction.

Farming by hand died hard in many parts of the country. A wooden seedlip, for sowing broadcast, was still being used in Berkshire in the 1930s. But, as the museum shows, machines were taking over elsewhere. There are early seed drills, a threshing machine, a horse-powered grain processor, a magnificent late 19th-century steam lawn-mower and the earliest-known surviving steam cultivating gear.

The museum houses the finest collection of wagons and ploughs in the country. They come from all over England and include a miller's wagon, a bow wagon and the 'hermaphrodite' – so called because it could be converted from a four-wheeled wagon to a two-wheeled cart. The museum also has the most comprehensive collection of baskets in Britain.

Displays of tools and products embrace a wide range of rural occupations – bee-keeping, animal husbandry, thatching, stonemasonry, saddlery, brick-making,

EARLY MOWER *Steam-powered machine of around 1890.*

blacksmithing and wheelwrighting. The hunter's display comprises an awesome array of instruments. It includes traps for badgers, otters, moles and men, and various alarm guns that were triggered by a trip wire.

University of Reading, Whiteknights, Reading, Berkshire. Tel. Reading 85123

Open Tues.–Fri., 10–4.30; Sat., 10–1 and 2–4.30. Closed on Bank Holidays and between Christmas and New Year.

PLOUGHING BY STEAM *A stationary engine and cable-drawn plough at work during the 19th century.*

RYE Map ref: Db
Rye Pottery, 77 Ferry Road, Rye.
Tel. Rye 3363
(Turning next to railway station. Pottery is close to Ferry Boat Inn. Parking in road.)

In the 17th century, Dutch potters introduced to England a form of decoration known as delftware, or majolica, whereby coloured oxides were painted on to a layer of opaque tin glaze before firing. This method is used at Rye Pottery to adorn a variety of tableware with cheerful floral motifs or stripes on a white background. Visitors can see the pottery being made in the workshop, which lies behind the showroom.

Showroom open Mon.–Sat., 9.30–5.30. Workshop open Mon.–Fri.; closed first two weeks in Aug.

RYE Map ref: Db
Rye Tiles, The Old Brewery, Wishward, Rye.
Tel. Rye 3038
(Wishward is a turning by the Pipemaker's Arms on main road through Rye. Parking near by.)

Hand-painted and silk-screened ceramic tiles are made by this small company, which belongs to the Cole family who own Rye Pottery. The range includes a series with flowers painted in soft colours on a white glaze. Customers may order tiles in any design and colour to match or complement their home decoration. The main showroom is in London, at 12 Connaught Street, W2, but callers to the Rye premises can buy small quantities of tiles and may sometimes see tiles being decorated.

Open Mon.–Fri., 9.30–5; Sat., 11–4.30.

RYE Map ref: Db
David Sharp (Ceramics), 55 The Mint, Rye.
Tel. Rye 2620
(Opposite Rye Tiles – see previous entry. Parking near by.)

In the past, when smuggling was rife, this building was used as a bonded store for contraband. Nowadays it houses a pottery which produces large porcelain animals, as well as making goblets and house-name plaques to order. The pottery is hand-thrown, or cast in moulds from original designs by David Sharp. Artists can be seen painting the pieces.

Open Mon.–Sat., 9–5.

SOUTH HEIGHTON Map ref: Cb
South Heighton Pottery, Grange Farm, South Heighton, Newhaven.
Tel. Newhaven 4408

(Just off the A26 at north-west end of village. Parking outside.)

A journey across the Sahara Desert and other parts of Africa has had a strong influence on the work of potters Ursula Mommens and Chris Lewis. This is reflected in the incised or painted ethnic patterns on many of their pieces. Most of the pottery, which ranges from casseroles to cider jars, is decorated with glazes containing wood ash from local apple orchards.

Open Mon.–Fri., 2–5, by appointment only.

MUSEUM

LEWES Map ref: Cb
Anne of Cleves House, 52 Southover High Street, Lewes.
Tel. Lewes 4610

When Henry VIII divorced Anne of Cleves he gave her this 16th-century house as part of the settlement. It now houses rooms furnished as they would have been at that time, and displays on local history, trades and crafts. One gallery is devoted to the Wealden iron industry.

The museum houses possibly the only surviving cannon-boring bar in the world. It is part of a reconstruction showing how a water-wheel would have rotated the bar in order to bore a hole for the barrel of a cannon. Another reconstruction shows a large water-driven tilt hammer. There is also a sectional model of a gun-casting pit of the 17th century.

Open mid-Feb.–Nov., Mon.–Sat., 10–5. From Apr.–Oct., also open Sun., 2–5.

GREATER LONDON

BARNET Map ref: Cc
Boosey & Hawkes (Musical Instruments) Ltd, Deansbrook Road, Edgware.
Tel. (01) 952 7711
(Deansbrook Road meets A5 from the east. Next to hospital. Street-side parking.)

Brass and woodwind instruments of all shapes, sizes and sounds are exported to the four corners of the earth from Boosey & Hawkes' Edgware factory. They are manufactured through a combination of the finest traditional craftsmanship with the most recent methods of engineering. On a two-hour tour of the company's multi-workshop industrial complex, visitors may see processes as diverse as the bending of brass tubes by means of hydraulic pressure and the hand-shaping of tuba bells.

Open Wed., 10–2 for group visits by musicians or for educational purposes. Appointment necessary. Closed last week of July and first week of Aug.

CAMDEN Map ref: Cc
Camden Lock (Craft Centre), Commercial Place, Camden Town, NW1.
Tel. (01) 485 7963
(Access by Commercial Place, which meets A502 [Chalk Farm Road] from west just north of lock and market. Near Camden Town Underground station.)

Skilled craftsmanship has flourished at North London's Camden Lock since 1971. In that year, craftsmen first moved into a collection of old timber-yard buildings congregated around a spur of the Regents Canal. Since then the lock has become London's leading craft centre.

Among the original craftsmen and women still there are Ivan Foster, who works in pine, and Janet Semmens, who decorates blinds by hand. However, the number and variety of crafts have increased considerably, and there are now about 30 different craftsmen covering – in addition – stained glass and engraved glass, weaving, jewellery, pottery, cane work, individually designed clothes, children's toys and games, architectural models, sculpture, knitwear, leatherwork, hand-painted silk, and musical instruments.

Advisable to telephone first to see individual craftsmen. The Lock Shop is open daily.

WALTHAM FOREST Map ref: Cc
The Handweavers Studio and Gallery Ltd, 29 Haroldstone Road, E17.
Tel. (01) 521 2281
(Haroldstone Road lies west of and parallel to Blackhorse Road [A1006], near St James's Street British Rail station.)

With a creak and a clatter, the spinning-wheels and looms of the Handweavers Studio and Gallery come to life at weekends. This is when small groups of students from all parts of London make their way to Walthamstow for instruction from two members of London's Guild of Spinners, Weavers and Dyers. Spinners may be using simple wooden spindles or wheels. Weavers learn on several small table-looms and a folding floor-loom.

Open Tues.–Thur. and Sat., 10–5; Fri., 10–9; Sun. by appointment.

WESTMINSTER Map ref: Cc
The Glasshouse, 65 Long Acre, Covent Garden, WC2.
Tel. (01) 836 9785
(On south side of Long Acre, near Covent Garden Underground station.)

Among the choice glass specimens blown by the five Glasshouse artists are distinctively shaped bottles, paperweights, drinking vessels and bowls. Each craftsman, employing his or her individual techniques, blows and shapes such pieces before a large double pot furnace in full view of visitors in the display gallery. From this Covent Garden studio, objets d'art go to homes and exhibitions throughout Europe and the United States.

Open Mon.–Fri., 10–5.30; Sat., 11–4. Closed Bank Holidays.

MUSEUM

HACKNEY Map ref: Cc
Geffrye Museum, Kingsland Road, London E2.
Tel. (01) 739 8368
(On east side of Kingsland Road [A10], which runs between eastern end of Old Street and Dalston Junction Station. Underground at Old Street station.)

The Geffrye Museum stands as an appropriate monument to the strong ties between Shoreditch and woodworking, which have extended from the Regency period to the present day. Situated in a shaded garden and occupying a terrace of early 18th-century almshouses, the museum holds a fine collection of English furniture and cabinet-making tools. Also on show are jewellery and portraits.

Immediately upon entering the museum, a Georgian shopfront, taken from Narrow Street, Limehouse, comes into view. Behind this façade an authentic woodworker's shop of the 1700s has been reconstructed. Scattered on the bench, wall and floor are many wooden hand tools of the carpenter's trade: a pole lathe, planes, gouges, saws and clamps.

In one corner rests the most treasured possession of the typical 18th-century woodworker – an inlaid tool chest. Until the 20th century, such boxes and tools, which were intended to last a lifetime, were made by all young apprentices aspiring to become master woodworkers.

The Geffrye Museum exhibits not only the tools of the English furniture maker, but also his handiwork. The row of almshouses have been faithfully converted into various period rooms, reflecting the evolution of English furniture from 1600 to the 1930s.

Open Tues.–Sat., 10–5; Sun. and Bank Holiday Mon., 2–5. Closed Dec. 24–26 and New Year's Day.

HAMPSHIRE

BASINGSTOKE Map ref: Bb
Viables Centre, Harrow Way, Basingstoke.
Tel. Basingstoke 3634
(Harrow Way is between A339 Alton road and A30 Winchester road. Car park on site.)

A part of old Basingstoke has been preserved at the Viables Centre, on the edge of this busy town. Converted farm buildings provide a natural and pleasant location for local craftsmen and women, producing pottery, gold and silver work, furniture, engraved glass, leatherwork, picture frames, woodturnery, screen-printed fabrics, paintings, model soldiers, carved candles, and metal engravings.

A craft fair is held usually in May. Craftsmen are invited from all over southern England to demonstrate their skills.

Centre open all year, Tues.–Sun., 2–5. The various craftsmen work at different times and on different days, but there is generally some activity in progress that is of interest to visitors.

BEAULIEU Map ref: Aa
Kristen Pottery, High Street, Beaulieu.
Tel. Beaulieu 612064
(Situated in main street. Car park behind main street.)

In these days of mass-production, many potteries turning out decorative figures use moulds to form the shapes. But at the Kristen Pottery each piece – clown, animal or bird – is made by hand. In the collection, hedgehogs, tortoises and birds are made to hold small posies of dried flowers. Piggy banks, hippo banks, pomanders and terracotta woodland lamps are also on display, together with a range of domestic ware.

Open daily, 10–5.30.

BISHOP'S WALTHAM Map ref: Bb
The Old Granary Art and Craft Centre, Bank Street, Bishop's Waltham, Southampton.
Tel. Bishop's Waltham 4700/4595
(Situated on corner of Brook Street and Bank Street. Free car park opposite the Craft Centre.)

During this building's 200 year history it has served as a wheelwright's shop, a wine cellar and a miller's store. The arched doorways were designed to admit a horse and cart. Today, more than a dozen craft workers use the old granary to demonstrate their skills. On three storeys, visitors can see hand-dyed knitwear, fashion and textile design, porcelain sculptures, patchwork, violin-making, gold and silver jewellery, models of trains and submarines, leatherwork and period dolls' houses. Part of the top floor has been partitioned off into a gallery, where frequent exhibitions of paintings and contemporary prints are on show. The products of cottage industries from a 30 mile radius are for sale in the craft shop next to the pottery.

Open all year, Tues.–Sat., 10–5.

EMSWORTH Map ref: Bb
Trevor Ellis (Woodcarver), Emsworth Yacht Harbour, Thorney Road, Emsworth.
Tel. Emsworth 2526
(Yacht Harbour signposted from A27 on Thorney Island turn-off. Parking available on site.)

In the days when Britannia ruled the waves, brightly painted figureheads took their proud place on the prows of sailing ships. Trevor Ellis claims to be one of only three woodcarvers in the country who still produce these masterpieces. One of his figureheads, a 4½ cwt. unicorn, resplendent in gold leaf and dazzling white paint, was made to grace the bow of the old frigate Unicorn. His other speciality is the ornately decorated prosceniums and figures for fairground organs. As well as doing large-scale carving, Mr Ellis works on rudderheads, sternboards, tillers and yacht name-boards.

Open all year, Mon.–Fri., 1–4. By appointment only.

GRAYSHOTT Map ref: Bb
Surrey Ceramic Co. Ltd, Grayshott Pottery, School Road, Grayshott, Hindhead.
Tel. Hindhead 4404
(Off main street through village. Car park on site.)

Robust country-style pottery is made in a large workshop by craftsmen using a variety of methods – wheel-throwing, slip-casting, jiggering, jolleying, and wet-clay pressing. The pots are decorated with painted designs or with transfers that are fixed on to the glaze during firing. The finished products are for sale in a showroom, beside those of many other crafts.

Pottery open all year except Bank Holidays, Mon.–Fri., 9–1 and 2–5. Shop open Mon.–Sat., 9–5. Parties by appointment only.

KING'S SOMBORNE Map ref: Ab
Barker and Geary Ltd, Arts, Crafts and Fencing Centre, Romsey Road, King's Somborne.
Tel. King's Somborne 205
(Situated in main street. Parking available.)

The weaving of wattle hurdles, to pen sheep and cattle, is one of the oldest woodland crafts in Britain. It has been going on for well over 1,000 years, and Barker and Geary follow the methods used by the Saxons. The fences are on show, but visitors are not able to see them being made as this is done on site, near the local hazel coppices. Members of the Barker family also carve stools, tables and wall plaques out of elm, and a small section of the showroom is divided off for this activity. Displayed around the room is a large assortment of craft products, including pottery, wrought iron, copper and brass items, wickerwork and baskets. Old pieces of horses' harness hang on the walls.

Open all year, Mon.–Fri., 9–5; Sat., 9–12; Sun., 2–5.

KINGSLEY Map ref: Bb
The Crystal Forge, Cold Harbour Farm, Kingsley, nr Bordon.
Tel. Bordon 4106
(Take road signposted Cold Harbour, off B3004 on common at Kingsley. Parking available on premises.)

Glass-making in Britain began in the south-east seven centuries ago. Ray and Lesley Gannon have brought it back to the region, after extensive research that took them to America, Sweden, Czechoslovakia, Italy and France. Mr Gannon re-learned the old techniques that had spread far afield. At the Crystal Forge he uses traditional methods to make clear crystal glass, creating a range of glass pieces, from perfume bottles and paperweights to sculpture.

Open by appointment only.

NORTH WARNBOROUGH Map ref: Bb
Bartley Heath Pottery, North Warnborough, Odiham.
Tel. Odiham 2163
(Take Junction 5 off M3, towards Odiham. First turning on left off first roundabout. Parking outside pottery.)

Casseroles, goblets, mugs, jugs, teapots, coffee sets and plant pots, and all the products of the potter's art, are on display at the Bartley Heath Pottery. The potters, Lesley and Michael Dixon, may be watched at work through a window when they are throwing pots. Most of the pieces have an oatmeal finish with a traditional glaze. They will make pottery to order.

Open all year, Mon.–Sat., 9.30–6. Other times by appointment.

PORTCHESTER Map ref: Bb
'Anahid' (Miniatures), 164 Castle Street, Portchester, Fareham.
Tel. Cosham 376289
(Situated on east side of Castle Street, near Portchester Castle. Unrestricted parking.)

Anahid, an Armenian, came to her unusual craft of decorating semi-precious stones with wildlife scenes by way of painting pebbles she picked up on the beach. Her miniatures have a delicacy that echoes the beauty of the materials she uses – agate, jade, turquoise, tiger's eye, mother of pearl and coral. Many of her paintings are less than ½ in. across, and they decorate pendants, ear-rings, cuff-links, brooches, paper knives, book markers, napkin rings and pill boxes. Larger slices of translucent agates are turned into ornamental plaques, and the play of light through the stone gives her wildlife scenes a unique beauty.

Open daily, except when away at exhibitions. Appointment necessary.

WHITCHURCH Map ref: Ab
James W. Potter & Sons (Cutlery), 10–12 Newbury Street, Whitchurch.
Tel. Whitchurch 2983
(From Market Square, turn north up Newbury Street. Shop situated 50 yds from square on right. Free car parks in town.)

Almost all British cutlery is nowadays factory-made. But at Whitchurch, the Potter family – three generations of cutlers – keep alive a centuries-old tradition of making forks and spoons by hand. The metal they use is sterling silver, and most of their work is done on commission. To turn a length of silver into, say, a spoon, involves beating, quenching, forging, shaping, decorating and polishing. Each piece is sent to the Assay Office in London to be hallmarked and tested for purity. The style of decoration depends on the wishes of the customer, but Georgian designs are among the most popular. The Potters also provide a repair service for antique cutlery.

Open all year. Shop: Mon.–Fri., 9–1 and 2–5.45. Closed all day Wed. Workshop: by appointment only.

MUSEUMS

ALTON Map ref: Bb
The Curtis Museum, High Street, Alton.
Tel. Alton 82802

Anyone interested in practical details of rural crafts is bound to enjoy a visit to the Curtis Museum. A gallery has been set aside to depict and explain how the cooper makes his barrels; how the glazier, making leaded lights, fits the glass into the lead cames which frame the panes; and how a wandering millstone dresser used to earn his living. There are also displays of the work of the clock maker, the mason, the brickmaker, the thatcher, the saddler, the shoe maker, the rake maker and the broom squire.

A cast-iron printing press, made in the early 1800s, dominates the room. It is magnificently ornate, and crowned with an eagle. Near by, there is a knife-sharpening machine that used to be wheeled about the streets by a cutler.

The museum also houses a saddler's flock-teasing machine to card the wool with which saddles were stuffed. Because of the tearing and rending noises emitted as the nails teased the wool, the machine was often known as a saddler's devil. A clay-pipe machine is on view, consisting of a vice, a mould and a plunger which was lowered to form the bowl of the pipe. A long, oiled needle was passed down the stem of the pipe to make the hole before the soft Cornish clay was fired.

Open Mon.–Sat., 10–5. Admission free.

BREAMORE Map ref: Ab
Breamore Countryside Museum, Breamore.
Tel. Downton 22468

Visitors to this imaginative museum are guided through the four seasons of the farming year. Each display consists of old hand tools and machines appropriate to the season – ploughs in winter, harrows and seed drills in spring, scythes and sickles in summer, threshing tools in autumn. The museum also houses a full-sized thatched cottage, a dairy, a brewery, a wheelwright's shop, a saddler's and bootmaker's shop, and a forge complete with tools. All have a truly authentic appearance, down to the smoke that has blackened the walls of the forge.

Opening times and other details may change. Check by telephone before making a special journey. 241

An enormous barn houses a collection of 20th-century agricultural machinery, including a 1926 'Dreadnought' – a general-purpose steam-powered traction engine – in its original livery.

Open Apr.–Sept., Tues., Wed., Thur., Sat. and Sun., 2–5.30. Charge for admission.

ISLE OF WIGHT

ARRETON   Map ref: Ba
The Haseley Pottery, Haseley Manor, Arreton, nr Newport.
Tel. Arreton 420
(Signposted off the A3056 south of Arreton. Parking on site.)

Haseley Manor dates back to Saxon times, and in its long history has been owned by four kings – Harold, William I, William II and Henry VIII. Ray and Krys Young have established their pottery in a long, low building near the house, used at one time as an open cart shed. All the pieces produced are both functional and decorative. Tea and coffee sets, mugs, jugs, bowls and flower pots are made in five basic colours and a limited number of combinations so that visitors can add to their existing sets over the years.

Open daily, Easter to end Oct., 10–6; rest of year, Mon.–Fri., 10–5.

ARRETON   Map ref: Ba
Isle of Wight Country Craft Workshops, Arreton Manor Farm, Arreton.
Tel. Newport 528353
(On main Newport-Sandown road [A3056] at Arreton. Car park on site.)

The old stone barns of Arreton Manor Farm – structures spanning some eight centuries – are being converted into workshops for local craftsmen. One barn is set out as a street of shops, where the crafts practised range from leather carving to the manufacture of rocking-horses. In the pottery shop, children can try their hand at throwing clay on a wheel. In another barn, visitors can see woodworkers, a blacksmith, and a boatbuilder who makes clinker-built dinghies – a construction method dating back to the Vikings.

Open all year, Mon.–Fri., 10–5.30; also Sun. afternoons, 2–5.30.

FRESHWATER   Map ref: Aa
Island Glass, London House, Queen's Road, Freshwater.
Tel. Freshwater 3473
(Queen's Road is off the main road through Freshwater at Moa Place. Parking in Queen's Road.)

Broad, swirling bands of colour lie trapped between layers of clear glass in the bottles, bowls and other glassware created by Michael Rayner. He uses a centuries-old technique to achieve this 'sandwich' effect. First he takes a gather of molten glass from the furnace on the end of a hollow pipe. He rolls the glass in brilliantly coloured powder, then returns the pipe to a crucible of molten glass in the furnace, where it is coated with another layer of clear glass. The glass is then ready to be blown, pulled and twisted into shape. Mr Rayner's showroom is an enchanted place, for his glassware is shot through with all the colours of the rainbow.

Open all year, Mon.–Sat., 9.30–1 and 2–5.30, excluding Bank Holidays. Glass making may be watched when in progress.

FRESHWATER   Map ref: Aa
Island Pottery Studio, School Green Road, Freshwater.
Tel. Freshwater 2356
(On main road through village [A3055] near library. Public car park near by. Private lay-by at studio.)

Joe Lester, later joined by his son Joe, revived craft pottery in the Isle of Wight when it was in the doldrums after the Second World War. In 1953 he set up a small studio where the public could watch him throwing pots. He trained other potters and established similar studios, which developed under his supervision, in other parts of the island. Working in white Devon clays, Mr Lester produces gift-ware such as mugs, jugs, bowls, goblets and ashtrays. Many of these are embellished with sea-horses or other animals, and glazed in bright translucent colours.

Open all year, Mon.–Fri., 10–12 and 2–4.

Appointment necessary for parties of more than six.

ST LAWRENCE   Map ref: Ba
Isle of Wight Studio Glass Limited, Old Park, St Lawrence, Ventnor.
Tel. Ventnor 853526
(Off A3055. Signposted from St Lawrence Inn, in village. Car park on site.)

In a 200-year-old barn, a small team of glass-blowers demonstrate their skills. Swirling colours follow the contours of delicately shaped vases, bowls and bottles. Other pieces are decorated with 22 carat gold and sterling silver leaf fused on to the glass in random patterns: a form of surface decoration unique to the studio.

Studio open all year, Mon.–Fri., 8.30–12 and 1–4. Showroom open all year, Mon.–Fri., 9–5; also June–Sept., Sat. and Sun., 10–1 and 2–5.

SHALCOMBE   Map ref: Aa
Chessell Pottery, Chessell, nr Yarmouth.
Tel. Calbourne 248
(On Newport-Freshwater road at junction of B3399 and B3401 at Shalcombe. Parking outside pottery.)

Sheila Francis was so struck by the myriad shapes and colours of the coral reefs, rock pools and fungi of Africa, where she lived for 15 years, that she now re-creates these natural forms in her pottery. Miniature water gardens, vases shaped like pebbles, table-lamps and candleholders all form part of her output of porcelain. Pieces from the Chessell Pottery are exported all over the world, as well as selling through outlets in the British Isles.

Open daily, 9–5; closed Sat. afternoons and Sun. from Oct.–Apr.

KENT

BAPCHILD   Map ref: Dc
Old Mill, Tonge, Sittingbourne.
Tel. Sittingbourne 78300
(Two miles east of Sittingbourne, north off the A2 at Bapchild. Car park on site.)

The weatherboarded mill stands beside the

stream that once powered it. But its outbuildings have taken on a new lease of life as the home of a number of craft shops. In the converted stables, visitors can see macrame lampshades and traditional patchwork cushions being made. They are for sale alongside pottery, jewellery and engraved glass by other Kent craftsmen. Goldwork panels are sewn in the mill house, and it is sometimes possible to see this demonstrated.

Open Easter to end Dec., Mon.–Fri., 1.30–5.30; Sat and during school holidays, 10–5.30.

BENOVER   Map ref: Db
JUDU Crafts (Spinning and weaving), The Old Granary, New Barns Farm, Benover, Yalding.
Tel. Collier Street 474
(Short way down lane to Hunton, which is signposted off B2162 between Collier Street and Yalding. Parking outside.)

The Wyatt family keep Romney sheep for their long, lustrous fleece, which is spun into a fine knitting yarn. They also keep Suffolks whose fleeces make a stronger wool more suitable for the rugs Mrs Wyatt weaves on an upright loom. As well as spinning and weaving, she produces enamelled copper jewellery, pictures and decorative boxes. Her mother makes colourful batik wall-hangings, and paints landscapes in oils and watercolours.

Open daily, May–Sept., 10–4. By appointment only.

BIDDENDEN   Map ref: Db
Wincraft Studio (Spinning and weaving), 20 High Street, Biddenden.
Tel. Biddenden 291339
(In centre of village. Car park signposted 30 yds away.)

In medieval and Tudor times, Biddenden was a centre for clothiers, and many of their timber-framed cottages still line the main village street. At Wincraft Studio, itself a much altered weaver's cottage, spinning and weaving are being practised once again. Fleeces from Jacob, Romney and Shetland sheep are spun into wool on an Ashford spinning-wheel. While some of the wool is sold as knitting yarn, it is used mainly for crochet shawls and general knitwear, and to add textural interest to wall-hangings and rugs. The textiles – chiefly skirt lengths and rugs – are woven on a four-shaft treadle-loom. Commissions are accepted. The studio also provides an outlet for a wide range of Kent crafts.

Open Mon.–Sat., 9–5.30; Sun., 2–5.30. Closed Wed. afternoon.

CANTERBURY   Map ref: Ec
Canterbury Pottery, 38A Burgate, Canterbury.
(Opposite main entrance to cathedral. Several car parks in city centre.)

Two contrasting methods of decorating pots are used at Canterbury Pottery. Wood-ash glazes give varied, muted tones to stoneware garden pots, tableware, umbrella stands and lamp bases, while a totally different effect is created for porcelain commemorative plates and mugs by painting them with lustrous enamels. The pottery is displayed on three floors of a tall, narrow building, and also in a small roof garden.

Open Mon.–Sat., 9.15–6; Sun. and Bank Holidays, 10.30–6.

CANTERBURY   Map ref: Ec
The Old Weavers House Ltd, 1 Kings Bridge, Canterbury.
Tel. Canterbury 62329
(In town centre where St Peter Street joins High Street. Public car park near by.)

This striking black-and-white timber-framed building, which fronts on to the River Stour, is believed to have been a centre for Flemish weavers who fled to the England of Elizabeth I to escape persecution by the Catholics. It is

---

Map ref: Cb

The Watermill Museum

HAXTED, SURREY

Created in 1949 inside a 300-year-old mill that was nearly derelict, this was the first water-mill museum to be established in Britain. Foundations of an even older 14th-century mill can still be seen. Now with everything restored to full working order, the air pulsates with the whirring of wheels, belts and mill-stones.

Upstream, three quarters of a mile of the River Eden is dammed up to around 10 ft above its normal level. As it cascades through the mill-race, it drives an overshot wheel, attached by a shaft to the pit wheel inside. Here, a farm mill, which would have been used for producing cattle feed, can be seen working.

Other exhibits include the original oak undershot wheel from a Sussex mill; engines that were used in larger commercial mills to supplement water power; tools for dressing the stones; wooden cogs from the days before the use of cast iron; and a hydraulic water-level control from Christmas Mill in Edenbridge.

Everything in this inventive museum illustrates beautifully the working of water-mills. At the touch of a button the visitor can operate a working model of Castle Mill at Dorking. Another model shows how grindstones work: as the upper stone revolves, the scissors action of its furrows grinds the corn, which is fed in at the centre, and sweeps the resulting flour to the outside of the stones and into the surrounding vat.

A slide show and commentary tells the history of water-

MATCHING EXTENSION *The left-hand wing was built on an oak frame in the 17th century. The other, framed in pitch pine, was completed a century later.*

mills and of the Wealden iron industry, to which a gallery of the museum is devoted. Several hundred years ago all the iron forges and furnaces were driven by water-wheels, and it was only in the 18th century, when the industry declined, that many water-mills became corn-mills.

Haxted Mill, Haxted, Surrey. Tel. Edenbridge 862914
(Two miles west of Edenbridge, on minor road to Lingfield.)

Open weekends and on Bank Holidays from Easter until end of Sept., 11–6. Also July–Sept., Mon.–Thur., 2–6. Small charge for admission.

Map ref: Bb

Old Kiln Museum

TILFORD, SURREY

In the 10 acres of garden, arboretum and woodland that comprise the museum, visitors can see and handle old agricultural implements and machines – now restored – from farms all over the country. There are several ancient buildings, including a smithy. Each year, on a Sunday in July, some 20 different craftsmen may be seen at work.

In a reconstructed farmhouse kitchen, the visitor gets the feeling of walking back into the early years of the century. Next door to the smithy, a hop-bagging machine, made in 1880, has been set up. Baskets of hops, together with wooden implements and sacking, infuse the room with the feel of the countryside.

The wheelwright's shop, full of wheels of every size, has a fine collection of tools, including a jarvis for shaping the spokes and a boxing engine for cutting out the centre of the hub.

A little corrugated-iron caravan is the home of a shepherd. The bed is lovingly made and the table laid; the boots stand by the stove and the sheep-shears, smock and a turnip knife hang on the wall.

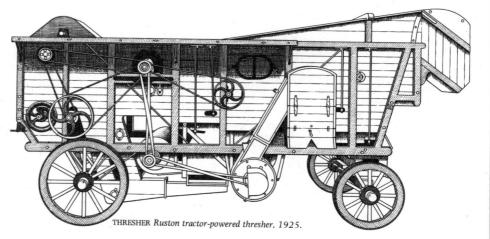

THRESHER *Ruston tractor-powered thresher, 1925.*

Numerous kinds of farm machines and hand tools are on display. Rows of hay rakes, harrows, ploughs, cultivators, tedders, potato lifters, winnowing machines, rollers and swathe-turners line one entire field. In another stands a wooden elevator, used to build corn and hay stacks.

Reeds Road, Tilford, Farnham, Surrey. Tel. Frensham 2300.
(On minor road off A287 Millbridge-Tilford road.)

Open Apr.–Sept., Wed.–Sun. and Bank Holidays, 11–6. Charge for admission.

---

now a craft centre which has revived its past traditions in a room equipped with old looms and spinning-wheels. Here, a weaver can often be seen at work. In another section, visitors can try their hand at brass rubbing from a choice of facsimile brasses. A craft shop on the ground floor of the building sells hand-woven clothing, brass rubbings, pottery and other craft goods.

Open daily in summer, 9.30–5.30; Mon.–Sat., in winter, 11.30–5. No brass rubbing from Nov. to Easter. Appointment necessary for parties of more than ten people.

FOLKESTONE Map ref: Eb
Prima Pottery, 19–21 The Old High Street, Folkestone.
Tel. Folkestone 56469
(Near the harbour front. Several car parks in town centre.)

In a narrow cobbled street which winds down towards the harbour, a glass-fronted studio displays an assortment of pots made by Marcus and Sally Goldberger. They can be seen throwing and decorating earthenware, ranging from coffee sets in green, blue, dark brown and sand colours to textured vases. These are painted whilst on the wheel to create a coloured 'ridge' effect.

Open May–Sept., Mon.–Sat., 9.30–6; Oct.–Apr., Mon.–Sat., 10–5.30, but closed on Wed. during winter.

KNOCKHOLT Map ref: Cc
The Forge, Panfield Cottage, Burlings Lane, Knockholt, Sevenoaks.
Tel. Knockholt 32068
(Burlings Lane is the first turning after the Tally Ho pub on the Knockholt–Cudham road, 2 miles from village centre. Parking in drive outside forge.)

Mr Knight makes mostly screens, house signs and fire-grates. Horses' heads, resembling the knight pieces in chess, decorate some of his firedogs. He works to commission, designing and forging traditional and more modern wrought ironwork – including fireplace screens which can be ordered with embroidery panels sewn by his wife.

Open Mon.–Fri., 8–6; Sat., 8–12. By appointment only.

MAIDSTONE Map ref: Dc
The John Solly Pottery, 36 London Road, Maidstone.

Tel. Maidstone 54623
(On A20 close to Maidstone West station, next to White Horse Inn. Room for five cars in drive.)

A whitewashed Victorian building, formerly a basket works, houses the pottery John Solly started 30 years ago. He makes slip-decorated high-fired earthenware, using 12 different glazes and slips to produce a wide colour range. Gallon-sized wine jars, goblets, large plates, bowls and vases are among the items for sale. Over the years he has passed on his skills to more than 1,200 students, who come from all over the world to learn the craft from him at the pottery.

Open Mon.–Fri., 9.30–6, when courses are not being held. Open Sat. all year. By appointment only. Maximum of six visitors at any one time.

PRESTON Map ref: Ec
Maureen Duck and Tony Benham (Potters), Preston House, Preston, Canterbury.
Tel. Preston (Kent) 324
(In main street of village, next to post office. Parking in street.)

The most primitive pottery technique is that of building or modelling clay by hand. It is also the most flexible method, and is used by Maureen Duck to create intricate waterfall sculptures and unusual textured containers for plants and grasses. She shares a spacious garden studio with Tony Benham, whose terrace pots, bonsai containers and large vases and bottles are thrown on a wheel. The pottery is fired in a wood-burning kiln and the ash gives it varied 'smoky' tones.

Open by appointment only.

SELLINDGE Map ref: Eb
Tim Huckstepp Pottery, 1 Hawthorn Barrow Hill, Sellindge.
Tel. Sellindge 2204
(On west side of A20 approaching Sellindge from Folkestone. Room for three cars in drive.)

A long, low stone building which used to be the village bakery nowadays serves as Tim Huckstepp's pottery studio. He makes a range of pottery, including vases decorated with flower motifs, clay clocks (clocks with pottery cases), and casseroles, plates, mugs and bowls in oatmeal glazed stoneware.

Open all year, Mon.–Fri., 9–6. Advisable to telephone first.

MERSHAM Map ref: Eb
Swanton Mill, Mersham, Ashford.
Tel. Aldington 223

The restoration work on this water-mill won a European architectural award for its owner, Mrs Christiansen. It had been derelict for years, but its exterior now presents a delightful cluster of red tiles and white-painted weatherboard. The mill stands at the edge of a garden, where the overflow from the mill-stream sometimes courses through the part set aside as a water garden.

Parts of Swanton Mill date from the Middle Ages, while an earlier mill on the same site is referred to in the Domesday survey. Since the East Stour River runs in a deep channel at this point, there is no need for a large mill-pond or artificial embankments. There are heavy wooden sluice gates of the old variety and, downstream, an eel trap where eels are caught in the spring and autumn.

Inside, strategically placed spotlights and transparent panes enable visitors to see exactly how the pit wheel, the gears and the machinery work. Mrs Christiansen grows and grinds her own wheat, and the flour can be purchased.

A collection of machines includes a wheat nibbler, an oat roller and a flour dresser. There are also tools, and old beams and bits of old buckets from the main wheel.

Visitors can compare a pair of French burr stones with a pair of the coarser Peak stones. A small exhibition explains the workings and the history of this and other mills.

Open at weekends, Apr.–Sept., 3–6, or by appointment. Charge for admission.

SITTINGBOURNE Map ref: Dc
Dolphin Yard Sailing Barge Museum, Crown Quay Lane, Sittingbourne.
Tel. Sittingbourne 24132

At the turn of the century it was possible to walk the length of Milton Creek from sailing barge to sailing barge, without stepping ashore. But with the decline of the barge industry, only one small shipbuilding yard lingered on at the end of this muddy, tidal inlet. It is now the site of the museum.

With its roof supported by ancient tillers, the building is still used for restoring sailing barges, such as the Oak and the Revival, that lie in the creek. For the museum not only traces the history of the industry, but is also dedicated to the working and preservation of

---

barges and to the revival of old crafts, including sailmaking and spar-making. Most of the exhibits are housed in a two-storey sail loft built from old ships' timbers.

The ground floor of the sail-loft building is dominated by a waterman's skiff, designed for up to eight passengers. There is a medley of shipwrights' tools, and photographs illustrating the techniques of the craft, such as caulking and rigging. Upstairs, where the red-brown sails were made and fitted on to the spars, there are small exhibitions of the crafts and industries on which the barges depended.

Open Easter to Oct., Sun. and Bank Holidays, 11–5. Small charge for admission.

SURREY

BLINDLEY HEATH Map ref: Cb
Sunhill Farmhouse Pottery, Sunhill Farmhouse, Blindley Heath.
Tel. Lingfield 833435
(Signposted on east side of main road [A22] through village – about 150 yds down farm track. Parking on site.)

Old dairy buildings overlooking a paved courtyard have been transformed into a pottery where Susan Tomkins is usually at work, wheel-throwing, glazing or kiln-packing. The versatility of her skills as a potter is reflected in the large display in the showroom. Besides her range of cooking pots and tableware, there are vases and pot-pourris carved with striking designs, small hand-painted pieces in porcelain and terracotta garden pots.

Open daily 10–7. An evening of demonstrations and talks can be arranged by appointment.

DORKING Map ref: Cb
Philip St Pier (Designer-craftsman in wood), The Lincoln Road Workshop, Lincoln Road, Dorking.
Tel. Dorking 880927
(Off A24, close to Dorking station.)

Using traditional methods and today's new techniques, Philip St Pier makes contemporary furniture of his own design to suit customers' requirements. Pieces include conference tables, dining tables, desks and cabinets. He also makes some smaller furniture. A selection of his work is displayed in a showcase in Dorking at 5 West Street. People wishing to commission furniture should make an appointment.

Opening times and other details may change. Check by telephone before making a special journey.

243

Open Mon.–Fri., 9–5; Sat., 9–12.30. By appointment only.

DORMANSLAND Map ref: Cb
Reddick Forge, The Forge, Plough Road, Dormansland, Lingfield.
Tel. Lingfield 832715
(Near The Plough Inn, just off the B2028. Parking in road.)

Visitors to Dormansland should look out for the village sign, a fine example of the work carried out at this small smithy. The blacksmiths concentrate on ornamental hand-wrought ironwork, and may be seen forging a range of fireside furniture and light fittings as well as larger, specially commissioned items such as gates, or fitments for churches. A room next to the forge has been converted into a display and sales area.

Open Mon.–Fri., 8–5; Sat., 8–12.

FARNCOMBE Map ref: Bb
The Wharf Pottery, 55 St John Street, Farncombe, Godalming.
Tel. Godalming 4097
(Follow sign from A3100 by Three Lions pub to Farncombe Parish Church, which is in St John Street. Parking in front of and behind shop.)

Mary Wondrausch makes hand-thrown commemorative plates and plaques in earthenware, decorated with lively folk designs under a rich honey glaze. She uses the traditional English method of slip trailing – decorating with liquid clay to form raised patterns – and the sgraffito technique of scoring designs into the clay. Although most of her work is to order, there is a range of traditional harvest jugs, owl jugs and pitchers which may be bought by anyone visiting the pottery.

Open Mon.–Fri., 9–1 and 2–5; Sat., 9–12. Maximum of five people at a time.

FARNHAM Map ref: Bb
The Hop Kilns Pottery, Weydon Lane, Farnham.
Tel. Farnham 725812
(Off the south side of the A31 Farnham by-pass, between the junctions with the A325 and A287. Parking available.)

The pottery is housed in a three-storey red-brick building, constructed in the 19th century as a hop kiln. Part of the ground floor has been converted into a showroom which displays hanging gardens and plant-pot containers. Visitors will also find a range of ovenproof stoneware, in oatmeal and speckled grey colours. A small team of potters may be seen throwing the pots in the adjoining workshop. Hand-woven rugs, shawls and lengths of fabric made on the premises are also for sale.

Open all year, Mon.–Sat., 9–6.

HASLEMERE Map ref: Bb
J. & M. Dolmetsch (Early musical instruments), 107, Blackdown Rural Industries, Haste Hill, Haslemere, Surrey.
Tel. Haslemere 3235
(From town centre take B2131 Petworth road. Haste Hill is a turning on the right, signposted to Blackdown Rural Industries.)

Early keyboard, stringed and woodwind musical instruments are made on the premises by a team of craftsmen, who apply ancient hand skills to exotic materials such as rosewood, satinwood and ivory. Guided tours are given, and visitors can spend an absorbing hour watching the instruments take shape from the initial woodturning and carving through to decorative inlaying. They will also see craftsmen fashioning mouthpieces for the recorders, and cutting keys for spinets, harpsichords and clavichords. Other craftsmen make and repair viols, guitars, rebecs, lutes, and other stringed instruments.

Open Mon.–Sat., by appointment only.

PUTTENHAM Map ref: Bb
Faith and David Winter (Sculptors), Venzers Studio, Puttenham.

Tel. Guildford 810300
(Signposted on north side of main village street. Parking in drive.)

Faith Winter is a sculptor who works to commission, carving figures in stone and wood. She also produces limited editions, modelled first in clay or plaster and then cast in bronze. Her son, David, makes miniature replicas of famous buildings which he casts in plaster, after first making a wax model, and then paints with great attention to detail. Visitors to the studio may watch him at work, and may commission a model of their home.

Open at most times, but an appointment is necessary.

SHERE Map ref: Cb
Shere Potter, The Square, Shere, Guildford.
Tel. Shere 2625
(Shop is in centre of Shere. Studio is 50 yds away in Lower Street, beside a stream. Parking in village square.)

Casseroles, coffee sets, lamp bases, salt and pepper pots are all hand-thrown in Chris Otway's glass-fronted studio. Traditional oatmeal and brown glazes are used in the decoration, producing interesting colour and tone variations where the glazes overlap. The pots are for sale in his shop, together with other locally made craft goods.

Open all year, Mon.–Fri., 9–1, and 1.30–5.30. Shop open daily, 10–6.

MUSEUMS

HAXTED Map ref: Cb
The Watermill Museum.
(See panel on p. 242)

TILFORD Map ref: Bb
Old Kiln Museum.
(See panel on p. 243)

WEST SUSSEX

BILLINGSHURST Map ref: Cb
Lannards Studio Pottery, Okehurst Lane, Billingshurst.
Tel. Billingshurst 2692
(1½ miles north of Billingshurst off A29. Room for about six cars outside.)

With clays and glazes that she mixes herself, Betty Sims produces attractive stoneware pottery ranging from sculptured pieces, textured lamp bases and vases to casseroles and coffee and wine sets. Two contrasting glazes decorate the pots – a matt stone colour, and a glossy, almost metallic rust and dark brown. They are displayed alongside a selection of work by other craftsmen and artists. Each year, at the end of November, Mrs Sims holds a craft exhibition at the studio.

Open most days, including Sun., by appointment only.

BOSHAM Map ref: Bb
Bosham Walk (Craft Centre), Old Bosham.
Tel. Bosham 572475
(Follow signs to quay. On right-hand side of road, opposite turning to car park.)

In a narrow street that leads straight down to the water at Bosham creek, a quaint two-storey building with a black weatherboarded front brings together a dozen little craft shops. Visitors can browse around the oak-beamed interior and see gold jewellery being made, together with spinning, weaving, glass engraving, and hand-painting on porcelain. They can also see the work of local artists, a clock restorer and a calligrapher. Other British-made goods may be bought from the centre's general craft shop.

Open daily, 10–5.30.

BURGESS HILL Map ref: Cb
Sheila Southwell (Artist on porcelain), 7 West Street, Burgess Hill.

Tel. Burgess Hill 44307
(At north-western end of town, off A273. Parking in street.)

Plain porcelain wall-plates, dressing-table sets and perfume bottles are transformed into decorative works of art when they pass through Sheila Southwell's hands. She paints them with colourful designs, ranging from flowers and berries to oriental motifs. Each piece is painted and fired several times to achieve the subtle background for which this artist is noted. Some are finished with 22 carat gold and mother-of-pearl lustre. Plates can be ordered with designs and personal inscriptions to celebrate any occasion. Wedding anniversary plates and christening cups are a speciality.

Open all year, Mon.–Fri., 10.30–4. By appointment only.

BURGESS HILL Map ref: Cb
Jack Trowbridge (Jewellery), 75 Royal George Road, Burgess Hill.
Tel. Burgess Hill 2208
(Turn off A273 by Royal George pub. Parking in road.)

Jack Trowbridge works in a wide variety of materials, ranging from slate and marble to bronze and gold. In his garden workshop he designs and makes pieces of modern jewellery, as well as small carved ornaments in stone or metal, and larger sculptures, lettered headstones and memorials for churches and public buildings. A selection of silver jewellery is for sale.

Open most days, by appointment only. Maximum of four people at a time.

DONNINGTON Map ref: Ba
Donnington Pottery, Blacksmiths' Cottages, Selsey Road, Donnington, nr Chichester.
Tel. Chichester 781880
(On B2201, a mile south of the Selsey Tram pub and almost opposite the Blacksmith's Arms. Parking in drive.)

Ornamental garden sculptures in the shape of primitive huts are an unusual feature of the work of potters Alison Sandeman and Sue Barker. Their studio occupies one of a row of four cottages, originally built for blacksmiths of a nearby forge. Besides outdoor pots of all shapes and sizes, they make a variety of pieces in porcelain, together with stoneware mugs, bowls, vases and large bread-crocks.

Open daily, 9–6, but advisable to telephone before weekend visits.

HORSHAM Map ref: Cb
Shal Design (Grace Hosking), 134 Brighton Road, Horsham.
Tel. Horsham 69844
(On A281, south-east of town centre between St Leonards Arms and Kerves Lane, hidden from road at end of garden path. Parking in road.)

Exquisite paintings on glass – on the reverse side of glass-topped tables – are the speciality of Grace Hosking. Working from original designs, she paints them individually in delicately graded colours. The panels, which take many days to complete, are made to order and the colours are adaptable to suit customers' requirements. One speciality is chess and coffee tables with a figurative design in 15th-century style.

Open Mon., Tues. and Thur., 10.30–4. By appointment only.

HORSTED KEYNES Map ref: Cb
J. B. Hoare-Ward, The Blacksmith's Shop, Horsted Keynes, nr Haywards Heath.
Tel. Sharpthorne 810292
(Opposite green in centre of Horsted Keynes village. Car park close by, next to recreation ground.)

There has been a smithy in the village for over 100 years, and for much of that time a farrier has worked in the small whitewashed building. Nowadays, the shoeing trade has declined, and visitors will find the present blacksmith

engaged in making ornamental ironwork. A small stock of hearthware and paper knives is displayed inside the forge but most of the work, especially such items as gates and weathervanes, is done to order.

Open all year, Tues.–Sat., 8.30–12.30 and 1.30–6; Sun., 10–12. Appointment necessary for two or more visitors at a time.

STEYNING Map ref: Cb
Geraldine St Aubyn Hubbard (Spinner and weaver), 2 Charlton Court Cottages, Mouse Lane, Steyning.
Tel. Steyning 814204
(Off A283 at north end of village by sharp bend. About ½ mile down lane on right. Room for parking two or three cars in lane.)

A tile-hung brick-and-flint cottage down a quiet country lane is the peaceful setting for Geraldine St Aubyn Hubbard's studio. She weaves fine silk, cashmere and woollen cloth on a large eight-shaft loom. She spins some of the silk she uses for weaving, and dyes most of the yarn with vegetable and chemical dyes. The finished cloth is made up into scarves, jackets, waistcoats and tunics.

Open most days by appointment. Maximum of ten people.

STORRINGTON Map ref: Cb
Storrington Pottery, 30 West Street, Storrington, nr Pulborough.
Tel. Storrington 3745
(On main road [A283] in centre of Storrington village.)

Visitors to the pottery may order plaques decorated with the name of their house, and plates and mugs to commemorate occasions such as christenings and weddings. Paula Appleby uses many different glazes, which she mixes herself in subtle colours. Her work also includes bowls, mugs, jugs, candleholders and planters.

Open Tues.–Sat., 10–1 and 2.30–5.30.

MUSEUMS

HORSHAM Map ref: Cb
Horsham Museum, 9 The Causeway, Horsham.
Tel. Horsham 4959

Flemish weavers were possibly the original occupants of this black-and-white timber-framed building, in the mid-16th century. It now houses bygones from Sussex homes, craft workshops and industries.

At the back of the house, a reconstructed street, with old signs and lamps, contains several craft workshops. Behind a bow-windowed front is William Albery's saddler's shop. The Albery family practised the craft locally from the late 18th century until the 1950s. The shop contains an extraordinary collection of many hundreds of different horse-bits.

Other shops in the reconstructed street are an old dairy, a wheelwright's shop from nearby Southwater, and a smithy. Each is jam-packed with the tools and products of its particular trade.

Upstairs, amongst a varied collection of bygones, a traditional Sussex farmhouse kitchen has been reconstructed. It includes a loom that belonged to a weaver who lived in Horsham from 1919 into the 1960s, and wove cloth for three English queens – Queen Mary, the Queen Mother, and Queen Elizabeth. It is still in working order, and available for the use of those who want to practise the craft of weaving.

Open Tues.–Fri., 1–5; Sat. 10–5. Admission free.

SINGLETON Map ref: Bb
The Weald and Downland Open Air Museum.
(See panel on facing page)

Map ref: Bb

The Weald and Downland Open Air Museum

SINGLETON, WEST SUSSEX

Sprawling over 40 acres of downland, this unique museum is devoted to the preservation of old buildings and to the illustration of traditional building techniques.

To save medieval Winkhurst House from destruction, the museum moved the timber-framed building from Kent and rebuilt it on the site. The acrid fumes of a fire now smouldering in the hall, and the blast of chill winds whistling through the unglazed windows and under the eaves, transport the visitor into the daily life of another age. Other buildings include a reconstructed Saxon hut, two re-sited farmhouses and an old market hall.

Each is a testimony to the craftsmanship and inventiveness of a different age. In Hambrook Barn, an exhibition explains the development of building techniques – from timber frames and wattle and daub, to tiling and bricklaying.

In a nearby wood, a charcoal-burner's camp has been built by Mr and Mrs Langridge, two retired charcoal burners from nearby Horsham. The visitor can see, stage by stage, how the kiln was made out of turf and pieces of timber. Because he had to watch the burning kilns night and day in case of a flare-up, the charcoal burner always lived on the site with his family. Until the age of 16, therefore, Mrs Langridge knew no home other than a hut covered in grass – similar to the one that stands beside the kiln.

Several of the buildings at Singleton are connected directly with rural crafts and industries. In a timber-framed house with a thatched roof and undaubed walls stands a tread-wheel from the village of Catherington, Hampshire. The wheel, which was built in about 1600, was used to raise water from a well reputed to be nearly 300 ft deep, and was driven by a man or a boy. It is now in working order again.

DOWNLAND COTTAGE *Built of flint rubble, it is one of two survivors from the deserted village of Hangleton.*

The museum contains four cattle sheds – or 'hovels', as they are sometimes called in the south-east. One of them houses a horse-powered chaff cutter, made in the late 19th century and used in Sussex until 1939.

Eighteenth-century weatherboarded stables contain tools which belonged to one of the few remaining wheelwrights in the south-east. Several times a week a carpenter gives a demonstration, as does a blacksmith in a reconstructed smithy. A working water-mill grinds flour daily.

Singleton, Chichester, West Sussex. Tel. Singleton 348.

Open daily, July–Aug., 11–5; Apr.–June and Sept.–Oct., Tues.–Sun., 11–5; Nov.–Mar., Sun., 11–4.

Wooden windpump from Pevensey, Kent.

PENDEAN FARMHOUSE *This half-timbered farmhouse was built in the 16th century, and moved from nearby Midhurst.*

Opening times and other details may change. Check by telephone before making a special journey.

245

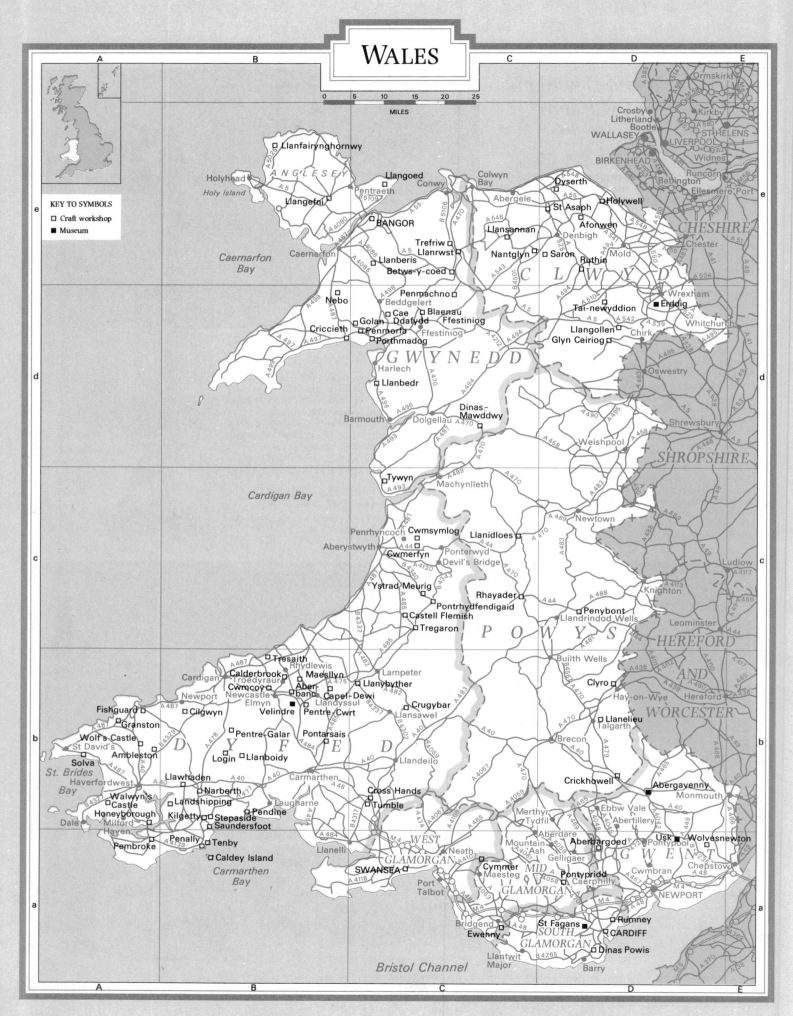

WALES

MILES
0 5 10 15 20 25

Llanfairynghornwy

ANGLESEY

Holyhead
Holy Island
Llangefni
Pentraeth
B5109
BANGOR
Caernarfon
Caernarfon Bay

Llangoed
Conwy
Colwyn Bay
Abergele
Llansannan
Trefriw
Llanrwst
Llanberis
Betws-y-coed
Nantglyn
Saron

Dyserth
St Asaph
Holywell
Afonwen
Denbigh
Ruthin
Mold

CHESHIRE
Chester

Nebo
Penmachno
Beddgelert
Cae Ddafydd
Blaenau Ffestiniog
Golan
Penmorfa
Porthmadog
Criccieth

Tai-newyddion
Wrexham
Erddig
Llangollen
Glyn Ceiriog
Chirk
Whitchurch

CLWYD

GWYNEDD

Harlech
Llanbedr
Barmouth

Dinas-Mawddwy
Dolgellau
Welshpool

Oswestry
Shrewsbury

SHROPSHIRE

Cardigan Bay

Tywyn
Machynlleth

Newtown

Penrhyncoch
Cwmsymlog
Aberystwyth
Cwmerfyn
Ponterwyd
Devil's Bridge
Llanidloes

Rhayader

Ludlow
Knighton

Ystrad Meurig
Pontrhydfendigaid
Castell Flemish
Tregaron

Penybont
Llandrindod Wells

Leominster

POWYS

HEREFORD
AND
WORCESTER

Tresaith
Rhydlewis
Calderbrook
Maesllyn
Troedyraur
Aber-
Cwmcoy
banc
Newcastle
Newport
Elmyn
Velindre
Pentre-Cwrt
Cilgwyn

Lampeter
Llanybyther
Capel-Dewi
Llandyssul
Crugybar
Liansawel

Builth Wells

Clyro
Hay-on-Wye
Hereford

Llanelieu
Talgarth

Fishguard
Granston
Wolf's Castle
St David's
Ambleston
Solva
St. Brides Bay
Haverfordwest

Pentre-Galar
Login
Llanboidy

Pontarsais
Llanbyther
Llandeilo

Brecon

Crickhowell
Abergavenny
Monmouth

DYFED

Walwyn's Castle
Honeyborough
Dale
Milford Haven
Llawhaden
Narberth
Landshipping
Kilgetty
Stepaside
Saundersfoot
Penally
Tenby
Pembroke
Caldey Island
Carmarthen Bay

Carmarthen
Laugharne
Pendine

Cross Hands
Tumble

Llanelli

WEST GLAMORGAN

Llandeilo

Merthyr Tydfil
Aberdare
Mountain Ash
Cymmer
Maesteg

Ebbw Vale
Abertillery
Aberbargoed
Gelligaer

GWENT

Usk
Wolvesnewton
Pontypool
Cwmbran
Chepstow

SWANSEA
Port Talbot
Neath

MID GLAMORGAN
Pontypridd
Caerphilly

NEWPORT

Bridgend
Ewenny
St Fagans
CARDIFF
Rumney
Dinas Powis

Llantwit Major
Barry

SOUTH GLAMORGAN

Bristol Channel

Crafts of many sorts are alive and well in Wales today. There is no better introduction to the rich heritage of Welsh craftsmanship than to take a step back in time at the St Fagans Folk Museum, where resident craftsmen ply their skills. Many other craftsmen, particularly potters, have sought the quieter parts of the Principality, where they derive inspiration for their designs from the ever-changing moods and colours of the mountains, and from masterpieces of Celtic folklore such as *The Mabinogion* and the *Book of Kells*. Often, they live alongside long-established craftsmen whose families have been following the same calling for centuries, perhaps still fashioning objects as traditional as Welsh love spoons – tokens of affection with a history that can be traced back to the Middle Ages. In some of the long-established woollen-mills that made 19th-century Wales prosperous, hand-looms and machine-operated looms stand side by side. It is a happy marriage of old and new.

CLWYD

AFONWEN Map ref: De
Afonwen Woollen Company, Afonwen, Mold.
Tel. Caerwys 427
(Clearly signposted from the A541 between Mold and Denbigh. Ample parking outside mill.)

Setting up any one of the mill's four looms can involve an entire working day, as more than 1,000 warps – the threads which run lengthwise – are fixed to the machines. The looms are powered by electricity, but nimble fingers and sharp eyes are needed by the craftworkers who tend them. Wool is woven into richly coloured and textured material used for making skirts, hats and other garments. It is also mixed with mohair to produce warm, soft rugs, scarves and stoles. Each loom takes up to two days to weave 75 yds of material. It is a noisy but fascinating process, which involves shuttles hurtling backwards and forwards at astonishing speed.

Open daily, May–Sept., 9–5; Oct.–Apr., Mon.–Fri., 9–5.

DYSERTH Map ref: De
Dyserth Home Weavers, Netherton, Elwy Avenue, Dyserth.
Tel. Dyserth 570256
(At the far end of Elwy Avenue, a narrow cul-de-sac on the south side of Dyserth. Limited parking outside.)

Hand-looms whose design has remained fundamentally unchanged since the Middle Ages are used by Cecil Rhodes, and his nephew Donald Lander. Craftworkers since 1951, they weave cotton and wool into lengths of skirt material, ties, trolley cloths, chair-back covers and other items. Mr Lander has made altar cloths for the cathedrals of Liverpool and St Asaph. The partners, both former teachers of hand-loom weaving, also make placemats to match customers' dinner services. This is a genuine cottage industry, which flourishes in a cheerfully cluttered and colourful bungalow overlooking the Vale of Clwyd.

Open daily, 10–6.

GLYN CEIRIOG Map ref: Dd
Ceiriog Crafts (Furniture makers), Argoed, Glyn Ceiriog.
Tel. Glyn Ceiriog 218
(In the centre of Glyn Ceiriog, a village west of the A5 as it runs through Chirk, on the England-Wales border. Parking in street.)

Theo Davies trained as a wheelwright and joiner, but now concentrates on furniture making. Kiln-dried oak is his favourite timber, but he and his fellow craftsmen – three experts and an apprentice – also use elm and mahogany. Working in an old, stone-built mill on the banks of the River Ceiriog, they make Welsh dressers, longcase clocks, corner cupboards, chairs and refectory tables which are displayed in a shop near by. A high degree of craftsmanship also goes into the 'standing frames' used by patients at the local orthopaedic hospital. Mr Davies and his team have worked on two of the area's most notable old houses – Plas Newydd, in Llangollen, and Erddig, a National Trust property near Wrexham. (See panel on p. 248.)

Workshop open by appointment Mon.–Fri., 9–5; Sat., 9–12. Shop open Mon.–Sat., 9–5, May–Sept. and by arrangement between Oct. and Apr.

HOLYWELL Map ref: De
Holywell Textile Mills, Greenfield Street, Holywell.
Tel. Holywell 712022
(North of town centre, near the parish church and next to St Winifred's Well. Parking in street outside mill.)

Cloth woven from the completely natural, undyed wool of the uncommon multi-horned Jacob sheep is one of this old-established mill's principal lines. The wool has to be carefully colour-sorted by hand before being made ready for the looms, which have been powered by electricity since just before the First World War. Other wool is made into flannel – a term derived from the Welsh word 'gwlanen'. Garments and lengths of cloth in many colours are sold in the mill shop and also exported to Europe, Japan and the USA. Holywell has been a weaving town since 1840; the present mill was built in 1884 after its predecessor had been gutted by fire.

Open Mon.–Fri., 10–12 and 2–4 for mill tours, but appointment essential. Shop open Mon.–Sat., 9–5.

LLANGOLLEN Map ref: Dd
Llangollen Pottery, Regent Street, Llangollen.
Tel. Llangollen 860249
(Opposite school in Regent Street, which is part of the A5 through Llangollen. Limited parking in street; large car park about 300 yds away, beyond traffic lights.)

The Llangollen Pottery, established in 1953, occupies a quiet courtyard off Regent Street. It produces cast or 'jollied' earthenware, finished with the potter's own glazes, and supplies many shops in Wales and the border counties. Models made in the pottery are sent to Stoke-on-Trent, where the plaster moulds are made. Although concentrating on domestic and decorative wares, the pottery has also produced such 'specials' as a limited edition of tankards to commemorate the 300th anniversary of a neighbouring town's charter.

Open Mon.–Sat., 9–5, and Sun. in summer.

LLANSANNAN Map ref: Ce
Alan Brunsdon Pottery, Aled Stores, Llansannan.
Tel. Llansannan 205
(In main street of Llansannan, a village on the A544 south of Abergele. Car park near by.)

The former village bakery, built about 1830, is Alan Brunsdon's cosy workshop and showroom. He hand-throws domestic stoneware, ranging from mugs to bread crocks and large cooking vessels. Mr Brunsdon uses a traditional kick wheel, rather than one powered by electricity, because it gives him a better feel for his clay. He also makes his own glazes on the premises, some featuring wood ash. The oil-fired kiln is big enough to hold about a month's output.

Open daily from May–Sept., 10–6.30. Appointment advisable Oct.–Apr.

NANTGLYN Map ref: Ce
Candles in the Rain (Leatherwork), Ty'r Efail, Nantglyn, Denbigh.
Tel. Nantglyn 389
(In centre of village, which is on the B5435 south-west of Denbigh. Parking in street.)

Despite the evocative name of their business, Bill and Val Norrington – American and Welsh respectively – actually make high-quality leatherwork. Candle-making was dropped several years ago. 'Wild West' and Celtic designs feature prominently on a range of hand-stitched goods, which include key fobs, belts, handbags and superb fly wallets for fishermen. Jewellery boxes and commemorative plates are among the couple's personal favourites. Ty'r Efail is a character-packed old smithy, complete with huge leather bellows, two forges, anvils and other interesting reminders of its history.

Open Mon.–Sat., 10–6. Sun. by arrangement.

RUTHIN Map ref: De
Geoffrey Barber, Studio 10, Ruthin Crafts Centre, Lon Parcwr, Ruthin.
Tel. Ruthin 4935
(At roundabout on A525 at edge of town. Car park.)

Hand-cut dovetail joints, hand-carved panels and chairs upholstered with oak-bark-tanned leather are examples of the traditional workmanship to be found in Geoffrey Barber's furniture-making craftshop. Working in North Wales' first purpose-built craft centre, Mr Barber makes commissioned furniture fashioned from English walnut, English oak, Canadian rock maple, elm, mahogany, pitch pine and other woods. Beautiful oak sideboards and Welsh dressers cost well over £1,000, but will be the antiques of tomorrow. Smaller items include wine tables, lamps and bowls. Many orders start as nothing more than an idea, or a rough sketch, which eventually becomes something of enduring beauty and character.

Open Tues.–Sun., 10–5.30.

ST ASAPH Map ref: De
Kentigern Studio Pottery, The Old Shop, Lower Street, St Asaph.
Tel. St Asaph 582412
(Next door to the Bull Inn, at south end of Lower Street. Car park 50 yds away.)

The name of the pottery recalls Kentigern, a Celtic monk who founded what eventually became St Asaph Cathedral. Dorothy Stopes and her son Ian devote most of their time to crafting modelled stoneware ideal for flower arrangements. Some of the goods are slab-sided while others are moulded around cylinders. These potters also model elephants in several sizes, all individually fashioned and glazed. Leaf-like motifs feature prominently, and the Stopes use many glazes which originated in China.

Open Apr.–Sept., Tues. and Fri., 9–5. But the potters live on the premises and will open at any time on request.

SARON Map ref: De
Acer Las Studio Pottery, Saron, Denbigh.
Tel. Llanynys 320
(Pass through Saron and take first turning on left after village. Pottery is ½ mile down lane. Very limited parking by house-cum-workshop.)

Tucked away down a tangle of steep, narrow lanes, the Acer Las pottery is extremely difficult to find without detailed instructions. Gottfried and Ann Gaugitsch therefore advise visitors to telephone in advance for a thorough briefing. Mr Gaugitsch, an Austrian, produces exceptionally fine earthenware which he finishes with his own glazes. His products range from mugs to bread crocks, with hosts of tiny mice making delightfully whimsical 'kiln fillers'. He also makes ceramic frames for the wild-flower pictures which his Welsh-born wife paints on parchment.

Open Mon.–Sat., 9–5. Sun. by arrangement.

TAI-NEWYDDION Map ref: Dd
Jim Malone Pottery, 2 Tai-newyddion, Llandegla.
Tel. Llandegla 397
(One of a cluster of cottages on the north side of the Horseshoe Pass, between Llangollen and Ruthin on the A542. Limited off-road parking.)

Clay collected from local streams, and wood ash from his own fireplace, provide Jim Malone with some of the raw materials for the traditional glazes used on his stoneware. He also mixes his own potting clay. Mr Malone was introduced to oriental motifs as a student, and his decorations still reflect strong Korean, Japanese and Chinese influences. Stoneware is his main line, but the pottery also produces beautiful teapots in porcelain, whose delicacy belies its inherent strength. Tai-newyddion is a tiny cluster of cottages, built for slate-quarry workers and their families, and stands more than 1,000 ft up on the north side of the spectacular Horseshoe Pass.

Open Mon.–Fri., 10–7, and at weekends by arrangement. Mr Malone advises telephoning first.

MUSEUM

ERDDIG Map ref: Dd
Erddig.
(See panel on p. 248)

DYFED

ABER-BANC Map ref: Bb
Yr Hen Ysgol (Craft workshop), Aber-banc, Llandyssul.
Tel. Velindre 370771
(Opposite war memorial in Aber-banc, a village on the A475 3½ miles east of Newcastle Emlyn. Parking outside craft shop.)

Yr Hen Ysgol – The Old School – was built in 1847 and had been empty for five years before John and Mary Lloyd Jones bought it in 1976. It is now a fascinating craft workshop, studio and art gallery where students can attend residential courses. Mrs Jones specialises in painting and tapestry weaving, while her husband – a member of the Welsh Arts Council's craft committee – weaves rugs on hand-looms. The couple dye their own wool and create 'natural' patterns inspired by the rich and varied colours of the lovely Teifi valley. It takes about a day to set a loom up, and rugs grow at approximately 6 in. an hour.

Open June–Oct., 10–5. By appointment at other times, and when courses are in operation.

AMBLESTON Map ref: Ab
Wallis Woollen Mill, Ambleston, Haverfordwest.
Tel. Clarbeston 297
(Signposted from the B4329, 8 miles north-east of Haverfordwest. Ample parking by mill.)

This attractive little mill, built of white-washed stone and nestling in a secluded valley, has been producing yarns and fabrics since 1812. The cast-iron flannel press used by the original weaver has survived intact. Powered and hand-operated looms are used by David and Margaret Redpath to produce a variety of woollen fabrics which are either sold in lengths or made up into skirts, dresses and other goods. Carn Meini carpet rugs – named after a peak in the nearby Preseli Hills – were evolved to commemorate a visit by Prince Charles in 1978. While there,

Map ref: Dd

Erddig

ERDDIG, CLWYD

Great houses such as Erddig, with its 1,870 acre estate, were once self-sufficient in terms of craft and building skills. The estate foreman commanded a staff of as many as 30 men, who would have seen to the upkeep of the buildings, roads and bridges on the estate. Today, visitors can wander around the grounds and gain an insight into the small world of the traditional country house, and the skills and resources at its disposal. Along one side of the estate yard are the blacksmith's shop, the joiner's shop and the sawpit. The outbuildings also include an old sawmill and a wagon shed.

Erddig, Wrexham, Clwyd. Tel. Wrexham 55314.

Open daily except Mon., 12–5.30, from Easter to end of Oct. Charge for admission.

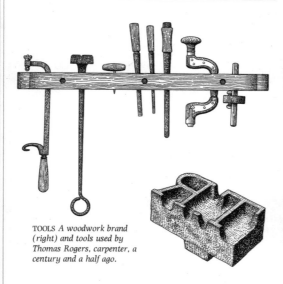

TOOLS A woodwork brand (right) and tools used by Thomas Rogers, carpenter, a century and a half ago.

JOINER'S SHOP A mortising machine is in the foreground, and templates for garden seats and other items made in the joiner's shop on the Erddig estate hang on the walls.

he re-opened the restored mill-pond, a few hundred yards upstream from the building.

Open Mon.–Fri., 10–6.

CALDERBROOK Map ref: Bb
Calderbrook Woodcraft, Calderbrook, Rhydlewis, Llandyssul.
Tel. Rhydlewis 494
(Two miles south-west of Rhydlewis, signposted off an unclassified road to Troedyraur. Parking by craft shop.)

A holiday amid the forests and log cabins of British Columbia, in western Canada, prompted Stephen and Meryl Thomas to become craftworkers in wood. Oak, sycamore, elm, ash, beech and other native timbers are turned into a selection of domestic goods, such as bowls, cheese boards and egg racks. They are hand-finished with beeswax, and some are decorated with pyrography (designs made by burning). The couple plant trees for the benefit of future generations, cut their own timber and season it in their own kiln. They sell their goods from their premises and also have a stall in Cardigan market.

Open Apr.–Sept., also in Dec., Mon.–Fri., 9–5. Appointment advisable at other times.

CALDEY ISLAND Map ref: Ba
Caldey Abbey, Caldey Island, Tenby.
Tel. Tenby 2879
(Two miles south of Tenby. Abbey is a five-minute walk from ferry's landing place. No cars.)

Caldey Island's golden abundance of gorse flowers provides one of the basic ingredients for

the perfumes and other fragrant toiletries blended and bottled by the abbey's dark-robed Cistercian monks. They also make chocolate, every bar of which is wrapped by hand, and sell other Welsh-made craft goods from the peaceful little island's well-stocked shop. The present community was founded in 1929, but Caldey's religious roots go all the way back to the 6th century AD.

Regular ferries run between Tenby and Caldey Island from the third week in May until mid-Sept.

CAPEL-DEWI Map ref: Bb
John Morgan and Son, Rock Mills, Capel-Dewi, Llandyssul.
Tel. Llandyssul 2356
(Well signposted from the A475 and B4336, and in Capel-Dewi itself. Ample parking by mill.)

Deep and wooded, the River Clettwr's enchanting valley is the setting for the stone-built, water-powered mill which John Morgan established in 1890. It is now run by his grandson, David, and his great-grandson, Donald. They spin, card and weave wool on machines driven by an impressive water-wheel which develops 12-15 hp, and was made in Cardigan. Tapestry bedspreads account for most of the work done by the father-and-son team, but many other craft goods are sold in the shop. The path down which sheep used to be driven for their pre-shearing wash can be seen at the old bridge a few yards upstream from this character-packed establishment.

Open Mon.–Fri., 9–5.30; Sat., 9–1.

CASTELL FLEMISH Map ref: Cc
Tregaron Pottery Ltd, Castell Flemish, Tregaron.
Tel. Bronant 639
(On the A485 to Aberystwyth, 3 miles north-west of Tregaron. Ample parking by pottery.)

The feathers of the red kite, a rare bird of prey which breeds only in central Wales, inspired the glazes which decorate some of the domestic stoneware made by Allan Baxter and his small team of potters at Castell Flemish. They work in a former school, built in 1879, and produce an attractive selection of goods, including hand-thrown mugs, and clocks which form parts of scenes featuring such things as churches and thatched cottages. Hand-painted Welsh dragons and Welsh words picked out in Celtic-style script are something of a speciality of Allan Baxter's establishment.

Open Mon.–Fri., 9–5.

CILGWYN Map ref: Bb
Greencroft Candles, 'Trefelin', Cilgwyn, Newport.
Tel. Newport (Dyfed) 820470
(Follow Cwm Gwaun signs from centre of Newport and continue along road for just over 2 miles. Greencroft Candles is on the right, immediately before a bridge. Limited parking by house.)

Clusters of colourful, hand-dipped candles hang like exotic plants from the roof of Inger John's small workshop in a tranquil valley at the foot of the Preseli Hills. Mrs John learned the ancient craft as a child in her native Sweden,

and now specialises in candles with graded colours. They are up to 2 ft in length, and their subtle shades are complemented by such fragrances as musk, jasmine, lilac, rose, honey and lemon. Mrs John sells her candles to visitors, and they are also available in many local craft shops.

Open all year; candles are generally made in the morning.

CROSS HANDS Map ref: Cb
The Woodland Craft Centre, 9 Woodlands, Cross Hands.
Tel. Cross Hands 842591
(In a row of terraced houses, off the A48 Swansea-Carmarthen road, in the centre of Cross Hands. Parking in street.)

An old spinning-wheel, brought in to be repaired, prompted Daniel Jenkins to start making replicas in a variety of hardwoods. Some are used as decorations and conversation pieces, but an increasing number of customers are keen amateur spinners interested in traditional techniques. The wheels are held together by wooden screws and have leather bearings. Mr Jenkins and his son, Geraint, also make miniature spinning-wheels and other scaled-down items such as rocking-chairs, harps, Welsh dressers and stools. What appear to be sand-filled egg-timers are in fact replicas of sermon-timers used by 19th-century clergymen to time their orations. Father and son work at their craft in a tiny building behind their home.

Open Mon.–Fri., 9–5.30; Sat., 9–10. Other times by appointment.

CRUGYBAR   Map ref: Cb
Glynborthyn Woodcrafts, Crugybar, Llanwrda.
Tel. Pumpsaint 281
(Craft shop combined with post office, 11 miles north of Llandeilo on B4302, near junction with A482. Parking on road.)

A woodcarver since childhood, Alan Hemming now concentrates his craftsmanship on love spoons – tokens of affection whose origins go back to medieval Wales. Working in sycamore, oak, ash and beech, he creates elaborate and beautiful spoons, whose designs are rich in ancient symbolism. Modern versions, made to order, tell much about the recipient; for instance a musical scholar celebrating her 21st birthday might be given a spoon featuring notes, a mortar board and 'the key of the door'.

Open normal business hours all year, and by appointment at any other time.

CWMCOY   Map ref: Bb
Felin Geri Mill, Cwmcoy, Newcastle Emlyn.
Tel. Newcastle Emlyn 710810
(Signposted from B4333 in Cwmcoy, a hamlet just over 1 mile north-west of Newcastle Emlyn. Parking by mill.)

This character-packed old mill, powered by a cast-iron water-wheel 12 ft in diameter, stood derelict for 30 years until it was treated to an award-winning restoration scheme in the mid-1970s. The huge mill-stones grind about 10 tons of wholemeal flour every week. Built in the 16th century, the mill is the focal point of a 30 acre smallholding, complete with pigs, goats, geese and ducks. One building is now a bakery, where bread made from Felin Geri flour is made and sold. Michael Heycock, who runs the mill, was previously the head of a London advertising agency.

Open daily, Easter to Oct., 9–6.

CWMERFYN   Map ref: Cc
Llettycaws Pottery, Cwmerfyn, Aberystwyth.
Tel. Aberystwyth 828537
(Cwmerfyn lies to the north of the A44, which runs inland from Aberystwyth towards Ponterwyd. Limited parking outside pottery.)

Seven miles east of Aberystwyth as the crow flies, Pip Koppel's pottery nestles in a remote and tranquil valley of great beauty. Here she produces a wide range of domestic stoneware and earthenware, but her personal favourites are 'picture' plates decorated with her own soft-hued glazes. Many are made to commemorate weddings, anniversaries and other notable occasions. House nameplates, inlaid with melted glass, are another product.

Open daily, 9–7; also in the evening by appointment.

CWMSYMLOG   Map ref: Cc
F. J. Walker (Furniture maker), Sunnyside, Cwmsymlog Mine, Aberystwyth.
Tel. Aberystwyth 828483
(Four miles from Penrhyncoch, north-east of Aberystwyth, off A487. Limited parking by workshop.)

Men once delved for lead in the area around this isolated hamlet amid the high hills of northern Dyfed. One of their cottages is now the home of John Walker, a maker of traditional-style furniture, who moved to Cwmsymlog in the mid-sixties. Working mainly in elm, mahogany and oak – his personal favourite – he makes tables, corner cupboards, dressers, bookcases and other items, nearly all of which are commissioned.

Open Mon.–Fri., 2–5.

FISHGUARD   Map ref: Ab
Workshop Wales, Glynymel Road, Lower Town, Fishguard.
Tel. Fishguard 872261
(About 500 yds along road which leaves the A487 near bridge at foot of steep hill in Lower Town. Ample parking close by.)

The River Gwaun's deep, wooded valley makes a beautiful setting for this busy crafts complex founded by John Cleal in 1970. Many different skills may be admired, but the accent is on high-quality goods made from leather and hardwoods. The two materials are often combined to create leather-topped tables, chess sets and boxes for writing paper and envelopes. Many of the products are one-off orders for customers from all over Britain and Europe. Workshop Wales also specialises in traditional 'tavern clocks' with gold numerals on a black background and a hand-painted scene beneath the face. Pictures by local artists are hung in a gallery near the large, well-stocked shop.

Open daily, Apr.–Oct., 10–6. Hours vary from Nov. to Mar., but proprietors live on the premises.

GRANSTON   Map ref: Ab
H. Griffiths and Son, Tregwynt Mill, Letterston.
Tel. St Nicholas 225
(Despite its postal address, the mill is near the hamlet of Granston. It is clearly signposted from the A487 south-west of Fishguard. Ample parking outside mill.)

Built midway through the 18th century, and run by the Griffiths family since 1912, the mill stands near a stream in a delightfully secluded valley near the sea. Its six looms are powered by electricity, but an old cast-iron water-wheel used until 1940 may still be seen. Visitors can watch wool being twisted, wound on to cones, put on a warping wheel and finally woven. Products range from knitting wools to flannel, tweed and tapestry. The fabrics, many of which feature traditional Welsh patterns, are sold as lengths or as tailor-made garments. The mill also has shops in Fishguard and St David's.

Open Mon.–Fri., 9–5.

HONEYBOROUGH   Map ref: Ab
Honeyborough Pottery, 5 Honeyborough Green, Neyland.
Tel. Neyland 600013
(Just off the A477, on north side of the bridge across Milford Haven, turn left at roundabout for Honeyborough. Parking on quiet road around green.)

Eileen Richards started potting as a hobby in the mid-1960s, and now produces stoneware in a single-storey craft shop built as a bakery in 1930. Her figures – notably boys with books and girls cradling doves or flowers – share the small but well-stocked shop area with unusual tile pictures, lidded boxes, pots embellished with landscape motifs and many other eye-catching creations.

Open Mon.–Sat., 10–6.

KILGETTY   Map ref: Bb
Avondale Glass, Carmarthen Road, Kilgetty.
Tel. Saundersfoot 813345
(Carmarthen Road is the A477. Avondale Glass is a few yards from the Pembrokeshire Coast National Park information centre. There is ample off-road parking near the workshop.)

'Gathers' of white-hot glass, heated in a gas-fired furnace, are transformed into decorative and functional goods when Vincenzo Speranza delights onlookers with his expertise. Born in Italy, he has been making, blowing and hand-forming glass since he was ten years old. Powdered glass and glass crystals are fused into the 'gather' or blob in another operation where split-second timing is essential. The display area contains a colourful array of paperweights, vases, birds, pigs, swans, mushrooms and many other creations.

Shop open Mon.–Fri., 8–5; Sat., 8–1. Glassmaking demonstrations on Mon., Thur., Fri., 8–2.30; Tues. and Wed., 8–1.

LANDSHIPPING   Map ref: Bb
Landshipping Pottery, Woodhouse Grange, Landshipping, Narberth.
Tel. Martletwy 225

(The pottery is 4½ miles from the Cross Hands Inn on the A4075, which links Pembroke to the A40 east of Haverfordwest, and is signposted from there. Ample parking outside pottery.)

John Vergette, a former paratrooper, makes a wide range of earthenware goods and mixes his own glazes to create beautiful finishes. There are many small, individual items, but Mr Vergette also produces 45-piece dinner services. The pottery stands in 70 acres of woodland in a superb setting, overlooking the broad Daucleddau estuary, at the end of a lane which runs past Landshipping Quay.

Open daily, May–Oct., 9–7. Also open Nov.–Apr., Mon.–Fri., 9–5.

LLANBOIDY   Map ref: Bb
J. Melfyn Davies, The Old Mill, Llanboidy, Whitland.
Tel. Whitland 520
(Opposite the church in centre of village. Llanboidy is 5 miles north of Whitland, which is on the A40 between Carmarthen and Haverfordwest. Parking in street.)

Milk from the lush local pastures used to be made into butter and cheese in the stone-built, 18th-century mill which now houses Llanboidy Country Furniture. The workshop specialises in such traditional furniture as Welsh dressers, Pembrokeshire 'coffer' sideboards, blanket chests, corner cupboards, tables and chairs. Templates are used to make standard items, but others are made to measure for individual customers. The timbers used range from pine to oak and mahogany.

Open Mon.–Fri., 9–5.30.

LLANYBYTHER   Map ref: Cb
Siwan Mills Ltd, Llansawel Road, Llanybyther.
Tel. Llanybyther 480722
(On outskirts of Llanybyther, beside B4337 signposted to Llansawel. Parking by mill.)

Several mills have flourished in and near Llanybyther – a small town famous for its monthly horse fairs – but the enterprise run by Martin and Yvonne Burton was not established until 1977. It occupies a 19th-century school building and has five looms, powered by electricity, which weave wool into fabrics ranging from light flannel to tweeds. The mill's well-stocked shop sells lengths of cloth, as well as ties, scarves, dresses, coats, bedspreads, purses and handbags.

Open Whitsun to Oct., Mon.–Fri., 9–5; Sat., 10–4.30. Oct. to Whitsun, Mon.–Fri., 9.30–4.

LLAWHADEN   Map ref: Bb
Ridgeway Pottery, Llawhaden.
Tel. Llawhaden 268
(Signposted off the road which links Llawhaden to the A40, 8 miles east of Haverfordwest. Limited parking by craft shop.)

John Baum, a self-taught American potter, became interested in his craft while working in South America during the 1950s. He later had a studio in Jerusalem, before moving to west Wales with his Swiss wife, Ingrid. Andean Indian motifs feature prominently on their stoneware goods, which include wind bells, large mirrors, elaborate candle holders, lamps and wall plaques. Although they do not concentrate on tableware, the couple do make such things as bread crocks and goblet sets. Their small pottery is close to Llawhaden, a village notable for its ruined medieval castle.

Open daily, 9–5.

LOGIN   Map ref: Bb
Village Hall Weavers, Studio-in-the-Church, Login, Whitland.
Tel. Clynderwen 676
(On unclassified road 2 miles south-east of Efailwen, a hamlet on the A478 between Crymych and Clynderwen. Parking for several cars.)

A church where pilgrims once rested on their way to St David's now houses the two traditional hand-looms used by Alan Hemmings, a weaver whose work has won national and international awards. Soft, fine wool from Angora goats is used either on its own or mixed with wool from Welsh Mountain sheep. From this is created the material for scarves, hats, stoles, rugs and other goods dyed in what Mr Hemmings calls his 'colours-of-the-countryside'. They range from delicate greys and fawns to rich blues and golds. Most garments are made in limited editions of not more than a dozen in each design. Alan Hemmings has been joined by Jane Harris, to develop other weaves.

Open Easter to Oct., Mon.–Fri., 9–5; Sat, 9–12.

MAESLLYN   Map ref: Bb
Maesllyn Woollen Mills and Museum, Maesllyn, Llandyssul.
Tel. Rhydlewis 251
(Off an unclassified road at Maesllyn, which is between the A486 and B4334, 4 miles north-west of Llandyssul. Ample parking by mill.)

Gwinnett Tyler, a wealthy landowner who lived in a mansion near Maesllyn, spared no expense when he built this large woollen-mill in 1881. He equipped it with the latest machinery – most of which has survived – and sent his sons to Yorkshire to learn the trade. Run by the Martin family since 1976, the mill now produces cloths which range from fine flannels to tweeds and are made into rugs and garments sold in the adjoining shop. Some fabric is woven on a hand-loom with a 'flying' shuttle. Although very much a working mill, Maesllyn is also a museum of industrial archaeology. An overshot water-wheel – of the type the mill once had – has been installed, and the dye-house is being restored.

Open Mon.–Sat., 10–6; Sun., 2–6.

NARBERTH   Map ref: Bb
The Narberth Pottery, 2 Market Street, Narberth.
Tel. Narberth 860732
(Market Street slopes away from the centre of Narberth. Ample car parking a few minutes' walk away.)

Although he uses an electric kiln, Simon Rich is very much a traditionalist who also fires his wide range of stoneware in a Japanese-style 'raku' kiln and another which burns wood. He makes his own glazes, using domestic ash as well as local riverbed clays and silts. Goods include tableware, delightful little cottages and a whimsical miniature zoo of crocodiles, mice, snails, ducks and other creatures. His wife, Susie, gives spinning-wheel demonstrations during the summer, and also makes sheepskin boots.

Open Mon.–Sat., 10–5.30.

PEMBROKE   Map ref: Aa
Heron Pottery, 62 Main Street, Pembroke.
Tel. Pembroke 2404
(Part of a raised terrace in the main street, a few hundred yards east of Pembroke Castle. Ample parking near by.)

Castles, fairy-tale turrets, town houses, toll houses and quaint little thatched cottages are among the many earthenware and stoneware goods modelled by Paul Roche. He also hand-throws relatively small quantities of jugs, mugs, parsley pots and other domestic items. Although designed as ornaments in their own right, the Heron Pottery's tall, slab-sided pots are also ideal for arrangers of bulrushes and other long, slender plants. Attractive pictures painted on fired clay were inspired by a pupil's painting when Mr Roche was an art teacher. The shop at the front of the premises sells artists' materials, in addition to a wide variety of hand-crafted goods.

Open Mon.–Sat., 9–5.30; Sun., 10–5. Workshop open by appointment.

Opening times and other details may change. Check by telephone before making a special journey.

249

PENALLY   Map ref: Ba
Penally Pottery, Llandsker House, Penally, Tenby.
Tel. Tenby 3796
(Just off A4139 Tenby-Pembroke coast road, between church and post office in village. Parking on road outside.)

Cartoon characters in old copies of Punch and other humorous publications delighted Peter Day when he was a boy. They also provided the early inspiration for many amusing figures which he now models in stoneware. Old codgers drinking at a bar or chatting on a park bench, piggy banks, 'barrel man' moneyboxes and tubby monks share the spacious shop's shelves with Heath Robinson lorries and many other whimsical creations. 'The old woman who lived in a shoe' inspired the very large but wonderfully detailed boots which take three days to make and stand almost 2 ft tall. Mushroom houses are also popular with visitors.

Open daily, Easter to Oct., 10–5.30, and until approximately 9 p.m. during July and Aug.

PENDINE   Map ref: Bb
Pendine Pottery, Pendine, Laugharne.
Tel. Pendine 233
(At entrance to Pendine Wildlife and Leisure Park. The village is on the coast, 5 miles south-west of Laugharne. Ample off-road parking outside pottery.)

Sarah Page and Leri Thomas were students together at the Dyfed College of Art in Carmarthen before they became professional potters in Pendine, a popular holiday village where the world's land-speed record was broken several times in the 1920s. They make flowerpots in terracotta, but devote most of their energy and skill to stoneware items, from small vases to large bowls. Mugs and storage jars are also popular. Terracotta nesting-boxes and bird-tables catch the eye in a large display area in which the Pendine Pottery's goods are on view, together with other items made by local craftsmen.

Open daily, Apr.–Sept., 9–6. Also open Oct.–Mar., Mon.–Fri., 9–5.

PENTRE-CWRT   Map ref: Bb
John Jones (Derw) Ltd, Derw Mills, Pentre-cwrt, Llandyssul.
Tel. Llandyssul 3361
(Signposted from A486 in Pentre-cwrt, a village just over 2 miles south-west of Llandyssul. Parking by mill.)

Travel rugs and fringed tapestry bedspreads are among the most popular goods produced from cloth made in this old-established mill on a tributary of the River Teifi. It was built by John Jones in 1880, and is still run by members of his family. As many as 12 electrically powered looms are available to weave wool into several fabrics, the finest of which is worsted flannel. Visitors may buy lengths of cloth, as well as ready-made items, and many other craft goods are sold in the shop.

Open Mon.–Fri., 9–5. Shop open June–Oct. on Sat., 10–4.30. Large groups wishing to tour the mill should make an appointment in advance.

PENTRE-GALAR   Map ref: Bb
Glyn-y-Fran Woodcraft, Pentre-Galar, Crymych.
Tel. Crymych 347
(Signposted off A478 Cardigan-Tenby road, 2 miles south of Crymych. Parking outside craft shop.)

Working in lime, ash, sycamore, elm, beech and other native woods, Peter Bossom and members of his family make an attractive range of functional domestic goods which include tiered racks for up to 30 eggs, 'trees' on which to hang mugs, and breadboards, bowls and platters. Some boards are decorated by pyrography – that is, the designs are burned into them. Glyn-y-Fran is a smallholding, in the heart of rural Dyfed.

Workshops open Jan.–Nov., Tues.–Fri., 9.30–1 and 2.30–5.30. Shop open Jan.–Nov., Mon.–Sat., 9–1 and 2–6.

PONTARSAIS   Map ref: Bb
Gwili Pottery, Bronwydd Road, Pontarsais, Carmarthen.
Tel. Llanpumsaint 449
(Signposted off the A485, 6 miles north of Carmarthen; 100 yds down B4301. Parking by pottery.)

Pru Green enjoys talking to visitors, because she appreciates their comments on her high-fired earthenware. Established in 1978, the Gwili Pottery is housed in a spacious old farm building and produces a wide range of domestic ware, from combined egg-cups and saucers to bread crocks, casseroles and storage jars. They are finished with a white glaze and then hand-painted with attractive designs in which flowers and leaf-like motifs feature prominently. Whimsical little mice appear on many items, and have become something of a trade mark for the pottery.

Open Mon.–Fri., 2–5; Sat., 9.30–5.

PONTRHYDFENDIGAID   Map ref: Cc
Abaty Pottery, Pontrhydfendigaid.
Tel. Pontrhydfendigaid 667
(By sign for Strata Florida Abbey in Pontrhydfendigaid, a village on the B4343 between Tregaron and Devil's Bridge. Parking in street.)

Almost 100 different items – from egg-cups and mugs to Stilton covers and large casseroles – are produced by this surprisingly large, bustling pottery in the heart of central Wales. Five full-time potters may be seen at work, shaping and decorating the high-fired stoneware which is sold in a shop a few yards away. Some goods are exported to markets as far afield as the USA.

Pottery open Mon.–Fri., 7.30–4. Shop open daily, 11–6, during July, Aug. and Sept., and 7.30–4 on weekdays during rest of year.

SAUNDERSFOOT   Map ref: Bb
Saundersfoot Pottery, Wogan Terrace, Saundersfoot.
Tel. Saundersfoot 812406
(In the centre of Saundersfoot, close to beach and harbour. Large car park near by.)

Corn dollies, baskets, candles and many other hand-crafted goods make this shop a browser's delight; but Carol Brinton, working at her wheel or tending a kiln filled with earthenware, is invariably the centre of attention. She first visited Saundersfoot as a child of two, and started the pottery in 1970. Her husband, Piet, is a graphic designer who does much of the decorative work and also dreamed up the pottery's four-toed Saundersfoot trade mark. Mrs Brinton hand-throws a wide selection of items, including combined plant pots and saucers, egg-cups, bowls and coffee sets. She also makes some of her own glazes.

Open daily, Easter to Sept., 10–5.30; and 8 p.m.–10 p.m. during the main holiday season.

SOLVA   Map ref: Ab
The Craftsman (Woodworker), Main Street, Solva.
Tel. St David's 721294
(Near the bridge in the lower part of Solva, a village on the A487, 3 miles east of St David's. Parking beside harbour at western end of Main Street.)

Once a busy little port, Solva has an atmosphere that is almost Cornish and provides a delightful setting for Hugh Loughborough's small shop and workshop. Ten years with the Forestry Commission gave him a sound knowledge of timber, and he uses only native hardwoods – mainly oak, elm, ash and beech – to make beautiful 'country' furniture. Mr Loughborough does everything from steam-bending timber to weaving the rushwork bottoms for chairs. More than half of his work

is specially commissioned, and he has also made a lectern and undertaken other work for St David's Cathedral. The shop stocks such things as pottery, hornwork from the Lake District and Suffolk basket and rush-work.

Open Mon.–Sat., 10.30–1 and 2–5.

STEPASIDE   Map ref: Bb
Stoney Park Woollen Weavers, Stepaside, Narberth.
Tel. Saundersfoot 813868
(Just over 1 mile up a narrow lane north of Stepaside, a village on the A477, 2 miles north of Saundersfoot. Parking area by craft shop.)

David and Linda Noon spent 30 months restoring Stoney Park, a small farm which had been derelict for more than a decade. The old grain loft, built in the 19th century, is now their snug and welcoming workshop-cum-showroom and stands amid sheep-grazed fields in an atmosphere of rural tranquillity. A small, domestic loom of the type used to make Harris Tweed produces beautiful cloth – made from machine-spun wool – for ties, rugs, dresses and light furnishings.
   The Noons create their own designs and favour soft, autumnal colours. Among their regular customers for tabards, rugs and a variety of other woven goods is a shop in Boston, Massachusetts.

Open Easter to Sept., Mon.–Fri., 10–1 and 2–6. By appointment in winter.

TENBY   Map ref: Ba
Tenby Pottery, 14 Upper Frog Street, Tenby.
Tel. Tenby 2890
(In the centre of Tenby, within the town's medieval walls. Very limited on-street parking near by; large car park overlooking sea about five minutes away.)

Tucked away down one of Tenby's typically narrow streets, this old-established pottery makes a wide variety of earthenware, including one-off plates to commemorate weddings, anniversaries and other special events. Casual callers have an excellent view of all the processes, including throwing on a traditional 'kick' wheel. Large plant pots are a popular choice, but Anthony and Mary Markes also make many smaller items. They were students together at a London art college, and in 1958 established what was then one of the very few potteries in west Wales. Mrs Markes concentrates on 'honey' glazing and painting the finished articles. Dark brown backgrounds with white motifs are typical.

Open Mon.–Fri., 10.15–1 and 2.15–5.30. Sat., 10.15–1.

TREGARON   Map ref: Cc
Clocsiau Caron (Clogs), Chapel Street, Tregaron.
Tel. Tregaron 8925
(Near crossroads in centre of Tregaron. Parking in street.)

Hywel Davies is probably the last full-time maker of traditional clogs left in Wales. He fells his own timber and prefers to use alder because it is both easy to work and hard-wearing. Three knives, each of a different size and shape, transform the rough-cut billets into smooth soles, most of which are made to order. It takes about half a day to make one pair. Mr Davies also carves limewood spoons with scenes depicting Arthurian legends and stories from The Mabinogion, the great treasury of Welsh folklore, together with statuettes, plaques and candleholders. He welcomes customers' commissions.

Open Easter to Sept., 9–7. During rest of year, 9–5.

TRESAITH   Map ref: Bb
The Studio Craftshop, Tresaith, Aberporth.
Tel. Aberporth 810512
(Just over 1 mile east of Aberporth, on left of steep hill leading down to Tresaith's beach. Parking by craft shop.)

Trevor and Valerie Green taught arts and crafts

in Leicestershire before they moved to this small seaside village in 1972. They are a versatile couple, whose interests include painting, dressmaking and enamelling on copper – but they specialise in pyrography, the old art of burning designs into wood. Mrs Green concentrates on wildlife and flowers, while her husband creates bold, elaborate designs inspired by such Celtic masterpieces as the 8th-century Book of Kells. The couple make three-legged 'milking' stools, breadboards, platters and other wooden items.

Open daily at Easter, and May–Sept., 9–6.

TUMBLE   Map ref: Cb
J. R. Thomas and Sons, The Forge, 76 Bethesda Road, Tumble.
Tel. Cross Hands 841612
(Behind bungalow in Bethesda Road [B4317] off lower end of Tumble's main street. Parking outside smithy.)

Roger Thomas, a member of the British Artist Blacksmiths' Association, is at least the third generation of his family to work with iron and steel, hammer and anvil. Considerable strength blends with inherited and acquired skills to create companion sets for fireplaces, dog grates, candlesticks, wall lights and other functional but decorative items. Most of his wares are made to order. One particularly memorable commission called for a pair of large gates which took eight weeks to forge, and another four weeks to decorate with leafwork and other embellishments.

Open Mon.–Fri., 8–5.

WALWYN'S CASTLE   Map ref: Ab
Tuson Ceramics, Barn Farmhouse, Walwyn's Castle, Haverfordwest.
Tel. Broad Haven 610
(Clearly signposted in small village off B4327, halfway between Haverfordwest and Dale. Parking by craft shop.)

It takes Clifford and Lynne Tuson anything up to two weeks to make the elaborate moulds for their vitreous whiteware. Among their most attractive products are large lamps, whose designs reflect strong Moorish and early Gothic influences. At the other end of the scale are pottery replicas of Victorian and Edwardian bottles which originally contained anything from poison to locally brewed beer. Sea-smoothed pebbles provide moulds for attractive ornaments which catch the eye in the small display area. Mr and Mrs Tuson taught craftwork at the Royal School for the Deaf in Birmingham before becoming professional potters.

Open Mon.–Sat., 10–8.

WOLF'S CASTLE   Map ref: Ab
Wolf's Castle Pottery, Wolf's Castle, Haverfordwest.
Tel. Treffgarne 609
(Clearly signposted off A40, halfway between Haverfordwest and Fishguard. Parking outside pottery.)

For a small fee, visitors to Philip and Madeline Cunningham's pottery can try their hand at the ancient craft. The couple also run residential courses for would-be potters. In business since 1972, the Cunninghams make a wide range of stoneware goods, most of which are intended for domestic use. Mrs Cunningham, a keen cook, tests all the new ovenware designs. Everything is fired in a large 'top hat' kiln, so called because it can be lifted off its base, revealing the way in which the contents are stacked.

Open daily, May–Oct., 9.30–6.

YSTRAD MEURIG   Map ref: Cc
T. D. Davies, The Smithy, Ystrad Meurig.
Tel. Pontrhydfendigaid 248
(On B4340, 1 mile north-west of Ystrad Meurig. Limited parking on road.)

Tom Davies, a blacksmith who learned his craft in the 1930s, transforms lengths of mild steel into what is still generally known as decorative

Museum of the Woollen Industry

VELINDRE, DYFED

From the Middle Ages until the middle of the 19th century, woollen manufacturing was the most important of the Welsh industries, first as a cottage industry and then as an aspect of the Industrial Revolution. In the second half of the 19th century the villages of the Teifi valley became major centres of textile manufacture, and Drefach-Felindre was one of these. Around the village the streams ran fast and deep enough to drive the machinery in the mills. The area was close to the wool-producing districts of what is now Dyfed, to the main markets in the industrial valleys of South Wales and to the fulling mills where the cloth was finished.

A legacy of industrial craftsmanship survived from the domestic industry which had flourished there previously – crucial to the success of the new undertakings.

Today, many of the mills have been converted to other uses, but the Cambrian Mill, which shares its premises with the museum, is still working, and glimpses can be caught of the weaving room. Visitors can also follow the Bargod stream up its small valley, and see a series of seven mills in the course of a few miles.

The museum traces the development of the industry and, with the aid of photographs, tools and captions, explains each stage of the manufacturing process. There is also a contemporary exhibition of products from other nearby mills. One room is full of sturdy old spinning-wheels, looms, drive-shafts and machinery that was originally driven by water, then by gas and finally by electricity. Upstairs there is an automatic mule – spinning machine – that was once used in the Cambrian Mill.

Drefach-Felindre, Llandyssul, Dyfed. Tel. Velindre 370453.
(Off the A484, 3 miles south-east of Newcastle Emlyn.)

Open Apr.–Sept., inclusive, Mon.–Sat., 10–5. Admission free.

MILL *Cambrian Mill, at Drefach-Eelindre, which flourished in the second half of the 19th century.*

SORTING WOOL *Work at Cambrian Mill in 1930.*

'ironwork'. Strength and skill combine to create hand-wrought goods which range from old-style candlesticks and gracefully elaborate peacocks to pairs of gates worthy of the most noble stately home. His craftsmanship has won a prize at the National Eisteddfod of Wales and prizes at the annual Royal Welsh Show. Mr Davies still does some repair work on agricultural implements, but has not made or fitted horseshoes since the mid-sixties.

Open Mon.–Fri., 9–5.30; Sat., 9–12.

MUSEUM

VELINDRE   Map ref: Bb
Museum of the Woollen Industry.
(Off the A484, 3 miles south-east of Newcastle Emlyn.)
(See panel above)

GWENT

ABERBARGOED   Map ref: Da
Stuart & Sons Ltd, Pengam Glassworks, Angel Lane, Aberbargoed, Bargoed.
Tel. Bargoed 831617
(Angel Lane is off A4049 on southern outskirts of Aberbargoed in the Rhymney Valley, near Bedwellty Comprehensive School. Parking on premises.)

When held up to the light a piece of cut crystal glass sparkles with a jewel-like brilliance. The mysteries of how this is achieved at Stuart & Sons are unfolded to visitors during a tour of the premises. A guide explains how the raw ingredients are mixed and melted in a furnace,

before being withdrawn as red-hot 'globs' on the end of steel rods and blown into graceful shapes. After cutting and trimming the glasses, the delicate art of incising diamond-sharp patterns is performed. In the showroom, slightly imperfect wine services, fruit bowls, vases and miniature gift items are for sale.

Tours arranged by appointment, Mon.–Thur., 10 and 2. Shop open daily, 9–5.

WOLVESNEWTON   Map ref: Da
Wolvesnewton Folk Collection and Craft Centre, nr Chepstow.
Tel. Wolvesnewton 231
(Turn off B4235 Usk-Chepstow road at Llangwm. Large car park.)

A huge, single-storey cruciform barn dominates a group of farm buildings which were built of local stone in the late 18th century for the Duke of Beaufort. No longer used for farming, they house a number of craft workshops, old agricultural implements, and a fascinating collection of unusual, often amusing, items used in everyday life from Victorian times onwards. The craftsmen who work here include a potter, a furniture maker, an antique restorer, a rug maker and a jeweller. There is also a corn-dolly workshop, and several times a year other craftsmen come to demonstrate their skills.

Open Good Friday to June 30, Sat.–Mon., 11–6; July–Sept., daily, 11–6; Oct.–Dec., Sun., 2–5.30.

MUSEUMS

ABERGAVENNY   Map ref: Db
Abergavenny Museum, The Castle, Castle Street, Abergavenny.
Tel. Abergavenny 4282

Surrounded by the ruins of a 12th-century castle, the museum occupies a commanding position. On one side it overlooks Abergavenny; on the other, the rolling farmland of the Borders. Small exhibitions include a display of traditional butter and cheese making, and a reconstructed saddler's workshop, the contents of which came from a business which closed down in 1924. In 1855 there were eight saddlers in Abergavenny, but today, despite a revival in the trade brought about by pony-trekking, there is only one.

Open Mar.–Oct., Mon.–Sat., 11–1 and 2–5; Sun., 2.30–5. Nov.–Feb., Mon.–Sat., 11–1 and 2–4; closed Sun. There is a charge for admission.

USK   Map ref: Da
Rural Crafts Museum, Newmarket Street, Usk.

Years ago, the village of Llanvapley – the original home of the Rural Crafts Museum – was self-sufficient. It had its own blacksmith's shop, water-mill, cobbler's shop, cider press and brew house. The museum commemorates the passing of these and other crafts, including thatching and coopering. At one time or another almost everyone in Llanvapley has contributed something to this collection. There are also two wagons, agricultural implements and countless hand-tools – all labelled, and their purposes explained.

Open daily, Apr.–Sept., 2–5 except Mon. and Wed.; in winter, Sun. only, 2–5. Other times by appointment (ring Llantilio 210).

GWYNEDD

BANGOR   Map ref: Ce
Doniau Cudd Pottery, 25 Garth Road, Bangor.
Tel. Bangor 2542
(Garth Road runs between the A5 and the pier, on the north side of Bangor. Parking near by.)

A friendly looking baby dragon, finished in a rich red glaze, is one of the most popular items made by this busy pottery, which supplies about 100 shops in Wales and England. Run by Patricia Joyce and David Frost, it specialises in casting from moulds and produces goods ranging from domestic ware to attractive ornaments. There is also a wheel on which small numbers of hand-thrown goods are made. The pottery makes extensive use of 'sgraffito' – a hand-engraving technique in which glaze is cut away to form a pattern.

Open daily, Easter to Oct., 10–6; rest of year Sat. and Sun., 11–5.

BETWS-Y-COED   Map ref: Ce
Pennant Crafts, The Pottery, Betws-y-coed.
Tel. Betws-y-coed 224
(On left of A5 as it heads out of Betws-y-coed towards Capel Curig. Limited parking on road outside craft shop; car park about 300 yds away, across bridge.)

Tom and Marjorie Edwards 'discovered' Snowdonia on walking holidays, and now run a thriving pottery and weaving business in the heart of the National Park. Mugs, goblets, decanters, vases, plant pots and many other items of earthenware are either cast or hand-

Opening times and other details may change. Check by telephone before making a special journey.

251

thrown by the couple and their sons, Jonathan and Peter. They also make attractive pomanders filled with a pot-pourri of local flowers. Two small 'domestic' looms are used to weave wool for ties, head squares and other goods as large as knee rugs. Potters and weavers share the building with a shop selling a good selection of craftwork.

Open Mon.–Sat., 9.30–5.30. Also Sun. in July and Aug.

BLAENAU FFESTINIOG Map ref: Cd
Ffestiniog Pottery, Blaenau Ffestiniog.
Tel. Blaenau Ffestiniog 601
(Two hundred yards down road, signposted for Tanygrisiau, which leaves the A470 on the north side of Blaenau Ffestiniog. Parking in street outside pottery.)

A traditionalist, steeped in the history of British pottery, Adrian Childs creates the sort of domestic earthenware produced by 'country' potters in the 19th century. Rich glazes and bold but simple slip-trailed decorations characterise his work, which ranges from mugs to casseroles, pancheons and large garden pots. As many as 1,000 large pieces can be stacked in what was probably the largest wood-fired kiln in Wales when it was completed in 1981. Considerably higher than a man, the kiln consumes around 1 ton of timber each time it is fired, and demands about 18 hours of dedicated stoking.

Open daily from 9 a.m. until 'late'.

BLAENAU FFESTINIOG Map ref: Cd
Gloddfa Ganol Slate Mine, Blaenau Ffestiniog.
Tel. Blaenau Ffestiniog 664
(Opposite Llechwedd Slate Products [see next entry]. Ample parking near workshop.)

Set on a man-made plateau, more than 1,000 ft above sea-level, Gloddfa Ganol's workshop forms part of what was once the world's largest slate mine. The mountain is riddled with more than 42 miles of tunnels, and hundreds of underground chambers blasted out with black powder. Machines and hand-tools are used to cut, split, plane and polish the slate, which is made into flower holders, ashtrays, place mats and clock cases; also traditional and functional items such as roofing slates and hearths. Visitors may also tour the old mine and see a terrace of cottages built for quarrymen and their families in the 1840s.

Open daily, Easter to Oct., 10–5.30.

BLAENAU FFESTINIOG Map ref: Cd
Llechwedd Slate Products, Blaenau Ffestiniog.
Tel. Blaenau Ffestiniog 343
(Off the A470, 1 mile north of Blaenau Ffestiniog. Ample parking near workshop.)

Llechwedd's blue-grey slate, formed 500 million years ago, was shipped all over the world when the industry was at its peak during the second half of the 19th century. The quarry still produces roofing slates, albeit on a much smaller scale, but they have been joined by clock and barometer cases, sundials, bookends, candle holders and many other hand-crafted products. Boards for chess, solitaire and shove ha'penny are also made in the workshop, together with a wide variety of screen-printed coasters. Visitors may also take a tram ride into the old slate caverns.

Open daily, Mar. to mid-Oct., 9.30–6. Also Mon.–Fri. during rest of year.

CAE DDAFYDD Map ref: Cd
Beddgelert Pottery, Cae Ddafydd, Llanfrothen, Penrhyndeudraeth.
Tel. Beddgelert 213
(Signposted off A4085 below Pass of Aberglasyn, 4 miles south-east of Beddgelert. Parking outside pottery.)

A narrow, tree-flanked lane takes visitors to this isolated pottery, whose grounds are patrolled by stately peacocks. Thirty acres of land provide Pauline Hancock with many of the ingredients for her secret pot-pourri recipe, which fills the pottery's pomanders with fragrance. Cast in earthenware, they come in many shapes and sizes including cats, owls, bears, elephants and a woman in traditional Welsh dress. The pottery also produces mugs, coffee sets and other domestic ware, and has a shop.

Open every day, 9.30–6. Parties should make an appointment.

CRICCIETH Map ref: Bd
Criccieth Slate Centre, Mona Terrace, Criccieth.
Tel. Criccieth 2867
(On road down to beach, just below and behind Seion chapel. Parking outside workshop.)

Five first-prize certificates from the National Eisteddfod, for craft goods made in slate, hang in Roy Williams's workshop, together with a number of other awards. Working in dark slate from Blaenau Ffestiniog and Corris, the craftsman produces an extensive collection of goods, from ashtrays and corkscrew handles to clock cases, which are finished with linseed oil. Mr Williams also makes elaborate coats of arms for individual customers. Small, screen-printed slates are popular souvenirs.

Open daily, Easter to Oct., 9–6; Mon.–Fri. during rest of year.

CRICCIETH Map ref: Bd
Woodcarving Workshop, East Promenade, Criccieth.
Tel. Criccieth 2833
(Near entrance to East Promenade car park, between railway line and beach.)

Working in blackthorn, apple, pear and cherry wood, together with some teak and mahogany, Charles Jones carves traditional Welsh love spoons – tokens of affection which date from the Middle Ages. Rich in symbolism and astonishingly detailed, they include such features as chains with more than 20 links, all of which are shaped from the same length of timber. Serpents, hearts, cages, initials and the 'vine of life' are among many other time-honoured decorations. Mr Jones also makes four-legged Welsh spinning stools in oak. They can be carved to illustrate the customer's family history.

Open Mon.–Sat., 9–6; Sun. by appointment.

DINAS-MAWDDWY Map ref: Cd
Meirion Mill, Dinas-Mawddwy.
Tel. Dinas Mawddwy 311
(Entrance opposite Buckley Arms Hotel in Dinas-Mawddwy, a village on the A470, 10 miles south-east of Dolgellau. Ample parking outside mill.)

Built in the 19th century as a storehouse for slate, the building became a woollen-mill in 1946 when it was acquired by a co-operative of local farmers. Their enterprise failed, but in 1966 the mill attracted Raymond Street, a Cheshire businessman, and Muriel, his Welsh wife. It is now a flourishing concern, visited by as many as 250,000 people each year, and weaves all types of woollen cloth from fine flannel to heavy tweed. A banner designed and woven in 1976 to commemorate the USA's 200th anniversary now hangs in the Library of Congress in Washington DC.

Mill open Mon.–Fri., 10–4.30. Shop open daily, 10–4.30, Apr.–Oct.

GOLAN Map ref: Cd
Brynkir Woollen Mill, Golan, Garn-Dolbenmaen.
Tel. Garn-Dolbenmaen 236
(On unclassified road, signposted from A487, about 2 miles north-west of Tremadog. Car park 50 yds from mill.)

This commendably complete mill does everything, from disentangling and blending its wool – a process known as 'willeying' – to weaving it into fabrics. These range from Welsh flannel to traditional tweeds and tapestries. Lengths are sold in a large shop on the mill's upper floor, together with bedspreads, blankets, a wide range of garments and many other goods made from Brynkir's cloth. The mill's history goes back to the Middle Ages, and its trade mark – based on a photograph taken about 1885 – depicts a spinning-wheel and a woman in traditional Welsh dress.

Open Mon.–Thur., 8–4.30; Fri., 8–4. Appointment needed for parties.

LLANBEDR Map ref: Cd
Maes Artro Craft Village, Llanbedr.
Tel. Llanbedr 467/497
(Alongside the main road on the south side of Llanbedr, a village on the A496 between Harlech and Barmouth. Ample parking in the village.)

Originally an RAF camp, Maes Artro was turned into a craft village by Brian Golding, a Welsh weaver, and has been open since Easter 1977. In 1979 about 150,000 people explored its craft workshops and other attractions, which include a re-created old Welsh street, an aquarium and a model village. Timber-clad workshops house candle makers, wood workers, garment makers, goldsmiths, jewellers, leatherworkers, potters, a signwriter, a clock-maker and other craftsmen. The village was specially commended by the British Tourist Authority in 1978, and gained a Prince of Wales Award in the course of the following year.

Most of the village is open daily from 9–6, and later during the holiday season. Parts may be closed Oct. to Easter. Charge for admission during season.

LLANBERIS Map ref: Ce
Llanberis Pottery, 2 Mur Mawr, Llanberis.
Tel. Llanberis 870700
(On south side of Llanberis, near waterfall and Snowdon Mountain Railway track. Reached by way of Victoria Terrace, which leaves Llanberis-Caernarfon road opposite Royal Victoria Hotel. Very limited parking near pottery.)

Superb views of Snowdon reward those who seek out Christopher Bourne's one-man pottery on the steep slopes above Llanberis. Greatly influenced by the beauty of his surroundings, he works in stoneware and mixes many glazes inspired by the mountain's ever-changing moods and colours. Raw materials include wood ash, and copper gleaned from abandoned workings. Mr Bourne produces a wide range of domestic and decorative goods, and works at a traditional 'kick' wheel which he built himself.

Gallery-cum-shop exhibits paintings and prints by Christopher Bourne. Open daily, Apr.–Oct., 9.30–5.30. Pottery workshop open on Tues.

LLANBERIS Map ref: Ce
Odyn Copr (Enamelling), High Street, Llanberis.
Tel. Padarn 366
(In main street of Llanberis, between Castle Hotel and post office. Car park about 100 yds away, off High Street.)

Sue Lowe's love of gardening is reflected by the flowing, flower-like designs which emerge from her kiln. Enamelling on copper, she creates key rings, pendants, sets of buttons, cuff-links, trinket boxes and many other attractive goods, most of which involve one base colour and three others. The finest enamel powders are ground with a pestle and mortar before being heated to about 1,520°F (825°C). A former geography teacher who took up enamelling as a hobby, Sue Lowe also does pokerwork and makes such things as paperweights featuring pressed 'cottage-garden' flowers.

Open all year, Mon.–Sat., 10–6. Workshop is behind a well-stocked shop and visitors must ask – or make an appointment in advance – if they want to see enamelling being done.

LLANFAIRYNGHORNWY Map ref: Be
Llywenan Pottery, Rhyd-y-Beddau, Llanfairynghornwy, Anglesey.
Tel. Llanfaethlu 693
(On minor road, ½ mile south-east of church in Llanfairynghornwy. Village is off the A5025 between Cemaes Bay and Llanrhyddlad. Parking outside pottery.)

Phil Hayes and Alison Fisher studied together in Stoke-on-Trent before opening their own pottery in the lovely north-west corner of Anglesey. Working in a converted farm building, they blend their own clay – using what was originally a baker's dough mixer – and also prepare their own glazes. The couple produce such things as cactus pots, teapots, soup bowls and other domestic ware as well as a delightful range of hand-modelled goods rich in detail and character. The latter include vintage cars, complete with Edwardian-style passengers, and whimsical figures in toppers and tails.

Open daily, May–Sept., 10.30–6. Also at other times when the potters are at work.

LLANGEFNI Map ref: Be
Bodeilio Weaving Centre, Talwrn, Llangefni, Anglesey.
Tel. Llangefni 722465
(Signposted off B5109, halfway between Llangefni and Pentraeth. Ample parking outside centre.)

Anglesey's last woollen-mill closed shortly after the Second World War, but the ancient craft of hand-loom weaving was revived at Bodeilio in 1974. Housed in the stone outbuildings of a handsome old farm, built at the start of the 17th century, the looms complement an exhibition which tells the story of hand-weaving from the earliest times until the advent of the Industrial Revolution. Special emphasis is paid to the craft in North Wales. The looms are worked by experts, but visitors are invited to try their hand at the craft. Bodeilio's other attractions include a craft gallery, shop and restaurant.

Open daily, Easter to Oct., 10–6. Other times by arrangement.

LLANGOED Map ref: Ce
Penmon Pottery, Dinmor Farmhouse, Penmon, Beaumaris, Anglesey.
Tel. Llangoed 270
(On south-eastern tip of Anglesey, almost 2 miles north-east of Llangoed village. Parking outside pottery.)

Tucked away near the end of a narrow lane, high on a headland above Conway Bay, this one-woman pottery produces a wide range of earthenware and stoneware. Ashtrays and other small items contrast with huge casseroles, while other products include decorative plaques and made-to-order nameplates for houses. Rowena Barnes's passion for underwater swimming shows in the fish, lobsters and other sea creatures which feature prominently among her motifs, many of which are painted by hand. Other decorative techniques used at Penmon include spraying and screen-printing.

Open at all reasonable hours, but visitors advised to telephone in advance.

LLANRWST Map ref: Ce
Snowdonia Taxidermy Studios, at Encounter! – The North Wales Museum of Wildlife, Fron Ganol, School Bank Road, Llanrwst.
Tel. Llanrwst 640664
(Museum is signposted from the main A470 on the south side of Llanrwst. Ample parking outside studio.)

Visitors can see the interesting techniques that Bob Reid uses to achieve realism in his work. He is an artistic sculptor-taxidermist whose artificial forms clad with skin, fur or feathers, enable creatures to be modelled in attractive and appropriate poses. They can be as small as a shrew or as large as a fully grown elephant. Mr Reid has also made model prehistoric animals, and bats for a horror film. Many types of birds and animals from all over the world are displayed in the museum. Visitors must pass through the collection to reach the taxidermist's studios.

Open Easter to Oct., Mon.–Fri., 10.30–5.30. Also open Sat. on Bank Holiday weekends. Charge for admission.

NEBO Map ref: Bd
Bryn Coch Pottery, Bryn Coch Mawr, Nebo, Caernarfon.
Tel. Penygroes 367
(Nebo is signposted off the A487, 8 miles south of Caernarfon. The pottery is about ¼ mile from the village school and post office, along Ffordd Cors-y-llyn. Parking outside pottery.)

Unlike many potters, Olga Kinsman concentrates most of her creative talents on modelling. Badgers, ducks, geese, goats, hedgehogs and many other creatures are made either individually or as part of scenes based around such central features as pools and gnarled tree trunks. Mugs with graceful 'animal' handles are also made, and the potter also creates wonderfully delicate stoneware leaves, fungi and 'pinch' pots. Young visitors are invariably delighted by the pottery-cum-farm's assortment of real-life animals.

Open Mon.–Fri., 11–6.30; Sun., 1–6.30.

PENMACHNO Map ref: Cd
Eric Boon, Bodafon, Penmachno, Betws-y-coed.
Tel. Penmachno 251
(Opposite the Machno Inn in Penmachno, a village on the B4406 south of Betws-y-coed. Limited parking outside workshop.)

It is fascinating to watch Eric Boon's nimble fingers transforming a bundle of cane or willow into anything from a small tray to a full-sized chair. Born in Lancashire, he has been making baskets since 1935 and is now one of the comparatively few people working at this ancient craft. Canes from the Far East are soaked in the nearby River Machno to make them pliable; willow comes from Somerset. Mr Boon also repairs rush-seated and cane-seated chairs.

Open daily, Easter to Oct., 9–7. Open 9–5 during rest of year.

PENMACHNO Map ref: Cd
Penmachno Woollen Mill, Penmachno, Betws-y-coed.
Tel. Betws-y-coed 545
(Half a mile along the B4406, signposted to Penmachno, which leaves the A5 2 miles south of Betws-y-coed. Ample parking outside the mill.)

A woollen-mill has been on this beautiful site in the River Machno's wooded valley since the 16th century. It was originally a 'pandy' or fulling-mill, but now concentrates on weaving with three electrically powered looms. Tapestry, tweed and other cloths are either sold in lengths or made into jackets, coats, hats and other garments. Cloth and garments are sold in the mill's shop, together with many other craft goods. An audio-visual display explains to visitors the story of wool and wool-processing.

Open Apr.–Oct., Mon.–Fri., 9–5.30, and until 6.30 in July and Aug. Tweed and craft shop open seven days a week.

PENMORFA Map ref: Cd
Tyn Llan Pottery, Penmorfa, Porthmadog.
Tel. Porthmadog 2514
(Signposted from A487 in Penmorfa, a village 2 miles north-west of Porthmadog. Parking outside pottery.)

Old beams, whitewashed stone walls and a slate-flagged floor combine to give this attractive pottery a great deal of character. Run by Trevor and Hazel Leese, it specialises in slip-cast earthenware and produces goods ranging from owls and trinket boxes to storage jars and coffee sets. Unlike some potters, Trevor Leese makes his own 'master' models and moulds. Celtic patterns, many inspired by the 8th-century Book of Kells, have been among the

couple's favourite decorations since they restored the derelict farm buildings in the mid-1970s. They also make embossed tiles in a press which Mr Leese designed and built with the help of an Arts Council research award.

Open Easter to Oct., Mon.–Fri., 10–5.30. Also open sometimes at weekends.

PORTHMADOG Map ref: Cd
Porthmadog Pottery, Snowdon Mill, Snowdon Street, Porthmadog.
Tel. Porthmadog 2785
(At the end of Snowdon Street, which leaves High Street opposite the post office. Parking outside pottery.)

'Throw a pot at Porthmadog' is the eye-catching slogan used to promote this big and bustling pottery housed in the basement of a 19th-century mill built to grind flour for ships' biscuits. Visitors may try their hand at a potter's wheel, but the resident experts use casting techniques to produce an extensive range of domestic and decorative earthenware. Iron, copper and cobalt oxides are used to create hand-painted decorations in yellows, greens and blues. Traditional motifs feature on the pottery's Celtic-style wares, which include soup bowls, cheese covers and milk jugs. Conducted tours take about 15 minutes, and enable visitors to see every stage from casting to glazing.

Open Apr.–Oct., Mon.–Fri., 9–5.30; June–Sept., weekends, 9–5.30. 'Seconds'

shop, and tweed and craft shop, open seven days a week all year.

TREFRIW Map ref: Ce
Trefriw Woollen Mills, Trefriw, Llanrwst.
Tel. Llanrwst 640462
(Alongside the main road through Trefriw, a village on the B5106 between Betws-y-coed and Conwy. Ample parking on opposite side of road.)

Thomas Williams bought this old-established woollen-mill in 1859, and it has been run by the same family ever since. One of the largest businesses of its kind in Wales, Trefriw employs almost 40 people and undertakes everything from blending the wool to making a wide selection of goods for the spacious, well-stocked shop on the ground floor. Each process is revealed and explained during a self-guided tour whose route is indicated by arrows. Craftworkers demonstrate hand-spinning and hand-loom weaving during the holiday season, but the machinery has been powered by hydro-electric turbines since the old water-wheels were dismantled about 1900. The oldest loom was installed in 1890.

Mill open Mon.–Fri., 8–12 and 1–4.45. Shop open Oct.–June, Mon.–Fri., 8–5; July–Sept., until 5.30. Open Sat., 10–4 all year, and Sun., 2–5, July and Aug.

TYWYN Map ref: Cc
The Pottery, 5 High Street, Tywyn.
Tel. Tywyn 710548

(In small lane behind crafts shop in town centre, on main street opposite post office. Limited parking in street; car park behind post office.)

Peter Roberts opened his pottery in 1980, and was swiftly commissioned to make plates commemorating the 1981 National Eisteddfod. Believed to be the only Welsh potter working with bone china, he makes such things as pomanders, dishes, trinket boxes, thimbles, china love spoons, and a range of animals and birds. Pitchers, mugs and other domestic earthenware are hand-thrown, but most of the goods are slip-cast. Requests to see Peter Roberts at work should be made at the crafts shop in the High Street.

Open Mon.–Sat., 9–5.30.

MID GLAMORGAN

EWENNY Map ref: Ca
Claypits Pottery, Ewenny, nr Bridgend.
Tel. Bridgend 61733
(Opposite Ewenny Pottery. Parking outside.)

Leonard Edger's skilled hands and inventive mind transform solid lumps of clay into lively sculptural forms of all descriptions. Among his most imaginative pieces are forms with spherical bases capped by clusters of whimsical buildings, and goldfish bowls – designed to enliven the dull existence of their occupants –

Love spoons

One of the most eye-catching exhibits in the Welsh Folk Museum at St Fagans, a few miles from Cardiff, is a large collection of remarkably ornate love spoons. The work of talented but anonymous amateurs rather than professional craftsmen, they recall the days when such spoons were a familiar feature of courtship, particularly in rural areas where young men often had little money but plenty of time.

Very little is known about the craft's history, but it is likely that the girl who accepted a love spoon carved by her suitor would then consider herself to be 'spoken for'. For that reason, love spoons are sometimes referred to in Wales as the 'poor man's engagement ring'.

Craft and custom may well be rooted in the Middle Ages, but the oldest dated love spoon was carved in 1667. That period until towards the end of the Victorian era is generally accepted as the golden age of the spoon-makers, whose

intricate workmanship was motivated more by romance than by practicality.

Early carvers probably beautified ordinary domestic utensils, such as the spoons used for drinking 'cawl', a broth of bacon, leeks and other vegetables which played an important part in the diet of western Wales. 'Cawl' spoons were generally made of sycamore felled during the winter when a low sap content ensured freedom from stains and other blemishes. The craftsman's traditional tools included the 'twca cam', a long-handled implement whose small, curved blade was used to scoop out the bowl of the spoon.

Known in Welsh as 'llwyau serch', love spoons developed into elaborate works of art which, in a great many cases, were no more functional than a knife without a blade. The bowl generally retained its familiar size, shape and lack of decoration, but handles were frequently enlarged to provide the carver with plenty of space to demonstrate his skill and imagination. Rectangular and cylindrical handles, for instance, were hollowed out to form cages containing wooden balls – all shaped from the same piece of wood – which symbolised either safe-keeping or the number of children wished for.

Flat-panel handles might have motifs cut into the surface, or be fretworked into bold, geometric patterns. Exceptionally patient and gifted suitors could transform a length of wood into a chain, none of whose many links were cut and re-joined in any way. Popular decorations included an anchor, which indicated a wish to settle down, and a ship to symbolise the hope of a smooth voyage through life. Hearts, locks, keys, lovers' knots, initials and houses were among many other favourites. Many love-spoon makers relied solely on the deftness of their blades, but others enhanced their craftsmanship with pokerwork patterns. Spoons with large 'panel' handles sometimes boasted two or even three bowls.

Experts are wary of pin-pointing regional specialities, but they do appear to have evolved. Love spoons with a small recess for the mounting of a picture seem to have been particularly popular in Caernarvonshire, just as twin-panel handles joined by a loop were fairly common in what used to be the county of Pembrokeshire.

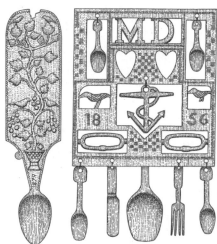

LOVE SPOONS *Examples of love spoons (above and right) at the Welsh Folk Museum, St Fagans, Cardiff.*

Opening times and other details may change. Check by telephone before making a special journey.

253

containing dozens of tiny figures modelled in playful stances. Mr Edger works in stoneware, using a variety of glazes made to his own recipes. His versatility as a potter is demonstrated by the variety of work on display, from tableware to carved mirror frames and miniature furniture.

Open daily, 9–1 and 2–5.30.

EWENNY Map ref: Ca
Ewenny Pottery, Ewenny, nr Bridgend.
Tel. Bridgend 3020
(On B4265 Bridgend-Llantwit Major road on outskirts of village. Large parking area on site.)

A document of 1610 recording a sale of tiles to Ewenny Priory is the earliest reference to this pottery, which for most of its long history has been owned by the Jenkins family. Originally, the local brown glacial clay was prepared by treading it with bare feet to detect the tiniest of stones. Nowadays, modern methods are used to mix the clay, some of which is still dug locally. Mr Alun Jenkins, using techniques passed down by his grandfather and father, produces a high-gloss glaze in distinctive greens, browns and blues. To produce these colours each item is dipped in one glaze, then another glaze is splashed on top. In the heat of the kiln, these two glazes fuse together to give the distinctive mottled effect.

Open Easter to Oct., Mon.–Sat., 9.30–5.30; Sun., 2–5. In winter months, Mon.–Fri., 9.30–5.30; Sat., 9.30–1.

PONTYPRIDD Map ref: Da
John Hughes Pottery, The Grogg Shop, Broadway, Pontypridd.
Tel. Pontypridd 405001
(From A470, join A4058 and follow signs to town centre. Pottery is on left-hand side before town is reached. Parking outside.)

Sports enthusiasts who step inside this pottery should have no difficulty in identifying the colourful ceramic models of famous rugby players, even though their features are amusingly caricatured. They are the creation of John Hughes who, with members of his family, imparts an element of humour to all the figures, known collectively as 'groggs'. Predominantly Welsh in character, they include coal miners, hill farmers and Celtic mythological creatures, as well as rugby and other sports personalities. Each piece is signed, and visitors may order personal caricature portraits.

Open all year, Mon.–Sat., 9–6.

POWYS

CLYRO Map ref: Db
Wye Pottery, Clyro, via Hereford.
Tel. Hay-on-Wye 820510
(On A438, opposite junction with B4351 to Hay-on-Wye. Parking outside.)

Adam Dworski, a self-taught potter, settled in the peaceful village of Clyro in the early 1950s to start his studio pottery. He throws mugs, jugs and bowls in earthenware, which he decorates by painting abstract patterns in coloured oxides over a tin glaze of white or grey. Using an even older technique, he models clay into wall plaques depicting colourful flowers, birds or town scenes, and romantic sculptures ranging from medieval knights on horseback to 'fairy-tale' castles. His work is displayed in a showroom alongside that of his wife, who brightens up old pine furniture with gaily painted designs inspired by traditional European peasant art.

Open Mon.–Sat., 9–1 and 3–6; Sun. by appointment. Mrs Dworski's workshop open by appointment.

CRICKHOWELL Map ref: Db
Grahame Amey Ltd (Furniture makers), Standard Street, Crickhowell.
Tel. Crickhowell 810540

(In town centre, off main A40, almost opposite High Street. Parking in street.)

Behind the mellow stone façade of a former medieval granary, a small team of craftsmen make solid, durable furniture from the 'king' and 'queen' of British hardwoods – oak and ash. Each craftsman is responsible for the completion of a piece of furniture, from selecting the timbers to signing his name on the finished article. The designs for the standard range of tables, chairs, benches, bookcases and dressers are notable for their classic lines, which emphasise the beauty of the wood.

Open Mon.–Fri., 8.30–5; Sat. and Bank Holidays, 9–4.30. Guided tours can be arranged for parties.

LLANELIEU Map ref: Db
Black Mountain Pottery, Llanelieu Court, nr Talgarth.
Tel. Talgarth 711518
(From Talgarth take road beside Tower Hotel. Turn right at T-junction. Bear right at first fork, left at next fork. Pottery is just before church, 2 miles from town. Room for several cars.)

A cobbled path leads to a lofty stone barn of medieval origin, one of several outbuildings attached to Llanelieu's old manor. It houses the pottery, which takes its name from the rugged mountains beyond. Inside, Pauline Paterson makes an attractive range of stoneware, including bread crocks, coffee sets and casseroles. She decorates them in relief with a sunflower motif before applying a warm, speckled glaze. Her husband, Trevor, is an artist, whose paintings line the walls of the barn, but he also produces highly decorative pottery. This includes ornamental masks made from elaborately looped and twisted coils of clay, carved mirror frames, and tiles painted with Egyptian designs.

Open most days, but advisable to telephone before visit.

LLANIDLOES Map ref: Cc
Black Sheep Weavers, 1 Great Oak Street, Llanidloes.
Tel. Llanidloes 2959
(In town centre, opposite Market Hall. Car park near by.)

Prosperity came to Llanidloes in the early 19th century when it became an important centre for the wool trade. Hundreds of weavers used to toil from dawn to dusk to meet the huge demand for cloth. Today, the craft has been revived by Irwin and Virginia Masterson, although on a much smaller scale. Using unspun fleeces from the hardy Welsh Mountain sheep that graze on the surrounding hills, they weave striking wall-hangings and rugs. Some of these incorporate motifs depicting such familiar local sights as a woodland owl and black sheep. They also weave a range of rugs, cushion covers and lamp shades in heavy woollen yarns in autumnal and wintry colours.

Open Apr.–Jan. inclusive, Mon.–Sat., 10–1 and 2–5.30.

PENYBONT Map ref: Dc
Penybont Pottery, Penybont, nr Llandrindod Wells.
(On A44 at east end of village opposite sheep market. Parking in lay-by adjoining pottery.)

Few visitors would guess that the charming Victorian residence of David Weake and his family once housed an assortment of local villains. For, until the First World War, it served as the village police station, complete with two cells. Mr Weake has turned part of the house into his pottery studio and showroom. His work reflects his interest in decorative techniques: for example, tableware with designs cut into the clay or painted over a background glaze; lamp bases from which protrude tree and rock sculptures; and ornamental boxes with jewel-like surfaces created by fusing tiny pieces of coloured glass with the glaze.

Showroom open Mon.–Sat., 9–7; Sun., 9–5. Studio open at weekends and during school holidays.

RHAYADER Map ref: Cc
Dragon Pottery Ltd, East Street, Rhayader.
Tel. Rhayader 810318
(At crossroads by town clock, take A44. Pottery ½ mile on right-hand side. Parking on site.)

At Dragon Pottery, visitors can watch craftsmen making pots by a method used in Britain since the mid-18th century. Known as slip-casting, the shapes of bowls, vases and jars are created by pouring slip (liquid clay) into plaster-of-Paris moulds. The excess water is absorbed by the moulds, leaving a 'skin' of clay behind. The clay pots are removed from the moulds and left to dry. They are then decorated by applying coloured glazes in contrasting bands of brown, yellow and green, through which a pattern, often a leaf motif, is incised. A large selection of pottery is displayed in the adjoining showroom.

Open by appointment, Mon.–Fri., 9–5. Showroom open Easter to Oct., Mon.–Sat., 9–5.

RHAYADER Map ref: Cc
Marston Pottery, Bridge Street, Rhayader.
Tel. Rhayader 810875
(At crossroads by town clock, take road to Elan Valley. Pottery is 400 yds on right-hand side. Off-street parking.)

In memory of his ancestors, who for many generations plied their trade as cobblers in Rhayader, Phil Rogers collects old tools and equipment associated with shoe-making, and displays them in his shop alongside his pottery. Visitors can see him throwing items of stoneware, including teapots, bread crocks, storage jars and decorative plates and vases. He uses local materials in his glazes – in particular, dust from a nearby shale quarry, which contains iron, and ash from elm and oak trees which enlivens the surfaces of the pots by heightening variations in colour.

Open daily, Easter to Oct., 9–6. Rest of year, Mon.–Sat., 9–5.

SOUTH GLAMORGAN

CARDIFF Map ref: Da
San Domenico Stringed Instruments, 177 King's Road, Cardiff.
Tel. Cardiff 35881
(West of city centre. Take fourth turning left off Cathedral Road into Sneyd Street. Shop is opposite end of street. Parking in Sneyd Street.)

Howard Morgan has named his business after a piazza in the Italian town of Cremona, renowned in the 17th and 18th centuries as the home of the finest violin makers, including the great Stradivari. Mr Morgan, who restores violins, violas and cellos, has travelled all over the world in search of fine quality, though neglected, instruments. In his small workshop he restores them to their original splendour and then sells them to musical-instrument collectors and musicians.

Open Mon.–Fri., 10–1 and 2–5.30; Sat., 10–1; but advisable to telephone before a visit.

DINAS POWIS Map ref: Da
Geoffrey Winter, MIMIT (Piano restorer), The Old Forge, Britway Road, Dinas Powis.
Tel. Dinas Powis 512394
(Britway Road is off main village square. Workshop is about 300 yds on left-hand side. Parking space in courtyard.)

Concealed under the glossy casework of elegant 'grand' and 'upright' pianos are over a thousand moving parts. Every one of these must be in perfect working order to attain pure, even notes with a harmonious ring. Geoffrey Winter is one of a very limited number of

craftsmen qualified to undertake their repair and restoration, a delicate task requiring infinite patience and absolute precision. His workshop usually contains four or five instruments needing attention, and visitors may see him engaged in re-stringing, renovating keyboards, tuning, or repairing the casework. Often he uses tools he has made himself.

Open Mon.–Fri., 9–5, by appointment only.

RUMNEY Map ref: Da
Rumney Pottery, Rumney, Cardiff.
Tel. Cardiff 78096
(On A48 at foot of Rumney Hill, at junction with Eastern Avenue. Parking on site.)

There has been a pottery at Rumney for hundreds of years. Successive potters dug the local red clay to make simple kitchen pots for the neighbouring community. The present owner, Robert Giles, specialises in presentation ware and finds a fine white earthenware clay from Staffordshire best for this purpose. His tankards, plates and bowls are inscribed by his wife with commemorative lettering, and decorated in relief with an appropriate motif. They are then coated with slips in bright, clear colours.

People interested in commissioning work should make an appointment to visit, Mon.–Fri., 9–5; or Sat., 9–1.

MUSEUM

ST FAGANS Map ref: Da
Welsh Folk Museum.
(See panel on facing page.)

WEST GLAMORGAN

CYMMER Map ref: Ca
Afandale Pottery Craftshop, Cymmer, nr Port Talbot.
Tel. Cymmer 850591
(Signposted from A4107 at bottom of steep hill. Street parking.)

An old Victorian pub stands in a sheltered wooded valley overlooking the spot where two rushing rivers converge. Their musical sound carries into the beer cellars, which have been converted into a pottery studio. Here, Mr Sterckx throws stoneware pots on a traditional 'kick' wheel. He decorates them by incising patterns in the wet clay and then glazing them in colours as varied as off-white, rust and a dark gun-metal blue.

Open Easter to Oct., 9.30–6. At other times by appointment.

SWANSEA Map ref: Ca
Celtic Studios, 5 Prospect Place, Swansea.
Tel. Swansea 54833
(Off A483. First left-hand turn at first roundabout when approaching from Cardiff. Car parks near by.)

One of the most isolated settlements in the world – an Indian village far north of the Arctic Circle – can boast a piece of British craftsmanship amongst its possessions. It is a decorative window of leaded stained glass, which enhances a little mission church. The window was designed and made at Celtic Studios. For over 40 years Mr Thomas and his assistants have created windows for cathedrals and churches, including several in Swansea. After a design has been approved, a full-size drawing, called a 'cartoon', is made. Using this as a guide, the craftsmen can be seen cutting and taping into position fragments of richly coloured glass. The finer details are then painted on and fused to the glass during a kiln firing. Finally the whole composition is given definition, and held in place, by soldering the glass into 'H'-section lead channels and the whole assembly is made waterproof with specially mixed cement.

Open Mon.–Fri., 8–5, by appointment only.

Map ref: Da

Welsh Folk Museum

ST FAGANS, SOUTH GLAMORGAN

This superb display of buildings and artefacts from the past, set in the grounds of 16th-century St Fagans Castle, reflects time-honoured skills in nearly every exhibit. A resident woodturner, miller and cooper demonstrate that craftsmanship remains alive and active today.

Most fascinating of all, perhaps, are some 18 old buildings from all parts of Wales – cottages and farmhouses, a watermill, a cockpit, a tannery, a smithy, a barn and pigsty, even a chapel. These are no mere replicas, but actual buildings that were dismantled on site, for rebuilding at St Fagans.

Neither are they mere shells. To walk through the doorway of Kennixton, a thatched farmhouse from the Gower, is to step back three centuries in time. The heavy oak furniture, sturdy equipment for kitchen and dairy, the children's bed constructed above a lower-floor 'charnel', or bacon store – all are just as they would have been in those distant days. The walls and ceilings are smoke-stained; a brace of pheasants awaits the pot.

Each building has its equivalent store of fascinating detail. There are attendants on hand to help, but visitors are free to wander as they will. They tend to linger in the kitchen, with its two massive fireplaces and such intriguing equipment as a dog-driven spit. Elsewhere, there are wood-carvings, tapestries, musical instruments and furniture.

The main museum block is a new building containing separate galleries for agriculture, agricultural vehicles, costume and everyday objects. Among a treasure hoard of exhibits is a collection of ploughs dating from the 18th century, a scold's bridle and other instruments of correction, delicately made harps and musical boxes, a collection of love spoons (carved by young men for their sweethearts) and an array of Welsh dressers.

Costumes of the past are displayed in a darkened gallery. In room-sized showcases, furnished in

COOPER *A resident cooper making barrels.*

period styles, family groups are seen going about their domestic affairs. Personal notes about the original owners of the costumes help to infuse life and credibility into the tableaux.

St Fagans, Cardiff, South Glamorgan. Tel. Cardiff 569441.
(Four miles west of Cardiff, off the A48.)

Open Mon.–Sat., 10–5; Sun., 2.30–5. Closed Good Friday, May Day, Christmas Eve, Christmas Day, Boxing Day and New Year's Day. Charge for admission.

CARAVAN *A gipsy caravan from South Wales.*

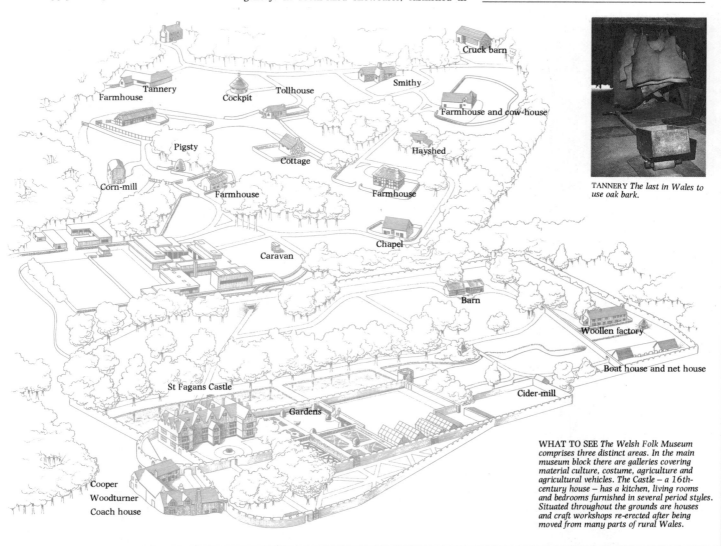

Cruck barn
Tannery
Farmhouse
Cockpit
Tollhouse
Smithy
Farmhouse and cow-house
Pigsty
Hayshed
Cottage
Corn-mill
Farmhouse
Farmhouse
Chapel
Caravan
Barn
Woollen factory
St Fagans Castle
Boat house and net house
Gardens
Cider-mill
Cooper
Woodturner
Coach house

TANNERY *The last in Wales to use oak bark.*

WHAT TO SEE *The Welsh Folk Museum comprises three distinct areas. In the main museum block there are galleries covering material culture, costume, agriculture and agricultural vehicles. The Castle – a 16th-century house – has a kitchen, living rooms and bedrooms furnished in several period styles. Situated throughout the grounds are houses and craft workshops re-erected after being moved from many parts of rural Wales.*

Opening times and other details may change. Check by telephone before making a special journey.

255

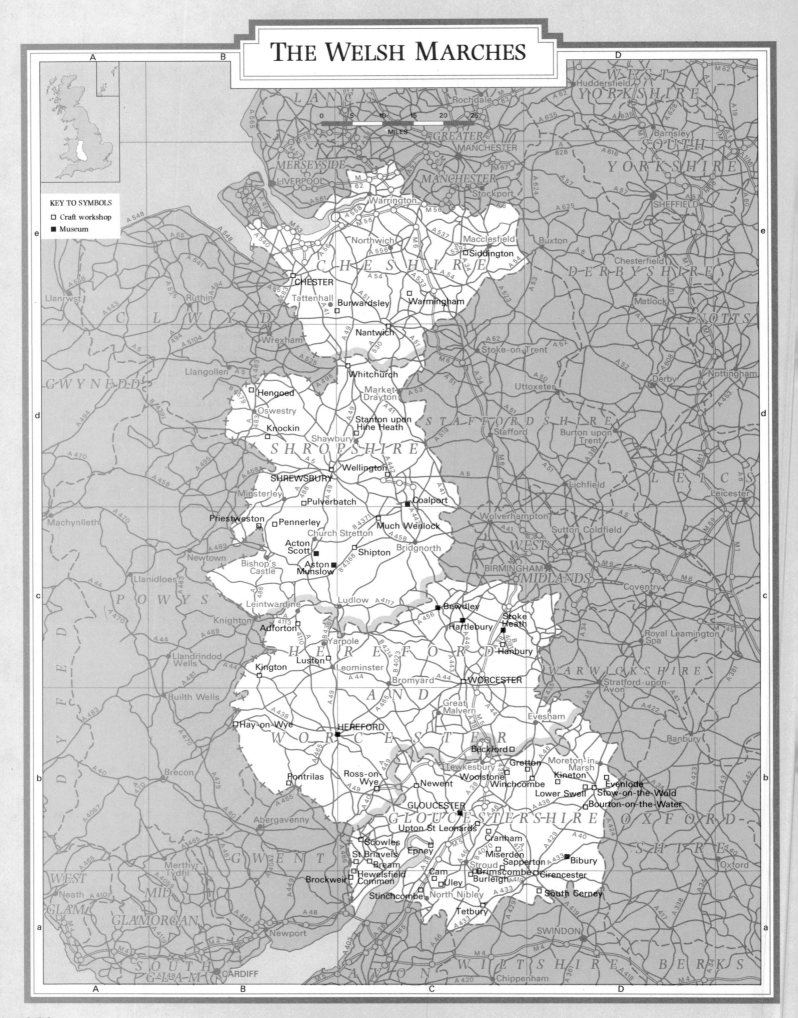

THE WELSH MARCHES

KEY TO SYMBOLS
□ Craft workshop
■ Museum

0 5 10 15 20 25
MILES

WEST YORKSHIRE
Huddersfield
Rochdale
Barnsley
SOUTH YORKSHIRE

LANCS
GREATER MANCHESTER
Warrington
Stockport
SHEFFIELD

MERSEYSIDE
LIVERPOOL
Northwich
Macclesfield
Buxton
Chesterfield
DERBYSHIRE

CHESHIRE
Siddington
Matlock
NOTTS

Llanrwst
Ruthin
CLWYD
CHESTER
Tattenhall
Burwardsley
Warmingham
Nantwich
Wrexham
Stoke-on-Trent
Derby
Nottingham

Llangollen
GWYNEDD
Whitchurch
Market Drayton
Uttoxeter
Hengoed
Oswestry
Knockin
Stanton upon Hine Heath
STAFFORDSHIRE
Stafford
Burton upon Trent
Lichfield
LEICS

Shawbury
SHROPSHIRE
Wellington
SHREWSBURY
Leicester
Minsterley
Pulverbatch
Coalport
Wolverhampton
Sutton Coldfield

Machynlleth
Priestweston
Pennerley
Church Stretton
Much Wenlock
Acton Scott
Shipton
Bridgnorth
WEST MIDLANDS
BIRMINGHAM
Newtown
Bishop's Castle
Aston Munslow
Coventry

Llanidloes
POWYS
Leintwardine
Ludlow
Bewdley
Stoke Heath
Royal Leamington Spa
Knighton
Adforton
Hartlebury
Hanbury
HEREFORD
Yarpole
Luston
Leominster
WARWICKSHIRE
Llandrindod Wells
Kington
Bromyard
WORCESTER
Stratford-upon-Avon

DYFED
Builth Wells
AND
Great Malvern
Evesham
Banbury
Hay-on-Wye
HEREFORD
WORCESTER
Beckford
Brecon
Pontrilas
Ross-on-Wye
Newent
Tewkesbury
Gretton
Moreton-in-Marsh
Kineton
Abergavenny
Woolstone
Winchcombe
Evenlode
Lower Swell
Stow-on-the-Wold
Bourton-on-the-Water
GLOUCESTER
GLOUCESTERSHIRE
OXFORD-SHIRE
Upton St Leonards
GWENT
Scowles
Cranham
St Briavels
Epney
Miserden
Sapperton
Bibury
Merthyr Tydfil
Bream
Brimscombe
Cirencester
WEST GLAM
Hewelsfield Common
Cam
Stroud
Oxford
MID GLAM
Brockweir
Uley
Burleigh
South Cerney
GLAMORGAN
Stinchcombe
North Nibley
Neath
Tetbury
Newport
SWINDON
CARDIFF
SOUTH GLAM
AVON
WILTSHIRE
BERKS
Chippenham

256

Opening times and other details may change. Check by telephone before making a special journey.

In the 1880s, a group of artist craftsmen – inspired by the romantic vision of William Morris and John Ruskin – fled the cities for the peace and quiet of the Cotswolds. In workshops set deep in the countryside, these pioneers of the Arts and Crafts Movement attempted to revive traditional handicrafts and improve contemporary standards of decorative design. A similar influx of new ideas can be detected today, for many furniture makers and potters in the Welsh Marches – the western border counties of England – have developed original designs and techniques. Specialising in ornamental ironwork or abstract steel sculptures, the village blacksmith of the 1980s is very different from his counterpart of 100 years ago. Other crafts, however, rooted in the timeless countryside, flourish as they always have. These include saddlery in the area around Cheltenham's famous racecourse, spinning and weaving, cider and cheese making, and basketry.

CHESHIRE

BURWARDSLEY Map ref: Ce
Cheshire Workshops, Burwardsley, nr Chester.
Tel. Tattenhall 70401
(Three miles south-east of Tattenhall. At Burwardsley post office turn left. At top of hill, turn right. Car park on site.)

Some of today's most elaborate and colourful candles are made at Cheshire Workshops, high up in the Peckforton Hills. The basic shapes are made by pouring liquid paraffin wax into moulds to set. They are then dipped into successive wax dye baths to build up layers of bright colours before being decorated. This is done by making diagonal cuts through the wax, then peeling and lopping it back into curls, twists and ribbons which reveal the richness of the colours beneath.

Open daily, 11–5, except Christmas Day and Boxing Day.

CHESTER Map ref: Be
Fabric Workshop, Chapel House, City Road, Chester.
Tel. Chester 319181
(At southern end of City Road, which leads northwards to Chester railway station. Restricted parking.)

Fiona Porteous finds inspiration for her abstract fabric designs in rocky landscapes. She specialises in appliqué work, which involves cutting fabrics into shapes and sewing them on to a background cloth. She uses rich materials, such as silk and velvet, in contrasting colour tones and makes them up into striking wall-hangings, bed covers and cushions. Examples of her work decorate the walls of her workshop, a converted chapel meeting-house.

Open Mon.–Fri., 10–4. Other times by arrangement. Appointment advisable.

CHESTER Map ref: Be
Three Kings Studios, 90–92 Lower Bridge Street, Chester.
Tel. Chester 317717
(To south of city centre, by city wall and River Dee. Several public car parks near by.)

Goods made by over 100 local craftsmen are displayed in the charming old building which is now Margaret and Tony Eaton's craft centre. They include jewellery, textiles, leaded glass, ironware and leatherwork. Tony Eaton makes ceramic table lamps resembling fairytale castles. Standing up to 24 in. high, they are sometimes decorated with enamels and lustres. Margaret Eaton embroiders decorative panels, in coloured silks and beads, depicting flowers and animals. On Saturdays she shares her studio with Elizabeth Meredith, who makes toys and restores rocking horses.

Open all year, Mon.–Sat., 10–6. Also Apr. to Christmas, Sun., 2.30–6.

NANTWICH Map ref: Cd
Nantwich Pottery, Poole Green, nr Nantwich.
Tel. Nantwich 624919
(Take road signposted to Poole and Cholmondeston off A51, 1 mile north-west of Nantwich. Follow road for 1½ miles. Pottery just beyond telephone kiosk.)

Inside Pete and Chris Clough's pottery workshops, the atmosphere is one of bustling activity as craftsmen work to meet the orders for their wide range of domestic ware and gift items. All the pots are hand-thrown in stoneware clay, and most are decorated with brushwork leaf motifs over glazes of blue-grey, oatmeal, speckled green or blackrust. For sale in the showroom are casseroles, coffee pots, mugs, vases and individual pieces in porcelain.

Workshop and showroom open daily, 9–5. Telephone for weekend visits.

SIDDINGTON Map ref: Ce
Raymond Rush, The Golden Cross, Siddington, nr Macclesfield.
Tel. Marton Heath 358
(Just off A34, beside church on B5392. Parking outside.)

At Harvest Festival the striking black-and-white church at Siddington is gaily decorated with hundreds of golden corn dollies, each one made for the occasion by Raymond Rush. He uses wheat straw to make the dollies, plaiting and weaving them into traditional designs with such names as Norfolk lantern, harvest rattle, Staffordshire knot, and Kentish ivy maid. These and many other shapes are for sale in his workshop, situated in a farm outbuilding.

Open daily.

WARMINGHAM Map ref: Ce
Warmingham Craft Workshops, The Mill, Warmingham, nr Sandbach.
Tel. Warmingham 246/304
(Near church in centre of village, which is 3 miles west of Sandbach, off A533. Parking on site.)

A former 19th-century corn-mill in the heart of this attractive village has been converted into a spacious craft centre. Although much altered externally, every effort has been made inside to re-create its original charm by using reclaimed bricks and Victorian cast-iron window frames to construct the craftsmen's studios. Visitors are likely to see pottery, silverware, picture frames, cabinets and musical instruments being made in the workshops.

Open Wed.–Sun., 11–5.30, and on Bank Holidays. Coach parties by appointment at any time.

GLOUCESTERSHIRE

BOURTON-ON-THE-WATER Map ref: Db
John and Judy Jelfs, Bourton-on-the-Water Pottery, Clapton Row, Bourton-on-the-Water.
Tel. Bourton-on-the-Water 20173
(From village green, cross river. Go south along Victoria Street, then left into Clapton Row. Pottery is on left in 100 yds, behind Birdland. Car parks in the Rissington road and in Station Road.)

The Jelfs throw and decorate their stoneware pots in a workshop adjoining their sale room. They use the wax-resist method of decorating pottery, as well as slip-trailing and brushwork.

Their range of functional household pottery includes wicker-handled teapots, jugs and casseroles.

Open daily, 10–5, all year.

BOURTON-ON-THE-WATER Map ref: Db
Ken Waterworth (Wood crafts), Clapton Row, Bourton-on-the-Water.
Tel. Bourton-on-the-Water 20892
(From village green, cross river. Go south along Victoria Street, then left into Clapton Row. Turn first right after church.)

Set in a picturesque Cotswold village, Ken Waterworth's workshop was built over a century ago. Working mainly with local elm, he builds bookcases, flower troughs, tables, garden seats, stools, chairs and bird-houses, and carves such images as shire horses on his tables.

Open daily, 9–5. Appointment necessary for workshop.

BREAM Map ref: Cb
The Forest of Dean Pottery and Gallery, High Street, Bream, nr Lydney.
Tel. Dean 562414
(In the main street of Bream, opposite school. Parking outside.)

The pottery supplies its own shop with hand-thrown domestic ware and sculptures. The potter, Peter Saysell, uses glazes that he mixes himself from clay, iron and wood ash. These melt and merge together in the kiln to form abstract designs in cobalt blues and coppery greens and browns.

Open daily, 9.30–1 and 2–5.30. Appointment necessary for conducted tour of workshop.

BRIMSCOMBE Map ref: Ca
Dennis French (Woodware), The Craft Shop, Brimscombe Hill, Brimscombe, nr Stroud.
Tel. Brimscombe 883054
(Half a mile south of A419, close by the parish church. Parking outside.)

Dennis French turns tableware, bowls, table lamps and other pieces. All are meticulously finished, with the wood polished to enhance its grain and colour. Goods made by other local craftsmen are on sale in his shop; they include pottery, leatherwork and wicker baskets.

Open Mon.–Sat., 9–5, but closed Thur. afternoon. Appointment necessary for workshop.

BROCKWEIR Map ref: Ca
Malthouse Pottery, Brockweir, Chepstow.
Tel. Tintern 291
(Brockweir is signposted from A466. Pottery is opposite Brockweir Inn. Parking space opposite in lay-by.)

This fine old building dates back to medieval times. A community of lay brothers lived and farmed here, supplying nearby Tintern Abbey with their produce. Part of the original fabric, a low-beamed room with 3 ft thick stone walls, has been turned into a pottery studio by Barrie Naylor and his son Peter. Most of their work is wheel-thrown tableware, slip-decorated with incised patterns.

Open Mon.–Sat., 9.30–6; Sun., 11.30–6.

BURLEIGH Map ref: Ca
Gordon Hodgson (Silversmith and jeweller), Woodside, Brimscombe Hill, Burleigh, nr Stroud.
Tel. Brimscombe 884350
(Turning south off the A419 into Burleigh, Woodside is first house after church.)

Most of Mr Hodgson's pieces are made by hand; the rest are either cast or pressed. As well as making rings, medallions and small picture frames, he has been commissioned to make trophies for national newspaper and television awards. Some of his work is made in co-operation with an enameller, and ranges from ear-rings to costly chess sets.

Open by appointment only.

CAM Map ref: Ca
The Snake Pottery, Green Street Cottage, Cam Green, Dursley.
Tel. Dursley 3260
(From Cam, follow signs towards Coaley. Green Street, with pottery at far end, is on left just after Cam Green playing field.)

From the River Severn and nearby clay deposits, Peter Brown obtains his materials to fashion wheel-thrown earthenware pottery. Both traditional and novelty pieces are made, including Toby jugs, fuddling cups (a group of small cups joined together), beer mugs with sculptured frogs in the bottom, and puzzle-jugs (a traditional trick drinking mug). He decorates the pottery with inscriptions and slip-trailed patterns, and fires it in a wood-burning kiln.

Open, by appointment only, at any reasonable time.

CIRENCESTER Map ref: Da
The Cirencester Workshops, Cricklade Street, Cirencester.
Tel. Cirencester 61566
(On east side of brewery car park.)

The Cotswold-stone buildings of an old brewery have been converted to make a craft centre. It contains a craft shop and craft workshops.

Tara McKee's domestic pottery is decorated with brushwork designs of bamboo and mice, and moulded impressions of birds. She also makes sculptured cats.

Philip Windsor-Stevens is an artist-craftsman who makes sculptured ornaments and jewellery to his own design in silver and gold. He also makes his own tools for his original 'metal quilting' technique, which gives a softly textured appearance.

Janet Gibbs makes tables and shelves with cane and glass, as well as re-caning all types of chairs – especially spider-backs, sofas and dining chairs.

Mike Smith uses English willow to make strong baskets, hampers and beds.

Stan Giles uses local woods, including pine, to make furniture and fitted units to meet individual commissions.

Hilary and Pasco Genillard make and restore fire bellows in modern and traditional designs, using hand-turned local hardwood and leather. They also hand-stitch the leather for bags, belts and wallets.

Neil Batchelor and Steve Hill restore antique furniture, and also make chairs, cabinets and tables in traditional and modern designs from English woods such as cherry and willow.

Margaret Smitten hand-weaves and embroiders wall-hangings and tapestries, often with pictures of clients' houses and gardens.

Ann Sharman uses natural wools and cottons to machine-knit brightly coloured clothes of original design.

Jennifer Whitehouse and Martin Griffiths high-fire hand-thrown earthenware pottery, carving local landscapes and birds out of the white slip-coatings.

Wendy Harding restores intricately painted dials of clocks dating back to the 1800s for museums and collectors all over the world. She also designs and makes new dials.

Open Mon.–Sat., 10–5.30. Appointment advisable to see specific craftsmen.

CIRENCESTER Map ref: Da
W. G. Hayes and Son Ltd (Saddlers), 6–8 Dyer Street, Cirencester.
Tel. Cirencester 3198/4459
(In town centre opposite the Fleece Hotel. Parking in Market Square opposite.)

The saddlery which Stephen Hayes' grandfather opened at the turn of the century now serves the surrounding stables of event horses and polo ponies. In an upstairs workshop, Martin Lee, Bill Ralph and a few trainees hand-stitch specialised saddles, suede riding chaps and bridles, repair side-saddles and riding boots, and replace the wooden heads of polo sticks. They use cowhides, pigskin and fleeces.

Shop open Mon.–Sat., 9–5.30. Workshop open Mon.–Fri., 9–5, by appointment only.

Opening times and other details may change. Check by telephone before making a special journey.

257

CRANHAM Map ref: Cb
Prinknash Pottery, Prinknash Abbey, Cranham.
Tel. Painswick 812239
(Five and a half miles north of Stroud on the western side of the A46. Parking outside.)

In 1939, when the new abbey was being built, a seam of clay was discovered. This led to a few monks starting a pottery. Since then it has developed into a commercial enterprise producing a wide variety of hand-thrown and moulded tableware, commemorative plates and tankards. From the viewing gallery, visitors can watch all the processes of throwing, casting and jiggering, and decorating with pewter and bronze-coloured glazes.

Workshop open Mon.–Sat., 10–12.30 and 1.30–5; Sun., 2–5. Shop open Mon.–Sat., 9–6; Sun., 9.30–6 (closes 5.30 in winter). Small charge (adults only) for viewing gallery.

EPNEY Map ref: Cb
Colin Squire and Janice Williams (Weaver and embroiderer), Sheldon Cottage, Epney, Saul.
Tel. Gloucester 740639
(At north end of village, which is 1 mile west of the A38. The cottage is up a drive towards river. Parking outside.)

On the bank of the River Severn, Colin Squire hand-weaves flat and pile rugs using linen and wool; also bags, double-weave cushions and furnishing fabrics, using natural fibres. His wife, Janice Williams, creates beautiful embroidery, using gold and silver threads and silks. She receives commissions for ecclesiastical soft furnishings and garments, and commemorative and heraldic work.

Usually open, but appointment necessary. No large parties.

EVENLODE Map ref: Db
Evenlode Pottery, Evenlode, nr Moreton-in-Marsh.
Tel. Moreton-in-Marsh 50804
(Travelling from Stow, the pottery is the first building on the right in Evenlode. Parking outside.)

The rich, autumnal colours of Dieter and Dinah Kunzemaan's pottery are obtained by firing the pots at a lower temperature than usual – about 2,000°F (1,100°C). The artistic slipware designs of birds, fish and wheat are applied with dyed clays, or with the local red clay.

Open all year, 8.30–6. Workshop on weekdays only, but showroom also open Sat. and Sun.

GRETTON Map ref: Db
W. Uedelhoven Ltd (Woodcrafts), Gretton, Cheltenham.
Tel. Winchcombe 602306
(Next to post office in village. Parking outside.)

As well as furniture, Willy Uedelhoven and Peter Campion work on original designs for smaller wooden items such as chess tables, cat-and-mouse-shaped cheeseboards, and bird-tables carved out of logs. Jeanne Uedelhoven does pokerwork and embroidery.

Open daily, 10–1 and 2–5. Appointment advisable at weekends.

HEWELSFIELD COMMON Map ref: Ca
Andrew Pyke (Craftsman in Wood), Grove Farm, Brockweir Lane, Hewelsfield Common, nr St Briavels.
Tel. Dean 530924
(A mile north-east of turning at Brockweir on A466. Workshop is behind pink bungalow. Parking outside.)

In a workshop with a magnificent view over the Wye Valley, Mr Pyke makes dressers, church furniture, old-fashioned boot-jacks and spinning-stools to individual commissions. He uses traditional dovetail and mortise-and-tenon joints, and all are designed to show the wood

grain to best advantage. The finished work is polished by his wife Susan. He also makes chairs with seats woven from rushes gathered from the River Avon. Small items, such as breadboards, table lamps and boot-jacks, are often in stock for visitors to purchase.

Open by appointment, at all reasonable hours.

KINETON Map ref: Db
Maurice Emtage (Saddler), Green Bank Cottage, Kineton, nr Guiting Power, Cheltenham.
Tel. Guiting Power 570
(At south end of village, almost opposite pub. Parking near by.)

The tack in many local racing and eventing stables is made by Mr Emtage, and he supplies hand-stitched leatherwork to a saddlery shop in Gloucester. He also makes the harnesses for the nearby Cotswold Farm Park's shire horses. His saddlery, bags and belts are shown at local craft exhibitions and sold at county agricultural shows.

Appointment necessary for workshop.

LOWER SWELL Map ref: Db
Austin Nicholls (Ornamental ironworker), The Old Smithy, Lower Swell, nr Stow-on-the-Wold.
Tel. Stow-on-the-Wold 30041
(Travelling from Stow on the B4068, the smithy is in the village on the right.)

An unusual wind-dial catches the visitor's eye on entering Austin Nicholls's workshop. Connected to a wind-vane outside, the dial is above a map of Britain which indicates exactly from where the wind came. Mr Nicholls makes a variety of wrought-iron and brass weather-vanes, lanterns, fire-baskets and water-clocks. Among his collection of bygones, on view to visitors, is a working display of kitchen implements – including a spit-engine and smoke spit-jack – from the time of George I to the Victorian era.

Open Mon.–Sat., 9–5. Appointment advisable.

MISERDEN Map ref: Cb
Michael E. Roberts (Ornamental ironworker), Anvil Barn, Miserden, nr Stroud.
Tel. Miserden 244
(South of Miserden, next to Lypiatt Farm. Parking outside.)

Michael Roberts is an enthusiast who uses both traditional and modern methods to make sculptural forge work of his own design. In a 17th-century Cotswold barn he hand-forges 'rope-twist' handles, ornamental gates, milk-skimmers, two-handled boot-scrapers and sculptured candlesticks. He forges in steel, brass, copper and aluminium, and he makes many of his own tools and the tools for his power hammer.

Open Mon.–Fri., 9–6. Also sometimes on Sat. and Sun. Appointment necessary.

NEWENT Map ref: Cb
Cowdy Glass Workshop Ltd, 27 Culver Street, Newent.
Tel. Newent 821173
(Turn off Broad Street by Barclays Bank into Culver Street. Workshop is 150 yds on right. Parking outside.)

Pauline Solven and Harry Cowdy and their four assistants hand-blow their glass, using traditional tools and applying colour by a variety of methods. Their work, distinctive for its contemporary design and use of colour, includes glass paperweights, wine glasses, goblets, bowls and vases, jugs and tumblers.

Open Mon.–Fri., 9–12.30 and 1.30–5. Closed Bank Holidays.

ST BRIAVELS Map ref: Cb
Gill and Rob McCubbin, The Pottery, St Briavels, nr Lydney.
Tel. Dean 530297

(In East Street, opposite the playing fields. Parking outside.)

Over 90 different items of domestic stoneware make up the range produced by Gill and Rob McCubbin. Their workshop walls are hung with sketches for Gill's creative designs, which include bowls and candle rings with pierced-work patterns of trees and viaducts.

Usually open, but appointment advisable.

SAPPERTON Map ref: Cb
Sherra (Handwoven fabrics), Tunley, Sapperton, nr Cirencester.
Tel. Frampton Mansell 259
(In a beechwood north-west of Sapperton, up the hill from Daneway. Parking outside.)

Gerald and Joan Carter use about ten different looms to weave wool, silk, worsted and mohair. They also do some of their own spinning and dyeing, and offer tuition in spinning and weaving. Visitors can watch the couple creating bold patterns on the rugs and tweeds that are their chief output.

Open Mon.–Sat., 10–1 and 2–4. Appointment necessary.

SCOWLES Map ref: Cb
Stuart Perkins Studio Pottery, The Old School, Scowles, Coleford.
Tel. Dean 33570
(Scowles is north-west of Coleford, ½ mile off the B4431. Parking outside.)

Earthenware pottery, in serviceable whites and browns, is hand-thrown in this small country workshop. Mr Perkins's standard lines include mugs, tea sets, tankards, casseroles and soup bowls. One highly original item is a 'Forest Miner mug', the design based on a local Forest of Dean miner on a 14th-century church brass. He also makes medallions for industrial promotions and clubs.

Open daily, except Wed. and on major show dates. Advisable to check by telephone.

SOUTH CERNEY Map ref: Da
South Cerney Pottery, School Lane, South Cerney.
Tel. Cirencester 860243 (after 6 p.m.)
(About 100 yds west of main street in village. Parking outside.)

Every day Rosemary Pasmore makes her delicate hand-thrown pottery, producing richly coloured domestic earthenware. Some of her work has painted or stencilled patterns, but her hallmark is an elegant tree design applied by a method which is a closely guarded secret.

Open Mon.–Sat., 9–1 and 2–5. Large parties by appointment only.

STINCHCOMBE Map ref: Ca
The Cider Mill Gallery, Blanchworth Farm, nr Stinchcombe, Dursley.
Tel. Dursley 2352
(Midway between North Nibley and the A38, 3 miles from Berkeley and 5 miles from Slimbridge. Parking on premises.)

For centuries, cider-making has been an annual autumn ritual at Blanchworth Farm. A horse still turns the farm's 200-year-old mill to crush locally grown apples. Juice is extracted from the pulp by means of a hand-operated press. In an adjoining gallery, such craft goods as pottery, patchwork, hand-woven fabrics and jewellery are for sale.

Depending on the supply of apples, cider-making generally takes place in Oct., Nov. and Dec. The premises are open Apr.–May and Sept.–Dec., Tues.–Sat., 11–5; June, July and Aug., Tues.–Sun., 11–5. Closed Jan., Feb. and Mar.

STOW-ON-THE-WOLD Map ref: Db
Judy Laws (Ceramist and sculptor), Sheep Street Studio, Sheep Street, Stow-on-the-Wold.
Tel. Stow 30120
(Sheep Street is in Stow on the eastern side of the A424. Car park at the bottom of Sheep Street.)

Beautiful colours and original designs are distinctive features of Judy Laws' jewellery. It is made from porcelain and terracotta, and decorated with combinations of enamel and glaze. The range includes pendants, ear-rings and bracelets.

Open Feb.–Dec., Tues.–Sat., 10–5. Appointment advisable.

TETBURY Map ref: Ca
Colin Clark (Furniture maker and wood turner), Wisteria Farm, Hampton Street, Tetbury.
Tel. Tetbury 53079
(North-west of Tetbury, just before the industrial estate on the B4014.)

Using his own traditional designs and brass fittings, Colin Clark makes dressers, chairs, tables – in fact any piece of furniture for which a commission comes his way. He has supplied both Harrods and the National Trust.

Open Mon.–Fri., 8.30–1 and 2–5. Appointment advisable.

ULEY Map ref: Ca
Old Chapel Antiques, Uley, nr Dursley.
Tel. Dursley 860656
(From Uley village follow signpost to Coaley. The chapel is on the right. Parking outside.)

In a converted 1803 chapel, where they sell antiques, Brian and Lou Narbeth restore 18th and 19th-century furniture with carefully matched woods. Among their collection of specialised tools are no fewer than 1,500 moulding planes, including the contents of a Victorian cabinet-maker's chest.

Open Mon.–Sat., 9–1 and 2–5. Closed Wed. afternoons.

UPTON ST LEONARDS Map ref: Cb
Taena Pottery, Whitley Court, Upton St Leonards.
Tel. Gloucester 60908
(Turning west off the A46 to Upton St Leonards, the pottery is on the left.)

High up on the edge of the Cotswolds, Sean and Vici Casserley throw personalised mugs and wedding plates, tableware, and horn-shaped plant and parsley pots in slip-decorated earthenware and stoneware. Visitors will also see porcelain vases carved with delicate floral designs, and terracotta garden pots, decorated with sculpted lizards.

Open all year, 10.30–4.30; closed Wed.

WINCHCOMBE Map ref: Db
Bryant Fedden (Letter cutter and glass engraver), 'Tanyard Bont', Castle Street, Winchcombe, nr Cheltenham.
Tel. Winchcombe 602782
(From main street in town, turn down Castle Street beside White Hart Inn. Go over bridge. House is first on left.)

In a converted barn and cowshed, Bryant Fedden cuts letters in stone, slate and wood. He and his wife Kate also engrave glass. Examples of their work can be seen in Manchester, Bristol and Gloucester cathedrals, Southwell Minster and Chelsea Royal Hospital, as well as in their own showroom.

Appointment necessary to watch work in progress.

WINCHCOMBE Map ref: Db
Magister Woodcraft, The Pottery, Becketts Lane, Winchcombe.
Tel. Winchcombe 603059
(Turning left off the A46 on the northern edge of Winchcombe, the workshop is immediately on the right, behind The Pottery. Parking outside.)

Using many different kinds of wood, Stephen Marchant turns anything from chess pieces to four-poster beds. Keith Jameson casts and models metal for such commissions as a cross for a church steeple, and bronze figures. Will Hall makes any type of furniture to order.

Open Mon.–Sat. Appointment necessary.

WINCHCOMBE Map ref: Db
Winchcombe Pottery, Becketts Lane, Winchcombe.
Tel. Winchcombe 602462
(Turning off the A46 to Greet, 1 mile north of Winchcombe. The pottery is at the junction. Parking outside.)

On the site of a 19th-century pottery, Ray and Mike Finch, and their assistants, make oil lamps, large cider jars and tableware. Outside, an old and now disused bottle kiln can be seen. Today's pottery is fired in a wood-burning kiln inside the barn, and there is also a special kiln for salt-glaze firing, and a small gas kiln.

Open all year except Sun. and Bank Holidays: Mon.–Fri., 9–4.30; Sat., 9–12.30. No large parties.

WOOLSTONE Map ref: Cb
Geoffrey Vivien Ltd (Picture-framers), The Grange, Woolstone, nr Cheltenham.
Tel. Bishop's Cleeve 2122
(Turn off A435 for Woolstone. Workshop is near church. Parking outside.)

Geoffrey and Vivien Evans frame old prints and pictures, some to private commissions. Near their 16th-century house is their workshop, an 18th-century cider-making barn in which some 160 kinds of wood and metal frames hang around the walls.

Visitors are welcome at any time by appointment.

MUSEUMS

BIBURY Map ref: Db
Cotswold Country Museum, Arlington Mill, Bibury.
Tel. Bibury 368

Although a mill was recorded at Arlington in the Domesday survey, the existing buildings date from the 17th century. During the 19th century, the mill was the largest and busiest in the district, but in 1914 the machinery was dismantled and sold as scrap. The machinery that visitors can now watch working was moved from a mill at North Cerney by the present owner. From the ground floor to the grinding stones, and from there to the chutes, storage bins and hoist machinery on the top floor, visitors can study how a mill works.

In addition to the mill, there are a weaving loom, a large Albion printing press and a collection of agricultural implements. In what was once a storage bin – its walls decorated with 19th-century graffiti – a cobbler's shop has been reconstructed.

The Cotswolds were a favourite resort of artists such as Ernest Gimson, who lived at nearby Sapperton. Enthusiasts of the Arts and Crafts Movement will be delighted by the furniture in the Exhibition Room, and by the plasterwork frieze cast from moulds by Gimson.

Open daily, Mar.–Oct. 10.30–7. Also open Nov.–Feb., Sat. and Sun. only, 10.30 to dusk. Charge for admission.

GLOUCESTER Map ref: Cb
Gloucester Folk Museum, 99–103 Westgate Street, Gloucester.
Tel. Gloucester 26467

Many of the displays are concerned with local crafts and industries, such as the horn trade. Gloucestershire was once famous for its dairy products, and the county's capital is still remembered in the names of two cheeses – Single and Double Gloucester. The dairy display contains many tools, including a magnificent gleaming copper vat which dates from the 18th century and is capable of holding 85 gallons of milk curds. A butter print – probably the gift of an ardent suitor to a dairymaid – bears the charming inscription 'Marry me'.

One gallery, which deals with fishing on the River Severn, contains basketwork traps for catching salmon, a description of net-making – one of the most ancient crafts – several model coracles, and a collection of spears for catching eels.

Beneath the low beams and timbered roof of the top floor there is a fine reconstruction of a wheelwright's shop and displays of the tools of the basket-maker, hurdle-maker and the tinsmith.

In 1820, Gloucester had no fewer than 11 pin factories, which employed many of the town's inhabitants. The museum describes how pins were made by hand, and has examples of the sorts of machine from Bristol and Birmingham that replaced hand methods. There are also many agricultural implements – seed drills, ploughs, a winnowing machine and threshing tools – which together occupy a whole gallery.

Open Mon.–Sat., 10–5. Also open on Sun. in Aug., 2–5. No charge for admission on weekdays.

HEREFORD AND WORCESTER

ADFORTON Map ref: Bc
Grace and Mary Whitehorn (Miniature dolls), Green Lane Cottage, Paytoe, Leintwardine, Craven Arms.
Tel. Wigmore 269
(Paytoe is 1 mile north-east of the A4110 at Adforton. The workshop is in Watling Street, at the south end of the village.)

Grace and Mary Whitehorn may take a fortnight to make one of their period miniature dolls. The dolls' bodies are simply wire, with plaster heads, but they are exquisitely clothed in leather and suede, and are complete with jewellery, fans or the tools of their calling. The Whitehorns' dolls represent famous people such as kings and queens of England, and ordinary workers too.

Open Tues.–Fri., 10–5.30; Sat. and Sun., 2–6. Advisable to telephone first. Closed first two weeks of Jan. Appointments necessary for parties of 10–20.

BECKFORD Map ref: Cb
Beckford Silk, The Old Vicarage, Beckford, nr Tewkesbury.
Tel. Evesham 881507
(From the A435, turn north-west for Beckford and bear left towards church. Workshop is just beyond. Parking outside.)

James Gardner and his local helpers hand-print silk scarves, ties and cushion covers. This involves several processes, from colour separation, screen-making and dye-making, to the final stages of ironing and packing. Visitors are most likely to see printing on Tuesday, Wednesday or Thursday afternoons. Items made on the premises may be bought in the adjoining Silk Store.

Workshop open Mon.–Fri., 9–1 and 2–6, except on Bank Holidays. Additionally, the Silk Store is open on Sat., 2–5.30.

HANBURY Map ref: Cc
Jinney Ring Craft Centre, Old House Farm, Hanbury, Bromsgrove.
Tel. Hanbury 272
(On B4091 at north end of village.)

A 200-year-old elm-beamed barn and a collection of antique agricultural machinery provide an attractive setting for the Jinney Ring Craft Centre. Working at his lathe, Richard Greatwood – the centre's founder – turns candlesticks, goblets, bowls, and legs for tables and chairs.

Porcelain and stoneware are the mediums through which Jim and Stella Webster express their creativity. They hand-throw pots and vases, and also make dolls and sculptures. Clothes for the dolls are skilfully embroidered.

Woodcarving is the craft of Bill Piper-Sprout. He fashions life-like animal and human figures from mahogany, lime and sycamore.

Open Apr.–Dec., Wed.–Sat., 10.30–5; Sun., 2.30–5.30. Jan.–Mar., weekends only.

HAY-ON-WYE Map ref: Bb
Spinning and Craft Centre, Tinto House, Broad Street, Hay-on-Wye.
Tel. Hay-on-Wye 820590
(Opposite stone clock-tower.)

In a charming Georgian house, Janet Clarke may be seen spinning Shetland, Welsh Black and local wools, some of which she colours with vegetable and flower dyes. Behind the house, Gordon Clarke designs and hand-turns spinning-wheels in a traditional style called Saxony, with a 26 in. wheel. Depending on the individual order, he uses English yew, sycamore, elm, Welsh ash or oak.

Open all year, 10–5.30, except Sun. morning and Tues.

KINGTON Map ref: Bc
Penrhos Project, Penrhos Court, Lyonshall, Kington.
Tel. Kington 230720
(On the A44, halfway between Kington and Lyonshall. Parking on premises.)

Penrhos Court is a centre for promoting the preservation of English rural skills and architecture. In its lovingly restored farm buildings – some of which date from the 13th century – craftsmen work on projects that will help to restore other old timber-framed buildings in the area. The Penrhos Brewery produces traditional ale.

Open Tues.–Sat., by appointment.

LUSTON Map ref: Bc
Kay Miles (Spinning, embroidery and patchwork), Roseneath, Luston, Leominster.
Tel. Yarpole 273
(In the lane between Luston and Yarpole, shortly after the fork just north of Luston.)

Kay Miles knits and crochets a variety of clothing, and usually she begins by spinning her own yarn. Needlework is another of her talents. Mrs Miles makes patchwork, which features intricate log-cabin patterns. In addition, she embroiders with wool, silk, raffia or cotton to make shoulder bags, belts and colourful covers for jewellery boxes.

By appointment only. No parties of more than six.

PONTRILAS Map ref: Bb
Graham Perkins (Ornamental ironwork), Paradise Forge, Pontrilas, nr Hereford.
Tel. Golden Valley 240374
(From the A465, turn west into the Rowlstone road. The forge is 1 mile from A465, on the right. Parking on premises.)

Graham Perkins shapes and welds all manner of hearth furniture, ornamental gates and candlesticks. They are made from mild steel, but he sometimes adds decorative finishes of copper or brass. Visitors can also see his 19th-century cheese-presses and ploughs.

Open daily, 9–5, by appointment. No large parties.

Map ref: Cc

Bewdley Museum

BEWDLEY, HEREFORD AND WORCESTER

An 18th-century cobbled arcade, called the Shambles, runs behind the elegant façade of Bewdley Town Hall, forming a charming setting for the museum's galleries.

One of the galleries is devoted to the traditional but disappearing coppice industries of the Wyre Forest. There are sections on basket-making, charcoal burning, besom-making and bark peeling – the bark being used in the tanning of leather. A ropewalk has been reconstructed as a reminder of the days when rope-making was an industry vital to Britain's maritime supremacy. There is also a cooper's workshop.

Small sections, each consisting of a few tools, photographs and informative captions, show local industries of the past and present. These include brass-making (with a working brass foundry), tanning, cap-making, wheelwrighting, cider-making and butchery – once there were 32 butchers with stalls in the Shambles.

Some of the rooms are now the workshops of practising craftsmen, and on occasions a woodworker, a glassblower and a pewterer can be seen at work.

Load Street, Bewdley, Hereford and Worcester.
Tel. Bewdley 403573

Open Mar.–Nov., Mon.–Sat., 10–5.30; Sun., 2–5.30. Small charge for admission.

ROPE-MAKING *A ropewalk at Wribbenhall in about 1900.*

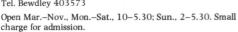

Opening times and other details may change. Check by telephone before making a special journey.

259

Map ref: Cc

Hereford and Worcester County Museum

HARTLEBURY, HEREFORD AND WORCESTER

Housed in the north wing of the 18th-century Bishop's Palace, the museum contains many items of historical, sartorial and archaeological interest. In addition, there is one room devoted to local crafts and industries of the past. There are sections on glassblowing, on the Belbroughton scythe makers, and on ironworking.

One exhibition commemorates the Bromsgrove Guild of the Applied Arts, a craft guild closely connected with the Arts and Crafts Movement. At one time it was famed for its stained glass, plaster models, woodwork, and decorative ironwork.

In an outside yard, a forge has been reconstructed. It also contains a number of tools of the wheelwright. There is a gallery which houses a fine collection of beautifully painted gipsy caravans, wagons and carts of the 19th century – an object lesson in the skill and art of the wheelwright. A cider mill has been moved from Hall Farm, Birlingham, and re-erected in the grounds. In this half-timbered building cider was produced for two and a half centuries, from around 1700 until 1960.

Hartlebury Castle, Hartlebury, Kidderminster, Hereford and Worcester.
Tel. Hartlebury 250416

Open Feb.–Nov., Mon.–Thur., 10–5; Sat. and Sun., 2–5. Charge for admission.

CIDER MILL *The massive stone wheel, for crushing cider apples, was drawn by a horse harnessed to the metal framework of the mill.*

painting, pottery, bobbin lace, batik, flower arranging, calligraphy and china painting. Of course, not all are present on a given day. The pottery includes thrown, coiled and sculptural pieces in earthenware and stoneware, with wax-resist and slip designs.

Open Wed. evening, 7–9; Thur., 10–3. Other times by appointment. No large parties.

MUSEUMS

BEWDLEY Map ref: Cc
Bewdley Museum.
(See panel on p. 259)

HARTLEBURY Map ref: Cc
Hereford and Worcester County Museum.
(See panel on left)

HEREFORD Map ref: Cb
The Museum of Cider, The Cider Mills, Ryelands Street, Hereford.
Tel. Hereford 54207

Britain's first museum of cider-making traces the development of the craft from early days on the farm to the factory of the 20th century. An 1830s farm cider house has been rebuilt, complete with 6 ton stone mill, press and casks. In the cellars, which once were filled with stacks of bottles of fermenting cider, a bottling line of the 1930s has been reconstructed. Further displays illustrate the cider trade out of Herefordshire, the old practice of supplying cider as part of agricultural wages, and the way in which cider was once used to adulterate foreign wines. The associated craft of coopering is also featured, with a working cooper on the premises.

Open Apr.–Oct., Wed.–Sun., 10–5.30. Open daily in July and Aug. Charge for admission.

STOKE HEATH Map ref: Cc
Avoncroft Museum of Buildings.
(See panel on facing page)

SHROPSHIRE

HENGOED Map ref: Bd
The Hengoed Pottery, Hilbre, Hengoed, Oswestry.
Tel. Oswestry 59782
(From Oswestry, take road north to Weston Rhyn for about 3 miles. Turn right at crossroads by The Last Inn. Pottery is just beyond next crossroads, on left. Parking in drive.)

Pheasants, partridges, herons and curlews are among the wild birds to be seen near the wooded brook which runs beside the pottery. Peggy Charlton spends many hours watching them and making sketches to use as studies for her range of ceramic wildlife. Hand-thrown tableware and vases, with a 'pebbly' glaze of soft grey, blue and brown, are also made.

Open all year, Mon.–Sat., 9–6.

KNOCKIN Map ref: Bd
Old Forge Taxidermy Studio, Knockin, nr Oswestry.
Tel. Knockin 394
(On main road through village beside the Bradford Arms pub. Parking outside.)

Mr Goss spent several years as a gamekeeper before becoming a taxidermist. This gave him the perfect opportunity to study animals and birds in their natural habitat, which explains why his mounted wildlife subjects are so lifelike. In his studio, he makes the body-frames over which the preserved skins are fitted. He uses wood straw for small birds, and clay or fibre-glass models for larger animals. Much of his work is commissioned by museums, but individuals often bring in specimens which range in size from red deer down to tiny wrens.

Open most days, by appointment only.

MUCH WENLOCK Map ref: Cc
Wenlock Pottery, Shineton Street, Much Wenlock.
Tel. Much Wenlock 727600
(Shineton Street is off High Street. Parking in driveway.)

With local clay from the beds at nearby Dawley, Mike and Marilyn Fletcher produce an attractive range of tableware and plant containers. They use a form of surface decoration known as 'sprigging', which involves applying a moulded clay motif to the side of a pot before it is fired. The pots are finished with an oatmeal glaze containing iron oxide, which gives the 'sprigs' a reddish hue.

Open daily, 9–5.

PENNERLEY Map ref: Bc
Tankerville Pottery, Tankerville, Pennerley, Minsterley.
Tel. Minsterley 580
(One mile south of Minsterley, turn left off A488 by telephone kiosk. Pottery is 3½ miles along this road. Parking outside.)

Behind the pottery the jagged outcrops of boulders known as the Stiperstones look out across acres of farmland towards the distant Welsh mountains. In these lovely surroundings, Roy Evans produces stoneware pottery – in particular, gallon cider jars, large casseroles and bread-crocks. The containers have an impressed decoration in the shape of an ear of corn, and are glazed only on the inside.

Open most days.

PRIESTWESTON Map ref: Bc
Priestweston Pottery, Priestweston, Chirbury, Montgomery.
Tel. Chirbury 618
(In village centre. Parking space next to pottery.)

Owen Thorpe's pottery workshop is housed in a Victorian chapel. In addition to a complete range of hand-thrown tableware, decorated with coloured slips and abstract designs, wedding and christening plates can be ordered. These are tin-glazed in white before being painted with blue floral or geometric patterns. Owen Thorpe's wife, Angela, is an artist who specialises in lithographic prints of landscapes and still life.

Pottery open Mon.–Fri., 10–6 (closed Wed. afternoons); Sat., 10–1. Advisable to telephone first. Printing studio open by appointment only.

PULVERBATCH Map ref: Bd
Witchcraft Designs, The Lawns Farmhouse, Pulverbatch.
Tel. Shrewsbury 790789
(Take Habberley turning to side of White Horse in village. First farm on left. Parking on site.)

In his 20 years as a woodturner, John Murtha has acquired the skills to design and make anything from a small toy to an elegant four-poster bed. Of particular interest among his turned kitchenware, toys and furniture are some engaging string puppets, and games which have amused children for hundreds of years – cup-and-ball sets, and whips and tops.

Workshop open by appointment.

SHIPTON Map ref: Cc
Cane and Rush Furniture, The Thatched Cottage, Shipton, Much Wenlock.
Tel. Brockton 673
(From B4368 turn left at Shipton, following signpost to Stanton Long. Workshop is about 100 yds down lane. Parking in drive.)

Bundles of cane and rush stacked in John Harriman's cottage workshop are used to renew the seats and backs of antique chairs. Before weaving can start, the cane (from Malaysia) and the rush (from the Fens and Thames Valley), have to be soaked for up to 12 hours to make them pliable. Mr Harriman also makes traditional rush log baskets by plaiting reeds into a rope, which can be coiled into any

ROSS-ON-WYE Map ref: Cb
Alpenhof Design (Candles), Old Gloucester Road, Ross-on-Wye.
Tel. Ross-on-Wye 63697
(Halfway along Old Gloucester Road.)

Colin Hughes and a few helpers make an extensive range of candles blended from around seven types of wax. Etched candles for souvenirs and promotions are one of the main lines, but some have coloured rings or pictorial patterns, or are in the shape of figurines.

Open Mon.–Fri., 9–5.

ROSS-ON-WYE Map ref: Cb
Multi-Crafts (Furniture makers), 25 High Street, Ross-on-Wye.
Tel. Ross-on-Wye 62438
(In town centre opposite the Rosswyn Hotel. Car park in western part of town, off A49.)

Gerry and Margaret Peckham make finely finished pine furniture – in particular, fitted kitchens, tables, dressers and basin stands. They turn some of the components on a lathe and finish many of the pieces with solid brass knobs, handles and locks. The workshop adjoins a retail craft shop selling locally made goods.

Open Mon.–Sat., 9–5.30 (closed Wed. afternoons).

ROSS-ON-WYE Map ref: Cb
A. W. Ursell Ltd (Stonemasons), Waterloo Monumental Works, Cantilupe Road, Ross-on-Wye.
Tel. Ross-on-Wye 62530
(Opposite the town bus station.)

Since 1885, this company has been making stone memorials, fireplaces, plaques and trophies. Today's craftsmen engrave lettering, pictures and designs on a variety of stone, which includes green slate from Westmorland, white Sicilian marble, a blue-grey stone from the Forest of Dean and a variety of granites. The inscriptions are often highlighted with gold leaf, black enamel or lead.

Open Mon.–Fri., 8–5; Sat., 9–12. No parties of more than six people.

WORCESTER Map ref: Cc
Bevere Vivis Group (Painting, ceramics and crafts), Bevere Knoll, Bevere, nr Worcester.
Tel. Worcester 51291
(Half a mile west of the A449. Car park in grounds.)

The Bevere Vivis Group was founded to foster enjoyment and experiment in handicrafts at a local level. The 200 members of the group – which includes the family of the founder, Heather Taylor – work at such crafts as

shape or size. Courses in either cane or rushwork are held at weekends.

Open Mon.–Fri., 9–5, but advisable to telephone first. Weekends by appointment only.

SHREWSBURY   Map ref: Bd
St Julian's Craft Centre for Shropshire, St Julian's Church, St Alkmund's Square, Shrewsbury.
Tel. Shrewsbury 53516
(Faces southern end of High Street. Several public car parks in town centre.)

A disused church in the heart of old Shrewsbury is the unusual setting for this craft centre. Many of the church furnishings have been retained, and the craft studios, which are arranged round the sides of the lofty nave, are partitioned off using the backs of the oak-panelled Victorian pews. Among the crafts practised here are printing, jewellery-making and spinning and weaving. Hand-made boots and shoes are made on the premises. Goods for sale range from pottery to wood turnery.

Open Tues.–Sat., 10–5.

STANTON UPON HINE HEATH
Map ref: Cd
Antony J. Robinson, The White House Forge, Stanton upon Hine Heath, Shrewsbury.
Tel. Shawbury 250681
(From village centre, follow signs to church. Forge is opposite a farm. Parking outside.)

Mr Robinson brings to his craft the imaginative and aesthetic qualities of an artist – so much so that two of his pieces have been acquired by the Victoria and Albert Museum in London. He works to commission only, designing and forging almost anything in mild or stainless steel. Examples are staircases, jewellery, gates, hearthware, sculptures, and even a canteen of cutlery. Visitors may see examples of his work.

Open Mon.–Fri., 9–5. Other times by appointment.

WELLINGTON   Map ref: Cd
Mrs Phillips, Dothill House, North Road, Wellington, Telford.
Tel. Telford 3829
(Half a mile north of town centre, at junction of North Road with A442.)

Three crafts are practised by Mrs Phillips in her elegant 18th-century home – spinning, weaving and knitting. Her chief interest is in spinning the soft fleeces of Shetland and Merino sheep into a very fine yarn, which she knits into exquisite evening and christening shawls following traditional lace knitting patterns. A much thicker wool, spun from the coarse fleeces of Herdwick or Scottish Black Face sheep, is ideal for weaving rugs.

Open most days, 9–5, by appointment only.

WHITCHURCH   Map ref: Cd
Hinton Bank Farm, nr Whitchurch.
Tel. Whitchurch 2631
(One mile north of Whitchurch on west side of A49. Parking on premises.)

'A cheese fit only for heroes' is how one connoisseur described the rich, creamy Farmhouse Blue Cheshire cheese made at Hinton Bank Farm. Over the centuries, the blue mould had shown up only 'accidentally' in batches of white Cheshire. But in 1968, production began here on a regular basis after the owners, Group Captain and Mrs Hutchinson-Smith, following years of research and experimentation, discovered the right conditions for the blue mould to grow consistently in the cheese. Visitors to the farmhouse cheese dairy will be shown the various processes, and may buy cheese.

Open by appointment only, to groups of at least six people.

WHITCHURCH   Map ref: Cd
The Shropshire Arts and Crafts Centre, Brownlow Street, Whitchurch.

Tel. Whitchurch 4232
(On A41/A49 trunk road through town. Car park on site.)

The building of mellowed brick which houses the craft gallery was once the local fire station. There is now a comprehensive display of locally made craft goods, which includes pottery, jewellery, hand-painted coral ware and candles. Here, David Reece, a craftsman in ceramics, can be seen creating decorative works.

Open daily, 9–5.30 (except Wed., Christmas Day, Boxing Day and New Year's Day).

MUSEUMS

ACTON SCOTT   Map ref: Bc
Acton Scott Working Farm Museum, Acton Scott, nr Church Stretton.
Tel. Marshbrook 306/7

Time has stopped still at Acton Scott – a working museum that illustrates life on a Shropshire upland farm at the turn of the century.

The Home Farm buildings are clustered around a cobbled farmyard pungent with smells that make visitors forget that they are wandering around a museum. Hens peck beneath the agricultural machinery on display in the yard and calves doze in the cowshed. The air is heavy with the rich countryside smells of straw, manure and fresh milk.

There is a display area consisting of tools and photographs, where insight is given into the daily life of the farm labourer in previous centuries. Every day there are demonstrations of butter and cheese-making in the dairy. The barn houses machinery that includes a chaff-cutter and an oil-cake breaker used to prepare concentrated nourishment for animal feed.

Every weekend there are demonstrations of such crafts as spinning, weaving, basket-making, woodturning and quilting.

Open Apr.–Oct. inclusive, Mon.–Sat., 10–5; Sun. and Bank Holidays, 10–6. Charge for admission.

ASTON MUNSLOW   Map ref: Bc
The White House, Aston Munslow.

For over 600 years the Stedman family lived in the White House, which consists of a 13th-century undercroft, a 14th-century cruck hall, a 16th-century timber-framed cross-wing and a Georgian addition. The house once commanded 2,000 acres of land; today, with its outbuildings, it remains a fine example of an ancient homestead and its equipment. Visitors may wander round the stables, the dairy, and a cider house with crusher and press. There is also a collection of old agricultural tools.

Open Easter to Oct., Wed. and Sat., 11–5.30.

Other times by written appointment. Charge for admission.

COALPORT   Map ref: Cd
Blists Hill Open Air Museum, Telford.
Tel. Telford 586309
(The Museum is situated at Coalport, about 7 miles south of Telford.)

In the days when Ironbridge Gorge was the most important ironmaking area in Britain, between 400 and 500 people were employed within the boundaries of today's museum. On a site of 42 acres, it sets out to reconstruct a 19th-century mining community and allows visitors to peer back into the days when Britain was the 'workshop of the world'.

Whenever possible, the museum has preserved buildings and machines, such as blast furnaces, where they stand. But some have been transferred from nearby sites; others, including the working saw-mill and candle factory, have been reconstructed from several sources. Near the railway sidings, a little town – typical of those to be found in Shropshire in the late 19th century – has been built. The buildings include a cobbler's shop, and a printing shop where a demonstrator can be seen producing Victorian notices and posters.

Open daily, 10–6, during British Summer Time. Closing is an hour earlier during the winter. Charge for admission.

Map ref: Cc

Avoncroft Museum of Buildings

STOKE HEATH, HEREFORD AND WORCESTER

Buildings that have been saved by the museum from destruction, and re-erected at Stoke Heath, include a 16th-century barn, a magnificent timber roof from a 14th-century hall, an 18th-century granary, one of the only three surviving post mills in the Midlands, and a 15th-century merchant's house.

Earlier this century, many citizens of Bromsgrove earned their living by manufacturing nails by hand. Nail and also chain workshops have been reconstructed, and occasionally visitors can watch chains being made. From time to time logs are converted into planks on the rack-saw that was transported from an estate near Warwick.

MERCHANT'S HOME *A reconstructed oak-framed house, built in the late 15th century.*

Stoke Heath, Bromsgrove, Hereford and Worcester.
Tel. Bromsgrove 31363

Open daily, Mar.–Nov., 10.30–5.30 (or dusk if earlier). Charge for admission.

CRUCK-FRAMED BARN *The spaces between the beams are filled with woven pales (stakes) of split oak.*

Opening times and other details may change. Check by telephone before making a special journey.

261

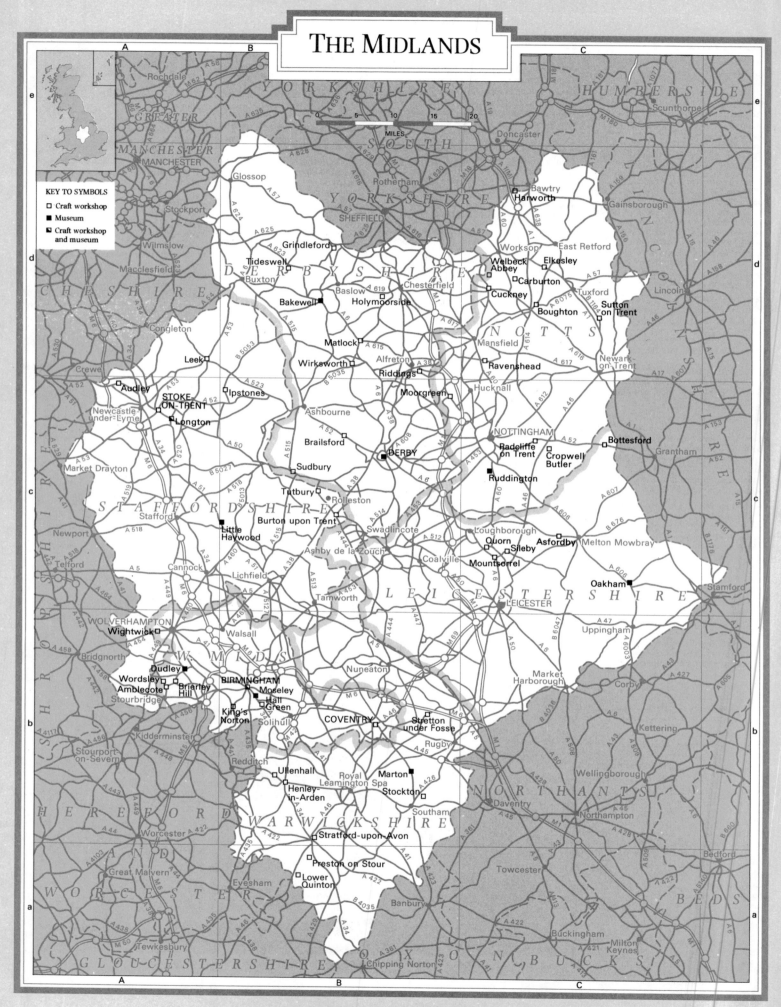

THE MIDLANDS

KEY TO SYMBOLS
- □ Craft workshop
- ■ Museum
- ◪ Craft workshop and museum

The Midlands helped to make 19th-century Britain the workshop of the world. The part they played was a portrait of a happy marriage between master craftsmanship and muscle, for it was the expertise of craftsmen that made the Industrial Revolution possible. Pottery, the best example of a trade poised between craft and industry, flourishes throughout the region – both in rural workshops and in factories with bottle ovens that dominate the skyline of Staffordshire's Six Towns. The same is true of the area's glassworks, whose fine crystal has graced many a royal table. But the Midlands offer the visitor more than the pounding heart of industrial Britain. Despite the common image, these counties also embrace mile upon mile of unspoiled landscape. As a result, country crafts still thrive – besom making, for example, the construction of traditional oak furniture, and the crafting of saddles, bits and bridles for prestigious hunts such as the Quorn and the Belvoir.

DERBYSHIRE

BRAILSFORD   Map ref: Bc
Cannon Craft, Sundial Farm, Brailsford.
Tel. Brailsford 480
(Signposted from main road through village. Parking on site.)

A 32-pounder cannon from Nelson's ship, Victory, and a 12-pounder field gun also used in the Napoleonic Wars are just two of the cannons that have been reproduced in miniature by Joe and Ida Platt in their workshop. The models, scaled down to one-eighth of their original size, are turned in brass and wood with meticulous attention to detail. The same precision goes into making sundials, and replicas of a later timepiece – a curious brass clock invented in the early 1800s by Sir William Congreve. A table beneath the clock contains a zigzag groove along which a ball rolls. When the ball reaches the end, the table tips and releases the spring that controls the time mechanism.

Open Mon.–Sat., 8.30–12.30 and 1.30–5.30. Usually open on Sun. afternoons.

BRAILSFORD   Map ref: Bc
Rupert Griffiths (Monastic Woodcraft Ltd), Saracen's Head Coaching House, Brailsford.
Tel. Brailsford 429
(On A52 in village centre. Parking on site.)

The period when the Tudors and early Stuarts were on the throne is known as the great age of oak. Trees in their thousands were felled to provide timber – not only for building ships and houses, but also for making sturdy furniture which was notable for its wealth of fine carving. Rupert Griffiths and his craftsmen produce furniture reminiscent of these early masterpieces. They use 'quartered' oak – a high-grade timber which is sliced radially from the centre of the trunk to minimise shrinkage and distortion.

Showroom open Mon.–Sat., 8–5.30. Workshop by appointment.

BRAILSFORD   Map ref: Bc
Barry C. Potter, The Forge, Brailsford.
Tel. Brailsford 368
(Next door to Rupert Griffiths [previous entry]. Parking on site.)

As Barry Potter fans the glowing fire in his smithy and begins work, the rhythmic sound of hammer striking steel fills the air. The results of his labours are displayed in his showroom next door – fire baskets, dog grates, fire irons, spark guards and light fittings. They are all simply designed, free from elaborate scrollwork, with the emphasis on graceful, balanced lines.

Open Tues.–Sat., 9–1 and 2–5.30.

GRINDLEFORD   Map ref: Bd
Andrew Lawton (Furniture maker), The Workshop, Goatscliff, Grindleford.
Tel. Chesterfield 202822 (Home)
(On B6001, at southern end of village. Parking outside.)

Ash, elm and oak have been used to make furniture for hundreds of years, because of their strength and durability. Andrew Lawton uses them for his furniture in modern, simple style. He prefers not to stain the wood, but just to protect its natural colour with a wax polish or polyurethane seal. In this way, the full beauty of the grain patterns and subtle variations in colour are clearly seen.

Open Mon.–Fri., 10–5.30.

HOLYMOORSIDE   Map ref: Bd
William R. Walker and Sons, Well Lane, Loads, Holymoorside, Chesterfield.
Tel. Chesterfield 6697
(From Holymoorside, take road west by the Lamb Inn. After 1½ miles take right turn, signposted Upper Loads. Premises are at bottom of lane. Parking on site.)

During the winter, when the trees have shed their leaves, Mr Tyson and his partners go out on the surrounding Chatsworth Estates or into Sherwood Forest to cut birch brushwood for making besoms. The firm was started over 100 years ago, but besoms have been made since at least Saxon times. After the twigs have been stored for several months to dry, they are grouped into bundles, secured tightly at the top with cane tags, and trimmed. Then a shaft of hazel is driven into the birch and nailed into place. Heather besoms are also made.

Open Mon.–Fri., 9–4, by appointment.

MATLOCK   Map ref: Bd
The Courtyard Pottery, The Courtyard, Dale Road, Matlock.
Tel. Matlock 4747
(At northern end of Dale Road – the A6 – opposite Midland Bank. Car park near by.)

Two potters share a workshop and showroom overlooking a pretty cobbled courtyard. Josie Walter spent six months working at a rural pottery in France, where she made a study of traditional French earthenware cooking pots. Terrines, gratinée dishes and poelons (bowls with handles) are among the items for sale, all glazed a rich golden-brown. She will also make special cooking pots to order. John Gibson's porcelain is notable for its varied decoration. He creates delicate 'impressionistic' patterns in soft, pastel shades by trailing, stamping or brushing the clay with coloured slips.

Open Mon.–Sat., 10–5, but closed Thur. afternoons. Open Sun. afternoons in summer.

MATLOCK   Map ref: Bd
Prisms (Glass engraving), 125 Dale Road, Matlock.
Tel. Matlock 2782
(On A6, at southern end of town, near railway bridge. Car park close by.)

Images on glass, so delicate that they appear to be seen through a fine mist, are created by David Prytherch using a technique called diamond-point engraving. He gradually builds up a picture by stippling the surface of the glass many times with a diamond-tipped stylus. For a more definite, linear design, he will use an electric drill. Any design, either pictorial or lettering, can be engraved on to glassware, ranging from goblets and bowls to mirrors and larger panels. Mr Prytherch runs weekend courses in his craft.

Open Mon., Tues., Wed., Fri. and Sat., 10–1.30 and 2.30–5.30.

MATLOCK   Map ref: Bd
Wheatsheaf House Pottery, Church Street, Matlock.
Tel. Matlock 55975
(Turn off A615 Alfreton Road opposite the Horseshoe pub. Pottery next to church.)

Wheatsheaf House, an attractive building of mellow stone and mullioned windows, dates back to the 17th century. John and Lynn Wheeldon have turned an outbuilding into a pottery studio where visitors can watch black basalt ware, porcelain and stoneware pots being thrown on the wheel. Sometimes Mr Wheeldon places a tiny pot of copper oxide in the kiln during firing porcelain to produce a delicate pink 'blush'. The more robust stoneware is glazed in an oatmeal colour with trailed patterns in green and a deep burned orange. The range of pottery for sale in the showroom includes ornamental boxes, lamp bases, pot-pourri bowls, bonsai pots and tableware.

Open Wed.–Sun., 10–6, or until dusk in summer.

RIDDINGS   Map ref: Bd
Riddings Pottery, Green Hill House, Green Hill Lane, Riddings.
Tel. Leabrooks 603181
(On corner of Green Hill Lane – the B6016 south of Alfreton – and South Street. Limited parking outside pottery.)

Madge Spencer had a remarkable stroke of luck when builders excavating a site opposite her home uncovered an unexpected source of clay. She prepares it herself, and makes a 'body' ideal for earthenware by mixing it with china clay from an outside supplier. Stoneware and porcelain are also made in this one-woman pottery housed in the former stables of Green Hill House. Goods range from small pieces of porcelain to large vases, more than 2 ft tall.

Open Fri., Sat. and Sun., 2–6. Also open at times during rest of week, when visitors are advised to telephone in advance.

SUDBURY   Map ref: Bc
Metwood Forge, School Lane, Sudbury.
Tel. Sudbury 232/589
(At end of lane, signposted as a No Through Road off main village street. Parking outside.)

Traditionally, a village blacksmith was skilled in all types of ironwork and would undertake any job from shoeing horses to making and repairing farm and domestic equipment. In Sudbury, today, there are two forges, each specialising in a different aspect of the craft. Decorative wrought ironwork, including fire grates, lights, weather-vanes and garden furniture, is made to order at Metwood Forge. Next door, Mr Lunnon forges shoes for hunters, ponies and workhorses.

Open Mon.–Fri., 7.30–4.30.

TIDESWELL   Map ref: Bd
Advent Hunstone (Woodcarver), Market Square, Tideswell, Buxton.
Tel. Tideswell 871571
(In market square, beside First Drop Inn. Parking in square.)

Visitors to Tideswell should take time to look round the parish church, known as the Cathedral of the Peak. For inside are some very fine furnishings, in particular the vicar's chair and the choir stalls, which were carved in oak by a talented local craftsman, Mr Advent Hunstone, in the 1880s. A century later, the business he started is continued by his great-nephew, Mr William Hunstone. Using many of his ancestor's tools, Mr Hunstone carries out commissions in English oak. His work ranges from spinning chairs, chests and fireplace surrounds, to lecterns and lych-gates.

Open Mon.–Sat., 9–5, by appointment.

TIDESWELL   Map ref: Bd
Tideswell Dale Rock Shop, Commercial Road, Tideswell, Buxton.
Tel. Tideswell 871606
(Opposite George Hotel, in town centre.)

Gem cutter and jeweller Don Edwards has revived the craft of black-marble inlay work for which Derbyshire became famous in the 18th and 19th centuries. It is exacting, detailed work which involves inlaying pieces of marble with gems, ivory and shells cut into delicate floral shapes. The rare Blue John stone has a pale translucence when polished, and is shot through with dark blue and purple bandings. From these stones, Mr Edwards makes exquisite pendants, brooches and rings.

Open Thur.–Sun., 9.30–5.30.

WIRKSWORTH   Map ref: Bd
T. C. Jones (Furniture maker), trading as Frank Pratt, Old Grammar School, Church Close, Wirksworth.
Tel. Wirksworth 2828
(From Market Place, take the Alfreton road – the B5035. Take second right-hand turn up Blind Lane. Workshop is halfway up.)

Founded during the reign of Elizabeth I, in 1576, the Old Grammar School was a place of learning for nearly 400 years. Here visitors will find Mr Jones, making traditional oak furniture. He learned his skills from Frank Pratt, who started the business in the 1930s, and under whose name he continues to trade. His work includes tables, dressers, bookcases and blanket chests. These incorporate beautiful carvings and are stained to the required shade before being given a wax finish.

Open Mon.–Sat., 9–5; Sun., by appointment.

MUSEUMS

BAKEWELL   Map ref: Bd
Old House Museum, Cunningham Place, Bakewell.
Tel. Bakewell 3647

In the 18th century Sir Richard Arkwright, the textile manufacturer and pioneer, converted the 16th-century limestone building that now houses the museum into six separate cottages for his workers at Lumford Mill. Oak-timbered rooms contain collections of farm equipment, samples of lace, and tools of the carpenter, wheelwright, leatherworker and saddler.

Open daily, Easter to Oct., 2.30–5. Charge for admission.

DERBY   Map ref: Bc
Elvaston Castle Museum, nr Derby.
Tel. Derby 71342

A fire blazes in the hearth, and gaslights flicker, as museum staff in traditional costume carry out the daily chores of decades ago. Every effort, including a detailed study of an inventory of 1881, has been made to create an atmosphere that is exactly right. As a result, visitors – fearing that they are intruding – have been heard to express embarrassment.

The country house and its estate formed a self-sufficient and flourishing community. At one time, 120 gardeners and 40 grooms were employed at Elvaston Castle. Ranged around a cobbled courtyard are the workshops where, on weekends from Easter to the end of October, craftsmen from time to time give demonstrations – a dairy, a laundry, saddler's, wheelwright's, plumber's, joiner's and cobbler's shops, and a blacksmith's forge.

Geese, game-fowl and Derbyshire Redcaps – a breed of chicken – rootle for food around the woodyard. Warrior, a shire horse born and bred in the county, carts logs that are cut up into planks on a large saw bench. Displays illustrate the importance of forestry and timber on the estate.

The museum's vast array of exhibits includes carts, wagons and coaches, together with

Opening times and other details may change. Check by telephone before making a special journey.

263

vintage engines – connected to overhead shafts – which power the saws. One inventive exhibition tells the agricultural history of the estate over the past 1,000 years by singling out the lives of people such as William Piggen, a farmer, and Mary Blackshaw, a dairymaid.

Open Easter to end Oct., Wed.–Sat., 1–5. Also open Sun. and Bank Holidays, 10–6. Charge for admission.

LEICESTERSHIRE

ASFORDBY Map ref: Cc
Timber Top Tables, 159 Main Street, Asfordby, Melton Mowbray.
Tel. Melton Mowbray 812320
(On corner of Mill Lane and main street, opposite Bluebell public house.)

From the Middle Ages up to the last century, the rolling green fields of Leicestershire supported vast flocks of sheep, and the wool trade flourished in the area. Mr Jim Williamson, whose workshop is in the garden of his mellow red-brick Georgian house, maintains a link with the past by making traditional spinning-wheels. Visitors to the workshop are greeted by the pleasant aromas of resins and varnishes as he works. Using English oak or yew, and shaping up to 100 different pieces on his lathe, Mr Williamson produces treadle-wheels in five basic designs.

Open all year, Mon.–Fri., 9–5, by appointment.

BOTTESFORD Map ref: Cc
Marcus Designs, Normanton Lane, Bottesford.
Tel. Bottesford 42519
(Normanton Lane leads on from Market Street, which leaves the A52 by the Bull Inn in centre of Bottesford. Parking outside workshop.)

The romantic age of chivalry is recalled in this busy workshop run by Dennis Morton and Brian Flannery. They and their team produce an extensive range of medieval-style reliefs and sculptures, featuring such subjects as warrior kings and princes, jousting and battles. Many hours of research are devoted to armour, coats of arms and other details before Dennis Morton is ready to sculpt the models from which moulds are made. Figures and scenes are then produced in cold-cast bronze, an ivory-like resin, and a type of stone composite. The entire range is displayed in a small shop.

Open Mon.–Thur., 9–12 and 1–4.30; Sat., 9.30–12.

MOUNTSORREL Map ref: Cc
Quorn Art Glass, 7a Loughborough Road, Mountsorrel.
Tel. Leicester 303663
(Opposite Nag's Head public house on the A6, in centre of Mountsorrel. Parking in streets near by, and in studio yard.)

Intense white flames, created by burning a mixture of natural gas and oxygen, are used to heat the glass rods and tubes which this small team of craftworkers transforms into delicate birds, trees and many other attractive ornaments. They include a special vase which recalls the time when local girls placed a flower in the front window to indicate that they were ready to be courted. Many pieces are decorated in beautifully subtle colours developed by Edward Hughes, the founder of Quorn Art Glass, and known as 'Shades of Charnwood'.

Open Mon.–Fri., 9–5; Sat. and Sun., 10.30–4.30. Appointment needed for workshop.

QUORN Map ref: Cc
Marshall Novelcrafts Ltd, 33 Freehold Street, Quorn, Loughborough.
Tel. Loughborough 63865 (Office); Loughborough 42418 (Workshop)
(From Leicester, turn right at Quorn crossroads. Follow road round to river. Freehold Street lies off to left of this road. Parking in street.)

The secret of how fully rigged models of sailing ships are put into bottles is a secret no more to those who have visited Marshall Novelcrafts. It is all done with a good eye, a steady hand and plenty of patience. The Marshall 'fleet' consists of more than 20 different models, among them Nelson's flagship HMS Victory, *Drake's* Golden Hind, *the* Mayflower *and the* Cutty Sark, *in a variety of bottles from 3 in. to 20 in. long. The meticulously built ships have their masts, spars and rigging folded flat against the decks and are carefully pushed through the neck of the bottle to sail on a sea of blue clay. Then drawstrings are gently pulled and the masts rise into place. Long probes are inserted through the neck of the bottle to straighten the sails.*

Open all year, Mon.–Fri., 9–5, by appointment.

SILEBY Map ref: Cc
Welford Pottery, Peashill Farm, Ratcliffe Road, Sileby.
Tel. Sileby 4102
(Signposted off Ratcliffe Road on eastern edge of Sileby. Parking outside pottery.)

John Weeks and Melanie Cunningham had a small pottery in Leicester before moving to Sileby in 1979. They converted a derelict, roofless cowshed into the snug building where white 'semi-porcelain' earthenware is slip-cast in plaster moulds made by Mr Weeks. Hand-painted planters, lamps, vases, trinket boxes and other wares are placed in two electric kilns, which are fired two or three times each week.

Open Mon.–Fri., 9–5, by appointment.

MUSEUM

OAKHAM Map ref: Cc
Rutland County Museum, Catmos Street, Oakham.
Tel. Oakham 3654

An indoor riding school built in 1794 for the local cavalry militia, the Rutland Fencibles, now houses the museum. Collections of tools illustrate trades and activities such as farming, stonemasonry, blacksmithing and cobbling. The cooper's tools came from Ruddles, the renowned local brewery; the wooden handles of the wheelwright's tools, which include a hand-made treadle lathe, are smooth from years of hard work. In the courtyard there is a fine collection of ploughs and carts.

Open all year, Tues.–Sat., 10–1 and 2–5; also Sun., Apr.–Oct., 2–5. Admission free.

NOTTINGHAMSHIRE

BOUGHTON Map ref: Cd
Wood Graphics, 39 Greenwood Crescent, Boughton.
Tel. Mansfield 860298
(Greenwood Crescent adjoins Tuxford Road – part of the A6075 – on eastern side of Boughton. Parking in street.)

A fitter by trade, Ray Cocking turned to craftwork after losing his sight in 1973. The workshop behind his home houses a 'braille-controlled' machine, specially imported from the USA, on which he carves domestic and commercial signs in yew, beech, elm, oak and other woods. Many are painted in black and gold, and then finished with a clear marine varnish to keep out the weather. Seven pieces of yew illustrate the various stages, from rough-cut to completion. Mr Cocking also uses cane and rush to restore old chairs, and co-operates with local craftsmen making traditional furniture.

Open Mon.–Fri., 9–5; Sat., 9–1. By appointment at other times.

CARBURTON Map ref: Cd
Wren Craftsmen in Oak, The Old School, Carburton, Worksop.
Tel. Worksop 731464
(On the B6005, 4 miles south of Worksop. Ample parking outside workshop.)

Mature oak, much of it from the Sherwood Forest area, is used by Thomas Rennocks and his son John, together with an assistant, to make the 'Wren' range of refectory tables, chairs, dressers, linen chests and corner cupboards. Staunch traditionalists who refuse to use veneers or plywoods, they even make drawer bottoms and cabinet backs from solid oak. Every item bears the delightful 'Wren' trade mark.

Open daily, 10–5.

CROPWELL BUTLER Map ref: Cc
Barratt and Swann (Furniture makers), Hardigate, Cropwell Butler.
Tel. Radcliffe on Trent 2642
(On edge of Cropwell Butler, a village between the A46 and A52 east of Nottingham. Parking outside workshop.)

Roy Barratt and Arthur Swann have spacious premises and employ about 16 people. Working in oak, ash, elm and cherry, plus a certain amount of pine, they produce a range of traditional furniture known as the 'Countryman's Collection', and specialise in made-to-measure pieces for individual customers. An appointment must be made to visit the workshops.

Open Mon.–Fri., 8–5.

CUCKNEY Map ref: Cd
Wood End Pottery, Woodend, Cuckney.
Tel. Mansfield 842599
(On the A616 towards Sheffield, just over 1 mile from Cuckney. Parking outside pottery.)

Tony O'Donovan traces his potting career back to an interest in archaeology which prompted him to start making replicas of Roman lamps for the museum in Doncaster. Designs and decorations inspired by craftsmen who worked in the Mediterranean area 2,000 years ago still feature prominently in his workshop. It takes almost two hours to paint some of the more elaborate pieces. Amateur potters may also be seen at work between Easter and October, when residential courses are organised.

Open daily from 9 a.m. until about 10 p.m.

ELKESLEY Map ref: Cd
Chris Aston Pottery, Yew Tree Cottage, 4 High Street, Elkesley.
Tel. Gamston 391
(Elkesley's High Street runs parallel to the northbound carriageway of the A1.)

Chris Aston and his wife, Phillippa, produce a full range of domestic stoneware, as well as many delightful decorative pieces. Visitors can see everything from the clay being processed to goods being packed carefully into one of the pottery's three kilns.

Open daily, 10–6.

HARWORTH Map ref: Cd
The Pottery, Tickhill Road, Harworth.
Tel. Doncaster 743838
(On the junction of Tickhill Road and Baulk Lane in Harworth, a village between Bawtry and the A1(M). Small car park available.)

Stoneware and porcelain are produced in this small, friendly pottery run by Robert Howard and his team of part-time assistants. The porcelain vases and bowls are decorated with a technique which raises the motifs and is then fired in a hand-built gas kiln. Hand-thrown tableware accounts for part of the pottery's output, but Mr Howard has also designed a range of whimsical little sheep, shaggy-coated Highland cattle and other ornaments, including a model of an old-style pottery.

Open Mon.–Fri., 10–5; Sat. and Sun., 12–5.

MOORGREEN Map ref: Bc
Oakcraft Hand-made Furniture, The Old Stables, Church Road, Moorgreen.
Tel. Langley Mill 66677
(Church Road is part of the B600 between Alfreton and Nottingham. Workshop is next to Horse and Groom public house. Limited parking outside.)

Corner cupboards, chairs, tables up to 10 ft long, dressers, fire surrounds and many other examples of made-to-order furniture are produced by Douglas Watchorn, a craftsman who works mainly in oak. Hand-cut joints and other traditional features help to explain why a single dining chair represents about ten hours of painstaking work. Finishing with boiled linseed oil gives the oak an enduring richness, and furniture can also be 'distressed' to create an illusion of age.

Open Mon.–Fri., 8–5; Sat., 8–12.

RADCLIFFE ON TRENT Map ref: Cc
Saddlecraft, 1a Cropwell Road, Radcliffe on Trent.
Tel. Radcliffe on Trent 2800
(From Nottingham take the A52 to Radcliffe on Trent. At Cropwell Road traffic lights turn left. Saddlecraft is on right near end of road, opposite Black Lion public house.)

Radcliffe on Trent is in the middle of some of the most famous hunting country in Britain – the domain of the Quorn and Belvoir hunts – so William and Lesley Cliff are constantly busy in their small workshop. The walls and shelves are packed with equipment for the horse, the horse owner, the casual rider and the countryman. There are bits for horses of all sizes – $3\frac{1}{2}$ in. bits, for small ponies, up to 6 in. long bits for the 17-hand hunters. Other items range from bridles to a complete manger.

Open all year, 9–12.45 and 2–5, except Wed., Sun. and Bank Holidays.

RAVENSHEAD Map ref: Cd
Longdale Rural Craft Centre, Longdale Lane, Ravenshead.
Tel. Blidworth 4858
(Longdale Lane leaves the A60 Nottingham–Mansfield road opposite entrance to Newstead Abbey. Craft centre about 1 mile down lane. Ample parking.)

This craft centre in what used to be the heart of Sherwood Forest was founded in the early 1970s by Gordon Brown, a gifted woodcarver who also makes furniture and restores antiques. The centre is the headquarters of the Nottinghamshire Craftsmen's Guild, and has displays ranging from corn dollies to wrought ironwork. A working museum of rural crafts has been developed. It includes a traditional smithy, a saddler's workshop, and a weaver.

Open Tues.–Sun., 9–6; also on Bank Holiday Mon. Coach parties should make an appointment.

RAVENSHEAD Map ref: Cd
Ravenshead Pottery, 23 Milton Drive, Ravenshead.
Tel. Blidworth 3178
(In centre of village, near village hall and shopping precinct. Parking in road.)

Ashtrays and pot knobs decorated with melted, multi-coloured glass catch the eye in this small, friendly pottery where Brian and Joan Marris, former schoolteachers who started potting as a hobby, make their attractive and functional stoneware. In addition to such goods as hand-thrown and hand-painted coffee sets, casseroles, planters and storage jars, they also make old-style punchbowls complete with 'dipper' mugs which hang from the rim.

Open at all times; but telephone in advance between May and Sept.

SUTTON ON TRENT Map ref: Cd
Trent Valley Potteries Ltd, Old Great North Road, Sutton on Trent.
Tel. Newark-on-Trent 821358
(On the B1164, about 6 miles north of Newark-on-Trent. Parking outside pottery.)

A huge 'top hat' kiln with a capacity of 300 cu. ft is used to fire the range of terracotta goods made in this big, bustling pottery. Chicken 'bricks', baking dishes, pots, jars, vases, bulb bowls and many other items are moulded in machines, 'fettled' and sponged by hand, and then placed in a rotating drier before being glazed and fired. Most combine a rough, natural finish with the traditional dark brown glaze of domestic earthenware.

Open Mon.–Fri., 8–5. Shop open Mon.–Sat., 10–4.

WELBECK ABBEY   Map ref: Cd
Hamlyn Lodge Cottage Industry (Furniture and pottery), Welbeck Abbey, Worksop.
Tel. Worksop 85252
(One mile down a private road, signposted for Welbeck College, off the A60 between Worksop and Cuckney. Parking outside workshop.)

The grounds of Welbeck Abbey – a huge estate once owned by the Dukes of Portland – provide a setting of rural elegance and tranquillity for Hamlyn Lodge's furniture and pottery business. Rex Barrows and his son, Norman, restore antiques and make superb reproduction furniture using English walnut and other high-quality woods. Another son, John, runs the pottery, where he hand-throws a range of mugs, piggy banks, storage jars and other items in hand-decorated stoneware. The partners also have a showroom at Station Road, Otterton (Tel. Mansfield 823600).

Open daily, 10–6.

MUSEUM

RUDDINGTON   Map ref: Cc
Ruddington Framework Knitters' Museum, Chapel Street, Ruddington.
Tel. Nottingham 212116 (Curator)

Two workshops and a block of cottages built in 1829 frame the courtyard where the knitters washed, grew vegetables and played impromptu games of cricket. Visitors to this enterprising museum can watch some of the 17 hand-frames in operation. Some are over 200 years old; others, built in 1954, are the last known to have been made in England. As the frames start clicking and clanking it is easy to imagine work here a century ago, with its cramped conditions, the fluff, the dust, the oil and the bustle. The museum also contains ties, scarves, shawls and stockings knitted in Ruddington when hosiery was the town's main industry.

Ring Curator for opening times. Small admission charge.

STAFFORDSHIRE

AUDLEY   Map ref: Ac
Audley Porcelain, Studio 'D', 18 Chapel Street, Bignall End, Audley, Stoke-on-Trent.
Tel. Stoke-on-Trent 720252
(Half a mile east of Audley Church, on the A52 between the M6 and Newcastle-under-Lyme. Parking on road outside pottery.)

Diana and Malcolm Keates have created a

whimsical world of 'mill meece' – delightful little mice whose quaint and colourful homes are actually children's lamps made of cast and hand-painted porcelain. Each lamp is accompanied by a tiny booklet which tells the story of Grandad Meece, Joseph the Vicar, Monty the Policeman and other characters in the 'village'. Established in 1977, the pottery also produces an attractive range of British garden birds, 'character' jugs, and bottle stoppers whose heads – such as a Cossack for the vodka – indicate contents. Diana Keates makes the models herself, then sends them to a craftsman who creates the plaster moulds.

Open Mon.–Sat., 9–5.30. Parties by appointment, to see the porcelain being made.

BURTON UPON TRENT   Map ref: Bc
Peter Halliday (Calligrapher), 26 Stapenhill Road, Burton upon Trent.
Tel. Burton upon Trent 68320
(Stapenhill Road runs parallel to the River Trent and is part of the A444, signposted to Nuneaton. Limited parking outside house.)

Quill pens and brushes of fine sable are used by Peter Halliday to transform sheets of vellum and paper into beautiful examples of the calligrapher's art. His 'bread and butter' items include commemorative scrolls and richly decorated coats of arms, but he also combines traditional techniques with modern concepts to illustrate poems and other literary works. John Donne and Dylan Thomas are among his favourite authors. Many methods used for

decorative work with paints and gold leaf have changed only in detail since the Middle Ages.

Open by appointment.

IPSTONES   Map ref: Bc
Rooke's Pottery, High Street, Ipstones.
Tel. Ipstones 606
(In centre of village, about 100 yds up hill from Ye Old Red Lion. Parking in street.)

David Rooke worked at the Gladstone Pottery Museum in Stoke-on-Trent, reproducing traditional wares, before starting his own pottery in 1977. He and his wife, Catherine, restored Ipstones' derelict smithy and now supply shops in London, Manchester, Chester and elsewhere. Coffee sets, parsley pots, trays, goblets and many other goods are hand-thrown in stoneware and terracotta. The couple mix their own glazes, and much of the decorative work is done by Catherine Rooke.

Open daily, 10–12 and 2–5. Open until 5.30 on summer weekends and Bank Holidays.

LEEK   Map ref: Ad
The Brindley Mill, Mill Street, Leek.
Tel. Leek 384195 (Secretary of The Brindley Mill Preservation Trust)
(Mill Street is part of the A523 from Leek to Macclesfield. Parking round corner in Abbey Green Road.)

Derelict for more than two decades, this enchanting old water-mill was restored by enthusiasts and rumbled back to life in 1974,

---

Map ref: Ac

Gladstone Pottery Museum

LONGTON, STAFFORDSHIRE

Bottle ovens dominate the skyline of Longton, one of the Six Towns of the Staffordshire Potteries. They loom above the cobbled yard of the Gladstone Pottery Museum, a typical early Victorian potbank that is now a working museum. Visitors can wander at leisure around the yard, which once would have been wreathed in smoke, and follow the various stages in the making of pottery.

Displays in converted warehouses and workshops tell the story of the rise of the Staffordshire Potteries and the history and techniques of applying colour to ceramics. There are also exhibitions of ceramic tiles and sanitary ware – from Sir John Harington's first proposal in 1596 for a flushing toilet to more recent models.

The kitchen and back bedroom of a typical potter at the turn of the century have been reconstructed, and sections on religion, housing and health give insights into the lives and preoccupations of the craftsmen who fashioned Britain's industrial history.

The factory, which was named after the statesman W. E. Gladstone in the 19th century, makes the perfect setting for this imaginative museum. Although the making of pottery is an industrial process, it requires expertise acquired over centuries. Several of the craftsmen who now demonstrate in the museum have had the benefit of disciplined training within a factory, and now have the opportunity to develop their own styles within the freedom of the museum. They can be seen making little china flowers, hand-painting delicate designs on plates, throwing, casting, sculpting and decorating.

Uttoxeter Road, Longton, Stoke-on-Trent, Staffordshire. Tel. Stoke-on-Trent 319232.

Open Mon.–Sat., 10.30–5.30; Sun. and Bank Holidays, 2–6. Closed Mon., Oct.–Mar.

BOTTLE OVENS The coal-fired ovens, dating from the 18th century, were in daily use until the 1960s.

Opening times and other details may change. Check by telephone before making a special journey.

265

when the Brindley Mill Preservation Trust first ground corn. Dating from 1752, the mill is believed to have been built by James Brindley, the 'father' of Britain's canal system, and its top floor has displays illustrating his life and times. Water from the River Churnet powers ancient machinery which drives two sets of millstones, the oldest dating from 1847. The flour is sold in small bags.

Open Easter to Oct., Sat., Sun. and Bank Holiday Mon., 2–5. Parties wishing to visit at other times must give the Preservation Trust's secretary at least two weeks' notice.

LONGTON Map ref: Ac
Royal Doulton Tableware Ltd, Gold Street, Longton, Stoke-on-Trent.
Tel. Stoke-on-Trent 313041
(Gold Street leads off The Strand, Longton's main street. Ample parking 200 yds away in Cook Street.)

The muscular elegance of Red Rum, Arkle, Nijinsky and other great horses is captured in the superbly detailed slip-cast figures made at this large, old-established pottery. They bear the Beswick 'backstamp', which recalls James Wright Beswick and his son – craftsmen who established their business in Longton in 1896. Other products include a wide range of delightful characters from the Beatrix Potter stories. A guided tour covers everything from casting to hand-painting.

Open Tues., Wed. and Thur. at 2 for guided tours. Appointment necessary.

STOKE-ON-TRENT Map ref: Ac
Spode Ltd, Church Street, Stoke-on-Trent.
Tel. Stoke-on-Trent 46011
(In centre of Stoke-on-Trent, ¼ mile south-west of railway station. Ample parking round corner in Eleanora Street.)

Born at Lane Delph, Staffordshire, in 1733, Josiah Spode was a pauper's son who started work in a local pottery when he was only seven years old. In 1776 he acquired the premises in Church Street, on what is now a 9 acre site, and founded a business whose wares were destined to become internationally famous. He evolved the formula for bone china – 50 per cent animal bone, 25 per cent china clay, 25 per cent Cornish stone – which his son, Josiah II, marketed. Spode now make a wide range of high-quality fine bone china and earthenware. A certain amount of modern machinery is used, but traditional craftsmanship features prominently on guided tours of the pottery. These take about 90 minutes. There is a spacious and comprehensively stocked shop.

Tours by appointment (small charge), Mon.–Fri., 10 and 2. 'Seconds' shop open Mon.–Fri., 8.30–5; Sat., 9–1.

TUTBURY Map ref: Bc
The Tutbury Sheepskin Shop, The Old Cornmill, Cornmill Lane, Tutbury, Burton upon Trent.
Tel. Burton upon Trent 813300
(Cornmill Lane, the road to Rolleston, leaves High Street in centre of Tutbury. Ample parking outside shop.)

The Chapman family had been making parchment for almost a century before Ernest Banks Chapman moved to Tutbury in 1914 and established a tannery in the 18th-century corn-mill. The mill now houses a shop and tearoom, while skins and hides are tanned in newer buildings near by. The skins of sheep, goats, deer and other animals, including lions, may be seen going through the various tanning processes. Gloves, slippers, handbags, rugs, coats and woollen goods are sold.

Shop open Tues.–Sat., 9–5.30. Tours of tannery, Apr.–Oct., by appointment.

MUSEUMS

LITTLE HAYWOOD Map ref: Bc
County Museum, Shugborough.
Tel. Little Haywood 881388

Shugborough, the ancestral home of the Earls of Lichfield, dates mainly from the 18th century. The museum block, which used to be called the 'backland' by the servants, consists of the laundry, the stables, the brewhouse and the coach-house. Fittingly, many of the displays illustrate the services and skills that were once demanded by a great house. The laundry, which gleams today with well-scrubbed pine, was in continuous use between the 1780s and the 1930s. Beer was brewed at Shugborough on a fairly large scale to provide an average personal allowance for the staff of a gallon a day. An exhibition of coachbuilding tools complements the fine collection of horse-drawn vehicles.

Other displays, both at the museum and at Shugborough Park Farm – a small working farm on the estate – are concerned with rural occupations such as poaching, ditching and harvesting. There are also a reconstructed tailor's shop and workroom, and a smithy.

Open mid-Mar.–Oct., Tues.–Fri., 10.30–5.30; Sat. and Sun., 2–5.30. Winter, 10.30–4.30; closed Sat.; open 1st and 3rd Sun., 2–4.30. Shugborough Park Farm open at weekends; other days by appointment.

LONGTON Map ref: Ac
Gladstone Pottery Museum.
(See panel on p. 265)

WARWICKSHIRE

HENLEY-IN-ARDEN Map ref: Bb
Torquil Pottery, 81 High Street, Henley-in-Arden.
Tel. Henley-in-Arden 2174
(In town centre. Parking in High Street.)

In Tudor times this small market town was surrounded by the densely wooded Forest of Arden. The forest has long since vanished, but some of its wood remains in the many timber-framed buildings which line Henley's broad, main street. One of these, a former coaching inn, belongs to Reg Moon, who runs the Torquil Pottery. He and his assistant, Louise, make pots in stoneware and porcelain which they decorate in a variety of ways, including abstract brushwork designs and 'piercing'. This technique is used on their range of hanging plant pots and nightlights, and involves cutting holes in the clay body to form open patterns in such shapes as circles and leaves. Visitors will see these displayed in the showroom.

Open Tues.–Sat., 9–6.

LOWER QUINTON Map ref: Ba
Stratford-upon-Avon Pottery, Firs Farmhouse, Lower Quinton, nr Stratford-upon-Avon.
Tel. Stratford-upon-Avon 720703
(At eastern end of village, almost opposite church. Parking on premises.)

On fine, sunny days, Gareth Richards often carries his pottery wheel on to the lawn outside his workshop so that he can work in the fresh country air in sight of the tall church spire and fields beyond. He makes stoneware, breadcrocks, casseroles, vases, tableware and, most popular of all, honey pots which are filled with honey from his own bees and those of other Warwickshire bee-keepers. He uses three basic glazes, which give an oatmeal, mustard or slate-blue colour. When the pots are fired, Mr Richards reduces the amount of oxygen in the kiln, causing the flames to draw out the iron oxides present in the clay. This produces dark flecks in the glaze.

Open daily, 10–5, except between Christmas and mid-Jan. Workshop closed Thur. and Sat. afternoons.

PRESTON ON STOUR Map ref: Ba
The Pottery, Old School House, Preston on Stour, nr Stratford-upon-Avon.
Tel. Alderminster 519
(Next door to post office. Car park behind building.)

Surrounded by fields, a gentle river and narrow country lanes, this picturesque village seems untouched by the bustle of the 20th century. Its peaceful atmosphere attracted Don Love some five years ago, when he started his pottery in the former school – a Victorian building of red brick, gables and diamond-leaded windows. He works in stoneware and porcelain, and among the more usual items displayed in his spacious showroom are whistles, wafer-thin dishes with 'curled' edges, and punch bowls designed to hold a dozen cups around the outer rim. Many of his pieces have dramatic splashes of dark green, purple or rust, achieved by spraying or brushing-on metal oxides.

Open most days, 10–6.

STOCKTON Map ref: Bb
Neville Neal, High Street, Stockton, nr Rugby.
Tel. Southam 3702 (Home)
(In village centre, next to newsagent's shop. Parking outside.)

The old rural craft of making spindle and ladder-back ash chairs with rush seats still thrives today in this tiny Warwickshire village. Neville Neal and his son, Lawrence, select strong but supple timbers cut from young ash trees, and gather rushes from local rivers, to make a range of dining, fireside and rocking chairs. One of the processes visitors might see is how the chair frames are curved. This is done by boiling them in a copper and then clamping them in a bending rack to dry. Mr Neal reproduces the graceful styles of the late-19th-century furniture designer Ernest Gimson, who sought to combine high standards of craftsmanship with simplicity.

Open Mon.–Fri., 8–5.30; Sat., 9–12.

STRATFORD-UPON-AVON Map ref: Bb
The Arden Pottery, 31 Henley Street, Stratford-upon-Avon.
Tel. Stratford-upon-Avon 4638
(Near Shakespeare's birthplace, at junction with Windsor Street. Car park in Windsor Street.)

As a founder member of the prestigious Craftsmen Potters Association back in the 1950s, Barbara Cass played an important role in the development of wood-ash glazes. She continues to produce high-quality stoneware, and mixes all her own clays, colours and glazes. The pots are fired for 30 hours in a large gas kiln, during which time she keeps a constant watch on the temperature and amount of oxygen feeding the flames. Her efforts are amply rewarded, for the reaction of the oxide washes and wood-ash glazes covering the pots forms beautiful surface patterns.

Open Mar.–Nov., Mon.–Sat., 10–5. Opening times in winter may vary slightly. Closed Jan.

STRATFORD-UPON-AVON Map ref: Bb
Robin Wade Ceramics, 21 Shakespeare Street, Stratford-upon-Avon.
Tel. Stratford-upon-Avon 69026
(At northern end of town, off Guild Street – the A34. Parking outside.)

Lamps disguised as merry-go-rounds; mirror surrounds in the form of miniature dressing tables; cheese dishes with pastoral figures sitting on their domed covers – these are just a few of the imaginative ceramics that visitors will find at Robin Wade's studio. She throws some of the basic shapes on her wheel, but most of her work is modelled by hand. This age-old method of working with clay is extremely versatile, lending itself to both low-relief decoration and sculptural pieces. She pays great attention to detail, texturing the clay to suggest such things as the movement of grass, or the pattern and folds of a dress.

Open Mon.–Fri., 11–5, by appointment.

STRETTON UNDER FOSSE Map ref: Bb
Yvonne Halton, The Cottage Pottery, Rose Narrow Boats, Stretton under Fosse, nr Rugby.

Tel. Rugby 833172
(Signposted off the A427 by Railway Inn. Parking outside.)

From the windows of her waterside studio, Yvonne Halton has a view of gaily painted narrow boats carrying holidaymakers along the Oxford Canal through a landscape of meadows and trees. Indeed, just as many of her visitors arrive by boat as by car. They will usually find her throwing earthenware pots on the wheel, which she decorates in relief with clay shapes inspired by the local scenery. Lamp bases, tea and coffee pots, plates and mugs, line the shelves of her studio, mostly glazed in soft green or grey.

Open all year, Mon.–Fri., 9–6. Also open Sat. in summer.

ULLENHALL Map ref: Bb
Stewart Silver, 1 Perrymill Cottage, Gentleman's Lane, Ullenhall, nr Henley-in-Arden.
Tel. Henley-in-Arden 4560
(In village centre, off Watery Lane.)

Methods of working silver, which comes in the form of wire, sheet or grains, have changed little down the centuries. Almost any shape can be made by beating, bending, cutting or casting the metal, while details are defined with engraving or punching tools. Visitors to Stewart Griffith's workshop may watch him making silverware, ranging from an elegant coffee pot polished to a mirror-like shine, to an eagle with finely textured, widespread wings. He will carry out commissions in silver and, sometimes, gold, and has a selection of candlesticks, pill boxes and goblets for sale.

Open Mon.–Fri., 9–5, by appointment.

MUSEUM

MARTON Map ref: Bb
Museum of Country Bygones, Louise Ward Close, Marton, nr Rugby.

When Mr George Tims showed his collection of family odds and ends and Victoriana to the villagers of Marton in 1965, they showed such interest that he was encouraged to start a museum. Everything now in the Museum of Country Bygones has been collected from farms and villages within a 10 mile radius. The exhibits include the hand tools of craftsmen such as the thatcher, the wheelwright and the blacksmith; dairying implements; lace-making equipment, agricultural machinery, and domestic items.

Open daily, 10–8, from Easter Mon. to end Oct. Charge for admission.

WEST MIDLANDS

AMBLECOTE Map ref: Ab
Thomas Webb Crystal, Dennis Hall, King William Street, Amblecote, Stourbridge.
Tel. Stourbridge 2521
(King William Street joins the A491 in Amblecote's high street, 1 mile north of centre of Stourbridge. Parking outside.)

Thomas Webb Crystal's long-standing reputation as makers of fine crystal is indicated by an impressive list of awards which goes back to the Great Exhibition held in London in 1851. Dennis Hall, a handsome 18th-century mansion, has been the heart of the company ever since Thomas Webb moved there in 1855, 15 years after establishing his own business near by. Conducted tours enable visitors to see the processes which have produced crystal masterpieces for many famous people, including royalty. The company's products, all shaped and decorated by means of traditional methods, range from small tumblers to large vases. Groups of ten or more should make an appointment in advance.

Guided tours, Mon.–Fri., start at 10.15, 11, 11.45, 2.15 and 3. Shop open Mon.–Fri., 9.15–4.30; Sat. 9.30–1.

Map ref: Bb

Sarehole Mill

MOSELEY, WEST MIDLANDS

J. R. R. Tolkien, author of *The Lord of the Rings*, spent much of his childhood close to 18th-century Sarehole Mill, and used to visit it. The mill has been used for grinding both corn and edge-tools, but today it is a museum. On each of the three storeys, visitors can see restored mill machinery. Parts of the building house displays of agricultural tools and machinery, and the reconstructed workshops of a cooper and a carpenter.

Colebank Road, Moseley, Birmingham, West Midlands. Tel. Birmingham 777 6612.

Open Easter to end Nov., Wed.–Sat., 1.30–5.30. Charge for admission.

CORN-GRINDING *The 200-year-old machinery is powered by a water-wheel.*

AMBLECOTE   Map ref: Ab
Webb Corbett, Coalbournhill Glassworks, High Street, Amblecote, Stourbridge.
Tel. Stourbridge 5281
(Just off main A491 through Amblecote, 1 mile north of centre of Stourbridge.)

Webb Corbett was founded in 1897, moved to its present site 16 years later – after the original glassworks was devastated by fire – and has been part of the Royal Doulton organisation since 1969. Men working in the glasshouse are grouped in small teams known as 'chairs'. The full-lead crystal is made into products from ornamental thimbles to hand-cut decanters and vases. The company's design team also creates many special pieces on commission.

Open for conducted tours Mon.–Fri., 9.30–12.30, by appointment. Shop open Mon.–Fri., 10–5; Sat., 10–1.

BIRMINGHAM   Map ref: Bb
Susan Vedadi (Jewellery), First Floor, 98 Spencer Street, Hockley, Birmingham.
Tel. Birmingham 523 4594
(Hockley is 1½ miles north-east of city centre. From Hockley clock-tower turn down Vyse Street. Turn right down Hockley Street, then left into Spencer Street. Car park in Hockley Street.)

The city of Birmingham has been a centre for the jewellery trade since the 1770s, when over 40 goldsmiths and silversmiths worked there. Susan Vedadi carries on this tradition at her workshop in the heart of the jewellery quarter. She makes delicately styled gold rings, pendants, ear-rings and bracelets, set with precious and semi-precious stones, including diamonds, opals, turquoise and coral. For commissions such as engagement rings, customers can make their own choice of the stone. She sends the finished pieces to Birmingham's Assay Office to be hallmarked.

Open Mon.–Fri., 10–5.30, by appointment.

BRIERLEY HILL   Map ref: Ab
Royal Brierley Crystal (Glassmakers), North Street, Brierley Hill.
Tel. Brierley Hill 70161
(Near junction of North Street and Moor Street, which runs due west from High Street, in centre of Brierley Hill.)

Hand-cut crystal from this old-established, family-run glassworks has graced royal households since Queen Victoria's reign, and the company has held an official royal warrant since 1919. The area's glassmaking traditions go back to the 17th century, and Royal Brierley's 'new' glassworks dates from 1870. Conducted tours enable visitors to see the 'metal', or raw materials, being heated in crucibles, shaped by teams of craftsmen and then cut to create traditional, diamond-bright

patterns. Products include decanters, vases, bowls and elegant drinking glasses.

Shop open Mon.–Sat., 9–4.30. Conducted tours (appointment necessary) at 11 (Mon.–Fri.) and 1 (Mon.–Thur.). Works not open to children under 18, student parties, or elderly or infirm.

COVENTRY   Map ref: Bb
Alec Marr (Woodcarver), 17 Wyke Road, Coventry.
Tel. Coventry 445313
(Off Wykeley Road, which leaves Leicester-bound A46 near Walsgrave Arms public house. Parking in street.)

Alec Marr is a veteran woodcarver, who worked on the ornate staircase in the vicarage of St James's Church in central London and carved the superb coat of arms for the Lord Mayor of Coventry's quarters in the city's Council House. Some of his tools are more than 200 years old; he made others when he was a boy, more than 50 years ago. A true master of his craft, Mr Marr can handle anything from a cabinet, mirror surround, table or fireplace to human figures, animals and birds. Small hedgehogs are his most popular line, but even they are put aside to season for about two years after the basic shape has been roughed out. Mr Marr uses lime, oak, mahogany, and other timbers.

Open by appointment.

HALL GREEN   Map ref: Bb
The Gem Box, 1541 Stratford Road, Robin Hood Island, Hall Green, Birmingham.
Tel. Birmingham 745 7911
(On A34, about 6 miles south-east of Birmingham, and just south of junction with A4040 ring road. Parking outside.)

As its name implies, the Gem Box is a treasure trove of sparkling, myriad-coloured precious and semi-precious stones. The man responsible for transforming them from their natural state – chunks of rough, rather lifeless rock – into satin-smooth gems is Robert Renfrey. Combining the skills of a lapidary with the craft of a silversmith, he also shapes the bracelets, rings, brooches, ear-rings and pendants in which the stones are set. A section of Mr Renfrey's workshop is occupied by another craftsman, Paul Osborne, who makes carriage clocks, glass dome and grandmother clocks (small grandfather clocks).

Open Mon.–Sat., 9–6.

KING'S NORTON   Map ref: Bb
Miss Truda Eloïse Lane (Calligrapher), 35 Heathcote Road, King's Norton, Birmingham.
Tel. Birmingham 458 2604
(Take A441 south of Birmingham. After about 5 miles, turn right down Dell Road just after the Breedon Cross public house. Heathcote Road is second on left.)

Truda Eloïse Lane combines the arts of calligraphy and painting to produce richly illuminated texts on subjects as varied as heraldry, literature and music. A permanent exhibition of some of her finest work adorns the walls of her home, and includes an illustrated poem on century-old vellum, large heraldic panels, decorative character studies, also dramatic and religious subjects. Particularly striking are the vibrant colours in the illustrations that accompany her flawless script. Their almost luminous quality is the result of many hours of painstaking work. Apart from her own collection, all her work is commissioned, and visitors will usually see a few pieces in progress in her studio.

Open weekday mornings, and weekend afternoons and evenings. Appointment necessary.

WIGHTWICK   Map ref: Ab
Wightwick Pottery, Wightwick Manor, Wightwick, Wolverhampton.
Tel. Wolverhampton 752169 (Home)
(Two hundred yards from the Mermaid Inn,

on the A454 Wolverhampton-Bridgnorth road. Parking in grounds.)

Wightwick Manor was built in 1887 by Theodore Mander, a wealthy Wolverhampton businessman, but the pottery run by Pat Mullett and Mary Smith is housed in a building which dates from the 17th century. Their floral motifs on pale blue backgrounds are particularly attractive. The partners produce a variety of hand-thrown earthenware and stoneware, ranging from whimsical owls and hedgehogs to bread crocks. Everything is decorated by hand, and the potters make some of their own glazes.

Open Mar.–Dec.: Tues., Wed. and Thur., 10–4.30; Sat., 2–6.

WORDSLEY   Map ref: Ab
Stuart and Sons Ltd, Red House Glassworks, Wordsley, Stourbridge.
Tel. Brierley Hill 71161
(Opposite the Vine public house on the A491 Stourbridge–Wolverhampton road.)

This famous, family owned company has links with the Red House Glassworks which go back to the early 19th century, when Frederick Stuart worked there as a boy of 11. The furnaces are now fired by gas instead of coal, but the methods used have changed only in detail since Stuart and Sons was established in 1881. Craftsmen create a magnificent assortment of hand-cut crystal wares, ranging from wine suites to giftware and tableware. Visitors see every stage, from mixing the raw materials to packing the finished products.

Guided tours start at 10.30 and 2, Mon.–Thur. Appointment necessary. Shop open Mon.–Sat., 9–4.45.

MUSEUMS

BIRMINGHAM   Map ref: Bb
City Museum and Art Gallery, Chamberlain Square, Birmingham.
Tel. Birmingham 235 2834

A gallery in the City Museum traces the origins and development of Birmingham with particular emphasis on its traditional crafts, trades and light industries. Such 18th-century trades as the manufacture of buttons, buckles, japanned ware, coins and medals, are well represented, and there are extensive collections showing the making of whips and brushes.

Open Mon.–Sat., 10–5.30; Sun., 2–5.30. Admission free.

DUDLEY   Map ref: Ab
Black Country Museum, Tipton Road, Dudley.
Tel. Birmingham 557 9643

The museum, on a 26 acre site, brings to life the past of the sprawling industrial area west of Birmingham known as the Black Country. Houses in the reconstructed village of the late 19th century are furnished, and sparks fly from the hammers of metalworkers who demonstrate trades once practised in the area. Bread is made in the bakehouse, and pills are rolled in the chemist's shop. In the boat dock, canal boats can sometimes be seen being repaired and painted.
The site itself is steeped in industrial history. Two sets of lime-kilns are still standing, and the steam-powered colliery is built over an existing pit shaft. One of the outstanding engineering achievements of the 18th century, the Dudley Canal Tunnel, takes the Dudley Canal under Castle Hill beside the museum site. The boats had to be propelled through nearly 1¾ miles of tunnel by men lying on their backs and pushing against the tunnel walls with their feet.

Open daily, Apr.–Sept., 10–5. Oct.–Mar., closing times may vary. Charge for admission.

MOSELEY   Map ref: Bb
Sarehole Mill.
(See panel on this page)

Opening times and other details may change. Check by telephone before making a special journey.

267

SOUTHERN CENTRAL ENGLAND

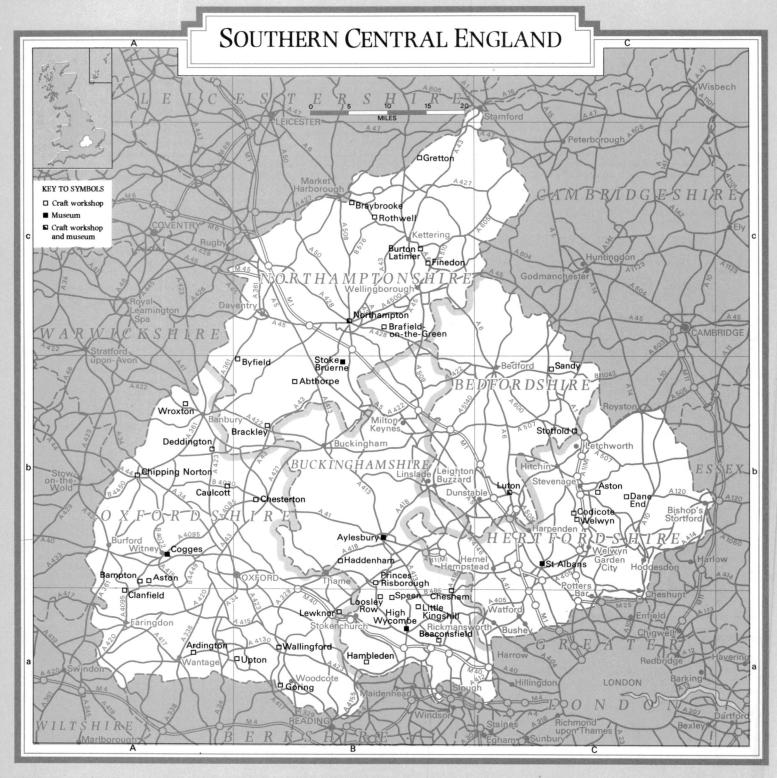

Victorian rocking-horses, 15th-century guitars, Welsh dressers and domestic furniture are just some of the articles still fashioned from wood by carpenters and cabinet makers in the group of counties that lies roughly between London and the industrial Midlands. But pride of place must go to the Windsor chair. Surrounded by acres of silent beechwoods, High Wycombe has for centuries been the home of this epitome of domestic comfort.

Northampton is still famous for its shoes, but a number of traditional skills, such as lace making and straw-plaiting, have all but disappeared from the region. With them have gone many of the long-established craftsmen who once supplied the everyday needs of small rural communities. Fortunately, they have been replaced in part by others who are not necessarily indigenous to the area – weavers, sculptors, glass workers and potters.

There has also been a change in the nature of some craftsmen's work.

Today's Hertfordshire blacksmith, for example, still sweats over a smoky hearth, but he produces sophisticated wrought ironwork rather than the rough-and-ready necessities of life.

BEDFORDSHIRE

LUTON Map ref: Cb
Younglass, Unit 39, 26/28 John Street, Luton.
Tel. Luton 29270
(John Street joins Church Street – the A505 – from the west, to the north of the Arndale Centre. Car park off Guildford Street, which is the next street to the north from John Street.)

Illuminated by the blue flame of an oxy-propane torch, Bill Young heats silica tubes and rods. On reaching a semi-molten state, the glass is shaped by being blown or modelled with simple tools. Flowers, jewellery, and tiny models for Victorian miniature houses are among examples of his work which are normally on display. Among the glass oddities that Mr Young has been called upon to create are a swan-shaped caviare bowl, an elegant slipper and a human finger.

Open any time by appointment.

SANDY Map ref: Cb
Charles J. Barr & Sons Ltd, Country Works, Sunderland Road, Sandy.
Tel. Sandy 81444
(Turn down Sunderland Road from Sandy's

B1042 roundabout. Follow for ¾ mile. Workshop is among last cluster of industrial buildings. Parking on premises.)

Chair making was the chosen trade of Charles J. Barr when he opened a modest workshop in the parish of Shoreditch in 1861. From this humble beginning the Barr enterprise has grown into a substantial company specialising in English-style furniture, with additional premises in London and at Peterborough. All the furniture is given an antique finish, while other finishing processes involve glazing, gold-tooling of hand-dyed leathers, and a limited amount of upholstery. Whenever possible, all these processes are carried out by hand, using methods employed by craftsmen of the period concerned.

Open Mon.–Fri., 9–5. Closed Bank Holidays. By appointment only.

STOTFOLD   Map ref: Cb
Ironcrafts (Stotfold) Ltd, Rook Tree Forge, Baldock Road, Stotfold, Hitchin.
Tel. Hitchin 730671
(At eastern end of Stotfold, on north side of A507. Parking on premises.)

A coke-fire forge is the focal point of Ironcrafts' busy workshop. Here, blacksmiths heat mild steel and hammer it into shape. Opposite the furnace, the welding and riveting takes place. Colin Day, the managing director, designs nearly all the articles produced at the forge. These range from simple fire pokers to elaborate gates, bound for stately homes.

Open by appointment Mon.–Fri., 8–5.30; Sat., 9.30–12. Closed Bank Holidays.

MUSEUM

LUTON   Map ref: Cb
Luton Museum and Art Gallery, Wardown Park, Luton.
Tel. Luton 36941

Lace making is well represented in the museum, for it used to be one of Bedfordshire's main cottage industries. The interior of a cottage has been reconstructed to show a farmworker's wife sitting at her lace pillow and using more than 150 bobbins to make a 'flounce', or wide border, of Buckinghamshire Point Ground lace. There are many samples of lace, and a fine collection of individually made lace bobbins bearing inscriptions that include names, blessings, admonitions and pious phrases.

Straw-plaiting is featured at the museum, too. A display shows how straw was plaited and sewn to make hats – a local craft that started on local farms and developed into a major industry.

Open Apr.–Sept., Mon.–Sat. 10–6; Sun. 2–6. Oct.–Mar., Mon.–Sat. 10–5; Sun. 2–5. Admission free.

BUCKINGHAMSHIRE

BEACONSFIELD   Map ref: Ba
Lake, Muckley & Co. Ltd (Blacksmiths),
1 Wycombe End, Beaconsfield.
Tel. Beaconsfield 3632
(On north side of A40, west of junction with B474. Parking on premises.)

Smoke first billowed from the Lake, Muckley forge in 1928. In those days, the community of old Beaconsfield was supplied with horseshoes, pig rings and agricultural implements from the smithy. Nowadays, such wares no longer make up a significant share of the forge's output. They have made way for a variety of ornate gates, lanterns and fireplace fittings. But the occasional tool is still repaired, and customers bring their own designs for wrought ironwork.

Open Mon.–Fri., 8–12.30 and 1.30–5. Sat., 8–12.30. Closed Bank Holidays.

CHESHAM   Map ref: Ba
Brown & Wakling Ltd (Woodturners),
Misbourne Works, Waterside, Chesham.

Tel. Chesham 783768
(South side of B485, 25 yds from junction with A416. Street-side parking.)

The smell of freshly cut timber and the buzz of machinery greet visitors to the workshops of Brown & Wakling. The firm's woodworkers are usually engaged in making turned kitchenware and furniture components for wholesalers and retailers. But they will also accept commissions.

Open by appointment, Mon.–Fri., 9–1 and 1.30–4.30. Closed Bank Holidays.

CHESHAM   Map ref: Ba
A. Rogers & Sons Woodware (Chesham) Ltd, 64 Higham Road, Chesham.
Tel. Chesham 785276
(Higham Road joins the A416 from the west in central Chesham. Street-side parking.)

Arthur Rogers has worked with wood for over 60 years. Today, working with two sons and a grandson, he is concerned principally with woodturning and joinery. In addition to making furniture parts and tableware, the Rogers family are often busy reproducing and repairing antique fittings for stately homes and churches.

Open by appointment, Mon.–Fri., 8.30–12.30 and 1.30–5.30. Sat., 9–12. Closed Bank Holidays.

HADDENHAM   Map ref: Bb
Ivor Newton & Son, Aston Road, Haddenham, Aylesbury.
Tel. Haddenham 291461
(One hundred yards east of church on south side of village. Parking opposite pond in Church Way.)

Nearly 200 years ago, wooden furnishings for church and manor house were made on the site where the carpenters of Ivor Newton & Son now work. As the church and nobility no longer command the furniture market, the present firm is engaged mainly in cabinet making and joinery for modern homes. Nevertheless, there is still a demand for reproduction furniture and the restoration of antiques.

Open Mon.–Fri., 8–5. Closed Bank Holidays.

HAMBLEDEN   Map ref: Ba
Craft Studio, Divine Mercy Mission, Fawley Court, Henley-on-Thames.
(Divine Mercy Mission is signposted on A4155 about 3 miles south-west of Hambleden and 1 mile north of Henley. Parking on premises.)

In the grounds of Fawley Court – a 17th-century manor house designed by Christopher Wren – stands the home and studio of Mr Czerwinski, who sculpts heads and busts in wood. Born in Poland, the son of a woodworker, Mr Czerwinski uses only hand-tools, many of them antiques. His work begins outside the studio under an evergreen tree, where he prepares and rough-cuts a block of wood. Then, indoors, he executes the more delicate stages of carving and finishing. Mr Czerwinski's designs include primitive, classical and modern works.

Open by appointment.

LITTLE KINGSHILL   Map ref: Ba
Haleacre Workshops, Watchet Lane, Little Kingshill, Great Missenden.
Tel. Great Missenden 4463
(Down an easy-to-miss rough-surfaced drive on the eastern side of Watchet Lane, 1 mile south of Little Kingshill's centre.)

Amid the rolling fields of southern Buckinghamshire stands a row of brick pig-styes. With the establishment of a community of craftsmen, the styes have been converted into workshops.

One of the craftsmen working there is Christopher Caris, a restorer of antiques. In his shop – habitually cluttered with broken chairs, tools and timber – he reconstructs, polishes and

gilds all sorts of antique furniture. These may be of any period from Georgian to Edwardian.

In the middle of the row is Ray Priem's glass-working enterprise. With a gas-lamp as the heat source, he models such items as perfume bottles, candle holders, vases and jewellery. Most of Ray's handiwork remains clear, but he colours some pieces, and sandblasts others to give an opaque finish.

Opening times of the different workshops vary, so it is advisable to telephone for an appointment.

LOOSLEY ROW   Map ref: Ba
Gommes Forge, Foundry Lane, Loosley Row, nr Aylesbury.
Tel. Princes Risborough 5546
(Half a mile east of A4010, 2 miles south of Princes Risborough. Parking on premises.)

Since the mid-19th century, decorative ironware for hearth and home has been wrought and cast at Gommes Forge. Over a small coal fire, mild steel is brought to a red glow and worked into shape on an anvil. Among the items made are gates, fire dogs and lanterns. A coke-fired furnace and a sooty wooden hoist stand as relics of the late Industrial Revolution in an adjoining foundry. Here, iron fire backs and brass dog irons are cast.

Open Mon.–Fri., 8–12.30 and 1–5. Sat., 8.30–12. Closed Bank Holidays and Christmas week.

PRINCES RISBOROUGH   Map ref: Bb
The Studio, Chiltern Retreat, Queens Road, Princes Risborough.
Tel. Princes Risborough 3115
(Off the A4010, on the north side of Princes Risborough. Queens Road is a quiet cul-de-sac, with parking at the side of the road.)

Ruth Reynolds, FRSA, MFPS, is a sculptor who works mainly in cold-cast bronze and in bronze. Visitors can see several examples of her work – small figures, heads, animals and birds. Since she has kept the moulds for many of her works, reproductions, as well as original commissions, can be made to order.

Open, by appointment only, Tues.–Fri. Mrs Reynolds prefers to see only potential buyers.

SPEEN   Map ref: Ba
Joyce Coleman, Spinning-wheel Cottage, Studridge Lane, Speen, Aylesbury.
Tel. Hampden Row 303
(Studridge Lane meets the Lacey Green–Speen road from the north just west of village centre. Street-side parking.)

Subtle colour combinations and delicate design have distinguished Joyce Coleman's silk, linen and wool handwovens for over 40 years. Working from a creeper-clad cottage, she produces tablecloths, rugs and scarves, cushions, blankets and tapestries on her floor looms. Some of her fabrics are woven with yarn which she herself has spun. Starting with raw fleece, she sorts and cards before spinning on two antique wheels.

Open daily, 3–6. Appointment needed for more than one or two visitors.

SPEEN   Map ref: Ba
Tessa Rubbra (Potter), Valley Cottage, Highwood Bottom, Speen, Aylesbury.
Tel. Hampden Row 206
(A quarter of a mile down a rough-surfaced drive which joins the Speen-Lacey Green road on the western outskirts of Speen. Parking on premises.)

Tessa Rubbra's pottery is in a valley between a grassy rise and a forested hill. Working alone, she throws, slip-casts and press-moulds clay into uncommonly light and decorative earthenware pots. Most are finished with hand-applied slip, but some of the moulded items, such as lamp bases and large eggs, bear unusual jasmine and fern-leaf motifs.

Open daily, 9–6. Appointment advisable.

MUSEUMS

AYLESBURY   Map ref: Bb
Buckinghamshire County Museum, Church Street, Aylesbury.
Tel. Aylesbury 82158

A handsome group of Georgian buildings in the old part of Aylesbury houses the museum. Its various local collections include small displays, consisting of tools and photographs, on such Buckinghamshire crafts as thatching and straw-plaiting. There are also samples of lace, and a collection of the decorative bobbins used by East Midlands lace makers. One gallery contains a fascinating array of agricultural hand-tools.

Open Mon.–Fri., 10–5; Sat., 10–12.30 and 1.30–5. Admission free.

HIGH WYCOMBE   Map ref: Ba
Wycombe Chair Museum.
(See panel on p. 270)

HERTFORDSHIRE

ASTON   Map ref: Cb
The Stables Studio, Dene Lane, Aston, Stevenage.
Tel. Shephall 271 and 308
(On west side of village, Dene Lane meets Broadwater Lane, Aston's main street.)

At a well-worn deal table, Mrs Betty Randles works with a sewing machine, scissors and needle and thread. With these few tools she tailors the patchwork and quilting that drape her studio walls. Made from cotton fabrics, many of which she designs herself, Mrs Randles's handiwork ranges from items as small as patchwork pincushions to quilts 9 ft square which take over 200 hours to complete.

Open Tues.–Sun., 11–4.

CODICOTE   Map ref: Cb
St Crispin's Glass, 28 St Albans Road, Codicote, Hitchin.
Tel. Stevenage 820335
(On east side of Codicote. Access to house and studio is through driveway between numbers 22 and 26. Street-side parking in St Albans Road.)

The name of Miss Charles's stained-glass window-making establishment derives from a reference to St Crispin in Shakespeare's Henry V. On the eve of the Battle of Agincourt, Henry holds St Crispin (whose feast day it was) as a symbol of brotherhood and honour – ideals represented in much of Miss Charles's work and especially in windows destined for churches. A former landscape and portrait painter, she makes all her windows from detailed water-colour patterns. These often take more time to paint than is required by the glasswork itself. An example of Miss Charles's finished work may be seen on the porch of Codicote's parish church.

Open by appointment, Mon.–Fri.

DANE END   Map ref: Cb
The Forge, Dane End, Ware.
Tel. Dane End 277
(In the centre of Dane End. Parking on premises.)

The first blacksmith of The Forge died in 1736. Since then, a continuous succession of smiths has sweated over the same brick hearth and under the same mossy, peg-tiled roof. Until the 1950s, Dane End's smiths produced mainly horseshoes and agricultural implements. Albert Springate, the present blacksmith, still takes on the occasional agricultural job, but in the main he forges ornate gates and domestic hearth furniture. As no sign hangs from The Forge, visitors should look out for two weatherworn, hand-powered petrol pumps of the 1930s that stand in front of Mr Springate's establishment.

Open Mon.–Fri., 8–12.30 and 1.30–5. Sat., 8–12. Closed Bank Holidays.

Opening times and other details may change. Check by telephone before making a special journey.

269

WELWYN Map ref: Cb
The Gemshop, R. H. Hill Promotions Ltd,
Prospect Place, Welwyn.
Tel. Welwyn 5021
(Twenty-five yards down Prospect Place
from London Road. Car park in London
Road.)

*Below the Gemshop, in a small brick cellar
which local legend associates with Dick
Turpin's Welwyn hideout, Jef Hill works with
gold, silver and gemstones. He uses only hand-
tools, including a mouth-blown gas torch, when
working with precious metals. The sole
machine found in his shop is used for gem
cutting. While his work is wide-ranging, he is
especially proud of his inlaid opals and
turquoise. In his own designs, he seeks to
combine modern and oriental traditions.*

Workshop open by appointment, Jan.–Oct.
Shop open all year, Tues.–Sat., 9.30–5.30.

MUSEUM

ST ALBANS Map ref: Cb
City Museum.
(See panel on facing page)

NORTHAMPTONSHIRE

ABTHORPE Map ref: Bb
Hendrik ten Bruggencate & Co. (Keyboard
Instruments Ltd), Silverstreet Workshops,
Abthorpe, Towcester.
Tel. Silverstone 857166

(West of parish church. Access along
driveway by Blossom Cottage at junction of
Main Street and Silverstreet.)

*Over 25 years ago a school teacher in
Poortugaal, Holland, advised one of his teenage
pupils to find some means of combining his
musical and technical interests. Today, this
former student can be found in his Abthorpe
workshop building pipe organs. Although
Hendrik ten Bruggencate constructs and
restores a variety of keyboard instruments, he
takes most pleasure in designing and making
magnificent pipe organs from English oak.
Organs made by him can be found in churches
throughout the country, including the Roman
Catholic Cathedral in Northampton.*

Open Mon.–Fri., 9.15–6. Closed Bank
Holidays. An appointment is necessary.

BRACKLEY Map ref: Bb
Duncan James, 33 High Street, Brackley.
Tel. Brackley 703060

*On the ground floor of a stone-fronted 18th-
century house, Duncan James can usually be
found at his bench, fashioning gold, silver and
gemstones into delicate pieces of jewellery. He
designs all the jewellery on display in his shop
and works at most aspects of the jeweller's
craft, including mould-making and gem-setting.
Nearly half of his ornaments are produced from
originals by means of the lost-wax casting
process.*

Open daily, 10–6, except Wed., Sun, and
Bank Holidays.

BRAFIELD-ON-THE-GREEN Map ref: Bc
Mildmay Pottery, 12 Bridle Path, Brafield-
on-the-Green, Northampton.
Tel. Northampton 891488
(Access to Bridle Path is from Church Lane,
which joins the A428 from the north.
Street-side parking in Church Lane.)

*Paul Ager makes pots of traditional design
using traditional methods. His ovenproof
stoneware, hand-thrown from Dorset ball clay,
is given a speckled appearance by the addition
of iron-bearing sand from nearby Leighton
Buzzard. Mildmay tableware is finished in a
range of three distinctive glazes: brown-black,
speckled cream and transparent green.*

Open Tues.–Sun., including Bank Holidays,
8.30–5.30.

BRAYBROOKE Map ref: Bc
Maggie Hartog (Pyrography), Old School
House Crafts, 7 School Lane, Braybrooke, nr
Market Harborough.
Tel. Market Harborough 65606
(Near Swan Inn. Parking outside house.)

*Instead of drawing with pen or pencil, former
art teacher Maggie Hartog uses a heat poker.
This is a special tool looking rather like a
dentist's drill, the tip of which is heated
electrically so that it will scorch wood. Mrs
Hartog decorates spoons, cheeseboards, tea
caddies, mirrors and other items with original
designs based on British wildlife and wild
flowers.*

Open any time, by appointment.

BRAYBROOKE Map ref: Bc
Sally Lewis, Braybrooke Pottery,
Braybrooke, nr Market Harborough.
Tel. Market Harborough 62313
(Two and a half miles south-east of Market
Harborough, opposite village church.
Parking on site.)

*Sally Lewis lives and works in a handsome red-
brick house of the 1830s between a gurgling
brook and the predominantly 14th and 15th-
century village church. Unlike many potters,
she produces both earthenware and stoneware.
Some of her pieces are decorated with fluting,
using a wire loop to scoop sections out of the
clay. For other pieces she achieves her effects
by using an old-fashioned school pen to cut out
entire sections before glazing and firing. In
1977 – Jubilee Year – when Prince Philip
visited neighbouring Leicestershire, Mrs Lewis
was chosen to make an enormous cheese bell in
which a 17 lb. Leicestershire cheese was
presented to the royal visitor.*

Open any time, by appointment.

BURTON LATIMER Map ref: Bc
D. J. Hornsby (Woodturner), 149 High
Street, Burton Latimer, Kettering.
Tel. Burton Latimer 2791
(On A6 opposite Burton Latimer Library
and Health Centre. Car park behind library.)

*Behind a former Wesleyan chapel, built 150
years ago, visitors will find a brick workshop
where 24 kinds of wood are shaped into
delicate lace bobbins for export around the
world. The woods include lignum vitae, ebony
and six types of rosewood. When time permits,
horse-pillows (stands upon which lace-making*

Map ref: Ba

Wycombe Chair Museum

HIGH WYCOMBE, BUCKINGHAMSHIRE

For over 200 years the chair industry in the Chilterns has
centred around High Wycombe and its outlying beech
woods. The museum, housed in an attractive flint-faced
residence, charts the history of this industry. Row upon
row of finely made chairs jostle for position, and the
exhibits include miniature chairs for dolls' houses and
small-scale apprentice pieces made to test the skills of
budding craftsmen.

But it is the Windsor chair for which High Wycombe is
justly famous. The Windsor room contains examples of
the various designs, from the traditional pattern of 1750,
through the 'Scroll-back', the one-armed 'Military' and
the 'Wycombe Windsor' to the modern version.

All these different types of Windsors have a common
characteristic which distinguishes them from cabinet-
makers' chairs. The legs are fitted into the underside of the
seat to form a stool; the back of the chair is then socketed
separately into the upper side of the seat.

Together with these finished chairs, there are displays of
the tools used by chair makers and a reconstruction of a
bodger's hut (see p. 222).

The Chiltern room has displays on crafts linked to chair
making, such as seat caning, and with other local
industries of the past and present, such as spinning,
thatching and straw-plaiting. A collection of lace bobbins
includes one inscribed 'Joseph Castle, hung 1860'. It was
sold at the public hanging of a man who had murdered his
wife.

Castle Hill House, Priory Avenue, High Wycombe,
Buckinghamshire. Tel. High Wycombe 23879.
(A quarter of a mile north of town, turn left off A404 just above
railway line.)

Open Mon., Tues., Thur., Fri., Sat., 10–1 and 2–5. Closed on Bank
Holidays. Admission free.

TRADITIONAL DESIGNS FOR SPLATS

'Feathers'

'Wheel'

'Prince of Wales' Feathers'

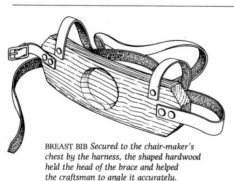

BREAST BIB *Secured to the chair-maker's
chest by the harness, the shaped hardwood
held the head of the brace and helped
the craftsman to angle it accurately.*

ELEGANT CARVING *A typical
lath-and-baluster Windsor
chair made out of beech.*

Map ref: Cb

City Museum

ST ALBANS, HERTFORDSHIRE

At first glance, visitors may be puzzled at the extent of the museum's remarkable collection of tools. The explanation is that many of the exhibits were acquired from Raphael Salaman, author of *The Dictionary of Tools* – a book that has become a bible for many museum curators.

Workshops have been reconstructed to recall the days when nearly every Hertfordshire village had its resident craftsmen, in particular a farrier and a blacksmith. A taped commentary in local dialect guides the visitor around the wheelwright's, the blacksmith's, the cooper's and the sawpit, describing how the work was done.

Tools and photographs illustrate the work of the tanner, the thatcher, the clock maker, the Lancashire clogger, the shipwright, the sailmaker, the chair bodger, the saddler, the joiner, and the makers of baskets and brushes. There are also small displays on the local rural crafts of hat making and straw-plaiting.

Hatfield Road, St Albans, Hertfordshire. Tel. St Albans 56679.
Open Mon.–Sat., 10–5. Admission free.

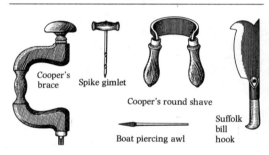

Cooper's brace   Spike gimlet

Cooper's round shave

Boat piercing awl   Suffolk bill hook

COOPER *Reconstruction of an 1840 cooper's workshop.*

---

pillows rest) and bobbin winders are made as well. The chapel itself serves as Mr Hornsby's home and office. When household chores are finished, Mrs Hornsby may be found taking her turn at the lathe.

Open daily, 9–6.

BYFIELD   Map ref: Bb
B. W. Pottery, 32 Banbury Lane, Byfield, Daventry.
Tel. Byfield 60630
(At junction of New Terrace and Banbury Lane, to west of A361. Street-side parking on New Terrace and Banbury Lane.)

An ironstone coaching inn of the 17th century now houses Nigel Buchanan-Wollaston's one-man pottery. Behind its fossil-riddled walls, he may be seen throwing West Country ball clay on an electric wheel, though for especially delicate work he uses a kick-wheel. Firing and glazing are performed in an old stone cottage on the other side of a narrow, paved patio – formerly the Daventry-Banbury road. A simple leaf design is the hallmark of much of the pottery.

Shop open Wed.–Sun., 10–6, including Bank Holidays. Workshop open by appointment only.

FINEDON   Map ref: Bc
D. A. Watts and Sons (Carpenter and wheelwright), 10 Millers Close, Finedon.
Tel. Wellingborough 680549
(On the north side of Finedon off the A510, ¼ mile from A6 junction. Parking outside workshop.)

Neatly stacked elm, ash and oak timbers line the workshop walls. From these timbers are fashioned glass-covered, carriage-wheel tables. Each consists of a hub, 12 oval or ornate spokes and a steel-tyred rim. The finished wheel is placed on a cylindrical base and covered with glass. Mr Watts and his two sons may be watched performing each stage of the operation,

including woodturning and shrink-fitting the steel tyres.

Open by appointment, Mon.–Fri., 8–6; Sat. 8–12.

GRETTON   Map ref: Bc
Elizabeth Palmer (Handweaver), Crown Cottage, 46 High Street, Gretton, Corby.
Tel. Rockingham 770303
(Between Baptist chapel and parish church. Limited parking in High Street.)

Fifty years ago, the residents of Gretton knew Crown Cottage as their local tavern – The Crown. Today, it is the home of Elizabeth Palmer, who weaves in an old stone barn, now converted into a comfortable workshop. Overlooked by brass-rubbings of figures from nearby village churches, she operates an assortment of looms, large and small. On these she produces a wide variety of tweeds, dress woollens, scarves and stoles. She also teaches the crafts of spinning, weaving and dyeing.

Open daily, including Bank Holidays, by appointment, 8.30–6.

NORTHAMPTON   Map ref: Bc
Fine Pine, 32 Tenter Road, Moulton Park Industrial Estate, Northampton.
Tel. Northampton 493620
(At northern section of Industrial Estate. Parking on premises.)

Craftsmanship of a bygone era exists at Fine Pine, in contrast with the typical industrial-estate premises in which the workshop is located. Here, Peter Tapehouse and Doug Allen make pine furniture by hand. Combining master woodworking with expertise in the world of antiques, they fashion second-hand pine timbers into furniture similar to that made by craftsmen in the 18th and 19th centuries.

Open by appointment, Mon.–Fri., 8.30–5. Closed Bank Holidays.

ROTHWELL   Map ref: Bc
The Glass Workshop, behind 1 Bridge Street, Rothwell, Kettering.
Tel. Kettering 760165 (Home)
(At junction of Bridge Street [B576] and A6. Parking in School Lane.)

The isolated workshop of R. J. Martin, glass modeller, is down an unpaved alley, behind a green gate. Over a workbench – barely visible beneath a multi-coloured sea of glass – Mr Martin models glass figures. Over 60 different ones are made, among which small, comic animals have proved especially popular. The most complex of Mr Martin's creations are sailing ships with delicate masts and rigging.

Open by appointment, Mon.–Fri., 9–12.30 and 1.40–5. Closed Bank Holidays.

MUSEUMS

NORTHAMPTON   Map ref: Bc
Museum of Leathercraft, Bridge Street, Northampton.
Tel. Northampton 34881

Only by understanding some of the processes of leatherworking is it possible to appreciate the craftsmanship involved. The museum explains what leather is, what its properties are, and how it is treated. Displays chart the history of leathercraft through the centuries and illustrate its development with masterpieces of craftsmanship from all over the world – a loin-cloth from ancient Egypt, shadow-puppets from Indonesia and buckskin breeches from 18th-century Britain. Some exhibits, such as the decorated caskets and pouches of the 18th century, are truly exquisite; others, including the leather oil seals used in industry today, are strictly functional.

Open Mon.–Sat., 10–1 and 2–5.30. Closed Christmas Eve, Christmas Day, Boxing Day and Good Friday. Admission free.

NORTHAMPTON   Map ref: Bc
Northampton Central Museum, Guildhall Road, Northampton.
Tel. Northampton 34881

Shoemaking has been Northampton's main industry for several centuries. Not surprisingly, the collection of shoes in this museum is one of the largest in the world. Exhibits range from the delicate slippers worn by Queen Victoria at her wedding in 1840, to the massive shoes of an Irish giant 8 ft 4 in. tall. There is also a collection of shoemaker's tools and a reconstruction of a traditional workshop.

Open Mon.–Sat., 10–6. Admission free.

STOKE BRUERNE   Map ref: Bb
The Waterways Museum.
(See panel on p. 272)

OXFORDSHIRE

ARDINGTON   Map ref: Aa
Ardington Craft Centre, Home Farm, School Lane, Ardington, Wantage.
(Signposted from A417, 1½ miles east of Wantage. Parking on premises.)

Since the 1970s, redundant buildings at Ardington's Home Farm have become a leading centre of traditional regional craftsmanship.

The farm's Victorian butter house is now occupied by Ardington Pottery (East Hendred 302). Here, hand-painted tiles depicting fish, flesh, fowl and the four classical elements – fire, water, air and earth – form an unusual backdrop for Les and Brenda Owens's stoneware pots. Among these are thrown, slab-built, coiled and moulded pots, many of which are of sturdy medieval shape and bear contemporary patterns.

Next to the pottery rises an elm-beamed water-mill where, in bygone days, Home Farm's corn was ground. Working alongside its heavy gears and mill-stone, Nigel Griffiths

Opening times and other details may change. Check by telephone before making a special journey.

271

(East Hendred 371) makes oak furniture which is in keeping with the premises in which he works. All the furniture is of original design, though in the English style of the 15th, 16th and 17th centuries. Great pains are taken to give the furniture a texture and finish appropriate to its period.

Adjoining Nigel's workshop is a tiny former wash-house where Christine Masterman (East Hendred 631) rebuilds and upholsters antique chairs and sofas. With only the simplest of tools, she brings to life tarnished and dilapidated furniture, largely of the 19th century. Christine honours tradition by using only horsehair packing and tacks, as opposed to synthetic foam and staples.

The aromatic scent of leather greets visitors to Sally Barnes's ex-granary workshop (East Hendred 719). She hand-stitches made-to-measure saddlery and harness, cut from cowhide and pig-skin. But she also designs and makes other leather goods, including a line of plain, suede-lined handbags and an assortment of belts, hair-slides and key cases.

Opening times of the different workshops vary, so it is advisable to telephone first.

ASTON   Map ref: Ab
Aston Woodcraft, Aston Works, Back Lane, Aston, nr Bampton.
Tel. Bampton Castle 850011
(On east side of Aston. Access by driveway at junction of B4449 and Back Lane.)

Where washerwomen once laboured over steaming cauldrons of laundry, the cheerful carpenters of Aston Woodcraft now reproduce and restore all manner of antique furniture, from Elizabethan to Victorian. In addition to basic woodworking skills, the craftsmen are experts at gilding, fine carving and inlaying.

Open Mon.–Fri., 9–4; Sat., 9–12.30. Closed on Bank Holidays.

BAMPTON   Map ref: Ab
Anthony Wakeham Potters, College Farmhouse, Bridge Street, Bampton.
Tel. Bampton Castle 850225
(On the south side of A4095 on the western outskirts of Bampton. Parking on premises.)

Tony Wakeham uses local clay and sand to create the traditional terracotta garden pots which line the drive leading to his old stone-walled pottery. Here, he makes a range of decorative terracotta garden furnishings, which include strawberry pots, bird houses and wall-hanging pots. Each vessel is thrown, and then decorated with a simple flower design. Leaving the thrown work to Tony, his wife Norma specialises in the moulding of slipware pie and flan dishes – each bearing a wheat-ear design applied by slip-trailer and feather.

Open Fri., 2–5; Sat., 9–5. Other times by appointment.

CAULCOTT   Map ref: Ab
Mr and Mrs M. E. Cowdy, Rectors Pottery, Green Way, Caulcott, Lower Heyford.
Tel. Middleton Stoney 289
(On north side of Caulcott's main street, about ½ mile off B4030.)

'Traditional earthenware with a touch of humour' is how Michael Cowdy describes the products of his pottery that are most popular with the public. These include gurgling-frog mugs and whistling pots. Such droll items are slip-cast by means of moulds designed by Michael's wife Catherine. Together with these amusing articles, she makes small sgraffito dishes – terracotta saucers with an animal figure etched on a surface of black slip. She also undertakes commissioned sculptures.

Open Mon.–Sat., 9.30–6. Advisable to telephone first.

CHESTERTON   Map ref: Bb
Chesterton Pottery, Chesterton, Bicester.
Tel. Bicester 41455
(Off the A4095, near church. Street-side parking.)

The autumnal tones of a clay-tiled roof, mottled

The Waterways Museum
STOKE BRUERNE, NORTHAMPTONSHIRE

A humpback bridge, an inn, a lock and the Waterways Museum form a picturesque cluster around the Grand Union Canal at Stoke Bruerne. Exhibits include a workshop display of tools once used by the canal men, and photographs which give a fascinating insight into the families who followed this traditional way of life, remote from the rest of the community. The gaily painted woodwork, furniture and jugs decorated with roses and castles are typical of the craftsmanship of the boat-folk.

Stoke Bruerne, nr Towcester, Northamptonshire. Tel. Northampton 862229.

Open daily, Easter to Oct., 10–6. Also Oct. to Easter, Tues.–Sun., 10–4.

JUG *Water vessel painted in traditional style.*

CANAL BOAT *Living accommodation in the* Sunny Valley, *a typical narrow boat.*

with moss and lichen, lend appropriate character to Tony Smythe's stone pottery. Sheltered by this singular roof, Tony hand-throws earthenware pots on a wheel at the head of his workshop. These are decorated with slip patterns, and then receive a rich, earthy glaze. Among Tony's varied stock, misshapen 'crazy mugs' and commemorative plates have caught the public's fancy.

Open Mon.–Fri. and most weekends, 9–6.

CHIPPING NORTON   Map ref: Ab
Paul Fischer (Luthier), West End Studio, West End, Chipping Norton.
Tel. Chipping Norton 2792
(On the west side of B4450, ½ mile from town centre. Parking on premises.)

Ebony, Brazilian rosewood, spruce and also mahogany timbers are stacked methodically at

one end of West End Studio. From these woods, Paul Fischer custom-builds reproductions of guitars dating from the 15th to the 20th centuries, as well as guitars of his own design. Working alone, he performs all stages of construction from cutting basic wooden components to carving intricate embellishments with a surgeon's scalpel. Mr Fischer's instruments are played by some leading classical guitarists.

Open by appointment, Mon.–Fri., 10–4. Closed Bank Holidays.

CLANFIELD   Map ref: Aa
Crowdys Wood Products Ltd, The Old Bakery, Clanfield.
Tel. Clanfield 216
(On east side of A4095, next to primary school. Parking on workshop premises.)

With a knowledge of timber gained by working in sawmills – in Borneo and Corsica, as well as in Britain – Tim Green set up in business as a woodworker in 1964, making mostly turned goods and small pieces of furniture. Today, he supervises eight skilled carpenters and wood-turners, whose products include contemporary domestic furniture, tableware, spinning-wheels and lace bobbins. No fewer than 47 varieties of wood are kept on hand. A 19th-century foot-powered lathe and a large collection of antique hand-tools are on display in the craft shop.

Open Mon.–Sat., 9–6. Closed Bank Holidays.

DEDDINGTON   Map ref: Ab
Michael and Heather Ackland, Coniston House, New Street, Deddington.
Tel. Deddington 38241
(On east side of A423, next to Russell Hotel. Street-side parking.)

Entomologist Michael Ackland has now turned his hand to the jeweller's craft. Producing an ever-developing range of modern jewellery, he hand-works gold, silver and unfaceted semi-precious stones in his three-room workshop. Many of the more popular creations are reproduced by lost-wax casting. Mr Ackland also makes silver-topped boxes by adding the craft of the silversmith to that of the wood-turner. His knowledge of entomology has led to an unusual series of insect-shaped pendants and necklaces.

Open weekdays (except Thur.) and Sat. 10–1 and 2–5. Closed Bank Holidays. Appointment advisable.

DEDDINGTON   Map ref: Ab
Goldford Furnishings, Hudson Street, Deddington.
Tel. Deddington 38165
(Fifty yards up Hudson Street, which meets the A423 from the east. Street-side parking.)

On display behind leaded windows stand just a few examples of the wide range of hand-upholstered furniture produced by Stuart Golding and Dave Langford. With a few simple hand-tools and a sewing machine, they painstakingly produce a line of upholstered chairs, couches and chaises longues, in both traditional and modern styles. The Goldford Furnishings craftsmen also take on antique restoration.

Open weekdays (except Tues.), 9.30–1 and 2–5; Sat., 9.30–12. Closed Bank Holidays.

GORING   Map ref: Ba
Quad Quilts, Elvendon Road, Goring.
Tel. Goring-on-Thames 872800
(Up long, rough-surfaced drive on north side of the Goring-Woodcote road, just outside Goring. Parking on premises.)

The soft floral patterns of Liberty lawn (a type of cotton fabric) are combined to produce subtle colour blends in the quilted patchwork of Quad Quilts, which operates from the home of Mrs Mhairi Armstrong. Assisted by several local quilters, Mrs Armstrong hand-quilts bedcovers, sewing baskets and a variety of cushions, most of which are made to commission. Her work draws freely from patchwork traditions.

Open by appointment any day, 10–4.

LEWKNOR   Map ref: Ba
Aston Woodware, Aston Hill, Lewknor.
Tel. Kingston Blount 51500
(On south side of A40, 2½ miles west of Stokenchurch. Parking on premises.)

Aston Woodware had its humble beginnings in the 1920s, when George Hunt began to make garden furniture at his filling station. The petrol pumps have long since gone, but furniture making continues under the management of his son, Michael. Aston craftsmen now specialise in furniture of classical design, ranging from elm chairs for children to massive oak dressers and refectory tables. One of the many designs of Windsor chair is also made in the Aston workshop.

Open Apr.–Oct., daily, 9–1 and 2–5.
Nov.–Mar., Mon.–Sat., 9–1 and 2–4.

UPTON Map ref: Ba
Studio Enamels, Springside Cottage, Stream
Road, Upton, Didcot.
Tel. Blewbury 850526
(On north side of Stream Road, at east end
of village. Limited street-side parking.)

*Mrs Barbara Price creates enamel mosaics in a
small pine studio overlooking her garden. For
this she employs three enamelling techniques:
sgrafitto, cloisonné and limoges painting. Each
of these involves a process of building up layers
of enamel on a base of copper or silver. Nature
and history provide rich sources for Mrs Price,
each finding expression in both natural and
stylised figures. Pride of place is given to small
wall-hangings, which offer a striking contrast
of rich, glossy motifs against a matt suede
background.*

Open daily by appointment, 10–3.30 and
7–9.

UPTON Map ref: Ba
Upton Craft, Upton Stores, Upton, Didcot.
Tel. Blewbury 850236
(In village centre, ¼ mile east of A417.
Street-side parking.)

*Old crafts remain an active part of the scene in
the tranquil village of Upton. Since 1978, a
local co-operative has produced an impressive
array of craft objects, including sea-grass and
twine chairs, patchwork, jewellery, knitting,
pottery and corn dollies. The 21 members of
the co-operative display their wares in the
upper room of Upton's general store. Each of
the crafts is demonstrated to the public on
special occasions, or when members are on
duty as sales staff.*

Open Mon.–Fri., 2–5.30. Open in evenings
by appointment.

WALLINGFORD Map ref: Ba
Haddon Rockers Ltd, Station Road
Industrial Estate, Wallingford.
Tel. Wallingford 36165
(Access by driveway at junction of A4130
and Charterway, at west end of
Wallingford. Parking on premises.)

*Each week, about 20 reproduction Victorian
rocking-horses emerge from John Labouchere's
two-storey workshop, destined for any of six
continents. On the first floor, his workers cut,
join and finish South American pine and
plywood for the bow rockers and pillar stands
on which the horses rest. In the wood shop
there is a pneumatic bow jig, designed and built
by the owner, for pressing together pine and
plywood when making the rockers. The
moulding, painting and assembly of the glass-
fibre horse bodies takes place on the ground
floor.*

Open Mon.–Fri., 9–1 and 2–5.30, Sat.
9–11.30. Closed Bank Holidays.

WROXTON Map ref: Ab
The Old Workshop, Church Walk, Wroxton,
nr Banbury.
Tel. Wroxton St Mary 362
(At east end of Wroxton, ¼ mile off A422.
Limited street-side parking.)

*Close by the mossy tombstones of All Saints'
parish church lies the reed-roofed woodworking shop of Nick and Rita Hodges. Nick,
who is the carpenter of the two, makes a
variety of furniture, which includes Welsh
dressers, refectory tables and mirror frames. He
is also a skilled carver, while his wife is a
talented pyrographer – that is, she burns
decorative designs into the wood. This craft is
also known as pokerwork.*

Open daily by appointment, 9–6.

MUSEUM

COGGES Map ref: Ab
Manor Farm Museum.
(See panel alongside)

Map ref: Ab

Manor Farm Museum
COGGES, OXFORDSHIRE

Cogges has had a continuous history since the Norman
invasion. Almost every century, a building has been
added to the mellow cluster inside the small, self-
sufficient world of the manor farm; yet nothing jars.

Today's visitor gets the impression that the farm and
its gardens have stood still, suspended in time, since the
Edwardian period. This is the era that the museum has
set out to re-create – a fascinating and (for the landowner) prosperous period when steam was as yet barely
challenged by the internal combustion engine, and
nearly all farm work was done by manual labour and
horses.

Displays in the barns and stables guide visitors
through the farming year. The functions of the agricultural tools and machinery – ploughs, harrows, hoes,
seedlips, harvesting tools, wagons and a winnowing
machine – are explained for those too young to
remember.

The house has a dairy, a laundry, a kitchen, and a
walled garden planted meticulously with the flowers
and vegetables that an Edwardian household would
have demanded.

During summer weekends, there are demonstrations
of domestic activities such as laundry work and dairying, and rural crafts such as blacksmithing and hurdle
making.

Cogges, nr Witney, Oxfordshire. Tel. Woodstock 811456.
(Off the B4022 between the A4095 at Witney and the A40
by-pass.)
Open daily, Apr. 18 to Sept. 27, 11–6. Charge for admission.

HOLLIS & SON, 17
Implement Works, High Coggs, Witney, Oxon,
MANUFACTURERS OF
Corn, Seed, and Manure Drills, Corn
Dressing Machines, &c.
Carts of every description made to order and all kinds
of Repairs. Makers of Hand Drag Rakes, Sheep
Racks and Troughs.
General Agents for all kinds of MACHINERY
and IMPLEMENTS.
PRICE LISTS ON APPLICATION.

CART MAKERS *Well known in
Oxfordshire for the excellence of
their carts, Hollis and Son
published this advertisement in
1904. It would be most unusual,
nowadays, to find a local
manufacturer making such a wide
range of farm equipment.*

RANGE *Above the 100-year-old coal-fired range at
Manor Farm are spit-racks left from an earlier
way of cooking.*

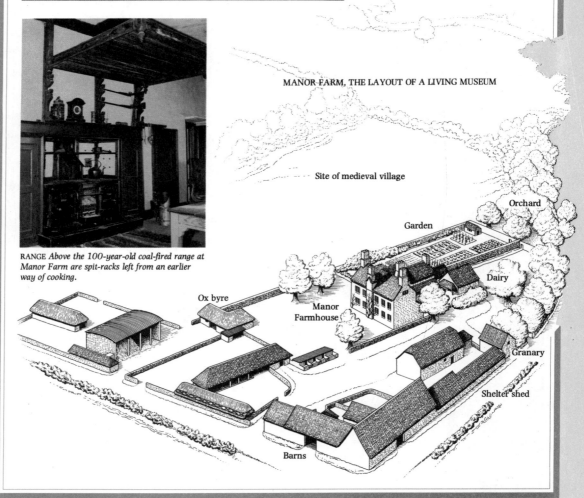

MANOR FARM, THE LAYOUT OF A LIVING MUSEUM

Site of medieval village

Orchard

Garden

Dairy

Ox byre

Manor
Farmhouse

Granary

Shelter shed

Barns

Opening times and other details may change. Check by telephone before making a special journey.

273

THE EASTERN COUNTIES

KEY TO SYMBOLS
□ Craft workshop
■ Museum
◪ Craft workshop and museum

MILES
0 5 10 15 20 25

Field after field, the rich farmlands of the Eastern Counties stretch into infinity, punctuated occasionally by the thrust of a church tower. The rural way of life and its crafts, such as thatching, have died hard in an area renowned for agriculture, good beer and, more recently, white wine. But it was wool which, in the Middle Ages, brought prosperity to the region. Today, weavers keep alive the memory of this ancient industry; and the churches and cathedrals, whose foundations were laid on the proceeds of the cloth trade, provide inspiration and commissions for stone engravers, stained-glass makers and blacksmiths specialising in wrought ironwork. Most rewarding of all is East Anglia's wide range of artefacts, ranging from English country furniture to models of stately homes; elegant boats for the Norfolk Broads to ceramic cars; ingenious Victorian toys to the taxidermist's stuffed birds. The quality they share is the expertise and loving care of the craftsmen who created them.

CAMBRIDGESHIRE

CAMBRIDGE   Map ref: Bc
Keith Bailey's Workshop, 63 Eden Street, Cambridge.
Tel. Cambridge 311870
(From Parkside, opposite Parkers Piece, turn into side-street next to police station. Then take the next left, right and left turns.)

Keith Bailey's memorial plaques and headstones may be found in cathedrals, churches and churchyards throughout the land. Working at an easel, he carves lettering and ornamentation in stone, slate and wood tablets, using a mallet and chisels. The scope of his work extends from carving architectural letters to detailed coats of arms. In addition to his memorial work, Mr Bailey carves and models figure sculpture, examples of which are in his studio.

Open daily, by appointment.

FORDHAM   Map ref: Cc
David English (Bookbinder), 225 Carter Street, Fordham, Ely.
Tel. Newmarket 720216
(Entering Fordham from the A142, turn left at the T-junction. Last house on the left. Street-side parking.)

As early as the 1400s, the Cambridge area was known to have two bookbinders – Walter Hatley and Gerard Wake. Following in their footsteps, David English binds antiquarian books, using many of the same techniques as were employed by his forerunners 500 years ago. Even the materials and tools of his craft have changed little through the ages. In restoring old books, most of which date from the 17th to the 19th centuries, Mr English makes every effort to preserve and make use of original materials.

Open daily, by appointment.

FORDHAM   Map ref: Cc
Fordham Pottery Co. Ltd, Muncey's Mill, 37 Mildenhall Road, Fordham, Ely.
Tel. Newmarket 720375
(On north side of B1102, on the eastern outskirts of Fordham. Parking on premises.)

A range of over 50 earthenware gift and souvenir items is made in the former corn-mill which now houses Fordham Pottery. At this small industrial pottery, all items are cast in plaster moulds which are individually made on the premises. After firing, the earthenware is glazed by dipping. Many objects – especially mugs, tankards and ash trays – are given promotional and commemorative motifs by means of transfers.

Open Mon.–Fri., 9–1 and 1.30–5.30. Closed Bank Holidays.

FULBOURN   Map ref: Cc
Richard Sell, 22 Station Road, Fulbourn, Cambridge.
Tel. Cambridge 880335
(On north-east side of Fulbourn. From A11, turn west into road to Fulbourn. Station Road is about 200 yds east of church.)

On a Victorian lithographic press, Richard Sell makes high-quality prints of his own original drawings. Trained at Chelsea School of Art, he paints and sketches topographical subjects. He then transfers these to blocks of limestone, using greasy chalk or ink – a technique used by the 19th-century pioneers of lithography. As a sideline to the lithographs, Mr Sell engraves small blocks of wood to make relief prints. He also does watercolours, and figure and portrait drawings.

Open Mon.–Sat., 9–5, by appointment.

ICKLETON   Map ref: Bb
David Whitaker, Frogge Cottage, 48 Frogge Street, Ickleton.
Tel. Saffron Walden 30304
(On B1379, on Ickleton's southern outskirts. Parking on premises.)

David Whitaker started working in wood by building racing dinghies in his early teens. He now runs a small workshop specialising in individual hand-made furniture, using English oak and elm. Work undertaken varies from a single chair to complete dining-room suites. An increasing number of ecclesiastical commissions are being received, and this is a feature of the workshop. His wife, Jean, is a woodturner in her own right, and produces a wide variety of domestic work, from bowls to stools.

Open Mon.–Fri., 8–6; Sat., 9–4.

KIMBOLTON   Map ref: Bc
Peter Roe Furniture, The Workshop, 12 East Street, Kimbolton, Huntingdon.
Tel. Tilbrook 229
(On A45, 8 miles from St Neots. Parking on premises.)

There is no doubting the maturity of the pine and oak used by Peter Roe and his team of carpenters. For the timber is second-hand, salvaged from old furniture and demolished buildings. After being de-nailed and cleaned, the second-hand wood is cut on power saws and assembled. The craftsmen hand-sand every piece of English country furniture that they make, giving a final finish with stain, two coats of polish, and wax. Excluding commissions, their main output consists of dressers, coffers, corner cupboards and refectory tables.

Open Mon.–Fri., 9–5.30; Sat., 9.30–4. Closed Bank Holidays.

MELDRETH   Map ref: Bb
M. David Gratch, The Maltings, 99 North End, Meldreth, Royston.
Tel. Royston 61615
(On minor road between Meldreth and Shepreth. Parking on premises.)

Where local barley was once kiln dried, David Gratch and his wife Betty turn British hardwoods, such as cherry, wych elm and ash, into modern furniture and tableware. Bowls, plates and rolling-pins are among the objects made at the 19th-century maltings, while Mr Gratch's laminated tables and lampstands bear witness to his considerable skill as a joiner.

Open daily by appointment, 8–6, including Bank Holidays.

PRICKWILLOW   Map ref: Cc
Prickwillow Pottery, 52 Main Street, Prickwillow, Ely.
Tel. Prickwillow 316
(On south side of B1382, by River Lark. Parking on premises.)

With a small team of local craftsmen, Derek and Margot Andrews make stoneware ceramics. On a potter's wheel, they hand-throw a variety of decorative vases, jugs and bowls in a blend of oriental and English styles. By slip-casting in moulds, the Andrews also make a wide range of kitchenware, and kits for Victorian-type dolls, these varying in height from 6 in. to 20 in.

Open Mon.–Sat., 9–5. Closed Christmas and New Year weeks.

ST NEOTS   Map ref: Bc
St Neots Pottery Ltd, The Old Chequers, 158 St Neots Road, Eaton Ford, St Neots.
Tel. Huntingdon 73207
(On east side of A428, just south of roundabout junction with A45. Parking on premises.)

The 16th-century timber-framed home of potter Tony Clark cannot fail to catch the eye of passers-by. In a long, stone-walled studio set behind the aged building, Mr Clark and a team of half-a-dozen craftsmen produce an extensive range of terracotta and glazed stoneware vessels – 72 regularly made items in all – for home and garden. Nearly all are thrown on the wheel, the exceptions being several kinds of moulded animals and also plant-pot holders. Most of the stoneware is dipped into tenmoku, dolomite, talc or tin glaze. The application of a hand-brushed, stylised leaf pattern – the hallmark of the pottery – completes the decoration.

Open daily, 9–5.30. It is advisable to telephone first at weekends and during holidays.

WILLINGHAM   Map ref: Bc
Den Young's Model Houses and Furniture, 63 Earith Road, Willingham.
Tel. Willingham 60015
(On west side of B1050, north of village centre. Parking on premises.)

Den Young started building wooden aeroplanes and locomotives in 1928, when, at the age of four, he was given his first miniature tool kit. While still using some of those tools, he has since graduated to constructing original dolls' houses and magnificent scale reproductions of stately homes. All aspects of the carpenter's craft are needed to build these detailed and precision-made masterpieces. Each major project requires perhaps 5,500 hours of labour, covering a period of several years. The finished houses come complete with articulated dolls and are fully furnished – including chandeliers and musical instruments. Everything is individually hand-crafted.

Open daily, by appointment.

WITCHFORD   Map ref: Cc
Fenweave (I. F. Allen), 37 Main Street, Witchford, nr Ely.
Tel. Ely 2150
(On south side of A142 on the eastern outskirts of Witchford. Parking on premises.)

Over 40 years ago, Mrs Ida Allen began weaving on a simple wooden-framed hand-loom. Since then, her work has belatedly been touched by the innovations of the Industrial Revolution – with the assistance of her husband, a retired engineer. Now in her 70s, Mrs Allen works a small mill, which includes seven massive cast-iron looms. They range from a semi-automatic Hattersley – much like those used by Victorian crofters – to a fully automatic rapier loom. On this equipment, Mrs Allen produces long bolts of woollen, cotton and linen cloth.

Open all year, Tues.–Sat., 9–12.30 and 1.30–5.

WOODDITTON   Map ref: Cc
Doreen Sanders (Handweaver), Pippin Cottage, Woodditton, Newmarket.
Tel. Stetchworth 357
(From Newmarket, take the B1061 Dullingham road. Almost immediately, take left fork for Woodditton – 2½ miles. At crossroads turn right; cottage is fifth on left. Parking in drive.)

Throughout the Middle Ages, sheep grazed on the gentle hills and along the quiet valleys of Suffolk, bringing prosperity to many villages and market towns. Doreen Sanders, in her charming 17th-century thatched cottage at Woodditton, maintains a link with these bygone days. Visitors can take a one week 'crash course' in spinning and weaving, or they can visit more briefly to admire her Navajo-style tapestries, her carpets, cushions and fleece rugs. For these she uses the fleece of Shetland and many other sheep in their natural colours – from almost chocolate-brown to creamy-white. She weaves unspun wool straight from the washed fleece into a warp of linen.

Open all year, by appointment, except Wed. and Sat.

MUSEUMS

CAMBRIDGE   Map ref: Bc
Cambridge and County Folk Museum, 2/3 Castle Street, Cambridge.
Tel. Cambridge 355159
(On junction of A604 and A45, on northern side of town.)

The well-seasoned timbers of the building that was once the White Horse Inn provide a perfect background for the museum's clutter of curiosities and everyday objects from the past. Small displays of tools illustrate the traditional trades of the area, such as thatching, brick-making and saddlery. One exhibit shows items that range from straw love tokens to horse's overshoes. It commemorates a breed of people that has all but vanished, for the people who lived in the Fens formed a community remote from the rest of East Anglia, having their own customs, games and folklore.

Open Tues.–Fri., 10.30–5; Sat., 10.30–1 and 2–5; Sun., 2.30–4.30. Charge for admission.

ELY   Map ref: Cc
The Stained Glass Museum, Ely Cathedral, Ely.

To reach the north gallery, where the museum is housed, visitors ascend a spiral staircase and wander through parts of the cathedral that they would not otherwise see. On the way, they can gaze down on the nave from an unaccustomed height. The museum was founded in order to rescue and preserve fine stained glass from disused churches and other buildings. It provides an opportunity not only to compare stained glass from the 14th century to the present day, but also to learn something about the craft itself. This can be done by studying models which show how stained-glass windows are designed and constructed.

Open Mar.–Oct., Mon.–Fri., 11–4; also Sat. and Bank Holidays, 11–4.30, and Sun. 12–3. Charge for admission.

ESSEX

BROADLEY COMMON   Map ref: Bb
Mr. T. Wheeley, Waterlane Forge, Water Lane, Tylers Cross, Roydon.
Tel. Roydon 2260
(Half a mile north of Broadley Common, turn into Water Lane – signposted Harlow. Forge is at the bottom of road on right-hand side before roundabout. Restricted parking.)

When television or film teams are working on historical dramas, they spare no pains to get every detail accurate. Craftsmen such as Mr Wheeley are called in to make the props. For

Opening times and other details may change. Check by telephone before making a special journey.

275

instance, he has constructed a well-head in Italian Renaissance style for the television series The Borgias. Another project has been a massive fire basket weighing 2 cwt for a film called Raiders of the Lost Ark. In his workshop, Mr Wheeley forges such items as mild-steel gates, fire baskets and smaller items of hearth furniture. One of his finest pieces is a 6 ft high arrow-and-ball weathervane on top of Nazeing Church.

Open all year, Mon.–Sat., 9–6.

CASTLE HEDINGHAM   Map ref: Cb
Castle Hedingham Handloom Weavers, DeVere Mill, Queen Street, Castle Hedingham, Halstead.
Tel. Hedingham 61193
(Clearly marked, in main street of village. Parking on site.)

In 1971, Warner and Sons, a long-established Braintree firm of weavers, closed down, and the ancient craft of silk handloom weaving was on the verge of extinction. However, Richard Humphries, the firm's last trainee designer, started his own company and moved into an old primary school at Castle Hedingham. Today, visitors can watch the fabrics being woven to order – many of them for stately homes and royal palaces. There is also a museum shop.

Open Easter Mon. to end Sept., Mon.–Fri., 2–4.30. Also Sat. and evening tours by appointment.

COLNE ENGAINE   Map ref: Cb
Colne Valley Workshop, Brooke Street, Colne Engaine, Colchester.
Tel. Earls Colne 2325
(Quarter of a mile west of village centre. Parking on site.)

Instead of producing the conventional vases, plates and bowls which are the stock in trade of most potters, the Godfrey family make ceramic cars. These tiny replicas, which include the 1945 MGTC and the 1970 Range Rover, are complete in almost every detail down to the windscreen wipers and side lights. They range in length from 5 in. for a Mini to 12 in. for a Jaguar 'E' type. Orders are received from collectors all over the world, the car in greatest demand being a 1970 Citröen. Mr John Godfrey and his son, Kevin, faithfully capture the individual character of each vehicle and will supply a personalised number-plate on request.

Open daily all year, 9–5.

PURLEIGH   Map ref: Ca
New Hall Vineyard, Chelmsford Road, Purleigh, Chelmsford.
Tel. Maldon 828343
(On the B1010 Chelmsford–Burnham-on-Crouch road, ¼ mile north of village. Parking on site.)

As far back as the 11th-century Domesday Survey there were 45 vineyards in Essex. The present-day New Hall Vineyard was founded in 1970, within 2 miles of two of these early vineyards at Mundon and Maldon. It forms part of Bill and Sheila Greenwood's 600 acre farm. At present, 22 acres are given over to vines, mostly German varieties but with some French Pinot grapes – a type introduced to Britain by the Romans in AD 280. 'Open Days' are held each year, usually during the last weekend in September. Visitors can see the vineyard at work, watch a film showing its operations throughout the year and taste the previous year's harvest. The bottles are stored in the cellars of the 14th-century farmhouse, and visitors may buy the wine at any time during the year. The New Hall wines, some of which are similar to a hock in flavour and bouquet, have won many awards in international competitions.

Cellars open all year, Mon.–Sat., 12–6; Sun., 10–1. Small charge for 'Open Days'.

RIDGEWELL   Map ref: Cb
Ridgewell Crafts, The Village Green, Ridgewell, Halstead.
Tel. Ridgewell 272

(On the A604, 6 miles south-east of Haverhill. Parking on site.)

The grand English elm, a tree that used to be plentiful along hedgerows in southern England, still grows in East Anglia. At Ridgewell Crafts, Patrick Crouch buys complete elm trunks which are sliced up and left to season for two years before they are used. The beauty of the grain, the generous width of the planks and the durability and strength of the wood make it an ideal timber for furniture. Dressers, sideboards, corner cupboards, garden furniture, blanket chests and Essex oyster stools are among the items made from the solid timber. Mr Crouch's uncle, Mr Arthur Godsell, who started the business, now runs the shop with his wife. Antiques, crafts and bric-à-brac fill the rooms. Of special interest are the antique clocks, and Mr Godsell offers a repair service for old clocks and watches.

Open daily except Wed., 10–6.30. Workshop by appointment.

THAXTED   Map ref: Cb
Jill Baines Ceramics, 'Coldhams Fee', Bardfield Road, Thaxted, nr Great Dunmow.
Tel. Thaxted 830867
(At south end of village, take road by school, signposted 'The Bardfields'. Second thatched cottage set back from road on right, and fifth cottage from fire station. Parking in road.)

Far more people have seen Jill Baines's pottery than have ever visited her workshop. For Mrs Baines is sometimes commissioned to make replicas of ancient Greek, Roman and Anglo-Saxon cooking and eating pots that are used in television plays and films. In her workshop she also makes more modern pieces: large bowls, garden pots, punch bowls and platters. Her smaller wares are often glazed in a glorious red, the recipe for which she keeps a closely guarded secret. Small, sculptured terracotta figures, and bulls covered in a shiny black glaze, are also on display.

Open most days, but it is advisable to telephone first.

WHITE RODING   Map ref: Cb
White Roding Pottery, White Roding, Great Dunmow.
Tel. White Roding 326
(At eastern end of village, on A1060. Car park on site.)

Every summer Deborah Baynes runs a series of week-long courses for aspiring potters. By the end of the week the students will have mastered some of the basic skills of throwing and firing pots. The highlight of the week is Raku night, when pots which the students have made are fired in a Japanese Raku kiln – spectacular with its leaping flames. The pots, glowing red, are lifted from the kiln with tongs and quenched in steaming water. White Roding Pottery is a working pottery as well, producing a range of stoneware for the kitchen and the table as well as larger pieces, such as bread-crocks and decorative planters.

Open most days, but it is advisable to telephone first.

LINCOLNSHIRE

ALVINGHAM   Map ref: Be
Alvingham Pottery, Alvingham, Louth.
Tel. South Cockerington 230
(Take Alvingham road from Louth via Keddington. At first junction in Alvingham, turn left into Yarburgh Road. Parking on premises.)

Bold in both colour and design, the earthenware vessels of Alvingham Pottery are made by half-a-dozen local craftsmen, who throw the pots on a number of electrically driven wheels. Once shaped and biscuit-fired, the earthenware receives background colour through glaze dipping. Abstract patterns or floral motifs are then hand-painted on the glaze.

Open Mon.–Sat., 9–5; Sun., 2–5. Closed Christmas Day and Boxing Day.

BRACEBOROUGH   Map ref: Bd
Art in Glass, Spa House, Braceborough, Stamford.
Tel. Greatford 310
(From A6121 turn east into road to Greatford. After 1½ miles turn left into the Braceborough road. Just beyond post office, turn left and follow road to end. Parking on premises.)

Born in Bavaria and apprenticed in Switzerland, Fritz Liebich makes leaded stained-glass windows at Braceborough's former Georgian spa. He produces multicoloured mosaics that find a place in both sacred and secular English architecture. Apart from church windows, Mr Liebich finds that the greatest demand is for coats of arms.

Open daily, 8–6.

CROWLAND   Map ref: Bd
S. W. Halford and Son, 10 South Street, Crowland, Peterborough.
Tel. Peterborough 210605
(In centre of village, just south of bridge. Parking in North Street.)

Four generations of Halfords have worked as saddlers since 1868. Today, the family tradition is continued by Stanley Halford and his son, Stephen. Still using many tools passed down by their forefathers, they make harness of every kind, suitable for heavy shire horses, Shetland ponies, hunters and racehorses.

Open Mon.–Sat., 7–12 and 1–7.

HOGSTHORPE   Map ref: Ce
Millstone Craft Centre, Mill House, West End, Hogsthorpe.
Tel. Skegness 72977
(On A52, on west side of Hogsthorpe.)

In bygone days the ovens of High Mill bakery supplied Hogsthorpe with fresh bread. Nowadays, baking of a different sort takes place – the firing of stoneware pots. Stuart MacDonald shapes pots either by throwing or modelling, and decorates with wax-resist, brushwork and also dipping.

Open daily, 9–5. Large parties by appointment only.

LINCOLN   Map ref: Ae
Richard Pullen (Silversmith), 64 Steep Hill, Lincoln.
Tel. Lincoln 37170
(From Broadgate [A158] turn into Clasketgate. Take first right [Danesgate] and continue to junction with Danes Terrace, where there is a car park. Follow Danes Terrace to Steep Hill.)

Richard Pullen's one-room workshop and showroom is tucked away between Lincoln's cathedral and city centre. In a setting steeped in history, it is appropriate that he should specialise in repairing and restoring antique silverware. He also fashions silver goblets, little caskets and plates in traditional styles.

Open Mon.–Sat., 10–5.30. Appointment advisable.

PINCHBECK WEST   Map ref: Bd
Tydd Pottery, Tydd Road, Pinchbeck West, Spalding.
Tel. Spalding 66120
(Tydd Road is a southern extension of Money Bridge Lane, which meets the B1180 just east of Pinchbeck West. Parking on premises.)

Terracotta pots for home and garden are produced by three craftsmen in this Fenland pottery. Ranging from 3 in. to 30 in. high, they are shaped on a wheel and decorated in a variety of styles. Many items of kitchenware and commemorative plates are dip-decorated with a transparent glaze, and are slip-trailed.

Open Mon.–Fri., 9–6. Other times by appointment.

SKEGNESS   Map ref: Ce
The Skegness Pottery, 17/25 Burgh Road, Skegness.
Tel. Skegness 2653
(On south side of A158, about 1 mile from sea. Parking on premises.)

Over 125,000 visitors annually pass through Skegness Pottery. A score of craftsmen are involved in producing domestic earthenware in over 100 different shapes and in seven basic patterns. All, with the exception of plates, are hand-thrown. Plates are shaped on a jig and jolley. The decorative process includes glaze dipping and the painting of stylised leaf motifs or abstract designs.

Open daily, 9–5. Closed Christmas week.

STAPLEFORD   Map ref: Ae
Country Craftsman, Brook Cottage, Newark Road, Stapleford.
Tel. Bassingham 640
(From A46 at Brough, south of Lincoln, turn east into road to Stapleford. Brook Cottage is first house in village.)

David Rawson is the 'Country Craftsman', and building classic furniture is his craft. Grandfather clock cases, dressers, tables and stereo cabinets are among his principal creations. Mr Rawson is particularly fond of working with oak, but he does use other woods, including sapele and pine. Much of his furniture bears hand-carved decorations, including complex scroll work and heraldic designs.

Open by appointment.

WOODHALL SPA   Map ref: Be
Edmund Czajkowski and Son (Cabinet makers and restorers), 96 Tor-O-Moor Road, Woodhall Spa.
Tel. Woodhall Spa 52895
(From B1191 in eastern Woodhall Spa turn south into Kirby Lane. Tor-O-Moor Road is first right. Parking on premises.)

Each piece of furniture bears the carved, oak-leaf hallmark of Edmund Czajkowski; an emblem that has now passed on to his son Michael, who performs much more than the basics of furniture making and restoration. Gilding, inlaying, oriental lacquering and carving are all skills that he practises with great expertise.

Open Mon.–Fri., 9–5.

WRAGBY   Map ref: Be
Christopher J. Maddison (Cabinet maker), Market Place, Wragby.
Tel. Wragby 858450 (workshop); Tealby 401 (home)
(Behind shops lining south side of Market Square – the village centre. Parking in square.)

In the solitude of a converted Victorian grain store, Christopher Maddison constructs and restores furniture. From oak and mahogany he reproduces the elegant creations of 18th and 19th-century designers. In addition to these reproductions, Mr Maddison also makes English farmhouse furniture of his own design mainly in timbers such as pine, chestnut, oak, and iroko.

Open Mon.–Fri., 9–6. Other times by appointment.

MUSEUM

LINCOLN   Map ref: Ae
Museum of Lincolnshire Life, Old Barracks, Burton Road, Lincoln.
Tel. Lincoln 28448
(Take A1102 for ½ mile from junction with A57 to west of city centre. Turn right into Upper Long Leys Road. Museum is on left.)

Collections covering all aspects of Lincolnshire life over the last 200 years emphasise the role played by agriculture in the history of the county, and by rural craftsmen such as the saddler, the cobbler, the blacksmith and the wheelwright. The museum actively encourages local crafts by holding regular demonstrations and by supplying local basket makers with home-grown willows from its own 1 acre willow holt.

Open Feb.–Nov., Mon.–Sat., 10–5.30; Sun., 2.30–6. Charge for admission.

NORFOLK

EAST RUNTON   Map ref: Dd
Valley Workshops, East Runton, Cromer.
Tel. Cromer 512049
(Take A148 out of Cromer and turn right after railway line. After ¾ mile take farm road to left. Parking on site.)

Arnold Zelter is a musician as well as a cabinet maker. It is natural, therefore, that he should specialise in making music-stands and cabinets for holding sheet music. He works mainly in English oak or Honduras mahogany, but yew, Indian rosewood, English walnut or Douglas fir is sometimes used for the furniture. His wife, Angie, is a potter who makes an attractive range of hand-thrown stoneware in shades of green or blue.

Open daily 10–6.

EDGEFIELD   Map ref: Dd
Edgefield Pottery, Rectory Lane, Edgefield, Melton Constable.
Tel. Saxthorpe 379
(Two miles from Holt on the B1149 Norwich road. Parking on site.)

Visitors to Edgefield Pottery can see pots being stacked in the kiln for firing – if they arrive on a Thursday. Once the final pot has been placed in position, the entrance to the kiln is bricked up and any gaps sealed with clay before firing. What potters call the 'breaking of the kiln' happens the following Tuesday, as the newly created pots are brought out for the first time into the light of day. All the work is glazed in a range of warm, autumnal colours. The pottery, in the heart of the Norfolk countryside, is housed in a barn and stables that date back to Tudor times.

Open daily 9–6, including Bank Holidays. Closed at Christmas.

ERPINGHAM   Map ref: Dd
Alby Crafts, Cromer Road, Erpingham, Norwich.
Tel. Hanworth 590
(On the A140 Norwich–Cromer road, 6 miles south of Cromer. Car park on site.)

Crafts from the four corners of the kingdom – glass, woodcarving, copper, ceramics, pewter, leather, wrought iron, jewellery – are on display at Alby Crafts. Up to a dozen craftsmen, including a harp maker, a picture framer, a signwriter and an embroiderer, work at the centre, housed in farm buildings that were originally built in 1850. During the summer, exhibitions and spinning and weaving classes are organised.

Open daily except Mon., Easter to Christmas, 10–5.

FELMINGHAM   Map ref: Dd
Belaugh Pottery, Church Road, Felmingham, North Walsham.
Tel. North Walsham 403967
(Near the church. Parking on site.)

Nestling in the shadow of Felmingham Church is the pottery of Bridget Graver and George Simmons. Visitors will see the two potters throwing stoneware for the kitchen and table. Their work is simple in shape and style, pleasing to the eye and finished in a white or oatmeal glaze.

Open daily except Wed., 10–5.

HEACHAM   Map ref: Cd
Norfolk Lavender Ltd, Caley Mill, Heacham, King's Lynn.
Tel. Heacham 70384
(On the A149 at Heacham. Parking on site.)

The lavender crop at Caley Mill is harvested in July and August, and visitors can see the oil being extracted in the distillery. The blooms are loaded into copper stills, and steam is passed through them from below. The heat turns the oil in the flower heads into vapour, and the mixture of steam and sweet-smelling vapour is passed into a condenser, where it liquifies into water and lavender oil. The mixture is passed to a separator where the oil, being lighter than water, floats to the top and is drawn off through a tap. From these lavender oils and from their own dried lavender, Norfolk Lavender make scented soaps, perfume, talcum powder, bath cubes and sachets.

Opening times: end May to end Sept., shop and tea-room 10.30–5 daily; Oct. to end May, shop only 8.30–4, Mon.–Fri. Distillery open during harvest (July–Aug.). Appointment necessary for large parties.

ICKBURGH   Map ref: Cc
Graham Wrench (Fine art woodturning), Thimble Cottage, Ickburgh, Thetford.
Tel. Mundford 379
(Off the A1065 at Ickburgh, 300 yds on left from 'No Through Road' sign by thatched cottage and small garage. Restricted parking by cottage.)

Whenever Graham Wrench selects a piece of wood for his work, he tries to give new life to the once-living wood as he fashions it into such items as goblets, chalices, single-bloom vases, candlesticks, platters and traditional hour-glasses. His workshop at Ickburgh is sweet with the aroma of exotic woods – paraking, putujumu, cocobolo, tulipwood, ebony and Indian rosewood. As well as specially commissioned pieces, he also produces restoration finials for clock cases and has collected something like 200 original patterns.

Open daily, May–Oct., 11 to dusk, by appointment.

KING'S LYNN   Map ref: Cd
Tim Clayton Jewellery, 5 Saturday Market Place, King's Lynn.
Tel. King's Lynn 2111
(Opposite St Margaret's Church. Car park in the market place.)

Between the years 1600 and 1696, King's Lynn had its own 'assay' mark stamped on all pieces of gold and silverware. It consisted of three dragons' heads, each pierced by a cross. A standard of fine craftsmanship was set in those years, and Tim Clayton works within that tradition making ear-rings, bracelets, rings and pendants, as well as larger items such as bowls, commemorative spoons and chalices. Many of these pieces are on display in his showroom.

Open all year, Mon.–Sat., 9–5.30. Closed Wed. Workshop by appointment only.

KING'S LYNN   Map ref: Cd
Wedgwood Glass, Oldmedow Road, King's Lynn.
Tel. King's Lynn 65111
(From town centre, take Hardwick Road to Hardwick Industrial Estate. Just before large roundabout, turn left by petrol station down Scania Way. Turn right into Oldmedow Road. Factory is a few hundred yards on right. Parking on site.)

When the Wedgwood glass factory opened in King's Lynn in 1967 it brought back a lost industry to a town that had a thriving glasshouse in the 17th century. In today's glasshouse, teams consisting of a pot boy or apprentice, a footmaker, a blower and a master craftsman, work closely together blowing and shaping the molten glass alongside the roar and fierce heat of the furnace. A 35 minute tour ends in the souvenir shop. Here, a wide selection of glass is displayed, from brilliant lead-crystal table glass to paperweights in the shapes of animals, fish and birds, candle-holders and vases.

Organised factory tours, Mon.–Fri., 9.30–2. Shop open all year, Mon.–Fri., 9–5; Sat., 9–4. Appointment necessary for organised tours.

NEW BUCKENHAM   Map ref: Dc
Bakehouse Pottery, King Street, New Buckenham, Norwich.
Tel. New Buckenham 512
(In the main street. Parking available outside pottery.)

Map ref: Cd

Norfolk Rural Life Museum

GRESSENHALL, NORFOLK

A handsome 18th-century workhouse, rising red-bricked and awesome from the flatness of the Norfolk landscape, now houses the Rural Life Museum. An extra range of buildings, added in the 19th century for tramps who trudged the countryside around, has been converted into a row of craftsmen's workshops. Existing workshops have been studied in detail in order to make these reconstructions as authentic as possible. As a consequence, it is easy to imagine craftsmen actually working in the shops of the blacksmith, baker, saddler, basket-maker and wheelwright.

For centuries, Norfolk has been renowned for its agriculture. It was the home of such pioneers as 'Turnip' Townshend, who popularised the four-course rotation of wheat, turnips, barley and clover that still provides a sound basis for farming practice. The aim of this ambitious museum is to preserve and present the life of people in the Norfolk countryside. Cherry Tree Cottage, where the workhouse officials used to live, has been renovated as a typical 19th-century farm-labourer's cottage with a garden to match. In one of the courtyards, a cattle ring and weighbridge from the town of Fakenham make up the market display.

Imaginatively arranged collections of machines, tools and photographs illustrate the work that would have been done in each month of the year – hedging, ploughing and drainage in October, for example, and barn work in December.

One particularly intriguing exhibit is a gate designed by Robert Marsham of Stratton Strawless Hall, and made exclusively from farm tools, such as pitchforks and scythes.

The museum also houses wagons, engines, part of an iron foundry and a display of cobbler's tools and shoes.

Gressenhall, East Dereham, Norfolk. Tel. Dereham 86053.
(To reach the museum, take the B1110 for 1½ miles north of East Dereham, then turn on to the B1146 Fakenham road. After ¾ mile turn left. Museum is on right.)

Open May–Sept., Tues.–Sat., 10–5; also Sun., 2–5.30. Bank Holidays, 10–5. Charge for admission.

SADDLER'S WORKSHOP *The tools and equipment for this convincing reconstruction come from a saddler who, until the 1960s, plied his trade in the nearby village of East Dereham, and from a harness maker who worked locally in Litcham.*

Opening times and other details may change. Check by telephone before making a special journey.

277

The first Elizabeth was on the throne when the small, thatched cottage where Dorothy and Bill Silk live and work was built. The range of stoneware on display – including house plates, large platters, punch bowls, tumblers, flower vases and pots, storage jars and lamps – is in combinations of four basic glazes. Some are decorated with wax-resist, others with sgraffito.

Open daily except Wed., 9–5.30.

REEDHAM   Map ref: Dd
Pettitts Rural Industries Ltd, Camp Hill, Reedham, Norwich.
Tel. Great Yarmouth 700243
(Signposted from the A47, near Reedham Church. Car park on site.)

The Victorian craft of taxidermy has never died out, and in some parts of the country it is even undergoing a revival. Brian Taylor and Neil Nichols use wire frames and wood wool to mount their birds and animals in naturalistic poses. Their main customers are theatres, artists and large department stores, for whom they have a hire service, but they also preserve a treasured pet.

The taxidermy house is part of a small ornamental park, with waterfowl and cages of ornamental birds and rare pheasants. Another building in the park is devoted to feathercraft. Here, the craftswomen use feathers to simulate flowers. They also build feathers into displays. One of the most remarkable is a windmill made up of 4,700 feathers.

Open all year, Mon.–Fri., 9–5. Also Sun., 12.30–5.30, during summer.

ROUGHTON   Map ref: Dd
The Old Forge Craft Gallery, Roughton, Norwich.
Tel. Hanworth 403
(Three miles south of Cromer on the A149 take the B1436 to Sheringham. Gallery is about 300 yds to west of the A140 junction at Roughton. Car park on site.)

Insects that lived millions of years ago are sometimes preserved for ever in the natural resin that seeped out of trees. In his workshop at the Old Forge Craft Gallery, Michael Kearns uses a synthetic resin to preserve the shapes of flowers and leaves from the Norfolk countryside. Each bloom or leaf is embedded in clear polyester resin, which hardens and turns the leaf into a man-made fossil. His creations are made into decorative door knobs, paperweights, finger plates and pen holders.

Mr Kearns works alongside more than 30 other craftsmen. These include woodworkers, ironsmiths, doll makers and basket weavers. Demonstrations of spinning, weaving and basket making take place in the studio gallery during the summer months.

Open daily June–Sept., 10–6. Oct.–Dec., Tues.–Sat., 10–6. Jan. to Easter by appointment only. Easter to end May, Tues.–Sat., 10–6. Also open Bank Holidays.

SHERINGHAM   Map ref: Dd
Sheringham Pottery, 30 Church Street, Sheringham.
Tel. Sheringham 823552
(Situated between putting green and parish church, 150 yds from North Norfolk Railway station. Restricted parking at the pottery.)

The Farncombe family make slab, coil and pinch pottery, using methods that pre-date the wheel. The clay pots, often decorated with tree, leaf or flower motifs, are fired twice. After the first firing, which takes 14 hours, they are covered first with an opaque glaze and then with iron oxides which supply the colour. During the second firing the oxides are fired into the glaze, forming haphazard but attractive patterns. A wide selection of lamps, vases, flower holders, hanging baskets, candle holders, bowls, plates and coffee and tea sets are on display in the showroom.

Open all year, Tues.–Sat., 10–5; also Sun., 10–1 and 2.30–5.

SNETTISHAM   Map ref: Cd
Snettisham Studio, 1 Lynn Road, Snettisham, King's Lynn.
Tel. Dersingham 41167
(On the main A149 in Snettisham. Parking available on forecourt.)

Carole Grace has painstakingly learned the technique of spinning a very fine thread on a 300-year-old spinning-wheel. She also has more modern wheels, on which she spins wool from local or Shetland sheep. Sometimes she colours the wool with natural dyes – elderberries, onion skins or oak bark – to produce satisfying, glowing colours in the finished garment. Mrs Grace weaves cloth on an array of looms, but she also turns her hand to bobbin lace, crochet and knitting.

Open most days Easter to Sept., but advisable to telephone first. Open Oct.–Mar. on Sat. Other days by appointment.

SUTTON   Map ref: Dd
Malcolm Flatman, Sutton Windmill Pottery, Church Road, Sutton, Norwich.
Tel. Stalham 80595
(Pottery is approximately ¼ mile south of village church. Parking on site.)

Malcolm Flatman built his pottery in sight of Sutton windmill, from which the pottery takes its name. Mr Flatman uses a windmill motif on all his work. He makes domestic stoneware – beakers, bowls, casseroles, jugs, plates, storage jars and vases. Many of these pieces have an attractive speckled finish, achieved in the firing by starving the kiln of oxygen. This draws iron oxides in the clay to the surface.

Open daily, but advisable to telephone before making special journey.

TATTERSETT   Map ref: Cd
Hewitt Alderson (Furniture restorer), Old School House, Tattersett, King's Lynn.
Tel. East Rudham 385
(About 5 miles west of Fakenham, turn left to Coxford off the A148. At T-junction [100 yds] turn left. First house on left. Parking available on site.)

When Hewitt Alderson restores a piece of antique furniture or an old musical instrument he makes sure that every detail is correct, even to the extent of using animal glue instead of modern epoxy resins. If he has to replace, say, a section of a walnut cabinet, he will look for walnut of the same age rather than use a piece of new wood. This, says Mr Alderson, is his way of keeping faith both with the past generations who made the furniture and with the future generations who will use it. He also undertakes commissions for new work that involve woodturning and delicate cabinet work. One of Mr Alderson's pieces, an American red oak display chest, was commissioned for presentation to the Royal Family and is now part of the furniture at Windsor Castle.

Open most days, any reasonable hour, by appointment.

TERRINGTON ST CLEMENT   Map ref: Cd
Tony Hodgson and Partners, The Forge, Wesley Road, Terrington St Clement, nr King's Lynn.
Tel. King's Lynn 828637
(Just north of the A17 in centre of village. Parking available outside forge.)

Four generations of the Hodgson family have worked as blacksmiths and farriers in the village of Terrington St Clement since the business was founded in 1918 by Mr John Hodgson. Today, two of his great-grandsons still continue the family tradition. They can tackle virtually any metalwork in any style, including fireside furniture and hand-beaten copper, together with brass or steel fire canopies. One of their most challenging and rewarding jobs has been to restore, section by section, the 20 ft high wrought-iron gate at Cliveden, a 19th-century mansion at Taplow, Buckinghamshire.

Open all year, Mon.–Fri., 8–5; Sat., 8–12.

WAYFORD BRIDGE   Map ref: Dd
Chippendale Craft Ltd, The Maltings, Wayford Bridge, nr Stalham, Norwich.
Tel. Stalham 81464
(About 1½ miles west of Stalham on the A149. Parking on site.)

One of the most famous sailors in Britain, former Prime Minister Edward Heath, once asked Jack Chippendale to build him a boat. He did – a 16 ft racing dinghy called Blue Heather II. The result, said Mr Heath, was 'a delight to the eye and a joy to sail ... it almost broke my heart to part with her, she was so beautifully built'. Mr Chippendale still builds beautiful boats, and he welcomes visitors to his workshop at Wayford Bridge.

Open all year, Mon.–Fri., 9–12 and 2–5; Sat., 9–12. By appointment only.

WELLS-NEXT-THE-SEA   Map ref: Cd
Holkham Pottery Ltd, Holkham Hall, Wells-next-the-Sea.
Tel. Fakenham 710424
(Two miles west of Wells, just south of the A149. Parking on site.)

Elizabeth, Countess of Leicester took up pottery as a hobby in 1951 and enjoyed it so much that she decided to set up a business at her home – Holkham Hall. In 1957, a small team of skilled potters began producing a range of fine stoneware. Today, visitors can watch vases, bowls, table lamps, jugs, wine goblets and decanters being thrown on the wheel, decorated and glazed in the studio section. These items, along with a wide variety of slip-cast stoneware, are on sale in the pottery and at the Ancient House in the village.

Pottery open late May to end Sept., Mon.–Fri., 9–5. Ancient House open daily, 10–5.

MUSEUMS

GRESSENHALL   Map ref: Cd
Norfolk Rural Life Museum.
(See panel on p. 277)

NORWICH   Map ref: Dd
Bridewell Museum, Bridewell Alley, Norwich.
Tel. Norwich 611277

Old Norwich prison is now a museum of Norwich trades and industries – the perfect urban complement to the Rural Life Museum at Gressenhall. A Jacquard loom is a feature of the room that commemorates 400 years of textile manufacture in the city. The industry declined in the 19th century, and today no wool or silk is woven in Norwich. Instead, the city is noted for its ladies' shoes, leather-working being one of Norwich's oldest trades. Displays in the museum consist of four centuries of shoes, a shoemaker's bench and tools, and a reconstructed saddler's shop.

Other trades represented include brewing and printing. In 1836 there were 26 breweries in Norwich, while in 1701 Norwich was one of the first provincial cities to produce a newspaper. Walls and roofs have been constructed by Norfolk craftsmen to show local materials and techniques. Since the county is very short of building stone, flint and pebbles were much used. The museum also houses a smithy, and examples of the intricate wrought and cast ironwork of 19th-century Norwich • foundries.

Open Mon.–Sat., 10–5. Charge for admission.

SUFFOLK

BECCLES   Map ref: Dc
Winter Flora, Hall Farm, Weston, Beccles.
Tel. Beccles 713346
(On west side of the A145, 1½ miles south of Beccles. Car park on site.)

People who visit Winter Flora during the drowsy days of late summer or early autumn

can keep the memory alive throughout the grey days of winter. For the flowers they will see, suspended from the ceilings of the packing sheds in a spectacular blaze of colour, are in the process of being dried to be made up into everlasting displays. The flowers grown in greatest numbers are helichrysum – gorgeous in their golds, pinks, oranges, whites and salmon tints – and statice, which comes in lavender, blue, purple, yellow, pink, apricot and white. Both are sown under glass in spring and planted out in the fields in May for harvesting in August. Bunches are hung upside-down in the sheds for up to a month, and are ready in September.

Open Sept.–Dec., and late Jan.–Mar., 10–5. Shop open all year, 10–5.

BURY ST EDMUNDS   Map ref: Cc
Chas. E. Cragg (Wood turner), 25A Garland Street, Bury St Edmunds.
Tel. Bury St Edmunds 62973 (evenings)
(From Angel Hill take Abbeygate Street. Turn first right along Lower Baxter Street. At crossroads, continue along Garland Street. Workshop is on left. Parking in Angel Hill.)

A rich bouquet of wood shavings, resins and polish fills the air as Charles Cragg skilfully brings out the full richness of grain and colouring of the woods on his lathe. Using English oak, mahogany, teak, sycamore and elm, Mr Cragg makes a range of bowls, lamps, decorative cheese-boards, wall plaques, mirrors and trivets. He is helped by his sister, who brings the turned pieces up to a high polish and adds decorative touches.

Open Tues., Wed. and Fri., 10.30–12.30 and 2.30–5; Sat., 10.30–12.30. Other times by appointment.

CAVENDISH   Map ref: Cb
Cavendish Manor Vineyards, Nether Hall Manor, Cavendish, Sudbury.
Tel. Glemsford 280221
(North of the green, beyond the church. Car park on site.)

There are two bonuses for visitors to Cavendish Manor Vineyards. Not only will they see extensive vine-growing on an English estate, but they can also browse among the estate's fine collection of country bygones. Parties of 25 or over are given a conducted tour of the vineyards and a welcoming talk on arrival. All visitors are welcome, for a small charge, to taste the refreshing dry white wine, which is similar to an Alsatian Hock. And, of course, bottles may be bought at the end of the tour. In a good year, Mr Basil Ambrose, who owns the vineyard, expects to produce 15,000 to 20,000 bottles of Cavendish Manor wine.

Among the bygones on display in the nearby barn are a man trap for use against poachers, a wolf trap, and a husband and wife plough in which the wife did the pulling and the husband at the back did the steering.

Open daily, Mar.–Oct., 11–5; Nov.–Feb., 11–4. Appointment necessary for group tours (25–100 people).

CLAYDON   Map ref: Db
Claydon Forge, Old Ipswich Road, Claydon.
Tel. Ipswich 831000
(Take first turning right off the B1113 after leaving roundabout junction on the A45 at Claydon. Parking outside forge.)

Stuart Hill brings the enquiring mind of an artist and the precision of an engineer to the blacksmith's craft. Instead of a traditional wrought-iron gate, for instance, with the usual ornamental scrollwork, he will produce one that is more like a painting, with writhing sunflowers framed in black steel. One of his most ambitious pieces is a design motif of a frog, forged from a single square bar of steel. The motif, showing the emergence of the frog in stages, has been incorporated in a table top. Called 'Metamorphosis', it is now in the Victoria and Albert Museum in London.

Open all year, Mon.–Sat., 9–5.

DEBENHAM Map ref: Dc
Kiln Cottage Pottery, Low Road, Debenham.
Tel. Debenham 860475
(Off the main street at south end of village.
Parking available outside pottery.)

*A cheese dish in the form of a fruit machine,
ashtrays in the shape of a pair of spectacles,
and a teapot that looks like a sandcastle are not
the usual products you would expect to find in
a pottery. But Tony and Anita Carter bring to
their work both imagination and a sense of fun.
Their designs are influenced by styles of the
1920s and 1930s, which is noticeable in their
unusual choice of materials. A ceramic money-
box, for instance, will be decorated with mother
of pearl and precious metals.*

Open all year, Mon.–Sat., 9–5.

GISLINGHAM Map ref: Dc
Edwin Turner (Furniture maker), Home
Farm, Mill Street, Gislingham, nr Eye.
Tel. Mellis 280
(Take lane by village hall – Mill Street.
Farm is about ¾ mile on left. Parking on
site.)

*To Edwin Turner the second half of the 18th
century – the period of Chippendale and
Sheraton, Adam and Hepplewhite – was the
golden age of furniture design. Many of the
sideboards, chairs and tables he makes in the
workshop behind his farmhouse are in the style
of these Georgian masters. As well as working
in these styles, he will undertake special
commissions to customers' own designs. He
also runs courses in furniture restoration.*

Open all year, Mon.–Fri., 8–6; also Sat.,
8–12. Open at other times by appointment.

GREAT BARTON Map ref: Cc
Felix White, The Flints, Livermere Road,
Great Barton, Bury St Edmunds.
Tel. Great Barton 675
(In village, turn left at crossroads by
telephone box [School Road]. At T-junction
turn left [Mill Lane]. At next crossroads
turn left [Livermere Road]. House is a few
hundred yards on left. Parking in drive.)

*Samples of Felix White's work have been
presented to the Queen, Prince Charles and
Princess Anne. Working in a flint-built
granary, he engraves trophies and presentation
pieces on high-quality lead-crystal glass with
diamond-point precision. Outside, the scene is
typically English – ducks on a pond and a fine
old 17th-century Suffolk farmhouse surrounded
by a large country garden. The scenes which
Mr White depicts on his glass in such brilliant
detail come from literature as much as from
nature. On one bowl he will etch pilgrims from
Chaucer's* Canterbury Tales; *on another a text
from the 8th-century* Book of Kells. *For other
themes Mr White goes to Dickens and* The
Pickwick Papers, *or to classical mythology.*

Open daily, but it is necessary to telephone
for appointment.

HELMINGHAM Map ref: Dc
The Workshop, Helmingham Forge,
Gosbeck Road, Helmingham.
Tel. Helmingham 485
(At the junction of the B1077 and Gosbeck
Road at Helmingham, about 8 miles north
of Ipswich. Parking available outside forge.)

*Rod Richens carries on a Suffolk tradition of
decorative ironwork at his forge at
Helmingham. He decorates hearth furniture
with one of the most ancient motifs in the
world – a ram's head. But he does not confine
himself to traditional forms, for he also enjoys
experimenting with metal tubes which he
presses and bends to make unusual fireside
tables.*

Open Mon.–Fri., 8.30–5.30. Also open Sun.
afternoons, Apr.–Sept.

LAXFIELD Map ref: Dc
Ron Fuller Toys, Willow Cottage, Laxfield,
Woodbridge.
Tel. Ubbeston 317
(Willow Cottage lies back a little from the
main street. Parking available in street.)

*To step into Ron Fuller's workshop is to step
into another world – the world of childhood
where wooden gymnasts turn somersaults,
where toy circus artistes ride tin-plate horses
round a miniscule ring, where wooden hens flap
their wings and lay eggs, where flying aces
pilot stubby-winged aeroplanes and where toy
submarines dive under the bath water. Mr
Fuller's brightly coloured models appeal to girls
as well as boys, for dolls' houses are included in
his extensive range.*

Open all year, Mon.–Sat., 10–5, by
appointment.

YOXFORD Map ref: Dc
Diana and Biddy Rose, Milestone House
Pottery, High Street, Yoxford, nr
Saxmundham.
Tel. Yoxford 465
(In the main street. Parking outside.)

*One of the most unusual buildings in this
charming Suffolk village houses the shop and
gallery of Diana and Biddy Rose. The pottery
takes its name from a 150-year-old milestone
in the road outside. Diana Rose makes large,
wheel-thrown stoneware and porcelain bowls
and vases, classically simple in shape and
sometimes decorated with brushwork or
sgraffito. Her daughter, Biddy, produces pots
for cooking in and eating from, as well as
pottery for the garden, sometimes altering the
basic shape by cutting, pressing or beating. As
well as selling their own work, the potters
display the products of other local craftsmen –
wooden toys, baskets, corn dollies – and give
exhibitions of the work of local artists.*

Open all year, Mon.–Sat., 9.30–6. Closed
Wed. Workshop by appointment only.

MUSEUMS

EASTON Map ref: Dc
Easton Farm Park, Easton, nr Wickham
Market.
Tel. Wickham Market 746475
(Half a mile north of Wickham Market on
the A12, take the B1116 and follow signs
for Easton.)

*It was local farmer James Kerr's interest in
collecting early farm machinery that provided
the inspiration for opening Easton Farm Park
in 1974. Today, however, there is something
for every visitor who wanders at leisure over
the park's 35 acres; vintage motor-cycles,
various breeds of farm animals, or the
opportunity to watch cows being milked in a
modern dairy. An older, octagonal dairy with
stained-glass windows, designed by an Italian
architect, is an unusual legacy from the 1870s
when the Duke of Hamilton built a model dairy
farm on his Easton estate. It contains butter-
making equipment. Elsewhere, tools and
products illustrate a host of other crafts, such
as thatching, malting, brewing, cobbling and
blacksmithing.*

Open daily, mid-Apr.–Sept., 10.30–6.
Charge for admission.

LAVENHAM Map ref: Cb
The Guildhall, Lavenham.
Tel. Lavenham 247646

*The beautifully preserved timber-framed
buildings of Lavenham survive to this day – a
legacy of the merchants who grew rich on the
wool and woollen cloth trade. The early 16th-
century Guildhall in the market place is now a
museum. In addition to a display of cooper's
tools in the cellar, there are exhibitions on the
history of the woollen cloth trade in East
Anglia and other local industries as well as a
display on local building methods. From this,
the visitor can learn how Lavenham's houses
have stood for over 500 years without
succumbing to old age.*

Open daily, Mar.–Nov., 10.30–12.30 and
2–5.30, but closed on Fri. in Mar. and Nov.
Charge for admission.

STOWMARKET Map ref: Dc
Museum of East Anglian Life.
(See panel below)

Map ref: Dc

Museum of East Anglian Life
STOWMARKET, SUFFOLK

Sprawling over 70 acres of the old Abbot's Hall estate,
the Museum of East Anglian Life chronicles the minutest
details of everyday life in the countryside over the last
few centuries. Among the countless exhibits there are
hundreds that will jog the memory of older visitors and
capture the imagination of all who go there.

Several of the museum's buildings, which include a
14th-century farmhouse, a 17th-century water-mill
and a 19th-century windpump, were saved from certain
decay when they were moved here from their original
sites. The timber-framed and weather-boarded smithy,
which dates from the 18th century, came from the
Suffolk village of Grundisburgh. Complete with tools,
furnace, bellows and anvil, it adjoins the 'traviss' into
which horses were led to be shod. There is a circular
tyring platform in front, where the blacksmith fitted iron
tyres on to wooden wagon wheels. Workshops of three
rural craftsmen – the wheelwright, the saddler and the
rake maker – have been reconstructed in one of the
museum blocks. Displays illustrate domestic life at the
turn of the century, and local trades and industries such
as malting, brewing and mussel fishing.

Until recently, farming was the principal occupation
in East Anglia, a fact reflected by the museum's
collection of farm tools and vehicles. These include
reapers, binders, threshing drums, tractors and – since
East Anglia was an area where travelling folk undertook

ANCIENT FORGE *This entire 18th-century smithy was moved from
a village 20 miles away.*

seasonal labour on farms – gipsy caravans. Abbot's Hall
barn, which is the oldest building on the site, houses old
fire-engines, horse-drawn hearses and biers. One of
these carries a pauper's coffin, distinguished by a hinged
lid that enabled it to be used again.

Stowmarket, Suffolk. Tel. Stowmarket 2229.

Open Apr.–Oct., Mon.–Sat., 11–5; also Sun., 12–5. Charge for
admission.

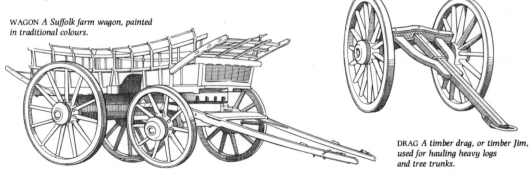

WAGON *A Suffolk farm wagon, painted
in traditional colours.*

DRAG *A timber drag, or timber Jim,
used for hauling heavy logs
and tree trunks.*

Opening times and other details may change. Check by telephone before making a special journey.

279

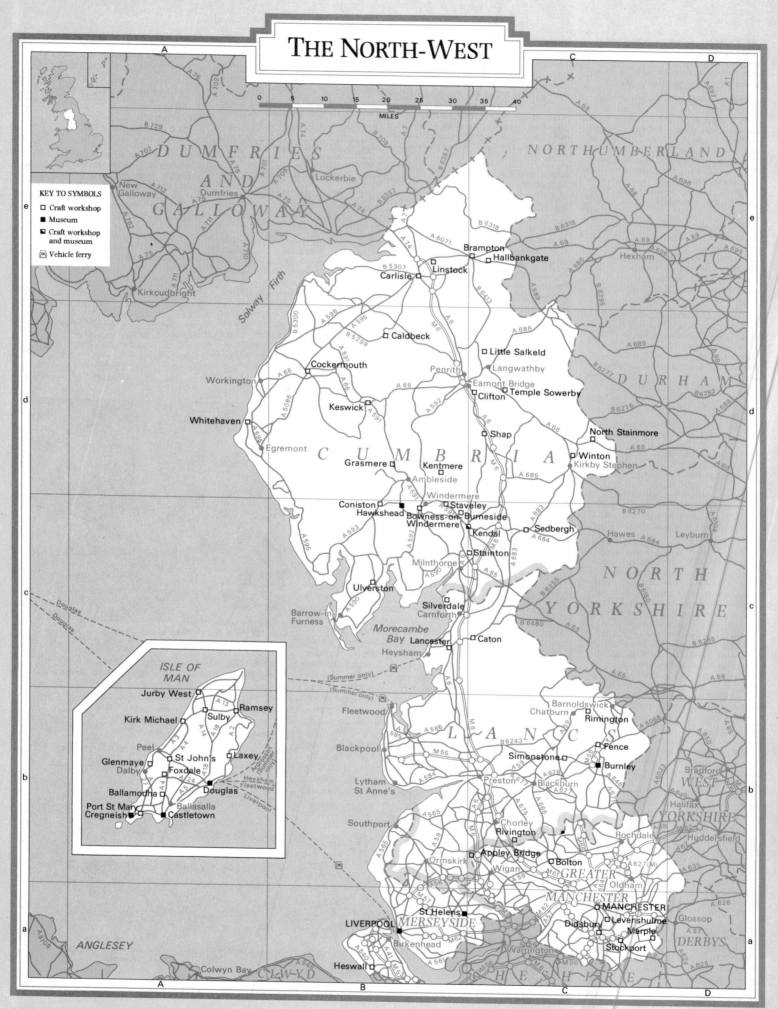

THE NORTH-WEST

MILES
0 5 10 15 20 25 30 35 40

DUMFRIES AND GALLOWAY

NORTHUMBERLAND

New Galloway
Dumfries
Lockerbie
Kirkcudbright
Solway Firth

Brampton
Hallbankgate
Linstock
Carlisle
Hexham

Caldbeck
Little Salkeld
Langwathby
Penrith
Cockermouth
Workington
Eamont Bridge
Temple Sowerby
Clifton
DURHAM
Keswick
Whitehaven
Shap
North Stainmore
Egremont
CUMBRIA
Winton
Kirkby Stephen
Grasmere
Kentmere
Ambleside
Windermere
Coniston
Staveley
Hawkshead
Bowness-on-Windermere
Burneside
Sedbergh
Kendal
Hawes
Leyburn
Stainton
Milnthorpe
Ulverston
NORTH YORKSHIRE
Silverdale
Carnforth
Barrow-in-Furness
Morecambe Bay
Caton
Lancaster
Heysham
(Summer only)
(Summer only)

ISLE OF MAN

Jurby West
Ramsey
Kirk Michael
Sulby
Peel
St John's
Laxey
Glenmaye
Dalby
Foxdale
Ballamodha
Douglas
Port St Mary
Cregneish
Ballasalla
Castletown

Fleetwood
Blackpool
Barnoldswick
Chatburn
Rimington
Fence
LANCS
Simonstone
Burnley
Lytham St Anne's
Preston
Blackburn
Southport
Chorley
Rivington
Rochdale
Halifax
WEST YORKSHIRE
Bradford
Huddersfield
Ormskirk
Appley Bridge
Bolton
Wigan
GREATER MANCHESTER
Oldham
St Helens
MANCHESTER
LIVERPOOL
MERSEYSIDE
Didsbury
Levenshulme
Marple
Glossop
Birkenhead
Stockport
DERBYS
ANGLESEY
Colwyn Bay
Heswall
CLWYD
CHESHIRE
Warrington

Opening times and other details may change. Check by telephone before making a special journey.

Vast areas of the North-West were untouched by the Industrial Revolution. They remain a forgotten country where crafts flourish, in the remote fastnesses of windswept moors. The fells are flecked with hardy breeds of sheep whose wool is still the livelihood of the region's knitters and weavers. On the Isle of Man, an independent sovereign country with its own parliament, laws and customs, many craftsmen – especially potters – use a variety of ancient Celtic and Viking designs, drawing on the inspiration of the island's rich folklore. A strong sense of tradition pervades the work of craftsmen throughout the region: the cabinet maker with his farmhouse dressers; the blacksmith with his decorative wrought iron-work, ranging from massive gates to intricate chandeliers; and the stained-glass maker, whose art is the product of skills acquired over the centuries.

CUMBRIA

BOWNESS-ON-WINDERMERE
Map ref: Bc
Craftsmen of Cumbria, The Craft Centre, Fallbarrow Road, Bowness-on-Windermere.
Tel. Windermere 2959
(From centre of Bowness, take lakeside road northwards. After 50 yds, turn left at far side of car park into Fallbarrow Road. Craft Centre is on right, just past end of parking area.)

Experts working at several different crafts may be seen in the course of a single visit. Although the crafts represented vary from year to year, there is always a range of activities for visitors to watch and even to try for themselves. Gold and silver jewellery is made. The centre also contains a working pottery, a leatherworker's bench and another workshop where the delicate, painstaking, but fascinating process of clock restoration takes place on anything from tiny carriage clocks to man-high long case clocks.

Open daily Apr.–Oct., 9.30–5.30. Open until 9.30 p.m. in school summer holidays. Open in winter daily except Thur., 9.30–5.30.

BOWNESS-ON-WINDERMERE
Map ref: Bc
Brian Johnson, Stone Craft Design, Longlands, Bowness-on-Windermere.
Tel. Windermere 3600
(Take main road uphill from Bowness pier towards Windermere. Longlands is on left after passing Royalty Cinema. Stone Craft Design is up short drive on right-hand side. Parking in Longlands.)

Lakeland stone in many shapes and hues – carved and polished into objects ranging from fireplaces and memorial panels to coffee tables, chess-boards, clocks and lamps – is the raw material of this small workshop in a backwater of Bowness. Visitors can see for themselves how the massive stone blocks are transformed, stage by stage, into finished pieces, and watch the process of carving names and numbers on plaques and panels to special order.

Open Mon.–Fri., 8–5; Sat. by appointment. Closed on Bank Holidays.

BRAMPTON
Map ref: Ce
Peter and Rosalind Whitaker (Furniture and pottery), Cambeck Bridge House, Brampton, nr Carlisle.
Tel. Brampton 3348
(Follow A6071 north-west from Brampton until road crosses River Irthing. Cambeck Bridge House is on right-hand side just before second bridge.)

The workshop shared by the Whitakers is in what was once a roadside inn. Here, Peter Whitaker makes furniture in traditional designs and to individual order – dressers, corner cupboards and ladderback chairs. His wife makes miniature pottery figures, including a range of bears and human heads, which are for sale on the premises.

Open all year, by appointment.

BURNESIDE
Map ref: Bc
W. & P. Turton, Fell View, Lower Crossings Cottage, Burneside, Kendal.
Tel. Kendal 25176
(Two miles north of Kendal off Windermere road, by railway crossing. Parking outside.)

Age-old skills are used by Mr Turton to serve an entirely new technology – much of his work involves carving patterns in wood for moulded plastic soles for the shoe trade. When not making patterns, Mr Turton carves smaller items to order, from house names and decorative panels to traditional utility objects, such as spoon racks. He also restores an assortment of wooden objects, from Victorian rocking-horses to gilt picture frames. Mrs Turton does upholstery and rush and cane seating.

Open most days 8–5, but advisable to telephone first.

CALDBECK
Map ref: Bd
Greenrigg Pottery, Caldbeck, nr Wigton.
Tel. Caldbeck 341
(Follow Keswick road – B5299 – from village of Caldbeck. After 2 miles the road crosses cattle-grid; ½ mile further on, look for sign at side of road and take track up to left. Parking close to pottery.)

Greenrigg Pottery is in a spectacular setting, an old fell farmhouse on the bleak moorland in the north of the Lake District National Park. Visitors are welcome to ask questions and to watch various stages in the making of pots. If they wish to buy, they can choose from a range of domestic stoneware including mugs, jugs, bowls and jam pots.

Open Easter to Oct., Mon.–Sat., 9 to sunset. By appointment in winter.

CALDBECK
Map ref: Bd
Greenrigg Cottage, Caldbeck, Wigton.
Tel. Caldbeck 679
(Greenrigg Cottage is on a fell, 3 miles from the village of Caldbeck. Follow road signposted Keswick, and after 3 miles turn left at sign for 'Greenhead'. Look out for sign at first turning left, and follow track to Greenrigg Cottage. Parking on fellside.)

Greenrigg Cottage was once lived in by shepherds who tended the flocks which roam these bleak Cumbrian fells. Now it is the home of journalist and weaver Anne Utting, who moved there from Suffolk but who now finds herself 'busier than ever', weaving thick, strong, reversible hearth rugs from the wool of the local Border sheep.

Open daily except Fri. Advisable to telephone first.

CARLISLE
Map ref: Be
Linton Tweeds Ltd, Shaddon Mills, Carlisle.
Tel. Carlisle 27569
(Linton Tweeds is in mill yard on corner of Shaddongate at foot of Dixons Chimney, a prominent landmark. Limited parking in mill yard, otherwise in nearby streets.)

Visitors will see hand-loom weaving in an unusual setting, for Linton Tweeds is alongside a yard belonging to one of the machine-driven mills that drove the original hand-loom

weavers out of business. But the company found itself a niche by supplying fine-quality tweeds to the Paris fashion houses of Chanel, Dior, Givenchy, Courrèges and Nina Ricci, and complex-patterned cloths for these demanding customers are still woven there by hand.

Mill open all year, except Christmas and New Year weeks: Mon.–Thur., 9–12.15 and 1–5; Fri., 9–12.30. Shop open Mon.–Fri., 9–5; Sat., 10–12.

CLIFTON
Map ref: Cd
Wetheriggs Country Pottery, Clifton Dykes, Penrith.
Tel. Penrith 62946
(Follow A6 south from Penrith. Look out for pottery signs on left-hand side between villages of Eamont Bridge and Clifton. Parking in front of pottery.)

Visitors to Wetheriggs will find no recently established craft workshop. The pottery was founded early in the last century to make pipes for land drainage, together with such everyday articles as flagons, bottles, baking dishes, hen feeders and beetle traps. It is one of the few remaining long-established country potteries. An ambitious ten-year restoration plan is virtually complete, and soon the pottery will clean and dry the raw clay, then throw, fire and glaze the finished pots, using traditional methods and machinery powered by a steam-engine, burning coal or wood. Already, glazed earthenware and slipware pots are made here in the old ways and decorated with the feather and frond patterns used by the Schofield and Thorburn families, who worked the pottery for over 150 years. The railway warehouse, once used for storing the finished pots, is now a gallery and weaving shed, where fleeces from the local Jacob and Herdwick sheep are woven on hand-looms into rugs and cushions.

Open daily, 10–5. Evening guided tours for large parties by appointment.

COCKERMOUTH
Map ref: Bd
Balnakeil Forge, Lamplugh Corner, Cockermouth.
Tel. Cockermouth 823169
(On the outskirts of Cockermouth at the junction of the A66 and the A5086. Parking space outside.)

Decorative wrought ironwork is the principal line at this busy working forge on the edge of the little town of Cockermouth. Visitors can see such items as large gates, screens and sculptures being made to special order, and they can choose from a wide variety of smaller examples of the smith's work, including fire irons and pokers with elegant ram's head and swan's head decorations.

Open Mon.–Fri., 8–5.30, with occasional days off. Also open Sat. mornings.

CONISTON
Map ref: Bc
Dunmail Studio, Waterhead, Coniston.
Tel. Coniston 312
(Take B5285 from Coniston. After ½ mile, in hamlet of Waterhead at edge of lake, turn up track to Thwaite Cottage. Dunmail Studio is building at end of slate track to left, just before cottage. Parking in field.)

Frank Shaw works in the greens and greys of Lakeland slate, cutting and shaping the blocks into garden ornaments, clock cases, lamps and barometers in a tiny workshop on the shore of Coniston Water. He also carves monumental headstones, but his most popular works are the made-to-measure fireplaces he builds in a variety of tones from the light greens of Broughton Moor and Tilberthwaite stone, through the darker greens of Honister, to the middle tones of slate from the quarries on the Old Man of Coniston.

Open daily, 8 a.m.–9 p.m., except for mealtimes.

GRASMERE
Map ref: Bd
Chris Reekie and Sons Ltd, The Old Coach House, Stock Lane, Grasmere.
Tel. Grasmere 221

(From A591 Ambleside–Keswick road, fork left at sign for Grasmere village. Workshop is on left-hand side of road on entering village. Private car park at rear, or public car park 50 yds back towards main road.)

The old hand-loom in a corner of the workshop is the one on which Chris Reekie served his apprenticeship in his native Selkirk, in Scotland. Although it is now almost 100 years old, it is still used by the Reekie family to turn out a range of brushed woollen rugs. They also make hand-woven skirt lengths and jackets, coats, capes and suits in mohair. All these are on display in the showroom, together with other craft goods by local workers.

Open daily, 9–5.30; but 10–4.30 on Sun. in winter.

HALLBANKGATE
Map ref: Ce
Frank Mercer (Hand-loom weaver), Eastern Cottage, Hallbankgate, Brampton.
Tel. Hallbankgate 309
(Follow A689 eastwards from Brampton to village of Hallbankgate. Take right fork past Belted Will Inn. After ½ mile, turn right along track in front of terrace of houses. Follow track for another ½ mile past lone cottage and gate. Eastern Cottage is first house at far end. Parking limited.)

On his loom Frank Mercer makes fine-quality cloth and tweed for men's suits, sports jackets and ties, ladies' clothes and table mats. He turns out between 130 and 140 yds of cloth a year in varying weights and patterns, some traditional and others of his own design.

Open Mon.–Fri., 9–5. Advisable to telephone first.

KENDAL
Map ref: Cc
Lene Bragger, Underfell, 17 Greenside, Kendal.
Tel. Kendal 23769
(Follow one-way system through Kendal and turn left at traffic lights opposite town hall. In about ¾ mile, after a green, turn up third drive on left. Parking outside house.)

Lene Bragger is an expert in batik and silk-screen printing. She produces batik designs on silk dresses and shirts, kimonos, and even on soft shoes; and hand-prints children's clothes, smocks and dresses. She also makes batik paintings, landscapes and plant studies.

Open by appointment to visitors who are genuinely interested.

KENDAL
Map ref: Cc
Susan Foster (Weaver), 9 Windermere Road, Kendal.
Tel. Kendal 26494
(Follow A5284 out of Kendal. House is on right-hand side on corner of Caroline Street, next to Kendal Green Hospital. Limited parking in nearby roads.)

The studio, in a downstairs room of Susan Foster's house, is devoted entirely to weaving. In the centre stands a small floor loom on which she weaves rugs, cushions, bags and an unusual series of wall-hangings, using wool from local sheep, including Jacob, Herdwick and Swaledale. One of her distinctive lines is a range of circular wall-pictures, woven on metal rings, in subjects ranging from Lakeland scenes to elegant abstracts. Since these do not need a loom (the metal ring provides its own frame to carry the warp and weft threads) they make an ideal introduction to weaving for beginners, and visitors can buy kits containing everything they need to make their own woven picture. For those who want to explore the craft further, Susan Foster runs a series of courses on spinning, frame weaving and loom weaving.

Open Sept.–July, Wed., Fri. and Sat., 10–5. Open Mon.–Sat., 10–5, during Aug. Other times by appointment.

KENDAL
Map ref: Cc
Jan Goodey (Jewellery Workshop), The Brewery Arts Centre, 122a Highgate, Kendal.
Tel. Kendal 25133

Opening times and other details may change. Check by telephone before making a special journey.

281

Map ref: Cc

Museum of Lakeland Life and Industry

KENDAL, CUMBRIA

Combining the 'convenience of a town house' with the 'stillness of rural retirement' is how *The Lonsdale Magazine* of 1821 described Abbot Hall. It has changed little since then. The house, which was designed in 1759 by John Carr, of York – the leading northern architect of the day – is now an art gallery; and the stable block is a museum.

In 1973 the Museum of Lakeland Life and Industry won the first 'Museum of the Year' award. Exhibits commemorating some of the trades of Kendal include a 19th-century hand-loom with a flying shuttle, a Columbia printing press once used for producing the *Westmorland Gazette*, and a length of material similar to Kendal green. This type of felted cloth, which was said to be impervious to arrows, was well enough known in Britain to rate a mention in Shakespeare's *Henry IV*. A half-made violin is one of the most recent artefacts; it came from the workshop of Bert Smith, the Coniston craftsman who has made violins for such virtuosi as Yehudi Menuhin.

Today, Kendal is the home of the large 'K' shoe-manufacturing firm. Tools from a clogger's shop are a reminder of the trade's earlier days, when there were nine small makers of boots and shoes in the town.

Other attractions include a reconstructed blacksmith's hearth, period rooms, a display of agricultural implements, and mining equipment from Cumbria's industrial past. The century-old 'spar box', or 'grotto' was made by a miner and his wife from rock crystals, as a parlour decoration.

Abbot Hall, Kendal, Cumbria. Tel. Kendal 22464.

Open Mon.–Fri., 10.30–5; Sat. and Sun., 2–5. Charge for admission.

WHEELWRIGHT'S SHOP *Tools that belonged to G. M. Jennings of Kendal, and a partly completed wheel, are displayed in the museum.*

This is still a working water-mill, a rare survivor of the many that once ground locally grown wheat. Visitors can see the water-wheel turning, and watch the mill machinery at work producing stone-ground wholewheat flour. Grain products produced by the mill are on sale.

Open on certain afternoons from Easter to end Oct. As these vary from year to year, visitors should write or telephone for details.

NORTH STAINMORE Map ref: Cd
Ian and Rhona Mathews, Local Stone Products, Dowgill Head, North Stainmore, Kirkby Stephen.
Tel. Brough 465
(Following the A66 eastwards past hamlet of North Stainmore, turn right after 1 mile down narrow road leading downhill. Take second entrance to left. Dowgill Head is at far end of road. Parking in farmyard.)

Greenish-grey Lakeland slate is used by the Mathews to make costume jewellery. Pieces of slate are cut and shaped into discs and ovals, then inset in metal to make ear-rings, cuff-links, pendants and brooches. Limestone is cut and polished to show the delicate tracery of fossils, such as the stalks of the sea-lily.

Open by appointment Apr.–Oct.

SEDBERGH Map ref: Cc
Pennine Tweeds, Farfield Mill, Sedbergh.
Tel. Sedbergh 20558
(Follow signposts for Hawes from centre of Sedbergh. After leaving town, pass Oakdene Hotel on left, then turn left at sign for Pennine Tweeds down long drive to group of mill buildings at end.)

Occupying one floor of a Victorian mill complex which used to make horse blankets, the company's three powered looms now make a wide range of tweeds, mohair and woollen blankets, rugs and lengths of cloth for making up into tailored clothing. Visitors can see the weaving in progress and choose from finished tweeds and mohairs in the mill's display area.

Open Mon.–Fri., 9.30–12 and 1.30–5; Sat. 9.30–12.

SHAP Map ref: Cd
Shap Pottery, 1 Central Buildings, Shap.
Tel. Shap 412
(Follow old main road through Shap village. Pottery is on corner of road signposted 'Crosby Ravensworth'. Parking in nearby streets or on edge of road.)

Shap Pottery, hidden away in an old corner shop, consists of a combined display area and workshop. The pots that visitors will see being made vary from standard ranges of domestic slipware to models of Lakeland houses and farm buildings in a semi-porcelain finish, and a series of cartoon caricatures of steam-engines.

Open in summer, Tues.–Sat., 9–5. Open in winter by appointment.

STAINTON Map ref: Cc
William Johnston (Restorer/cabinet maker), Field End Barn, Stainton, Kendal.
Tel. Sedgwick 60581
(Following A6 north from Carnforth, turn right at Milnthorpe on to B6385. After crossing over A591 dual carriageway, turn left, signposted 'Stainton'. One mile further on, look for sign of wood-worker on right, by entrance to Field End. Limited parking beside barn.)

Mr Johnston works on antique furniture, repairing the ravages of time, neglect or accident and tackling anything from a Georgian bureau, which arrived in pieces on the back of a cattle wagon, to a long case clock which had been rescued from a fire. He also makes new furniture, but using as far as possible the methods and the materials of the 18th century and the styles of Sheraton or Hepplewhite.

Workshop open Mon.–Fri., 8.30–6, by appointment.

(At southern end of Highgate, set back from road. Look for Brewery Arts Centre sign over a gateway next to the Royal Insurance offices. Parking in nearby car parks.)

A resident craftswoman at the Arts Centre, Jan Goodey makes 'one-off' pieces of jewellery for galleries in London and for customers countrywide. She works in silver and gold, with other metals chosen mainly for their colour effects. These include various coloured golds, copper, and more unusual metals such as tantalum and niobium, which give a range of brilliant peacock hues.

Jan Goodey has recently formed a partnership called 'Brewers' with Melanie Sproat, a silversmith also resident at the Arts Centre.

Open Mon.–Fri., 8–6; also some Sat. and Sun. opening. By appointment only.

KENDAL Map ref: Cc
Kendal Studio Pottery, 2/3 Wildman Street, Kendal.
Tel. Kendal 23291
(Wildman Street is on the main A6 road through Kendal. Follow one-way system, and turn right by railway station. Pottery is long, low building opposite Castle Dairy.)

The Studio Pottery is housed in a rambling old building called Sleddall Hall, built about 1600 as the manor house of the hamlet of Doodleshire – quite distinct and separate from Kendal across the river. The pottery turns out a variety of Lakeland domestic stoneware, including several unusual pieces. These range from salt jars in a shape that has been traditional since Roman times, to pomanders, lamp bases decorated with wood-ash glazes and tall and elegant bread crocks.

Open Mon.–Sat., 10.30–1 and 3–7.

KENDAL Map ref: Cc
The Silversmith (A. F. Kelly), 11 Lowther Street, Kendal.
Tel. Kendal 24547

(Lowther Street runs eastwards along the south side of the town hall, which is situated on Highgate in the centre of Kendal. Parking in nearby off-street car parks.)

A standard shopfront in a narrow Kendal side-street is the surprising setting for a workshop where rare and beautiful articles in silver, from cuff-links to coffee pots, take shape at an open bench. From the detailed sketches and drawings which form the basis of each commission, to the painstaking work itself, the whole process may be viewed by visitors.

Open daily except Thur. and Sun., 9.30–12 and 1–5.30.

KENTMERE Map ref: Bd
Saw Mill Cottage, Kentmere.
Tel. Staveley 821621
(From Staveley, on main road from Kendal to Windermere, take road up valley to Kentmere. After 2 miles look out for works entrance on left, and sign for Saw Mill Cottage. Turn into works approach, then through left-hand gate and down drive to pottery. Limited parking.)

Visitors to Saw Mill Cottage can browse round shelves of earthenware – coffee sets, tea sets, jugs, mugs and beer and cider sets – and, through windows, look into the workshop and watch the whole pottery process. The tableware is finished in a variety of styles. Some of the pieces have a delicate porcelain finish, with panels bearing floral patterns stamped into the clay; others are embossed with Victorian seals.

Open daily, but telephone before visiting.

KESWICK Map ref: Bd
Lakeland Stone Craft Ltd, 13 High Hill, Keswick.
Tel. Keswick 72994
(Follow road for Cockermouth from centre of Keswick. Where road crosses a bridge, Lakeland Stone Craft is behind the small white cottage on the left at the end of a

greystone terrace. Parking in yard behind cottage.)

Lakeland stone is cut and shaped by Lakeland Stone Craft to make such varied objects as fireplaces, name and number-plates for houses, memorial panels, bird-tables and sundials. Shaping the stone is noisy, dusty work, but carving the finer patterns and inscriptions can be fascinating to watch. Small items are on sale in the showroom.

Open Mon.–Fri., 8–4.30. Appointment necessary for parties.

LINSTOCK Map ref: Be
Carlisle Pottery, Close House, Linstock, Carlisle.
Tel. Carlisle 26833
(Close House is at the end of a track from the centre of the village of Linstock. Travelling from Carlisle, turn right alongside village green and look out for pottery sign. Parking in pottery yard.)

The pottery is made in a studio set up in an old barn attached to Close House, a farmhouse that dates from 1720. The wide range of traditional earthenware includes salt jars, goblets, coffee sets and a steadily increasing range of small animals, such as mice, frogs, hippos, elephants, owls and rabbits. A popular mug has a pottery frog in the bottom. The sudden appearance of the realistic frog as the drinker drained his mug was believed by the Victorians to be an effective cure for hiccoughs.

Studio open Mon.–Sat., 10–4. Shop and showroom open Mon.–Fri. until 7.

LITTLE SALKELD Map ref: Cd
The Watermill, Little Salkeld, Penrith.
Tel. Langwathby 523
(From centre of Langwathby, on A686 north-east of Penrith, follow road northwards to Little Salkeld. Mill is at bottom of hill where road crosses bridge on approach to village. Parking behind mill.)

STAVELEY Map ref: Bc
Peter Hall Woodcraft, Danes Road, Staveley,
nr Kendal.
Tel. Kendal 821633
(Workshop is on left-hand side of A591
Kendal–Windermere road on leaving
Staveley. Parking in grounds of workshop.)

*A cabinet maker in the old style, working
principally in such timbers as oak and
mahogany, Peter Hall is at ease with both
traditional and modern designs. The wood he
uses is stored for several years before being
further dried in a dehumidifier. To make even a
modern hi-fi cabinet, he still fashions the
drawers with hand-cut dovetails and bottoms
grooved into slips. Other furniture includes oak
dining chairs and oak chests with hand-carved
rails and panels. Mr Hall also restores antique
pieces.*

Open Mon.–Fri., 8.30–5; Sat. by
appointment.

TEMPLE SOWERBY Map ref: Cd
Newbiggin Forge, Newbiggin Hall,
Newbiggin, Temple Sowerby, Penrith.
Tel. Kirkby Thore 574 (Newbiggin Hall)
(Forge is in grounds of Newbiggin Hall, in
centre of village of Newbiggin which is near
Temple Sowerby. Parking at forge and in
village.)

*The forge stands next to the mellow sandstone
towers of Newbiggin Hall. The ironwork is
appropriate to the setting, for the smith, Mr
Miller, specialises in baroque decorative
ironwork. Wrought-iron gates, screens, railings
and balustrades are built to order, using
extravagent scrolls, leaves and curlicues in
classic, traditional patterns.*

Open all year by appointment, Mon.–Sat.,
10–6.

ULVERSTON Map ref: Bc
Cumbria Crystal Ltd, Lightburn Road,
Ulverston.
Tel. Ulverston 54400
(Follow A590 Barrow road westwards
round edge of town. After roundabout, turn
left at traffic lights into Victoria Road.
Factory is first left, behind church in

Lightburn Road. Parking in nearby streets.)

*In a small glassworks that was once the town's
sheep and cattle market, lead-crystal glass is
made by hand in the traditional way. Visitors
can watch the whole process, then study the
range of finished glass in the showroom. The
most unusual designs are reproductions of the
work of William and Mary Beilby, who
pioneered hand-enamelling on glass in
Newcastle upon Tyne in the 18th century.
These compositions of trees and landscapes,
leaves and fruit, are reproductions based on the
originals, using enamels, and the glasses are
decorated with 24 carat gold rims.*

Glassworks open Mon.–Fri., 8–4.
Showroom open Mon.–Fri., 9–5.30; Sat.,
9–12.

ULVERSTON Map ref: Bc
Wendy Todd Textiles, Corn Mill Galleries,
Town Mill, Ulverston.
Tel. Ulverston 54600
(From Market Square in centre of town,
follow King Street northwards 200 yds to
Kings Arms. Turn left. Town Mill is stone
building facing. Parking in Gill car park
beyond mill.)

*Town Mill is a 17th-century corn-mill where
the original water-wheel has been restored and
put back into operation, driving the wooden
gears to turn the sets of grinding stones. In this
spectacular setting there is a large workshop
where Wendy Todd hand-prints textiles: ties,
scarves, day and evening clothes, cushions,
bedspreads and table linen. There is also a
gallery where regular craft exhibitions are held,
as well as a display and sales area for the work
of other craftsmen – jewellers, glassmakers,
potters, weavers, embroiderers and painters.*

Open Tues.–Sat., 9.30–5.30.

WHITEHAVEN Map ref: Ad
Whitehaven Workshop, 48–49 Roper
Street, Whitehaven.
Tel. Whitehaven 63310
(Roper Street runs south-east from Market
Place and Tourist Information Office, close
to old South Harbour. Parking in nearby
streets.)

*Pottery and hand-printed fabrics are made on
the premises and are sold along with other local
crafts. Visitors can watch the pottery-making
in progress in the workshop attached to the
shop.*

Open 10–5.30, except Wed. and Sun.

WINTON Map ref: Cd
Langrigg Pottery, Winton, Kirkby Stephen.
Tel. Kirkby Stephen 71542
(Pottery faces the more westerly of two
short lanes entering Winton from the
A685, north of Kirkby Stephen. Parking in
pottery yard.)

*The pottery is situated in an old hay barn.
There are coffee mugs, bowls, jugs, plates,
casseroles, and a wide range of plant pots with
matching bases for indoor plants. Visitors can
watch whichever part of the process is going on
at the time – throwing, turning, glazing,
decorating and so on. Finished pots are on sale
in a display area in the studio.*

Open all year, Tues.–Sat., 9–5, and at most
times in summer.

MUSEUMS

HAWKSHEAD Map ref: Bc
Hawkshead Courthouse Museum,
Hawkshead.
Tel. Kendal 22464 (No. of Abbot Hall)

*Before the dissolution of the monastery in
1537, the monks of Furness Abbey used the
room above the arched entrance as a manor
court. Today, it contains displays which
introduce visitors to the area and encourage
them to go out and look for themselves.
Exhibits range from sheep-shearing tools to a
piano which once belonged to Beatrix Potter.
Coppice industries, such as besom making, are
well illustrated; as is the making of swills –
baskets of hazel and oak.*

Open May–Sept., Tues.–Fri. and Sun., 2–5.
Closed Mon. and Sat. Charge for admission.

KENDAL Map ref: Cc
Museum of Lakeland Life and Industry.
(See panel on p. 282)

GREATER MANCHESTER

DIDSBURY Map ref: Ca
Studio Pottery, 39 Dalston Drive, Didsbury.
Tel. Manchester 445 9200
(Follow Wilmslow road from city centre to
Didsbury. Go through village and take left
turn into Didsbury Park. Dalston Drive is
second turning on right. Parking in side
roads.)

*Rhian Templeman's individual style of eggshell
finishes and pastel shades attracts attention at
exhibitions and in local craft shops, but visitors
who would like to see both decorative and
domestic pots being made can visit the studio.*

Open Mar.–July and Sept.–Dec., Mon.,
Thur. and Fri., 9–3.30. Appointment
necessary.

LEVENSHULME Map ref: Ca
Gordon Cooke (Porcelain), 2 Limefield
Terrace, Levenshulme.
Tel. Manchester 225 5349
(Directions will be given when making an
appointment. Parking in side roads.)

*Gordon Cooke makes unusual porcelain in the
cellar workshop of his Victorian house in a
quiet corner of suburban Manchester. He builds
up his elegant plaques, bottles and boxes from
sheets of clay. These he decorates with metallic
oxides, which he first brushes on to the clay
before scoring and scratching the surface to
produce a varied texture. The coloured clay is
then assembled into shape before firing.*

Open at most times by appointment.

MANCHESTER Map ref: Ca
Andrew Coomber and Kathryn Wantling
(Jewellery), St Margaret's Chambers,
5 Newton Street, Piccadilly.
Tel. Manchester 236 0589
(Newton Street runs north-east from
eastern corner of Piccadilly, in centre of
Manchester. St Margaret's Chambers are
close to Piccadilly end of street. Parking
limited to meters in nearby side streets.)

*Much of the work of Andrew Coomber and
Kathryn Wantling involves batch-produced
silver jewellery, but they also make individual
items to order. Visitors are welcome to see the
range of finished jewellery and also to watch
work in progress.*

Open Mon.–Fri., 9.30–5, by appointment.

MARPLE Map ref: Ca
Bees Pottery and Crafts, 36 Town Street,
Marple Bridge, Stockport.
Tel. Manchester 449 8998
(From Marple, follow signs for Marple
Bridge or Glossop. At bottom of hill, cross
bridge over River Goyt, and turn right at T-
junction into Town Street. Bees is on left-
hand side. Limited parking in Town Street,
or in nearby car parks.)

*Here, overlooking the River Goyt, stands Bees
– named after its proprietors, Pru Barron and
Ben Bates. The craft shop offers a wide range of
pottery, prints, paintings, jewellery and
textiles. In the workshops, visitors can watch
stoneware pottery being made (by
appointment), and will also see the painstaking
care that goes into the cutting and stitching of
patchwork cushions and quilts.*

Open all year, Mon., Tues., Thur., Fri. and
Sat., 10–5.

STOCKPORT Map ref: Ca
Kerrand Pottery, 2 Portland Grove, Heaton
Moor, Stockport.
Tel. Manchester 442 8024
(Portland Grove is a side street off Heaton
Moor Road, the main shopping street of the
Stockport suburb of Heaton Moor. Limited
parking; some spaces on main road, others
in side streets.)

*This unassuming craft centre hides at the top of
a narrow flight of stairs behind a butcher's
shop. In one room a leather-worker makes*

Map ref: Ab

The Manx Open-Air Folk Museum

CREGNEISH, ISLE OF MAN

Prevailing winds, whistling up from the Calf Sound,
frequently buffet Cregneish – a straggling village where,
for centuries before the opening of the museum in 1938,
crofters won a hard living from the acid upland soil and
from the sea. This type of settlement, which consisted of
half-a-dozen small farmers and their families, is a rare
survivor from the Celtic past. Within living memory the
community formed a small world of its own, with Manx
Gaelic as its mother-tongue.

The cottage of Harry Kelly, who died in 1934, is a fine
example of the squat, sturdy and simple abodes of the
crofters. In the garden, herbs that were once used as cures
for illness are still grown – vervain for fits, comfrey for
sprains and bruises, feverfew for earache, and mugwort to
ward off evil spirits. Inside, the furniture, the spinning-
wheel, the turned wooden bowls and the horn beakers
were all made locally. The ruined crofts, which pepper the
uplands of the Isle of Man, bear silent witness to the
passing of a way of life. It is fortunate, therefore, that the
museum has also preserved the little group of thatched
stone buildings which, together with about 30 acres of
arable fields and grazing, comprised the Karran farm.

Traditional crafts are brought back to life as well.
Despite the fact that there are not many days in the year
when it is calm enough in Cregneish for thatching, the
museum preserves this dying craft. There is a recon-

CROFTER'S COTTAGE *In the garden of Harry Kelly's cottage at
Cregneish, herbs to treat many ills grow.*

structed smithy, and a turner's shed where the tools and
treadle-lathe were used, in particular, for making
spinning-wheels. In the loom-shed of the weaver's cottage
a hand-loom has been preserved. Demonstrations of
spinning, weaving and the smith's craft are given weekly
throughout the season.

Cregneish, Isle of Man. Tel. Douglas 5522.

Open May–Sept., Mon.–Sat., 10–1 and 2–5. Also Sun., 2–5.
Charge for admission.

Opening times and other details may change. Check by telephone before making a special journey.

283

personalised cases for cameras and radios, as well as hand-tooled belts and bags. In another is a pottery, turning out domestic stoneware and earthenware. Evening and weekend courses are given in such crafts as pottery, spinning and weaving.

Open Thur., Fri. and Sat., 10–5.

ISLE OF MAN

BALLAMODHA   Map ref: Ab
Shebeg Gallery, nr Ballasalla.
Tel. Castletown 3497
(From Douglas, take the A5 to Ballasalla – about 8 miles. Turn right on to A34 for Ballamodha. Pottery is 300 yds on left after right turn on to A4. Parking on premises.)

John Harper, a farmer's son, has channelled his agricultural interest into making porcelain models of cattle. Over the years he has so perfected the craft that a number of his models are now approved by breed societies, and he supplies them for the British Friesian Society's silver award. They are also given regularly as prizes at Danish farm shows. John Harper and his wife Patricia also model a variety of agricultural and rural characters, the most popular being a shepherd and his dog.

Open Mon.–Fri., 9–5.30. Closed for two weeks at Christmas.

FOXDALE   Map ref: Ab
Foxdale Craft Centre Limited, Foxdale House, Foxdale.
Tel. St John's 293 and 353
(From Douglas, take A24 for 6 miles to Foxdale. Craft Centre is on right just before junction with A4. Parking on site.)

Foxdale Craft Centre offers instruction and design services in a remarkably wide range of crafts. Products of local workshops are on sale to visitors. The activities include calligraphy, cane and basketwork, ceramics, drawing and painting, pewter and copper work, graphics, embroidery, spinning and weaving, wood carving and upholstery. The centre is housed in a 150-year-old barn attached to the stone-walled house where the Captain, or manager, of a nearby lead and silver mine used to live.

Open daily, 10–4.30.

GLENMAYE   Map ref: Ab
Glen Maye Pottery, Waterfall House, Glenmaye, Peel.
Tel. Peel 2647
(From Peel, take Dalby road south for 3 miles to Glenmaye. Halfway down steep hill, turn right into 'Waterfall' car park. Pottery is next to pub. Parking outside.)

The individual styles of the two potters at Glenmaye account for the refreshing variety of pieces on offer. Marjorie Cringle concentrates on the traditional shapes of Mexican peasant pottery, with Mexican Indian decorations. Cheryl Wilde makes sculptural porcelain, together with functional stoneware engraved with Celtic designs or the natural shapes of grasses, reeds and flowers.

Open Sun.–Thur., 1–5. Appointment advisable in winter.

JURBY WEST   Map ref: Ab
Kelly Souvenirs Ltd, Jurby.
Tel. Sulby 7506
(Take A13 from Ramsey to Sandygate crossroads – about 7 miles. Turn right for Jurby aerodrome, where workshop is located. Parking alongside.)

About 20 years ago, it occurred to Ewan Kelly that local traditions were in danger of being forgotten. Souvenirs were being imported and not enough made of the island's own colourful heritage – its tradition, folklore and language. To help redress the balance he began making thatched-cottage musical boxes which play traditional Manx tunes. Individually thatched, each musical box is a miniature replica of the old-style Manx cottages. Now, he also makes

cottage furniture from local sycamore.

Open Mon.–Sat., 8.30–5.30. Also open Sun., Apr.–Oct.

KIRK MICHAEL   Map ref: Ab
Barnacle Products, Laurel Dene, Rhencullen, Kirk Michael.
Tel. Kirk Michael 363
(Seven miles from Peel on the A3. Workshop is ½ mile north of Kirk Michael, on seaward side of road. Parking in driveway, or on main road 30 yds south of property.)

John Place works mainly to commission making custom-built furniture, but he also restores antique furniture and clocks, cuts and facets gems, and fashions fine jewellery with them. He also provides a consultancy service on matters as diverse as precision instruments for machinery, and problems associated with furniture design.

Open on weekdays, 10–6, but an appointment is preferred.

LAXEY   Map ref: Ab
The Mariners, South Cape, Laxey.
Tel. Laxey 781170
(From Douglas, take Laxey road. Just past Fairy Cottage, fork left to first bungalow on left. Parking in drive.)

Spinning-wheels and Lancashire spindleback chairs, as well as table lamps, boxes and bowls, are among the items created in the garden workshop of wood turner Mike Sainsbury. All his work, including polishing, takes place on the lathe. Visitors can buy finished pieces on the spot.

Open 10–4 most days. Appointment necessary.

PORT ST MARY   Map ref: Ab
Ballabrara Arts, 2 The Promenade, Port St Mary.
Tel. Port St Mary 832656
(Port St Mary is at south-western tip of island, 8½ miles from Douglas. Workshop is at western end of Promenade. Parking near by.)

Ancient Manx crosses have been the inspiration behind the unusual craft of Maureen Richards. In her combined workshop and shop she can be seen carving the maurite, Manx slate and serpentine stone into the intricate and historic patterns. Whole crosses, pendants, rings, brooches, cuff-links, spoons and key-rings are on sale.

Open all year, Mon.–Sat.

RAMSEY   Map ref: Ab
Quayside Pottery and Craft Centre, 16 West Quay, Ramsey.
Tel. Ramsey 812581
(On quayside, opposite swing bridge. Parking on quay, or in town car parks.)

Here, Roger McDonald and his two assistants produce slip-cast and hand-thrown carafes and goblets, salt and pepper sets, coffee sets and plant-pot holders. Some of the slip-cast ware has a golden glaze, with a red-brown iron-oxide patterning; other pieces are given a black-brown glaze, with the glaze scraped off to create the pattern.

Open daily, May–Aug., 9–5.30; weekdays only Sept.–Apr.

ST JOHN'S   Map ref: Ab
Tynwald Craft Centre, St John's.
Tel. St John's 213
(Take A20 from Peel. After 3 miles, turn right on to A4. Take first turning right on to minor road, signposted Tynwald Mill. Parking next to premises.)

Close to St John's National Park and less than a mile from Tynwald, where the Manx Parliament sits, is an old single-storey woollen-mill in an enclosed river valley. During the 1970s the mill was renovated, the existing machinery modernised, and production methods re-thought. Since 1975 other craftsmen have

joined the establishment to fill the space created by modernisation. Crafts now include glass blowing, doll making, silversmithing, pottery and screen printing.

Open Mon.–Sat., 9–5.30. Appointment necessary for large parties.

SULBY   Map ref: Ab
Celtic Craft Centre, The Barn, Tholt-y-Will, Sulby Glen, Lezayre.
Tel. Sulby 7447
(From Douglas, take A18 north for 7½ miles to junction at Bungalow Tram Station with A14. Turn left on to A14 for 3 miles to Tholt-y-Will. Craft Centre on right, past hotel. Parking near by.)

In the heart of the island's largest glen is a slate-roofed, stone-built barn. Here, Juan Vernon and his two sons make enamelled pendants, brooches, key-rings and necklaces decorated with Celtic designs. They also spin, using a hand-built wheel and wool from the rare Manx Loughton sheep. Other locally made craft goods are sold at the Centre.

Open daily, July–Aug., 10.30–5.30. Weekends only, June and Sept. Evening visits for groups can be arranged by telephone.

MUSEUMS

CASTLETOWN   Map ref: Ab
The Nautical Museum, Castletown.
Tel. Douglas 5522

In 1791, Captain George Quayle, a member of a prominent Castletown family, enlarged his boathouse in order to accommodate Peggy, his schooner-rigged yacht. Her sailing days over, she lay there for more than a century, undisturbed and almost forgotten. Now that Peggy has been restored and the boathouse established as a museum, visitors have the rare opportunity of seeing a small coastal craft typical of the period. Other exhibits illustrate the island's nautical life in the days of sail, together with its fishing industry. A sailmaker's workshop has been reconstructed in the loft of the old boathouse.

Open May–Sept., Mon.–Sat., 10–1 and 2–5; also Sun., 2–5. Charge for admission.

CREGNEISH   Map ref: Ab
The Manx Open-Air Folk Museum.
(See panel on p. 283)

DOUGLAS   Map ref: Ab
The Manx Museum, Crellin's Hill, Douglas.
Tel. Douglas 5522

The Manx Museum illustrates all aspects of Manx history, archaeology and natural history, but in particular its well-displayed collections of folk life illustrate a variety of local crafts and industries such as weaving, farming, fishing, mining and dairying. The displays include reconstructions of a farmhouse, a barn, a dairy and a fisherman's shed.

Open Mon.–Sat., 10–5.

LANCASHIRE

APPLEY BRIDGE   Map ref: Cb
Orbit Crafts, 23–25 Appley Lane North, Appley Bridge, nr Wigan.
Tel. Appley Bridge 2249
(On main road in village between railway line and bridge over River Douglas. Limited parking in front of garage next door.)

Orbit Crafts hand-make high-quality furniture and a variety of other wooden articles, from crossbows to miniature long case clocks. Most striking of all are the workshop's beautiful wooden tables, ranging from a dining table with four different size combinations (using removable sections) to a magnificent round table in mahogany and rosewood.

Open Mon.–Sat., 9–5, by appointment.

BOLTON   Map ref: Cb
Edith Norris Stained Glass, Weighbridge Studio, 12a Ulleswater Street, Bolton.
Tel. Bolton 26777
(Ulleswater Street is off Blackburn Road, leading north from town centre. Studio is at far end, in red-brick building.)

A genuine interest in stained glass is needed to make a visit worthwhile, for it is necessary to write for an appointment. But those who do arrange a visit can see all the intricacies of a craft that goes back to the building of the great cathedrals. They can watch the drawing, the cutting, the painting, the firing and the leading of the memorial and heraldic panels that Edith Norris fashions with loving care. She is training young men in glass painting and firing, and her work is seen in local churches.

Open to visitors Mon. only, by written appointment.

CATON   Map ref: Cc
The Lunesdale Pottery, Farrier's Yard, Caton, nr Lancaster.
Tel. Caton 770284
(Pottery is behind Ship Hotel in main street of village. Parking in front of nearby shops.)

Audrey and Barry Gregson's highly individual work includes delicate bowls made from as many as half-a-dozen types of clay – ranging from smooth porcelain to rough fireclay – and inlaid with patterns resembling the rocks of the Lune Valley and nearby Morecambe Bay. Other mixtures of clays are moulded into pebble shapes and built up into abstract sculptures. Special hollow forms are pierced with holes so that, lit from inside, they glow vividly and splash patterned light on walls and ceilings.

Open most of the year, including weekends, but appointment advisable.

FENCE   Map ref: Cb
Slate Age (Fence) Ltd, Fence Gate, Fence, nr Burnley.
Tel. Burnley 66952
(Workshop is at west end of village, opposite Fence Gate Restaurant.)

This one-time farm houses a workshop where slabs of green Westmorland slate are fashioned into articles that range from simple ashtrays, book-ends, pen-stands and plaques to more elaborate lamps and pendulum clock cases. The workshop also makes name-plates and decorative panels for houses and public buildings, together with shaped blocks for making into doorsteps or fireplaces. Visitors can see the various stages in progress, from cutting the slate (under water to reduce the dust) to the hand-finishing and engraving.

Open Mon.–Fri., 8–4.30; Sat., 8–4.

LANCASTER   Map ref: Bc
Hornsea Pottery Co. Ltd, Wyresdale Road, Lancaster.
Tel. Lancaster 68444
(Follow 'Hornsea Pottery' signs from city centre along road for Trough of Bowland. Pottery is approximately 1 mile from city centre. Parking on premises.)

This is not so much a craft workshop as a factory in a garden setting. Even so, it is a splendid spot for a day out, with guided tours of the production lines, and a shop where 'seconds' are sold at bargain prices. The main interest lies in several ranges of high-quality pottery decorated with a variety of designs which are printed or modelled in relief.

Open daily, 10–5 (10–6 during July and Aug.), including Bank Holidays. Closed Christmas week.

RIMINGTON   Map ref: Cb
Holme Lea Crafts (Leatherwork), Holme Lea, Rimington, nr Clitheroe.
Tel. Gisburn 423
(From Chatburn take Downham road. Turn left at signpost to Rimington. Craft shop is in main street. Parking at roadside.)

Behind a conventional shopfront is a leather

workshop where a wide range of goods is made – from key fobs and bracelets to belts and handbags. Elaborate patterning, together with careful use of different dyes and colouring inks, produces some beautiful decorative effects.

Open Wed.–Sun., 10 a.m. to dusk.

RIVINGTON   Map ref: Cb
'Windy Rannets' (Jewellery), Horrobin Lane, Anderton, Chorley.
Tel. Adlington 481815
(Directions will be given when telephoning for an appointment.)

A wide range of jewellery is made in a workshop housed in one of the old buildings attached to this thatched farmhouse. Elisabeth Batley's work is of individual design, using gold and silver, mother-of-pearl, and many precious and semi-precious stones including diamonds, rubies, sapphires and opals. Visitors can watch the various processes, and see finished pieces.

Opening hours vary. By appointment only.

SILVERDALE   Map ref: Bc
Ingleton Crafts, Main Street, Ingleton, nr Carnforth.
Tel. Ingleton 41352
(From A65 follow signs for village centre. Main Street starts at Bridge Inn, and craft shop is opposite the church.)

In this small craft shop in a narrow, winding village street, visitors can see pottery being made on the spot, and there are changing displays of individual craftsmen's work during the summer. The shop stocks leatherwork, paper sculptures, walking sticks with deer-horn handles, and pottery figures and animals.

Open Tues.–Sun., 10–12 and 1–6, in summer. Open Tues.–Sat., 10–12 and 1–5, and Sun. 12–5, in winter.

SILVERDALE   Map ref: Bc
Wolf House Gallery and Studio, Gibraltar, Silverdale, Carnforth.
Tel. Silverdale 701405
(Follow signs for Silverdale, and turn left at signpost for gallery. Parking in yard.)

In the old shippon (cowshed) of this former working farm is a gallery containing work from craftsmen all over the country. Some is made on the spot, for there is a working pottery in the old dairy, turning out earthenware decorated with patterns inspired by the surrounding countryside, for example, brambles and apples. Items made elsewhere include unusual plant holders built up from stained-glass panels, screen-printed coloured-glass pictures, leather belts, bags and bellows, and hand-carved hardwood birds. Courses and demonstrations are given by local craftsmen.

Open all year: June to mid-Sept., Tues.–Sun., 10.30–1 and 2–5.30; mid-Sept. to Christmas, and Easter to June, open Tues.–Fri. afternoons and all day weekends. New Year to Easter, weekends only.

SIMONSTONE   Map ref: Cb
Trapp Forge, Simonstone, nr Burnley.
Tel. Padiham 71025
(Take road from A678 to Simonstone, and follow road through village. Forge is on left-hand side just below Higher Trapp Hotel.)

Ron Carter's traditional wrought ironwork ranges from small domestic items, such as door-catches, fire irons and toasting forks – some decorated with a ram's head, based on the extravagant curled horns of the local 'Lonk' breed – to massive creations such as a crown-of-thorns chandelier for a local church. Visitors are welcome to watch the work – and even to try their hand, under supervision.

Open daily.

MUSEUM

BURNLEY   Map ref: Cb
Museum of Local Crafts and Industries, Towneley Hall, Burnley.
Tel. Burnley 24213

In the early 1970s, Burnley made a conscious effort to abandon its old mill-town image and move into the future. At the same time, the Museum of Local Crafts and Industries was established to preserve the memory of the town's vanishing craftsmen and declining textile and coal-mining industries. As a result, exhibits include the tools of the last signwriter, brush maker, woodcarver and oatcake maker to have worked in the area. A small clogger's workshop is a reminder of the clogs worn by mill workers as protection against damp and draughty mill floors.

Open Easter to Oct., Mon.–Fri., 10–5.30; open in winter, Mon.–Fri., 10–5.15. Also open Sun., 12–5, all year.

MERSEYSIDE

HESWALL   Map ref: Ba
Heswell Crafts, The Old Smithy, Village Road, Lower Heswall, Wirral.
Tel. Liverpool 342 1817
(Follow A540 to centre of Heswall, then turn downhill towards River Dee to reach old village of Lower Heswall. Go right through village. Smithy is on main village road, opposite Roscote Close. Parking in smithy yard.)

This working pottery and craft workshop is situated in a long, open-plan room on the ground floor of a 17th-century smithy. Visitors can watch Jacaranda pots being made, which, with their delicate floral relief decoration, are mainly ornamental. But the pottery also produces its 'Harvest' range of kitchenware, decorated with a wheatsheaf motif. There is a range of paperweights made from local flowers preserved in resin, including roses from the smithy wall.

Open daily, 10–1 and 2.15–5, including Bank Holidays.

MUSEUMS

LIVERPOOL   Map ref: Ba
Merseyside Maritime Museum, Pier Head, Liverpool.
Tel. Liverpool 236 1492

The opening of a maritime museum in the heart of the city's historic dockland reflects the pride Merseyside still takes in its past, and the hope that it has for the future. Visitors can wander round the restored quayside; study an assortment of craft – including Lively Lady, the yacht in which Sir Alec Rose sailed round the world – and learn for themselves how the original dock fittings, such as capstans and winches, worked. There are demonstrations of coopering, net making and boat repair.

Open daily, end May to early Nov., 10.30–5.30. Charge for admission.

ST HELENS   Map ref: Ba
Pilkington Glass Museum.
(See panel on left)

Map ref: Ba

Pilkington Glass Museum

ST HELENS, MERSEYSIDE

Glass-making techniques from ancient Egyptian times are demonstrated by lifelike models in this large and fascinating museum at the headquarters of the giant Pilkington company. Workshop scenes have been skilfully re-created in miniature, and housed in dramatically lit glass cases. Glass-blowers are seen in the several stages of making a goblet; others are making 'cylinder glass' – large cylinders which were sheared lengthwise, then reheated and flattened for use in windows. 'Crown' glass, another window glass, is made by blowing a glass globule which is then opened out. After reheating, the opened globule is made into a flat disc by spinning it rapidly on the end of a metal rod known as a punty. The disc, called a table and having the traditional 'bull's eye' in the centre, is then cut into rectangles for windows.

The museum, which is on two spacious floors, houses also a magnificent collection of glassware, including Egyptian and Persian, Roman and Venetian, German, Bohemian and, of course, British.

Other artefacts include early microscopes, spectacles and lamps, right through to holographic, laser and photochromic exhibits demonstrating craftsmanship at increasingly advanced levels.

Prescot Road, St Helens, Merseyside. Tel. St Helens 28882.

Open weekdays, 10–5 (Mar.–Oct., Wed., 10–9). Sat.–Sun., 2–4.30. Also on Bank Holidays (except Christmas and New Year), 2–4.30.

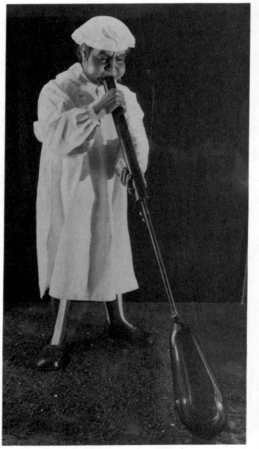

AN ANCIENT CRAFT A model glass-blower creates a cylinder from which window glass was made.

GLASS SHIP A sailing ship made of glass about 1880.

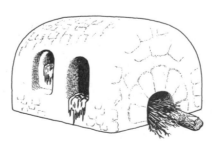

GLASS KILN In the 16th century, glass was fired in wood-fuelled kilns.

Opening times and other details may change. Check by telephone before making a special journey.

285

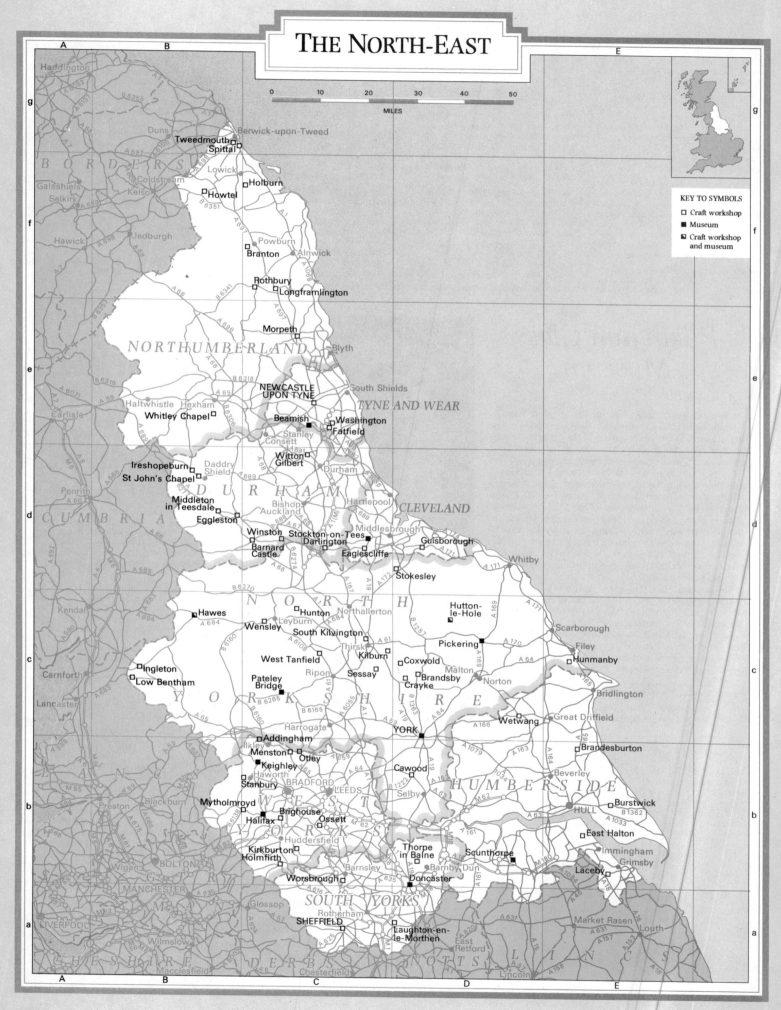

THE NORTH-EAST

MILES
0 10 20 30 40 50

KEY TO SYMBOLS
□ Craft workshop
■ Museum
◪ Craft workshop and museum

Haddington
BORDERS
Duns
Berwick-upon-Tweed
Tweedmouth
Spittal
Coldstream
Galashiels
Selkirk
Kelso
Lowick
Holburn
Howtel
Hawick
Jedburgh
Powburn
Branton
Alnwick
Rothbury
Longframlington
NORTHUMBERLAND
Morpeth
Blyth
Penrith
CUMBRIA
Haltwhistle
Hexham
NEWCASTLE UPON TYNE
South Shields
TYNE AND WEAR
Whitley Chapel
Beamish
Washington
Fatfield
Carlisle
Stanley
Consett
Witton Gilbert
Durham
Ireshopeburn
Daddry Shield
St John's Chapel
DURHAM
Middleton in Teesdale
Bishop Auckland
Hartlepool
CLEVELAND
Eggleston
Winston
Stockton-on-Tees
Darlington
Middlesbrough
Barnard Castle
Eaglescliffe
Guisborough
Whitby
Stokesley
Hawes
Hunton
Northallerton
Hutton-le-Hole
Leyburn
Wensley
South Kilvington
Scarborough
Thirsk
Pickering
Filey
Ingleton
West Tanfield
Kilburn
Coxwold
Hunmanby
Low Bentham
Sessay
Brandsby
Malton
Norton
Carnforth
Ripon
Crayke
Lancaster
Pateley Bridge
YORKSHIRE
Bridlington
Harrogate
Wetwang
Great Driffield
Addingham
YORK
Ilkley
Menston
Otley
Brandesburton
Keighley
Cawood
Beverley
Haworth
BRADFORD
Selby
HUMBERSIDE
Stanbury
LEEDS
HULL
Mytholmroyd
Brighouse
WEST
Burstwick
Preston
Blackburn
Halifax
Ossett
YORKS
East Halton
Huddersfield
Immingham
Grimsby
BOLTON
Kirkburton
Holmfirth
Thorpe in Balne
Scunthorpe
Barnsley
Barnby Dun
Laceby
MANCHESTER
Worsbrough
Doncaster
LIVERPOOL
SOUTH YORKS
SHEFFIELD
Rotherham
Market Rasen
Louth
Laughton-en-le-Morthen
East Retford
Lincoln
CHESHIRE
DERBYS
NOTTS
LINCS
Macclesfield
Chesterfield

286

Opening times and other details may change. Check by telephone before making a special journey.

The people of the North-East are very proud of their heritage as the backbone of Britain. It is not surprising that they get annoyed when the vast tract of living history and unspoiled countryside on their doorstep is branded a desert of dark satanic mills, flat caps and clogs. In a conscious attempt to destroy this myth they have set up museums and craft centres, all of which are entirely different. Although Northumberland, Durham and Yorkshire were once part of the Saxon kingdom of Northumbria, and although together they have shared a history as turbulent as that of any other region in Britain, every dale in the north has preserved its distinctive character and crafts. As a result, a fresh surprise lurks around every fold in the landscape. There are endless opportunities to learn about crafts both past and present; these include weaving and the making of traditional oak furniture, Northumbrian smallpipes and County Durham's famous quilts.

CLEVELAND

EAGLESCLIFFE   Map ref: Cd
Mrs I. E. Burnell (Lace maker), 2 Clarence Road, Eaglescliffe, Stockton-on-Tees.
Tel. Eaglescliffe 780647
(From A135 turn west into Victoria Road, near Parkmoor Hotel. At T-junction turn left into Clarence Road. Street-side parking.)

Using bobbins of wood, bone and ivory, wound with linen thread, Mrs Evelyn Burnell works her lace on a pillow. The patterns are mostly traditional, but some are her own design. They range from delicate flowers and butterflies of Honiton lace, to thicker Torchon mats.

Open daily, 9–5, by appointment.

GUISBOROUGH   Map ref: Dd
'Margaret Gray' (Silk-screen printer), 3 Rectory Lane, Guisborough.
Tel. Guisborough 37091
(At junction of Rectory Lane and New Road, which meets High Street [A171] from the south. Parking in Rectory Lane.)

Paddy Hutton and Marjorie Parkin are serigraphers, or silk-screen printers. Their 'Margaret Gray' headscarves, table linen and accessories are distinguished by detailed wild-flower scenes and art nouveau patterns.

Open Mon.–Fri., 9–5, by appointment.

MUSEUM

STOCKTON-ON-TEES   Map ref: Cd
Preston Hall Museum, Yarm Road, Stockton-on-Tees.
Tel. Stockton-on-Tees 781184
(On east side of A135 at northern end of Eaglescliffe. Parking on premises.)

Preston Hall Museum stands in the midst of 50 acres of parkland, with a children's playground and quiet walks along the River Tees. With over 400,000 visitors annually, the hall – an imposing mansion of the early 19th century – is the area's most popular attraction after Durham Cathedral.
The museum specialises in Victoriana of Teesside, which has been brought to life in the form of a reconstructed 19th-century high street. Beyond the many period shopfronts that line the sett-paved street, Peter Oberon and Jack Summer work the Preston Hall smithy. To fan the flames of his coal fire, Mr Oberon employs antique, double-action bellows.
Besides those wielded by Messrs. Oberon and Summer, antiquated tools are exhibited in the museum's craft gallery. Among them are the implements of bookbinders, stonemasons, coopers and clay-pipe makers.

Open Mon.–Sat., 10–6: Sun., 2–6. Closed Good Friday, Easter, Christmas Day and Boxing Day. Craftsmen at work Fri.–Sun.

DURHAM

BARNARD CASTLE   Map ref: Cd
Barnard Castle Pottery, 12 The Bank, Barnard Castle.
Tel. Teesdale 37850
(On east side of The Bank [A688], just below Market Cross. Street-side parking.)

A potter for 20 years, Brian Goodwin makes traditional domestic items in rich, warm-coloured stoneware. His casserole stands, toast racks, plates and plaques are hand-built, and have pierced or wax-resist designs inspired by the rugged landscape of the area.

Showroom open Apr.–Oct., Wed., Fri., Sat. and Sun., 10–5.30. Other times by appointment.

DARLINGTON   Map ref: Cd
Artistic Eggs, Mowden Pines, 86 Lunedale Road, Darlington.
Tel. Darlington 61620
(From A67 on western outskirts of Darlington, turn north into Edinburgh Drive. At a T-junction, turn left into Lunedale Road. Street-side parking.)

Lawrence Walker designs and fashions brilliantly ornamented eggs in the style of the renowned Russian jeweller Fabergé. He mostly uses goose eggs, but sometimes his creations demand the size and shape of an ostrich, parrot or chicken egg. First, he cuts a door in the egg. Then, after he has drained and cleaned it, he sprays the shell with four or five coats of enamel and decorates it with small beads and semi-precious stones.

Open daily, by appointment.

DARLINGTON   Map ref: Cd
Darlington Arts Centre, Vane Terrace, Darlington.
Tel. Darlington 483168
(Vane Terrace meets the A68 from the south, ¾ mile from city centre.)

As well as promoting drama, music, literature and painting, Darlington Arts Centre – one of England's largest regional centres of creative activity – provides workshops for craftsmen.
The stoneware ceramics of Angus Ferguson have a strong north-eastern flavour. His sculptures, which are unique, depict working men of the region, such as miners, blacksmiths and fishermen, in days gone by.
Old-fashioned methods characterise Claire Oates's spinning, dyeing and weaving. To concoct natural dyes she combs the countryside for roots, berries and herbs. All of her material is woven by hand on a floor-loom and on an assortment of tapestry frames.
Made-to-measure musical-instrument cases and bags for photographic gadgets are the stock-in-trade of leather worker Austin Winstanley. Mr Winstanley uses vegetable-tanned cowhide.
The inspiration for Gerry Wilmer's miniature embroideries comes from her work as a writer and illustrator of children's stories. Each of the embroideries is a detail of one of her water-colour illustrations.

Opening times of the different workshops vary, so it is advisable to telephone first.

EGGLESTON   Map ref: Bd
Tom Neal's Pewter Studio, Eggleshope House, Eggleston.
Tel. Teesdale 50235
(From B6278 turn west into lane just north of village centre. Follow the lane to end.)

In a hillside studio overlooking the wooded Tees valley, Tom Neal crafts pewterware. His most popular pieces are goblets, candlesticks, tankards and coasters in both contemporary and traditional designs. His three basic methods of shaping the pewter are to cast it in aluminium or rubber moulds, to spin it on a lathe, and to sculpt it with a flame.

Open daily, by appointment.

IRESHOPEBURN   Map ref: Bd
Weavers Forge Cottage, Ireshopeburn, Weardale.
Tel. Wearhead 346
(On south side of A689, about 1 mile west of St John's Chapel. Street-side parking.)

In a 200-year-old stone smithy, Mary Crompton and her husband Michael spin yarn from fleece that they have sorted and carded. The yarn, which is generally used for knitting, is then sold in hanks, or else woven in Forge Cottage. Mrs Crompton weaves twill rugs, blankets and garment fabrics on an oak floor-loom. Mr Crompton's special domain is a high-warp tapestry loom, where he weaves tapestries with designs incorporating themes from local landscapes.

Open Mon.–Wed. and Fri.–Sun., 10–4.

MIDDLETON IN TEESDALE   Map ref: Bd
The Woodsmith, Hude Works, Middleton in Teesdale.
Tel. Middleton in Teesdale 593 or 731
(From B6277 turn north-west into lane by working-men's club. Then turn into narrow drive just before Middleton House.)

Behind the imposing structure of Middleton House – the 19th-century headquarters of the London Lead Company – stands The Woodsmith's workshops. Here, several cabinet-makers fashion unstained oak and pine furnishings. Their work revolves around the construction of made-to-order kitchen units, but they also make small items, including stools, spice racks, and coffee tables.

Open Mon.–Fri., by appointment. Closed Bank Holidays.

ST JOHN'S CHAPEL   Map ref: Bd
A. Emms (Quilter), 'Wayside', Huntshield Ford, St John's Chapel.
Tel. Wearhead 356
(Just north of the bridge at Daddry Shield [½ mile east of St John's Chapel] turn west from A689 into lane that runs parallel to river. 'Wayside' is about ¾ mile from bridge.)

Since 1918, Mrs Amy Emms has been quilting in the traditional County Durham fashion. The rose, feather, cable and wheat-sheaf patterns that she stitches were taught to her by her mother and grandmother. To keep her craft alive, Mrs Emms teaches a class of learners.

Open by appointment.

WINSTON   Map ref: Cd
Dalton Leathercraft, 'Holme Lea', Winston, Darlington.
Tel. Darlington 730259
(In centre of Winston, opposite B6274.)

From sheets of English cowhide, Ian Dalton makes belts, handbags, cigar boxes and a decorative inlay for wooden lamp bases. He stains his leather with autumnal-coloured dyes of his own recipe, and finishes it with a home-made wax. His leather goods are then meticulously stitched, or thonged, by hand.

Open Mon.–Sat., 10–5, by appointment.

WITTON GILBERT   Map ref: Cd
David Reynolds (Wood sculpture), 17–18 Front Street, Witton Gilbert.
Tel. Durham 710512
(On south side of A691, opposite road to Sacriston. Street-side parking.)

A true country craftsman, David Reynolds started his woodcarving career by dressing walking sticks. From this age-old rural pastime, his scope has broadened to the carving of both religious and secular sculptures – wildlife and human figures from lifelike to abstract, and from humorous to solemn.

Open Mon., and Wed.–Sat., 10–5.30; also Sun., 2–5.30, from Easter to Christmas. Other times by appointment.

MUSEUM

BEAMISH   Map ref: Ce
North of England Open Air Museum, Beamish, Stanley.
Tel. Stanley 31811

England's first open-air museum provides a rare opportunity to view the past in action. At Beamish, visitors can savour for themselves the life and work of people in the north-east during the last century. They can wander around farms teeming with animals and rich with the smell of hay, straw and manure; they can ride on trams and go underground in a drift mine to see how coal was worked.
Old buildings, which include a railway station and a colliery, have been transported to Beamish from all over the region and equipped with appropriate furniture or machinery.
The 200 acres of rolling countryside now occupied by the museum once belonged to the Beamish estate. The Home Farm, which is still working, contains a blacksmith's shop and collections of agricultural and craftsmen's tools; and the hall itself, dating from 1630, now houses an exhibition which includes a collection of 'Durham Quilts'. In the stable block, visitors can occasionally watch a potter, a printer and a weaver of coconut mats at work.

Open daily, Apr.–Sept., 10–6; Oct.–Mar., Tues.–Sun., 10–5. Charge for entrance.

HUMBERSIDE

BRANDESBURTON   Map ref: Eb
Cottage Crafts (Pokerwork), Main Street, Brandesburton, Great Driffield.
Tel. Leven 43203
(Main Street meets A165 from west.)

George Cundill uses hot pokers to burn detailed pictures in leather and wood – a craft known as pokerwork. He finds his inspiration in wildlife and the countryside, and so his subjects include pheasants, foxes, horses and eagles. The pokerwork is generally used to decorate hardwood coffee-tables or leather pictures.

Open Tues.–Sat., 9.30–5.30; Sun., 10.30–5.30. Other times by appointment.

BURSTWICK   Map ref: Eb
John L. Corlyon (Furniture) Ltd, The Workshop, Burstwick, Hull.
Tel. Patrington 70701
(On north side of B1362.)

Reproduction Georgian and Regency furniture is hand-made by John Corlyon's team of woodworkers. The firm specialises in re-creating famous Chippendale, Hepplewhite and Sheraton designs. All of the skills associated with the Golden Age of furniture making – carving, inlaying, turning and polishing – are performed by specialists.

Open by appointment, Mon.–Fri., 8.30–5.

EAST HALTON   Map ref: Eb
White Cottage Pottery and Gallery, King Street, East Halton, Grimsby.
Tel. Killingholme 40308
(From centre of East Halton, on minor road 4 miles north-west of Immingham, follow signs to pottery. Parking on premises.)

A collection of farm buildings next to a 16th-century cottage houses Arthur Watson's pottery and craft shop. Most of his pots are decorated with geometric and abstract sgraffito patterns, which he etches into slips concocted from clay found in the pottery's grounds.

Open daily except Wed., 10–6.

Opening times and other details may change. Check by telephone before making a special journey.

287

LACEBY Map ref: Eb
David and Avril Morris (Potters), Archways, Caistor Road, Laceby, Grimsby.
Tel. Grimsby 72341
(Caistor Road joins A18 from north-east, ¼ mile from roundabout junction with A46. Street-side parking.)

Both David and Avril Morris produce stoneware, but there the similarity ends. Mr Morris fashions functional hand-thrown pottery which he decorates with brown or blue floral patterns, commemorative lettering or abstract lines on a white background. Mrs Morris creates wall plaques, miniature flower arrangements and animals.

Open Wed.–Sun., 10–6. Appointment advisable.

WETWANG Map ref: Dc
Oak Rabbit Crafts (Furniture), Main Street, Wetwang, Great Driffield.
Tel. Driffield 86257
(On north side of A166. Street-side parking.)

A tiny carved rabbit is the trade mark used by Peter Heap to identify his hand-crafted furniture. Chairs, cupboards and tables form most of his output, but he also furnishes churches, schools and boardrooms.

Open Mon.–Fri., 8–5; Sat. and Sun., 11–1 and 2–5.

MUSEUM

SCUNTHORPE Map ref: Db
Scunthorpe Museum and Art Gallery, Oswald Road, Scunthorpe.
Tel. Scunthorpe 843533

Wide-ranging displays in the museum include collections of agricultural implements and tools belonging to country craftsmen such as the saddler, the wheelwright and the joiner. The museum has a branch at Normanby Hall, a Regency mansion 4 miles north of Scunthorpe, where a blacksmith's forge can be seen, and a potter gives demonstrations.

Open Mon.–Sat., 10–5; Sun., 2–5. Charge for admission on Sat. and Sun.

NORTHUMBERLAND

BRANTON Map ref: Cf
Breamish Valley Pottery, Branton, Powburn, Alnwick.
Tel. Powburn 263
(From A697 turn west into road to Branton and Fawdon, about 600 yds north of Powburn. Pottery is 1 mile down this road.)

Stoneware pots are made on the upper floor of Alastair Hardie's rustic pottery. Some of them are immersed in brown, green or white glazes, whereas others remain partially, or even entirely, unglazed. Mr Hardie completes the decorative process by firing his pots in a wood-burning kiln. The circulation of the wood ash inside the kiln gives the unglazed surfaces a toasted, reddish-brown tint.

Open usually daily, 10–6. It is advisable to telephone before calling.

HOLBURN Map ref: Cf
John Suthern (Woodworker), 9 Holburn Village, Lowick, Berwick-upon-Tweed.
Tel. Berwick-upon-Tweed 88695
(Turn south into road to Holburn and Hazelrigg, which meets B6353 1½ miles east of Lowick. Workshop just south of Holburn T-junction. Parking on premises.)

All his adult life John Suthern has been a woodworker. Nowadays he specialises in cases for grandfather clocks. Mr Suthern makes these by hand, and mostly from mahogany and oak.

Open Mon.–Fri., 8.30–5, by appointment.

HOWTEL Map ref: Bf
Bowmont Crafts, Bowmont House, Howtel, Mindrum.

Castle Museum
YORK, NORTH YORKSHIRE

Each year more than 800,000 visitors wander round England's largest and most popular folk museum. They have the foresight and determination of one man to thank. At the turn of the century, as Dr John Kirk visited sickbeds in the farms and cottages of the North York Moors, he realised that the old ways of life were changing. And so he began to collect items that were at the time considered to be little more than junk. With remarkable persuasiveness he talked his patients out of anything that caught his fancy, often in lieu of fees.

The Castle Museum was founded in order to house his collection. And this prompted some more original thinking on the part of Dr Kirk. Disliking the old-fashioned and unimaginative method of displaying museum exhibits in glass cases, he suggested showing them off instead in settings as lively and authentic as possible. The results of his inspiration are period rooms – a Victorian parlour, a Jacobean dining-room, a moor-land cottage bedroom and the reconstructed workshops and streets for which the museum is famous.

There is something for everyone in this pioneer of folk museums. Exhibits range from police truncheons to ploughs, gingerbread moulds to fire insurance company marks, locks and keys to samples of lace, military costumes to children's toys. They are all housed in two imposing 18th-century prisons – one built for women, the other for debtors. Evidence of the buildings' former use haunts the visitor wherever he goes; grilles in the windows, streets laid out in old exercise yards, and craft workshops reconstructed in the cells. Dick Turpin, the notorious highwayman, spent the night in one of these before his execution.

The contents of the workshops came from old crafts-men of the area. Those represented include a picture framer, a clogger, a comb maker, a cooper, a cutler, a clay-pipe maker, a brush maker, a wheelwright, a blacksmith, an engraver and, of course, a jet worker. The jet, found on the Yorkshire coast at Whitby, is the finest in the world, and has been fashioned by man ever since Celtic times. During the last century, when lathes were first used for turning it, the stone became very popular. At one time, ladies presented to Queen Victoria were requested to wear no other form of jewellery.

York, North Yorkshire. Tel. York 53611.

Open Apr.–Sept., Mon.–Sat., 9.30–6; Sun., 10–6. Also open Oct.–Mar., Mon.–Sat., 9.30–4.30; Sun., 10–4.30. Charge for admission.

YORKSHIRE CRAFT *A Halifax clog maker at work.*

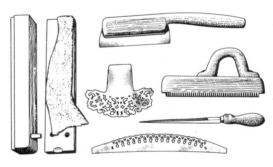

COMB-MAKER'S TOOLS *They were used in the early 19th century to make combs out of horn.*

Map ref: Dc

Tel. Mindrum 222
(On north side of B6352, about 3 miles west of junction with A697. Parking on premises.)

Inside the thick stone walls of Howtel's old Presbyterian chapel, Peter Mossop hand-throws stoneware pottery. He does not usually biscuit-fire his ceramics but immediately dips the unfired clay, or 'greenware', into brown, cream or blue glazes. Mr Mossop decorates many of his pots with simple, hand-brushed leaf designs.

Open daily, Apr.–Oct., 11–6; Nov.–Mar., by appointment.

LONGFRAMLINGTON Map ref: Cf
D. G. Burleigh (Smallpipe maker), Rothbury Road, Longframlington, Morpeth.
Tel. Longframlington 635
(On north side of Rothbury Road by junction with A697. Street-side parking.)

It was the piper to the Duke of Northumberland who taught David Burleigh how to master the art of making Northumbrian smallpipes –

blown by bellows. The basic smallpipes consist of chanter and drones – of African blackwood or ivory, keywork in brass or silver, reeds of Spanish cane, and a hand-stitched leather bag and bellows. Silver or brass and ivory are then used as decoration. To promote an appreciation of his craft, Mr Burleigh maintains an exhibition of pictures which illustrate the various stages of smallpipe construction and portray Northumberland pipers past and present.

Open Tues.–Sat., by appointment.

MORPETH Map ref: Ce
Phil Headland's Silver Studio, 7A Oldgate, Morpeth.
Tel. Morpeth 58385
(In an alley on the south side of Oldgate, which meets A192 at Morpeth's old clock-tower. Street-side parking.)

Phil Headland finds that his modern jewellery, with its art nouveau and art deco influences, has a special appeal for young people. He makes a variety of pieces, including rings, ear-rings, bracelets, pendants and jewellery boxes. Many

of the larger items are decorated with an enamelled floral motif.

Open Mon.–Sat., 9.30–1 and 2–5.30. Closed Thur. in winter, except Dec.

ROTHBURY Map ref: Cf
The Rothbury Pottery, Studio Keramos, High Street, Rothbury.
Tel. Rothbury 20691
(On south side of B6341.)

Norman and Joyce Salkeld fashion contemporary stoneware ceramics. They glaze their pots with a unique, rust-coloured slip which they make from clay found only a few miles away. The Salkelds have established a special reputation for originally designed lamps and lamp shades. These are often decorated with abstract engravings.

Open Mon.–Sat., 9–6; Sun., 12–6.

SPITTAL Map ref: Bg
Spittal Pottery, East Street, Spittal, Berwick-upon-Tweed.
Tel. Berwick-upon-Tweed 6708

(From Spittal's main street turn east into Sandstell Road, then right into East Street.)

On a home-made kick-wheel, Arthur Wood shapes both domestic and decorative stoneware. After biscuit-firing, he decorates his pots with an underglaze of hand-brushed oxides. They are then dipped into glazes, which may contain wood ash for a speckled effect, or stone dust from a local quarry to create a green tint.

Open May–Sept., Mon.–Fri., 10–1; Sat., 10–5. Rest of the year by appointment.

TWEEDMOUTH Map ref: Bg
Meadow Cottage Workshops, Knowehead, Tweedmouth, Berwick-upon-Tweed.
Tel. Berwick-upon-Tweed 7314
(From A1 turn west into Knowehead. Meadow Cottage stands beyond the square, at the end of Knowehead.)

The traditions and terrain of Northumberland have left a strong mark on the work of the two craftsmen at Meadow Cottage.

Hand-thrown Northumbrian slipware forms a large part of Peter Thomas's pottery. Such pots bear simple, slip-trailed motifs of the sort that have been used in the region for centuries. In recent years, Mr Thomas has developed a line of picture pots decorated with detailed sgraffito engravings or brush-applied oxides.

On a large, pine loom Margaret Wilson weaves woollen rugs, in which she evokes the colours and shades of local land and seascapes. Her patchwork quilts, on the other hand, use bold colours and contemporary patterns.

Open daily, 10–4, by appointment.

WHITLEY CHAPEL Map ref: Be
Stefan Sobell Musical Instruments, The Old School, Whitley Chapel, nr Hexham.
Tel. Slaley 338
(From B6306 turn west into road to Whitley Chapel. Workshop is at crossroads by call box. Street-side parking.)

Over the past decade, Stefan Sobell has acquired an international reputation as a maker of stringed musical instruments. He built his first instrument – an Appalachian dulcimer – as an experiment when he was a professional folk musician. He makes guitars, but mandolins and citterns are his special interest.

Open Mon.–Sat., by appointment.

NORTH YORKSHIRE

BRANDSBY Map ref: Dc
Acorn Industries, Brandsby, York.
Tel. Brandsby 217
(On west side of B1363, just north of post office. Street-side parking.)

For over 55 years George Grainger has been making furniture in his native village. With his son and several other experienced craftsmen, he now produces a regular line of traditional furniture from English oak. All of their furniture bears a small acorn emblem.

Open Mon.–Fri., 8.15–5.15; Sat., 8.30–12.15. Other times by appointment. Closed Bank Holidays and at Christmas.

CAWOOD Map ref: Db
Charlotte Hargreaves (Potter), 8 Market Place, Cawood, Selby.
Tel. Cawood 585
(In centre of Cawood on west side of B1222.)

In the historic village of Cawood, where Cardinal Wolsey was arrested in 1529, Charlotte Hargreaves produces stoneware pottery. She throws a variety of dinner services, garden pots, flowerpot holders and floor vases. Many items are given sgraffito decorations that require slip made from local clay. Others are dipped into wood-ash glazes and bear fine lines or wax-resist patterns.

Showroom open daily, 10–6. Small charge for admission to workshop (refundable on purchase). Appointment advisable.

COXWOLD Map ref: Dc
Coxwold Pottery, Coxwold, York.
Tel. Coxwold 344
(On south side of Coxwold's main street.)

Peter Dick and his wife produce domestic slipware, stoneware and terracotta ceramics. Their slipware is decorated with bold floral motifs, whereas the terracotta garden pots are often embellished with African-inspired engravings and applied decorations. The mottled, greenish-copper surfaces of the stoneware vessels are left unglazed.

Open Mon.–Fri., 10–5. Other times by appointment.

CRAYKE Map ref: Dc
Woodcarvers of Crayke, Crayke, York.
Tel. Easingwold 21512
(Just south of Crayke on road to Stillington Grange. Parking on premises.)

Derek Slater and his team of skilled cabinet-makers produce solid oak furniture. They craft dining-room and office furniture, and also bookcases and small tables.

Open Mon.–Fri., 8.30–5. Other times by appointment.

HAWES Map ref: Bc
W. R. Outhwaite and Son (Rope makers), Town Foot, Hawes.
Tel. Hawes 487
(On the north side of A684 by Upper Dales Folk Museum and car park, and opposite children's playground.)

It is known that agricultural ropes have been made in the market town of Hawes, Wensleydale, for at least 200 years. To this day they remain the staple products of this rope-making business. To make a rope, the rope maker twists strands of natural yarn, such as sisal, flax and cotton, or man-made fibres, such as nylon and polypropylene. Three or four strands are then twisted together to make the rope. Products include cattle and horse halters, dog leads, tow ropes and skipping ropes.

Open Mon.–Fri., 9–12.30 and 1–5.30; Sat., 10–12 in winter, 10–4 in summer.

HUNMANBY Map ref: Ec
The Village Craft Centre and Forge, 3 Hungate Lane, Hunmanby, Filey.
Tel. Scarborough 890453
(Hungate Lane meets Hunmanby's main street from the east. Parking on premises.)

When John Hill served his apprenticeship over 20 years ago, he spent most of his time shoeing horses and repairing agricultural implements. Now that he works his own smithy, he designs and makes articles that range from small, classic candelabras to huge ornamental gates of contemporary design. Mr Hill's assistant, Geoff Bayes, makes pendants and wall plaques from horseshoe nails.

Open Mon.–Fri., 8.30–12 and 1–5; Sat., 8.30–12. Open Sun. in holiday season.

HUNTON Map ref: Cc
Robin Watson Signs, Robin's Return, Hunton, Bedale.
Tel. Bedale 50388
(In western outskirts of Hunton.)

Signs and wall hangings fashioned from pine and an assortment of hardwoods are made by Robin Watson and his craftsmen. Mr Watson started the enterprise by carving name and number plates, but now his firm also produces a large number of wall clocks.

Open Mon.–Fri., 8.30–5. Closed Bank Holidays and for two weeks at Christmas.

HUTTON-LE-HOLE Map ref: Dc
Wold Pottery, Hutton-le-Hole.
Tel. Lastingham 527
(Opposite the inn on west side of stream.)

One of the North York Moors' most picturesque and popular villages – Hutton-le-Hole – is the home of Aidan Dixon's Wold Pottery. Working in an old stone schoolhouse by the banks of Hutton Beck, Mr Dixon hand-throws red earthenware pots. Some bear impressions of ferns or of sycamore and oak leaves.

Open daily, Easter to Oct., 9–5. Nov. to Easter, Mon.–Fri., by appointment.

INGLETON Map ref: Bc
Ingleton Crafts, Main Street, Ingleton, nr Carnforth.
Tel. Ingleton 41352
(From A65 follow signs for village centre. Main Street starts at Bridge Inn, and craft shop is opposite the church. Parking 150 yds away, at Community Centre.)

In this small craft shop, visitors can see pottery being made on the spot, and there are occasional displays of individual craftsmen's work during the summer. The shop also stocks leatherwork, paper sculptures, and walking sticks with deer-horn handles.

Open Mon.–Sat., 10–12 and 1–6 in summer; Tues.–Sat., 10–12 and 1–5 in winter.

KILBURN Map ref: Cc
Robert Thompson's Craftsmen Ltd, Kilburn, York.
Tel. Coxwold 218
(On Kilburn's main street by Forester's Arms public house. Parking on premises.)

The carved mouse hallmark of Robert Thompson is renowned throughout the world as a symbol of outstanding craftsmanship in English oak. By the time of his death, in 1955, his simple furniture and elaborate carvings could be seen in countless homes and in over 700 churches, including Westminster Abbey and York Minster. Today, the Thompson tradition is continued by his two grandsons and by a team of over 30 craftsmen, who still carve the ubiquitous mouse on every piece they make.

Open Mon.–Thur., 8–12 and 12.45–5; Fri., 8–12 and 12.45–3.45; Sat., 10.30–12. Closed Bank Holidays, Easter week and Christmas fortnight. No coaches.

LOW BENTHAM Map ref: Bc
Bentham Pottery, Oysterber Farm, Low Bentham, Lancaster.
Tel. Bentham 61567
(From Low Bentham village, take road next to Sundial Inn for Burton in Lonsdale. Oysterber Farm is at top of hill out of village, on left. Parking in old farmyard.)

In the stalls which used to house Jersey cows, Kathy Cartledge now makes hand-thrown stoneware pots, vases, cups, mugs and bowls. All are on sale in the old haybarn above, together with grotesque figures, and sculpted animals and birds. Wall plaques bear the weirdly beautiful shapes of fungi.

Open daily, 10–5.30, in summer; weekdays only in winter.

SESSAY Map ref: Cc
Albert Jeffray (Woodcarver and cabinet-maker), Sessay, Thirsk.
Tel. Hutton Sessay 323
(At northern end of Sessay's main street, near junction with road to Dalton.)

The English oak furnishings made by Albert Jeffray range from full-sized Welsh dressers to small napkin rings. Many pieces feature panelling, undulating surfaces and a carved Yorkshire rose.

Open Mon.–Fri., 8–5. Other times by appointment.

SOUTH KILVINGTON Map ref: Cc
Kilvington Studio (Woodwork), South Kilvington, Thirsk.
Tel. Thirsk 22328
(On east side of A61, about 1 mile north of Thirsk. Parking on premises.)

Variety is the essence of Kenneth Wilkinson's craftsmanship. In over 40 years of cabinet-making he has used all sorts of timber and constructed furniture for almost every function. Moreover, he designs pieces influenced by styles from the late 18th century to the present.

Open daily, 9–5. Appointment advisable.

STOKESLEY Map ref: Dd
Stokesley Spinning Wheel, 64 High Street, Stokesley.
Tel. Middlesbrough 592693 (evenings)
(At western end of High Street near village green. Street-side parking.)

The mother-and-daughter team of Mary Williams and Dolly Dunton produce the Spinning Wheel's woollen Shetland-lace shawls. Untreated fleece, and luxury fibres such as alpaca and mohair, are carded and sorted by Mrs Williams, who then spins the wool into thin strands of yarn on a Hebridean wheel. Once the yarn has been prepared, Mrs Dunton painstakingly knits the delicate shawls.

Open Mon.–Sat., 10–4, except Wed. Other times by appointment.

WENSLEY Map ref: Cc
White Rose Candles, Wensley Mill, Wensley, Leyburn.
Tel. Wensleydale 23544
(Just off A684 by Three Horseshoes Inn.)

In a 17th-century water-mill beside Wensley Beck, Mick and Jen White make candles to the music of a tumbling waterfall. Long candles are produced in the traditional way by dipping wicks repeatedly into a container of molten wax. They also cast candles in an assortment of shapes in moulds which they also make.

Open Easter Holidays, and daily except Wed., June–Sept., 10–5. Oct. to Christmas, weekends only, 10–5.

WEST TANFIELD Map ref: Cc
John Burford (Stained glass), West Tanfield, Ripon.
Tel. Bedale 70341
(Just off A6108, on west side of village.)

John Burford works with stained glass in a picturesque village on the banks of the River Ure. He designs and assembles art deco terrariums, mirror frames, jewel boxes and window hangings. The production process involves cutting clear or marbled glass, applying copper tape to its edges and, finally, soldering the pieces together.

Open daily, Easter to Christmas, 9–5. Other times by appointment.

MUSEUMS

HAWES Map ref: Bc
Upper Dales Folk Museum, Station Yard, Hawes.
Tel. Hawes 494

The fields and moors of North Yorkshire are still flecked with the sheep that have for centuries provided the dales' wealth. Related crafts, which include hand-knitting and weaving, are remembered in the museum – a former warehouse on the old Wensleydale railway line. There are also collections of dairying equipment, used to produce Wensleydale cheese, and peat-cutting tools.

Open Apr.–Sept., Mon.–Sat., 11–1 and 2–5; Sun., 2–5. Also open on Tues., Sat. and Sun. in Oct. Charge for admission.

HUTTON-LE-HOLE Map ref: Dc
Ryedale Folk Museum, Hutton-le-Hole.
Tel. Lastingham 367

The 17th-century manor house, a cruck-framed cottage some 500 years old, and the other buildings which cluster round the 'village' green of Ryedale's folk museum, could have been there for centuries. In fact, one by one and brick by brick, they have been moved there from local villages.

The museum illustrates the daily life of people who once lived around Hutton-le-Hole. Reconstructed craft workshops in the museum include a forge where a blacksmith can occasionally be seen at work, a saddler's shop

Opening times and other details may change. Check by telephone before making a special journey.

289

Map ref: Cb

West Yorkshire Folk Museum

HALIFAX, WEST YORKSHIRE

One of the aims of the West Yorkshire Folk Museum is to immerse its visitors in the lives of people who once worked in the area. To achieve this, standards at Shibden Hall have to be exacting. When all the research into authentic ways of reconstructing a workshop has been done, craftsmen are invited to put it to the test. If they do not think that it would be possible actually to work there, the project is scrapped and started afresh. As a result, the workshops always look as real as if a craftsman had just downed tools for lunch.

Shibden Hall, set in the middle of 85 acres of rolling parkland, dates from the 15th century and is furnished in the styles of four distinctive periods. A cluster of outlying farm buildings houses the workshops, which include a blacksmith's, a wheelwright's and a cooper's. The clogger's shop is a reminder of the days when the streets of Halifax echoed with the ring and scuff of clog-irons on the stone pavings. A basket-maker's shop has been reconstructed, too; in the 19th century there were several such workshops in and around the town, where baskets were made from willows grown along the banks of the River Calder. Every year there is a craft weekend in July when visitors can watch demonstrations of such crafts as pottery, lace making, wheelwrighting, spinning and clogging.

Another of the museum's reconstructions is the bar-room of an old Halifax inn. Named after the patron saint of leather workers, Crispin Inn was where the Luddites met in 1812 to decide which mill to attack first. The 17th-century Pennine barn contains a fine collection of horse-drawn vehicles, ranging from stately hearses and sedan chairs to gipsy caravans and farm carts. Most large halls used to have a brewhouse to cater for the needs of the household and its guests. Shibden Hall was no exception. Its brewhouse still stands, fitted with a brick-cased vat, and with the tools of the trade.

OLD BREWHOUSE *The building dates from 1718, but the equipment came from a local inn.*

Shibden Hall, Halifax, West Yorkshire. Tel. Halifax 52246.

Open Apr.–Sept., Mon.–Sat., 10–6; Sun., 2–5. Also open Oct., Nov. and Mar., Mon.–Sat., 10–5; Sun., 2–5. Open on Sun. in Feb., 2–5. Charge for admission.

---

and a joiner's shop. But scattered throughout the museum there is a mass of other tools and agricultural implements. For instance, an apprentice cabinet-maker made the fine inlaid chest holding around 300 tools. Also on display are the tools of the thatcher, the tinker, the cooper, the bootmaker, the besom maker, the mason and the rope maker.

An Elizabethan glass furnace, a mid-13th-century pottery and an iron foundry typical of Ryedale in the 1820s, have all been reconstructed.

Open daily, end Mar. to end Oct., 11–6. Last admission 5.15. Charge for admission.

PATELEY BRIDGE Map ref: Cc
Nidderdale Museum, Pateley Bridge.
Tel. Harrogate 711225

A Victorian workhouse which held German prisoners during the First World War has been transformed into this delightfully old-fashioned museum. Several rooms are devoted to trades and industries. A cobbler's shop has been reconstructed to look just as it did when a Coverdale man, named Chris Binks, ran it. There are also displays on quarrying, lead-mining and the making of twine.

Open daily, Spring Bank Holiday to Sept., 2–5; Sat. and Sun., Easter to Spring Bank Holiday; Sun., Oct. to Easter.

PICKERING Map ref: Dc
Beck Isle Museum, Pickering.
Tel. Pickering 73653

It is appropriate that the house of William Marshall, an early 19th-century agriculturalist, should now be a museum devoted to the rural life of Ryedale. The yard at the back of this handsome stone building is full

of carts, ploughs, harrows and cultivators, many of them rescued from local ditches and nettlebeds. Inside, old photographs accompany displays of agricultural implements and tools of country craftsmen.

Open Easter to mid-Oct., 10.30–12.30 and 2–5; Aug., 10.30–7.

YORK Map ref: Dc
Castle Museum.
(See panel on p. 288)

SOUTH YORKSHIRE

LAUGHTON-EN-LE-MORTHEN
Map ref: Da
Pear Tree Pottery, Firbeck Lane, Laughton-en-le-Morthen, Dinnington.
Tel. Dinnington 564788
(Firbeck Lane is just east of village crossroads. Street-side parking.)

Roy and Paul Newman practise their craft surrounded by a large and colourful display of tableware, kitchenware and decorative knick-knacks. Every one of their products is individually hand-thrown or modelled. But it is the use of rich glazes, spanning the full colour spectrum, which distinguishes their work.

Open daily, 10–5. Evening parties by appointment.

SHEFFIELD Map ref: Ca
Ron Butterfield, Taurus Studio, 205 Shirebrook Road, Meersbrook, Sheffield.
Tel. c/o Sheffield 662352 (Studio)
(Studio is in Harland Road, which meets Ecclesall Road – the A625 – from south.)

Since 1934 Ron Butterfield has been a sculptor of clay, wood, bronze and silver in his native Sheffield. Nowadays, however, almost all his works are hand-carved from oak, mahogany or lime. Most of his carvings are destined for churches, pubs and stately homes.

Open Mon.–Fri., by appointment.

THORPE IN BALNE Map ref: Db
Robin Pottery and Craft Centre, Spring Acre Farm, Thorpe in Balne, Doncaster.
Tel. Doncaster 882565 and 882444
(From Barnby Dun follow signposts to Thorpe in Balne. Craft centre is 1 mile north of power station.)

Restored farm buildings standing in 9 acres of land house the Robin Pottery and Craft Centre – a craft-orientated leisure park. The centre's resident potter is Mrs Audrey Robinson. She specialises in small hand-thrown bowls, mugs and vases. Among the people who regularly demonstrate their crafts at the centre are Sheila Wilson and Jenny Sheppard, who both make corn dollies, and the tapestry weavers Bill and Jean Skidmore.

Open Easter to Christmas: Sat. and Sun., 2–6.

WORSBROUGH Map ref: Cb
Jill Watts (Tapestry weaving), Worsbrough Mill House, Worsbrough.
Tel. Barnsley 203961
(On west side of A61, 1 mile north of Birdwell. Parking on premises.)

Jill Watts weaves tapestries in an old, stone mill-house by Worsbrough Mill Museum – a water-powered flour-mill which dates from the 17th century. The themes of her tapestries are drawn largely from nature, and may be represented either pictorially or as abstract images. She prefers to weave wool, cotton or linen, some of which she spins and dyes.

Open Mon.–Fri., 9–5, by appointment.

MUSEUM

DONCASTER Map ref: Db
Cusworth Hall Museum, Cusworth Lane, Doncaster.
Tel. Doncaster 782342

Displays in a handsome early Georgian mansion illustrate some vanished rural crafts. They include the tools of the cooper, the clog maker, the wheelwright and the blacksmith. Coopers were so skilled that, without written measurements or patterns, they could produce a barrel that was absolutely watertight.

Open Mar.–Oct., Mon.–Thur. and Sat., 11–5; Sun., 1–5. Also open Nov.–Feb., Mon.–Thur. and Sat., 11–4; Sun. 1–4. Closed Fri. Admission free.

TYNE AND WEAR

FATFIELD Map ref: Ce
Biddick Farm Arts Centre, Biddick Lane, Fatfield, Washington.
Tel. Washington 466440
(On east side of Biddick Lane, which runs from Washington village to Fatfield.)

The reconstructed buildings of 130-year-old Biddick Farm now house an arts centre. This fosters an appreciation of arts and crafts through the sponsorship of a theatre, an art gallery and several workshops.

Opening times and other details may change. Check by telephone before making a special journey.

The first resident craftsman at Biddick Farm was Barry Oliver, who constructs violins in the old Italian tradition.

Opposite the violin workshop stands the ceramics studio of Alan Ball, who hand-throws both functional and experimental pottery.

Decorative tuning pegs for stringed instruments were Phill Brown's first creations as a woodturner. He still produces pegs – some of which are commissioned for Barry Oliver's violins. But now he also turns goblets, furniture components, tiny jewellery boxes and bowls.

Margaret Alderton, a harpsichord and furniture maker, shares a workshop with Phill Brown. Most of Miss Alderton's harpsichords are copies of outstanding 18th-century masterpieces.

Open all year except Christmas Day and New Year's Day. Opening times of the different workshops vary.

NEWCASTLE UPON TYNE   Map ref: Ce
Blackfriars Craft Centre, Stowell Street, Newcastle upon Tyne.
Tel. Newcastle upon Tyne 328630
(From Newgate Street [A6127] turn west into Crook Street, then left into Stowell Street. Car park is next to craft centre.)

Blackfriars – a 13th-century Dominican priory – has become a tranquil haven for an association of Newcastle craftsmen. After the Dissolution of the Monasteries in the 1530s it served for centuries as the meeting place for Newcastle's nine craft guilds. Today the craft centre preserves the priory's 400-year connection with the crafts.

Peter Dickenson combined his two interests – chess and woodwork – when he started to specialise in making ornamental chess sets for collectors. He uses ebony for the black chess men, and boxwood for the white.

Craft shops from Brighton to the Orkneys market Stuart Hails' leatherwork. He specialises in making classic handbags, but he also produces belts and small leather goods.

All kinds of silver jewellery are hand-crafted by Jadwiga Billewicz. Much of her work, which is often abstract in design, incorporates ivory or unusual stones.

Soft toys that range from tiny finger puppets to motor vehicles and wild animals are produced by Claire Bennett. The toys are made from calico, hessian, tweed or corduroy.

With a collection of simple, home-made chisels, Peter Henry cuts figures and designs into wood, linoleum and metal, including gold and silver commemorative plates.

James Williamson-Bell is internationally renowned for his wildlife sculptures in bronze and solid metals. He sculpts a figure in wax; this he covers in plaster of Paris to make a mould, which he fills with molten metal.

Opening times of the different workshops vary, so it is advisable to telephone first.

NEWCASTLE UPON TYNE   Map ref: Ce
Charlotte Press Ltd, 5 Charlotte Square, Newcastle upon Tyne.
Tel. Newcastle upon Tyne 327531
(Charlotte Square is just north of Westgate Road, by the junction with Clayton Street. Car park in square.)

Assisted by several craftsmen, artists from all over the north-east use the Charlotte Press to print limited editions of their works. Its range of hand-powered presses is used for the production of lithographic, relief, intaglio and silk-screen prints. A number of antique presses are in regular use as well.

Open Mon.–Fri., 9.30–5.30. Closed Bank Holidays. Appointment advisable.

NEWCASTLE UPON TYNE   Map ref: Ce
Newcastle Potters Workshop, The Pottery, Westgate Hill Terrace, Westgate Hill, Newcastle upon Tyne.
Tel. Newcastle upon Tyne 326573
(Near the end of Westgate Hill Terrace, which meets Westgate Road from south.)

Rob Davis produces individually designed

ceramics and a range of kitchenware. His kitchen pots are made from stoneware and are mostly bottle-shaped. For decoration he merely dips them into one of several glazes – a creamy-brown glaze being the most popular. His decorative ceramics – vases, jewellery boxes and small bowls – are made from stoneware or porcelain, and tend to be modern in design and decoration. Unlike the kitchenware, the decorative pieces are spray-glazed.

Open Mon.–Sat., 10–4. Appointment advisable from mid-July to end Aug. Closed last two weeks in Dec.

WASHINGTON   Map ref: Ce
Washington Studio Pottery, Old Hall Smithy, The Green, Washington.
Tel. Washington 460960
(In centre of village. Street-side parking.)

In a stone pottery by Washington Old Hall – the ancestral home of America's first president – David Gibson makes both thrown and slab-built stoneware pots. His pots are coated with earthy green and brown glazes. Many of his lamp bases and vases bear press-moulded Saxon and Celtic patterns.

Open Mon.–Sat., 9.15–5.15; Sun., 1–5.30. Parties of more than ten by appointment.

WEST YORKSHIRE

ADDINGHAM   Map ref: Cb
Helyg Pottery, 2 Bolton Road, Addingham.
Tel. Addingham 830165
(On west side of B6160, by junction with A65. Car park opposite pottery.)

As well as a range of tableware, Eric Stockl hand-throws many individual pieces. He gives much attention to the colour composition of his pottery, using ten different glazes which range from off-white to dark brown. The ceramics are glazed by means of dipping, and many of them are decorated with wax-resist patterns.

Open Mon.–Fri., 9–5. Also open Sat., 9–5, Easter to Christmas.

BRIGHOUSE   Map ref: Cb
Shelf Pottery Ltd, Spout House Lane, Hove Edge, Brighouse.
Tel. Brighouse 710618
(From A641 turn east into Upper Green Lane, then left into Spout House Lane.)

More than 15 craftsmen are engaged in manufacturing contemporary ceramics at Shelf Pottery. They produce kitchenware, sculptural lamp bases, vases and animals. After the basic shapes have been cast in home-made moulds, the hands of the craftsmen provide the finishing touches. Oatmeal and brown glazes are then applied by brushing, dipping and pouring.

Open Mon.–Fri., 9.30–3.30. Parties of more than ten by appointment.

HOLMFIRTH   Map ref: Cb
Booth House Gallery (Pottery), 3 Booth House Lane, Holmfirth.
Tel. Holmfirth 5270
(On western outskirts of Holmfirth. Booth House Lane meets A6024 from the north about 500 yds west of Jet Service Station.)

Jim Robison's ceramics studio and showroom are housed in an 18th-century, oak-beamed barn. As well as producing functional items, he makes large slab-built, abstract sculptures. He is American by birth, and his work frequently captures the rugged landscapes and open spaces of his native land.

Open Sat. and Sun., 2–6. Other times by appointment.

HOLMFIRTH   Map ref: Cb
Dave Roberts, Raku Ceramics, Cressfield House, 44 Upperthong Lane, Holmfirth.
Tel. Holmfirth 5110
(From A6024 turn north-west into narrow Upperthong Lane.)

Raku pottery, which originated in 17th-

century Japan, is the speciality of Dave Roberts. The raku techniques he uses are low-temperature firing of earthenware clay, rapid cooling to craze the glaze and the envelopment of pots in smoke and wood ash.

Open at weekends, by appointment.

KIRKBURTON   Map ref: Cb
T. K. Matthews (Clog maker), 7 Riley Park, Kirkburton, Huddersfield.
Tel. Huddersfield 603102
(From B6116 turn west into road next to The Royal public house. Then turn left by the cricket club into Riley Park.)

In a small workshop with a fine view of Kirkburton's 13th-century parish church, Kevin Matthews constructs a variety of hand-stitched Yorkshire clogs. The uppers are cut and shaped from black and brown saddlers' bridle leather, and then nailed to carved blocks of alder, sycamore or beech. The soles and heels are equipped with hard rubber pads or traditional horseshoe-shaped irons.

Open by appointment. No groups of more than four.

MENSTON   Map ref: Cb
Menston Pottery, Four Lane Ends, Menston, Ilkley.
Tel. Menston 77985
(From Menston's main street turn north into Burley Lane. Pottery is behind hairdresser's premises on right of road.)

On a motor-assisted kick-wheel, Peter Robinson throws earthenware vessels for the kitchen and dining-room. Most of his pottery is decorated with slip, which he applies with brushes, fingers and trailers. His wife, Denise, coats many pots with a honey-coloured glaze.

Open Mon., Tues. and Sat., 10–5. Appointment advisable.

MYTHOLMROYD   Map ref: Cb
Pot Luck, The Old Fire Station, Cragg Road, Mytholmroyd, Hebden Bridge.
Tel. Halifax 883651
(On west side of B6138, opposite textile mill. Street-side parking.)

Ted and Stella Underhill manufacture stoneware ceramics in Mytholmroyd's old fire station. Through a large glass partition bounded by mementoes of the building's past, visitors can watch them making mugs, plant pots, soup bowls and plates by jiggering and jolleying – a machine process.

Retail shop and pottery showroom open Mon.–Sat., 9.30–5.30. Closed Christmas week. Appointment advisable.

OSSETT   Map ref: Cb
J. Burdekin Ltd, Basket Works, Wakefield Road, Ossett.
Tel. Ossett 273103
(From roundabout junction of M1 and A638 follow Ossett signs. Basket Works is by junction of A638 and Wakefield Road.)

In 1870, Joseph Burdekin started making cane and willow baskets for local textile mills. Today, about half-a-dozen craftsmen sit on the cane-strewn floor of the Burdekin workroom and deftly weave fishing baskets, linen baskets, balloon baskets, laundry hampers and textile skips. Besides items made on the premises, baskets and cane furniture from all over the world are displayed in the Burdekin showroom.

Open Mon.–Fri., 7.30–12 and 12.45–5.

OTLEY   Map ref: Cb
Duncan Craft Workshops, Ackroyd's Mill, Ilkley Road, Otley.
Tel. Otley 461700
(On north side of A660, on Otley's western outskirts. Car park at side of mill.)

On the banks of the River Wharfe stands Ackroyd's textile mill – a monument to Yorkshire's industrial revolution. Since the establishment of the Duncan Craft Workshops, in 1980, one wing of the mill has been given over to the promotion of traditional crafts.

Chris Porritt and Judith Stonier weave rugs and cloth on a collection of wooden-framed hand-looms. They use only natural fibres.

A keen rock climber, Michael Sims knows very well the curious geological formation of the Pennines' gritstone outcrops. From these he finds inspiration for his slab-built, abstract sculptures. Most are designed to accommodate living plants that colonise the clay just as moorland foliage colonises the outcrops.

The craftsmen of Laurence Pianos can tune, repair, restore or build almost any strung keyboard instrument. But they spend most of their time restoring pianos that date from the 18th century to the present day.

Individual pieces of stoneware and porcelain are hand-thrown on a kick-wheel by Dianne Cross. When throwing stoneware pots, she seeks to emphasise the plasticity of the clay by fashioning it into slightly asymmetrical shapes.

Opening times of the different workshops vary, so it is advisable to telephone first.

STANBURY   Map ref: Cb
Ponden Hall Hand-loom Weavers (Brontë Tapestries), Ponden Hall, Stanbury, Keighley.
Tel. Haworth 44154
(From Haworth travel west on the Stanbury-Colne road. Continue through Stanbury. Turn south at Ponden Reservoir.)

In the Georgian wing of an Elizabethan manor house, Roderick Taylor and Jenny Coats work an assortment of hand-looms. These include home-made, wooden-framed floor-looms and a cast-iron Hattersley pedal-loom. The weavers specialise in producing rugs and abstract tapestries from natural fibres. During the autumn and spring, they hold residential spinning, dyeing and weaving courses.

Open daily, 10–5. Appointment advisable in winter, and for party visits.

MUSEUMS

HALIFAX   Map ref: Cb
The Piece Hall Industrial Museum, Halifax.
Tel. Halifax 59031

Piece Hall, a massive classical building crowned on one side by a Golden Fleece, was opened amidst great pomp and ceremony on January 1, 1779. It had been built so that hand-loom weavers, who produced cloth at home for their manufacturers, could bring their pieces to one centre and meet buyers from all over England and Europe. Today, prints, tools and machinery in one of the building's many galleries trace the processes involved in textile manufacture. At every stage, from wool sorting to the baling of the finished cloth, visitors can compare the old methods of the 18th century and before with techniques introduced during the 19th century.

Open Apr.–Sept., Mon.–Sat., 10–6; Sun., 10–5. Oct.–Mar., daily, 10–5.

HALIFAX   Map ref: Cb
West Yorkshire Folk Museum.
(See panel on facing page)

KEIGHLEY   Map ref: Cb
Cliffe Castle Museum, Keighley.
Tel. Keighley 64184

In the second half of the 19th century, Henry Isaac Butterfield, a wealthy local textile manufacturer, built Cliffe Castle, a turreted mansion in the Victorian baronial style. The building now houses the museum. Some of the reception rooms have been reconstructed as craft workshops: a clog-iron maker's shop from the village of Silsden, a wheelwright's shop from Arncliffe-in-Littondale, and a muffin bakery from Haworth. The museum also contains nail-making tools, spinning-wheels, shuttles, tools for wool combing, and the loom used by 'Timmy Feather', the last hand-loom weaver in the Keighley area.

Open all year, Tues.–Sun., Apr.–Sept., 10–6; Oct.–Mar., 10–5. Admission free.

Opening times and other details may change. Check by telephone before making a special journey.

291

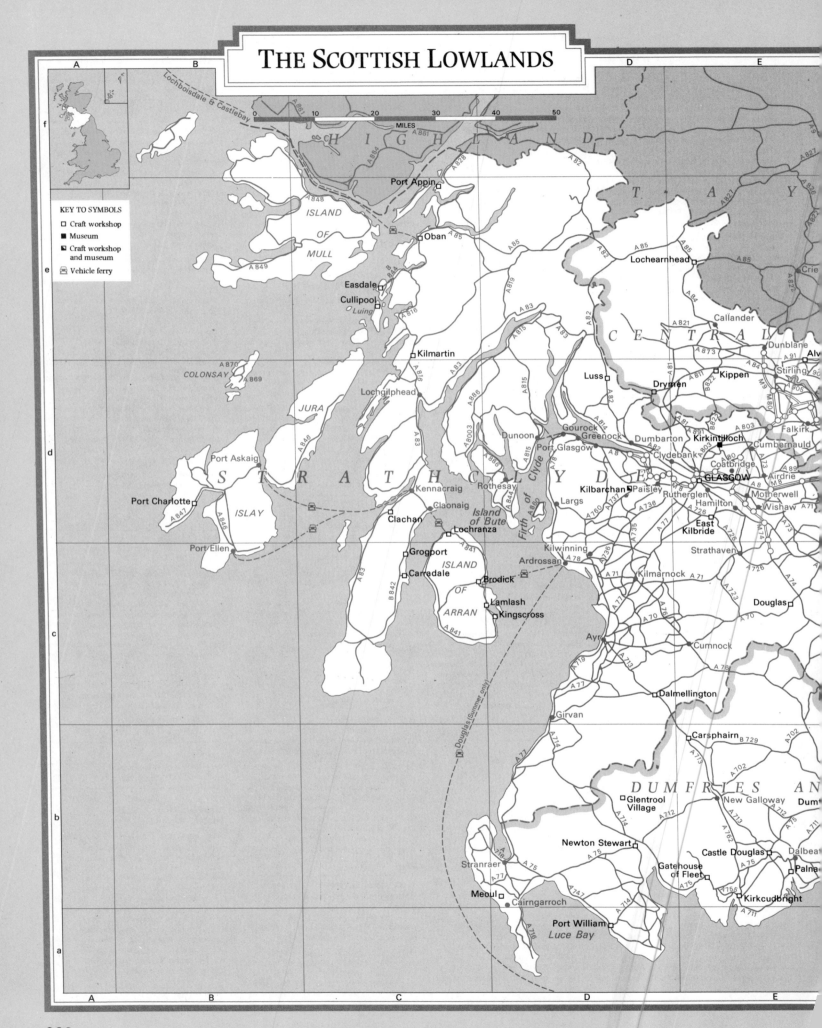

THE SCOTTISH LOWLANDS

Opening times and other details may change. Check by telephone before making a special journey.

The workshops of Lowland craftsmen, which range from old cattle-sheds to stately homes, are as full of surprises as the crafts which they practise. Some of these skills, such as weaving, bagpipe making, embroidery and cheese making, have been perfected over many generations, often by members of the same family. Others are more recent inventions, or revivals. A trip to the Lowlands can be a rare chance to meet craftsmen who have rediscovered techniques and objects that have been forgotten by time: 17th-century puzzle jugs ingeniously designed to thwart even the most determined drinker; looms similar to those used hundreds of years ago in Peru; stained-glass windows for the home, similar to those in vogue during the 16th century; and ceramics with the iridescent lustre of the pots made in Iraq and Persia over 1,000 years ago. In the past, the Lowlands' changing panorama of pines, peaks and pastures, and the turbulent history of the Borders, have inspired such great writers as Sir Walter Scott and Robert Burns. They continue to serve as an inspiration; only now it is to 20th-century craftsmen.

BORDERS

BONJEDWARD Map ref: Gc
John and Judy Strachan (Loom makers),
Jerdonfield, nr Jedburgh.
Tel. Ancrum 393
(Off A68, 2½ miles north of Jedburgh and ½ mile from the Bonjedward filling station, down a farm track. Parking outside workshop.)

In his rural workshop, Mr Strachan constructs simple yet ingenious backstrap looms similar to those used hundreds of years ago by the Incas of Peru. They consist of two rods cut from a very hard, straight-grain wood – Mr Strachan uses Malayan ramin – between which the warp is stretched. A jute strap attached to one bar is worn round the weaver's waist, while the other bar is fixed to a suitable stable object. The looms are sold in kits, complete with instructions for weaving a waistcoat, hat, and a pair of slippers.

Open Mon.–Sat., 9–6. Appointment advisable.

ETTRICKBRIDGE Map ref: Fc
Ettrickbridge Pottery, Main Street,
Ettrickbridge.
Tel. Ettrickbridge 247
(On B7009 in centre of village. Parking outside.)

Beneath forested hills, a low whitewashed building lies near the banks of a lazy river. It houses Tom McCarthy's pottery, where he practises a traditional technique known as 'raw glazing'. In this method the glazes are applied to the clay pots without first firing them to a 'biscuit'-hard state. Judging the right balance of ingredients is critical to ensure that the glaze shrinks at the same rate as the clay during the single firing. The rustic tableware he produces is decorated in soft, natural shades.

Open all year, 9–6. End May–end Aug., daily; rest of year, Mon.–Fri. Advisable to telephone first in winter.

INNERLEITHEN Map ref: Fc
Traquair House (Craft workshops),
Innerleithen, nr Peebles.
Tel. Innerleithen 830323
(Signposted from A72 at Innerleithen, off B709. Car park in grounds.)

Many English and Scottish monarchs have stayed in this romantic old mansion, whose many treasures reflect over 800 years of history. Attached to the main house is a restored 18th-century brewhouse where the Laird makes, and is licensed to sell, Traquair Ale. Visitors will see the mash tun in which crushed malted barley is steeped in hot water; a large copper for boiling the extract with hops; draining coolers; and fermenting vessels. In the spacious grounds, some outbuildings, called 'bothies', have been turned into craft workshops where pottery, candle making, wood turnery, paintings and screen-printing of fabrics are carried on. An annual craft fair is held in the

summer, during the second weekend in August.

House and grounds open daily from Easter Sat. to end Oct. 1.30–5.30 (July and Aug., 10.30–5.30). Last admission 5. Charge for admission.

KELSO Map ref: Gc
The Kelso Pottery, The Knowes, Kelso.
Tel. Kelso 24027
(Behind the abbey. Public car park opposite pottery.)

The 'Pictish Eye', a curious symbol found carved on ancient Scottish stones, has been adopted as a seal by Ian & Elizabeth Hird and is impressed on the underside of their pottery. Tableware ranging from whisky tots to tall vases is thrown by Ian Hird and colourfully decorated with scenes from the Border landscapes. His wife accepts commissions for modelling miniature replicas of buildings, and makes candleholders, hen and piggy banks, and Christmas nightlights with illuminated nativity scenes.

Open Mon.–Sat., 10–1 and 2–5. Appointment necessary for parties of more than six.

NISBET Map ref: Gc
Monteviot Woodcraft, Harestanes Mill,
Nisbet, nr Jedburgh.
Tel. Denholm 446
(On B6400, 300 yds from A68, next to Visitors' Centre. Parking outside workshop, beyond Visitors' Centre car park where fee is charged.)

Comprising an attractive converted outbuilding beside a saw-mill in the heart of the Lothian Estates, which embrace acres of forest and farmland, the surroundings of Jack Torbet's workshop provide an appropriate setting for his craft of woodturning. Timbers from the estate account for most of the wood that he uses, among it ash, oak, beech and pine. From these he turns many items, ranging from children's games, such as tops and whips, to pieces of furniture that include cleverly designed, old-fashioned box-stools. Next door to his workshop is a Visitors' Centre where information on the estate and details of nearby forest walks are available.

Open all year, Mon.–Fri., 9–5; Sun., 2–5. Visitors' Centre open Easter–Oct., Tues.–Sun., 1.30–5.

OXNAM Map ref: Gc
Oxnam Pottery, Oxnam, Jedburgh.
Tel. Campton 217
(The pottery is signposted about 1 mile south of Oxnam post office. It is at the end of a farm track, where there is a parking space.)

*'This jug is made your wit to try
And you may drink if you are dry.
But if you cannot find the way
Without good liquor you must stay.'
So went a rhyme which adorned the sides of 17th-century puzzle jugs, cunningly designed with several pouring outlets to thwart the most*

Opening times and other details may change. Check by telephone before making a special journey.

293

determined drinker. Reproductions of these intriguing vessels are made by Peter Fishley Holland, a seventh-generation potter, who promises to disclose their secret to customers. Like his forefathers he works in earthenware clay, which he decorates with coloured slips and fires in a wood-burning kiln. He also makes 'pilgrim' flasks, chess sets, an attractive range of tableware, and garden pots.

Open daily 10–6; evenings by appointment.

SKIRLING   Map ref: Fc
Douglas Davies (Potter), Loanfoot, Skirling, Biggar.
Tel. Skirling 254
(Beside village green. Parking outside.)

Many of the stoneware and porcelain pots made by Douglas Davies have been exhibited in galleries up and down Britain, as well as further afield in France, Austria and Switzerland. In his studio, an old stone byre, may be seen many large decorative pieces, including vases, dishes, planters and candleholders. These are usually thrown on the wheel and then adorned with chunky, slab-built decoration. The more ornamental pieces are painted with shiny gold, platinum and mother-of-pearl lustres.

Open by appointment, at weekends and during college holidays, 9.30 a.m.–10 p.m.

MUSEUM

WALKERBURN   Map ref: Fc
The Scottish Museum of Wool Textiles.
(See panel on this page)

CENTRAL

ALVA   Map ref: Ed
Derick M. Sanderson (Musical instruments), 151 Brook Street, Alva.
Tel. Alva 60334
(On east side of B908, beside primary school. Street-side parking.)

Formerly a violinist with the BBC Scottish Symphony Orchestra, Derick Sanderson and his two skilled associates work at the delicate craft of constructing and repairing all manner of stringed instruments. From time to time a harp or lute will be the subject of Mr Sanderson's attention, but violins, violas, cellos and double basses in various stages of construction and states of repair are found with greater frequency upon his workbenches.

Open Mon.–Sat., 9–5. Closed Bank Holidays and Tues. during Mar., Apr. and Oct.

DRYMEN   Map ref: Dd
Drymen Pottery, The Square, Drymen, by Glasgow.
Tel. Drymen 60458
(In village centre opposite The Winnock Hotel. Parking across The Square.)

In the red-sandstone pottery at Drymen – long associated with legends of Rob Roy MacGregor – the sensitive fingers of Shirley Bracewell and Alice MacFarlane work Stoke-on-Trent clay into functional and decorative objects for the home. These are thrown in traditional shapes and receive a natural glaze of oatmeal and temoku. Oxides and slips are applied to create contemporary designs.

Open Mon.–Sat., 9.30–5.30. Also on Sun., from 1.30.

KIPPEN   Map ref: Ed
The Tryst (Leather and woodwork), Kippen Station, by Stirling.
Tel. Kippen 295
(Not in village but on east side of B822, 300 yds north of A811. Parking on premises.)

Suitably named The Tryst – a commercial meeting place in old Scotland – Kippen Station's retail craft shop markets the wares of local craftsmen, as well as the wooden and leather handiwork of its proprietor, Eric Lewis. Using only hand tools, and an interesting old foot-powered stitching machine, Mr Lewis produces the key rings, belts and hair-grips on display in his shop. Occasionally he may be found cutting and stitching such singular items as medieval costumes and all-leather chess sets. In addition to his leatherwork, Mr Lewis carves silhouette sculptures from laminated woods.

Open daily, 10–5.

LOCHEARNHEAD   Map ref: Ee
Bran Clay Pottery, Lochearnhead.
Tel. Strathyre 274
(On east side of A84, off Balquhidder road. Parking on premises.)

Nestling between mottled, brush-covered hills at the head of Balquhidder Glen stands Bran Collingwood's one-man, one-room pottery. With this landscape as a backdrop, he throws and models a 50-piece range of decorative and functional earthenware, in addition to specially commissioned work. Most of his handiwork is of contemporary design, and decorated with at least one of eight glazes. His original 'Scottish Blue' glaze was inspired by patches of blue sky seen through breaks in the mist above the lochs.

Open Apr. to end Oct., Mon.–Sat., 9.30–5.30. Closed on Tues. during Mar., Apr. and Oct.

DUMFRIES AND GALLOWAY

CARSPHAIRN   Map ref: Eb
P. C. Walker (Carpenter), Burnfoot, Carsphairn, Castle Douglas.
Tel. Carsphairn 665
(A mile and a half east of Carsphairn. Turn at drive signposted Marbrack on north side of B729.)

The carpentry needs of the Carsphairn community are served by the woodwork enterprise of Patrick Walker. He undertakes jobs of all sorts, from repairing window-frames to constructing solid dining suites. Most of his furniture is built from oak, pine, sycamore and mahogany. When working to his own designs, Mr Walker combines modern and more traditional styles.

Open daily by appointment, 9–9.

CASTLE DOUGLAS   Map ref: Eb
Galloway Gems, 5A Church Street, Castle Douglas.
Tel. Castle Douglas 2295, after 6 p.m.
(West of A75 in centre of Castle Douglas. Street-side parking.)

Precious and semi-precious cabochon gemstones from all quarters of the globe glisten beneath glass in Galloway Gems' spacious showroom. In a workshop behind this exotic display area works the lapidarist, Joan Lawson. On one side, modern gem-cutting and polishing equipment lines the long wall. Opposite hang the simple silversmithing tools used to make settings. Much of the jewellery reveals an ancient Celtic quality, though Joan Lawson does occasionally produce modern pieces.

Open Mon.–Fri., 9–5.30; Sat., 10–5.

DALTON   Map ref: Fb
The Stained Glass Studio, Dalton, by Lockerbie.
Tel. Carrutherstown 688
(On south side of B725 in village of Dalton. Street-side parking.)

Before the 17th century, small stained-glass pictures were not uncommon in the windows of British houses. By producing leaded stained glass almost exclusively for the home, the Studio seeks to promote this largely forgotten custom. The stained-glass pictures are made by kiln-firing enamels and traditional pigments, which are painted on hand-blown glass. Heraldry and nature provide the subject matter

for much of the Studio's glasswork. The artistic styles range from that of the 16th century to those in vogue today.

Open all year, Mon.–Fri., 9.30–5.30.

DORNOCK   Map ref: Fb
Solway Pottery, Dornock, nr Annan.
Tel. Eastriggs 456
(Signposted off A75 between Dornock and Annan.)

The whitewashed stone structure of Solway Pottery is built on a grassy slope that runs gently to the tidal waters of the Solway Firth. Solway's potters, Brian and Susan Brittleton, throw, mould and build stoneware coffee sets, goblets, table lamps and vases. Designs range from traditional shapes with simple floral decoration to more contemporary forms bearing complex abstract patterns.

Open Mar. to end Dec., Tues.–Sun., 10–5.

GATEHOUSE OF FLEET   Map ref: Eb
Bridget Drakeford (Potter), The Drill Hall, Castramont Road, Gatehouse of Fleet.
Tel. Gatehouse of Fleet 695
(A quarter of a mile down Castramont Road, which joins A75 from north at eastern end of town. Street-side parking.)

Tucked away in a corner of her small studio, Bridget Drakeford throws stoneware and porcelain pottery of a functional nature, including tea and coffee sets, bowls and jugs. But most of her porcelain pieces, such as mirror frames, scent bottles and table lamps, are primarily decorative. In both the stoneware and porcelain ranges she seeks to expose the qualities of clay, and to emphasise shape by using the simplest of patterns in her decoration.

Open daily, 10–4.

GLENTROOL VILLAGE   Map ref: Db
Minniwick Pottery, Glentrool Village, Newton Stewart.
Tel. Bargrennan 274

Map ref: Fc

The Scottish Museum of Wool Textiles

WALKERBURN, BORDERS

The latest technology has been adopted by the firm of Henry Ballantyne and Sons, which runs the Scottish Museum of Wool Textiles in its mills at Walkerburn. But the museum commemorates centuries of craftsmanship, stretching back long before the rapid developments of the last 100 years transformed the manufacture of textiles from a handicraft into an industry.

Visitors can watch demonstrations of hand-carding, hand-spinning and hand-loom weaving. Spinning, either with a spindle – the technique used by the Egyptians – or on a treadle-wheel, is a laborious process. In the 17th century, spinning was such an accepted occupation for unmarried women that the word 'spinster' passed into the English language with the meaning that we usually give it. There is also a collection of some of the materials that the weaver would have used: samples of fleece from different breeds of sheep, various plants used to dye the wool, and equipment such as shuttles. A fascinating assortment of odds and ends includes old pattern books, and a piece of the original Balmoral Tartan designed by Prince Albert and made in Walkerburn in 1857.

A letter from a Parisian firm of tailors had to be sent to a firm in nearby Langholm had to be sent by balloon because, at the time – 1870 – Paris was under siege; it took only a day to reach England, from where it was sent on by normal post. The museum also acknowledges the debt that the tweed trade owes to Sir Walter Scott. Borderers did not wear tartan until he set a fashion by adopting the black and white shepherd check as the tartan of the Scott clan.

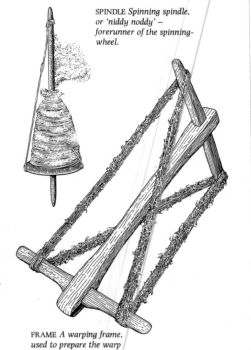

SPINDLE *Spinning spindle, or 'niddy noddy' – forerunner of the spinning-wheel.*

FRAME *A warping frame, used to prepare the warp for hand-weaving.*

Tweedvale Mill, Walkerburn, Borders. Tel. Walkerburn 281.
(Two miles east of Innerleithen on the A72.)

Open Mon.–Fri., 10–5, from Mar. to end of Oct. Charge for admission.

(Departing north from Glentrool Village, take first right turning outside village. Then turn sharp right at next intersection. Pottery is 1 mile down this track. Parking on premises.)

In a cobblestoned byre, surrounded by a panorama of peaks and woodland, hand-thrown stoneware pots are made by Rosey and Andy Priestman. These are largely functional jugs, mugs, bowls and lidded pots. Their work is characterised by soft, subtle colour combinations and intricate patterns. The Priestmans also produce a small quantity of delicate porcelain bowls and vases.

Open daily by appointment, Apr.–Oct.

KIRKCUDBRIGHT   Map ref: Eb
David Gulland Engraved Glass,
'Skairkilndale', 6 Barrhill Road,
Kirkcudbright.
Tel. Kirkcudbright 31072
(Barrhill Road is an extension of St Mary's Place, which meets the A711 from the east, at the south end of town. Street-side parking.)

The art of copper-wheel engraving on rock crystal was first practised in ancient times. Today, David Gulland perpetuates this craft on hand-made crystal glass. With a collection of lathe-turned wheels and carborundum paste, he abrades a host of stylised and natural subjects, among which human forms and wildlife predominate. He also engraves windows, and decorated panels and mirrors, for home and church by means of sand-blasting. Five such windows, bearing coastal scenes, may be seen between his workshop and showroom.

Open by appointment, Mon.–Fri., 10–1 and 2–5.

KIRKCUDBRIGHT   Map ref: Eb
Old Mill Pottery, Millburn Street,
Kirkcudbright.
Tel. Kirkcudbright 30468
(At north end of Millburn Street, which lies east of, and parallel to, the A711. Street-side parking.)

The burn that for 300 years powered Kirkcudbright's corn-mill still provides an audible background for the mill's present occupants, Thomas Lochhead and his son Wilson. They hand-throw stoneware pots of many shapes and sizes. For decoration, Thomas composes patterns by means of hand-brushed oxides. His son prefers the wax-resist method. Many of the pots are decorated with abstract leaf patterns.

Open Mon.–Sat., 9–1 and 2–5.

MEOUL   Map ref: Db
Invergyle Jewellery, Meoul, Stranraer.
Tel. Sandhead 349
(Turn south off B7042 on to Cairngarroch road. Meoul is 1½ miles down this road on right. Parking on premises.)

At a remote workshop, bound on all sides by a sea of rolling grassland, Glen Kelso Frame fashions sterling silver and 18 carat gold jewellery. Using basic hand-tools, he imposes both modern and time-honoured classic designs on these precious metals. Most of his designs call for the use of gemstones, and these he sets himself.

Open daily, May–Oct., 10–9; Nov.–Apr., 10–5.30.

MOFFAT   Map ref: Fc
Moffat Pottery, Ladyknowe, Moffat.
Tel. Moffat 20568
(Access by drive meeting A708 from south, ¼ mile east of village centre. Parking on premises.)

Rack after rack of drying pots dominate the workshop of Moffat Pottery. Alongside, craftsmen hand-throw stoneware clay into vases, bowls, jugs, plant pots and lampstands. The pots are decorated with white and green glazes, and given simple but prominent abstract patterns before firing.

Open daily, May–Sept., 9–9; Oct.–Apr., 9–5.

MOFFAT   Map ref: Fc
Moffat Weavers, Ladyknowe, Moffat.
Tel. Moffat 20134
(Access by drive meeting A701 from east, just south of A708 junction. Parking on premises.)

A strong stone's throw from the village pottery stands Moffat Weavers. Weaving is no longer performed on the premises, but woollen garments are still made there. Tweeds and tartans are cut, stitched and pressed by several tailors and seamstresses. They exercise their skills opposite a display of antique cast-iron weaving equipment, which includes a loom from the last century.

Open daily, Apr.–Oct., 9–5; Oct.–Mar., Mon.–Fri., 9–5.

NEWTON STEWART   Map ref: Db
Glen Cree Ltd (Weavers), Cree Mills,
Newton Stewart.
Tel. Newton Stewart 2990
(On east side of A714, in town's northern outskirts. Parking on premises.)

Cree Mills was established beside the banks of the swift-flowing River Cree at the turn of the century. At that time its heavy cast-iron looms turned out traditional Scottish woollens. More recently, high-quality mohair blankets, rugs, scarves and stoles have been the mill's exclusive products. Special attention is given to producing a soft, luxurious pile by means of brushing woven lengths against the prickly heads of teasel plants.

Admission Mon.–Fri. at 10, 10.30, 11, 11.30, 2.30 and 3. Advisable to telephone first for parties.

PALNACKIE   Map ref: Eb
North Glen Gallery, Palnackie, Castle Douglas.
Tel. Palnackie 200
(Half a mile south-east of Palnackie on the Glen Isle road.)

A wide variety of decorated glass objects are blown by Ed Iglehart in his workshop overlooking the Urr estuary. These range from a multitude of glass vessels to an assortment of mushroom figures. Drawing from early Mediterranean, art nouveau, and Japanese artistic traditions, he gives his work colour through the application of oxides. Most of Mr Iglehart's creations are shaped from laboratory tubing, fired for blowing in the flame of an oxypropane torch. The remainder emerge from molten spirit bottles, blown traditionally on a

---

long pipe. For certain decorative items, he uses his own homemade glass.

Open Mon.–Fri., 10–6, but advisable to telephone. Other times by arrangement. Charge for admission.

PORT WILLIAM   Map ref: Da
Shieling Crafts (Embroidery), South Street,
Port William.
Tel. Port William 510
(On west side of A747, just south of The Square. Parking in The Square.)

Seated snugly in a comfortable rocking-chair before a simple pine table, Dorothy Harris works with needle and thread to make embroidery. On Irish linen and on cotton-linen fabrics, Dorothy hand-embroiders table-cloths and handkerchiefs. Her patterns range from non-representational designs to elaborate floral compositions. Cotton and wool lengths for dressmaking are sold, and hand-knitting is done to commission.

Open daily during holiday season, 9–12.30 and 2–5. Closed on third Tues. of each month and all other Tues. afternoons.

MUSEUM

DUMFRIES   Map ref: Eb
Dumfries Museum.
(See panel above)

LOTHIAN

ABERLADY   Map ref: Fd
The Quill Gallery, Aberlady.
Tel. Aberlady 405
(On coastal side of main street.)

Centuries ago, Celtic monks painstakingly inscribed and illustrated manuscripts as lavishly decorated as the sumptuous Book of Kells. *The materials they used – quill pens, Chinese inks, gold leaf and calf-skin vellum – are similar to those used by Beryl Tittensor to create richly illuminated texts and heraldic documents. In her light, confident hand, the quill seems to flow effortlessly over the vellum, forming fine, even script embellished with elegant flourishes. Most of her work is commissioned by The Court of the Lord Lyon, Scotland's official heraldic office, and comprises detailed family trees, decorative coats of arms and related legal documents. She also reproduces poems with ornamental borders, and designs book plates.*

Open Apr.–Sept., weekdays (except Wed.) and Sat., 11–5. Oct.–Mar., 2–5.

DUNBAR   Map ref: Gd
Patricia Hassall Ceramics, Woodbush Brae,
Dunbar.
Tel. Dunbar 63724
(At east end of Dunbar, by beach. Parking outside.)

Patricia Hassall injects an element of surprise into many of her thrown and sculptural pots. Concealed lids in large 'egg' ornaments open to reveal tiny modelled figures; rounded vases with side openings for flowers or grasses are topped with tree and plant forms; and little country figures recline on the rims or handles of mugs. These and many other original pieces are attractively displayed in her waterside studio.

Open Mon.–Sat., 9–12.30 and 2–5.
Sun., 2–5.

EAST LINTON   Map ref: Gd
Preston Mill, East Linton.
Tel. East Linton 426
(Signposted from B1407. Parking space beside mill.)

In a beautiful riverside setting of trees and meadows, one of Scotland's oldest and smallest water-mills has been restored to working order. Visitors can wander through the mill and inspect the antiquated machinery. There are three buildings: an oasthouse-type kiln where grain was formerly dried on a perforated iron floor over a fire, the mill, and a barn which contains historical murals. The mill is in the care of the National Trust for Scotland.

Open Mon.–Sat., 10–12.30 and 2–6.30.
Sun., 2–6.30 from Apr.–Sept.; 2–4.30 for rest of year. Charge for admission.

EDINBURGH   Map ref: Fd
Ace Knitwear, 250 Canongate, Edinburgh.
Tel. Edinburgh 557 0104
(In Canongate at eastern end of the Royal Mile. Parking meters in street.)

Scotland is renowned for its distinctive Fair Isle knitwear, once the chief occupation of women living in isolated crofts during the long winter months. At Ace, these traditional multi-patterned jerseys are fashioned on hand-operated machines, each one incorporating up to eight complementary colours. Jumpers with picture designs in vibrant colours are also made.

Open Mon.–Sat., 1–5.

EDINBURGH   Map ref: Fd
Canonmills Pottery, 5 Warriston Road,
Edinburgh.
Tel. Edinburgh 556 5904 (evenings or before 9 a.m.)

Map ref: Eb

Dumfries Museum
DUMFRIES, DUMFRIES AND GALLOWAY

The 18th-century stone windmill which houses part of the museum commands magnificent views of Dumfries and the River Nith. Its Egyptian-style windows are a fanciful legacy from the 1830s, when the museum doubled as an observatory; visitors can still see the camera obscura – forerunner of the pinhole camera – on the top floor.

The second floor contains the craft collection – saddles, man-traps, agricultural hand-tools, woodworking tools and baskets from the 19th century, when a basket-making industry thrived on the willows that grow along the banks of the River Nith. There are also cloggers' tools, for in the 19th century Dumfries supplied clogs for the whole of Scotland. Cheese-making equipment dates from the days when most farms in Dumfries and Galloway produced their own cheese in a dairy.

Further craft material can be seen in the museum's large new extension.

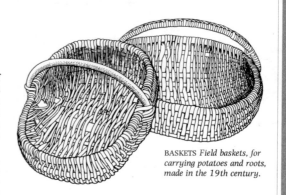

BASKETS *Field baskets, for carrying potatoes and roots, made in the 19th century.*

The Observatory, Dumfries, Dumfries and Galloway.
Tel. Dumfries 3374.
(In Church Street, west of River Nith.)

Open 10–1 and 2–5, from Mon.–Sat., but closed on Tues. Also open 2–5 on Sun. from Apr.–Sept.

Opening times and other details may change. Check by telephone before making a special journey.

295

(A quarter of a mile south-east of Royal Botanic Gardens, 100 yds from Canonmills clock. Parking at back of pottery.)

Although less than a mile away, the bustle of the city centre has not invaded the peace of this quiet little backwater where Janet Adam works. In her studio, a converted farm cottage overlooking the clear Water of Leith, she throws stoneware pots. They are decorated in glazes imparting rich blue and red-brown hues, as well as the more traditional earthy tones. Some of the more unusual pieces include lidded jars, and urns with applied leaf decorations.

Open Mon.–Sat., 1–6; usually mornings as well, but telephone first.

EDINBURGH Map ref: Fd
The Society Port, 44 Candlemaker Row, Edinburgh.
Tel. Edinburgh 225 2075
(Off Grassmarket, near the statue of Greyfriars Bobby. Parking meters close by.)

A co-operative of five craftsmen has set up studios in a part of Edinburgh which has a strong craft tradition. In the Middle Ages, when craftsmen and tradesmen were forming themselves into guilds, many chose this area for their headquarters. The studios occupy a three-storey building. On the ground floor a leather worker makes equipment for sports such as archery, besides tooling and stitching bags, belts and purses. Other craftsmen repair jewellery, and make silver and gold jewellery set with precious and semi-precious stones. Upstairs, tartan kilts are skilfully pleated and sewn by hand, and a versatile signwriter accepts commissions for decorating anything from shop fronts to tee-shirts.

Open Mon.–Sat., 10–6. Advisable to telephone to check when a particular craftsman will be there.

GIFFORD Map ref: Gd
Adrian Gardiner, Bolton Muir Lodge, Gifford.
Tel. Gifford 228
(On B6355, 1 mile west of Gifford, next to large thatched house.)

Adrian Gardiner's pots are all hand-thrown, mostly in stoneware, with celadon (grey-green) and tenmoku (black-rust) glazes and occasionally decorated with slim bands of gold lustre. Besides tableware, 'flattened' flasks and jardinières, he creates ceramic mirrors and panels, and makes bases for tables and fashions tops for them in English hardwoods.

Open at most times by appointment. Maximum of six people. No selling from premises, but details will be given of retail outlets in the area.

HADDINGTON Map ref: Fd
Margery Clinton Ceramics, The Pottery, Newton Port, Haddington.
Tel. Haddington 3584
(Off Market Street in town centre. Parking outside.)

Ceramics with an iridescent lustre were being made in Iraq and Iran more than 1,000 years ago. The technique was lost over the centuries, but after much research it has been revived and developed by Margery Clinton at her studio. Glazes containing silver, copper and colouring oxides are poured over the pots. During a reduction, or smoked, firing the metals are drawn to the surface, where they produce a rich, lustrous finish. Her work includes decorative bowls, boxes, goblets, candleholders and a range of art nouveau hanging lamps in the shape of harebells, fuchsias and lilies.

Studio open Sat., 10–1. At other times by appointment. Showroom open Tues.–Sat., 10–1 and 2.30–5.30.

PENICUIK Map ref: Fd
The Edinburgh Crystal Glass Company, Eastfield, Penicuik.
Tel. Penicuik 72244
(At north-east end of town, Eastfield is signposted from A701.)

Edinburgh lead-crystal glass has been made since the early 1800s, and visitors can watch the fascinating process during a tour of the works. From a viewing platform above the glowing furnaces, craftsmen can be seen taking 'gathers' of molten glass on the ends of long steel pipes, then deftly twisting and blowing them into over 100 different shapes of glasses or decanters. The characteristic sharp-edged patterns are precision-cut on revolving diamond-impregnated or stone wheels. At this stage the glass has a dull opaqueness, but after an acid bath and thorough polish its sparkling brilliance is revealed.

Tours, preferably booked in advance, on Mon.–Fri., available between 9.15 and 11, and between 1.15 and 3, excluding public holidays.

STRATHCLYDE

BRODICK Map ref: Cc
Dunifion Workshop, Corriegills, Isle of Arran.
Tel. Brodick 2393
(Half a mile south of Brodick, off the A841, take second turning on left. Follow this road for a further ½ mile. Walk to workshop from parking space provided.)

The three craftsmen who staff this furniture and cabinet workshop share a simple enthusiasm for the material that they handle every day. They work mainly in oak, ash and elm – local hardwoods from the west coast of Scotland – although they occasionally use mahogany and teak. Guided by their knowledge and love of wood, they pick the timber for each job, be it for furniture, spinning-wheels, kitchen utensils or carved birds and animals. Each is meticulously finished, with hand-made joints and delicate carvings where appropriate. The work can be bought at a craft co-operative at nearby Lamlash.

Open Mon.–Fri., 9–5. Appointment necessary.

BRODICK Map ref: Cc
A. D. Mackenzie, Cladach, Brodick, Isle of Arran.
Tel. Brodick 2311
(One mile north of Brodick, off the A841. Turn left before sawmill at National Trust signpost 'Footpath to Goatfell'. Parking outside.)

Four leather workers now work on the edge of Brodick Country Park in the stables that once belonged to Brodick Castle. Each of the craftsmen – including Alan Mackenzie, who started the business six years ago – can turn their hand to any branch of the work, although each has his own speciality. They make a variety of leather goods: saddles, bridlework, harness, shoulder bags and, to a lesser extent, belts and chess-boards. With the continuing interest in pony-trekking among visitors, their commissions come mainly from the islanders themselves.

Open Feb.–Dec., 11–6.

CARRADALE Map ref: Cc
Wallis Hunter Design, The Steading, Carradale.
Tel. Carradale 683
(At end of road that joins B879, beside village hall. Parking on premises.)

A solar-panelled roof covering a stone cowshed-turned-studio symbolises the meeting of old-fashioned craftsmanship with the modern methods of jewellery production found at Wallis Hunter Design. Silver prototypes of all manner of jewellery are hand-crafted by Mike and Trish Hurst. These are then reproduced through the most up-to-date lost-wax casting process. Also in modern vein are Mr Hurst's original designs, many of which carry the flavour of the art nouveau and art deco styles.

Open Apr.–Sept., Mon.–Sat., 8–5.30. Oct.–Mar., closed Sat.

CLACHAN Map ref: Cd
Fiadh Mor Antlercraft, Battery Point, Clachan, Tarbert.
Tel. Clachan 226
(At the end of rough-surfaced track, signposted Battery Point, ¾ mile south of Clachan off A83. Parking on premises.)

'Fiadh Mor' – meaning 'big stag' in Gaelic – is an appropriate name for the antlercraft enterprise of Highlander Alec Dale. The antlers of red deer are annually collected from the island of Islay, which also provides a fine prospect from his seaside premises. For the most part using woodworking tools, the antlers are cut into shapes suitable for lampstands, cutlery and walking-stick handles, and various household articles. The objects are then sanded and given a wax polish.

Open daily, 9–4.

CULLIPOOL Map ref: Ce
Longhouse Buttery and Gallery, Cullipool, Isle of Luing, nr Oban.
Tel. Luing 209
(About 12 miles south-west of Oban, cross to the Isle of Seil by Clachan Bridge, then take ferry to Isle of Luing.)

It requires determined effort to arrive on the Isle of Luing. There is one signpost only from the mainland to point the visitor in the direction of this small (population 150) but beautiful island. Edna Whyte came to live on the island in 1972, after spending many summer holidays there. Having converted a house into a workshop, miniature gallery and buttery (where she and her partner serve food) she now draws and paints the landscape and the people around her. With pen and brush she creates fine, detailed country scenes in black on white and white on black. These are for sale.

Open Easter to end Oct., 10.30–5. Appointment preferred July–Aug.

DALMELLINGTON Map ref: Dc
Charles Fairns Horncraft, Ayr Road, Dalmellington.
Tel. Dalmellington 550265
(On south-west side of A713, at western fringe of village next to petrol station.)

Sleek, square-rigged model sailing ships adorn the display window of Charles Fairns Horncraft. These, and his other creations – hunting-horns, spoons and shoe-horns – are all made from imported raw ox-horn. In a workshop cloudy with dust, the horn is cut and ground into shape. Objects, such as spoons and shoe-horns, requiring additional shaping are dipped into a cauldron of hot oil to soften them before moulding. Finally, the horn is given a brilliant sheen by burnishing and waxing.

Open Mon.–Fri., 8.30–12.30 and 1.30–4.30.

DOUGLAS Map ref: Ec
Douglas Valley Forge, Gardens House, Castle Grounds, Douglas.
Tel. Douglas (Lanark) 394
(Castle Grounds lie at northern end of Main Street. Continue along estate road to T-junction at base of ruined tower. Turn left and cross iron bridge. Gardens House stands isolated on left. Parking on premises.)

The sight of ascending smoke, and the sound of steel striking steel in the small smithy in the park of ruined Douglas Castle, signify that Dick Standring is hard at work. He forges many traditional furnishings for hearth and garden, but takes special pleasure in shaping mild steel to his own contemporary designs. Unusual among his work are a series of horseshoe-nail sporting figures and a variety of wood-burning fire grates and stoves.

Open daily, 9.30–5. Closed Bank Holidays.

EASDALE Map ref: Ce
Isle of Seil Pottery, The Old Engineering Works, Ellanabeich, Easdale, Oban.
Tel. Balvicar 333
(Access by signposted track that meets B844 just east of Easdale Harbour.)

One hundred years ago, floods from a tempest-tossed sea forced the permanent closure of one of Ellanabeich's slate quarries. The others have shut down during the years between. However, the quarries' whitewashed engineering works is once again in use – though now as Janette Borwick's pottery. Her hand-thrown domestic stoneware is characterised by the use of muted brown and green glazes and the application of simple abstract floral patterns by means of brush-applied oxides.

Open daily in peak season; off season, Mon.–Fri. After 5 p.m. by appointment.

EAST KILBRIDE Map ref: Ed
Laura Grant Products (Dolls), 31 Tennant Avenue, College Milton South, East Kilbride.
Tel. East Kilbride 34613
(On industrial estate south of A726 in western outskirts of East Kilbride. Take first left, then right, after entering estate. Parking on premises.)

Old-fashioned story-book dolls are made by several craftswomen seated around adjacent work tables. The dolls' bodies are simply round wooden balls attached to the points of yarn cones. Faces are hand-painted on the wooden balls, and the cones covered with cotton dresses made on the premises. A range of tartan-attired dolls has proved successful as a Scottish novelty. Besides being decorative, most of the dolls function as spice and soap containers.

Open by appointment, Mon.–Fri., 9.15–4.45. Closed Bank Holidays.

GLASGOW Map ref: Ed
Saltoun Pottery, Saltoun Lane, 24 Ruthven Street, Glasgow.
Tel. Glasgow 334 4240
(Ruthven Street meets Byres Road from the west, near Hillhead Underground station. Limited street-side parking.)

Neatly arranged pots in all stages of production fill the studio shelves of Nancy Smillie's pottery. Working in a quiet backwater of Glasgow, she throws a broad range of functional and ornamental stoneware. For the most part these have glazes with earthy tones and simple hand-brushed patterns. To supplement her line of stoneware, she has taken increasingly to making delicate, decorative objects in porcelain.

Open Mon.–Fri., 9.30–5.30; Sat. 10–5.30.

GROGPORT Map ref: Cc
Grogport Rugs, Grogport Old Manse, Carradale.
Tel. Carradale 255
(A quarter of a mile south of Grogport, 4 miles north of Carradale. Access by long drive that joins B842 from east. Parking on premises.)

Molly Arthur first acquired the tanner's craft on the small, remote island of Soay, off the coast of Skye. Today, on an isolated 35 acre glebe, she uses her skills to transform raw sheepskin into finished rugs. The process begins by scraping and washing the woolly hides. Then they are immersed in tubs of tanning liquid, where they remain for seven to ten days, with daily attention. Finally, the tanned skins are dried on wooden frames and brushed, the leather is softened and finally the wool is brushed out.

Open daily, by appointment, 9–9.

KILBARCHAN Map ref: Dd
Anne Clare Graham (Jewellery), 41 High Barholm, Kilbarchan.
Tel. Kilbarchan 4814
(Set behind hedges on north side of Kilbarchan's main street. Street-side parking.)

In a cottage annexe, where hand-looms of a bygone age once manufactured woven woollens, Anne Clare Graham now designs and makes modern gold and silver jewellery. Seated at a tool-lined pine workbench, she makes all her pieces by hand from start to finish. Her work is usually figurative or geometric in design.

Open Mon.–Fri., 9–5.30. Appointment advisable.

KILMARTIN Map ref: Ce

Kilmartin Crafts (Woodturning), Kilmartin.
Tel. Kilmartin 270
(Access by signposted drive on east side of A816, opposite church. Parking on premises.)

The faint odour of wood chips and sawdust permeates the stone workshop of the brothers Mike and John Thornton. With the division of labour well defined, Mike turns such exotic woods as ebony and iroka, in addition to local species including sycamore and yew. Among his varied handiworks are bowls, lampstands, ornamental eggs and ring boxes. John is wedded to the craft of furniture restoration. His skills have been called upon to mend furniture dating from as early as the 1600s.

Open daily, June–Sept., 10–7. Oct.–May, Mon.–Sat., 10–6.

KINGSCROSS Map ref: Dc

The Pottery, Kingscross, Isle of Arran.
Tel. Whiting Bay 323
(Two and a half miles south of Lamlash take the signposted turning on left to Kingscross. Take third turning off this road and park 100 yds from pottery at bottom of track.)

Alasdair Dunn has worked with clay for 35 years. Previously a lecturer in sculpture, he gave this up ten years ago to concentrate on ceramics, which has enabled him to live and work on Arran. His previous experience has influenced his pottery which uses designs based on the animals, birds and landscapes around him. Of particular note are his 'Arran Chuckie-Stanes'. Inspired by the round, concentric markings of the local Arran stones, these are made from a sandwich of three different clays, thrown on the wheel and remodelled to form spirally whorled 'stones'. Mr Dunn's work is for sale at nearby Lamlash.

Open daily. By appointment only.

LAMLASH Map ref: Dc

Arran Candlemaker, Spion Kop, Lamlash, Isle of Arran.
Tel. Lamlash 474
(One and a half miles south of Lamlash on A841. The workshop is signposted on right. Parking 100 yds away in small lay-by.)

Jo Morgan began making candles in 1970, two years after coming to Arran. Starting as a hobby on a trial-and-error basis, the enterprise has become a thriving business. Her candles come in many shapes and sizes, and in bright reds, oranges, greens, blues and purples. Particularly popular are candles decorated with heather and wild flowers from the surrounding countryside.

Open Tues., Wed. and Thur., 10–1 and 2–5.

LOCHRANZA Map ref: Cd

Arran Stonemen, 'The Whins', Lochranza, Isle of Arran.
Tel. Lochranza 650
(Off the A841 at Lochranza. Take public footpath on north side of harbour. Park at bottom of footpath near boats.)

Arran stonemen are not indigenous to Scotland. They have close relatives on the Continent – Norwegian trolls and German stein menne. Mr Reginald Scott Morgan, a bookbinder by trade, started making animals and men from stones only four years ago. He collects the stones from local beaches, cements them together, and then paints and varnishes the figures. These may be anything from doctors, dentists, builders or joiners, to cats, frogs, owls and hedgehogs.

Open daily, Mar.–Sept., 10–6. Appointment necessary for large parties. Maximum of ten visitors.

LUSS Map ref: Dd

Thistle Bagpipe Works, Luss, Loch Lomond.
Tel. Luss 250

(Just off the main A82, ½ mile south of Luss.)

Clad in traditional Highland attire, Mr James Kirkpatrick constructs bagpipes in the same way as did his forefathers several generations ago. The basic wooden components – the mouth pipe, the chanter and drones – are shaped by turning African blackwood, and are sometimes embellished with silver and ivory. Mr Kirkpatrick and his craftsmen secure these to airtight sheepskin bags, which they hand-stitch themselves. With the addition of a tartan, the finished bagpipe is ready to become a piper's most treasured possession.

Open Mon.–Sat., 9.30–4.30. Closed at Christmas and for three days at the New Year.

OBAN Map ref: Ce

MacDonald's Tweeds Ltd, Soroba Road, Oban.
Tel. Oban 63081
(Half a mile south of town centre on A816. Parking on premises.)

Haunting photographs of Highland crofting scenes, antique apparatus and written expositions are combined to tell the story of Scottish spinning and weaving at MacDonald's mill. The exhibition is brought to life by Mr Dugie MacColl's spinning and weaving. Operating a 100-year-old wheel of Outer Hebrides origin, he spins yarn, which he then colours with vegetable dyes. On a foot-powered Hattersley hand-loom he weaves this yarn into tweeds – sold in lengths in MacDonald's large retail shop.

Open Mon.–Fri., 9–12.30 and 1.30–5.30; Sat., 9.30–12.

OBAN Map ref: Ce

Oban Glassworks, Lochanvullin Estate, Oban.
Tel. Oban 63186
(Half a mile south of Argyll Square. Signposted access from Combie Street. Parking on premises.)

Multicoloured glass paperweights are exported to 49 countries. Contemporary in design, these fancy objects hold largely abstract patterns. Visitors to the glassworks can see a team of craftsmen going through the complex and fascinating routine of moulding and polishing, having gathered the molten glass from brick furnaces and blown it.

Open Mon.–Fri., 9–5, Sat. 9–12. Closed Christmas week, and on Bank Holidays during off-peak season.

PORT APPIN Map ref: Ce

Pat Cheney Craft Gallery and Workshop, Port Appin Pier, Port Appin.
Tel. Appin 375
(Two and a half miles west of A828. Opposite pier, behind tea room. Parking in adjacent public car park.)

The craggy cliffs of Clack Thoull rise to the rear of Pat Cheney's small, whitewashed premises. In front stretch the salt waters of Loch Linnhe. Working in the midst of all this beauty, she designs and, with a brush, hand-paints jewellery destined for fashionable shops in London and Glasgow. Her many stylised designs are of the art nouveau tradition. The craft of the silversmith is practised by her colleague, Robin Mackie, who fashions prototypes of small personal ornaments.

Open by appointment from Mar.–Oct., Mon.–Sat., 10–5; Sun., 2–5.

PORT CHARLOTTE Map ref: Bd

Islay Creamery Co. Ltd, Port Charlotte, Islay.
Tel. Port Charlotte 229
(Sixteen miles from Port Askaig on A847, via Bridgend. In Port Charlotte take first turning on right after museum. Parking near Creamery.)

An average of a ton of cheese is made daily at the Islay Creamery, yet the process is not

---

dissimilar to the one that used to be employed on crofts – and neither is the product. It is a white cheese (though sometimes given a yellow tinge by the addition of a vegetable dye) and is slightly sweeter and smoother than Cheddar cheese. The various stages of making it can be seen throughout the day. The milk is pasteurised into 1,000 gallon vats, then set with rennet. Paddles with knives attached cut the curds to release the whey. After the whey has been drained off, the remaining curds are mixed with salt and put into moulds overnight. The cheese can then be wrapped and packed.

Creamery open 8–5. Shop open 9–5.

MUSEUMS

BIGGAR Map ref: Fc

Gladstone Court Museum, Biggar.
Tel. Biggar 20005
(In a lane off 113 High Street.)

Street scenes and shops reconstructed in the museum ring true down to the last telling detail. Carefully arranged shop-fronts lure the visitor into Aladdin's caves of yesterday, jam-packed with everything that the inhabitants of a small town would have needed. Many of these goods depended on the work of local craftsmen – the clock maker, the joiner and the printer. All the articles are brought to life with imagination and charm, and are rendered with

---

very careful attention to local detail.

Open Mon.–Sat., 10–12.30 and 2–5. Also 2–5 on Sun., Easter to Oct. Charge for admission.

KILBARCHAN Map ref: Dd

The Weaver's Cottage.
(See panel below)

KIRKINTILLOCH Map ref: Ed

Auld Kirk Museum, Cowgate, Kirkintilloch.
Tel. Glasgow 775 1185

Kirkintilloch's old Town Hall, crowned by an impressive clock-tower, once housed the courtroom, schoolroom and gaol. Today, it contains the museum's craft exhibits. These highlight the major activities of the town in the 19th century, and describe how the district grew up. A reconstruction of a typical hand-loom, examples of locally woven material, and a banner carried by weavers in 1832 demanding 'Reform, Redress and Relief', commemorate the days when weaving was Kirkintilloch's leading industry and the town's womenfolk were famed for their hand-spinning.

There are also tools and examples of work from local iron foundries, and a display on boat-building. Kirkintilloch was once renowned as the birthplace of its 'puffers' – little tugs that plied along Scotland's canals and coasts.

Open Tues.–Sat. afternoons.

Map ref: Dd

The Weaver's Cottage
KILBARCHAN, STRATHCLYDE

In the 1830s, 800 hand-looms were in use in the small village of Kilbarchan, but production declined because of competition from power looms. The Weaver's Cottage, with cruck-beams supporting its roof, was built in 1723 and is one of Kilbarchan's original houses. So little has been altered that it is easy to imagine how weaving families of as many as 12 lived and worked in such cottages, sleeping in box-beds (built into a wall, or with boarded sides) and guarded from evil spirits by the glass 'witch-ball' that hung in the window. Exhibits record the history of the local weaving industry. These include wool-winders, a muckle wheel (a type of spinning-wheel) and a hand-loom.

The Cross, Kilbarchan, Strathclyde. Tel. Kilbarchan 5234 (ask for Custodian).

Open daily, 2–5, June–Aug., also 2–5 on Tues., Thur., Sat. and Sun. in May, Sept. and Oct. Charge for admission.

SPINNING-WHEEL *A muckle (great) wheel made in Scotland about 200 years ago.*

Opening times and other details may change. Check by telephone before making a special journey.

297

THE SCOTTISH HIGHLANDS AND ISLANDS

MILES

KEY TO SYMBOLS

□ Craft workshop
■ Museum
◪ Craft workshop and museum
🚗 Vehicle ferry

ORKNEY

Pierowall
Westray
Surrigarth
Rousay
Hullion
Sandwick   Bimbister
Grimeston   Finstown
Stromness   Kirkwall

Pentland Firth

Scarfskerry   W.Mey
Brough   Ham
Scrabster
Durness   Thurso   Keiss
Talmine   Wick
Tongue

DUNE

Ness
Borve   Tolsta
Carloway
Stornoway   Coll
Gisla
Lochinver
Balaglas   Tarbert   Drinishader   Melvaig   Lairg   Kinbrace
Plocrapool   Badachro   Gairloch   Ullapool   Helmsdale
Rodel   Kilmuir   Dornoch
Lochmaddy   Geary   Uig   Tain
Gillen   Alness   Cromarty   Lossiemouth
Muir of Aird   Hallin   Edinbane   Conon Bridge   Forres   Elgin   Portso
Glendale   Dunvegan   North Kessock   Nairn   Keith
Uiginish   Portree   Leachkin   INVERNESS   Gollanfield   Craigellachie
Eochar   Strathcarron   Huntly
Lochboisdale   Lochcarron   Tomatin   Grantown-on-Spey
Mid-Strome   Tomintoul   Strathdon   Heugh-head
Kyle of Lochalsh   Kingussie   Lumphan
Broadford   Kyleakin   Shiel Bridge
Isleornsay   Braemar   Ballater
Tangasdale   Teangue
Castlebay   Mallaig
Fort William   Pitlochry
Tobermory   Aberfeldy   Blairgowrie   Glamis
Dunkeld   Forfar
ISLAND OF MULL   Craignure   Comrie   Crieff   PERTH   St Andrews
Oban   Lochearnhead   Cupar
Callander   Lundin Links   Lower Largo
Lochgilphead   Glenrothes
Stirling   Kirkcaldy

Despite the Act of Union, which in 1707 finally joined the two countries, Scotland and England are nations apart in spirit. The Highlands, in turn, are very different from the Lowlands, from which they are separated by mountain ranges and centuries of independent existence. This difference is reflected in the unique range of Highland crafts. Most of the artefacts for which the region is renowned, such as Harris Tweed, Fair Isle jerseys and malt whisky, were originally everyday goods made from local materials. Their principal purpose has been to protect this race of fishermen, crofters and soldiers from the savagery of the elements; and their character has come from the wealth of tradition which the Highlanders prize so fiercely. Tartans, targes, sporrans and bagpipes are still made today. In addition, the decorative crafts have flourished. There are many potters, glass engravers and silversmiths in the area who, inspired by the majesty of this wild and lonely land, are creating objects that are more than merely functional – they can be imaginative, original and beautiful.

FIFE

CRAIL   Map ref: Fa
Crail Pottery, Crail.
Tel. Crail 413
(Follow signs from chemist in High Street, down Rose Wynd off Castle Street, towards sea. Parking in street.)

Few pieces of hand-thrown pottery made by Stephen Grieve take more than two or three minutes to throw, mainly because he keeps all his shapes simple. His wife, Carol, makes up many of the glazes, mixing in wood ash, a crushed blue stone from St Andrews and a volcanic stone from nearby Elie.

Open Apr. 15–Sept. 30: weekdays 9–1 and 2–5; weekends 2–5. Workshop open, but not in operation, from end June to middle Aug.

CUPAR   Map ref: Fa
Eddergoll Studios, Eddergoll House, 29 Bonnygate, Cupar.
Tel. Cupar 54757
(In main street of Cupar, 100 yds from Mercat Cross. Car park near by.)

As well as being one of Scotland's leading leather-carvers, Raymond Morris is a laird, or landed proprietor. With such a background it is no surprise that Morris of Eddergoll (to use his full title) should carve heraldic beasts, medieval caskets, and targes – or Scottish war shields. Even his smaller pieces, such as coasters, are ingrained with history, for he carves on them designs from the 8th-century Book of Kells, one of the finest artistic achievements of Celtic Christianity. Many of the targes are carved with tools similar to those used in medieval times, and made by the laird himself. His wife, Margaret, demonstrates metal-thread embroidery and tapestry weaving.

Open all year, Mon.–Sat., 10.30–5.30.

LOWER LARGO   Map ref: Fa
Largo Pottery, Main Street, Lower Largo.
Tel. Lundin Links 320686
(Off the A915, towards harbour. Turn left at harbour. Pottery situated near end of main street. Parking in road.)

Local people believe that the site of Largo Pottery has a connection with one of the most sinister figures in medical history – Dr Robert Knox of Edinburgh. Dr Knox was an anatomist who, in the early 19th century, needed a supply of corpses for his lectures. His main suppliers were the bodysnatchers Burke and Hare, but the story goes that an extra source was a Dr Goodsir, who owned the row of cottages that now form the pottery. The local name for the cottages is the Doctor's Vennel – a vennel being a path that leads nowhere.
Today, the resident potter, Anne Lightwood, glazes her stoneware pieces in earthy greens and browns – colours that are influenced by the fossils and sea shells found near by. Among the items on display are colanders, lemon squeezers, ramekins, casseroles, bowls and plates, vases and hanging pots for plants.

Workshop open June–Sept., in business hours. Advisable to telephone in advance. Shop open at same times between Apr. and Oct.

LUNDIN LINKS   Map ref: Fa
Dust Jewellery Ltd, Studio/Workshop, 7 Mill Wynd, Lundin Links, Leven.
Tel. Lundin Links 320742
(Off the A915. Parking available outside studio.)

Titanium is an enormously strong, heat-resistant metal used in the construction of spacecraft. Though normally a dull grey, it comes alive with a spectrum of colours – blues, pinks, purples, greens, yellows and oranges – when an electric charge is passed through it. Norman Grant, the designer at Dust Jewellery, makes full use of this effect in his necklaces, ear-rings and brooches. He also designs with more traditional materials, such as gold, silver and enamel, in styles dating from the turn of the century.

Open all year, Mon.–Fri., 8.30–5.30; Sat., 10–4 (showroom only). Closed for a fortnight over Christmas.

GRAMPIAN

BRAEMAR   Map ref: Ec
James and Isobel Crichton, The Woodcraft Shop, Invercauld Road, Braemar.
Tel. Braemar 657
(Just off A93 in centre of village, opposite garage. Car park in village.)

In Robert Burns's day, whisky tots were made of wood, not glass. James Crichton would have won the poet's approval, for his whisky tots are made of oak and turned on a lathe. Mr Crichton, who concentrates on wooden items of kitchenware, carves shortbread and butter moulds out of sycamore, using a thistle motif. His spirtles, for stirring porridge, are of turned beech.

Open all year, Apr.–Oct. 9–8; Nov.–Mar. 10–5.

BRAEMAR   Map ref: Ec
McLean of Braemar, The Horn Shop, 10–12 Invercauld Road, Braemar.
Tel. Braemar 602
(Just off A93 in centre of village, next to garage. Car park in village.)

As far back as the Stone Age, man used animal horns for making weapons and tools. At the Horn Shop visitors can watch as the tough, hollow horns from stag, sheep or ram are split into flexible slices, heated, and shaped in a vice or turned on a lathe. Among the many items on display are shoe-horns, ornamental handles for knives, spoons, buttons, reading lamps and shepherds' crooks. There are also pieces in their more natural state, cleaned and polished to be used as ornaments.

Open all year, 8–5; winter months, Mon.–Sat.; summer months, daily.

COLPY   Map ref: Fc
Glenfoundland Products, Colpy.
Tel. Colpy 337
(Three-quarters of a mile north of Colpy, on A96. Parking at the Foundland Roadhouse.)

The hamlet of Colpy lies in the shadow of the Hill of Foundland, whose brooding face bears the scars of old slate workings. The quarries closed about 1870, but Michael and Wendy Mann still use blocks and small slabs of slate that were discarded and abandoned by the quarrymen. The blocks are sliced on a diamond saw, then sanded and highly polished. The minerals and oxides in the slate produce autumnal colours in some strata. The slate is now used to make items ranging from engraved clockfaces and table lamps, to ring-boxes and pendants.

Open all year, May–Sept., 9.30–5.30; Oct.–Apr., 10.30–4.30.

FORRES   Map ref: Ed
Harold Gordon (Glass engraver), Greywalls Studio, Forres.
Tel. Forres 72395
(Entering Forres on A96 from Nairn, turn right down Pilmuir Road. Greywalls Studio is a converted stables on right.)

As he deftly manipulates the crystal under the revolving copper wheel, Harold Gordon makes glass engraving seem simple. He makes all his own wheels, which total 150 and are in varying sizes and thicknesses. These, in turn, are fed with an abrasive and light oil. This method gives both depth and delicacy to his work. His designs range from intricate coats of arms to subjects from the countryside – among them flowers, game birds, leaping salmon and fishing flies.

Open by appointment, Mon.–Fri., 9–5; Sat., 9–12.

HEUGH-HEAD   Map ref: Fc
Strathdon Pottery, Heugh-head, Strathdon.
Tel. Strathdon 241
(Signposted off the B973, about 2 miles east of Strathdon. Parking on site.)

Salt-glazing is a special feature of Strathdon Pottery, which was once a romantic old coaching inn. Zelda Mowatt applies a thin skin of coloured slip before stacking the pots in a high-temperature kiln. During the firing, she throws handfuls of salt into the kiln. This vaporises in the intense heat and is carried through the kiln by the flames and the draught. The result is rewarding – a pitted 'orange peel' effect beneath a deep gloss that brings out the full, autumnal richness of the surface colours.

Shop open daily, 9–5. Workshop by appointment only.

INVERURIE   Map ref: Fc
'Mr Clay' Studio Potters, 125 High Street, Inverurie.
Tel. Inverurie 20515
(In the main street. Parking in street.)

Between them, the versatile team of Frances and David Jamieson, will undertake to make anything in pottery, from giant earthenware strawberry pots to a complete dinner service. Most of their work is to order, and as well as undertaking entirely new projects they will re-create broken pieces in the original style to complete a set. Pottery classes are held, four days a week, in the charming old bakery that now serves as the pottery.

Open all year, Mon.–Fri., 9.30 a.m. to 10 p.m. (approx.); Sat. 10–6, Sun. 12–6.

KEITH   Map ref: Fd
Chivas Brothers Ltd, Strathisla Distillery, Keith.
Tel. Keith 7471
(Situated in Seafield Avenue, the road leading to the railway station in Keith. Parking in street.)

Only the Scots can distil Scotch malt whisky. For only they have the essential ingredients,

Opening times and other details may change. Check by telephone before making a special journey.

299

including pure burn water and the skills born of centuries of experience. Those centuries roll back for the visitor to Strathisla Distillery – the oldest in the Highlands, founded in 1786 when George III was on the throne.

The basic method of whisky making is the same as it was nearly 200 years ago. A 20 minute tour is provided for visitors.

The whisky begins its life as colourless, plain spirit, cocooned in oak casks as it lies maturing in a warehouse for at least three years. During this time the whisky becomes mellow and acquires a gold hue. No visitor leaves without the opportunity to sample 'a wee dram'; and the company also sells its products on the premises.

Guided tours are given (9–4) between mid-June and end of Aug. (If distillery is not in operation, visitors can see a film of the process.) Group visits limited to ten.

LUMPHANAN   Map ref: Fc
Foggieley Sheepskin Rugs, Foggieley Croft, Craigievar, Alford.
Tel. Lumphanan 317
(Four miles north-west of Lumphanan and 1 mile north of B9119. Look for 'sheepskin' signs. Parking on site.)

At Foggieley Croft, visitors can watch George Wilson transform sheepskins into finished rugs. He begins by immersing the skins in a tanning vat, where they stay for a week for the preservative liquid to soak into them. The skins are then stretched on a frame to dry at room temperature. Mr Wilson beats the leather to make it soft and pliable; then he buffs the backs of the skins to make them smooth. Finally, the skins are combed. All the finished rugs have natural colours, for Mr Wilson uses no dyes. The colour variations come from the different breeds of sheep whose skins are used – shaggy Scottish Blackface, Jacob, Scottish halfbreeds, brown and white Cheviots, Welsh blacks and Shetlands.

Open all year, summer months 9–9, winter months 9–6.

OLDMELDRUM   Map ref: Fc
Donald and Fiona Fraser, Pennyfeu, Doulies Crofts, Oldmeldrum.
Tel. Udny 2419
(From Oldmeldrum take the A920 east towards Pitmedden. At crossroads [about 3 miles] turn left at signpost 'Tarves'. Second house on right. Parking in lay-by outside.)

Tartans are as traditional to Scotland as a haggis on Burns night. And so are what have become known as district checks. In the 19th century, when sporting Victorians streamed to the Highlands to stalk deer, they were looked after by shepherds, ghillies and gamekeepers wearing the traditional checks of the district or estate. And so these became the uniform of sportsmen. At Pennyfeu, Donald Fraser weaves both traditional checks and fashion fabrics he has designed himself. With these fabrics, his wife, Fiona, designs and creates stylish clothes. She will undertake commissions, to customers' specifications.

Open all year, by appointment. Tues.–Sat., 10–6; Sun., 2–6.

PORTSOY   Map ref: Fd
The Marble Workshop and Portsoy Pottery, by the old harbour, Portsoy.
Tel. Portsoy 2404
(Take any road off main street towards sea and turn left by harbour. Parking on site.)

So sought after was 'Portsoy marble' in the 17th century that a harbour was built to export it to France. There, it was used in the Palace of Versailles. The quarry has long been abandoned, but the harbour is still there, alongside a 'new' harbour built in 1840. Fragments of the 'marble' – not true marble but an attractively flecked green or red waxy stone known as serpentine – are still collected from the beach. At the workshop, a few hundred yards away, they are cut to size, ground and polished. The small pieces of serpentine, which are rich in grain colouring,

are made into jewellery and desk ornaments.

Next door, in a former grain store that dominates the tiny harbour, is the Portsoy Pottery. Here, Brian Shand uses the three basic techniques of pottery manufacture – slab, coil and throwing on a wheel – to produce a range of stoneware for the kitchen and dining-room. His work is notable for its bright and cheerful glazes.

Both the Marble Workshop and Portsoy Pottery are open all year, Mon.–Fri., 9–5. The Workshop is also open most Saturdays.

TURRIFF   Map ref: Fc
Russell Gurney Weavers, Brae Croft, Muiresk, Turriff.
Tel. Turriff 3544
(Three miles south-west of Turriff off the B9024. Restricted parking on site or at roadside.)

Russell Gurney welcomes visitors, and demonstrates the traditional methods of spinning and weaving. He works out his own designs with mathematical precision. Most weavers work to a diagrammatic plan, but Mr Gurney has trained his memory to hold all the strings of numbers that tell when to change the weft colours to produce intricate woven patterns. The yarn is either pure wool, or a blend of wool and silk. No pattern is repeated, and he weaves lengths of cloth as well as making shawls and ties.

Open all year, Mon.–Sat., 9.30–5.30.

HIGHLAND

ALNESS   Map ref: Dd
Mill Pottery, Cuillich Mill, Ardross, Alness.
Tel. Alness 882981
(Mill Pottery is in a log cabin off the A836, 3 miles north of Alness.)

On his kick-wheel, John Day throws domestic pottery in traditional English designs. His output includes milk-jugs, tankards complete with thumb-stops, salt-pigs and pitchers. Some of the designs use the wax-resist technique, allowing the colour of the clay body to show through the design.

Open during normal shop hours throughout the summer; winter by appointment.

BADACHRO   Map ref: Cd
Elizabeth Duvill, Dry Island, Badachro, Gairloch.
Tel. Badachro 263
(Half a mile north of B8056. Access via Aird Road. Street-side parking.)

Secluded, on a rocky, tidal island, from the fishing village of Badachro, Elizabeth Duvill makes tapestry wall-hangings on a great iron loom. Painstakingly she weaves wool, silk and hessian threads through a warp of cotton fisherman's twine at the rate of 1 sq. ft every eight hours. Many a subject for the tapestry is provided by the rugged Ross and Cromarty landscape. Some of the woollen weft in the tapestries is spun on one or other of her own two wooden wheels. One is a relatively new Hebridean model; the other – her favourite – is a Shetland wheel built in 1841.

Open Mon.–Sat., by appointment.

BROUGH   Map ref: Ef
David Glass (Hand-loom weaver), Ivy Cottage, Brough, Thurso.
Tel. Barrock 695
(Signposted on Ham–Brough road near junction with B855. Parking on premises.)

Two looms – an ageing foot-powered Hattersley and a four-box fly shuttle – dominate the workroom of David Glass. From the foot-powered loom come heavy tweeds in traditional patterns, while on the fly shuttle he weaves overshot woollens. Most of his material is sold in the form of bolts, skirt lengths or tablecloths. The remainder is made into garments by his wife, Joan. She also contributes to the family enterprise by spinning and knitting.

Open daily, 10–6. Appointment advisable Oct.–Apr.

BROUGH   Map ref: Ef
Michael O'Donnell (Woodturner), The Croft, Brough, Thurso.
Tel. Barrock 605
(On B855 next to Brough Post Office. Street-side parking.)

In a rustic stone byre, Michael O'Donnell turns exotic African woods – among them afrormosia and sapele – and several domestic hardwoods. Bowls are his main item, for which he uses native woods such as holly, laurel and tulip-wood. He also turns a wide variety of finely finished, light domestic furnishings and a range of kitchenware.

Open Mon.–Fri., 10–1 and 2–6; Sun., 2–6.

BROUGH   Map ref: Ef
Allen Whitehead (Leather craftsman), Candleberry Cottage, Brough, Dunnet.
Tel. Barrock 333
(On north side of cul-de-sac which joins B855 from east, just north of junction with road to Ham. Parking on premises.)

Two work benches line opposite walls of Allen Whitehead's studio, which faces the distant pink cliffs of Hoy. At one, he drafts blueprints in his capacity as an architect. At the other, he cuts, stitches and dyes thick cowhide – all by hand. Handbags, shoulder-bags, belts and briefcases are among Mr Whitehead's products. These he embosses with simple geometric patterns.

Open daily, 2–6, by appointment.

CONON BRIDGE   Map ref: Dd
The Post Office and Craft Shop (Woodturner), Conon Bridge.
Tel. Conon Bridge 2201
(Post Office is in main street; workshop is behind it.)

Derek McLay can turn his hand to anything connected with woodworking – boats, chairs, oars, the restoration of antique furniture, the turned handles on his vast array of tools, and wooden minnows used by fishermen to lure salmon. Pieces of wood in every stage of crafting lie about his workshop, from massive planks being seasoned, to the finished and polished articles.

Usually open during normal shop hours.

CROMARTY   Map ref: Ed
Cromarty Design Workshop (Pottery), Shore Street, Fishertown, Cromarty.
Tel. Cromarty 254
(Shore Street runs beside the sea. Workshop is marked Fishertown Craft Centre.)

The pottery is housed in a row of 17th-century fishermen's cottages. Most of Alison Dunn's earthenware bowls, vases and pots are hand-thrown or hand-built, and many have distinctive friezes of applied clay decorated with majolica glazes. Even the slip-cast or jiggered pots are individually decorated with designs inspired by local colours and forms – the sea, Celtic designs, flowers, even pieces of driftwood.

Open daily by appointment, May–Sept., 10–5.

DORNOCH   Map ref: Ed
Town Jail Craft Centre (Weavers), Town Jail, Castle Street, Dornoch.
Tel. Dornoch 555
(Craft Centre is close to Castle Hotel in centre of town.)

Whereas modern textile manufacturers use high technology, machines in the Town Jail work on the same principle as hand-looms and have changed little since Victorian times. Kilt cloth is made to order, and over 1,000 different tartan designs have been produced so far. This vast array of tartans is a result of the Victorians' conscious revival of a tradition that was banned after the 1745 Jacobite rebellion.

Open Mon.–Fri., 9–5. Closed for lunch.

EDINBANE   Map ref: Bd
Edinbane Pottery, Edinbane, Isle of Skye.
Tel. Edinbane 234
(On A850 opposite Edinbane Hotel. Parking on premises.)

At the head of Loch Greshornish, four craftsmen make stoneware pots ranging in size from tiny egg-cups to sturdy 2 ft high cider flagons, and in design from traditional mugs to contemporary goblets. They are dip decorated, and some of the larger pots are given abstract patterns by glaze splashing. Subtle textures are achieved in many of the pots made here through the use of wood ash and salt in the glazing process.

Open daily, July–Sept., 9–6; Oct.–June, Mon.–Sat.

GILLEN   Map ref: Bd
The Knitwear Workshop, 12 Gillen, Waternish, Dunvegan, Isle of Skye.
Tel. Waternish 267
(From end of B886 take Hallin–Geary road. Gillen is 1½ miles east of Hallin. Street-side parking.)

On several hand machines, and one that is electrically powered, Mr and Mrs Morris knit wool sweaters of classic design. They also manufacture all kinds of hosiery, ranging from ankle socks to knee-length kilt hose, on automatic equipment. But an antique hand-powered sock-knitting machine is retained for demonstration purposes.

Open Apr.–Oct., Mon.–Sat., 2–8. Nov.–Mar. by appointment.

GLENDALE   Map ref: Bc
Skye Venture Cottage Industry, 18 Holmisdale, Glendale, by Dunvegan, Isle of Skye.
Tel. Glendale 316
(One and three-quarter miles from Glendale, on Holmisdale road. Parking on premises.)

Behind the thick stone walls of Barrie and Sue Evason's 'black house', pure wool is knitted into garments by hand and by machine. These garments include Fair Isle and Arran sweaters, cardigans, waistcoats and an exclusive range of Vargan oiled sweaters. The use of undyed wool of several colours is a special feature of many items in the Evasons' range. Their son, Jonathan, weaves hearth rugs from undyed wool on a simple tapestry loom.

Open Easter to mid-Oct., Mon.–Sat., 10–6. Winter months by appointment.

GOLLANFIELD   Map ref: Ed
Culloden Pottery, The Old Smiddy, Gollanfield, by Inverness.
Tel. Ardersier 2340
(A large white building with blue shutters at the crossroads of the A96 with the B9006, 10 miles north-east of Inverness.)

If Bob Park wanted to use local clay he would have to dig it himself, for no one excavates it on a commercial scale. Being a busy man, he orders his clay from Stoke-on-Trent. He believes that this explains why there are so few potters in the Highlands. He produces a wide range of hand-thrown domestic pottery – mugs, butter dishes, goblets, vases, casseroles and coffee-pots. As well as the more conventional opaque glazes, he uses the wax-resist method to decorate many of his pots; this allows the natural texture of the clay to show through.

Open daily, 9.30–5 from Easter to end Oct. Tues.–Sun. from end Oct. to Christmas.

INVERNESS   Map ref: Dc
E. and D. J. Wilson (Plume makers), No. 2 The Coach House, Bught Drive, Inverness.
(Take the west bank of the River Ness past the Royal Northern Infirmary and follow signs to Municipal Caravan Park. The Coach House is between ice-rink and caravan site.)

Traditionally, feather plumes were worn as a decoration on kilt pins by men and on lapels by women. Nowadays, they tend to be used

The Great Highland bagpipe

The low harmonic hum of the bagpipe inevitably brings to mind kilt-clad, sporran-sporting Highlanders, perhaps massed for war, or dancing a Highland reel. No instrument is more closely associated with Scotland.

A shroud of mystery veils their origins, but bagpipes were, without doubt, played in ancient times throughout the Mediterranean world. The Emperor Nero himself was a renowned piper. Yet the first document to link the bagpipe with Scotland dates no earlier than the 12th century. At this time the bagpipe was simply a pig's bladder, inflated by a mouth pipe and with another pipe – the chanter – attached for playing the melody. The chanter contained a reed and had fingerholes for varying the note. This crude instrument, known as a *chorus*, was gradually developed by Highland pipers until the 18th century, when the Great Highland bagpipe, as we know it today, came into being. The Great Highland bagpipe has a hide bag, and in addition to a chanter has one bass and two tenor drones – long, reeded pipes that provide a continuing harmony.

One present-day maker of Great Highland pipes is Gillanders and McLeod Ltd., of Forfar. Most of the bagpipe-maker's labour revolves around African blackwood – the favourite wood of pipers and pipe-makers alike – and a lathe. At Gillanders and McLeod's workshop, the initial step in construction is the boring of rough shafts through the lengths of blackwood blocks. Following the drilling, each of the bagpipe's 14 wooden components are hand-turned to shape. Traditionally, bagpipe-makers decorated drones and chanters with their own distinctive turned markings. Chanters and drones may also be decorated with silver, nickel or ivory fittings.

Perhaps the most important stage of the woodwork is enlarging the shafts of chanters and drones. This operation requires great precision, for the shafts must be straight as an arrow and smooth as glass if the instrument is to produce the desired tones.

The Gillanders and McLeod craftsmen fashion bags from cowhide or the traditional sheepskin. These are made airtight by rubbing a seasoning into the leather. In bygone days all sorts of natural materials, such as honey and egg whites, were used as seasoning, but these have since given way to more reliable synthetic sealants.

GREAT HIGHLAND BAGPIPE *Its three drones create a majestic and intimidating sound.*

Besides a mastery of woodturning and leatherwork, an expertise in reed-making is required. The material most commonly used is *Arundo donax* cane. Drone reeds are made from a 2 in. piece of cane by sealing one end with wax, cutting a long tongue into one side, and binding the tongue with waxed hemp near its base. Chanter reeds comprise slices of cane that are bound and stapled together.

With the completion of the woodwork, leatherwork and reed-making, the bagpipe-maker is ready to assemble his handiwork. This process involves tying the stocks – hollow sockets – into the bag, inserting reeds into the chanter and drones, sliding the drone sections together and, finally, fitting the chanter, drones and mouth pipe into the stocks. Now in working condition, the Great Highland bagpipe is gloriously wreathed with a tartan bag cover and colourful cords.

---

wherever a touch of colour and decoration is needed. Over the 50 years that the Wilsons have been in business they have established 40 successful designs. These include sprays of brightly coloured feathers mounted on a background of roe-deer skin, and exotic feather brooches shaped like flying birds. Part of their skill lies in the careful selection and shaping of the feathers, the rest in the deft assembling, gluing and binding of the plumes.

Open Mon.–Fri., 9–5.

ISLEORNSAY   Map ref: Cc
Muileann Beag a' Chrotail, Camascross, Isle of Skye.
Tel. Isleornsay 271/2
(On A851, by junction with road to Isleornsay. Street-side parking.)

At Muileann Beag a' Chrotail – meaning, in Gaelic, Little Crotal Mill – sweaters of Harris, Shetland and Gotland wools are knitted on several hand flat machines. Several of the colours used – elderberry, bracken and heather – are accurate reproductions of the tones achieved with vegetable dyes by Skye crofters.

Open Mon.–Fri., 8.30–5.30.

KEISS   Map ref: Fe
Mona Larsen Weavers, Whitehill, South Keiss, by Wick.

Tel. Keiss 335
(A quarter of a mile south of Keiss, on road meeting A9 from the west. Parking on premises.)

Danish-born Mona Larsen and her husband John produce tweeds and floor rugs. Many of their colour schemes reflect the local landscape, while Mona's designs suggest a strong Scandinavian influence. Their materials are sold by the yard, and also in the form of garments tailored by Mona herself.

Open daily, May–Sept., 10–6.

KILDONAN   Map ref: Bd
Skye-Lytes, 2 Kildonan, Arnisort, Isle of Skye.
Tel. Edinbane 286
(On east side of Kildonan road, which meets A850 from north. Street-side parking.)

Colourful candles are made in a converted croft, which rises high above the deep waters of Loch Greshornish. The makers, Brenda and Barrie Creed, use several production techniques, among them sand casting, block moulding and dipping. In colour and design the candles reflect the local landscape and Celtic tradition. Most are engraved with patterns carved with small wood-cutting tools.

Open Mon.–Sat., 10–5.30; Sun., 12–5.30.

KINGUSSIE   Map ref: Ec
Highland China (Scotland) Ltd, Station Yard, Kingussie.
Tel. Kingussie 576
(In a small industrial estate near Kingussie Station.)

From the slip-house at one end of the factory to the store-room at the other, visitors can watch every process in the mass-manufacture of both bone china and earthenware. The stages include the mixing of the slip, the casting in plaster-of-Paris moulds and a sequence of firings, glazing and decoration. It is a rare opportunity to see exactly how the sacks of raw clay and burned animal bones are transformed into glazed and finished products, among them thimbles, beakers and animals – even models of the Loch Ness monster.

Open Mon.–Fri., 8–4.30.

LEACHKIN   Map ref: Dc
Highland Capital Crafts (Sporran maker), Cruachan, Leachkin Brae, Inverness.
Tel. Inverness 33655
(Take Fort William road out of Inverness. After canal, turn right on General Booth Road. At sign for hospital and Leachkin, turn left. Turn right to Upper Leachkin; workshop is on left.)

Originally, sporrans were bags in which the

Scots put their iron rations of oatmeal and salt. Alex Robertson's sporrans, nowadays used for decoration and as purses, are more sophisticated. He cures the skins of foxes and wildcats from the nearby hills, and cuts the brass cantles, from which the sporrans hang, in four basic designs. He also makes kilt belts with brass buckles, plaid brooches, kilt pins and 'pieteans' – traditional thonged leather doublets.

Open daily, 10–12 and 2–4.

LOCHCARRON   Map ref: Cc
Loch Carron Weavers Ltd, North Strome, Lochcarron.
Tel. Lochcarron 212
(Two and a half miles west of Lochcarron, on road to Mid-Strome. Parking on premises.)

Many years of practical experience lie behind every bolt woven in this long-established waterside mill. At one time, production centred on tweeds, but nowadays only woollen tartans roll off the mill's four, semi-automatic hand-looms. Though only a small enterprise, Loch Carron Weavers produces a remarkably large range of patterns.

Workshop open Mon.–Fri., 9–12 and 1.30–5. Shop open Mon.–Sat., 9–5.

LOCHINVER   Map ref: De
Highland Stoneware (Scotland) Ltd, Lochinver.
Tel. Lochinver 376
(On road to Baddidarach, ¾ mile from A837. Parking on premises.)

Sets of soft blue celadon tableware, decorated with a simple iron band, are supplemented by a range of ornate tableware and wall tiles. These are decorated with stylised motifs drawn from nature – wild flowers, birds, fish and landscapes. The decoration is carried out by several craftsmen, who hand-paint each item. Most pieces are shaped by jiggering and jolleying techniques, but some are thrown on a wooden kick-wheel.

Open Mon.–Fri., 8.30–5.30; also Sat., June–Sept.

MELVAIG   Map ref: Cd
Melvaig Pottery, The Old School, Melvaig, by Gairloch.
Tel. North Erradale 248
(On B8021, 9 miles north-west of Gairloch. Parking on premises.)

A disused school provides premises for this one-man pottery, where Philip Gulliver hand-throws a variety of stoneware vessels for the home. Occasionally, he models ceramic sculpture. Both thrown and modelled objects are decorated by glaze dipping, dribbling and splashing. The glazes are his own concoctions and, for some, he uses wood ash and clay from local beaches.

Open May–Sept., Mon.–Sat., 9.30–5.30. Oct.–Apr. by appointment.

NAIRN   Map ref: Ed
M.A.C. Designs (Goldsmith), 115 High Street, Nairn.
Tel. Nairn 53573

Alan McKechnie is one of the few goldsmiths in the Highlands who will carry out work not only to his own designs and specifications, but also to those of his customers. Behind the shop are ranged the jeweller's workbenches. Here, he and his assistant, Tony Snelson, produce rings, pendants, brooches, ear-rings and bracelets. They fashion their own delicate designs – flowers, veined leaves and flies with feather-light wings.

Open Mon.–Sat., 9–6.

NAIRN   Map ref: Ed
Nairn Ceramics, Viewfield Street, Nairn.
Tel. Nairn 53119
(Viewfield Street is off Seafield Street, near the Marine Parade and next to the Clifton Hotel.)

Opening times and other details may change. Check by telephone before making a special journey.

301

Muriel Macintyre believes that a good potter should be able to turn his or her hand to anything – earthenware, porcelain, even sculpture. She specialises in majolica – a type of brightly coloured, tin-glazed pottery that got its name from the island of Mallorca. Her designs are inspired by the sea, by local legends, books and plants, and are executed with great imagination.

Open daily in summer, 10–6. By appointment in winter.

NORTH KESSOCK   Map ref: Dc
Janet Dalgety (Silversmith), Sligo, North Kessock, Inverness.
Tel. Kessock 613
(Take A9 north from Inverness. Half a mile north of the bridge over the Firth, turn right, signpost to Drumsmital. In ¼ mile, turn right, signpost to Kilmuir. At end of tarmac road fork left, and left again in 300 yds. Workshop is on right in 200 yds.)

At one stage of his life Frederick Dalgety was a shepherd on the Isle of Mull. During the long winter evenings he learned his craft from an old lady who lived near by. He and his wife, Janet, now make beautiful silver boxes, pocket knives, lockets and crosses engraved with great attention to detail. Most of their work is commissioned, and they have even been asked to engrave on cuff-links the paws of a customer's favourite dog. They have also made exquisite boxes on which are mounted tiny, hinged silver shells that open and close.

Open by appointment, Apr.–Sept., Mon.–Fri., 2–4.

SCARFSKERRY   Map ref: Ef
Matheson The Boatbuilder, The Boatyard, Scarfskerry, by Thurso.
Tel. Barrock 332
(At western end of Scarfskerry, near call-box. Parking on premises.)

On most days Peter Mathieson may be found constructing a fishing boat or small pleasure craft from oak and larch timbers. When boatbuilding does not demand his attention, he is likely to turn his hand to making simple, hand-finished country furniture in pine – or to catching fish or lobsters.

Open Mon.–Sat., 8–5.

SCARFSKERRY   Map ref: Ef
Scarfskerry Pottery, The Moorings, Scarfskerry, by Thurso.
Tel. Barrock 324
(At eastern end of Scarfskerry, 1½ miles off A836 via West Mey. Parking on premises.)

Manned by David and Sally Body, Scarfskerry produces hand-thrown stoneware pots for the kitchen. They are simply decorated by being dipped in glossy brown, matt ochre and matt off-white glazes. Some pots receive a press-moulded design. The Bodys also make one-off hand-decorated pieces, which bear detailed pictures inspired by local scenery.

Workshop visits by appointment only. Showroom open Mon.–Fri., 10–5; Sat., 10–1.

STRATHCARRON   Map ref: Cc
Carron Pottery and Craft Shop, Cam-Allt, Strathcarron.
Tel. Lochcarron 321
(One mile south of Strathcarron, on A890. Parking on premises.)

In a workshop that has splendid views of the mountain-bound Loch Carron, Barry Jones shapes clay into domestic stoneware. The pieces that he throws are dipped into buckets of glaze, and coated in various shades of white, blue and green. Before dipping, some pieces are decorated with simple wax-resist patterns.

Open Mon.–Sat., 9.30–6.30 in summer; 10–5 in winter.

TAIN   Map ref: Ed
Highland Fine Cheeses Ltd, Blarliath, Tain.
Tel. Tain 2034

(Take the road north-west from town and turn right down Shore Road. Take left-hand bend and continue straight on to gates of Highland Fine Cheeses.)

'Crowdie', a type of cottage cheese peculiar to Scotland and the Islands, is perhaps the oldest cheese in the British Isles, with a history that can be traced back to the Vikings. Highland Fine Cheeses use the special Highland recipe which requires that the skimmed milk should be semi-cooked in a vat. The other speciality is 'caboc' – a rich and delicately flavoured double-cream cheese rolled in pin-head oatmeal. This is made from an ancient recipe that has been handed down from mother to daughter ever since the 15th century.

Open Mon.–Fri., 9.30–12.30 and 2–5. Appointment advisable.

TALMINE   Map ref: De
Achnahuaig Hand-Embroideries, Talmine, by Lairg.
Tel. Talmine 277 (home)
(By call-box 2½ miles north of Kyle of Tongue causeway [A838]. Parking on premises.)

Maggi Thomason combines artistic talent and needlework skills in making intricate embroidery. Using satin-stitch techniques, she embroiders original designs on cotton backgrounds. Most of her embroidery embellishes smocks, blouses, dresses and pill-box tops.

Open Easter to Oct., Tues.–Sat., 2–5.

TEANGUE   Map ref: Cc
Westman's Pottery, Teangue, Sleat, Isle of Skye.
Tel. Isleornsay 264
(On road to Upper Teangue, which joins A851 in Teangue. Parking on premises.)

Tom and Elizabeth Westman hand-throw and model tableware and decorative pieces from stoneware clay. Their pots are decorated through combinations of sprigs, slip-trailing and dipping. Many of the Westmans' works bear intricate designs from ancient Celtic manuscripts and stone carvings.

Open Mon.–Sat., 9–5. Advisable to telephone first. No groups of more than eight.

THURSO   Map ref: Ee
Fisherbiggin Pottery Studio, Riverside, Thurso.
Tel. Thurso 3318
(Riverside runs along western bank of River Thurso, north of A836. Pottery stands by church ruins. Street-side parking.)

Using both kick and electric wheels, Mary Barclay gives form and function to lumps of stoneware clay. In decorating her pots, she achieves striking colour combinations by using unique glazes, the recipes for which call for peat ash, local sand and seaweed. Several methods of decorating are employed to create the abstract designs of her work.

Open Apr.–Sept., Mon.–Sat., 10–12, 2–4 and 7–9. Also Oct.–Mar., Mon.–Sat., 10–12 and 2–4.

TOMATIN   Map ref: Ec
James Scarlett (Weaver), Milton of Moy, Tomatin.
Tel. Tomatin 321
(Take the turning to Ruthven off the A9. Do not follow the road over humped-back bridge, but carry on along track to only house in sight.)

James Scarlett has studied tartans for nearly 20 years and has written four books on the subject. The colours he has chosen are from early-19th-century specimens discovered in museums, and not the garish reds and yellows that the Victorians introduced. He designs new tartans in the traditional mode, and he specialises in individual commissions.

Open Apr.–Oct., by appointment.

TONGUE   Map ref: De
M. Sutherland (Weaver), Woodend, Tongue.
Tel. Tongue 235
(On western side of A836, 2 miles north of Tongue. Parking on premises.)

In the old granite schoolhouse where Murdo Sutherland received his primary education, he runs a craft shop and exercises his weaving skills. Using dyed yarn, he weaves tweeds and tartans in 50 yd lengths on two foot-powered Hattersley looms. After being sent away for washing and shrinking, the bolts are returned to his shop for sale.

Open Mon.–Sat., 9–6.

UIGINISH   Map ref: Bc
Skyeramics Pottery, Uiginish, Dunvegan, Isle of Skye.
Tel. Dunvegan 348
(One mile north of B884 on road to Uiginish. Parking on premises.)

Earthenware pots in 80 different shapes and 70 different colours are produced by Morris Manson and his associates. The great majority of pieces are coated in rich, bold glazes by double dipping. Certain ceramics, however, are further enhanced by pressing – a technique dating from the 16th century – intricate sgraffito and slip-trailing.

Open daily Mar.–Oct., 10–7.30; Nov.–Feb., Mon.–Fri., 10–5.

WICK   Map ref: Fe
Caithness Glass Ltd, Harrowhill Wick.
Tel. Wick 2286
(Signposted on A9 in southern outskirts of Wick. Parking on premises.)

Glass tableware and ornaments for the home and export markets are blown in the Caithness glasshouse. Blowers inflate molten glass gobs into moulds to make vases, goblets, decanters and tankards. Once shaped, each item embarks on a two hour journey through a 70 ft oven. The oven's conveyor belt transfers the glass from the glasshouse to the finishing room, where it is cut, ground and polished ready for buyers.

Open Mon.–Fri., 8–12 and 12.30–4.30. Closed for two weeks at Christmas and New Year.

WICK   Map ref: Fe
J. McCaughey (Boatbuilders) Ltd, Harbour Quay, Wick.
Tel. Wick 2858
(Overlooking inner harbour on south side of Wick Bay. Street-side parking.)

Boats large and small ply between Wick's inner harbour and the fishing grounds of the North Sea. Some of these vessels were built in Mr McCaughey's quayside boatyard. At most times his men are busily building and overhauling several different boats. Many are wooden, with home-grown Scottish larch planks, and oak keels and frames. But Mr McCaughey's small engineering works also constructs steel craft.

Open Mon.–Fri., 8–1 and 1.30–5. Closed Bank Holidays.

MUSEUMS

KILMUIR   Map ref: Bd
Kilmuir Croft Museum, Kilmuir, Isle of Skye.
Tel. Duntulm 213
(Five miles north of Uig, on A856.)

Beside the coast road is a cluster of thatched houses which have been renovated over the last 20 years by Jonathon MacDonald to re-create the crofter's way of life. This is the Kilmuir Croft Museum – four thatched, 100-year-old 'black houses', comprising a main dwelling house, a weaving house, a smithy and a Ceilidh house (or meeting house). All except the Ceilidh house have been furnished with the original, rough, hand-made furniture and the tools that were used by the crofters of long ago. The smithy contains the mass of tools required

by any farrier – together with an anvil, hearth and bellows. Only the Ceilidh house has a change of role, for it is now filled with pictures, documents and letters recording the Isle of Skye's past.

Open daily, Apr. to mid-Oct.

KINGUSSIE   Map ref: Ec
Highland Folk Museum.
(See panel on facing page)

WICK   Map ref: Fe
Wick Heritage Centre, Bank Row, Wick.
Tel. Wick 4179

In its heyday, 100 years ago, Wick was one of the herring industry's main centres in northern Europe. The Centre – a complex of four houses designed by the famous civil engineer Thomas Telford – brings the industry back to life. Displays include a full-scale reconstruction of a harbour scene and of a cooper's shop with a fine collection of tools. A 'skaffie' – the type of fishing boat used in the area during the last century – is berthed five minutes' walk from the museum in the harbour.

Open June–Oct., 10–12 and 2–5. Charge for admission.

ORKNEY

BIMBISTER   Map ref: Ff
Fursbreck Pottery, Harray.
Tel. Harray 419
(Take A965 eastwards from Kirkwall. Beyond Finstown turn on to A986. The pottery is signposted 2½ miles later at Bimbister, near the Corrigal Farm Museum. Parking outside.)

With five helpers, Andrew Appleby makes fine, colourful but practical porcelain. Fursbreck Pottery is the largest pottery in Orkney and the largest producer of hand-made porcelain in Scotland. Hand-painted flowers, dragons, birds and fish are among the most common decorations.

Open daily, 10–6. Closed Sun. in winter.

FINSTOWN   Map ref: Ff
Lindor Sheepskins, Braevilla, Rendall.
Tel. Finstown 356
(Take A965 from Kirkwall to Finstown, then turn on to A966 to Evie. The workshop is on the left after 4 miles, just over a stream. Parking outside the workshop.)

Mr and Mrs Plant cure on average about six fleeces a week, a process that takes up to three weeks. First they are cleaned of all blood and fat, then salted, rolled up and stored until they are needed. They are then washed, stretched out on wooden frames and left to dry in the fresh air. When dry, the skins are rubbed with the curing agent – a chrome solution – and again left to dry. Finally, the fleece is rubbed to soften the skin, the wool is brushed, and the rug is ready for sale.

Open Mon.–Fri., 11–4. Small parties of up to four only.

GRIMESTON   Map ref: Ff
HT Wood Craft Signs, Coney Hall, Grimeston, Harray.
(Take the A965 westwards from Kirkwall. Beyond Finstown turn on to the A986. A mile later follow sign to workshop. Parking both sides of building.)

Square, simple but practical, this workshop started life as a cowshed. Hardwoods are used for the signs, which are made to order. The words are marked out in the required script, then each is carved, sanded and finally varnished with eight or nine coats. The name stands out – not through paint, but because of the depth of the lettering, and different colours of the wood.

Open Wed.–Sun., 10–7.

Map ref: Ec

Highland Folk Museum

KINGUSSIE, HIGHLAND

When Dr I. F. Grant, a social and economic historian, opened her museum on Iona in 1934, people thought she was a crank. At the time, specialist folk museums were a new idea; until then, the study of other cultures had been considered more worthwhile than the study of our own. As a result, the Highland Folk Museum, which comprises Dr Grant's collection from Iona, can claim to be the oldest folk museum in Britain.

The exhibits embrace every aspect of Highland life. The fine collection of local furniture demonstrates the craftsman's ingenuity in making the most of his raw materials; there is a dresser made from driftwood and chairs roughly hewn from slabs of wood. Forked branches were often used in the construction of furniture because they were stronger than jointed pieces.

Textiles have been made in the Highlands from prehistoric times to the present day. Some of the costumes, tartans and tweeds in the museum date back to the 18th century. The collection of equipment includes spindles, spinning-wheels and looms, and a huge range of dye samples produced from a myriad different plants.

Among over 1,000 tools in the blacksmith's collection there are some that were made in a local foundry which closed down early in the 18th century. The rope-maker's display includes a length of rope made from horsehair. It comes from the deserted island of St Kilda, where it was once used for scaling cliffs in order to take birds' eggs.

As can be seen from the horse collars made from marram grass, craftsmen such as the saddler made full use of local materials. Tools and products make up displays on a wide range of other crafts, including basket making, shoe making, butter making, stone masonry, wheelwrighting and wood working.

The museum also resurrects a little-known craftsman who, before the days of the village shop,

MASON'S SKILLS *Clock housing in stone, and mason's mallets.*

fulfilled a vital role in the local economy – the 'Cairdean'. Jack of all trades – silversmith, jeweller, basket maker and lamp maker – he travelled the Highlands, living in a tent or caravan. He was jealous of his secret techniques, and would not allow strangers to watch him at work.

The agricultural exhibits include hand-tools, ploughs, carts and Patrick Bell's reaper, the world's first mechanical corn reaper, which was made in 1826. During the summer there are occasionally displays of hay-making and the building of corn stacks.

Traditional building methods are also well represented. The walls of a turf-built house have been reconstructed. So has an entire 'black house' from the Isle of Lewis – a low, dry-stone building with thick walls and a thatched roof of oat straw. It is divided into three sections, with the byre at one end, the living quarters and kitchen in the middle and the 'good room' at the other end. Despite the cramped conditions of the rest of the house this room was used, before the 19th century, only on special occasions such as births, marriages and for the laying out of the dead.

Duke Street, Kingussie, Highland. Tel. Kingussie 307.

Open Apr.–Oct., Mon.–Sat., 10–6; Sun., 2–6. Nov.–Mar., Mon.–Fri., 10–3. Charge for admission.

DRIFTWOOD *Dresser made from driftwood on South Uist.*

ONE-PIECE CHAIR *Seat made from a single piece of wood found on the Island of Harris.*

CROFTER'S COTTAGE *Reconstructed 'black house' from the Isle of Lewis. Rain from the thatch drains away through a core of sand between the inner and outer skins of the wall.*

Opening times and other details may change. Check by telephone before making a special journey.

303

HULLION Map ref: Ff

The Orkney Pottery, Rousay.
Tel. Rousay 266
(From ferry follow B9064 to the west for 2½ miles to Hullion. Pottery is on right of the road. Parking outside.)

Frank Harris, Christine Campbell and Katherine Peace form a hard-working team making decorative and functional stoneware, as well as hand-thrown porcelain. Much of the pottery is glazed with plain colours; some has designs painted with coloured oxides, and a transparent glaze over the top; in yet other cases the patterns are incised by hand. Many of these designs are of Celtic origin, derived from those on the standing stones around the islands.

Open all year, 9–6.

KIRKWALL Map ref: Ff

Ola M. Gorie, 11 Broad Street, Kirkwall.
Tel. Kirkwall 3251
(Situated behind the Longship, opposite cathedral.)

From becoming Orkney's first professional jeweller in the 1960s, Ola Gorie now has a staff of ten assistants. The Nordic influence is evident in his designs: longships, crosses, and the animals and birds depicted on archaeological ruins. These are copied on to pendants, rings, bracelets and cufflinks. Each design has history and folklore attached, and the story is given away with each item sold. Modern designs also form a part of the range.

Workshop open by appointment, Mon.–Fri., 8–1 and 2–5. Shop open Mon.–Sat., 9–5; Wed., 9–1.

KIRKWALL Map ref: Ff

D. M. Kirkness, 14 Palace Road, Kirkwall.
Tel. Kirkwall 2429
(Near the cathedral. Parking outside.)

Mrs Maureen Lennie makes traditional Orkney chairs and stools out of Japanese oak. The wood is fumed and treated with linseed oil for protection, and the joints are mortised and tenoned. The seats are made of sea-grass, and the backs are of local straw. The straw is either woven straight on to the chair backs, or on to frames which are attached later. These three raw materials complete the low, sturdy Orkney chair that looks much the same now as in the days when it was fashioned out of driftwood.

Open Mon., Tues. and Thur., 8–5.

KIRKWALL Map ref: Ff

Ortak, Hatston Industrial Estate, Kirkwall.
Tel. Kirkwall 2224
(Follow A965 for ¼ mile round bay to west of Kirkwall, then turn right on minor road and take first left. Parking outside workshop entrance.)

Malcolm Gray claims to be the largest jewellery manufacturer in Scotland. Working with gold, silver, precious and semi-precious stones, Ortak produces over 600 designs, ranging from traditional Celtic to modern. Mr Gray has built up a thriving industry employing a staff of 26 in his workshop.

Workshop open Mon.–Fri., 9–1 and 2–4.30. Shop open Mon.–Sat.

KIRKWALL Map ref: Ff

Robert H. Towers, 'Rosegarth', St Ola, Kirkwall.
Tel. Kirkwall 3521
(On A964, 1½ miles south-west from Kirkwall. Parking close to workshop.)

Mr Towers is one of a handful of craftsmen who continue to make the traditional Orkney chair – long made by crofters for their personal needs. It used to be fashioned from driftwood, because timber has always been scarce on the island. One of its features is a low seat, so that its occupant's head was below the haze of smoke that tended to linger from the open fire.

The chair evolved from a straw-covered stool into a straw-backed chair, and some acquired a hood. Robert Towers makes his chairs from pine or walnut, and the seats are – like those of

much older chairs – contain a drawer. The curved backs are still made from local straw. The one difference in recent years has been a sea-grass or cord seat, but even this is in part a reversion to the original straw seat.

Open all year, Mon.–Fri. Appointment preferred. Room for up to four visitors.

SANDWICK Map ref: Ef

Knowtoo Pottery, Knowtoo Cottage, Sandwick.
(From Stromness, take the A965 Kirkwall road. Turn left at B9055 Brodgar road. Pottery is in about 3 miles. Parking outside.)

Situated on a spit of land between two lochs, this converted threshing-mill still has its cast-iron wheel as evidence of its past. Sidney Smith, the potter, is an artist/potter of considerable experience. Making stoneware and earthenware, he throws bowls and vases, and casts such items as trinket boxes and candle holders. He creates the glazes himself, and his methods of making and decorating ensure great variety in shape and colour. Hand-painting, which gives the finishing touches, is based on Viking, Celtic and Pictish designs found locally. Mr Smith experiments occasionally with local clay, which is coarse and rather difficult to work.

Open May–Sept., 10–6.

SANDWICK Map ref: Ef

A. H. & J. D. Yates, Keldroseed, Sandwick, Stromness.
Tel. Sandwick 628
(Take the A965, then A967, north from Stromness for almost 5 miles. Turn right on road immediately after crossing the end of Loch of Stenness. Keldroseed in on left after ½ mile. Park by house.)

From behind her traditional loom, Jennefer Yates enjoys spectacular views of the surrounding countryside. She weaves Brora and Orkney yarns into natural-coloured scarves. Rugs, curtains, bedspreads, scarves and cloth for clothes are woven in natural shades of brown, green and rust.

No set opening times, and an appointment is necessary. Small groups welcome – up to six. Residential spinning and weaving courses are given.

SURRIGARTH Map ref: Fg

Westray Strawback Chair Producers, Surrigarth, Westray.
Tel. Westray 323
(Take B9066 south-east from Pierowall. After 4 miles turn on to minor road to Surrigarth. Parking outside.)

All the craftsmen in this co-operative of five or six chair-makers are part-timers. James Fergus, for instance, combines his furniture making with running a 40 acre farm, though visitors can usually see another chair-maker at work if he is out on the land. It was a demand for the original Orkney chair – which has a low seat and a straw back – that first started him mixing furniture with farming. Now the chairs are distributed to the mainland, and sold all over the world.

Open by appointment all year, Mon.–Sat., 9–5. Room for up to four visitors.

SHETLAND

WEISDALE Map ref: Ge

Shetland Silvercraft, Soudside, Weisdale.
Tel. Weisdale 275
(On the A971, 10½ miles north-west of Lerwick on the eastern side of Weisdale Voe.)

The beautiful seascape of Weisdale Voe provides a memorable setting for this island workshop, where gold and silver jewellery is made. The designs are simple, showing a Scandinavian and Celtic influence. Local wildlife has been depicted on the pendants, brooches,

necklaces, bracelets and ear-rings, together with figures from Norse legends. One such is Odin Sleipnir, a magical horse which had eight legs and could gallop through the air. Craftsmen can be seen at work casting the silver in moulds, cutting silver, soldering and polishing.

Open Mon.–Fri., 9–1 and 2–5.

WHITENESS Map ref: Ge

Hjaltasteyn, Whiteness.
Tel. Gott 351
(On A971, 9 miles north-west of Lerwick. Parking at workshop.)

The company name is in old Norn – the spoken language in Shetland 150 years ago – and means Shetland stone. It is appropriate, since the only gemstones used in their jewellery are local Shetland stones. A team of six skilled craftsmen can be seen making a variety of silver, gold and enamel jewellery – sawing, grinding, sanding and polishing the stones; making the settings by hand; cutting sheet metal; making filigree wire work; soldering and polishing the metals.

Workshop open Mon.–Fri., 11–12.30 and 2.30–4.30. Shop open 9–1 and 2–5.

MUSEUM

VEENSGARTH Map ref: Ge

Tingwall Valley Agricultural Museum, Veensgarth.
Tel. Gott 344
(Off A971, 5 miles north-west of Lerwick.)

Over the years Mrs Jean Sandison has gathered over 800 bygones from Shetland's yesterdays. The collection is housed in farm buildings that date from 1750. There is a typically furnished

Shetland bedroom. Mrs Sandison conducts guided tours through the different rooms where hand-operated agricultural tools vie for attention beside butter-making equipment and spinning-wheels. There are Shetland chairs, an old threshing machine and a pony cart.

Open May to end Sept., Tues., Thur. and Sat., 10–5.

TAYSIDE

BLAIRGOWRIE Map ref: Eb

Piob Mhor, 39–43 High Street, Blairgowrie.
Tel. Blairgowrie 2131
(In the main street. Parking available in side streets.)

It takes 14 hours and about 8 yds of pure woollen cloth to make a kilt for a Scottish piper at Piob Mhor. The Milne family make complete outfits for pipe bands in many parts of the world – feather bonnets, jackets and, of course, sporrans, which are traditionally made of pigskin. The bags of the bagpipes are made from sheepskin or cowhide, hand-sewn with thread of a wider diameter than the needle so that all of the seams will be airtight. The pipes themselves are of African blackwood, and in the more expensive sets the mountings can be of silver or ivory.

Open all year, May–Oct., daily, 9–5.30; Nov.–Apr., Mon.–Sat., 9–5.30. Early closing Thur.

CRIEFF Map ref: Ea

Thistle Potteries, 13 Muthill Road, Crieff.
Tel. Crieff 3515
(About 1 mile south of Crieff on the A822. Car park on site.)

Map ref: Ea

Museum of Scottish Tartans

COMRIE, TAYSIDE

The museum's record of every known tartan makes it the most comprehensive collection in the world. Among over 1,300 samples are tartans that have been to the moon and back, pieces from royal tartans, and a magnificent 'double bar' plaid dated 1726. A wealth of documentation includes orders for cheap tartans for negro slaves in Jamaica – in order, it is said, to make them more conspicuous and easier to shoot if they escaped. Woven into this fascinating display are tales of daring and deceit from the Highlands, and insights into the history of tartan. A weaver's cottage, typical of early 18th-century Perthshire, has been reconstructed outside. Here, traditional methods of dyeing, spinning and hand-loom weaving are demonstrated occasionally.

Comrie, Tayside. Tel. Comrie 779.

Open Mon.–Sat., 9–5; Sun., 2–4, from Easter to Nov. In winter, open Mon.–Fri., 10–4; 10–1 on Sat. Closed for lunch 1–2 throughout year. Charge for admission.

WEAVER'S HOME *Reconstruction of an 18th-century weaver's cottage.*

The Buchan family have produced fine stoneware here since 1867. Each of the pieces is decorated by hand on a background of grey-blue, reminiscent of the Highland mist, so that every design, though confining itself to only three traditional Scottish plants, is subtly different. Guided tours are arranged for visitors, and a large selection of seconds is available.

Open all year, Mon.–Fri. Shop, 9.30–5; also summer weekends, 10–5. Factory tours Mon.–Thur., mornings and afternoons; also Fri. mornings.

DUNKELD   Map ref: Eb
Jeremy Law Ltd (Leatherwork), City Hall, Dunkeld.
Tel. Dunkeld 569
(Next to the Royal Hotel in main street. Parking in nearby free car park.)

A grey-stone building in the heart of Dunkeld, the City Hall now houses Jeremy Law's team of four leatherworkers. Using deerskin for everything except the linings, they make hand-bags, purses, wallets and other leather goods that are sent all over the world. Visitors may purchase from a varied selection of factory rejects and travellers' samples.

Open all year, Mon.–Sat., 8–5; closed 12.30–1.30.

PERTH   Map ref: Ea
Caithness Glass Ltd, Inveralmond Industrial Estate, Perth.
Tel. Perth 37373
(Off the A9 at a roundabout 2 miles north of Perth. Car park on site.)

The recipe for Caithness glass is 65% sand (from Lochaline on the west coast of Scotland), 14% soda ash, 6% calcium carbonate, 6% potassium carbonate, 4% lead oxide, 4% sodium nitrate and 1% arsenic. In addition, small quantities of metallic oxides are added to give the required colours. Behind large picture windows, visitors can watch glass blowers at work, following each stage of the process with the aid of explanatory captions. On display is a large selection of glasses, decanters, goblets, vases and bowls – some sand-sculpted with birds, butterflies and flowers. Note the paperweights, in colourful abstract designs.

Open all year. Viewing gallery, Mon.–Fri., 9–4.30. Shop, Mon.–Sat., 9–5; Sun., 1–5.

PITLOCHRY   Map ref: Eb
Kasinga Woodcraft, Kasinga, Well Brae, Pitlochry.
Tel. Pitlochry 2373
(Near Pitlochry Hydro Hotel. Parking in road outside house.)

Mr James Hislop lived in the Far East, where he built up a collection of ornamental tropical hardwoods – woods with exotic names such as machang, sepetir, padouk, setambun and many others. Now Mr Hislop devotes himself to his great love – woodturning. In his bowls, lamp bases, plates and other items he brings out the full beauty of grain and colour in these Oriental timbers.

Open all year, Mon.–Sat., 10–4.

MUSEUMS

COMRIE   Map ref: Ea
Museum of Scottish Tartans.
(See panel on facing page)

GLAMIS   Map ref: Fb
Angus Folk Museum, Kirkwynd Cottages, Glamis.

In a long, low row of five old estate cottages and a wash-house, visitors can see how country people lived in the 19th century. Exhibits include spinning-wheels and shuttles. There is a Jacquard loom, in working order. The tools and displays in the agricultural hall and smithy show almost every aspect of Angus rural life in days gone by, including the lathe on which Patrick Bell made the parts for the world's first reaping machine in 1826.

Open daily, 12–5 (last entry 4.30), May–Sept. Charge for admission.

WESTERN ISLES

BALAGLAS   Map ref: Ad
Lachlan MacDonald, Cnoc Ard, Grimsay, North Uist.
Tel. Benbecula 2418
(Off the A865, north of the island of Benbecula, take second exit on Grimsay circular road at Balaglas. Workshop is a short distance down road on right. Parking outside.)

Lachlan MacDonald works in a spot he describes as 'one of the wildest, most remote, unspoilt areas left in Britain'. Here, using only Scottish wool, he weaves Harris Tweed. Several years ago, when Harris Tweed was thought of as suitable only for men, Mr MacDonald devised colours and patterns suitable for women's clothes and soft furnishings.

Open daily, but advisable to telephone first in winter to make sure that weaving will be in progress. Shop open Mon.–Sat.

BORVE   Map ref: Be
Stornoway Pottery Ltd, Borve, Isle of Lewis.
Tel. Borve 345
(Take the A857 north towards Ness from Stornoway. After 17 miles, take first turning on left after Borve Post Office. Parking outside pottery.)

Alex and Susan Blair make stoneware pottery that is attractive, practical and always functional. It comes mainly in natural colours – browns, oatmeals and pale blue. Of particular interest are their tree and abstract designs on lamp bases and storage jars, which are applied in raw clay when the pots are 'leather hard'. They are then treated so that, at the second firing, they do not take the glaze, and so stand out from the rest of the surface.

Open all year, Mon.–Sat.

COLL   Map ref: Ce
Coll Pottery/Fear an eich, 22a Coll Back, Isle of Lewis.
Tel. Back 219

(Seven miles from Stornoway on B895 Stornoway–Tolsta road. Workshop is in Coll on north side of road. Parking on premises.)

During the last 30 years Marjorie Maclennan has listened to countless stories about how life was lived on the island over 100 years ago, and has chosen to re-create the characters of those days in pottery. Using strong, solid glazes – browns, golds and greens – she brings to life these delightful characters: ladies making butter, spinning wool, carrying peat, cleaning fish; fishermen at work, or a man catching a ram by its horns.

Open all year, 10–5.

DRINISHADER   Map ref: Bd
Mrs Annie Morrison (Weaver), Post Office House, Drinishader, Isle of Harris.
Tel. Drinishader 200
(From Tarbert take the A859 Tarbert–Rodel road. Turn left after 2 miles on to Golden Road to Drinishader. Parking at gate.)

Mrs Annie Morrison was brought up with Harris wool. Her mother was a weaver and knitter before her, and since leaving school she has carried on the family tradition. She dyes the wool herself, using local, natural dyes that produce soft heather colours – browns, greens and blues. Mrs Morrison has two looms, and can be seen warping up and weaving Harris Tweed. She also plies the yarns into 3-ply knitting wools, and hand-knits Harris jerseys, scarves, socks and ski caps. The wool she uses is produced virtually on her own doorstep, for her husband is a farmer who owns a large flock of sheep.

Open May–Sept., 9–6. Space available for groups of up to ten.

EOCHAR   Map ref: Ac
Hebridean Jewellery, Garrieganichy, Iochdar (Eochar), South Uist.
Tel. Carnan 288
(Workshop is signposted from main road, about 1½ miles from it.)

From this remote island Mr and Mrs Hart sell their jewellery worldwide through their mail-order catalogue. John Hart was trained by his father, and has been designing and making jewellery for 15 years in silver, gold and semi-precious stones. His designs are mainly traditional, strongly influenced by Celtic and Scottish motifs and styles. He can be seen making the jewellery by hand, hand-sawing, filing, soldering, polishing, setting the stones and engraving.

Open all year, Mon.–Sat., 9–5.

GISLA   Map ref: Be
Gisla Woodcraft, Gisla, Uig, Isle of Lewis.
Tel. Timsgarry 371
(Twenty-five miles west of Stornoway. Turn left off the A858 on to the B8011. Workshop is near the small power station in Gisla. Parking outside.)

Jenny Daniel sells her large range of turned wood – bowls, dishes, lamps, boxes, barometers and mirrors – on the mainland in Scotland and England as well as from her own workshop.

She uses ash, elm, beech, oak and laburnum, which comes either from Lord Leverhulme's plantation at Stornoway Castle, or from the Scottish mainland.

Open daily.

MUIR OF AIRD   Map ref: Ad
D. Macgillivray & Co., Muir of Aird, Benbecula.
Tel. Benbecula 2204
(Situated near the airport, on opposite side of road to army camp off the B892. Parking available.)

Donald Macgillivray began his business in 1943 employing local outworkers, and still does so. Local crofters' wives weave, spin and knit the wool from the island's sheep into tweeds, tartans and knitwear. However, spinning and weaving is also done at the workshop, and visitors may see it in progress. They may even try their hand at the looms and spinning-wheels. Besides the company-produced items, perfume, carvings and other local craft goods can be bought.

Open daily, except Sun.

PLOCRAPOOL   Map ref: Bd
'Croft Crafts Harris', 4 Plocrapool, Drinishader, Isle of Harris.
Tel. Drinishader 217
(From Tarbert take the A859 Tarbert–Rodel road. Turn left after 2 miles on to Golden Road to Plocrapool, via Drinishader. Parking at workshop.)

Alistair Campbell's parents were weavers, and he and his family now continue the business. They weave the cloth to their own designs on foot-propelled Hattersley looms. (Harris Tweed may not be woven on mechanical looms if it is to bear the Orb mark, the sign of its authenticity.) The Campbells also ply the Harris yarn on a twisting machine, to produce 3-ply knitting wools. These, and the Harris Tweed, are for sale in the shop, all in the island 'heather' colours of brown, green, blue and white.

Open all year, Mon.–Sat., 9–9.

TANGASDALE   Map ref: Ac
The Hebridean Perfume Co. (Barra) Ltd, Tangasdale, Castlebay, Isle of Barra.
Tel. Castlebay 216
(Half a mile north of Castlebay on the A888.)

Iain Campbell and Lenora Bond started this perfume business in 1967 with just three perfumes. Now they have eight, and since then Mr Campbell has learned a great deal about the public's likes and dislikes. He finds perfume 'rather like wine': some people like it dry or semi-dry; others prefer it sweet, woody or musky. To visitors he will explain the composition of his perfumes, in this case high-quality essential oils. All the perfume is hand-blended in small batches of about ¼ gallon at a time, bottled and finally boxed. Visitors who wish to buy a particular perfume can have it made up for them on the spot.

Open all year, Mon.–Sat., 9–5.

Opening times and other details may change. Check by telephone before making a special journey.

305

ANNUAL CRAFT EVENTS IN BRITAIN

A regional calendar of the major shows and exhibitions throughout the country where craftsmen and their work can be seen.

The South-West

CORNWALL

June Royal Cornwall Show, Wadebridge. Thur.–Sat. in early June. Tel. A. H. Riddle (Sec.), Wadebridge 2183.

DEVON

May Devon County Show, Whipton, Exeter. 3rd Thur. in May for 3 days. Tel. C. F. J. Hocken (Sec.), Exeter 77316.

July Totnes and District Show, Berry Pomeroy, nr Totnes. Last Thur. in July. Tel. W. C. Stephens (Sec.), Totnes 863888 or Newton Abbot 3881.

August Honiton and District Show, Honiton. 1st Thur. in Aug. Tel. C. R. S. Birch (Sec.), Up Ottery 433.

August West Country Craft Show, Rolle College, Exmouth. Sun.–Wed. of 2nd week in Aug. Tel. Christine Pankhurst (Organiser), Exmouth 272010.

DORSET

July Dorset Craft Guild Exhibition and Market, Milton Abbey School, Milton Abbas. 3 weeks end July to beginning Aug. Tel. Mavis Hollingworth (Sec.), Chideock 462 (before 7 p.m.).

August Dorset Craft Guild Exhibition and Market, Youth Centre, Gundry Lane, Bridport. Fri.–Wed. in mid-Aug. Tel. Mavis Hollingworth, Chideock 462 (before 7 p.m.).

August Gillingham and Shaftesbury Show: Gillingham in even-numbered years, Shaftesbury in odd-numbered years. 4th Wed. in Aug. Tel. Col. A. W. Gough-Allen, Gillingham 3955.

August Melplash Show, Bridport. Last Thur. in Aug. Tel. Secretary, Bridport 23337.

September Dorchester Show, Came Park, Dorchester. 1st Sat. in Sept. Tel. Mrs M. Tomblin, Dorchester 64249.

SOMERSET

June Royal Bath and West Show, Shepton Mallet. Wed.–Sat., 1st week in June. Tel. John W. Davis, MBE (Sec.), Shepton Mallet 82211.

June–September Craft demonstrations held at Somerset Rural Life Museum, Abbey Farm, Chilkwell Street, Glastonbury. Most weekends in summer. Programme of events available from Feb. each year. Tel. Glastonbury 32903.

July Summer Exhibition of the Somerset Guild of Craftsmen, Town Hall, Wells. Last week in July, 1st week in Aug. Tel. Taunton 81222.

WILTSHIRE

May Lacock and Chippenham Folk Festival: at Chippenham for 3 days before Spring Bank Holiday, and at Lacock on Spring Bank Holiday. Tel. Bradenstoke 890726 or Chippenham 50760.

May–December Local Craft of Wessex Exhibitions held at several venues in Avon and Wilts. Tel. Mrs Collett (Sec.), Castle Combe 782441.

November Christmas Craft Fair, St Edmund's Art Centre, Bedwin Street, Salisbury. 2 days at end Nov. to beginning Dec. Tel. Salisbury 20379.

The South-East

BERKSHIRE

September Newbury Fair, Shaw Showground, Newbury. 3rd weekend in Sept. Tel. Richard Pettit-Mills (Organiser), Woolhampton 2345.

December Craft Fair, South Hill Park Arts Centre, Bracknell. 1st weekend in Dec. Tel. Alastair Snow, Bracknell 27272.

EAST SUSSEX

Guild of Sussex Craftsmen organise about four craft markets a year at different venues. Tel. Michael Pryke (Publicity Officer), Hassocks 5246.

August Sussex Crafts and Small Industries Exhibition, Michelham Priory, Upper Dicker, nr Hailsham. 1st Wed. in Aug. for 5 days. Tel. COSIRA, Lewes 3422.

GREATER LONDON

Annual exhibition of traditional crafts, British Craft Centre, 43 Earlham Street, Covent Garden, London WC2. Lasts for 5 weeks; time of year varies. Tel. 01 836 6993.

April London Crafts Fair, Camden Arts Centre, Arkwright Road, London NW3. Fri.–Sun. in Apr. Tel. 01 435 2643.

June Putney Weekend and Horse Show, Putney Lower Common, London SW15. 3rd weekend in June. Tel. Dena Bedborough or Molly Simpson, 01 223 9311.

July Lambeth Country Show, Brockwell Park, Herne Hill, London SE24. Weekend in mid-July. Tel. Press and Publicity Office, 01 274 7722.

July Wandsworth Weekend, King George's Park, Garratt Lane, London SW18. 3rd weekend in July. Tel. Dena Bedborough or Molly Simpson, 01 223 9311.

August International Craft and Hobby Fair, Wembley Conference Centre, Wembley, Middx. Sun.–Wed., last week in Aug. Tel. ICHF Ltd, Highcliffe 72711.

September The British Craft Show, Syon Park, Brentford, Middx. Thur.–Sat., mid-Sept. Tel. ICHF Ltd, Highcliffe 72711.

HAMPSHIRE

May Viables Annual Craft Fair, Viables Centre, Harrow Way, Basingstoke. Sat.–Mon., May Day weekend. Tel. Basingstoke 3634 (mornings only).

May Wessex Craft Show, Breamor House, Fordingbridge. Spring Bank Holiday, Sun.–Tues. Tel. ICHF Ltd, Highcliffe 72711.

June Braishfield Country Fair, Braishfield. Weekend in early June. Tel. Miss Saunders (Hon. Sec.), Braishfield 68391.

July Country Fair, Queen Elizabeth Country Park, Gravel Hill, Horndean, nr Portsmouth. Sat.–Sun. in mid-July. Craft demonstrations are also held here at weekends, Apr.–Oct. Tel. Horndean 595040.

July New Forest Show, New Park, Brockenhurst. Last Wed.–Thur. in July. Tel. Mr Shanks (Sec.), Lymington 22400/22470.

August Beaulieu Country Sports and Crafts Fair. Grounds adjacent to National Motor Museum, Beaulieu. Sun. in mid-Aug. Tel. Fair Organiser, Beaulieu 612345.

August Wessex Guild of Craftsmen's Annual Show, Queen Elizabeth Country Park, Gravel Hill, Horndean, nr Portsmouth. Sat. in mid-Aug. Tel. Anahid Thomas (Hon. Sec.), Cosham 376289.

August Mid-Southern Counties Show, Rushmoor Arena, Aldershot. Weekend before Aug. Bank Holiday. Tel. Mrs Westcombe (Sec.), Basingstoke 21017.

September Romsey Show, Broadlands Park, Romsey. 2nd Sat. in Sept. Tel. Romsey 517521.

November Portsmouth Craft Fair, The Guildhall, Portsmouth. Fri.–Sun. in early Nov. Tel. Ursula Norton, Portsmouth 834146.

KENT

June Allington Castle Medieval Market, Allington Castle, Maidstone. Sat. in mid-June. Tel. Mrs M. Kelly, Maidstone 65684.

July Kent County Show, Detling, Maidstone. Thur.–Sat. of 2nd week in July. Tel. J. C. Hendry (Sec.), Maidstone 37030.

November Bonfire, Fireworks and Crafts, Allington Castle, Maidstone. Sat. in early Nov. Tel. Mrs M. Kelly, Maidstone 65684.

December Christmas Craft Market, Allington Castle, Maidstone. 1st Sun. in Dec. Tel. Mrs M. Kelly, Maidstone 65684.

SURREY

May Southern Counties Craft Market, The Maltings, Farnham. Fri.–Sun. of 3rd week in May. Tel. Farnham 725887.

May Surrey Show, Stoke Park, Guildford. Spring Bank Holiday Mon. Tel. Stephen Lance (Chief Exec. and Sec.), Godalming 4651.

July Rustic Sunday, Old Kiln Museum, Reeds Road, Tilford, Farnham. Last Sun. in July. Tel. Frensham 2300.

October Southern Counties Craft Market, The Maltings, Farnham. Fri.–Sun., end of Oct. Tel. Farnham 725887.

WEST SUSSEX

April Craft Fair, Chalk Pits Museum, Houghton Bridge, Amberley. Sun. in late April. Tel. Bury 370.

June South of England Show, Ardingly, nr Haywards Heath. Thur.–Sat. in early June. Tel. Haywards Heath 892245.

September Craft Fair, Chalk Pits Museum, Houghton Bridge, Amberley. 3rd Sat.–Sun. in Sept. Tel. Bury 370.

November Craft Exhibition, Lannards Studio Pottery, Okehurst Road, Billingshurst. Last weekend of Nov. Tel. Billingshurst 2692.

Wales

August Royal National Eisteddfod of Wales is held during 1st full week of Aug. It includes demonstrations of crafts and craft competitions. Venue changes. Details from Central Office, Cardiff.

CLWYD

Summer Series of craft demonstrations at Erddig, Wrexham, during summer. Tel. National Trust Regional Information Officer, Betws-y-Coed 636.

DYFED

May Biennial exhibition of Pembrokeshire Craftsmen's Circle, Library Hall, Haverfordwest. Last 2 weeks of May in odd-numbered years. Tel. Mrs Jill Holden (Hon. Sec.), Lamphey 672339.

August Pembrokeshire Show, Withybush Airfield, Haverfordwest. Mon.–Wed., 3rd week in Aug. Tel. John W. Cole (Sec.), Haverfordwest 4331.

GWENT

July Abergavenny and Border Counties Show, Llanwenarth, nr Abergavenny. Last Sat. in July. Tel. Mrs Fiona Jenkins (Sec.), Abergavenny 3152.

August Newport Show, Tredegar House Country Park, Newport. Fri.–Sun. after August Bank Holiday. Tel. J. W. Gibbon (Organiser), Newport 277566.

GWYNEDD

May–June North Wales Show, Bethel, nr Caernarfon. Thur.–Fri. before Whit Sunday. Tel. Mrs R. Jones, Lanwnda 830382.

MID GLAMORGAN

July Bridgend Show, Newbridge Fields, Bridgend. 2nd weekend in July. Tel. M. R. Margetts, Bridgend 50110.

POWYS

July Royal Welsh Show, Builth Wells. Mon.–Thur. of 3rd week in July. Tel. Secretary, Builth Wells 553683.

SOUTH GLAMORGAN

May–September Series of craft demonstrations at Welsh Folk Museum, St Fagans, Cardiff. Sat. from end May–Sept. Programme of events available Apr.–May. Tel. Cardiff 569441.

The Welsh Marches

CHESHIRE

June Cheshire Show, Tatton Park, Knutsford. 3rd Wed. in June. Tel. Knutsford 3155.

June Tatton Weekend Show, Tatton Park, Knutsford. Weekend in June. Tel. Knutsford 3155.

October Country Park Craft Show, Tatton Hall, Knutsford. Weekend in mid-Oct. Tel. Knutsford 3155.

GLOUCESTERSHIRE

July The Craftsmen of Gloucestershire Annual Exhibition, Tithe Barn, Southam, nr Cheltenham. 10 days in mid-July. Tel. Marjorie Smith (Sec.), Cheltenham 512782 (day only).

HEREFORD AND WORCESTER

June Craft Fair, Bewdley Museum, Load Street, Bewdley. 1st weekend in June. Tel. Bewdley 403573.

June Three Counties Show, Malvern, Tues.–Thur. in mid-June. Tel. Lyn M. Downes (Director), Malvern 61731, or Malvern Tourist Board, Malvern 4700.

SHROPSHIRE

May Shropshire and West Midlands Show, Berwick Road, Shrewsbury. Wed.–Thur. of 3rd week in May. Tel. Shrewsbury 62824.

May Whitchurch Festival, Whitchurch Civic Centre, Whitchurch. 1st 10 days in May. Tel. Mrs Forrester, Whitchurch 3403.

June Ludlow Festival. Craft Market in Town Hall. Weekend in early July. Tel. Mr B. L. Mundy, Ludlow 2150.

August Shrewsbury Flower Show, The Quarry, Shrewsbury. Fri.–Sat. in mid-Aug. Tel. Miss Salt, Shrewsbury 64051.

The Midlands

DERBYSHIRE

April–November Series of craft events at Sudbury Hall, nr Derby. Programme available in Feb. each year. Tel. Curator, Sudbury 305.

May Craft Demonstration Day, Elvaston Castle Museum, nr Derby. May Day Bank Holiday. Tel. Maggie Heath, Matlock 3411, ext. 7397.

May Derbyshire County Show, Elvaston Castle Country Park, nr Derby. Spring Bank Holiday Mon. Tel. B. G. Daykin, Derby 512170.

August Bakewell Show, Bakewell. 1st Wed.–Thur. in Aug. Tel. Bakewell 2736/7.

August Chatsworth Country Fair, Chatsworth. 1st weekend after August Bank Holiday. Tel. Mr Cuthbert, Binham 367.

September Great Grandfather's Harvest Home, Elvaston Castle Museum, nr Derby. Last weekend in Sept. Tel. Maggie Heath, Matlock 3411, ext. 7397.

LEICESTERSHIRE

June Leicestershire Show, Derby Road Playing Fields, Loughborough. 2nd weekend in June. Tel. P. Wilkinson (Show Director), Wymeswold 880208.

August Rutland Show, Burley on the Hill, Oakham. 1st Sun. in Aug. Tel. Mrs L. A. Blake, Oakham 2018.

NOTTINGHAMSHIRE

August Craftworks Craft Fair, Brewhouse Yard Museum, The Castle, Nottingham. Sun.–Mon. of August Bank Holiday. Denise Kitchener (Sec.), Nottingham 700987.

STAFFORDSHIRE

October The Heart of England Craft Market, University of Keele, nr Stoke-on-Trent. Fri.–Sun. at beginning of Oct. Tel. Patricia Beswick, Ware 870040 (day only).

WARWICKSHIRE

July Royal Agricultural Show, Stoneleigh, Kenilworth. 1st Mon.–Thur. in July. Tel. Coventry 555100.

August Town and Country Festival, Royal Showground, Stoneleigh, Kenilworth. August Bank Holiday weekend. Tel. Coventry 555100.

WEST MIDLANDS

April The Heart of England Craft Market, University of Warwick, nr Coventry. Fri.–Sun. in Apr. Tel. Patricia Beswick, Ware 870040 (day only).

May Craft weekend at Black Country Museum, Tipton Road, Dudley. Sat.–Sun. of Spring Bank Holiday. Tel. Birmingham 557 9643.

Southern Central England

BUCKINGHAMSHIRE

September Bucks County Show, Hartwell Park, nr Aylesbury. 1st Thur. in Sept. Tel. Aylesbury 83734.

HERTFORDSHIRE

May Living Crafts, Hatfield House, Hatfield. Thur.–Sun. following May Day Holiday. Tel. Jean Younger (Organiser), Harpenden 61235.

May Hertfordshire Show, Friar's Wash, Redbourn, nr St Albans. Sat.–Sun. of Spring Bank Holiday weekend. Tel. Org. Sec., St Albans 55525.

August Knebworth Country Craft Show, Knebworth. 1st weekend in Aug. Tel. Stevenage 812661.

November Eastern Counties Craft Market, Rhodes Centre, Bishop's Stortford. Fri.–Sun. in Nov. Tel. Patricia Beswick, Ware 870040 (day only).

NORTHAMPTONSHIRE

Easter East of England Craft Expo, Lilford Park, Oundle. Sat.–Mon. of Easter weekend. Tel. Mrs Pamela Dennis, Kettering 511533.

July Northampton Show, Abington Park, Northampton. Fri.–Sun., end of July. Tel. Org. Sec., Northampton 34734, ext. 543/544.

OXFORDSHIRE

July Art in Action, Waterperry House, nr Wheatley, Oxford. Wed.–Sun. in early July. Tel. Mrs K. Watson (Org. Sec.), 01 998 1043 (day only).

September Thame Show, Thame. 3rd Thur. in Sept. Tel. Org. Sec., Thame 2737.

October Abingdon Crafts Festival, Abbey Buildings, Abingdon. Fri. for 10 days in mid-Oct. Tel. Pauline Burren, Abingdon 21873.

The Eastern Counties

CAMBRIDGESHIRE

May British Pecheron Horse Show, Midsummer Common, Cambridge. Last Sat. in May. Tel. Mr D. G. Maskell, Cambridge 356778.

July East of England Show, Alwalton, Peterborough. Tues.–Thur. of 3rd week in July. Tel. Peterborough 234451.

August Expo Steam Transport and Country Fair, Alwalton, Peterborough. August Bank Holiday weekend. Tel. Peterborough 234451.

ESSEX

June Essex Show, Great Leighs, nr Chelmsford. Fri.–Sat. in mid-June. Tel. Great Leighs 259.

LINCOLNSHIRE

April 'Crafternoon' at Museum of Lincolnshire Life, Old Barracks, Burton Road, Lincoln. Sun. afternoon at end Apr. Also 1st Sun. afternoon in Sept. Tel. Lincoln 28448.

June Lincolnshire Show, Lincoln. Wed.–Thur., or 3rd week in June. Tel. Lincoln 22900/24240.

NORFOLK

June Royal Norfolk Show, Dereham Road, New Costessey, Norwich. Wed.–Thur. at end June. Tel. Norwich 742000.

September Town and Country Weekend, Dereham Road, New Costessey, Norwich. Mid-Sept. Tel. Norwich 742000.

SUFFOLK

May Suffolk Show, Bucklesham Road, Ipswich. Wed.–Thur. after Spring Bank Holiday. Tel. Ipswich 76847.

September Country Fair, Museum of East Anglian Life, Stowmarket. Weekend in mid-Sept. Also weekend craft demonstrations Apr.–Sept. Tel. Stowmarket 2229.

The North-West

CUMBRIA

July–August Guild of Lakeland Craftsmen Summer Exhibition, Ladyholme Centre, Windermere. 2nd Sat. in July until last Sat. in Aug. Craft demonstrations given on Sat. and Wed. during this period. Tel. Rosemary Russell (Sec.), Kendal 27917.

ISLE OF MAN

July Yn Chruinnaght (The Gathering), annual festival of island crafts and Celtic culture in Ramsey. 3rd week in July. Tel. Mr G. Fehle, Ramsey 812986.

LANCASHIRE

July Royal Lancashire Show, Witton Park, Blackburn. Last Tues.–Thur. in July. Tel. Preston 21626.

August Great Northern Show, Moor Park, Preston. August Bank Holiday Monday. Tel. Mrs Simpson, Preston 35595.

MERSEYSIDE

August Southport Flower Show, Victoria Park, Rotten Row, Southport. Thur.–Sat. of 3rd week in Aug. Tel. Mr J. F. Drittler (Sec.), Southport 33133, ext. 234.

The North-East

HUMBERSIDE

June Cottingham Show, Priory Road, Cottingham. 1st Sat. in June. Tel. Mr J. P. Fluck, Hull 847302.

NORTHUMBERLAND

June Alnwick Fair, Market Place, Alnwick. Last Sun. in June for 1 week. Tel. Alan Lawson, Alnwick 603490.

November Christmas Craft Fair of the Society of Northumbrian Craftsmen, The Guildhall, Newcastle Quayside, Newcastle upon Tyne. Late Sat. in Nov. Tel. Mr R. Houghton, Newcastle upn Tyne 614307.

NORTH YORKSHIRE

June Midsummer Celebration (folk-dancing and craft demonstrations) at Ryedale Folk Museum, Hutton-le-Hole. 3rd Sat. afternoon in June. Tel. Lastingham 367.

July Great Yorkshire Show, Wetherby Road, Harrogate. 2nd Tues.–Thur. in July. Tel. Harrogate 61536.

August North Yorkshire Show, Pasture House, Thornton-le-Moor, nr Northallerton. 1st Thur. in Aug. Tel. Mr Pybus (Organiser), Northallerton 3429.

SOUTH YORKSHIRE

Worsbrough Mill Museum usually organises three craft events at Easter, Spring and August Bank Holidays. Tel. Barnsley 203961.

June Country Fair, Worsbrough Country Park, nr Barnsley. A Sun. in late June on alternate even-numbered years. Tel. Recreation Department, Barnsley 82216.

June Craftsman's Fair, Abbeydale Industrial Hamlet, Abbeydale Road South, Sheffield. 2nd week in June for 9 days. Tel. Sheffield 367731.

September Craft Day at Cusworth Hall Museum, Cusworth Lane, Doncaster. Sun. in Sept. Tel. Doncaster 782342.

WEST YORKSHIRE

April and October Two craft weekends at Colne Valley Museum, Golcar, Huddersfield. End of Apr. and beginning of Oct. Tel. Huddersfield 659762.

Summer Nostell Priory Craft Show, Nostell Priory, Wakefield. Weekend in summer (no set date). Tel. Wakefield 863892.

July Craft weekend at West Yorkshire Folk Museum, Shibden Hall, Halifax. 1st weekend in July. Tel. Halifax 52246.

August Harewood and District Show, Harewood Park, nr Leeds. 1st Tues. in Aug. Tel. Mrs D. J. Townson (Organiser), Harrogate 63539.

The Scottish Lowlands

BORDERS

May Borders Country Fair, The Hirsel, Coldstream. Last weekend in May. Tel. Tourism Division of Borders Regional Council, St Boswells 3301.

August Berwickshire County Show, Duns Castle, Duns. 1st Sat. in Aug. Tel. Mr Candlish (Sec.), Duns 2752.

August Annual Craft Fair, Traquair House, Innerleithen, nr Peebles. Early weekend in Aug. Tel. Innerleithen 830323.

August The Borders Show, Whithaugh Park, Newcastleton. August Bank Holiday weekend. Tel. Mr K. Welters, Liddesdale 220.

CENTRAL

July Doune and Dunblane Show. Keir Mains, Dunblane. 1st Sat. in July. Tel. C. C. Carrick-Anderson, Dunblane 822296.

DUMFRIES AND GALLOWAY

August Dumfries and Lockerbie Show, The Showfield, Park Farm, Dumfries. 1st Sat. in Aug. Tel. R. Hamilton, Dumfries 3425.

LOTHIAN

June Royal Highland Show, Ingliston, Newbridge. Mon.–Thur., 3rd week in June. Tel. Edinburgh 333 2444.

The Scottish Highlands

HIGHLAND

June–September Major exhibition of Scottish crafts, including occasional craft demonstrations and tours of workshops, organised by Highland Craftpoint, Beauly, nr Inverness. Other craft events are held throughout the year. Tel. Beauly 2578.

ACKNOWLEDGMENTS

The publishers would like to thank the individuals and organisations whose names appear in the first part of the book – *The Craftsman's Art* – for their help in its preparation. Valuable assistance was also provided by the following:

Agricultural Training Board; Area Museum Service for South-East England; Mrs Henry Barnet; J. and A. Beare Ltd; The Brewers' Society; Bridon Ltd; Peter Brockett (CoSIRA); Castle House Restorations; Mrs Gillian Curtis; Curtis and Pape Ltd; Hall and Ryan Ltd; Hereford Cider Museum Trust; Mrs Inger John; S. Learoyd MBE; Raymond Lister; Llechwedd Slate Caverns; Long John International Ltd; F. de Lotbinière; Mrs Nenia Lovesey; Peter Middleton; Nazeing Glass Works Ltd; New Forest Wagon Centre; Peak Park Planning Board; Michael St John; Brian Scrivener; Percy H. Sissons and Sons Ltd; Towy Pottery; Watford Glass Co. Ltd; J. Willetts; Wycombe Chair Museum.

Many organisations helped in the preparation of the regional guide – *Craftsmen at Work*. The publishers would like to thank them all, including:

British Craft Centre; Cornwall Crafts Association; Council for Small Industries in Rural Areas; Crafts Council; Craftsmen of Gloucestershire; Devon Guild of Craftsmen; Dorset County Arts and Crafts Association; Dorset Craft Guild; English Tourist Board; Galloway Guild of Craftsmen; Guild of Gloucestershire Craftsmen; Guild of Herefordshire Craftsmen; Guild of Lakeland Craftsmen; Guild of Master Craftsmen; Guild of Sussex Craftsmen; Guild of Yorkshire Craftsmen; Harris Tweed Association; Highland Craftpoint; Isle of Man Craft Association; Local Crafts of Wessex; Mid Northumberland Arts Group; National Farmers' Union; North-West Arts; Pembrokeshire Craftsmen's Circle; Red Rose Guild of Designer Craftsmen; Royal Agricultural Society of England; Rural Crafts Association; Scottish Development Agency; Scottish Tourist Board; Society of Northumbrian Craftsmen; Somerset Guild of Craftsmen; Surrey Crafts Association; Mrs Sheila G. Tarr; Wales Craft Council; Wales Tourist Board; Wessex Guild of Craftsmen; Western Isles Crafts Association.

The illustrations in this book were provided by the following artists, photographers and agencies.

Except where stated credits read from left to right down the page. Work commissioned by Reader's Digest is shown in italics. All artwork from pages 229 to 304 is credited to Hayward and Martin.

8 artists *Hayward and Martin*: artists *Hayward and Martin*: both, artists *Hayward and Martin* after A. Nicholls, Clocks in Colour, Blandford Press: 9 both *Colin Molyneux*: 10 The Mansell Collection: artist *Brian Delf* after R. W. Symonds, Thomas Thompion, his Life and his Work, Spring Books: 11 *Colin Molyneux*: artists *Hayward and Martin*: 12 artists *Hayward and Martin*: University of Reading, Institute of Agricultural History and Museum of English Rural Life: 13 *Jon Wyand*: artist *Brian Delf*: 14 all *Jon Wyand*: 15 artist *Brian Delf*: artist *Colin Emberson*: 16 source unknown, taken from N. Wymer, English Town Crafts, B. T. Batsford Ltd: 17 Central Office of Information: from Jarrolds, The Church Bells of Buckinghamshire, A. H. Cocks MA: 18 Michael St Maur Sheil: *Andrew Lawson*: 19 source unknown, taken from The Oxford Companion to Music, Oxford University Press: artists *Hayward and Martin*: 20–21 both *Colin Molyneux*: artist *Steve Sturgess*: 22 artist *Steve Sturgess*: source unknown, taken from J. Irvine, Victorian and Edwardian Dorset, B. T. Batsford Ltd: 23 artist *Launcelot Jones*: 24 all *Colin Molyneux*: top, artists *Hayward and Martin*: bottom, artist *Steve Sturgess*: 25 both *Colin Molyneux*: artist *Brian Delf*: 26–27 artist *Norman Lacey*: Ray Green/Camera Press: top inset, Ray Green/Camera Press: bottom inset, *Jon Wyand*: 28 Merseyside County Museums: from D. Phillips-Burt, The Building of Boats, Stanford Marine: *Jon Wyand*: 29 *Jon Wyand*: artist *Norman Lacey*: 30 *Malkolm Warrington*: centre *Jon Wyand*: 31 artists *Hayward and Martin*: 32 artist *Brian Delf*: all *Jon Wyand*: 33 *Jon Wyand*: artists *Hayward and Martin*: 34 *Andrew Lawson*: 35 both *Andrew Lawson*: artists *Hayward and Martin*: 36–37 artist *Brian Delf*: all *Andrew Lawson*:

artist *Brian Delf*: 38 artists *Hayward and Martin*: *Colin Molyneux*: 39 *Colin Molyneux*: artist *Andrew Aloof*: 40 J. E. Manners: 41 all University of Reading, Institute of Agricultural History and Museum of English Rural Life: artist *Colin Emberson*: 42 *Andrew Lawson*: 43 Donald Jackson: *Andrew Lawson*: artist *Donald Jackson*: *Andrew Lawson*: from 'L'Encyclopédie de Diderot et Le Rond L'Alembert': 44 artists *Hayward and Martin*: Reader's Digest: 45 artist *Andrew Aloof*: 46–47 Picturepoint-London: artist *Andrew Aloof*: both J. Fleming: 48 artists *Hayward and Martin*: 49 artists *Hayward and Martin*: artist John Rignall: 50–51 artist *Rachel Birkett*: all *Colin Molyneux*: 52–53 artist *Norman Lacey*: both *Colin Molyneux*: 54 Mary Evans Picture Library: 55 *Colin Molyneux*: Museum of Cider, Hereford: 56 courtesy National Museum of Wales (Welsh Folk Museum): 57 artist *Launcelot Jones*: both National Museum of Wales (Welsh Folk Museum): 58 Mary Evans Picture Library: *Jon Wyand*: artists *Hayward and Martin*: 59 *Jon Wyand*: 60 from 'L'Encyclopédie de Diderot et Le Rond L'Alembert': artist *Brian Delf*: 62 artist *Brian Delf*: Jon Wyand: 63 National Museum of Wales (Welsh Folk Museum): artist *Brian Delf*: Jon Wyand: 64 top and bottom left, artists *Hayward and Martin*: right, artist *Andrew Aloof*: 65 University of Reading, Institute of Agricultural History and Museum of English Rural Life: artists *Hayward and Martin*: 66 artists *Hayward and Martin*: 67 all *Colin Molyneux*: 68–69 John Cook: artist *Brian Delf*: artist *Andrew Aloof*: John Cook: 70 Michael Burgess: 71 University of Reading, Institute of Agricultural History and Museum of English Rural Life: Reader's Digest: 72 artists *Hayward and Martin*: artist *Launcelot Jones*: 73 all *Colin Molyneux*: 74 artists *Hayward and Martin*: *Jon Wyand*: 75 both *Jon Wyand*: artist *Colin Emberson*: 76 Illustrated London News: Long John International: 77 artist *Andrew Aloof*: 78 Long John International: artists *Hayward and Martin*: 79 left *Jon Wyand*: Long John International: artists *Hayward and Martin*: 80 artist *Brian Delf*: artist *Andrew Aloof*: 81 *Colin Molyneux*: artist *Brian Delf*: 82 all *Andrew Lawson*: artist *Norman Lacey*: 83 all *Andrew Lawson*: 84–85 all *Andrew Lawson*: 86 both *Colin Molyneux*: 87 *Colin Molyneux*: artist *Brian Delf*: 88 Reader's Digest: artists *Hayward and Martin*: Suffolk Photographic Survey, County Hall, Ipswich: 89 Suffolk Photographic Survey, County Hall, Ipswich: artists *Hayward and Martin*: 90 Michael Burgess: 91 Michael Burgess: P. H. Ward/Natural Science Photos: artist *Richard Lewington*: 92 artists *Hayward and Martin*: from 1,800 Woodcuts by Thomas Bewick and His School, Dover Publications: 93 *Colin Molyneux*: artist *Launcelot Jones*: 94 left, artists *Hayward and Martin*: right, artist *Ted Williams*: 95 both *Colin Molyneux*: artists *Hayward and Martin*: 96 both *Colin Molyneux*: 97 *Colin Molyneux*: artist *Brian Delf*: 98–101 all *Andrew Lawson*: 102–3 *Colin Molyneux*: artists *Hayward and Martin*: artist *Colin Molyneux*: Laurence Whistler: both Laurence Whistler: 104 John Vigurs: Ronan Picture Library: 105 top right, artist *Andrew Aloof*: bottom left, artists *Hayward and Martin*: 106–7 all John Cook: artist *Andrew Aloof*: artists *Hayward and Martin*: 108 all *Colin Molyneux*: 109 artist *Brian Delf*: 110–11 artist *Brian Delf*: *Colin Molyneux*: 112 *Colin Molyneux*: 113 artist *Brian Delf* after W. J. Zucherman, The Modern Harpsichord, Peter Owen: artist *Brian Delf* based on material from The Harpsichord and Clavichord by Raymond Russell: 114 by courtesy of Dr Carl Dolmetsch: Popperfoto: 115 all *Colin Molyneux*: 116–17 top right, artists *Hayward and Martin*: left, artist *Norman Lacey*: all The Agricultural Training Board/William Waddilove: 118 artists *Hayward and Martin*: artist *Brian Delf*: 119 all *Andrew Lawson*: 120 both *Jon Wyand*: 121 both *Jon Wyand*: Georgios M. Hadjigeorgiou: 122 *Jon Wyand*: 123 both *Jon Wyand*: artists *Hayward and Martin*: 124 Wycombe Chair Museum: 125 John Topham Picture Library: inset, all *Michael Burgess*: 126 Michael Burgess: 127 both Michael Burgess: artist *Brian Delf*: 128 artist *Norman Lacey*: both *Jon Wyand*: 129 Raymond Morris of Eddergoll: 130 artist *Andrew Aloof*: Jon Wyand: 131 both *Jon Wyand*: artist *Launcelot Jones*: 132 Graham Herbert: 133 *Jon Wyand*: artists *Hayward and Martin*: 134–5 artist *Colin Emberson*: Jon Wyand: inset, John Cook: 136 John Cook: Hampshire County Museum Service: Turner Photographics, Stamford: 137 artist *Andrew Aloof*: 138–9 artist *Brian Delf*: both *Jon Wyand*: 140 artist *Brian Delf*: Smithsonian Institution, Photo No. 44029-A: 141 *Jon Wyand*: artist *Brian Delf*: 142–3 artist *Norman Lacey*: both *Andrew Lawson*: 144 both *Andrew Lawson*: 145 both *Colin Molyneux*: 146 artist *Norman Lacey*: Bridport Museum and Art Gallery: 147 top right and left, artist *Norman Lacey*: centre and bottom right, artists *Hayward and Martin*: 148 artists *Hayward and Martin*: 149 artist *Norman Lacey*: 150 *Jon Wyand*: 151 both

Jon Wyand: 152 artist *Brian Delf*: *Colin Molyneux*: 153 all *Colin Molyneux*: 154 artist *Brian Delf*: 155 both *Colin Molyneux*: 156 all The Bridgeman Art Library: artist *Norman Lacey*: 157 British Tourist Authority: 158 bottom left, Mr Curtis: both *Colin Molyneux*: 159 all *Colin Molyneux*: 160 Tate Gallery, London: 161 artist *Andrew Aloof*: 162 artist *Colin Emberson*: from 'L'Encyclopédie de Diderot et Le Rond L'Alembert': 163 Christine Pearcey/Daily Telegraph Colour Library: artists *Hayward and Martin*: 164 The Beaford Archive: 165 Jon Wyand: artist *Les Smith*: 166 artists *Hayward and Martin*: both *Jon Wyand*: artists *Hayward and Martin*: 167 artist *Les Smith*: 168 artists *Hayward and Martin*: both *Jon Wyand*: 169 artist *Norman Lacey*: 170 artists *Hayward and Martin*: North Yorkshire County Library: 171 *Jon Wyand*: artist *Launcelot Jones*: 172–3 left, artist *Steve Sturgess*: right, artists *Hayward and Martin*: all *Jon Wyand*: 174 Colour Centre Slides: artists *Hayward and Martin*: 175 *Jon Wyand*: artist *Launcelot Jones*: 176 both *Colin Molyneux*: 177 artists *Hayward and Martin*: *Colin Molyneux*: 178 *Colin Molyneux*: The National Museum of Wales: 179 artist *Brian Delf*: 180 F. E. Gibson: 181 artist *Launcelot Jones*: 182 artist *Brian Delf*: *Colin Molyneux*: 183 *Colin Molyneux*: artists *Hayward and Martin* from J. Arnold, Shell Book of Country Crafts, John Baker: artist *Norman Lacey*: 184 Sonia Halliday Photographs: 185 artist *Colin Emberson*: 186 artist *Andrew Aloof*: 187 Angelo Hornak: 188 both *Jon Wyand*: 189 *Jon Wyand*: artist *Brian Delf*: 190 *Jon Wyand*: 191 artist *Barbara Brown*: 192 both *Jon Wyand*: 193 both *Jon Wyand*: artists *Hayward and Martin*: 194–5 artists *Hayward and Martin*: *Jon Wyand*: 196 *Colin Emberson*: University of Reading, Institute of Agricultural History and Museum of English Rural Life: 197 *Jon Wyand*: artist *Colin Emberson*: 198 *Colin Molyneux*: artist *Norman Lacey*: 199 *Colin Molyneux*: from L. Upcott Gill, Practical Taxidermy, Montague Brown: 200 J. E. Manners: 201 artist *Norman Lacey*: 202 artist *Norman Lacey*: 203 John Tarlton: artists *Hayward and Martin*: 204 Victoria and Albert Museum: artists *Hayward and Martin*: 205 all University of Reading, Institute of Agricultural History and Museum of English Rural Life: artist *Andrew Aloof*: 206 *Jon Wyand*: from 'L'Encyclopédie de Diderot et Le Rond L'Alembert': 207 artist *Launcelot Jones*: 208 all *Jon Wyand*: 209 all *Jon Wyand*: artist *Launcelot Jones*: 210 all CoSIRA: 211 artist *Colin Emberson*: artist *Andrew Aloof*: 212 artists *Hayward and Martin*: 213 all *Jon Wyand*: 214 artist *Launcelot Jones*: 215 both *Jon Wyand*: 216 University of Reading, Institute of Agricultural History and Museum of English Rural Life/Eric Guy Collection: 217 artist *Launcelot Jones*: 218–19 *Malkolm Warrington*: top, artists *Hayward and Martin*: bottom, artist *Andrew Aloof*: 220 John Marmaras/Daily Telegraph Colour Library: 221 both *Colin Molyneux*: 222 artist *Launcelot Jones*: 223 *Jon Wyand*: artist *Norman Lacey*: 224 *Colin Molyneux*: 229 St Ives Museum: 231 *Colin Molyneux*: 232 Tiverton Museum: 235 English Life Publications Ltd: Somerset County Museum: 236 both, Street Shoe Museum: 240 both, University of Reading, Institute of Agricultural History and Museum of English Rural Life: 242 photo, Clive Friend, FIIP, Woodmansterne Ltd: 245 both, Weald & Downland Open-Air Museum: 248 *Colin Molyneux*: 251 both, Welsh Folk Museum, St Fagans: 225 all, Philip Evans: 259 Bewdley Museum: 260 Hereford and Worcester County Museum: 261 Avonscroft Museum of Buildings: 265 Gladstone Pottery Museum: 267 Birmingham Museum and Art Gallery: 271 City Museum, St Albans: 272 British Waterways Board: 273 both, Oxfordshire Museum Services: 277 Norfolk Museum Services: 279 Museum of East Anglian Life: 282 Museum of Lakeland Life and Industry, Abbot Hall: 283 Manx Open-Air Folk Museum: 285 both, Pilkington Museum: 288 Castle Museum, York: 290 West Yorkshire Folk Museum: 303 all, Rick Beattie.

The publishers also acknowledge their indebtedness to the authors and publishers of the following books, which were consulted for reference:

Country Crafts Today J. E. Manners (David and Charles); *The Craftsman's Directory* (Stephen and Jean Lance); *Handbook of English Crafts and Craftsmen* June R. Lewis (Robert Hale); *See Britain at Work* Angela Lansbury (Exley Publications); *The Shell Book of Country Crafts* James Arnold (John Baker); *The Showman's Directory* (Stephen and Jean Lance); *Traditional Country Craftsmen* J. Geraint Jenkins (Routledge and Kegan Paul).

Maps drawn by Clyde Surveys Ltd
Composition in Photina by Filmtype Services Limited, Scarborough, North Yorkshire
Colour separations Mullis Morgan Ltd, London and Gilchrist Bros. Leeds
Printing and binding Arnoldo Mondadori Editore, Verona, Italy

41.026.1